Jeremy Howard-Williams was born on the Isle of Wight in 1922. He joined the Royal Air Force during the Second World War as a night fighter pilot and stayed in the Service until 1958. On leaving the RAF, he entered the sailing industry and wrote a number of books about sailing and related topics. From 1974 until he retired in 1982, Howard-Williams was the Editor of Adlard Coles Ltd.

He has been a devotee of the crossword puzzle since childhood; while working at Adlard Coles Ltd he read of an American crossword dictionary which had sold over a million copies, and decided to try his hand. From then on he noted down interesting clues as he did the crosswords in the newspapers – the *Daily Telegraph*, *The Times* and the *Sunday Times* to name but three – and he has tried to include an example of each one in this fascinating volume.

JEREMY HOWARD-WILLIAMS

The Complete Crossword Companion

Third Edition

GRAFTON BOOKS

A Division of the Collins Publishing Group

LONDON GLASGOW
TORONTO SYDNEY AUCKLAND

Grafton Books
A Division of the Collins Publishing Group
8 Grafton Street, London W1X 3LA

Published in paperback by Grafton Books 1989

First published by Granada Publishing 1984
Second edition published by Grafton Books 1986
Third edition 1988

Copyright © Jeremy Howard-Williams 1984, 1986, 1988

A CIP catalogue record for this book is available
from the British Library

ISBN 0-586-20519-5

Printed and bound in Great Britain by
Collins, Glasgow

Set in Times

The Complete Crossword Companion

Contents

Preface to the Third Edition

The warm reception given to the first appearance of this *Companion* confirmed my original faith in the idea behind it, and encouraged the Publishers to ask me to prepare a second edition. I nearly doubled the number of items in the various lists, and added many new individual entries; the opportunity was also taken to correct one or two errors which had crept into the first printing (excusably, perhaps, when it is remembered that the book is the work of one hand rather than that of a committee, as is more usual with most reference books).

Heartened by a continuing success, I was recently persuaded that an even more thorough enlargement was justified, and this third edition is the result. Many kind readers have suggested various subjects and words for inclusion; most of these have been followed up, many of them leading to further lines of investigation.

Diversions and side-issues are among the fascinations of a book of this nature — let us take the mini-biography of Absolom as an example. His death came about because his hair got entangled in an oak tree while he was fleeing on an ass or mule from the battlefield; this enabled Joab's men to catch and kill him. Crossword puzzlers, however, can find this out from the Bible, or else from most reference books which have an entry on Absolom. But his name may not be given in the clue — indeed, it may be the very word which is being sought, and the clue may only refer to 'ass', which might be indicated by **Assassinated after running on the first (or second) three** (7) = ABSOLOM, or else to 'hair', which could be implied by **Locked into the branch, he was eventually found and killed** (7) = ABSOLOM. There are many obvious similar parallels: the entry **DANCE** in this book, besides listing some 75 of the better-known names of specific dances, also points to *Salome*, which gives a further reference to *Herod* and thus to John the Baptist's sad demise. Equally, **SHOWER** reminds the reader that Zeus used his magical powers to transform himself into a shower of gold in order to sneak up on the fair Danae in her prison cell, where, as they say, he took advantage of her (a girl really wasn't safe when he was around — half a dozen transformations for this purpose are listed under the entry **ZEUS**); Danae became the mother of Perseus nine months later. That information is contained under **DANAE** in most of the right reference books (and also possibly under **PERSEUS** or **ZEUS**), but if the clue only refers to 'shower', as in **He showered down in the lock-up** (4) = ZEUS, or else to 'gold', which might say **Falling gold caused her downfall** (5) = DANAE, then the solver will be hard put to it to get a lead — unless he or she has a copy of this book, where both **SHOWER** and **GOLD** offer *Danae* as a line of enquiry, and where the information is given to those who follow up the cross reference. Incidentally, **SHOWER** also gives *demonstrator* and *exhibitor* in case the puzzler should forget.

Among the new lists now included are Chinese dynasties (and their calendar); famous country houses of fiction; emperors; furniture of various kinds; cartoonists; captains, majors and colonels of fact and fiction; circuses; metals; minerals; painters; poets; strong men; and theatre names. Nearly all of these have been suggested by readers. I have also expanded the already extensive range of antelopes and of rivers (both of which seem to have an inexhaustible supply of names); composers; writers and assemblies of animals. The entries on games of all kinds have now been divided into ball games, board ~s, card ~s, ~s as such, and sports, which in turn have been subdivided into outdoor sports, indoor ~s, water ~s and winter ~s. Music terms and tempi have been similarly improved.

I have derived particular enjoyment from collecting words that describe specific collectors, where I was encouraged by a reader who lives in Gwent, and with whom I had a lively and stimulating correspondence. The Rev. Clifford Warren offered to send me a fresh 'collector' for each new one I could suggest to him, which was exactly the spur needed to send me hastening to my reference books and other sources; he eventually provided me with no fewer than eight, including deltiologist, ephemerist, notaphilist and tegestologist (I wouldn't let him have elephantalist, and he refused me gramma-tologist). I am incidentally also indebted to the same kind reader for the boxed palindrome, which I have taken pleasure in putting on the first page of the Introduction, instead of my original four-word palindrome (which I may now confess I concocted myself). Clifford Warren offers as a translation 'Arepo the sower holds the wheels at work', and has even managed to juggle the letters to produce 'paternoster'; he tells me that it is found throughout the Christian world, and was scratched on a Roman wall at Cirencester. It's much better to have the real thing, and who am I to disbelieve a man of the cloth? But I have tried my hand at coining a word to fill what seems to be a strange gap; as far as I am aware, a collector of autographs had no noun of its own until this edition appeared.

One or two surviving errors have been corrected (no doubt there are still some left, waiting to be spotted by the eagle-eyed), and some surprising omissions have been filled in: the George Cross (GC) was not among the **MEDALS**; gunter, lug and sprit were not mentioned under **RIG** or **SAIL** (surprising lapses these, considering my long association with the sailing business); some well-known **RIVERS** were missing; the **CAPITAL** of Bulgaria was conspicuous by its absence; and Qantas did not figure among the instances of **Q** being used without a following **U** — my elder son spotted this one (it is, perhaps, interesting to note here that an author who wishes to remain up to date needs to keep his eyes open. In the autumn of 1986, a number of well-known places in northern Canada were officially renamed in the Inuit language — and some of them had Qs without Us); and, finally, I found to my astonishment that the two pages which I had devoted to summarising the plots of all the Dickens novels made no mention, above all things, of the story of David Copperfield!

Some people seem to have failed to appreciate fully the use made of italics in this book. Specifically, I have been taken to task for not listing Red Indian tribes and, it so happens, the labours of Hercules. For the benefit of anyone having this trouble, I have varied the system slightly for the third edition, as far as these and one or two other entries are concerned. In the first two editions, **REDSKIN** did no more than list *AMERICAN INDIAN* in its text, on the assumption that the italic letters would be sufficient in themselves to tell the reader to cross refer to that entry for further details (I was assuming that readers would have taken in the section *How to Use this Companion* which follows the *Introduction*). **RED INDIAN** now comes right out with it and says 'See *AMERICAN INDIAN* for tribes.' I have, in fact, done the same sort of thing in some other entries, where an italicised word might not be enough to emphasise the long lists which are available under another entry (Swiss cantons, chairs, Gilbert, Sullivan, music tempi, etc.); in yet others, I have made use of the abbreviation (q.v.) to help draw the reader's attention better than the more elusive use of italics.

In the case of Hercules' labours, as with Red Indians, there is not enough room in the book to give all the information on the subject under both Greek and Roman names; one entry has to be selected as the master, and to contain the major information, if duplication is to be avoided. I should explain here that this *Companion* normally gives priority in the classics to the Attic rather than the Latin mythology (it was, after all, earlier), so that most Greek entries will be found to contain more information than their Roman counterparts. But I recognise that more people refer to the Roman Hercules than to the Greek Heracles, so, for those particular entries, this edition finally admits this, and the latter merely refers the reader to the former, rather than vice versa as previously.

I would not, of course, have been able to complete a work of this nature from my own memory. Besides the kind help of readers, the following works of reference have been used with advantage (but any remaining errors are mine alone):

Bibliography

The Bible (King James Authorised Version)
Brewer's Dictionary of Phrase and Fable (Evans) Cassell 1986
Cambridge Guide to English Literature (Stapleton) CUP (Newnes) 1985
Classified Quotations (Benham) Cassell 1921
Collins English Dictionary (Hanks) Collins 1985
Collins Thesaurus (ed. W. T. McLeod) Collins 1986
Complete Works of William Shakespeare (ed. Alexander) Collins 1966
Concise Oxford Dictionary (Fowler) OUP 1958 and 1979
Crossword Dictionary (Ace/Stoneshire 1984) Dawn Gorrick, Aus 1981
Dictionary of the Bible (Hyamson) George Routledge c.1940
Dictionary for Crossword Puzzles (Newman) Doubleday, USA 1967
Dictionary of the English Language (Dr Johnson) Longman 1786
Everyman's Factfinder (Dempsey) Dent 1982
Halliwell's Film Guide (Halliwell) Granada 1979
Jack's Reference Book (was Pannell's) TC & EC Jack Ltd 1921
Library of Modern Knowledge (3 vols) Reader's Digest 1979
New Age Encyclopedia (Maine & Foreman) Collins 1958
Oxford Companion to Music (Scholes) OUP 1950
Oxford Companion to Ships and the Sea (Kemp) OUP 1979
Oxford Companion to Sports and Games (Arlott) OUP 1977
Oxford Dictionary of Quotations (Darwin) OUP 1979
Quickway Crossword Dictionary (Hill) Warne & Co 1958
Roget's International Thesaurus (Chapman) Harper & Row, USA 1984
Smaller Classical Dictionary (Marindin) Murray 1910
Thesaurus of Book Digests (Haydn & Fuller) Avenal, USA 1977
Thesaurus of English Words and Phrases (Roget) Longman 1958

Introduction

History

Playing with words has captured man's imagination since shortly after he learned to write; indeed, it has been an integral part of the art of calligraphy, as can be traced in the development of Coptic hieroglyphs in ancient Egypt. From a later period, the poet Samonicus, who lived during the second century A.D., has left a record of the use of the word Abracadabra as a charm against agues and fevers. Written on parchment in a triangular form, the amulet was then folded into a cross and hung round the sufferer's neck for nine days before being cast into a stream:

<pre>
        ABRACADABRA
        BRACADABR
        RACADAB
        ACADA
        CAD
        A
</pre>

It will be noted that it reads round the outside as well as across the top (and through the middle). Not surprisingly, the amulet was eventually found to be ineffective, so that the word came to imply contempt for useless mumbo-jumbo.

Simple squares, where across and down words read the same, have been around for at least the same length of time; in some cases, the square will also read backwards:

<pre>
        S A T O R
        A R E P O
        T E N E T
        O P E R A
        R O T A S
</pre>

The Crossword Proper

It was not until 1913, however, that one Arthur Wynne suggested to the New York *Sunday World* that the paper should adopt a novel form of diversion for its readers. The first true crossword was diamond-shaped, and its inventor called it a *Word Cross*. The idea took the better part of ten years to travel to England, but in August 1982, G. E. Cousins was to have a letter published in the *Daily Telegraph*, wherein he commented on the diamond jubilee of the crossword in the UK. It seems that in March 1922 he was a junior reporter in august company, listening with some respect as his superiors discussed the new craze. The judgement of his boss was that it would be 'a nine days' wonder'. This somewhat sweeping condemnation was supported by contemporary medical opinion, which held that the dazzling patterns could eventually lead to neuroses and eye trouble; it said nothing about brain fatigue.

Two years later, however, a book of crossword puzzles was published, and the habit took a firm hold in this country. It is, perhaps, interesting to look back at some of the clues and answers from the novelty's first appearance in the *Daily Telegraph* (30 July 1925):

Traveller's haven (3)	INN
Beverage (4)	BEER
Consider (4)	DEEM
A people with unalterable laws (5)	MEDES
The germ of a building (4)	PLAN

The last two were about the only clues to go any further than a dictionary definition. Since those days, the cult has developed to the point where two distinct forms have emerged. The first of these requires some etymology and a store of synonyms, together with a grounding in general knowledge (or else a dictionary and a good encyclopaedia); the second needs a more convoluted mind, where homonyms are more important than synonyms, and where clues have to be dissected, examined, twisted and even repunctuated. The latter, more cryptic, form took a number of years to appear, and was eventually developed by some of the more serious newspapers, while the popular tabloids continued to pursue the more direct line, which became known as the 'quick' crossword. During the Second World War the Germans even turned the quick crossword into a weapon: in 1944 they literally fired it at Britain by means of the V1 flying bomb as a crude form of propaganda. (**He is your enemy too** (9) gave BOLSHEVIK; **This is the beginning of a German victory** (2) was VI. The black squares of the grid were in the shape VI.) Not many of them reached the general public.

In this *Companion* we are concerned with both forms. For the quick puzzler there are lists of synonyms for many of the more popular clue words, so that the book acts as a kind of thesaurus; there are also a lot of groups of words listed either alphabetically (where the number is small enough to allow easy reference), or else broken down into groups each containing 3, 4, 5, 6 etc letters. For instance, **ANTELOPE** is a word which often appears in clues, and there are over 60 breeds listed; there are 2 dozen words meaning **SALMON**; under **CASTLE** we find not only a dozen words connected with military architecture (bailey, motte, rampart etc), but also the names of more than 350 castles in the UK, broken down into groups of 3-lettered names, 4, 5, 6, up to 9 letters, and then those with 10 or more.

These classifications are, of course, also of use to the cryptic puzzler, but he or she is more likely to need help in lateral thinking. For instance **ARROW** not only lists synonyms, but also suggests that *bowman* might be a useful line of enquiry, under which we read of *fiddler* and *cellist*, each with its own entry; we also see that **ARROW** is a kind of *grass* (which has over seventy entries of its own). Besides its connection with love, **COURTED** suggests the law courts (*judged*, *sued*) and *tennis* (which in turn lists the more popular venues, together with some terms from real tennis). The Greek and Roman gods, so beloved of puzzle setters, receive full coverage.

The Art of the Setter

The Crossword Editor of *The Times* is on record (31 December 1981) as warning would-be solvers to distrust every word in a clue, because the puzzle setter's aim is to say one thing while meaning another.

Once the ruthless nature of the setter has been established, the solver is half-way towards success. The master-craftsman of the setting world is devious, inventive, clever, impudent, and extremely cunning, but always scrupulously fair (well, nearly always). An average cryptic clue will usually have two indications or pointers to its solution, both twisted and often deliberately mingled. If the attention of the solver can be directed on to a false trail, then the setter will consider that he has won a partial victory. To this end he will adopt many stratagems but, in the final analysis, the solver should be able to tip his hat and say 'Oh, I see; well done', even if, once the answer is known, he or she adds 'What a nerve!'

Asterisks and Brackets

Before embarking on explanations and examples of different forms of cryptic clue and answer, it should be pointed out that the asterisk is used throughout this *Companion* to indicate where a letter has been omitted or two words joined to form one. Brackets in an answer show where a letter or word has been inserted. This is purely a mechanical aid to understanding how an answer is reached, and the solver should read such words as though the intruders were not there. Thus **It is forbidden to have a girl in a bed** (6) = B(ANN)ED, should be read as BANNED; in **The boy loses some time** (3) = TIM*, the asterisk should be ignored.

Anagrams

In the more esoteric puzzles, a clue will not be so brash as to say baldly *Anag*; the solver will be left to deduce, not only that an anagram is intended, but also which words form the letters to be shuffled. It is not too much to say that ten per cent of all adjectives, verbs and adverbs, and many nouns, can be interpreted as intending an anagram, even if the reasoning is sometimes rather cryptic. Words such as 'stew', 'badly', 'twisted' and 'replaced' are fairly easy indicators, while 'grim', 'wry' and 'horrible' are, perhaps, less obvious. An example is: **Wrong vote blocks the decision** (4) = VETO; it will be seen that there are the requisite two indicators to the solution, which is reached by the anagram of **vote** (**wrongly** written) forming an answer meaning something which **blocks a decision**.

To help identify some of the many indications that letters should be shuffled, use of the word *Anag* in this *Companion* implies that an entry may intend this interpretation. It should be noted, however, that 'anagram' is taken to mean any rearrangement of letters, even if in their new form they do not make a proper word in themselves. Thus, **Escaping, the wayward nun is caught by the gang** (7) = R(UNN)ING; the word **nun** is reordered to UNN and placed in, or **caught by**, a synonym for **gang**, which is RING, to give the answer which means **escaping**. This may be termed a loose anagram of **nun** and is restricted to one which forms only part of the solution. **WAYWARD** would have *Anag* written after it if it were an entry in the *Companion*; we may take the word 'wrong' as another example, and a typical clue might read **The Redcap has gone wrong, and gets into hot water**. This could give the solution SP*ONGE, where SP stands for 'service policeman' (slang = **Redcap**) and ONGE is a loose anagram of **gone**; a sponge is often used in **hot water**. Note that **wrong** here could also refer to **Redcap**, whose anag might give us CARPED — but this does not conform with the second half of the clue which, to justify such an interpretation, would have to read something like **The Redcap has gone wrong and found fault**. See also **SCRAMBLED EGG** in the main text, which can give GGE as a cryptic answer. This, of course, is not a word in itself, but it might be used in the make-up of a solution, as in **The king's got scrambled egg covering the roe — quite properly sent back** = G*EOR*GE (GGE is **scrambled egg** and it is round, or **covering**, EOR which is **roe** backwards without any other alteration — **quite properly sent back**. The whole is the name of a **king**). The reader is referred to **Anag** in the main text for further information.

Hidden Word

There are plenty of underhand ways of showing that the answer is formed by letters which appear consecutively in the clue, even though they may form parts of two or more words in that clue. 'Holds', 'contains' and 'part of' are self-evident indications; 'betrays', 'we see', 'carries' and 'is evident' are less direct: **To go unceremoniously carries weight** (5) = O*UNCE.

Sometimes the clue has to be modified before the word can be made. **The best tray à la carte, without a good man, will yield** treachery (8) = BE*TRAY*A*L. This involves removing the letters **st** from the second word (so that it is without a saint, or **good man**) before running the next six letters on to it, to give (or **yield**) a synonym for **treachery**. See entry **Hidden word** for further discussion.

Punctuation

It is considered fair play to change punctuation of a clue so that a different meaning is conveyed. Thus, **Gad! Wall-joint gets the bird** (7) = GAD*WALL (which is a duck), because it should be read **Gad/wall joint, gets the bird**. Alternatively, **Thanks to the French, a sacked part of Old England** (6) should be read **Thanks (to the French), a; sacked part of old England**, which gives us MERCI*A.

A slightly more abstruse misuse of punctuation is shown by the clue **Forty-nine out for a duck** (3, 5). This should be read as **Forty. Nine out**

for a duck, to give TWO SCORE (implying not only the quantity 40, but also that only two batsmen scored any runs from a cricket team of eleven, so that nine of them made nought). Note that there are still two pointers to the solution.

The reader should beware how punctuation is rearranged. Take an innocent short part-clue such as **I left in South Africa**. This can be read in four ways, depending where the comma is mentally placed (some of the results of this example are a bit unwieldy, but it should be remembered that this is a hypothetical example to demonstrate a principle).

1. **I, left in South Africa** requires the letter I to be written, followed by the letter L for **left** placed in an abbreviation for **South Africa** = I*S(L)A.
2. **I left, in South Africa** requires letters for I and **left** put into the abbreviation for **South Africa** = S(I*L)A.
3. **I left in, South Africa** requires the letter i to leave the word **in**, and to be followed by SA = N*SA.
4. **I left in south, Africa** requires the letters I and L to be placed in an abbreviation for **south**, and followed by one for **Africa** = S(I*L)O*AF ('so' being an abbreviation for south, and 'Af' one for Africa).

See also the entry **Question Mark** in the main text.

Split Words
If the foregoing is enough to show that many switches can be played within a clue to give a wide range of interpretation, the following will demonstrate how the answer itself has sometimes to be read in different ways in order to satisfy both halves of the clue. **Play some role in dismantling** (4, 5) provides the usual two pointers, and from the first half we get TAKE A PART (4, 1, 4); if this is read as TAKE APART (4, 5), it becomes **dismantling**. Similarly, we may have **Piece on board or back all right** (4) to give ROOK, which is a castle on a chess board, and can also be read as **or back** (RO) plus **all right** (OK).

A word may also be split and then tampered with. **Influence me to replace the head of Victoria, say** (7) should be started with a close look at **say** which, in this case, means 'for instance'. Victoria is often given as an instance of a railway station, a queen or an empress; here 'me' or 'I' should replace her 'head' or first letter. ME*TATION, I*TATION, ME*UEEN and I*UEEN get us nowhere, but ME*MPRESS or I*MPRESS look better, for the latter rings the bell with a word which also means **influence**. See also **Spelling** in the text.

Pronunciation

Another weapon in the setter's armoury is brainwashing. If he can persuade the solver that a particular (wrong) meaning should be given to a clue, he will go happily on his way, satisfied that he has fairly misled his opponent (for be under no illusions — solver and setter are deadly enemies in this war of words). **Draw from this water-tower** (3) encourages a train of thought which conjures up a large tank of water on top of a pillar or column, with someone drawing water from it by means of a pipe with a tap. In fact, the water-tower refers to something which is water-borne and pulls or **tows**; the answer is TUG. Another common deception is use of the word 'flower', intended to make the solver think of daffodils and roses whereas, pronounced in a different way, it can also mean something which 'flows' — usually a river. Thus, **Flower of England** (4) is designed to conjure up the word ROSE, and the spectre of the setter will chortle with glee if this is written in; to be fair, the usual secondary clue should help identify the answer and, in this case, it might be **A single flower of England** (4), which would give A*RUN (referring to a single run at cricket, and to the river Arun).

Note how the mind is programmed to think along the wrong lines, and look for a pronunciation which is different from the obvious; be prepared for any word in the clue to have a meaning other than one which is associated with the obvious pronunciation. If **Sewer cover** comes into the clue, don't think immediately of drains and inspection pits, but consider the alternative pronunciation of **sewer** and a seamstress should come to mind; her **cover** might be a THIMBLE.

When we turn to words which are pronounced the same but spelled differently, a whole new range of possibilities is opened up. These have been indicated in the text of the *Companion* by abbreviating the words 'sounds like . . .' to 's/l . . .' and adding the word in question. Thus, the entry **SOURCE** (s/l *sauce*) will encourage the reader to branch off into thoughts of impudence or ketchup, if he or she is confronted by a clue which starts **Sound source of** . . .

Warning that such a meaning is intended may not be conveyed so obviously as this; the word 'hear' is often used for this purpose, so that we get **It's boring to hear you in a wild rage** (5) = A(U)GER, in which the letter U is heard as **you**, and is placed in a loose anagram (**wild**) of **rage**; the whole word means something which can be used for **boring** a hole.

Before we leave pronunciation, a few final words of warning are in order. Always keep your mind open to further deception (as you should do at all times): **Sounds like a sheep** = BLEATS or BAA; **Sound asleep** =

SNORE or ZZ. **Sound** here is being used in onomatopoeic form to indicate the noise being suggested. Compare also: **Food said to raise a smile** (6) = CHEESE (in front of the portrait camera).

Homonyms

The *OED* tells us that a homonym is a word of the same form as another, but with a different sense. The setter is therefore faced with a similar pronunciation for the two meanings of the word he is using; if he wants to brainwash his opponent into thinking of the wrong one, he must resort to other means. If we read **Get rid of the batter and wash the dish** (5, 4), beware of being persuaded by the second part of the clue that the whole of it refers to cooking; **batter** here is another way of saying 'batsman' and refers to cricket, so that the solution is CLEAN BOWL (**get rid of**, or 'bowl out' the batsman) and **wash** or CLEAN the **dish** or BOWL).

The setter is also apt to invent his own cryptic homonyms (or, more likely, to use any of a series of conventionally accepted ones, such as have already been suggested, e.g. **bloomer** for FLOWER, **operator** for SURGEON, and so on). **Swiss banker** (5) might encourage the answer GNOME, being one of the celebrated financial wizards known as the gnomes of Zurich; but **banker** is more likely to mean 'river' (it flows between banks), so that the answer required is RHONE. A really nasty setter might give easy clues for the words which produce the intersecting O and E, thereby further encouraging GNOME, to the detriment of the answer which runs across the beginning of the word. The correct solution would depend on the secondary clue which, in this instance, could well bring in the word 'currency' — another cryptic homonym which seems to support the GNOME and his financial dealings but which, in this instance, is a second reference to a river (which has a 'current').

One final example under this heading will serve to reveal a further series of pitfalls which lie in wait for the unwary. The setter takes a word like 'distressed' and throws it into the clue somewhere. The tyro could be forgiven for seizing triumphantly on it with a cry of 'Anagram!' Indeed, a part-clue like **distressed hair-net** may intend an anagram (THE RAIN), but it is more likely to require a synonym for 'tress' (curl, hair, lock etc) to be removed from the word, leaving ****NET in this case. Many words starting 'de-' or 'dis-' can be used in this way, thus 'disrobed' can require the removal of a synonym for clothes, 'disgrace' takes away 'grace' or any of its alternatives, and so on.

Inversion

I term it an inversion where the word to be written into the grid is, in effect, the clue; the answer to this clue is given by the setter as the clue. This may sound complicated, but can quickly be explained by an example. Presented in the usual way, **Wild rose is hurt** (4) could expect SORE as an answer (being **rose** written **wildly** or in anagram form, and meaning **hurt**). But if the clue were to read, **Sore, perhaps, for not being cultivated** (4, 4), we should get the answer WILD ROSE (an instance of **rose** written **wildly** could be **sore**, and the whole thing is **uncultivated**). Similarly **Cat ham** (3, 5) could become ACT BADLY (**act** written **badly** is **cat**, and to act badly is to 'ham' it up). Note that the words 'wild' and 'badly', each denoting an anagram, now appear in the answer.

A related example, which switches only part of the clue into the answer, is furnished by **The young cow plays into the hands of Alfred** (4). This requires C*ALF, because the second part of the clue can be turned into 'is caught at cricket by Alf', which would be written into the score-book as c. Alf.

If the words 'perhaps' or 'for instance' are included in the clue, the implication is that a quote or meaning from the answer has been given in the clue, and this can be used in a number of ways other than the one instanced above with the **wild rose** clue. **Immoral, perhaps, he might say paradoxically** (5) = PRUDE (because a prude might say 'I'm moral', and it would be paradoxical for a prude to be immoral); and see **IMPERFECT** in the entries. In a similar vein, **I, for instance, represent investment** (7) = CAPITAL, because the letter **I** as written in the clue is an **instance** of a capital letter; the answer also means money, or **investment**. See also example about **Victoria, say** under *Split Words* above.

Alphabet

There are, of course, literally hundreds of different ways of suggesting a single letter. Because the answer will form only part of the final solution, the pointer will be a part-clue and must, of necessity, be short and snappy if the whole clue is not to become long and unwieldy. In the following examples, I have given each clue a second indication (which is put in brackets); either may be used indepen-dently of the other, or they may be joined together.

A	First (across).	N	Name (the ultimate sin).
B	A follower (is born).	O	Love (a duck).
C	A hundred (Centigrade).	P	Quiet (president).
D	Five hundred (died).	Q	Cue for sound (question).
E	Final score (for bridge player).	R	Royal (year end).
F	Feminine (mid-off).	S	Stop-start (bender).
G	German (third degree).	T	Square (car).
H	Beethoven's fifth (is hot).	U	Acceptable (you hear).
I	One (island).	V	Five (against).
J	Judge (James the First).	W	With (raw edge).
K	Cork tip (king).	X	Ten (wrong).
L	Second class (lake).	Y	Fourth of July (in Yugoslavia).
M	A thousand (married).	Z	Last (model gauge).

Test Your Skill

If you have read this far, you should now be ready to try your hand at a few tests of varying complexity. The following represent examples of the more common cryptic clues, some of which have been taken from puzzles appearing in the more serious newspapers, some have been adapted, and some have been concocted specially.

1. A pinch added to tuck at a pinch (3).
2. Extremes of cold seize a blackguard (3).
3. Rotten starters of banquets and dinners (3).
4. Unmatched in the food department (3).
5. Crazy about you finally being asked into the garden (4).
6. Small mechanical device to alleviate child-bearing (4).
7. Dog food (4).
8. Pop wine (4).
9. The case for a sewer (4).
10. The way a land measure is brought out (4).
11. Spirit in which there's a profit (4).
12. Backroom for Othello, perhaps (4).
13. Doctor leaves the capital by boat (4).
14. Quiet time for bookmaker (4).
15. Country starting with a long Eisteddfod session (5).

16. Peach under the tree (5).
17. Can a sty hold such unpleasantness for a pig? (5).
18. Makes war pay (5).
19. Change for one pound in old money (5).
20. Some of one's energies misplaced in the Alps (5).
21. Not smiling at the back (5).
22. Conclude there's not much information you can give the Queen (5).
23. Feeling one's lost direction in Austen Abbey (5).
24. Vehicle transport with no French iron to convey (5).
25. Secure kind of delivery (6).
26. See the old fool dodder — not half — grabbing a sailor (6).
27. Getting through in a U-boat is magnificent (6).
28. Stick a suitable notice in the agony column (6).
29. Where one presents one's case in Calais (6).
30. Setting music is nothing, leaving out Beethoven's fifth (6).
31. Cut off-licence tax (6).
32. Greek island ways, they say (6).
33. Deny entry on Tyneside (6).
34. Second class ways in Norfolk (6).
35. Proverbially tearful, Misses Bo-Peep and Lockett? (6).
36. Gas about a Spanish region (6).
37. Reassure a number in solitary confinement (6).
38. Not the same appeal by the Royal Society (6).
39. Pious man, having the last word, makes a bit of a bloomer (6).
40. Begins to get sour on board (6).
41. A prisoner in the string section (7).
42. A thunderous immortal described by American men of letters (7).
43. Not free to wed? (7).
44. Whip a Chinese coin out in Mexico (7).
45. Tried putting a politician into a toboggan (7).
46. Bone found by archaeological research party (7).
47. Rush to get river payment from tenant (7).
48. A boat for every customer present (7).
49. Supporter on the blower in Italy (7).
50. Seconds out, in ten days from starting this find (7).
51. When forming path around pound this (7).
52. Simple but callous as the Cockney said (7).
53. Obscures setting of Indian city-figures (8).
54. A house, many springing up here (8).
55. We hear the French after self-satisfied duty-dodger (8).
56. Saving money eagerly for those who post bills (8).

57. Disregarding gold in mixed double gin (8).
58. Teddy's family goes on ahead in the army (8).
59. Happy-go-lucky, but it's said he wasn't so well off (8).
60. Enclosed, we turn on her and hit out (8).
61. Wild pig, dressed in its own fat and old port (8).
62. Billy's mad on mountain butter (4, 4).
63. Shows consideration for ladies, but not for his date (6, 2).
64. They form part of the family accounts (9).
65. Like a measure in a volume for stargazers (9).
66. Unknown partner is a shade before time (5, 4).
67. Suitable confection for a hen-party? (5, 4).
68. A stiff examination (4, 6).
69. Dogmatic French governor, legislator and party man (10).
70. He would stick up for his employer (10).
71. Some bounder going to seed? (6-4).
72. Traitor gets pass to unfinished test centre (12).
73. Tell it, for instance, much the same (6, 6).
74. Information broadcast from all directions getting round at home (4, 8).
75. He should provide relaxation, atmosphere and true cooking (12).

Answers to Test Clues

1. NIP. Not only does the answer mean **pinch**, but, when paired with **tuck** to give 'nip and tuck', means **at a pinch**. See also the entry **ACCOMPANIST** in the main text.
2. C(A)D. The extremes of a word are often taken as the first and last letters. When they **seize**, or enfold, the letter **a**, the result means **blackguard**.
3. BAD. The answer is formed by the **starters**, or initials, of the second half of the clue; it means **rotten**.
4. ODD. Besides meaning **unmatched**, this word is hidden in the clue (fo**OD D**epartment).
5. MA(U)D. **Crazy** often implies an anagram, but not here; a synonym is MAD, which when placed **about you finally**, or about the final letter of **you** (U), gives the name of the young lady whom Tennyson asked to come **into the garden**.

6. PRAM. **Child-bearing** here means baby-carriage rather than child-birth. **Small** means abbreviation in this case, and the shortened version of perambulator gives the answer.

7. CHOW. A short snappy clue, where the solution responds to each word individually, being a breed of **dog** as well as a slang for **food**.

8. HOCK. Here again the solution can mean either half of this short clue.

9. ETUI. No drain intended here, but a seamstress, whose hold-all provides the answer.

10. RO(A)D. A **way** or ROAD is formed by the letter A with ROD, or a **land measure**, outside it.

11. G(A)IN. **Spirit** can mean any one of elf, pixie, goblin or, as here, liquor (rum and gin are popular, because they are conveniently short words). GIN, **in which there's** A, means **profit**.

12. MOOR. Almost too easy, this one. **Perhaps** can mean anagram (as can 'for instance' or 'say') but they are all more likely to mean 'is an example of . . .' Shakespeare's character is an example of a MOOR, which is **backroom**, or room written backwards.

13. (mo)SCOW. If the **doctor**, or MO, **leaves the capital** (of Russia, as it happens), a form of **boat** remains.

14. P*AGE. This is a nice one, and I wish I had thought it up. P is the letter for pianissimo or **quiet** which, when added to AGE (or **time**), gives part of the make-up of a book.

15. WALES. **Eisteddfod** should be enough to give us the **country** we are seeking, and this is confirmed by the knowledge that it is formed by the letters **starting** the words which follow.

16. GRASS. The clue is designed to make the solver think of a fruit-tree; but the **peach** we want means 'betray', for which another slang word provides the answer.

17. N*A*STY. The clue **holds** the answer, which is thus a hidden word meaning **unpleasantness.**

18. WAGES. If a comma is mentally placed after **war**, each part of this clue points to the answer.

19. NOBLE. This **pound** is not one of currency but of weight, despite appearances. ONE LB (**one pound**) is **changed**, or put into anagram, to give the name of an old coin.

20. EIGER. This is an example of the kind of somewhat naughty clue which sometimes creeps in unfairly. Five letters (or **some**) of the word **energies** are put into anagram (**misplaced**) to give the solution.

21. STERN. Place a comma mentally after **smiling**, and each part of the

clue then points independently to the solution.

22. INF*ER. An abbreviation (**not much**) for **information** is placed next to the royal cypher to give a word meaning deduce or **conclude**.

23. ANGER. Jane **Austen** wrote about Northanger Abbey. If a meaning for **direction** (north, in this case) is removed (or **lost**) the result is a **feeling**.

24. CAR(fer)RY. A **vehicle transport** here is a car ferry. If the **French** word for **iron** is removed, the result is CARRY which means **convey**.

25. RESCUE. The words **kind of** imply both anagram and synonym. In this case the anag is of **secure** and the synonym for **delivery**.

26. DO(TAR)D. The word **dodder** which has **not half** its letters is either DOD or DER; these are put round (**grabbing**) another word for **sailor**, and a process of elimination brings the answer which means **old fool**.

27. SU(PER)B. A mechanical make-up, of a word for **through** which is **getting in** a word for **U-boat** or submarine.

28. AD*HERE. The **agony column** might announce 'Place your small-ad here'; the whole means **stick**.

29. DOUANE. The cryptic part of this clue is provided by **presents one's case**, but here it concerns presenting a suit-case to the French Customs, not a court case to a judge.

30. NOT*ING. This should present no difficulty once **Beethoven's fifth** has been established as the letter H. Leaving this out of the word **nothing** provides the answer, which is a cryptic way of describing **setting music**, or composing.

31. EXCISE. Before the answer is attempted, the hyphen in this clue should be read as a dash. Each half then provides the answer separately.

32. RHODES. **Ways, they say** requires that the answer, when said aloud, should sound like **ways** or a synonym, 'roads' in this case.

33. NE*GATE. **Tyneside** is usually NE, much as 'home counties' or 'Kent' is SE. Add a synonym for **entry** to give an answer which means **deny**.

34. B*ROADS. If you got RHODES above, this one should present little problem; it is self-evident when the answer is split as shown.

35. LOSERS. A working acquaintance with proverbs and sayings is useful. Here, 'finders keepers, losers weepers' is the one which links the two young ladies in the clue, who lost respectively sheep and a pocket.

36. AR(A)GON. ARGON (**gas**) placed about A, giving a **Spanish region**.

37. SOL(A*C)E. **A number** can be any Roman single-letter figure (V, X, L, C, D or M; the last three may be clued as 'many'). Here the letters for a hundred (including the indefinite article) are **confined** in a word for **solitary**, all meaning **reassure**.

38. O*THE*RS. An **appeal** is often written as the exclamation O or OH; here it is written **by**, or next to, **the** and also (letters for) **Royal Society**. Put together, it means **not the same**.

39. ST*AMEN. A **pious man**, like a 'good man', is usually ST (being 'saint'). **The last word** can be either OMEGA or AMEN. The answer is **a bit of a bloomer** (i.e. part of a flower — which blooms).

40. S(TART)S. **Sour** can be 'acid' or, as here, TART which, when placed in letters for a boat (i.e. in a steam ship or **on board**), gives a word meaning **begins**.

41. CELLIST. Someone who inhabits a cell is a **prisoner**.

42. A*U(THOR)S. THOR was the Norse god of **thunder**; when **described** (surrounded) by a synonym for **American**, we get U(THOR)S. The clue starts with the indefinite article, and A should be put first, so that it all means **men of letters**.

43. ENGAGED. It is usually necessary to split a clue into two, and then find an answer which satisfies both parts. **Not free** suggests being sold rather than given away, or a prisoner, or restricted or occupied; **to wed** conjures up marriage, groom, church and fiancée. A question mark is often a hint from the setter that he is being devious; here it signals that the clue, in fact, means just the opposite. ENGAGED satisfies all the pointers.

44. YU(CAT)AN. Another word-split. **Whip** = CAT; **Chinese coin** = YUAN; when the latter is **out**, or outside of, the former, it all means a city **in Mexico**.

45. S(A*MP)LED. It all means **tried**. **A politician** (A*MP) is put into a SLED. Note the indefinite article is sometimes included in the answer and sometimes not.

46. SHIN*DIG. A simple joining of types of **bone** and **archaeological research** produces a synonym for **party**.

47. TO*R*RENT. TO **gets** the abbreviation for **river** and then **payment from tenant**, to form a word meaning **rush**. To be ethical, a clue should mean something as a sentence; it must be confessed that this one doesn't mean a lot.

48. SH(ALL)OP. In this case, **every customer present** requires slightly more thought that we have needed so far: 'all who are in the shop'. Put together in the way shown, the answer means **a boat**.

49. LEG*HORN. Use of the slang word **blower** in the clue implies an equally slang word in the answer, which gives us a choice between 'phone' and 'horn' or possibly use of 'buzz' or 'bell'. A **supporter** is often a 'foot' or 'leg' (or a 'fan', but not in this instance). A process of selection produces the only combination which forms a place **in Italy**.

50. UNEARTH. **Seconds** can be 'secs' or, as here, the second letters of the appropriate words. This clue needs mentally repunctuating, by deleting the comma, putting a colon after **Seconds** and a full stop before **find**. The second letters of the phrase between these stops then form the answer, meaning **find** (as a verb, not the noun implied by the clue).

51. AS*PHA(L)T. **When** = AS, followed by anag of (**forming**) **path** placed **around** L (= **pound**).

52. ARTLESS. The answer means **Simple**. **Callous** = heartless, and the usual implication of **Cockney** is to drop an initial aitch; **said** means 'sounds like', so the first 'e' goes as well (**Cockney** can also mean rhyming slang, but not in this case).

53. DI(AGRA)MS. **Setting** implies one word in another. In this clue we take DIMS for the word **obscures**; an **Indian city** (AGRA is often a safe bet) is **set** inside to produce a word meaning **figures**. Note that the hyphen should be read as a dash.

54. D*WELLING. **Many** is often a Roman letter meaning 100, 500 or 1,000 (C, D, or M). If things are **springing up** they are WELLING; when you get 500 of them, the answer means **a house**.

55. SMUGGLER. This is a good illustration of the use of pronunciation. **The French** is 'le'; **we hear** tells us that it is a question of 'sounds like . . .' Someone who is **self-satisfied** is 'smug', and this is also governed by **we hear** to give SMUGG. Put together, it means **duty-dodger**.

56. HOARDING. If a comma is mentally placed after **eagerly**, the answer responds directly to each part of the clue.

57. IGN(OR)ING. **Gold** is often either the chemical symbol AU or, as here, the heraldic OR (it can also imply an Olympic winner). The reader who has reached this far should need no explanation of **mixed double gin**.

58. BEARS*KIN. **Family** can be either KITH or KIN. **Teddy's family** is now obvious. Put together, it goes on a head (not **ahead**) in **the army**.

59. HEED*LESS. **It's said** (or 'we hear') nearly always implies pronunciation in one form or another. Use of contractions in the clue implies an

equal and opposite use of contractions in the answer. In this case, **not so well off** could be expressed as 'he had less'; this could be contracted to 'he'd less', which in turn could sound like HEED*LESS. This also means **happy-go-lucky**.

60. HER*EW*ITH. This one is built up literally through and through. **We turn** gives EW; **on her** means 'added to her' = HER*EW; **hit out** could mean place HIT outside the result, but this gives us nothing; or else add an anagram of **hit** = ITH. The word **enclosed** points towards the answer as a whole.

61. LAR(BOAR)D. **Wild pig** could either require a loose anagram of 'pig' or else be literal and mean BOAR. The comma needs to be mentally moved from after **pig** to after **fat**, so that **dressed in** = enclosed in; **its own fat** = LARD. The result is an old word for **port** (as opposed to starboard).

62. WILD GOAT. **Butter** often requires GOAT (one who butts), as opposed to margarine or fat of any kind. **Billy** is also a GOAT.

63. STANDS UP. This is more literal, but derives its cryptic meaning from interpretation of the answer rather than the clue. One who STANDS UP for ladies, gives up his seat **considerately**; if he STANDS UP **his date**, he fails to keep a tryst, and is thus not **considerate**.

64. RELATIONS. **Accounts** = narrations or RELATIONS; **family** = kith, kin or RELATIONS.

65. AS*T(ROD)OME. **A volume** is either a quantity, or a vol, a book or a tome; use of the word **measure** is designed to distract the solver towards the first of these. But this should be ignored, for we have TOME, which has ROD (a **measure**) in it, preceded by AS (**like** in the clue) to give something for **stargazers**.

66. BLIND DATE. A **shade** = BLIND (or awning), and it is placed **before** a word for **time**; the whole meaning **unknown partner**.

67. LAYER CAKE. Responds to both **confection** and **hen** (which lays).

68. POST MORTEM. This is an example of a single pointer to the solution. Given the licence of calling a dead body a **stiff**, it is a literal interpretation of the clue. It was quoted on BBC Radio 4 in February 1983 by logophile and inveterate puzzle setter Roger Squires as one of his favourite clues.

69. PERE*MP*TORY. Licence is also required here to render **French governor** as PERE by way of 'father' (for which **governor** is an archaic term). From there, addition of MP and TORY are short steps to a **dogmatic** answer.

70. BILLPOSTER. This requires two meanings for **stick up**.

71. TENNIS-BALL. **Bounder** means 'ball' as often as it means 'cad'. **Seed** refers here to tennis tournament handicapping.

72. COL*LABORATOR(y). A **pass** is often a COL; a **test centre** can be a LABORATORY which, if it is **unfinished**, loses its last letter(s), to complete the word for **traitor**.

73. LITTLE CHANGE. An example of the answer being partly a clue. **Tell it** is an **instance** of LITTLE being **changed**, or anagrammed.

74. NEWS BULLETIN. **All directions** indicates north, east, west and south (NEWS); **round** can be a BULLET; and **at home** = IN (i.e. not out). It all means **information broadcast**.

75. REST*AURA*TEUR. **Relaxation** = REST; **atmosphere** = AURA; **true cooking** = anag **true**. The whole clue also relates to the answer.

How to Use This Companion

The puzzle setter uses devious methods of saying one thing while meaning another, thereby hoping to distract the would-be solver's mind from the correct line of approach to a clue. This *Companion* uses different type-faces to encourage the reader into lateral thinking, and thus to avoid the traps with which most cryptic clues abound. The reader must usually expect to refer to a second entry, suggested either [by square brackets] as an associated idea, or else (*by italics*) as an alternative meaning with its own entry.

CAPITALS
Capitals are used for words which are either entries or answers.

BOLD CAPITALS. All main entries are in bold capital letters.

PLAIN CAPITALS. A word suitable as an answer to the entry against which it appears is in plain capital letters.

ITALIC CAPITALS. A word suitable as an answer, which is also an entry in its own right (having further possible answers with different connotations), is in italic capital letters.

SMALL CAPITALS. Answers to example clues within an explanation are printed in small capital letters. They are largely used to demonstrate clue construction, and therefore are not direct answers to the entry under which they appear.

ITALICS
Italic letters are used to show that the word concerned forms an entry elsewhere in the *Companion*, either as it stands, or else in allied form (thus *relative* appears as **RELATED** and **RELATION**, and *lovely* as **LOVE** and **LOVER**).

ITALIC CAPITALS. Since the letters are capitals, they show a possible answer to the entry against which they appear. Since they are italic, they also show that the word has an entry in its own right.

Italic lower case. Because the word is not in capital letters, it does not form a direct answer to the entry against which it appears. But its italic lettering shows that it has an entry in its own right, which could lead to a different train of thought and a possible answer.

To save space, an entry with several synonyms will only give any list under one synonym; the others will refer to it by using italics as just described or, in important cases, will tell the reader directly where to 'see' any list, or will use 'q.v.'.

BOLD LETTERING

Bold lettering is reserved for clue-words in one form or another.

BOLD CAPITALS. Bold capitals are used for main entries, which are normally words taken directly from the clue being examined.

Bold lower case. Bold lower case letters are used for example clues within an explanation. They are also used for sub-entries within an explanation, thus the entry **VICTORY** has a sub-entry **Goddesses**, giving the names of the Greek and Roman goddesses of victory.

Order and Punctuation

Different meanings of a particular entry obey no hard and fast rule as to the order in which they appear in the explanation. In broad terms, abbreviations tend to come first, and the rest follow in alphabetical order. Commas divide words of similar meaning within an explana-tion; semi-colons make a bigger difference, perhaps between nouns and verbs of the same meaning. Colons introduce a list of words: breeds of dog, characters from Shakespeare, rivers of the world etc. An equals sign shows a direct link with the preceding word(s), thus **VICTORY** has **Goddesses: Gk** = NIKE; **Rom** = VICTORIA.

A full stop signifies that the meaning changes completely, thus **BOOT** has SHOE; WELLINGTON. DISMISS, FIRE, SACK. TRUNK (US). AVAIL. Where an entry has textual as well as one-word explanations, these are differentiated by use of 1, 2, 3 etc.

( ) Round brackets enclose words which augment an explanation. When used in an answer to an example clue (which therefore has small capital letters), they reveal where a letter or letters have been inserted in the cryptic make-up of that answer, and they should be mentally dismissed when reading such a word. Thus, **All at sea, I'm in the hill** = T(IM)OR shows that the letters IM have been inserted in TOR, and it should be read as TIMOR.

[ ] Square brackets enclose words which suggest further avenues for possible investigation. The words are not answers in themselves, but are an encouragement to lateral thinking.

* An asterisk shows where a word has been split, or else letters have been removed, to form a cryptic answer. Asterisks should be mentally ignored when reading the word concerned because, like round brackets, they are purely a mechanical method of showing how an answer has been reached. Thus, **A quiet time for the attendant** = P*AGE, shows that the letter P represents **quiet**, while AGE = **time** but, when read as PAGE, the word means **attendant**.

~   A tilde signifies repetition of the entry word, or of the word immediately preceding the sign itself; identification will be evident from the sense of the text.

Registered Trade Names

Many proprietary names and trade marks have passed into the language as everyday terms. Where such words have been knowingly included in this *Companion*, they are indicated by the symbol ®. Unwitting inclusion of further unidentified trade marks does not imply that they have necessarily acquired a general significance in the legal sense; their omission is regretted, as is any wrong attribution which may have been made. Corrections will be made in subsequent reprints, if substantiated objections are made with adequate notice.

Cross-Reference

If an entry fails to satisfy, don't give up! Any word in italics has its own entry, so the reader should cross-refer. For instance, when wanting to know Red Indian tribes, the reader who looks up any one of those three words will find *AMERICAN INDIAN* (in italics); the entry **AMERICAN INDIAN** lists over 70 tribes. Equally, the entry **SHIP** gives (among others) *BOAT*; the entry **BOAT** gives 80 different types of ship or boat. *Cross-refer to words in italics.*

Abbreviations

The following abbreviations are used in this *Companion*. They are not necessarily such as may appear in clues or solutions, although inevitably some of them might do so.

A	Austria, ~n	celeb	celebrated
abbr	abbreviated	Celt	Celtic
aero	aeronautical	cent	century
Af	Africa, ~n	Ch	China, ~ese
Afghan	Afghanistan	ch	church
A-Hung	Austro-Hungary, ~ian	chem	chemical
anag	anagram	CI	Channel Islands
anon	anonymous	coaln	coalition
Arab	Arab, ~ian, ~y	coll	collector
arch	archaic; architecture	comm	commercial
Arg	Argentina, ~ian	comp	companion
A-Sax	Anglo-Saxon	Cong	Congo, ~lese
ass	assassinated	Cons	Conservative
Aus	Australia, ~n	cook	cookery, ~ing
av	aviation	crypt	cryptic
		Cz	Czechoslovakia, ~n
Bab	Babylon, ~ian		
Belg	Belgium, ~ian	d	daughter; died
bibl	biblical	Dem	Democrat
Bol	Bolivia, ~n	dial	dialect
bot	botanical	div	divorced
Br	Britain, ~ish	dn	down clue only
br	brother		
Braz	Brazil, ~ian	E	east
Bud	Buddha, ~ist	eccles	ecclesiastic, ~al
Bur	Burma, ~ese	e.g.	for example
		Egy	Egypt, ~ian
C	Cambridge	elect	electrical
Cam	Cambodia, ~n	Eng	England, ~ish
Can	Canada, ~ian	Eq	Equatorial

esp	especially	Jor	Jordan, ~ian
Eur	Europe, ~an	jun	junior
ex	dead, extinct, former		
		k	killed
f	father		
fem	female	Lab	Labour
fict	fictional	Lat	Latin
fig	figurative	leg	legal
Finn	Finland, ~nish	Lib	Liberal
Fr	France, French	lit	literal, ~ly
Gab	Gabon	m	mother of
Gam	Gambia	mar	married
G and S	Gilbert & Sullivan	math	mathematics
geog	geographical	mech	mechanical
Ger	German, ~y	med	medical
Gk	Greece, Greek	Med	Mediterranean
gram	grammatical	met	meteorological
Guy	Guyana, ~anian	Mex	Mexico, ~an
		mil	military
h	husband	Mong	Mongolia
Heb	Hebrew	Mos	Moslem
herald	heraldry	Moz	Mozambique
Hind	Hindu, ~i	Ms	manuscript
hist	historical	mus	musical
HK	Hong Kong	myth	mythology, ~ical
Hung	Hungary, ~ian		
		N	north
i.e.	that is	naut	nautical
incl	include(d), inclusive	Nig	Nigeria, ~n
Ind	India, ~n	NL	Netherlands, Dutch
int	international	Nor	Norse, Norway
IOM	Isle of Man	NT	New Testament
Ire	Ireland, Irish	NZ	New Zealand
IS	Isles of Scilly		
Is	island	O	Oxford
Isr	Israel, ~i	OE	Old English
It	Italy, ~ian	ON	Old Norse
		opp	opposite
Jap	Japan, ~ese	Ork	Orkneys
Jew	Jewish	OT	Old Testament

Pac	Pacific	sis	sister
Pak	Pakistan, ~i	sl	slang
Para	Paraguay, ~n	s/l	sounds like
para	paratroop	Som	Somalia
parl	parliament, ~ary	Sp	Spain, Spanish
Pers	Persia, ~n	sui	suicide
	Iran, ~ian	Swe	Sweden, ~ish
Phil	Philistine	Swi	Switzerland, Swiss
Phoen	Phoenicia, ~n		
photo	photography, ~ic	Tanz	Tanzania
Pl	plural	tech	technical
Pol	Poland, ~ish	theat	theatrical
polit	political	trad	traditional
Port	Portugal, ~uese	trans	translate, ~ion
print	printing	Turk	Turkey, ~ish
		TV	television
q.v.	which see		
		UK	United Kingdom
Rep	Republic, ~an	US	United States of
rh sl	rhyming slang		America
rly	railway	USSR	Soviet Russia, ~n
Rom	Roman		
Rum	Romania, ~n	Venez	Venezuela, ~n
Russ	Russia, ~n	Viet	Vietnam, ~ese
S	south	W	west
s	son	w	wife
SA	South Africa, ~n	Wal	Wales, Welsh
Sax	Saxon		
Sc	Scotland, Scottish	Y	Yugoslavia, ~n
Scand	Scandinavia, ~n		
Shak	Shakespeare	Z	Zanzibar
Sh	Shetlands	Zam	Zambia, ~n
sig	signature	Zod	Zodiac
Sing	Singapore	zool	zoological

Mini-biographies

Fact

Aaron	Esau	Nebuchadnezzar
Abraham	Galahad	Nero
Absolom	Guinevere	Paul
Alban	Herod	Peter
Antony	Hippocrates	Pilate
Archimedes	Homer	Plato
Artemisia	Horace	Pompey
Attila	Incitatus	Ptolemy
Belshazzar	Isaac	Pytheas
Boadicea	Jacob	Rehoboam
Caesar	Jehu	Ruth
Caligula	Jeroboam	Salmanazar
Cato	Jesus	Salome
Chaucer	Joab	Samson
Claudius	Joan of Arc	Samuel
Cleopatra	Joseph	Saul
Daniel	Joshua	Sheba, Queen of
David, King	Judas	Socrates
Eli	King Arthur	Solomon
Elijah	Lancelot	Terpander
Elisha	Mohammed	Xanthippe
Enoch	Moses	Xerxes

Fiction

Acheron	Aesculapius	Anubis
Achilles	Agamemnon	Aphrodite
Actaeon	Amazons	Apollo
Adonis	Amphitrite	Argonauts
Aeneas	Amphitryon	Argus
Aeolus	Andromeda	Ariadne

Artemis
Asclepius
Astarte
Atalanta
Athene
Atlas
Augeas
Aurora
Autolycus
Baal
Bacchus
Balder
Bellerophon
Cassandra
Castor
Cercyon
Charon
Chiron
Clytemnestra
Daedalus
Danae
Daphne
Demeter
Deucalion
Diana
Dido
Doris
Echo
Electra
Eris
Eurydice
Frey
Freya
Frigg
Galatea
Ganymede
Grundy, Solomon
Hades
Hebe
Hecate
Hector

Hecuba
Hel
Helen
Helios
Helle
Hera
Hercules
Hermes
Hero
Hiawatha
Hippolyte
Holmes, Sherlock
Hyperion
Icarus
Isis
Janus
Jason
Job
Juno
Jupiter
Kali
Leander
Leda
Loki
Maia
Mars
Medea
Medusa
Mercury
Methuselah
Midas
Minerva
Minos
Minotaur
Narcissus
Neptune
Nereus
Nimrod
Niobe
Noah
Nyx

Oceanus
Odin
Oedipus
Orcus
Orestes
Orion
Orpheus
Osiris
Pallas
Pandora
Paris
Penelope
Periphites
Persephone
Perseus
Phaeton
Pluto
Poseidon
Priam
Procrustes
Prometheus
Psyche
Pygmalion
Python
Remus
Rhea
Romulus
Saturn
Sciron
Selene
Sisyphus
Tantalus
Terpsichore
Theseus
Thor
Typhon
Ulysses
Uranids
Uranus
Woden
Zeus

Authors' works

Andersen, Hans
Austen, Jane
Brontës, the
Chaucer, Geoffrey
Cicero
Conan Doyle, Sir
  Arthur
Dickens, Charles
Gilbert, W. S.
  (G & S)
Grahame, Kenneth

Haggard, Rider
Homer
Hope, Sir Anthony
Horace
Kipling, Rudyard
Lear, Edward
Lofting, Hugh
Milne, A. A.
Orwell, George
Potter, Beatrix
Scott, Sir Walter

Shakespeare,
  William
Shaw, G. B.
Stevenson, R. L.
Sullivan, see
  Gilbert
Swift, Jonathan
Tacitus
Twain, Mark
Wilde, Oscar
Wodehouse, P. G.

Heading Lists

African tribes
Aircraft
Airlines
Airports
Alice in Wonderland characters
American Indians
Andersen, Hans
Anniversaries
Antelopes
Apples
Architectural terms
Argonauts
Assemblies, nouns of
Austen, Jane, books
Aversions
Awards (theat)
Ballet terms, companies
Ball games
Bath deaths etc.
Battles, air, land, sea
Bears
Beetles
Bell-ringing, changes
Bells
Biblical towns
Big game
Birds
Birthstones
Board games
Boat types
Bones of the body
Bottle sizes
Brontës, the, books
Butterflies, see Lepidoptera
Capital cities

Captains (fict)
Card games
Car plates (countries)
Carriages
Cartoonists
Castles in the UK
Cathedrals in the UK
Cats
Cattle
Ceramics
Chairs, see Furniture
Chaucer characters
Cheeses
Chemical elements
Chiltern Hundreds
Chinese calendar
Chinese dynasties
Church dress
Churchmen
Cigarette brands
Circuses
Clerks
Clocks, see Furniture
Clowns, see Jesters
Clubs, London
Coins
Collectors
Colonels (fict)
Colours
Comics
Commonwealth countries
Composers
Companies, City livery
Companions, celebrated
Constellations

Counties, see Divisions
Country houses (fict)
Cricket grounds
Currencies
Dances
Deer
Deserts
Desks, see Furniture
Detectives
Dickens characters
Dinosaurs
Discoveries
Dive positions
Dive types
Divisions of the UK
Doctors, celebrated
Dog breeds
Drinks
Ducks
Dwarfs
Eagles
Ear parts
Emperors
Empresses
Epicureans
Episcopal signatures
Explorers
Eye parts and disorders
Fairies
Fates
Fishes
Five towns
Flowers
Football teams and grounds
Forests
French Revolutionary calendar
Friars
Fruit
Furniture terms
Gaols
Games, indoors
Games, outdoors

Gates of London
Gems
Ghosts
Gilbert & Sullivan, see G and S
Gods
Goddesses
Governesses
Grahame, Kenneth, characters
Grasses
Guards (mil)
Gulfs
Habitations
Haggard, Rider, books
Hats
Heraldic terms
Herbs
Hercules' labours
Holmes, Sherlock, cases
Horses
Hunchbacks
Indian provinces
Insects
Instruments (mus)
International units
Inventions
Islands of the UK
Japanese words
Jesters/clowns
Jews
Kings, biblical
Kings, fict
Kings, early Eur
Kipling, Rudyard, books
Knighthood, orders of
Knots
Lakes, principal
Landladies (fict)
Landlords (fict)
Law practitioners (fict)
Lear, Edward, books
Legislative assemblies
Lemurs

Lepidoptera
Liqueurs
'Little' people (fict)
Lizards
Lovers, celebrated
Lovers of . . . (-ophiles)
Maids (fict)
Majors (fict)
Male and female animals
Many-armed, -eyed, -headed, -legged
Markets (London)
Materials
Measures
Metals
Military leaders
Milne, A. A., characters
Minerals
Mister (forms of address)
Models for fict characters (places)
Monarchies of the world
Monarchs of Eng/UK
Monkeys
Monsters
Moths, see Lepidoptera
Muses
Musical instruments, see Instruments (mus)
Music terms
Nicknames
Nine angelic orders
Nine worthies
Nobles
Numbers, specific
Nurses, celebrated
Obsessions
Offspring
One-armed, -eyed, -legged
Organ parts (mus)
Orwell characters

Outlaws
Owls
Oxen
Painters
Palaces
Palms
Parasites
Parrots
Parsons (fict)
Patron saints
Pears
Philosophers
Pigs
Pirates
Planets
Plants
Poets
Potter, Beatrix, books
Presidents of the USA
Prime Ministers of the UK
Prisoners
Prophets
Provinces of Canada
Public schools
Q without U, words
Rabbits
Racetracks, horses
Racetracks, motor cars
Reactors
Red Indians, see American ~
Reference books
Religion
Rhyming slang
Rivers of the world
Robbers, celebrated
Roman place names, UK
Roman roads in England
Round table knights
Royal families
Rugby grounds
Sailors

Sails
Salmon
Satirists
Schoolmasters
Schools (fict)
Scott, Sir Walter, books
Seas
Seaweeds
Secret police
Servants (fict)
Seven ages of man
Seven deadly sins
Seven hills
Seven sages
Seven seas
Seven wonders of the world
Shakespeare characters
Shakespeare plays
Sharks
Shaw, G. B., plays
Sheep
Shells (zool)
Shoes
Slaves
Snakes
Soldiers
Songs
Spacecraft
Space travellers
Spices
Spirits (drink)
Sports, outdoor (ball)
Sports, water
Sports, winter
Stately homes
States of the USA
Stevenson, R. L., books
Stoics
Straits of the world
Street markets
Study of . . . (-ology)

Swift, Jonathan, books
Swiss cantons
Tables, see Furniture
Tarot cards
Taverns (fict)
Teeth, see Bones
Tempi (mus)
Ten commandments
Tennis venues
Thames bridges
Theatres
Titans
Trees
Tribes (Roman Britain)
Tribes (World)
Twins, celebrated
Typefaces
Underworlds
Unions, initials
Universities
Unseen characters (fict)
Vegetables
Violin parts
Waterfalls
Weapons
Weights in boxing
Whales
Wild plants/weeds
Windows
Winds, local, celebrated
Winds, Gk and Rom
Wines
Winter sports
Wodehouse, P. G., books
Woodpeckers
World girdlers
Writers
Zodiac, signs of

This represents over 300 lists
with a total number of interpretations which exceeds 15,000.

The Companion
A - Z

A (s/l *eh*). *ABOUT*. ACROSS. ADULTS ONLY, ADVISORY, PARENTAL GUIDANCE (film *censorship*). ALPHA. AREA. ARGON (*chem*). AUSTRIA (*car plate*). Austria, ~n. *BEST*. *KEY*; *NOTE*.

AA ALCOHOLICS ANONYMOUS. ANTI-AIRCRAFT; FLAK. AUTOMOBILE ASSOCIATION; CAR CLUB. *MILNE*. FILM *CENSORSHIP*. *LAVA*.

AARON Bibl br of *Moses*, his rod (with that of *Moses*) was transformed into a *serpent* when cast down before *Pharaoh*; it later sprouted to bear almonds. ~d on Mt Horeb.

AB *SAILOR*. BACKWARD SCHOLAR (crypt). Heb month.

ABACK 1. BACKWARDS, BEHIND. DISCONCERTED, SURPRISED. MOUNTED, RIDER. 2. Word/answer reversed, e.g. **Little Trevor's taken aback and green** (4) = VERT.

ABBEY MONASTIC BUILDING; **celeb**: BATTLE, BUCKFAST, FOUNTAINS, FURNESS, GLASTONBURY, KIRKSTALL, MELROSE, ROMSEY, TINTERN, TITCHFIELD; [Abbess, Abbot]. NORTHANGER (*Austen*).

ABC ALPHABET [Reading]. RATING. *BROADCASTING* (*Aus*; *US*). *REFERENCE WORK* (rly).

ABCDEFGHIJKLM A*TO*M (crypt).

ABEL (s/l *able*). s of *Adam*; *Adamson*, FIRST VICTIM, THIRD PERSON; [Garden of Eden; murder]. **Comp** = *Cain*. Bibl town.

ABERDEEN *UNIVERSITY*. **Episcopal sig** = ABERDON. [Granite]. THE DONS (*football*).

ABERDON *Episcopal sig* of ABERDEEN.

ABET AID, *ASSIST*, EGG, ENCOURAGE, URGE; (**opp** = hinder). A*WAGER (crypt).

ABIGAIL 1. MAID (The Scornful Lady, Beaumont and Fletcher). 'FATHER'S DELIGHT'. 2. Brought food to *David* who later mar her.

ABLE (s/l *abel*). ADROIT, CLEVER, SKILLED (**opp** = inept).

ABOARD ON BOARD, SHIPPED; hence put S*S round, e.g. **Very French aboard leads to an accent** (6) = S*TRES*S. A*PLANK (crypt).

ABOMINABLE SNOWMAN *MONSTER* (Himalayan), YETI; BIG-FOOT (Can; US); BUNYIP (Aus); SASQUATCH (US); YAMINSKAY (S Andes).

ABOUT 1. A, C, CA, RE. ON, NEAR, *ROUND*, TURN. A*FIGHT (crypt). 2. Reverse word. 3. Put word round another, e.g. **It's about the backward writer, and incompetent** (5) = I*NEP*T.

ABRAHAM Bibl founder of the Jewish nation, f of *Isaac* whom God reprieved from sacrifice. Also known to Mahommedans, who believe he was cast into fire which turned into a bed of *roses*.

ABROAD 1. FOREIGN. OUTDOORS; WIDELY. 2. Translate, e.g. **I'm abroad** = JE or ICH etc.

ABSOLOM 1. Bibl s of *David*, who rebelled against his f; fled from battle of Wood of Ephraim on an ass or mule, but became *entangled* in an oak tree by his *hair* and k (against orders) by *Joab*. 2. Duke of Monmouth in Dryden's satire '~ and Achitophel' (Lord Shaftesbury).

ABSORB ENGROSS. BLOT, MOP UP (**Dn** = POM), SOAK.

ABSTAINER *AA*, *TT*. MUSLIM; RECHABITE; [drink, *pussyfoot*, Johnson, *Turner*].

ABSTRACT ABSTRUSE, IDEALISTIC (**comps** = animal, *vegetable*, *mineral*). DEDUCT, DISENGAGE, REMOVE, SEPARATE; SUMMARY; [legal evidence].

AC *ACCOUNT*, ~ANT, BILL, *SETTLEMENT*. ACROSS. ACTINIUM (chem). AIRMAN. ALTERNATING CURRENT, hence CURRENCY (crypt); **Comp** = DC.

ACCENT PRONUNCIATION; STRESS. Such a mark: ACUTE (´), *BREVE* (˘), *CEDILLA* (¸), *CIRCUMFLEX* (ˆ), *DIAERESIS* (¨), *GRAVE* (`), *MACRON* (¯), *TILDE* (~), UMLAUT (¨).

ACCEPTABLE U. PLEASING, TOLERABLE, WELCOME.

ACCOMPANIST 1. APPENDAGE, ESCORT, SUPPORTER (**opp** = loner). 2. Word which often goes with another, e.g. **Bill's accompanist** (3) = COO.

ACCOUNT AC. NARRATIVE, *REPORT*, STATEMENT, STORY. CONSIDER, ESTIMATE; PROFIT, REGARD, RECKONING. ALLOW, JUSTIFY. [money].

ACCOUNTANT CA, FCA. CASHIER. AUTHOR, *REPORTER*, STORY-TELLER, *WRITER*; [Scheherazade].

ACCUMULATOR *COLLECTOR*, GATHERER. *BET*. *BATTERY*, *CELL* (elect). COMPUTER, *MEMORY*, RETRIEVAL *BANK*.

ACE I, MONAD, ONE. BEST, CHAMPION, EXPERT, TOP.

CARD, ONE CARD. SERVICE (*tennis*).

ACELDAMA BLOODSHED, SLAUGHTER (bibl).

ACHERON Gk myth s of *Ceres*. He was changed into a river across which (with the *Styx*) *Charon* ferried the souls of the dead.

ACHILLES Gk myth s of Peleus and Thetis. Invulnerable except in his heel, where he was killed in the war of *Troy* by an arrow shot by *Paris*. His *horse* was *Xanthus* (*Shak*, T and C).

ACID BITING, SEVERE, SHARP, SOUR; [PH, silica] (**opp** = alkali). *DRUG*, LSD (sl).

ACOLITE (s/l *acolyte*). BRIDGE PLAYER (crypt).

ACOLYTE (s/l *acolite*). ATTENDANT (eccles), BEGINNER, *CHURCHMAN*.

ACT *DEED*, OPERATION; BEHAVE, PERFORM, PORTRAY. LAW.

ACTAEON Gk myth hunter trained by *Chiron*. He spied on *Artemis* (**Rom** = *Diana*) bathing, and was *transformed* into a *stag* which was killed by his own dogs.

ACTION ACT, *DEED*, EVENT, EXERTION (**opp** = inertia). ENGAGEMENT, FIGHTING, OPERATIONS (mil). CASE, LEGAL PROCESS, SUIT. MECHANISM, WORKS. INACTION, STRIKE.

ACTOR PERFORMER, PLAYER, THESPIAN; OLIVIER, IRVING, TREE etc. [*stage*].

ACUTE CRITICAL. KEEN, POINTED, SHARP (**opp** = blunt). HIGH, SHRILL. *ACCENT*.

AD (s/l *add*). ANNO DOMINI, NOWADAYS, YEAR . . . ADVERT (~ISEMENT), HOARDING, NOTICE, POSTER. TO.

ADAM FIRST FALLER, FIRST PERSON, FIRST GARDENER; **comp** = *Eve* [Eden]. A*BARRIER; A*MARE (crypt). *ARCHITECT*, CABINET MAKER [Fireplace]. COMPOSER (Giselle; *mad*). *ISLAND*. SERVANT (*Shak*).

ADAMSON ABEL, CAIN, SETH (crypt).

ADD (s/l *ad*). SUM, TOT, TOTAL (**opp** = subtract). INCLUDE.

ADDER *SNAKE*, VIPER [*Wyvern*]. CALCULATOR, COUNTER, TELLER; *SUMMER* (crypt).

ADDITIONALLY ADDED, SUPPLEMENTARY. Add to word.

ADDRESS HOME. POISE, PRESENCE (**opp** = gaucherie). SPEAK TO, SPEECH, AIM AT, APPLY.

ADD UP CALCULATE, COMPUTE, SUM, TOTAL, TOT UP. MAKE SENSE. DDA (dn).

ADJUST *Anag.* ADAPT, ARRANGE, *ORDER*.

ADMIT CONCEDE, CONFESS, OWN (**opp** = deny). ALLOW, LET IN.

ADMIX ADD, MINGLE, STIR IN. YEAR 1009 (crypt — Lat).

ADONIS 1. PHEASANT'S EYE (*flower*). 2. Gk myth handsome youth loved by *Aphrodite* (**Rom** = Venus). After he was killed by a boar, he was allowed by the Gods to spend half of each year with her. The *flower* anemone sprang from his blood in the earth. [Good looks].

ADORN BEDECK, *DECK*, ORNAMENT.

ADRIFT *Anag* (e.g. **Gone adrift** = NEGO, ONGE etc).
ILL-INFORMED, OUT OF ORDER, OUT OF TOUCH.
DRIFTING, UNFASTENED [flotsam, jetsam, lagan].

ADVANCE GO FORWARD, GO ON (**opp** = retreat). FLOAT, LEND, LOAN, PAY ON ACCOUNT, RAISE A LOAN.
PROMOTE, PROGRESS.

ADVERTISEMENT AD, PR. ANNOUNCEMENT, *NOTICE*, PUBLICITY.

AEGIS 1. COVER, DEFENCE, PROTECTION. 2. The shield of *Athene* and *Zeus*.

AENEAS Rom hero of *Troy*; founder of the Roman state.
Companion = Achates. (*Shak*, T and C). Loved in vain by *Dido*.

AEOLUS Gk myth king of Aeolia, god of the *winds*, which he kept shut up in a *cave* [harp, *instrument* (mus)].

AESCULAPIUS Rom equivalent of *ASCLEPIUS* (Gk), *god* of medicine [*Hippocrates*].

AESIR Chief Nor gods, dwelt in Asgard.

Af Africa.

A FRENCH UN, UNE.

AFRESH *Anag.* ANEW.

AFRICAN ASHANTI, BANTU, BERBER, BOER, HOTTENTOT, IBO, KIKUYU, MASAI, MOOR [Othello], TAUREG, XHOSA, ZOUAVE, ZULU etc. [*tribe*].

AFRICUS Rom myth SW *WIND* (**Gk** = LIPS).

AFTERTHOUGHT PS. ADDED; CODICIL. LATER CHILD.

AG *SILVER* (chem). LIMITED COMPANY (Ger).

AGAIN *Anag.* BESIDES, FURTHER, ONCE MORE, RE-.
A*PROFIT (crypt).

AGAINST V, VS, VERSUS. ANTI, *CON* (**opp** = for, *pro*).

AGAMEMNON Gk myth hero, who led the Greeks to *Troy*.
Quarrelled with *Achilles* over slave-girl Briseis. Killed in his *bath*

by his unfaithful wife *Clytemnestra* on his return to Argos. Father of
Electra. (*Shak*, T and C).

AGATE *GEM*, SEMI-PRECIOUS *STONE*, *CHALCEDONY*:
CORNELIAN, ONYX, SCOTCH PEBBLE; *Birthstone* (June).
MARBLE, TAW. *WRITER*. *TYPEFACE* (US). A*BARRIER,
AN*ENTRANCE, AN*OPENING, A*MOUTH (crypt).

AGE GET ON, GROW OLD. [Picture of Dorian Gray (Wilde)].
PERIOD (in hist order): *STONE*, EOLITHIC, PALAEOLITHIC,
MESOLITHIC, NEOLITHIC, *COPPER*, *BRONZE*, *IRON*. **Pl** =
Seven ~s (*Shak*).

AGENT FACTOR. A*GENTLEMAN (crypt). MOLE, SPY;
celebrated (fact): NURSE EDITH CAVELL, ODETTE
CHURCHILL, MATA HARI, VIOLETTE SZABO; (fiction):
DICK BARTON, JAMES BOND, BULLDOG DRUMMOND,
THE SAINT, SMILEY, SIMON TEMPLAR.

A GERMAN EIN, EINE.

AGORAPHOBIA *Aversion* to open places.

AGREE CONCUR, CONFORM, CONSENT, GET ON (**opp** =
dissent). AT*ONE (crypt).

AHAB *SAILOR*, *WHALER* (Moby Dick, Herman Melville; *ship* =
Pequod). Bibl *king* who mar Jezebel.

AHEAD ON. IN FRONT (**opp** = behind). A*HEAD (crypt).

AHEM COUGH, HESITATION. A*BORDER (crypt).

AI BEST, FIRST CLASS [*Lloyds*]. 3-TOED *SLOTH* (S Am). *Bibl
town*.

AIM DESIGN, END, GOAL, INTENT, OBJECT, TARGET;
DIRECT, POINT.

AIRBORNE FLYING (**opp** = *grounded*). PARA, RED BERET,
RED DEVIL, SAS. [AWACS; Huma, myth bird which never
lands].

AIRCRAFT FLYING MACHINE: AEROPLANE, AIRPLANE
(US), AIRSHIP, BALLOON, GLIDER, HANG-GLIDER,
HOVERCRAFT, MICRO-LIGHT, UFO.

Celeb (fighters)®:

BEAUFIGHTER (UK)	HELLCAT (US)
BUCCANEER (UK)	*HUNTER* (UK)
CAMEL (UK)	*HURRICANE* (UK)
CORSAIR (US)	*LIGHTNING* (UK)
HARRIER (UK)	MIG (USSR)
HAWK (UK)	*MOSQUITO* (UK)

MUSTANG (UK/US)	SPITFIRE (UK)
PHANTOM (UK/US)	*TEMPEST* (UK)
PUP (UK)	*THUNDERBOLT* (US)
SABRE (UK/US)	*TYPHOON* (UK)

Celeb (bombers)®:

AVENGER (US)	*LINCOLN* (UK)
BADGER (USSR)	*MOSQUITO* (UK)
BEAR (USSR)	STIRLING (UK)
BOSTON (UK/US)	SUPERFORTRESS (US)
FLYING FORTRESS (US)	VALIANT (UK)
GOTHA (Ger)	VICTOR (UK)
HALIFAX (UK)	*VULCAN* (UK)
HUSTLER (US)	*WELLINGTON* (UK)
LANCASTER (UK)	WHITLEY (UK)
LIBERATOR (UK/US)	

AIRFIELD AERODROME, *AIRPORT*.

AIRLINE BREATHING TUBE, TRACHEA, WINDPIPE (all crypt). AIR SERVICE, CIVIL AIR-CARRIER; **celeb** (all ®): AEROFLOT (USSR), *BA* (UK), BEA (ex-UK), BOAC (ex-UK), CAC (Ch), EL AL (Isr), IBERIA (Sp), KLM (NL), *LOT* (Pol), PAN-AM (US), QANTAS (Aus), SABENA (Belg), *SAS* (Scand), *TAP* (Port), TWA (US).

AIRMAN AC, FO, PO. BALLOONIST, FLYER, *PILOT*. *DAEDALUS*, *ICARUS* (myth). BARITONE, *BASS*, BUGLER, FLAUTIST, OBOIST, ORGANIST, *SINGER*, TENOR, TRUMPETER (crypt). SHOW-OFF, SWANKER.

AIRPORT NOSTRIL, MOUTH (crypt). AERODROME, AIRFIELD; **celebrated**:

Aberdeen, DYCE; **Amsterdam**, SCHIP(H)OL; **Ayr**, PRESTWICK; **Azores**, SANTA MARIA; **Berlin**, SCHONEFELD, TEGEL, TEMPELHOF; **Birmingham**, ELMDON; **Blackpool**, SQUIRES GATE; **Boston**, LOGAN; **Bournemouth**, HURN; **Buenos Aires**, EZEIZA, JORGE NEWBERY; **Cardiff**, RHOOSE; **Chicago**, O'HARE; **Copenhagen**, KASTRUP; **Corfu**, KERKYRA; **Dallas**, FORT WORTH; **Frankfurt**, RHEIN MAIN; **Fiji**, NADI; **Geneva**, COINTRIN; **Hamburg**, FUHLSBUTTEL; **Hong Kong**, KAI TAK; **Isle of Man**, RONALDSWAY; **Leeds**, YEADON; **Limerick**, SHANNON; **Liverpool**, SPEKE; **London**, CROYDON (ex), GATWICK, HEATHROW, HOUNSLOW (ex), MAPLIN, NORTHOLT, STANSTED; **Lydd**, FERRYFIELD; **Malta**, VALETTA; **Marseilles**, MARIGNANE; **Melbourne**, TULLAMARINE; **Middlesbrough**, TEES-SIDE; **Minneapolis**, ST PAUL; **Montreal**, DORVAL, MIRABEL; **Moscow**, BYKOVO, DOMODEDOVO, SHEREMETYEVO, VNUKOVO; **New York**, IDLEWILD, JFK, KENNEDY, LA GUARDIA; **Oslo**, FORNEBU; **Paris**, DE GAULLE, LE BOURGET, ORLY, ROISSY; **Peking**, BEIJING; **Rio de Janeiro**, SANTOS DUMONT; **Rome**, CIAMPINO, FIUMICINO, LEONARDO DA VINCI; **Rotterdam**, WAALHAVEN; **Saigon**, TAN-SON-NHUT; **Seattle**, TACOMA; **Southampton**, EASTLEIGH; **Stockholm**, ARLANDA, BROMMA; **Sydney**, KINGSFORD SMITH; **Tel Aviv**, LOD; **Tokyo**, NARITA; **Washington**, DULLES.

AL ALUMINIUM (chem). CAPONE, GANGSTER. ALBERT, ALEC (abbr). ALABAMA (US *state*). ALBANIA (*car plate*). ALBERTA (*province*, Can).

ALAS PITY! WOE! (Yorick, Hamlet, *Shak*). ALASKA (US *state*).

ALBAN 1. Roman soldier who was first Christian martyr in Britain, AD 304; canonized. 2. *Episcopal sig* of ST ALBANS.

ALBATROSS *BIRD*, PETREL [Ill-omen]. Three under *par* on *golf course*.

ALECTO One of the *FURIES*.

ALEXANDER BEETLE (*A. A. Milne*). THE GREAT (Bucephalus, horse). FIELD MARSHAL. *MILITARY LEADER*. [Antipater (Macedonia); *battles*].

ALGOPHILE *Lover* of pain.

ALGOPHOBIA *Aversion* to pain.

ALIAS OTHERWISE. NOM DE PLUME, PEN NAME.

ALIBI ELSEWHERE (**opp** = ibid). EXCUSE [crime].

ALICE 1. Girl's name, especially character by Lewis Carroll (Rev Charles Lutwidge Dodgson) in '~ in Wonderland'; drawings by John Tenniel; **other characters**: Dinah the *cat*, the White *Rabbit*, Bill the *lizard* (curiouser and curiouser!); Dodo, *Dory, Duck*, Eaglet, Mouse (Caucus-race); Caterpillar (hookah, mushroom, Father William); Dormouse, Mad Hatter, March Hare (tea-party); King, Queen and Knave of *Hearts*, 1–10 of *Hearts* (children), 2, 5 and 7 of *Spades* (*gardeners*), courtiers (*Diamonds*), *soldiers* (*Clubs*), Duchess, Cheshire *Cat* (vanished but for its smile), hedgehogs, flamingos and soldiers (respectively, croquet balls, mallets and hoops; 'off with his head'); Mock Turtle, Gryphon (arithmetic: ambition, distraction, uglification, derision; mystery ancient and modern; sea-ography; drawling, stretching and fainting in coils; laughing and grief; lobster quadrille, porpoise, snail, whiting). Also 'Through the Looking-Glass (and what Alice Found There)'; **other characters**: Red and White Kings, Queens and Knights; Dinah the *cat*; Tiger-Lily; Jabberwock, Tove, Borogrove, Mome Rath, Jubjub Bird, Bandersnatch, Tumtum Tree, Vorpal Sword, Tulgey Wood; Tweedledum, Tweedledee, Humpty Dumpty; Gnat, Goat, *Beetle*, Rocking-horse fly, *Walrus*, *Carpenter*, *Oysters*, *Lion*, Unicorn; Haigha, Hatta (*messengers*). *Model* = Alice Liddell. 2. *Nanny* of Christopher Robin (*Milne*), *modelled* on Olive Brockwell.

ALIGNMENT DRESSING, *ROW*.

ALIVE ACTIVE, BRISK, RESPONSIVE; SWITCHED ON, WORKING, LIVING, QUICK (**opp** = *dead*).

ALKALINITY PH (**opp** = acidity).

ALL 1. (s/l *awl*). WHOLE, WHOLLY (**opp** = none). BOTH SIDES, EACH, EVERYBODY. *SUM*, TOTAL (**opp** = *part*). ENTIRELY, QUITE. *HUNDRED*, C (crypt); A*FIFTY*FIFTY (crypt, hence A HALF). 2. Start antonym with O, e.g. **All female sign** (4) = OMEN.

ALLOCATED *Anag*. ALLOTTED, ASSIGNED, DEVOTED, PUT IN PLACE; APPORTIONED.

ALLIGATOR *CROCODILE* (q.v.) [~ pear; avocado]. CLIP, GRIP (mech).

ALLOW ADMIT, CONCEDE (**opp** = deny). *LET*, PERMIT, TOLERATE (**opp** = *refuse*). ASSERT, CONSIDER. ADVANCE, GIVE.

ALLOY *Anag*. DEBASE, MIX, MODERATE.

ALMOND BIRD, PIGEON, TUMBLER. COLOUR (yellow/brown). TREE; KERNEL, NUT. NARROW, OVAL SHAPED [~ eyed (Ch, Jap); *Aaron's* rod; dragee; marchpane, marzipan; tipsy cake].

ALMOST 1. NEARLY, NIGH. 2. Word less one or two letters, e.g. **Almost dinner on target** (5) = *INNER.

ALONE 1. EXCLUSIVELY, ONLY. APART, NOT WITH OTHERS, SOLO. 2. 'One is one and all alone' in *song*.

ALPH 1. Sacred Gk *river*. 2. First half of alphabet, i.e. A*TO*M.

ALPHA A, FIRST, GOOD. CHIEF STAR.

ALSO-RAN FAILURE, UNPLACED (**opp** = *first*, winner).

ALTERNATING *Anag.* CHOICE, OR. DEPUTY, SUBSTITUTE; INTERCHANGING.

~ **CURRENT** AC.

ALUMINIUM *AL* (*chem*). LIGHT *ALLOY*, *METAL*.

ALWAYS EER, EVER, REPEATEDLY (**opp** = *never*). NESW or any *anag* (crypt).

AM AMERICUM (*chem*). Amplitude modulation (radio). ANTE MERIDIEM, MORNING. I EXIST. FIRST AID MAN (crypt).

A—M A*TO*M (crypt); hence *ALPH* (crypt).

AMAZON 1. WARRIOR (fem); masculine woman (butch). 2. Legendary female warrior tribe of S Am, said to have removed the right breast to aid drawing their bows. 3. In Gk myth, race of fem warriors, the d's of *Ares*, living in Scythia; **queens**: *Hippolyte* (sis to Antiope), Penthesilea (*Troy*); Philostrate (MND, *Shak*). 4. *River* of S Am. PARROT.

AMERICAN INDIAN BRAVE, REDSKIN, TRIBESMAN (**opp** = paleface); HIAWATHA, MINIHAHA (Longfellow); INJUN JOE (*Twain*); POCAHONTAS [squaw, kloo(t)ch, teepee, wigwam]; **celeb**:

3-letters
FOX (N)
WEA (N)

4-letters
CREE (N)
CROW (N)
ERIE (N)
HOPI (N)
INCA (S)
MAYA (S)
TUPI (S)
ZUNI (N)

5-letters
ADENA (N)
AZTEC (S)
CREEK (N)
HAIDA (N)
HURON (N)
MIAMI (N)

NAZCA (S)
OLMEC (Mex)
OMAHA (N)
OSAGE (N)
PONCA (N)
SIOUX (N)
YAQUI (N)

6-letters
APACHE (N)
APINAI (S)
ATOARA (S)
CAYUGA (N)[6]
DAKOTA (N)
KAYOPO (S)
LENAPE (N)
MICMAC (N)
MOHAVE (N)
MOHAWK (N)[6]
MOJAVE (N)
NOOTKA (N)

ONEIDA (N)[6]
OTTAWA (N)
PANARE (S)
PAWNEE (N)
SENECA (N)[6]
SIWASH (N)
TOLTEC (N)
TUPIAN (S)

7-letters
ARAPAHO(E) (N)
ARAUCAN (S)
CATAWBA (N)
CHIBCHA (S)
CHOCTAW (N)
FUEGIAN (S)
MOHICAN (N)
OJIBWAY (N)
QUECHUA (S)
SHAWNEE (N)
TLINGIT (N)

WAIMIRI (S)
WYANDOT (N)
ZAPOTEC (S)

8-letters
ARAPAHO(E) (N)
ARIKAREE (N)
CHEROKEE (N)
CHEYENNE (N)
CHIBCHAN (S)
CHIPPEWA (N)

COMANCHE (N)
DELAWARE (N)
IROQUOIS (N)
MESQUITO (S)
ONONDAGA (N)[6]
PUEBLOAN (N)
QUICHUAN (S)
SEMINOLE (N)
SHOSHONE (N)
SIHASAPA (N)
SILKSIKA (N)

9+ letters
ALACALUFAN (S)
ALGONQUIAN (N)
ATHABASCAN (N)
BLACKFOOT (N)
CHICKASAW (N)
GUARANIAN (S)
HOOCHINOO (N)
MICCOSUKEE (N)
PATAGONIAN (S)
PUELCHEAN (S)
TUSCARORA (N)[6]

[6] = One of the Confederation of Six Nations.

AMETHYST *GEM*, PRECIOUS STONE; *Birthstone* (February).
  COLOUR (purple).

AMISS *Anag.* INAPPROPRIATE, OFFENCE, WRONG.
  A*GIRL, A*SPINSTER (crypt).

AMONG AMID, AMIDST. Hidden word.

AMOR = *CUPID*, Rom *god* of *LOVE*; (**Gk** = EROS).

AMP AMPERE (elect). A member (crypt).

AMPHITRITE Gk myth *Nereid* or Oceanid, goddess of the sea. The
  d of *Nereus*, mar to *Poseidon*, she was m of Triton.

AMPHITRYON In order to seduce ~'s wife Alcmena, *Zeus* gave a
  party in ~'s house in his absence. ~ returned home and claimed to
  be the *host* but, as Molière put it, he who gives the party is
  reckoned to be the host (the other is presumably the *servant*). In
  Gk myth, Alcmena subsequently gave birth to *Heracles*.

AN Article. IF (arch).

ANAESTHETIC *Drug*, DULLER, GAS, NEEDLE; NUMBER
  (crypt). [hospital, operation].

Anag ANAGRAM. ADJUST, ARRANGE, *ORDER*,
  RE-ORDER. About ten per cent of all clues are capable of being
  interpreted as intending an anagram. To give just a few examples
  from the first letter of the alphabet, of words which can be so
  interpreted: adrift, afresh, allocated, alloy, altered, alternate,
  amiss, angled, annoyed, anyway, arranged, awful, awkward. All
  those can be construed in another way (both 'construed' and 'in
  another way' are also candidates). In this *Companion*, the word
  'anagram' is taken to mean any re-ordering of letters, even if they
  do not in themselves make a word — they may form only part of

the final word. So, if a clue is troublesome, try looking for an anagram somewhere — and the word or words giving the letters may not necessarily be actually in the clue. Thus: **I cut a deep ditch arranged for defensive purposes** (9) gives: **I cut a moat** (anag) = AUTOMATIC. The anagram indicator may appear in the answer, i.e. **Ham for cat** = ACT BADLY.

ANAPAEST *FOOT*.

ANATOLE *FRANCE*.

ANDERSEN Hans Christian ∼, Danish writer; **stories**: Emperor's New Clothes (*Nude*); Inchelina (Maja); Little Mermaid; *Nightingale* (clockwork); Princess and the Pea (*bed*); Red Shoes (*dancing*); Snowman (stove); Snow Queen; Tinderbox (*dogs*); Tin Soldier (ballerina, steadfast); Ugly Duckling (*swan*); Wild Swans (Elisa).

AND NOT 1. NOR. 2. Add NOT before or after word, e.g. **Cold and not remarked** (7) = NOT*ICED.

ANDREW *PATRON SAINT* (Sc) [Apostle, Fisherman, 30 Nov]. SWORD.

ANDROMEDA 1. Gk myth heroine who was chained to a rock as sacrifice to a *monster* sent by the *Nereids*, who were angry at her beauty. *Perseus* turned the monster to stone by exhibiting the head of *Medusa*, and he then married Andromeda. 2. A *constellation* in N hemisphere.

ANGEL *BACKER* (theat). *CAKE. COIN.* CHERUB, SAINT, ST. ITHURIEL (Paradise Lost, Milton). [*Nine* angelic orders]. *SHARK. WATERFALL.* **Pl** = HEIGHT (RAF sl).

ANGER DISPLEASURE, DISTEMPER, ENRAGE, HEAT, *INCENSE*, IRE, RILE, *TEMPER*, WRATH (**opp** = pleasure).

ANGLE ARRANGE, CONTRIVE. ASPECT, *BEARING*, POINT OF VIEW. *FISH. TRIBESMAN* (Eur).

ANGLOMANIA *Love* of English ways.

ANGLOPHOBIA *Aversion* to English ways.

ANNA *COIN* (1/6th of A RUPEE, hence any one of those six letters, crypt). *GOVERNESS*.

ANNIVERSARY DATE (yearly return); CELEBRATION.

(1) *PAPER*	(7) *WOOL* or *COPPER*
(2) *COTTON*	(8) *BRONZE*
(3) *FEATHER*	(9) *POTTERY*
(4) *FLOWER*	(10) *TIN*
(5) *WOOD*	(11) *STEEL*
(6) *CANDY*	(12) *SILK*

(13) *LACE*   (45) *SAPPHIRE*
(14) *IVORY*   (50) *GOLD*
(15) *CRYSTAL*   (55) *EMERALD*
(20) *CHINA*   (60) *DIAMOND*
(25) *SILVER*   (65) BLUE *SAPPHIRE*
(30) *PEARL*   (70) *PLATINUM*
(35) *CORAL*   (75) *(DIAMOND)*
(40) *RUBY*

ANNO DOMINI AD, NOWADAYS. TO (if allied to 'shortly' or similar word indicating abbreviation to A.D.; crypt).

ANNOY *Anag.* GALL, HARASS, IRRITATE, MOLEST, RILE (**opp** = *please*).

ANNUAL *FLOWER*. YEARLY. *BOOK*, DIARY.

ANON *SOON*; **comp** = ever. ANONYMOUS, UNKNOWN.

ANT INSECT; EMMET, TERMITE; **assembly**: colony; WORKER, **pl** = TUC (crypt) [Myrmidons]. ARE NOT, IF IT (arch).

ANTE (s/l *anti*). BEFORE, PRE. *BET*, STAKE, WAGER.

ANTELOPE Ruminant quadruped, like a *deer*; **breeds**:

3-letters	GORAL	DZEREN
GNU	GUEVI	DZERON
GOA	IZARD	IMPALA
KOB	KAAMA	INDIAN ~
NYL	KEMAS	NILGAI
	KONZE	OTEROP
4-letters	NAGOR	PALLAH
HART	NYALA	PYGARG (bibl)
KUDU	OKAPI	QUREBI
ORYX	ORIBI	REEBOK
THAR	*ROYAL* ~	
TORA	SAIGA	**7-letters**
	SASIN	BLESBOK
5-letters	SEROW	BUBALIS
ADDAX	TAKIN	BUSHBUK
AUDAX	WANTO	CHAMOIS
BEISA	YAKIN	CHIKARA
BONGO		GAZELLE
BUBAL	**6-letters**	GEMSBOK
CHIRU	DIK-DIK	GRYSBOK
ELAND	DUIKER	SASSABY

TARTARY	BONTEBOK	REEDBUCK
UNICORN (myth)	CHOUSINGHA	*SPRINGBOK*
	HARTEBEEST	STEINBOK
8+ letters	KLIPSPRINGER	WILDEBEEST
BLACKBUCK	PRONGHORN	

ANTE MERIDIEM *AM*, FORENOON, MORNING.

ANTEPENULTIMATE LAST BUT TWO, SECOND FROM LAST, CHI (Gr), X.

ANTHONY (s/l *Antony*). HOPE. PATRON OF SWINEHERDS. RUNT.

ANTI (s/l *ante*). AGAINST, VERSUS, V, VS (**opp** = *pro*).

ANTI-AIRCRAFT *AA*, FLAK. V-BOMBER (crypt).

ANTICIPATE 1. EXPECT, FORESTALL. 2. Come before in a word, e.g. **He anticipates the record to be of assistance** (4) = HE*LP.

ANTONY (s/l *Anthony*). 1. MARK ~, lived 83–30 B.C. Ally of *Caesar*, mar (1) Fulvia, (2) Octavia, (3) Cleopatra (paramour). Triumvirate 43 B.C. Infatuated with Cleopatra, he forsook *Rome* and turned Egyptian. Beaten at sea by Octavian (his br-in-law) at Actium, he committed suicide in Alexandria. 2. ~ and Cleopatra (*Shak*).

ANUBIS Gk rendering of Egy *conductor* of souls to *Osiris*; it had a *hyena's* head (sometimes jackal).

ANVIL BLOCK, SHAPE [*smith*]. BONE (*ear*). *INSTRUMENT* (mus).

ANYWAY *Anag*. IN ANY WAY, IN ANY CASE, AT ANY RATE, REGARDLESS.

AOC AIR OFFICER COMMANDING (mil).

AP ASSOCIATED PRESS; *PRESS, REPORTERS*. SON OF (Wal).

APE COPY, IMITATE, MIMIC, TAKE OFF. TAILLESS *MONKEY* (hence MONKE, crypt); **breeds**: BARBARY, CHIMPANZEE, GIBBON, GORILLA, MAGOT, ORANG-(O)UTANG.

APELIOTES Gk myth EAST *WIND* (**Rom** = SUBSOLANUS).

APHRODITE Gk *goddess* of LOVE (**Rom** = *VENUS*), d of *Zeus* and Dione; mar Hephaestus (**Rom** = *Vulcan*), and m of *Eros* by *Ares*. [*ASTARTE, FREYA, ISHTAR, ISIS*].

APOLLO 1. Gk *god* of beauty, music, prophecy, sun etc; s of *Zeus* and Leto, *twin* of *Artemis* and f of many gods, including *Asclepius*. **Rom** = *PHOEBUS*. 2. *SPACECRAFT. THEATRE.*

APOSTLE MESSENGER. **12 of Christ**: ANDREW, BARTHOLOMEW, JAMES, JAMES THE LESS, JOHN, JUDAS ISCARIOT, MATTHEW, PHILIP, SIMON PETER, SIMON THE CANAANITE, THADDEUS, THOMAS; **later**: BARNABAS, ST PAUL, MATTHIAS: also the 70 disciples. *Song*.

APOSTROPHE 1. Sign of omission of letter(s). An ~ often denotes the possessive case, as in Shakespeare's writing (an elision of 'Shakespeare, his writing'), meaning the work of the Bard. But an alternative interpretation can be 'Shakespeare is writing', and the puzzle setter can adopt this in order to confuse the issue.

It avoids the somewhat clumsy construction shown by the clue **Silver in the church is a lock-up** (4); this not only reads better as **Silver in the church's lock-up** (4), but also distracts some attention from **lock-up** as the principal synonym; = C(AG)E. The opposite application is exampled by the clue **Countryman's against a trap** (4); this looks as though a rustic peasant is against, or does not hold with, the use of traps. In fact, it should be read in the possessive sense to imply the form or sound of 'against' as used by a countryman, which = AGIN (also meaning a trap when split A*GIN). 2. Dropping the letter H from the start of a word is indicated by substitution of an apostrophe. This implies either a Cockney or slang interpretation or, more likely, an equal omission of H from the answer, e.g. **'E's fit to drink** (3) = (h)ALE. 3. ~ can be an answer in itself, and a suitable clue might refer to the omission of the letter I from 'Who is Who' as follows: **Indicates I am not in Who's Who** (10) = APOSTROPHE. 4. ADDRESS, SPEECH (to an absent or imaginary person).

APPEAL ATTRACT, PLEASE. RETRIAL [judge]. ASK, BEG, IMPLORE, IMPORTUNE [umpire (cricket)]; HOW'S THAT? HEY, HOY, O, OH.

APPEAR 1. MANIFEST (**opp** = *vanish*) [ghost]. SEEM. 2. Read as . . ., or include word mentioned, e.g. **It appears to me on reflection** (4) = IT*EM.

APPLE FRUIT; TREE (genus Malus). NEW YORK (sl). [*Adam, Atalanta, Eris, Heracles, Hesperides, Paris*]; **types**:

BRAMLEY'S SEEDLINGS, CAPE DELICIOUS, COX'S ORANGE PIPPIN, DISCOVERY, EGREMONT, ELLISON'S ORANGE, EPICURE, GEORGE CAVE, GOLDEN DELICIOUS, GOLDEN NOBLE, GRANNY SMITH,

GRENADIER, HOWGATE WONDER, IDARED, JAMES
GRIEVE, KIDD'S ORANGE RED, LANE'S PRINCE
ALBERT, LAXTON'S FORTUNE, LORD DERBY, LORD
LAMBOURNE, MERTON KNAVE, NON PAREIL, ORLEANS
REINETTE, RUSSET, SPARTAN, ST EDMUND'S RUSSET,
SUNSET, WORCESTER PEARMAIN. **Pl** = *STAIRS* (rh sl).
Isle of ~s = Avalon (King Arthur).

APPOINTMENT ASSIGNATION, *DATE*, *ENGAGEMENT*,
MEETING, TRYST. *DEGREE*, *OFFICE*, ORDINANCE,
POSITION, POSTING. EQUIPMENT, FITTING;
FURNISHING, OUTFIT (and pl).
APRIL (4th) MONTH, M, APR (Rom Aprilis, bud-opening);
  (**birthstone** = *diamond*) [~ fool; ~ showers]. Girl's name.
APT APPROPRIATE, SUITABLE. CLEVER, QUICK-WITTED.
  TEND. ADVANCED PASSENGER TRAIN (rly).
AQUAMARINE *GEM*; *BERYL*. *COLOUR* (blue-green).
AQUILO Rom myth NE *WIND* (**Gk** = KAIKAS).
ARACHNE Gk myth d of Idmon, weaver who turned into a *spider*.
ARCH *BRIDGE*, SPAN, VAULT. *COY*, PERT, PLAYFUL,
  SAUCY, *SHY*, *TEASING* (**opp** = *modest*). CHIEF, SUPERIOR.
  ARCHAIC (abbr). ARCHITECTURE (abbr).
ARCHER 1. *BRIDGE*, SPAN, VAULT (crypt). *BOWMAN*,
  TOXOPHILIST; **celeb**: *CUPID*, DAN (radio), ROBIN *HOOD*,
  WILLIAM TELL. *PAINTER*. *WRITER*. 2. *Constellation*
  (Sagittarius); (9th) sign of *Zodiac*.
ARCHIMEDES Gk mathematician (287–212 B.C.) who invented the
  screw for pumping water (cochlea); also discovered the principle of
  water displacement [eureka!], and the use of the lever.
ARCHITECT THE CREATOR, GOD. ACHIEVER, SCHEMER.
  BUILDER, DESIGNER, PLANNER; **celebrated**: *ADAM*,
  INIGO JONES, LE CORBUSIER, LUTYENS, SIR GILES
  GILBERT SCOTT, SIR JOHN SOANE, *WREN* [si monumentum
  requiris, circumspice].
ARCHITECTURE BUILDING ART, ~ CONSTRUCTION,
  ~ LAYOUT, ~ SCIENCE; **styles**: Arenated, Byzantine,
  Decorated, Early English, Eastern, Egyptian, Gothic, Grecian,
  Jacobean, Minoan, Norman, Perpendicular, Pointed, Rectilinear,
  Renaissance, Romanesque, Sumerian, Superimposed, Trabeated,
  Transitional; **Five Orders**: Composite, Corinthian, Doric, Ionic,
  Tuscan. **Terms** (and see *Cathedral parts*; *castle*; *temple*; *window*):

4-letters
ARCH (cinquefoil, elliptical, gothic, horseshoe, ogee, norman, pointed, segmented, semi-circular, trefoil)
DADO (body of a pedestal)
JAMB (side of a chimney, door or window)
OGEE (round and hollow moulding; type of arch)
STOA (portico, roofed colonnade)

5-letters
AMBRY (niche)
GABLE (triangular upper part of wall)
NICHE (recess for statue, vessel or ornament)
OGIVE (gothic arch)
OVOLO (convex moulding)
SHAFT (main part of column)
SOCLE (plinth)
TORUS (semi-circular moulding)

6-letters
ABACUS (upper part of capital)
ALMERY (niche)
ARCADE (series of arches [colonnade])
ASHLAR, -ER (hewn stone)
AUMBRY (niche)
AUMERY (niche)
COLUMN (vertical pillar comprising plinth, foot, base, dado, cornice and capital)
CORBEL (projecting frame support)
CUPOLA (ceiling of a dome)
FINIAL (pinnacle or spire ornament)
FLECHE (spire)
FRIEZE (relief band on entablature)
IMPOST (top of pillar)
LANCET (arch)
LIERNE (cross rib)
LINTEL (top of doorway)
METOPE (recess in frieze [*intaglio*])
PILLAR (vertical support or ornament)
PLINTH (projecting base of column)
SCREEN (partition)

SOFFIT (undersurface of arch or ceiling)
VOLUTE (spiral scroll)

7-letters
CALOTTE (concavity in niche)
CAPITAL (head of column)
CORNICE (top of column)
ECHINUS (egg and anchor ornament)
ENTASIS (swelling column)
PORTICO (range of columns)
TRANSOM (horizontal bar in window)

8-letters
ABUTMENT (pier, wall of arch)
ASTRAGAL (beading)
ATLANTES (male supporting figures [Caryatides])
BUTTRESS (support)
GARGOYLE (grotesque animal forming water spout)
KEYSTONE (topmost voussoir)
PEDESTAL (base of column; specially, a whole Classical column)
PEDIMENT (triangular gable)
PILASTER (square supporting column)
TRIGLYPH (projection on frieze [*cameo*])
VOUSSOIR (tapered archstone)

9+ letters
ARCHITRAVE (ornamental door moulding)
BALUSTRADE (parapet)
COLONNADE (series of columns [arcade])
ENTABLATURE (superstructure across two columns)
CARYATIDES (female supporting figures [Atlantes])
STANCHION (vertical bar in window)
TRIFORIUM (gallery)

ARENA RING, SPHERE, ZONE.
ARE NOT AINT, ANT, ARENT.
ARES Gk *god* of WAR (**Rom** = *MARS*); s of *Zeus* and *Hera*.
Arg Argentina, ~ian.
ARGENT AG (*chem*); *SILVER* (*herald*). FRENCH MONEY (crypt).
ARGON A (*chem*); GAS (inert).

ARGONAUT CEPHALOPOD, NAUTILUS (zool). **Pl** = Gk myth
adventurers who sailed in the Argo under *Jason* in search of the
golden fleece: ADMETUS (mar Alcestis), AMPHIARUS (a
prophet), CALAIS (s of *Boreas*), *CASTOR*, GLAUCUS (builder,
but see *Argus*, and *steersman* of the Argo), *HERACLES*,
MOPSUS (a *prophet*), NESTOR (a *sage*), *ORPHEUS* (a *singer*),
PELEUS (f of *Achilles*), PHILAMON (a *poet*), *POLLUX*,
THESEUS, TYDEUS (f of Diomedes), ZETES (s of *Boreas*).

ARGUS 1. Gk myth *god* with 100 eyes, set by *Hera* to watch *Io*.
Stolen by *Hermes*, his eyes were placed on the peacock's tail. 2.
Ulysses' dog (also ARGOS). 3. Some say builder of the Argo (but
see *Argonaut*); s of Phrixus. 4. PHEASANT.

ARIADNE 1. Gk myth d of *Minos*, who mar *Dionysus*. Helped
Theseus to escape from the *labyrinth* by means of a silken thread,
and then went to Naxos. 2. A minor *PLANET*.

ARIEL (s/l aerial). SPRITE, *SPIRIT*. Character in Temp (*Shak*).

ARMOUR MAIL, PROTECTION (chain ~, plate ~); **parts**:
ACTON (jacket), BEAVER (jaws), BREASTPLATE (breast),
CUIRASS (body), CUISSE (thigh), GORGET (neck), GREAVE
(shin), HABERGEON (coat), HAUBERK (coat), HELM (head),
PANOPLY (suit), PAULDRON (shoulders), TASSET (hip),
VAMBRACE (arm), VISOR (eyes). [*patron saint*].

ARMS (s/l alms). LIMBS, MEMBERS (*bone*). SLEEVES.
BRANCHES. *WEAPONS. HERALDRY*.

ARMY 1. *SA. TA*. CORPS, HOST, *SOLDIERS* [~ and Navy
Club/Stores; Fred Karno's ~; Salvation ~]. *KALI* (crypt). 2. Of
the arm, e.g. **army cover** = SLEEVE; **army connections** =
SHOULDERS.

AROUND 1. ABOUT. A*ROUND q.v. A*BULLET (crypt).
2. Reverse the word, e.g. **Idol to follow around** (3) = GOD.

ARRIVAL TIME ETA. BIRTHDAY (crypt).

ARRIVED CAME, HERE. MADE.

ARRIVES ARR. COMES. (**opp** = *leaves*).

ARROW *DART*, FLECHETTE, FLIGHT, QUARREL; *MISSILE*,
WEAPON [*Bowman*; St Sebastian] **comp** = *bow*; **pl** = *game*
(*darts*). *GRASS*. DIRECTION INDICATOR, POINTER,
SIGNPOST. ~ ROOT.

ARSENIC MINERAL; AS (*chem*). POISON, SEMI-METALLIC
ELEMENT. [Old Lace].

ARSON FIRE-RAISING, INCENDIARISM; LIGHT CRIME
(Pyro-*mania*).

ARSONIST BLAZER, FIREMAN, PYRO-*MANIAC*.

ART 1. CRAFT, KNACK, SKILL. ARTICLE. ARE (arch). ARTHUR (abbr). PAINTING, SCULPTURE. 2. **Goddess: Gk** = *ATHENE*, **Rom** = MINERVA.

ARTEMIS 1. Gk virgin *goddess* of *nature* and *hunting*; CYNTHIA (**Rom** = *DIANA*); d of *Zeus* and Leto, and *twin* of *Apollo* [UPIS, *HECATE*, SELENE]. A minor *PLANET*.

ARTEMISIA Queen of Halicarnassus; mar Mausolus and built the *Mausoleum* as his tomb [*Daedalus*, *Minos*].

ARTHUR *ART*. See also *KING* ~.

ARTICLE A, AN, ART, THE. ITEM, THING. CLAUSE, PARTICULAR. LITERARY PIECE, WRITING. **Pl** = APPRENTICESHIP.

ARTILLERY *RA*; GUNS, ORDNANCE, *WEAPONS*.

ARTIST (s/l *Artiste*). *RA*; *PAINTER* (q.v. for list). CRAFTSMAN, DEVOTEE; THESPIAN.

ARTISTE (s/l *Artist*). DANCER, PERFORMER, SINGER, THESPIAN [*stage*].

ARTS MAN BA, MA.

AS *ARSENIC* (*chem*). ROMAN *COIN*. BECAUSE; LIKE. WHEN. FRENCH *ACE*.

AS AT QUA.

A-Sax Anglo-Saxon.

ASCENT 1. CLIMB, MOUNTING, RISE. 2. Word reads upwards (dn).

ASCLEPIUS Gk *god* of medicine, s of *Apollo*; mar Epione and f of *Hygieia*; killed by *Zeus* with a *thunderbolt*. His attribution is a *staff* with entwined winged serpent (caduceus). *Hippocrates* was one of his supposed descendants (the Asclepidae) [*Oath*]. **Rom** = AESCULAPIUS.

ASP *SNAKE* [A and C, *Shak*]. AS SOON AS POSSIBLE.

ASPIRATION AMBITION, HOPE. Sound the letter H. BREATHING, VENTILATION.

ASS ASSASSINATED, ~ION. BURRO (US). DONKEY, MOKE; NEDDY [mule; *Absolom*; Balaam; *Bottom*; Poppaea; *Silenus*]; **breeds**: CHIGETAI, DZIGGETAI, ONAGER; **male** = *JACK*, **female** = *JENNY*; [hinny]. FOOL ABOUT. BACKSIDE (US).

ASSEMBLY DELIBERATIVE BODY, *LEGISLATIVE* COUNCIL. FITTING TOGETHER, MANUFACTURING, PRODUCTION. *MUSTER* (mil); CONCOURSE, *CROWD*, *GATHERING*, MEETING; COLLECTION OF ANIMALS as:

Antelope	TROOP
Apes	SHREWDNESS
Badgers	CETE
Bears	SLEUTH
Bees	SWARM
Card players	*SCHOOL*
Cats	CLOWDER, CLUSTER
Cattle	DROVE, *HERD*
Chickens	*FLOCK*
Choughs	CHATTERING
Clans	*GATHERING*
Crows	MURDER
Deer	*HERD*
Doves	*FLIGHT*
Draught animals	*TEAM*
Ducks	*FLIGHT*, PADDLING
Elephants	*HERD*
Finches	*CHARM*
Fish	*SCHOOL*, SHOAL
Foxes	SKULK
Geese (domestic)	*FLOCK*, GAGGLE
Geese (wild)	SKEIN
Goats	*FLOCK*, *HERD*
Grouse	PACK
Gulls	COLONY
Hares	*DOWN*
Hawks	*CAST*
Hens	BROOD, CLUTCH
Herons	COLONY, SEDGE
Hounds	KENNEL, PACK
Hyenas	*PACK*
Jellyfish	SMUCK
Kangaroos	*MOB*
Kine	DROVE
Kittens	KINDLE
Lapwings	*DESERT*
Larks	*BEVY, EXALTATION*
Leopards	LEPE
Lions	PRIDE
Mallards	*FLUSH*
Monkeys	TROOP

Nightingales	*WATCH*
Oxen	*TEAM*
Partridges	COVEY
Peacocks	*MUSTER*
Penguins	ROOKERY
Pheasants	NIDE, NYE
Pigs	DROVE, *HERD*
Pigeons	*FLOCK*, LOFT
Plovers	CONGREGATION
Porpoises	*SCHOOL*
Quails	*BEVY*
Rabbits	WARREN
Rhinos	CRASH
Rooks	BUILDING, *ROOKERY*
Seals	POD, *ROOKERY*
Sheep	*FLOCK*, *HERD*
Snipe	*WISP*
Starlings	MURMURATION
Swans	*HERD*, *WEDGE*
Swine	*HERD*, *SOUNDER*
Teal	*SPRING*
Whales	POD, *SCHOOL*
Witches	COVEN
Wolves	*PACK*
Woodcocks	*FALL*
Young *ducks*	*TEAM*
Bevy	*LARKS, QUAILS*
Brood	HENS
Building	*ROOKS*
Cast	HAWKS
Cete	*BADGERS*
Charm	FINCHES
Chattering	CHOUGHS
Clowder	*CATS*
Cluster	*CATS*
Clutch	HENS
Colony	GULLS, HERONS
Congregation	PLOVERS
Coven	*WITCHES*
Covey	PARTRIDGES

Crash	*RHINOS*
Desert	LAPWINGS
Down	HARES
Drove	*CATTLE*, KINE, *PIGS*
Exaltation	*LARKS*
Fall	WOODCOCK
Flight	DOVES, *DUCKS*
Flock	*CHICKENS, GEESE, GOATS, PIGEONS, SHEEP*
Flush	MALLARDS
Gaggle	*GEESE*
Gathering	CLANS
Herd	CATTLE, *DEER, ELEPHANTS, GOATS, PIGS, SHEEP, SWANS, SWINE*
Kennel	*HOUNDS*
Kindle	KITTENS
Lepe	*LEOPARDS*
Loft	*PIGEONS*
Mob	*KANGAROOS*
Murder	*CROWS*
Murmuration	STARLINGS
Muster	PEACOCKS
Nide	PHEASANTS
Nye	PHEASANTS
Pack	*GROUSE, HOUNDS*, HYENAS, *WOLVES*
Paddling	*DUCKS*
Pod	SEALS, *WHALES*
Pride	*LIONS*
Rookery	PENGUINS, *ROOKS*, SEALS
School	CARD PLAYERS, *FISH*, PORPOISES, *WHALES*
Sedge	HERONS
Shoal	*FISH*
Shrewdness	APES
Skein	*GEESE*
Skulk	*FOXES*
Sleuth	*BEARS*
Smuck	JELLYFISH
Sounder	*SWINE*

Spring	TEAL
Swarm	BEES
Team	DRAUGHT ANIMALS, OXEN, YOUNG *DUCKS*
Troop	*ANTELOPES*, MONKEYS
Warren	RABBITS
Watch	NIGHTINGALES
Wedge	*SWANS*
Wisp	*SNIPE*

ASSESS ESTIMATE, VALUE. JENNY, SHE-MULE.

ASSIST *ABET*, AID, GUIDE, HELP. BE PRESENT, TAKE PART. MULETEER (crypt).

ASSOCIATION FRIENDSHIP. CONNECTION. CLUB, ORGANIZATION. [*Football*].

ASSUME POSIT, POSTULATE. DON, PUT ON. SIMULATE. ARROGANT. UNDERTAKE.

ASSUMPTION 1. ARROGANCE, SIMULATION, TAKING, UNDERTAKING. CLOTHING (crypt). 2. Reception of Virgin Mary in Heaven.

ASTARTE 1. MOLLUSC. 2. Phoen *goddess* of *LOVE*; **Gk** = *APHRODITE*; **Rom** = *VENUS*. 3. Heroine of Byron's poem 'Manfred'.

ASTRONOMY STARGAZING, STUDY OF THE HEAVENS. **Gk Muse** = *URANIA*.

ATALANTA Gk myth maiden who avoided mar by *refusing* suitors who could not beat her in a race; she killed the unsuccessful. Eventually Milanion (or Hippomenes) distracted her by dropping golden *apples* given him by *Aphrodite*, and he won.

ATE 1. CONSUMED. 2. Gk *goddess*, d of *Zeus*; personification of *RETRIBUTION*. 3. A minor *PLANET*.

ATHENE = PALLAS. Gk *goddess* of *ART*, *WAR*, and *WISDOM*; d of *Zeus*, her *shield* was called *Aegis*. **Rom** = *MINERVA*.

ATHENIAN ATTIC, GREEK [TIMON (*Shak*)].

ATHLETE *BLUE*; COMPETITOR; RUNNER.

ATHLETIC AGILE, SUPPLE; FIT, MUSCULAR, STRONG. **Pl** = EXERCISES, *SPORTS* EVENTS, e.g. **field events**: discus, hammer, high jump, hop-step-jump, javelin, long jump, pole vault, shot put; **track events**: hurdles, marathon, long distance, middle distance, sprint, steeplechase. And see *SPORT*.

AT HOME IN, NOT OUT (**opp** = *out*). COMFORTABLE.

ATHOS MUSKETEER (Dumas; Aramis, Porthos [d'Artagnan]).
  MOUNTAIN (Gk holy).
ATLAS 1. MOUNTAIN RANGE. *BONE*, FIRST VERTEBRA.
  WORLD MAP. CHARLES ~ (*strength*). 2. Gk myth *TITAN*,
  who bore the universe on his shoulders; he was turned by *Perseus*
  into *stone* (and thus became the Atlas mountains).
  3. *SPACECRAFT*.
ATOM 1. PARTICLE. SMALL PORTION/QUANTITY. 2. First
  half of alphabet (i.e. A*to*M) hence *ALPH* (crypt).
ATOMIC NUMBER 1 = HYDROGEN. **92** = URANIUM.
~ WEIGHT 1 = HYDROGEN. **238** = URANIUM.
ATONE 1. ABY(E), EXPIATE, MAKE AMENDS, RECONCILE.
  2. A sound (**a*tone**, mus); agree (**at*one**); both crypt.
ATTEMPT ENDEAVOUR, ESSAY, *GO*, *TRY*, *TURN*.
ATTENDANT AIDE DE CAMP, PAGE, *SECOND*, SERVANT;
  WAITING. CONCOMITANT.
ATTENTION HARK, HEED, *LIST*, LISTEN. ERECT, READY,
  SHUN. CARE, CONSIDERATION.
ATTIC LOFT, TOP ROOM. ATHENIAN, GREEK. *ELEGANT*,
  PURE, *SIMPLE*.
ATTILA King of the *Huns*. He sacked eastern Europe and extorted
  tribute from Emperor Theodorus. Advancing into *Gaul*, he was
  defeated in A.D. 451 near Châlons-sur-Marne. He died advancing
  on Rome two years later.
ATTRACT *DRAW*, PULL (**opp** = *repel*).
ATTRACTIVE ARRESTING, GOOD LOOKING, PRETTY,
  TAKING (**opp** = *ugly*); MAGNETIC.
AU *GOLD* (*chem*). TO THE FRENCH (crypt).
AUC AB URBE CONDITA (foundation of *Rome*).
AUGEAS Gk legendary king of Elis. Owned stables housing 3,000
  oxen, which were cleansed by *Hercules* in one day, when he
  diverted two rivers for the purpose.
AUGUST IMPRESSIVE, MAJESTIC, NOBLE, VENERABLE.
  (8th) MONTH, M, AUG (Augustus *Caesar*); **birthstone** =
  sardonyx.
AUK SEABIRD; **breeds**: GUILLEMOT, GREAT ~ (ex), LITTLE
  ~, PUFFIN, RAZORBILL [cormorant, shag].
AUNT SALLY *SHY*. Tom Sawyer's aunt (Mark Twain).
AURAL (s/l *oral*). AUDITORY, BY *EAR*.
AURORA 1. Rom *goddess* of *DAWN* (**Gk** = EOS). She rose in the
  east at the end of night, and crossed the sky in a chariot drawn by

two horses; m by Astraeus of the beneficial *winds*. 2. A minor
PLANET.

Aus Australia, ~n; and *car plate*.

AUSTEN CHAMBERLAIN (polit). JANE, WRITER; books:
Emma (Hartfield, Highbury; Emma Woodhouse, Mr Knightley,
Frank Churchill); Mansfield Park (Northampton; Lady Bertram,
Fanny Price); Northanger Abbey (Wiltshire; Morlands, Thorpes,
Tilneys); Persuasion (Kellynch Hall, Somerset; Sir Walter Elliot,
Anne Elliot, Capt Wentworth); Pride and Prejudice, ex First
Impressions (Longbourn, Netherfield Park, Herts; Elizabeth
Bennet, Mr Darcy; Jane Bennet, Mr Bingley; Lydia Bennet, Mr
Wickham); Sense and Sensibility (Norland Park, Barton Park,
Sussex; Dashwoods, Ferrars, Lucy Steele); The Watsons
(unfinished).

AUSTER Rom myth SOUTH *WIND* (**Gk** = NOTOS). AIRCRAFT.

AUSTRIA A; and *car plate*.

AUTHOR *ACCOUNTANT* (crypt). CRIME WRITER,
DRAMATIST, NOVELIST, PLAYWRIGHT; ORIGINATOR.
See *poets* and also *writers* for list.

AUTHORITY POWER, SAY-SO, *SEAL*. EXPERT. *BOOK*.

AUTOLYCUS 1. Gk myth s of *Hermes*; a *robber* who could change all
he touched, and so avoid detection. Trapped by *Sisyphus* who
marked under the hooves of cattle. 2. Gk astronomer of 4th
century B.C. 3. A salesman in the Winter's Tale (*Shak*); 'a snapper-
up of unconsidered trifles'.

AUTOMATIC MECHANICAL, NECESSARY, SELF-ACTING,
UNCONSCIOUS (**opp** = *contrived*). BREN, BROWNING,
COLT, LUGER, STEN, *WEAPON*.

AUTOMATICALLY MECHANICALLY, UNCONSCIOUSLY. OF
GUNS, ORDNANCE.

AV AUTHORIZED VERSION, BIBLE. AVIATION.

AVAILABLE DISPOSABLE, ON OFFER, UP FOR GRABS.
APPROACHABLE.

AVE HAIL, WELCOME. ALOHA, FAREWELL. AVENUE.

AVENGER EXACTOR OF
RETALIATION/RETRIBUTION/SATISFACTION.
AIRCRAFT.

AVER AFFIRM, ASSERT, DECLARE. PART MEANS
(AVERage; crypt).

AVERAGE ESTIMATE, *MEAN*, ORDINARY, *PAR*. DAMAGE,
LOSS.

AVERSION 1. ANTIPATHY, DISLIKE, FEAR, *HATRED*,
PHOBIA (**opp** = *lover*), as:

Beards	POGONOPHOBIA
Dogs	CYNOPHOBIA
Enclosed spaces	CLAUSTROPHOBIA
English customs	ANGLOPHOBIA
Feet	PODOPHOBIA
Fire	PYROPHOBIA
Foreigners	XENOPHOBIA
French customs	GALLOPHOBIA
Heights	ACROPHOBIA
Horses	HIPPOPHOBIA
Marriage	GAMETOPHOBIA
No 13	TRISKAIDEKAPHOBIA
Open places	AGORAPHOBIA
Pain	ALGOPHOBIA
People/races	GENOPHOBIA
Poisons	TOXIPHOBIA
Russian customs	RUSSOPHOBIA
Sleep	HYPNOPHOBIA
Spiders	ARACHNEPHOBIA
Strangers	XENOPHOBIA
Teeth	ODONTOPHOBIA
Travel	(H)ODOPHOBIA
Water	HYDROPHOBIA
Women	GYNOPHOBIA
Work	ERGOPHOBIA

2. AN*ACCOUNT, A*BOOK, A*TRANSLATION;
A*TURNING (crypt).

AWARD ASSIGN, GRANT, PAYMENT, PENALTY. JUDICIAL
DECISION. *HONOUR*, *PRIZE*, TROPHY (theat) most ®:
BAFTA (Br film, TV), CEZAR (Fr *Oscar*), *EMMY* (US TV),
GOLDEN GLOBE (Hollywood Foreign Press Association),
GOLDEN PALM (Cannes film), GOLDEN ROOSTER (Ch film),
GOLDEN ROSE (Montreux film), GRAMMY (US popular
music), IVOR NOVELLO (US music), OLIVIER (ex SWET, UK
West End theat), *OSCAR* (US film), STELLA (UK film), TONY
(US stage).

AWFUL *Anag.* IMPRESSIVE, NOTABLE. *BAD*;
FRIGHTENING.

AWKWARD *Anag*. BUNGLING, CALLOW, CLUMSY;
EMBARRASSED, *SHY*.
AWL (s/l *all*). AUGER, *DRILL*.
AZURE *BLUE* (*herald*). CLOUDLESS, SERENE.

B BARON. BEFORE. BELGIUM (*car plate*). BETA. BLACK.
BORN. BORON (*chem*). BOWLED. KEY, NOTE. SECOND
CLASS. SOFT (pencil). 300 (Rom).
b born.
BA ARTMAN: BACHELOR OF ARTS. BARIUM (*chem*).
AIRLINE (UK).
BAAL Chief *god*; god of *SUN* (Phoen). FALSE *GOD*.
Bab Babylonia, ~n.
BACCHUS (s/l *back us*). Rom *god* of *WINE* and *FERTILITY*; also
IACCHUS. mar *Ariadne* and was worshipped in drunken orgies
(**Gk** = DIONYSUS) [*drink*].
BACHELOR BA, MB. UNMARRIED [*Lear*].
~ OF ARTS BA.
~ OF MEDICINE MB.
BACK 1. BET ON, WAGER. SECOND, SUPPORT. GO BACK,
REVERSE. RIVER (Can). **Pl** = *GROUNDS* (C). 2. Reads
backwards, e.g. **Backward** = DRAW. **Back seat** = DEB (crypt; but
beware, it can also = SADDLE!).
BACKED WAGERED. SUPPORTED. REVERSED, WENT
ASTERN. MOUNTED, RIDING, SADDLED [*horse*] (crypt).
DE (crypt).
BACKER BETTER, PUNTER. SECOND, SUPPORTER;
ANGEL. LORD CHANCELLOR (ceremonial). RE (crypt).
BACKWARD 1. ASTERN, REARWARD. UNDEVELOPED.
DRAW (crypt). 2. Word reversed, e.g. **Backward scholar** = AB.
BACKWATER CUL DE SAC, DEAD END, STAGNATION
POINT. WAKE, WASH. RETAW, OOH (H_2O backwards,
crypt — but *chem* inaccurate).
BAD(LY) *Anag*. AWFUL. COUNTERFEIT, DEFICIENT, DUD,
FOUL, INFERIOR, NO GOOD, ROTTEN, UNPLEASANT,
WORTHLESS (**opp** = *good, well*).
BADGER WORRY, *TEASE*. ANIMAL [*assembly* (cete); *habitation*
(sett)]. SHAVING BRUSH. *AIRCRAFT* (USSR). *ISLAND*.
BAD PRESS CRITICISM, POOR PUBLICITY. *RAG*. SPERS etc
(*anag*).

BAFFLED *Anag*. FRUSTRATED, PERPLEXED. DAMPED, SILENCED.

BAG *BOOK*, DEMAND, RESERVE. KILL. CASE; *SACK*; **types**: ATTACHE CASE, BRIEF CASE, CARPET ~, DESPATCH CASE, DIPLOMATIC ~, DITTY ~, ETUI, GLADSTONE ~, KIT ~, PORTFOLIO, POUCH, RETICULE, RUCK-SACK, SADDLE ~, SA(T)CHEL, SCRIP, VANITY ~, WALLET. **Comp** = *baggage*. **Pl** = *BAGGAGE*. TROUSERS; PANTS (US).

BAGGAGE BAGS, CASE, EQUIPMENT, GEAR, GRIP, KIT, LUGGAGE, *TRAPS*, TRUNK; **comp** = *bag*. HUSSY, JADE, MINX, SAUCY PIECE.

BAGPIPE INSTRUMENT (mus; Ire, Sc); MUSETTE (Fr); **parts**: bag, bellows, blowpipe, bourdon, chanter, drone.

BAIL (s/l *bale*). SECURITY, SURETY. LIBERATE, RELEASE. CASTLE WALL. WICKET TOP (cricket). HOOP HANDLE. ACCOST, BUTTONHOLE (Aus). PUMP OUT, SCOOP OUT (and *BALE*; naut). [parachute].

BALD BLUNT, PLAIN, SIMPLE. BARE, HAIRLESS, (CLEAN) SHAVEN [Brynner, Charles the ~, coot, ~ eagle, *Elisha*, Kojak]. ~ money = spignel (*plant*).

BALDER 1. LESS HAIR, SMOOTHER [Brynner; coot; *Elisha*; Kojak]. 2. *God* of *SUN* (Nor), s of *Odin* and *Frigg(a)*, mar Nanna; slain by his blind br Hod, who unwittingly used a poisoned mistletoe dart supplied by *Loki*.

BALE (s/l *bail*). DESTRUCTION, EVIL, MISERY, PAIN, WOE. PACK, WRAP. *MEASURE* (paper). PUMP OUT, SCOOP OUT (and *BAIL*; naut). [parachute].

BALL (s/l *bawl*). *DANCE*. PILL; BEAMER, BOUNCER, DELIVERY, FULL TOSS, LEG BREAK, LONG HOP, OFF BREAK, YORKER; BOUNDER (crypt). [baseball, billiards, *cricket*, *football*, hockey, *rugby*, *snooker*, *squash*, *tennis*].

BALLET *DANCE* (classical, mime, Fr, Russ); **terms**: arabesque (position), ballerina, -o (dancer, fem, male), barre (exercise bar), battement (leg movement), batterie (crossing feet), chasse (step), coda (dance section), coryphee (junior ballerina), coupe (step), elevation (jump), entrechat (leap), fouette (whip turn), glissade (glide), jete (leap), *leotard* (exercise costume), pas (step; ~ de basque, ~ de chat, ~ de deux, ~ glisse, ~ seule), pirouette (spin), plie (bend), pointe (tip-toe), prima ballerina assoluta (principal star), repetiteur (rehearsal teacher), ronds de jambe (leg

movements), tutu (stiff skirt). [Noel Streatfeild]; **celeb companies**:
Bolshoi (Moscow), Festival ~, Kirov (Kiev), New York, Rambert,
Royal ~, Sadler's Wells; **celeb personalities**: Ashton, Diaghilev,
Dolin, Dowell, Fokine, Fonteyn, Grey, Markova, Massine,
Nijinsky, Nureyev, Pavlova, Rambert, Shearer, Sibley, Soames,
de Valois.

BALL GAME Any game played with a ball (usually out of doors);
types: *BASEBALL* (US), BILLIARDS, *CRICKET*, CROQUET,
FIVES, *FOOTBALL* (Association, Am, Aus Rules, Gaelic,
Rugby, ~ League), *GOLF*, HANDBALL, HOCKEY, HURLING
(Ire), LACROSSE, NETBALL, PALL MALL, PELOTA
(Basque), POLO, *RACKETS*, ROUNDERS, *RUGBY*, SHINTY
(Sc), *SNOOKER*, SOFTBALL, SQUASH, *TENNIS* (lawn,
real/royal, table), VOLLEYBALL, WATER POLO (and see
board game, *game*, *sport*).

BALTHAZAR 1. *BOTTLE* (wine *measure* = 16 normal ~s). 2. Bibl;
one of the *Magi* [Caspar, Melchior (Matthew 2)]. 3. *SERVANT* (R
& J, *Shak*). 4. Variant of Belshazzar.

BAN *BAR*, FORBID, VETO.

BAND (s/l *banned*). BOND, OBI (Jap), SASH, STRIP, TIE.
CARTEL, CLIQUE, COTERIE, GANG. HOOP, LOOP,
STREAK, STRIPE. ORCHESTRA, *PLAYERS*.

BANG DIN, EXPLOSION, NOISE. *FIRE*, *SHOOT*. BUMP,
KNOCK. CURL, FRINGE.

BANGER AUTOMATIC, *GUN*, *REVOLVER*, *ROCKET*, *SHELL*.
FIRECRACKER, *FIREWORK*; *REPORTER* (crypt). CAR,
OLD CROCK (sl). SAUSAGE (sl).

BANK EDGE, *LEAN*, *TILT*. RIVERSIDE, SLOPE; BUND.
PANEL, *ROW*. RELY ON. MONEY BOX, SAFE DEPOSIT;
LODGE (Barclays, *Lloyds*, Midland, NatWest, Tellson's [2 Cities,
Dickens]). MUD ~, SAND ~ (naut). **Pl** = *STRAIT*.

~ CHARGES INTEREST, COMMISSION. FERRY TOLL,
RIVER TOLL (crypt).

BANKER CASHIER. ROTHSCHILD. DEALER (cards).
AILERON (aero). *RIVER* (crypt) e.g. **London banker** = THAMES.
[football pools].

BANNED (s/l *band*). FORBIDDEN, TABOO, TABU (**opp** =
allowed).

BAR (s/l baa). BISTRO, *DIVE*, INN, *PUB*, SNUG, *TAVERN*;
COUNTER [*drink*]. REST (mus). ESTOP, OBJECT,
PREVENT, SHUT, *STOP*. BAN, FORBID, VETO. GRILLE,

GRATING. LEVER. EXCEPT, SAVE. SANDBANK. Pl =
PRISON.

BARABBAS *Robber* released by Pilate instead of Jesus.

BARGE CHARGE, LURCH, PUSH, SHOVE. *BOAT*: CANAL
BOAT, FREIGHTER, HOY, THAMES, WHERRY;
HOUSEBOAT; STATE CRAFT.

BARIUM BA (*chem*). *METAL*.

BARK (s/l barque). HOWL, YAP. RIND, SKIN. ABRADE,
GRAZE. *CRY*, *HAWK*, PEDDLE, TOUT. *BOAT*, CLIPPER,
SAILING SHIP.

BARKER CRIER, PEDLAR, TOUT. *DOG*. [Actor's benevolent
fund].

BARMAID 1. SERVING WENCH, HOSTESS. ALTO,
CONTRALTO, SOPRANO (crypt). 2. Gk myth *HEBE*, cup-
bearer to the *gods* (**Rom** = JUVENTAS).

BARMAN *HOST*, INNKEEPER, *LANDLORD*, PUBLICAN
[*Ganymede*]. MUSICIAN (crypt).

BARNET Place (UK). HAIR (*rh sl*).

BARON B. LORD, *NOBLE*. [Richthofen; Rothschild].
MERCHANT. *JOINT* (meat).

BARONET BT, BART, KT; KNIGHT; SIR.

BARREL CASK, *MEASURE* (beer). CYLINDER, DRUM
(capstan, winch). GUN PART.

BARRIE JM, *WRITER* [Peter Pan; **characters**: *Crocodile*, *Darlings*,
Capt *Hook*, Lost boys, Nana, *Peter*, *Smee*, Tiger-Lily, Tinkerbell,
Wendy; Never-Never Land].

BARRIER *FENCE*, *GATE*, RAILING; BOUNDARY,
OBSTACLE. DAM. *LISTS*, PALISADE (jousting).
DIVIDER; *NET* (*tennis*).

BART BARONET. BARTHOLOMEW. *PIRATE*.

BASE (s/l *bass*). *BOTTOM* (opp = *top*); FOUNDATION,
GROUNDWORK, PRINCIPLE [~ on, see *model*]. ARMY
CAMP, SUPPORT AREA. ESTABLISH. RELY.
COWARDLY, DESPICABLE, LOW, *MEAN*, MENIAL.

BASEBALL FOOTBALL GROUND (Derby County). GAME
(**originator**: Cartwright) [Joe di Maggio, Babe Ruth, rounders,
softball]; **celeb teams (US)**: Boston Red Sox, Brooklyn Dodgers,
Chicago Cubs, Knickerbockers, New York Giants, New York
Yankees, Phillies; **venue**: Houston Astrodome.

BASHFUL COY, DIFFIDENT, *MODEST*, SHEEPISH, *SHY* (opp
= arrogant). *DWARF* (Snow White).

BASIC EDUCATION RRR (crypt).
BASKERVILLE *TYPEFACE*. **Pl** = Hound of ~ (*Holmes*).
BASS (s/l *base*). DEEP-SOUNDING, LOW (**opp** = alto). *FISH*,
PERCH, SEA-DACE, SEA-WOLF. *STRAIT*. *BEER®*, *DRINK*.
FIBRE, LIME-BARK, TIER [*raffia*].
BAT 1. IMPLEMENT; RACKET, RACQUET; **comp** = *ball*.
STRIKE; BATSMAN. PACE, *RATE*, WINK. BINGE, SPREE.
2. Nocturnal flying mammal: Barbastelle, Bechstein's ~,
Daubenton's ~, Diadem ~, Flittermouse, Flying Fox, Fruit ~,
Horseshoe ~, Kalong (largest), Pipistrelle, Pteropus, Serotine,
Vampire. 3. BAGGAGE (arch mil). **Pl** = CRAZY, *MAD*.
BATH 1. DECORATION, ORDER. CITY, SPA; AQUAE SULIS
(Rom); ~ and Wells (eccl See). BATHE, LAVE, RINSE, SOAK,
WASH; LAVATORY, TUB, VESSEL, WASH-TUB, JACUZZI,
SAUNA, STEAM ~, TURKISH ~. **Pl** = SWIMMING ~;
HAMMAM (Turk). 2. **Celeb** ~ **connections**: Agamemnon (k in ~
by *Clytemnestra*; *Archimedes* (discovered displacement in his ~;
Eureka!); Diogenes (lived in a tub; crypt); Marak (k in ~ by
Charlotte Corday); Poppaea (~ of asses' milk for complexion);
Anthony Perkins (as Norman Bates in Hitchcock film Psycho,
murdered girl in *shower* ~).
BATTALION BN, MEN, *SOLDIERS*, TROOPS.
BATTER BEAT, BREAK, BRUISE, HAMMER, HIT, *STRIKE*.
COOKING MIX. PLAYER AT BAT (*baseball*, *cricket*).
BATTERY ASSAULT, BEATING. *GUNS* (crypt).
ACCUMULATOR, PILE. COOP, HENHOUSE. INNING(S)
(*baseball*, *cricket*; crypt).
BATTING WINKING. AT STRIKE, *IN*, STRIKING (*baseball*,
cricket).
BATTLE STRUGGLE. ARGUMENT. TOWN. *FIGHT*, *WAR*:
celebrated:

Air	MALTA
ATLANTIC	MATAPAN
BERLIN	MIDWAY
BLITZ	MOHNE DAM
BRITAIN	PEARL HARBOR
CORAL SEA	PLOESTI
GUERNICA	RUHR
LEYTE GULF	SCHWEINFURT
LONDON	TARANTO

Sea
ACTIUM
ARMADA
ATLANTIC
CAPE ST VINCENT
COPENHAGEN
CORAL SEA
FALKLANDS
GUADALCANAL
JUTLAND
LEPANTO
LEYTE GULF
MATAPAN
MIDWAY
NILE
PEARL HARBOR
RIVER PLATE
SALAMIS
TARANTO
TRAFALGAR

Nelson
BASTIA (siege)
CALVI (lost eye)
COPENHAGEN
  ('I see no signal')
CAPE ST VINCENT
NILE (Aboukir Bay)
TENERIFE (lost arm)
TOULON
TRAFALGAR (death)

Land
ALAMEIN
ANZIO
ARDENNES
ARNHEM
AUSTERLITZ
BALACLAVA
BORODINO
BULGE

BULL RUN
BURMA
CASSINO
CORUNNA
CRETE
DIEN BIEN PHU
DIEPPE
DUNKIRK
FALKLANDS
FLANDERS
GALLIPOLI
GETTYSBURG
HASTINGS
IWO-JIMA
JENA
LITTLE BIG HORN
MARNE
MONS
OKINAWA
SHILOH
SOMME
STALINGRAD
TOBRUK
VERDUN
VIMY RIDGE
WATERLOO
YPRES

Civil War
ADWALTON MOOR
CHALGROVE FIELD
CROPREDY BRIDGE
DUNBAR
EDGE HILL (first)
GAINSBOROUGH
LANSDOWN
LOSTWITHIEL
MARSTON MOOR
NASEBY (last)
NEWBURY
PRESTON

ROUNDWAY DOWN
SELBY
TURNHAM GREEN
WINNINGTON BRIDGE
WORCESTER (final)

Alfred the Great
ALDERSHOT
ASHDOWN (first)
BENFLEET (last)
CHICHESTER
CHIPPENHAM
EDDINGTON (Ethandun)
EXETER
LONDON
RIVER STOUR

ROCHESTER
WAREHAM

Wars of the Roses
BARNET
BOSWORTH FIELD (last)
EDGECOT
HEDGLEY MOOR
HEXHAM
LOSECOAT FIELD
MORTIMER'S CROSS
ST ALBANS (first)
TEWKESBURY
TOWTON
WAKEFIELD

Classical

Megiddo	1479 B.C.	Deborah & Barok	beat Sisera (Armageddon)
Troy	1250 B.C.	Agamemnon (Gk)	beat Paris (Trojan)
Marathon	491 B.C.	Miltiades (Gk)	beat Datis (Pers)
Thermopylae	480 B.C.	Xerxes (Pers)	beat Leonidas (Sparta)
Salamis	480 B.C.	Themistocles (Gk)	beat Xerxes (Pers)
Plataea	479 B.C.	Themistocles (Gk)	beat Mardonius (Pers)
Granicus	334 B.C.	Alexander	beat Memnon (Pers)
Issus	333 B.C.	Alexander	beat Darius (Pers)
Arbela	331 B.C.	Alexander	beat Darius (Pers)
Hydaspes	326 B.C.	Alexander	beat Darius (Pers)
Cannae	216 B.C.	Hannibal	beat Romans
Zama	202 B.C.	Scipio (Rom)	beat Hannibal
Philippi	42 B.C.	Octavian & Antony	beat Brutus & Cassius
Actium	31 B.C.	Octavian	beat Antony & Cleopatra
Masada	A.D. 73	Romans	beat Jews

American War of Independence
Brandywine River
Brooklyn
Bunker Hill
Camden
Charleston
Concord
Cowperis
Germantown
Guilford Court House
Heights of Abraham

Lexington (1st)
Saratoga
Trenton
White Plains
Yorktown (last)

American Civil War
Antietam
Appomatox (last)
Atlanta
Bull Run

Chancellorsville
Chattanooga
Cold Harbor
Fort Hudson
Fredericksburg
Harper's Ferry (1st skirmish)
Fort Sumter (1st)
Gettysburg
Vicksburg
Shilo
Wilderness

BATTLESHIP HMS, USS. DREADNOUGHT. CAPITAL SHIP, IRONCLAD. SHIP OF THE LINE. *WEAPON*.

BATTLE ZONE ARENA, FIELD, FRONT, *THEATRE*, WAR ZONE.

BAWL (s/l *ball*). CRY, HOWL, SHOUT, WAIL. REPRIMAND.

BAY (s/l *Bey*). BARK, HOWL [*dog, hound*]. *LAUREL TREE*. *HERB*. *HORSE*. BIGHT, *GULF*, INLET. RECESS, *SIDELINE*. BROWN *COLOUR*.

BB BOYS BRIGADE, CADETS. BARDOT (theat). BIG BROTHER (*Orwell*). VERY SOFT (pencil).

BBC BROADCASTING, RADIO, TV. AUNTIE.

BC BEFORE CHRIST. BRITISH COLUMBIA (*Province*, Can).

BDS DENTIST.

BEACHCOMBER LONGSHOREMAN, SCAVENGER, VAGRANT. *WAVE*. HUMORIST.

BEAK *BILL*, NEB (Sc), PECKER (mandible). *MASTER*, TEACHER (sl).

BEAKER BRONZE *AGE* FOLK, PRIMITIVE MAN. EWER, JAR, JUG, POT, URN. *BIRD*, HEN, LAYER (crypt).

BEAM LIGHT, RAY, SHAFT, SPOT. SMILE. JOIST, RAFTER, *SUMMER*, *TIMBER*. BREADTH, WIDTH (naut).

BEAR (s/l bare). ANIMAL; URSA, URSUS; BRUIN; ['Exit, pursued by a ~' W Tale, *Shak*; *Elisha*]; **assembly**: sleuth; **breeds**: BLACK, BROWN, BRUANG, GIANT PANDA, GRIZZLY, HIMALAYAN, HONEY, KOALA, KODIAK, POLAR, *SLOTH*, SPECTACLED, SUN [**Offspring** = cub]; **celeb**: BALOO, BOOBOO, MARY PLAIN, PADDINGTON, POOH, RUPERT, THREE BEARS (Goldilocks), YOGI, ARCAS (his m changed to a ~ by Zeus). *AIRCRAFT* (USSR). CARRY, GIVE

BIRTH. ENDURE, SUPPORT. OVERLOOK, SUBTEND.
ISLAND. CONSTELLATION. SPECULATOR (*comm*; **opp** =
bull). **Pl** = *Football team* (US).
BEARD *BEAVER*. BRISTLES, GROWTH. AWN, EAR (wheat).
DEFY.
BEARER *BED*. CARRIER, *MESSENGER*. *MOTHER* (crypt).
BEARING 1. E, N, S, W (or NE, SW etc); HEADING. AIR,
APPEARANCE, ASPECT, *CARRIAGE*, *LOOK*, MIEN; PORT,
PORTAGE. ACCOUCHEMENT, CHILDBIRTH, LYING-IN
(crypt). BALL-RACE, ROLLER. LEANING, PUSHING,
RELATION, REFERENCE. CHARGE, DEVICE (*herald*).
2. Word attached to or 'bearing' another, e.g. **Harsh south wind
bearing east** (7) = AUSTER*E.
BEAT BEST, CHASTISE, LATHER, LICK, OVERCOME,
WORST; SLIPPER, *TAN*, THRASH, WHIP (**opp** = *lose*).
WHISK (cook). PULSE, RHYTHM. PERPLEX. DEFORM,
SHAPE (metal). CLOSE-HAUL, WORK TO WINDWARD
(naut).
BEATER (s/l *beta*). CONQUEROR, *VICTOR*. GAME ROUSER
(shooting). CARPET DUSTER. MIXER, WHIPPER, WHISK.
HEART, PULSATOR. TANNER. DRUMMER (crypt).
BEAT UP COSH, MUG [GBH]. TAEB (dn).
BEAUTY 1. PULCHRITUDE, GOOD LOOKS. 2. **Gods: Gk and
Rom** = *APOLLO*; **goddesses: Gk** = *APHRODITE*, **Rom** =
VENUS. [*Adonis*, Antineus, *Aphrodite*, *Apollo*, *Ganymede*,
Helen, *Paris*, *Psyche*, *Venus* (de Milo)].
BEAUTY SPOT FACE-PATCH. DELL, PANORAMA, VISTA.
BEAVER *BEARD*. FUR. RODENT (*habitation*). WORK AT.
FACEGUARD, VISOR [*armour*].
BECAUSE AS, FOR, SINCE.
BECK *BROOK*, *RIVER*, STREAM. NOD, SIGNAL; **comp** =
CALL.
BECOME TURN INTO. BEFIT, FLATTER, *SUIT*.
BED COUCH, DIVAN, *LITTER*, MATTRESS (and see *furniture*
for types); **comp** = board, breakfast [*Hans Andersen. Procrustes*].
BASE, FOUNDATION, *SEAT*, STRATUM. *PLANT*. *PLOT*.
SEABOTTOM.
BEDDING BEDCLOTHES, BEDLINEN, DUVET; TUCKING UP.
GARDENING (crypt).
BEE (s/l *B*, *be*). *INSECT*; (BUSY) WORKER (**Pl** = TUC);
COMBER (crypt); **assembly** = hive, swarm. 'DEBORAH'

[*Potter*. Queen ~. **comps** = birds, knees].

BEER (s/l *bier*). ALE, *BASS*®, BITTER, *DRINK*, LAGER, MILD, OCTOBER. MUG, PINT (*measure*) [**comp** = skittles]. PIG'S EAR (*rh sl*) [*inventor* = Gambrinus].

BEES AND *MONEY* (*rh sl*).

BEETLE 1. BUG, INSECT (coleopter) [*collector*; *study*]; **breeds**: BEECHAFER, BLACK ~, BOMBARDIER ~, BUPRESTID, (COCK)CHAFER, COCKROACH, DEATH WATCH ~, DOR, DUNG ~, GLOW-WORM, RAM ~, SCARAB, TIGER ~, WILLOW ~: **celeb (fict)**: Arthur Corkran, M'Turk and ~ (Stalky & Co, *Kipling*); ALEXANDER ~ (*Milne*); JABIZRI (*Lofting*); Through the Looking-Glass (*Alice*). 2. ANASTIGMATIC. DICE GAME. OVERHANGING, PROJECTING; SCOWLING, SHAGGY. RUN, SCURRY. CAR (VW, VOLKSWAGEN®).

BEFORE ANTE, B, ERE, PRE (**opp** = after).

~ CHRIST BC.

BEGETTER WH (Shakespeare). *FATHER*, SIRE.

BEGGAR MENDICANT [*friar*, *patron saint*]. BREAK; EXHAUST.

BEGINNER 1. L; DEB, LEARNER, TYRO. *STARTER*. **Pl** = opening actors of new scene (theat). 2. Use first letter of word concerned, e.g. **Circus beginner** = C.

BEHEAD 1. DECAPITATE, EXECUTE, GUILLOTINE. 2. Omit first letter, e.g. **Behead them on the edge** (3) = (*)HEM.

BEHIND TIME 1. *LATE*. 2. Word after synonym for time, e.g. **Under age or behind time** (5) = MIN*OR.

Belg Belgium, ~ian.

BELGIUM B (*car plate*).

BELL (s/l belle). DINGALING, DING-DONG, *RINGER*; *INSTRUMENT* (mus) [campanology: ANGELUS, SANCTUS, Quasimodo (Dumas)]; **celeb**: BIG BEN (Westminster), BOOM (RAF ch), CENTENNIAL (US 1976), CZAR KOLOKOL (Moscow), GREAT TOM (Oxford), GT PAUL (St Paul's), LIBERTY (US 1752), LUTINE (*Lloyd's*), SEBASTOPOL (Windsor). INVENTOR (Alexander Graham ~, telephone). *PAINTER*. *Model* (*Holmes*). WRITER (Brontë). **Pl** = TIME (naut watchkeeping).

BELLEROPHON 1. Gk myth hero who rode *Pegasus* and slew the *monster Chim(a)era*. 2. Br warship which took Napoleon's surrender.

BELLOWS MAKER *BULL*, *COW*, OX; *LOWER* (crypt). FLUTE (*Shak* MND).

BELL RINGING CAMPANOLOGY; **changes**: Bob Major, Bob
Maximus, Bob Minor, Bob Royal, Bob Triple, Grandsire Triple,
Great Tom, Nine Tailors, Oxford Treble Bob, Treble Bob,
Yorkshire Surprise Major [Quasimodo]. TINNITUS.
TINTINABULATION.

BELONG *FIT*, GO WITH, *SUIT*. OWNED BY.
PROCRASTINATE, TARRY (crypt).

BELSHAZZAR Variant spelling of *BALTHAZAR*. The bibl s of
Nebuchadnezzar, at ~'s feast a moving hand wrote 'Mene mene
tekel upharsin'. *Daniel* interpreted as 'You are weighed in the
balances and found wanting'. That night ~ was k.

BEM BRITISH EMPIRE MEDAL: *DECORATION*, *MEDAL*.

BEND *S*; *U*; CURVE. *BOW*, STOOP, SUBMIT. APPLY (to task).
KNOT (*fisherman's* ~, sheet ~). PERVERT. SPREE. STRIPE
(*herald*) [dexter; sinister (bastardy)]. **Pl** = Decompression sickness
(astronauts, divers).

BENDER BINGE, SPREE. STOOP. PERVERTER. HINGE,
JOINT; ELBOW, KNEE, KNUCKLE (crypt). *S*, *U* (crypt).

BENT *BOWED*, CRANKED, CURVED, OUT OF TRUE,
TWISTED (**opp** = straight). DISHONEST.

BERMUDA ISLAND. *TRIANGLE*. **Pl** = *SHORTS*. London
district (arch).

BERRY DOLLAR (US), POUND (sl). *FRUIT* (without stone); also
HIP, HAW, SLOE. [Dornford Yates].

BERYL *GEM*, PRECIOUS STONE; AQUAMARINE, EMERALD
(blue, green, white, yellow). GREY, REID (theat).

BESIDES *AGAIN*, AS WELL, ELSE, MOREOVER,
OTHERWISE. ALONGSIDE.

BE SORRY APOLOGIZE, CARE, MOPE, REGRET.

BEST A, AI, *ACE*, NO I; CHOICE, FIRST RATE, TOPS (**opp** =
worst). *BEAT*; WORST.

BET ANTE, STAKE. GAMBLE, PUNT, RISK, SPECULATE,
WAGER; **types**: *ACCUMULATOR*, CANADIAN, DOUBLE,
HEINZ, TREBLE, TRI-CAST, YANKEE.

BETA (s/l *beater*). B, *SECOND* (LETTER). ELECTRON.

BETRAY(ER) GIVE AWAY, *GRASS*, INFORM, NARK, PEACH,
SHOP, SING, SNEAK, SPLIT, SQUEAL, STOOL PIGEON,
TELL-TALE(S).

BETTER IMPROVED, SUPERIOR. GAMBLER, PUNTER,
SPECULATOR; LAYER (crypt).

BETTING ODDS, SP. GAMBLING (and see *bet*).

BEVY *ASSEMBLY*, COMPANY (of beauty, ladies, *larks*, *quails*).
BEY (s/l *bay*). GOVERNOR, *NOBLE*, OFFICIAL (*Turk*).
BIBLE AV, RV; NT, OT. BOOK OF BOOKS. LAST WORD,
MANUAL. [~ *King*].
BIBLICAL TOWN AERE, *AI*, APHEK, BETHEL, CANA, DAN,
DOR, ENDOR, GATH, GAZA, GEBA, JAHAZ, JERICHO,
NAIN, NEVE, NOB, SIDON, *TYRE*, UR, ZIPH.
BIBLIOMANIA *Obsession* with books.
BIBLIOPHILE *Lover* of books.
BIER (s/l *beer*). FUNERAL LITTER, HEARSE, LAST
TRIP/VEHICLE.
BIG OS, LARGE (**opp** = little, small); TIDY (sl). BOASTFUL.
BIG GAME 1. CHAMPIONSHIP, (CUP) FINAL, (TEST) MATCH
(all crypt). 2. BEASTS, JUNGLE DWELLERS, WILD
ANIMALS, -LIFE, e.g. *ANTELOPE* (q.v.), *BEAR*, *CAT* (q.v.),
CROCODILE, ELEPHANT, ELP, GIRAFFE,
HIPPOPOTAMUS, HYENA, JACKAL, *KANGAROO*,
MAMMOTH (ex), *MONKEY* (q.v.), RHINOCEROS, WOLF,
ZEBRA [*deer*, *dolphin*, *shark*, *whale*].
BIGHT (s/l *bite*, byte). *BAY*, *GULF*, INLET. COIL, LOOP (naut).
BIKE RACE *TT* [Isle of Man]. TOUR DE FRANCE.
BILL *AC*, *ACCOUNT*, *CHECK*, INVOICE, *NOTE*,
RECKONING, *SETTLEMENT*, TAB. BANKNOTE.
POSTER; ANNOUNCE. *MEASURE* (parl). HALBERD,
PIKE, *WEAPON*. WILLIAM, WM [Old ~ (Bairnsfather)].
BEAK; PECK; **comp** = coo; Mary (William and ~). *LIZARD*
(*Alice*). **Pl** = *Football team* (US).
BILLIARDS *GAME* [*Cleopatra*; '. . . elliptical ~ balls' (Mikado, *G
and S*); cannon; *snooker*, spot].
BILLYCOCK BOWLER *HAT*.
BIRD *GIRL*, YOUNG WOMAN (sl). RASPBERRY (sl). PRISON
SENTENCE, *TIME* (sl). *WRITER*. FEATHERED
VERTEBRATE; BEAKER, DICKY, LAYER [Audubon, *Male
& female*, *offspring*, *study*]; **comp** = bees; **breeds:**

2-letters	COB	KAE
KA	ELK	KEA
OO	*EMU*	MAO
	ERN	*MOA* (ex)
3-letters	HEN	*NUN*
AUK (ex)	JAY	OWL

PAU
PEN
PIE
POE
ROC (myth)
ROK (myth)
RUC (myth)
TIT
TUI
WRY

4-letters
BAYA
BUBO
CIRL
COCK
COOT
CRAX
CROW
DODO (ex)
DOVE
DUCK
ERNE
EYAS
FOWL
GAWK
GOWK
GUAN
GULL
HAWK
HERN (arch)
HUMA (myth)
IBIS
KAGU
KAKA
KITE
KIWI
KNOT
KOEL
LARK
LOON

LORY
MINA
MYNA
NENE
NIAS
NYAS
PAUW
PAVO
PERN
PICA
PIET
POLL
RAIL
RHEA
ROOK
RUFF
RYPE
SHAG
SKUA
SMEE
SMEW
SWAN
TAHA
TEAL
TERN
TODY
URIA
WEKA
WREN
XEMA
YAUP
YITE
YOIT
YUNX
ZATI

5-letters
AGAMI
AMSEL
ANNET
ARGUS

BIDDY
BOOBY
BOWET
BRENT
BUCCO
CAPON
CHICK
CLAIK
COLIN
CRAKE
CRANE
CURRE
DAKER
DIVER
DUNNE
EAGLE
EGRET
EIDER
FINCH
FRANK
GLEDE
GOOSE
GREBE
HERON
HOBBY
HOMER
IMBER
JAGER
JUNCO
LAYER
LOXIA
LYRIE
MACAW
MADGE
MAVIS
MERLE
MOLLY
MONAL
MURRE
MYNAH
NANDU

NODDY
ORNIS
ORTYX
OUSEL
OUZEL
PAAUW
PEWIT
PICUS
PIPIT
POKER
POLLY
POULT
PURRE
QUAIL
RALPH
RAVEN
REEVE
ROBIN
RODGE
RUDGE
RYPER
SAKER
SALLY
SCAUP
SCOBY
SCOPS
SCOUT
SCULL
SENEX
SERIN
SITTA
SKITE
SNIPE
STILT
STINT
STORK
STRIX
SWIFT
TARIN
TEREK
TIDDY

TOPAU
TOPET
TWITE
URILE
URUBU
VEERY
VIREO
WADER
WHAUP
WHILK
WONGA
YACOU

6-letters
ADELIE
AIGLET
ANANAS
ANCONA
ARGALA
AVOCET
BOWESS
BULBUL
CANARY
CHOUGH
CONDOR
CORBIE
CORVUS
CUCKOO
CULVER
CURLEW
CUSHAT
CYGNET
DARTER
DIPPER
DRONGO
DUNLIN
EAGLET
FALCON
FULMAR
GANDER
GANNET

GENTOO
GODWIT
GRAKLE
GROUSE
GUINEA
HOOPOE
HOOPOO
JABIRU
JACANA
JERKIN
KELTIS
KONDOR
LANNER
LINNET
LORIOT
MAGPIE
MARROT
MARTIN
MERLIN
MERULA
MISSEL
MISTLE
MOPOKE
MOT-MOT
NANDOO
NESTOR
NICKER
ORIOLE
OSPREY
OUZLEM (myth)
OXBIRD
PARROT
PARSON
PASTOR
PAVONE (arch)
PEAHEN
PEEWIT
PETREL
PHENIX (myth)
PHOEBE
PIGEON

PLOVER
POUTER
PUFFIN
PULLET
QUEEST
QUELEA
QUEZAL
RAPTOR
REDCAP
ROLLER
RUDDOC
SCOTER
SEAHEN
SEAMEW
SERULA
SHRIKE
SICSAC
SIMBIL
SIMURG (Pers myth)
SISKIN
SOLAND
SPARVE
SULTAN
SURREY
TATLER
TERCEL
TEWHIT
THRUSH
TOM-TIT
TOUCAN
TROGON
TURBIT
TURKEY
TURNER
TYSTIE
WEAVER
WIGEON
WILLET
WITWAL
XENOPS
YAFFLE

YAFFIL
YUCKER
ZICSAC
ZOO-ZOO

7-letters
AWL-BIRD
BEE-BIRD
BITTERN
BLUE-CAP
BLUE-JAY
BLUE-TIT
BUNTING
BUSHTIT
BUSTARD
BUTCHER
BUZZARD
CHICKEN
COAL-TIT
COLIBRI
COW-BIRD
CREEPER
DIDIDAE
DOTTREL
DUNNOCK
FEN-DUCK
FERN-OWL
FLUSHER
GADWALL
GOBBLER
GORCOCK
GOSHAWK
GRAY-LAG
GRAY-OWL
GREY-HEN
GREY-LAG
HALCYON (myth)
HARRIER
HAWK-OWL
HICKWAY
HOATZIN

JACAMAR
JACKDAW
KESTREL
LAPWING
LAVROCK
MALLARD
MARABOU
MAY-BIRD
MOORHEN
ORTOLAN
OSTRICH
OVEN-TIT
PEACOCK
PELICAN
PENGUIN
PETEREL
PHAETON
PHOENIX (myth)
PINNOCK
PINTADO
PINTAIL
POCHARD
POULTRY
QUABIRD
RADDOCK
RATITAE
REDPOLL
REDTAIL
REDWING
ROOSTER
ROSELLA
ROYSTON
RUDDOCK
SAWBILL
SAWWHET
SCOOPER
SEA-CROW
SEA-DOVE
SEA-DUCK
SEAGULL
SEA-HAWK

SKIMMER
SKYLARK
SNOW-OWL
SPARROW
SUNBIRD
SWALLOW
TANAGER
TARROCK
TIERCEL
TITLARK
TOURACO
TUMBLER
VULTURE
WAGTAIL
WARBLER
WAXWING
WHOOPER
WIDGEON
WILLOCK
WIMBREL
WOOD-OWL
WRYBILL
WRYNECK
WYANDOT
YELDRIN

8-letters
ACCENTOR
ADJUTANT
ALCATRAS
AMADAVAT
BARNACLE
BEE-EATER
BELL-BIRD
BLACKCAP
BLUEBIRD
BOATBILL
BOBOLINK
CHURN-OWL
CURASSOW
DABCHICK

DINORNIS
DOTTEREL
DUCKLING
DUN-DIVER
EAGLE-OWL
FALCONET
FENGOOSE
FIRETAIL
FISH-HAWK
FLAMINGO
FORKTAIL
HACKBOLT
HAWFINCH
HEATH-HEN
HOACTZIN
HORNBILL
LANDRAIL
LANNERET
LINGBIRD
LOVEBIRD
LYRE-BIRD
MARABOUT
MARSH-HEN
MARSH-TIT
MIRE-CROW
MOORCOCK
MOREPORK
NESTLING
NUTHATCH
OVEN-BIRD
OX-PECKER
PARAKEET
PARAQUET
PAROQUET
PENELOPE
PHEASANT
PHILOMER
PICKEREL
PUFF-BIRD
RAINBIRD
REDSHANK

REEDBIRD
REEDLING
RICE-BIRD
RING-BILL
RING-DOVE
RINGTAIL
ROCKDOVE
RUBECULA
SAND-BIRD
SAND-COCK
SAND-LARK
SARCELLE
SARDELLE
SCREAMER
SEA-EAGLE
SEA-QUAIL
SEA-RAVEN
SEDGE-HEN
SHELDUCK
SHOEBILL
SNOWBIRD
SONGBIRD
SONGSTER
STARLING
THRESHER
THROSTLE
TITMOUSE
TITTEREL
WATER-HEN
WHEATEAR
WHIMBREL
WHINCHAT
WILDFOWL
WOODCOCK
WOODLARK
WRANNOCK
XANTHURA
YELDRING
YELDROCK
ZOPILOTE

9-letters
ALBATROSS
BALTIMORE
BECCAFICO
BLACKBIRD
BLACKCOCK
BLACK SWAN
BOWERBIRD
BRAMBLING
BULLFINCH
CASSOWARY
CHAFFINCH
CHICKADEE
COCKATIEL
CORMORANT
CORNCRAKE
CROSSBILL
FIELDFARE
FIRECREST
GALLINULE
GERFALCON
GOLDCREST
GOLDENEYE
GOLDFINCH
GOOSANDER
GUILLEMOT
GYRFALCON
HIRUNDINE
KITTIWAKE
LORRIKEET
MERGANSER
NIGHTHAWK
PARDALOTE
PARTRIDGE
PEREGRINE
PHALAROPE
PTARMIGAN
RAZORBILL
REDBREAST
RED GROUSE
RING OUSEL

ROSSIGNOL
SANDPIPER
SAPSUCKER
SECRETARY
SHELDRAKE
SNOW GOOSE
SOOTY TERN
SPOONBILL
STONECHAT
TROCHILUS
TRUMPETER
TURNSTONE
WATERFOWL
WIDOWBIRD

10+ letters
ARCHAEOPTERYX (ex)
BALTIMORE BIRD
BIRD OF PARADISE
BISHOPBIRD
BLACK GROUSE
BLACKTHROAT
BUDGERIGAR
BLUETHROAT
BRENT GOOSE
BUSH CREEPER
BUTCHERBIRD
CANADA GOOSE
CANVAS-BACK
CAPERCAILLIE
CARRION CROW
CHANTICLEER
CHIFFCHAFF
CORNBUNTING
CRESTED GREBE
CRESTED PIGEON
CRESTED TIT
DEMOISELLE
DISHWASHER
EMPEROR PENGUIN
FANTAIL PIGEON

FLYCATCHER
GOLDEN EAGLE
GOLDEN ORIOLE
GOLDEN PHEASANT
GREENFINCH
GUINEAFOWL
HERRING GULL
HOUSEMARTIN
HUMMINGBIRD
KINGFISHER
KING PENGUIN
KOOKABURRA
LAMMERGEIER
MARSH WARBLER
MEADOW PIPIT
MISSELTHRUSH
MOCKINGBIRD
MUTTONBIRD
NIGHTINGALE
NUTCRACKER
REED WARBLER
RIFLE WARBLER
ROADRUNNER
ROCK PIGEON
SANDERLING

SAND GROUSE
SAND MARTIN
SCISSORBILL
SEA SWALLOW
SECRETARY BIRD
SHEARWATER
SNOW BUNTING
SOLAN GOOSE
SONG THRUSH
SPARROWHAWK
STORMY PETREL
TURTLEDOVE
WATERWAGTAIL
WEAVERBIRD
WHIP-POOR-WILL
WHITETHROAT
WILLOW WARBLER
WHOOPER SWAN
WOODPECKER
WOODPIGEON
YAFFINGALE
YELLOW BUNTING
YELLOWHAMMER
ZEBRA FINCH

BIRDIE One under par on a *golf-course*, hence PAR*I or PAR*ONE (dn). [camera].

BIRTHSTONE Jan = *GARNET*; **Feb** = *AMETHYST*; **Mar** = *BLOODSTONE*; **Apr** = *DIAMOND*; **May** = *EMERALD*; **Jun** = *AGATE*; **Jul** = *CORNELIAN*; **Aug** = *SARDONYX*; **Sep** = *CHRYSOLITE*; **Oct** = *OPAL*; **Nov** = *TOPAZ*; **Dec** = *TURQUOISE*.

BISHOP *CHURCHMAN*, CLERGYMAN [*episcopal sig*; *see*]; RR, Rt Rev. CHESSPIECE, *ROOK*. *Military leader* (air). *POET*.

BIT *BORE*, CUTTING IRON, *HEAD*, PIECE. CHEWED, GRIPPED, NIPPED. BRIDLE, HACKAMORE, SNAFFLE (*harness*). MORSEL. SOMEWHAT. CONTRIBUTION. BINARY DIGIT, COMPUTER INFORMATION. **Pl comp** = *pieces*.

BITCH *FEMALE* DOG/FOX/OTTER/WOLF. MALICIOUS

WOMAN, TERMAGANT, *VIXEN*. GRUMBLE, MUDDLE.
BITE (s/l *bight*, byte). CHEW, NIP; FOOD, MEAL. BORROW,
EXTORT. STING. GRIP. INFECT.
BL BRITISH LEGION. BRITISH LEYLAND.
BLACK B; *COLOUR*; DARK; SABLE (*herald*); [~ Rod, Garter].
SEA. SNOOKER BALL (score 7). **Comp** = *blue*; *white*.
BLACKBIRD SONGBIRD (turdus merula; thrush family); MERLE
(arch Sc) [24 ~s baked in a pie]. NEGRO SLAVE. SPY-PLANE
(US mil).
BLACKFRIARS DOMINICANS, PREACHING *FRIARS*.
THAMES BRIDGE.
BLACKSMITH FARRIER, FORGER, METAL-WORKER
[*Company* (livery)]; **celeb**: JAMES BURTON (Kingsley), JOE
GARGERY (Great Ex, *Dickens*), THE VILLAGE ~
(Longfellow).
BLADE LEAF. CHISEL, KNIFE, SWORD. DASHING
FELLOW. Part of bat, oar, paddle wheel, propeller, spade,
turbine.
BLAZE BRIGHT FLAME, BURN, *FIRE*. *COLOUR*, EMIT
LIGHT. PROCLAIM. MARK ON HORSE; SLASH A TREE.
BLAZER COLOURED JACKET, SCHOOL COAT. ARSONIST;
FIREMAN (crypt).
BLEND(ED) *Anag*. *ADMIX*, AMALGAM, MIX, MIXTURE.
BLEW (s/l *blue*). WAFTED. BURST. SPENT. SQUANDERED.
BLIND RASH, RECKLESS, UNSWERVING. CONCEALED,
DEAD-END, PLAIN, WALLED-UP. DAZZLE, DECEIVE.
ANOPTIC, SIGHTLESS, UNSEEING; **celeb**: *Balder* (Nor myth);
Earl of Gloucester (Lear, *Shak*); Edward *Rochester* (Jane Eyre,
Brontë); *Isaac* (bibl); Helen Keller (US); King John of Bohemia
(hist); Nydia (Bulwer Lytton); *Oedipus* (Gk myth); ~ Pew
(*Stevenson*); Phineus (Gk myth); *Samson* (bibl); Tiresias (Gk
myth); Milton (*poet*); bat, mole, owl. And see *one-eyed*.
AWNING, CURTAIN, SCREEN, SHUTTER, SUNSHADE.
DUMMY, MASK, PRETEXT, SMOKE-SCREEN, STALKING-
HORSE, SUBTERFUGE, VEIL. DRUNK (sl).
BLONDEL MINSTREL [*Lionheart*, ransom, Richard].
BLOODSTONE *GEM*, SEMI-PRECIOUS STONE.
CHALCEDONY (green/red). *Birthstone* (Mar).
BLOODSUCKER LEECH, *MOSQUITO*, *TICK*, VAMPIRE.
GOLD-DIGGER (sl).
BLOOMER BLUNDER, ERROR, MISTAKE. FLOWER (crypt).

Pl = *DRAWERS*, KNICKERS, UNDERWEAR.

BLOOMING FLOWERING, *OUT*. DASHED, WRETCHED.

BLOW PANT, PUFF, VENT, *WIND*. EXPLODE, PUNCTURE. BREAK, FUSE, MELT. *BETRAY*. FLY'S EGGS. HIT, KNOCK, ONER, *SMACK*. DISASTER, SHOCK. SPEND, SQUANDER. *COMPOSER*.

BLOWER *WIND*. ENGINE, PUFFER, STEAM-TRAIN. SUPERCHARGER (sl). TELEPHONE (sl).

BLOW-OUT PUNCTURE; FUSED. VOLCANO (crypt). MEAL. *Anag* 'blow'.

BLUE (s/l *blew*). *COLOUR*, AZURE (*herald*), INDIGO (anil, woad); **comp** = *black*. SNOOKER BALL (score 5). COLD, DEPRESSED, DISCONSOLATE, DISPIRITED, DOWN, LOW. BRUISED. FEAR. INDECENT, SALTY. LEARNED. *GRASS*. *OXFORD* or *CAMBRIDGE ATHLETE* or *PLAYER*. SPEND. **Pl** = DEPRESSION, DUMPS. HORSEGUARDS, HOUSEHOLD CAVALRY. UNIVERSITY TEAM (O and C).

BLUSH *COLOUR*, FLUSH, REDDEN. GLANCE, GLIMPSE.

BM BRITISH MUSEUM.

BMA BRITISH MEDICAL ASSOCIATION.

B MUS MUSICIAN.

BN BATTALION, *SOLDIERS*, TROOPS.

BO BODY ODOUR [perspiration, sweat]. Sacred tree of Buddha.

BOADICEA BOUDICCA. Queen of the *Iceni*, she withstood the *Romans*, defeating them at Camulodunum (*Colchester*) and London, where she slew 50,000. Was finally defeated by Suetonius Paulinus, and committed suicide in A.D. 61.

BOAR (s/l *bore*). *MALE PIG*/GUINEA-PIG. [Labour of *Hercules*].

BOARD (s/l *bored*). *FOOD*, KEEP, MEALS; *TABLE*; **comp** = bed; lodging. PLANK, SLAB. COVER OVER. EMBARK, GET ABOARD/ON. SHIP'S SIDE, TACK. *DIRECTORS*. **Pl** = *STAGE, THEATRE*.

BOARD GAME Game played on a board: **types**: L'ATTAQUE®, BACKGAMMON, BINGO (Housey Housey, Keno, Lotto, Tombola), CHECKERS (US), CHESS, CLUEDO®, CROWN & ANCHOR, DRAUGHTS, GO(H) (Jap), HALMA, LUDO®, MAH JONGG (Ch), MONOPOLY®, RISK®, SCRABBLE®, SEPTEMBER®, SHOVE HA'PENNY, SNAKES & LADDERS, SOLITAIRE, TRIVIAL PURSUIT®; CRIBBAGE, DARTS, DECK HOCKEY/TENNIS (all crypt).

BOARD, ON 1. EMBARKED. 2. Word with S . . . S round it, e.g. **I**

go on board to find my little sister (3) = S*I*S.   3. Game played on a board, any *board game* (q.v. for **types**).   4. AT TABLE, DINING.
BOAT ARGO(SY), *CRAFT*, PACKET, SHIP, SS, *VESSEL*; **types**:

3-letters
ARK
CAT
COB
FLY
GIG
HOY
MTB (mil)
TUG

4-letters
BARK
BRIG
BUSS
DORY
JUNK
KOFF
PINK
PRAM
PRAU
PROA
PUNT
SCOW
SHIP
SKIP
SNOW
YAWL

5-letters
BALSA
BARGE
CANOE
DANDY
E-BOAT (mil)
FUNNY
KETCH
LINER

PARDO
PRAAM
PRAHU
SKIFF
SLOOP
SMACK
U-BOAT (mil)
XEBEC
YACHT

6-letters
ARGOSY
BARQUE
BIREME
CUTTER
DINGHY
DOGGER
DUGOUT
GALLEY
HOOKER
HOWKER
LAUNCH
LORCHA
LUGGER
PACKET
RANDAN
ROWING
SAMPAN
SETTEE
SURFER
TARTAN
TENDER
VESSEL
WHALER
WHERRY

7-letters
BEAN-COD
BUGALET
CARRIER (mil)
CHAMPAN
CLIPPER
CORACLE
CRUISER (mil)
DRIFTER
FELUCCA
FRIGATE (mil)
GALLEAS (mil)
GALLEON
GALLIOT
HOUARIO
LIGHTER
LYMPHAD (*herald*)
PIROGUE
POLACRE
SHALLOP
TRIREME

8+ letters
BATTLESHIP (mil)
CARACORE
CATAMARAN
CORACORE
DESTROYER (mil)
HERRINGBUSS
OTAHEITE
PERIAGUA
SAILBOARD
SCHOONER
SUBMARINE (mil)
TRIMARAN
WINDSURFER®

BOAT-GIRL FLORA (MacDonald). STEWARDESS. WAVE
(US), WREN, WRNS.

BOB S, SHILLING, VP, XIID. HAIRSTYLE, PAGEBOY,
TASSEL. SLED, SLEDGE, SLEIGH. BOUNCE, CURTSEY,
DANCE, DUCK, JERK, WEAVE. PLUMB, WEIGHT.
CHANGE (*bell ringing*). ETONIAN (**dry** ~ = cricketer, **wet** ~ =
rower).

BOBBY ROBERT. *POLICEMAN* (*Peel*). *CALF*.

BOFFIN 1. BACKROOM BOY, SCIENTIST (sl). 2. NICODEMUS
~ (*Dickens* character, Mutual F; dustman who became rich).

BOGEY BUGBEAR. GOBLIN, *SPIRIT*. PAR (golf). *Colonel* ~
(Sousa, mus). SWIM (Aus). Unidentified aircraft (mil).

BOIL *Anag*. BUBBLE, SEETHE, STEW, UNDULATE (all of
which also mean *anag*). GATHERING, TUMOUR (med).

BOMBER *AIRCRAFT*.

BONDED DUTY-FREE, EX-CUSTOMS, SCOT-FREE,
TAX-FREE. GLUED, SEALED, TIED UP.
[Ian Fleming; 007].

BONE *ROB*, *STEAL* (sl). *PAINTER*. FILLET. STIFFEN.
HARD TISSUE, DENTINE, IVORY, WHALEBONE
[scrimshaw, *study*]. ~s of the body: **head**: CRANIUM (skull)
[antrum, sinus], ALVEOLUS, MANDIBLE, MAXILLA (jaw);
BICUSPID, CANINE, EYETOOTH, INCISOR, MILKTOOTH,
MOLAR, PREMOLAR, WISDOM TOOTH (teeth); **neck**:
ATLAS, AXIS; **shoulder**: CLAVICLE (collar ~), CORACOID,
SCAPULA (shoulderblade); **spine**: COCCYX, SACRUM,
VERTEBRA [cervical, thoracic, lumbar]; **arm**: HUMERUS
(upper), ELBOW, RADIUS, ULNA (forearm); **hand**: CARPUS
(wrist), METACARPUS, *PHALANX* (finger), TRAPEZIUM;
chest: RIB, STERNUM (breastbone); **hip**: ILIUM, PELVIS,
SACRUM; **leg**: FEMUR (thigh), PATELLA (kneecap), FIBULA,
TIBIA (shin) [Pott's fracture]; **foot**: TALUS (ankle),
CALCANEUM (heel), *PHALANX* (toe), METATARSUS,
TARSUS; [calcium, marrow, necrosis, ossify]. **Comp** = rag. **Pl** =
DICE (sl); SKELETON. ESSENTIALS, FRAMEWORK.
CASTANETS, *INSTRUMENT* (mus).

BOOK ENTER, LIST, LOG. BAG, *ENGAGE*, RESERVE.
BETTING. *ANNUAL*, EDITION, ISSUE, PUBLICATION,
VOL(UME), TOME. BIBLE. [*measure* (paper size)]. **Comp** =
bell and candle.

BOOKED ENTERED, LISTED, LOGGED. BAGGED,

ENGAGED, RESERVED. BOUND, ISSUED, PUBLISHED, WRITTEN ABOUT (crypt).

BOOKLET BK, ED, VO, VOL.

BOOKMAKER AUTHOR, COMPILER, EDITOR, PAGE(S), PUBLISHER, *WRITER* (all crypt). [*patron saint*]. BETTING MAN, BOOKIE [*racetrack*, tote].

BOOT *SHOE*; *WELLINGTON*. *DISMISS*, *FIRE*, *SACK*. TRUNK (US). AVAIL.

BORACIC LINT BROKE, SKINT (*rh sl*).

BORE (s/l *boar*). MINE, WELL. AUGER, AWL, DRILL; *MISER*. CALIBRE. EAGRE, (TIDAL) *WAVE*. TIRE (**opp** = *enchant*). BEGAT.

BOREAS Gk myth NORTH *WIND*.

BORED (s/l *board*). DRILLED. RIFLED. *TIRED*.

BORING DRILLING. ENNUI, TEDIOUS, TIRING; *DRY*, DULL.

BORN (s/l *borne*, *bourn*). B, NE, NEE. DESTINED. *NATIVE*, ORIGINATED. **Comp** = bred.

BORNE (s/l *born*, *bourn*). *CARRIED*. NARROW MINDED.

BORON B (*chem*).

BORROW 1. INCUR DEBT, RAISE (money, the *wind* [IOU]); **opp** = lend; ADOPT, APPROPRIATE. *COPY*, *IMITATE*, *PIRATE*, PLAGIARISE. UPHILL, SLOPE; DEVIATION, SWERVE (golf putting). George ~, Eng *writer*.

BOSIE LORD *ALFRED* DOUGLAS. *CHINAMAN* (Bosanquet, *cricket*).

BOSPHORUS *STRAIT*; *OX-FORD* [*Io*].

BOSS EMPLOYER, FOREMAN, MANAGER, OVERMAN, OVERSEER; M (Bond's ~). KNOB, STUD, UMBO. *SECRET POLICE* (S Af).

BOTHER CONFOUND, DAMN, DRAT. ADO, FUSS, TODO. IRRITATE, *NETTLE*, WORRY.

BOTH SIDES 1. EW, LR (crypt). 2. Word at start and end, e.g. **One on both sides** (5) = ON*I*ON.

BOTTLE RESTRAIN, STOP UP (hence POTS, dn) (**opp** = decant; release). ELAN, NERVE; DUTCH COURAGE (crypt). *JAR*. *ISLAND*. CONTAINER, *MEASURE*, VIAL [~d = place word in ~ (or synonym), e.g. **Lively bottled car** (5) = VI(T)AL]; **types:** *SPLIT* (¼ bot), HALF-BOTTLE, BOTTLE (80 cl), MAGNUM (2 bots), *JEROBOAM* (4 bots), *REHOBOAM* (6 bots), *METHUSELAH* (8 bots), *SALMANAZAR* (12 bots),

BALTHAZAR (16 bots), *NEBUCHADNEZZAR* (20 bots); DEMIJOHN. CARAFE. [ten green ~s].

BOTTOM 1. *BASE*, BASIC, FUNDAMENTAL, LOWEST, NADIR, NETHERMOST, UNDERNEATH. BACKSIDE, BEHIND, BUTTOCKS, SIT-UPON. RIVERBED, SEABED; RUN AGROUND. *BOAT* (arch; q.v. for list), HULL, SHIP, *VESSEL* (q.v. for **celeb**). HOLLOW, VALLEY. 2. A *weaver* in MND (*Shak*), whose head was *transformed* into that of an *ass*, and with whom Titania was made to fall in love on waking.

BOUDICCA *BOADICEA*.

BOUGH (s/l *bow*). BRANCH, STEM.

BOUNCER CHUCKER-OUT, DOORMAN. BUMPER, SHORT BALL (hence *BAL*, crypt, cricket). DUD CHEQUE. *BOUNDER*, *JUMPER*, LEAPER; **celeb**: Mrs ~ (*landlady*, Box and Cox, Morton); *GORGON*; TIGGER (*Milne*).

BOUND BOUNCE, JUMP, LEAP, RECOIL, SPRING. TIED, LIMIT(ED). *BOOK*, PUBLISHED (crypt). CERTAIN, DESTINED, SURE.

BOUNDARY BARRIER, EDGE, LIMIT, PALE; MARCH. FOUR (*cricket*). TRAMPOLINE (crypt). **Rom god** = TERMINUS.

BOUNDED DELINEATED, EDGED, LIMITED. JUMPED, LEAPED, SPRANG. TIED UP.

BOUNDER *HOPPER*, *JUMPER* [*Gorgon*]; *CRICKET*, FROG, GOAT, GRASSHOPPER, KANGAROO (all crypt). CAD. *BALL* (crypt).

BOURN (s/l *born*, *borne*). *BROOK*. GOAL, LIMIT.

BOVINE COWLIKE, OX-LIKE, STUPID.

BOW (s/l *bough*). NOD, OBEISANCE, SALUTE, SUBMIT. FRONT, STEM (naut); ROWER. SLIPKNOT. *ARCH*, CURVE. LONGBOW, *WEAPON* [black ~ of Euryatus (*Ulysses*)]; **comp** = *arrow*. RAINBOW. PLAY *FIDDLE*/VIOLIN etc.

BOWED *ARCHED*, BENT, CURVED, HUNCHED. NODDED, SALUTED. FIDDLED, PLAYED (crypt). SHOT ARROW (archery, crypt).

BOWER *CELLIST*, FIDDLER, VIOLINIST (crypt). ARCHER, ROBIN *HOOD*, WILLIAM TELL (crypt). ARBOUR. CONSENTER, NODDER, SUBMITTER: COURTIER, LACKEY, USHER. ANCHOR. *CARD* (euchre, knave).

BOWERY 1. OBEISANCE (crypt). ARBOUR. 2. District of New York.

BOWL BASIN, DISH. DELIVER, TAKE OVER (*cricket*).
TRUNDLE. BIASED BALL, JACK, WOOD [bowls, skittles].

BOWLED B, DELIVERED, SENT DOWN (*cricket*). SALAD
(crypt).

BOWLER CRICKETER, DELIVERY MAN, PITCHER. DRAKE
(crypt). BILLYCOCK, *HAT*. POTTER (crypt).

BOWMAN ARCHER; CUPID, ROBIN *HOOD*, WILLIAM TELL.
CELLIST, *FIDDLER*, VIOLINIST (crypt).

BOX *FIGHT*, *SPAR* [pugilism]. CARTON, CASE, *CHEST*.
TELLY, TV. *TREE*. *MEASURE* (fish). *PLANT*. **Comp** = Cox
(Mrs *Bouncer*).

BOXER *FIGHTER*, PUGILIST; *POLLUX*. *HORSE* (Animal
Farm, *Orwell*). CASE-MAKER, PACKER. CHINAMAN.
LETTER-SENDER/POSTER (crypt). SENTRY (crypt).

BOXING 1. FISTICUFFS, PUNCHING; BAREKNUCKLE, THE
FIGHT GAME; THAI ~ [Queensberry Rules]; **weights**: fly ~,
bantam ~, feather ~, junior light ~, light ~, junior welter ~,
welter ~, light heavy ~, heavy ~. 2. ENCASING, WRAPPING
(presents [~ Day]). UNDERTAKING, LAYING OUT (sl).
Planting a hedge, shrub; HEDGING (crypt). Reciting compass
points in order. CUFFING, SLAPPING (ears).

BOY 1. KID, LAD, NIPPER. DICK, ED, JACK, SAM, TOM etc.
2. Three lily-white ~, in *song*. [~ **and girl** = pigeon pair].

~s BRIGADE BB, CADETS.

BR BRAZIL (*car plate*). *BRIDGE*. BRITISH *RAIL*. BROMINE
(*chem*). *BROTHER*.

Br Britain, ~ish. Brother.

BRAG BOAST, SHOW OFF (**opp** = *modest*). *CARDS*. Nor *god*.

BRAHMA Principal Indian *god*.

BRAKE (s/l *break*). BROKE (OE). BRACKEN, BRUSHWOOD.
SKID, SLIPPER (tech); CHECK, CRUSH, RETARD.
CARRIAGE, ESTATE CAR, WAGON.

BRANCH STEM [tree: *Absolom*]. OFFSHOOT, SUB-OFFICE.
JUMP.

BRAND BURN, CHAR. MARK, STIGMA. LABEL,
TRADEMARK; HOT IRON. SWORD. BLIGHT.

BRASS 1. *MONEY*; **comp** = muck. BUGLE, TROMBONE,
TRUMPET, TUBA etc. STAFF OFFICERS. 2. Copper/Zinc
alloy, hence CU*ZN.

BRAVE FACE UP TO; BOLD, FEARLESS, *GAME*. *AMERICAN
INDIAN* (q.v. for tribes; **opp** = paleface).

Braz Brazil, ~ian.

BREAD CRUST, *LOAF*, ROLL; DOUGH [~ into *roses* (St
  Elizabeth)]; **comp** = *butter*, *cheese*. *MONEY* (sl).

BREAK (s/l *brake*). *Anag.* BUST, *CRACK*, FRACTURE,
  SEPARATE, SHATTER, SNAP. GAP, INTERVAL. ESCAPE;
  EXHAUST. TAME. **Comp** = *make*.

BREAKER KEG. *COMBER*, SURF, *WAVE*. CRACKSMAN,
  ROBBER. CB ENTHUSIAST (radio, sl).

BREAKING Word in another, e.g. **We are breaking the collection,
  Honey** (5) = S*WE*ET.

BREAKPOINT CRUNCH. PUBERTY (crypt).

BREATHER *REST*. *GILL*, LUNG, MOUTH, *NOSE*, WEASAND,
  WINDPIPE. VENT.

BREED RAISE, REAR. RACE, STOCK, TYPE.

BREEDING GROUND ATOMIC/NUCLEAR *REACTOR* (crypt).
  INCUBATOR, NURSERY, STOCK/STUD FARM.

BREVE *NOTE*. *ACCENT* (˘ = short). AUTHORITY, *LETTER*
  (papal, royal).

BREW *Anag.* CONCOCT, INFUSE. MAKE BEER/TEA
  [*Company* (livery)]. FESTER.

BRIBE GREASE, OIL (palm); PALM-OIL (crypt). INDUCE,
  SQUARE.

BRIDGE BR. ARCH, ARCHER, SPAN(NER) (crypt); RIALTO,
  THAMES. CONNING TOWER/DECK. *CARD GAME*,
  TRUMPERY (auction, contract) [Acol, Blackwood]. LOAN.
  REST (snooker). **Pl** = *POET*, *WRITER*.

~ **GAME** *CARDS*. TRUMPERY (crypt). POOHSTICKS (A. A.
  Milne).

BRIDGEHEAD INROAD, SALIENT. CARD BUFF (Acolite;
  crypt).

BRIDGE PLAYER E, N, S or W; EAST, NORTH, SOUTH, WEST;
  BRIDGER, WE, THEY.

BRIDGER *BRIDGE PLAYER* (crypt). CAPTAIN, NAVIGATOR
  (crypt). HORATIO (crypt).

BRIDGING TEAM RE, SAPPERS. BRIDGE PLAYERS, EW, NS,
  WE/THEY (crypt). APPEASERS, CONCILIATORS, ACAS
  (crypt).

BRIG BRASSHAT, BRIGADIER, SOLDIER. *BOAT*. *GAOL*
  (naut). BRIDGE (Sc).

BRISTOL BREAST (*rh sl*). *UNIVERSITY*.

BRITISH LEGION BL.

BRITISH LEYLAND BL.
  MUSEUM BM.
~ **RAIL** BR, RLY, RY, LINES.
BROADCAST SCATTER, SOW. AIR(ING), RADIATE,
  TRANSMIT; BBC, IBA, ITA, ITV (UK); ABC, CBS, NBC (US).
BROKE BANKRUPT, INSOLVENT, PENNILESS, RUINED;
  BORACIC LINT (*rh sl*) **opp** = *rich*. DID *BREAK*, BUST.
  [Evans].
BROKEN *Anag* e.g. **Heartbroken** (5) = HATER. WAS BROKE.
  SNAPPED. TAMED.
BROKEN FUSE BLOWN OUT, FUSED. Anag 'fuse' i.e. FUES.
BRONTË 1. *WRITER*; ANNE ~ = Acton Bell (Agnes Grey; *Tenant*
  of Wildfell Hall). CHARLOTTE ~ = Mrs Nicholls = Currer Bell
  (Jane Eyre; The Professor; Shirley; Villette; Land of Angria).
  EMILY ~ = Ellis Bell (Wuthering Heights; Land of Gondal).
  PATRICK BRANWELL ~ 2. Lord Nelson and ~ (*military*
  leader; Emma Hamilton). 3. Gk myth THUNDER [blacksmith].
  Pl = CYCLOP.
BRONZE 1. *AGE*. THIRD PRIZE. *Anniversary* (8th).
  2. Copper/Tin alloy, hence CU*SN.
BROOK BECK, *BOURN*, BURN, CREEK, RILL, *RIVER*,
  RIVULET, STREAM. TOLERATE.
BROTHER BR, *SIB*. FRIAR, *MONK*. ASSOCIATE, EQUAL.
  [Jonathan]. **Pl** = TUC.
BROTHERHOOD ASSOCIATION, FRATERNITY. COWL
  (crypt).
BROWN ROAST; *TAN*. *COLOUR*. *PAINTER*. *SNOOKER*
  BALL (score 4). FATHER ~ (*Chesterton*). Lancelot 'Capability'
  ~ (*gardener*). TOM. SHOOT HAPHAZARDLY (hence
  HOOTS etc). [Queen Victoria]. **Pl** = *Football team* (US).
BROWNE *SAM* (belt). *CARTOONIST* (Phiz, *Dickens*).
BROWNIE GOBLIN. YOUNG GUIDE. CAMERA®.
BROWNING AUTOMATIC, *WEAPON*®. DYE, TANNING.
  FIRING WILDLY. GRAVY. *WRITER*.
BRS BRITISH ROAD SERVICES. Pl of BR.
BRUNHILDA (BRUNNHILDE) 1. Nor myth Chief of the *Valkyries*.
  2. A minor *PLANET*.
BRUTUS *CONSPIRATOR*; *STOIC* [honourable; Caesar's ghost,
  (*Shak*)].
BT BARONET.
BTU BRITISH THERMAL UNIT (heat).

BUCCANEER *PIRATE. AIRCRAFT*.

BUCEPHALUS ALEXANDER'S HORSE.

BUCK *DOLLAR*. JUMP, THROW. DANDY, FOP. CART.
SAW-HORSE. PEARL (films). *WRITER. DOG. Male* deer,
hare etc.

BUFF ENTHUSIAST. POLISH. NUDE, SKIN. *COLOUR*. **Pl** =
EAST KENT REGIMENT. ['Steady the ~s' (*Kipling*)].

BUG *BEETLE*, PARASITE. EAVESDROPPER, LISTENER,
TRANSMITTER. RIVER (Pol).

BUILD *Anag*. CONSTRUCT, COMPOSE, MAKE.
PROPORTIONS, SHAPE.

BULL 1. ROT, RUBBISH. CENTRE, GOLD (archery). DECK
GAME. PAPAL EDICT. DRINK. PRICE RAISER (**opp** =
bear). TAURUS; *male* cow, elephant etc; SIRE. 2. Gk myth
EUROPA [*Minos*, Seventh labour of *Hercules*]. APIS (Egy god).
3. *Constellation* (Taurus); sign of *Zodiac* (2nd).

~ AND COW *ROW* (*rh sl*).

BULLETHOLE BARREL, CHAMBER, RIFLING (all crypt).

BULLSEYE CENTRE, *GOLD* [inner, magpie, outer]. LANTERN.
COMIC. CANDY, GOBSTOPPER, SWEET. *DOG* (Bill Sikes).

BULLY BRAVO! EXCELLENT! FIRST RATE! CORNED BEEF.
START (hockey). OPPRESSOR, THUG, TYRANT; **celeb**:
CERCYON (myth), FLASHMAN (Tom Brown's Schooldays),
FRONT DE BOEUF (Ivanhoe, Scott), JOSIAH BOUNDERBY
(Hard Times, *Dickens*), SIR JOHN CHESTER (Rudge, *Dickens*),
LEGREE (Uncle Tom's Cabin, Harriet Beecher *Stowe*).

BUN HAIRPIECE; UPBRAIDED (crypt). BREAD ROLL:
BATH, CHELSEA, CURRANT, HOT CROSS etc.

BUND *BANK*; QUAY.

BUNTER SCHOOLBOY, OWL OF THE REMOVE (*Greyfriars*
School, Richards). *SERVANT* (to Lord Peter Wimsey, Dorothy
L. Sayers).

BUNTING *BIRD. FLAG*, WORSTED (*material*).

BURDEN LOAD, OPPRESS, SADDLE; OBLIGATION,
LIABILITY, PASSENGER. TONNAGE. CHORUS,
REFRAIN, THEME.

BURGLAR *ROBBER*, THIEF, YEGG. Raffles (Hornung).

BURLAP CANVAS, JUTE, *MATERIAL*.

BURLINGTON HOUSE RA, (ROYAL) ACADEMY [*painters*].

BURN *BROOK*. BLISTER, SORE; *BLAZE, CHAR*, CONSUME,
FIRE, PARCH, SCORCH, TAN. **Pl** = RABBIE, POET (Sc).

BURRO (s/l *burrow*). *DONKEY*.

BURROW (s/l *burro*). MINE. RABBIT
WARREN/*HABITATION*. ISLAND (Eng).

BUSH *PLANT* (q.v. for list), SHRUB; FOREST, WOODLAND.
HAIR. *PIG*. LINING, SLEEVE, WASHER. RIVER (Ire).

BUSINESS *CO*, FIRM, TRADE. AFFAIR, CONCERN, DUTY,
OCCUPATION, TASK. AGENDA.

BUT (s/l *butt*, *butte*). EXCEPT, HOWEVER, ONLY. WITHOUT.
YET. *UTTER*. **Pl comp** = ifs.

BUTCHER MEAT TRADER [*Company* (livery)]. SLAUGHTER.
CUMBERLAND. *BIRD*. **Pl** = *LOOK* (*rh sl*).

BUTT (s/l *but*, *butte*). CASK, KEG, *MEASURE*. AIM, OBJECT,
RANGE, STAND (shooting). HANDLE; ABUT(MENT).
FISH: FLATFISH, PLAICE, SOLE. STUB, TREE TRUNK.
CUE (snooker). NUDGE (with head). TARGET (for jokes).

BUTTE (s/l *but*, *butt*). *HILL*.

BUTTER FAT. ADULATE, PRAISE. GUNNEL (*fish*). GOAT
(crypt, nudge). LANDLORD (crypt, cask). MARKSMAN
(crypt, range). SNOOKER PLAYER (crypt, cue). SMOKER
(crypt, stub). COASTER (crypt, Masefield). **Comp** = *bread*; *toast*.

BUTTERFLY *LEPIDOPTERA*; **coll** = LEPIDOPTERIST.
MADAM ~ (Puccini; Nagasaki; Cho Cho San, Lt *Pinkerton*).
[*Psyche*]. *Swimming* style (q.v.).

BUTTER UP FLATTER, PRAISE. RETTUB (dn, crypt).

BUTTRESS PIER, PROP, SUPPORT (*architecture* term, q.v.). Part
of horse's hoof. Fem goat (crypt), hence *NANNY*.

BUZZ BOMB DOODLEBUG, FLYING BOMB, V1 [revenge].

BY (s/l *bye*). *NEAR*, NEXT, PER, THROUGH. SECONDARY,
SIDE. SECRET. FATHERED/SIRED BY . . . **Comp** = *large*.

BYE (s/l *by*). *PASS*. *EXTRA* (cricket). INCIDENTAL. SIDE.
SECRET.

BYE-BYE *FAREWELL*. **Pl** = SLEEP.

BYGONE ANTIQUE. PAST.

C *CAMBRIDGE*. CARBON (*chem*). *CAUGHT*. CELSIUS,
CENTIGRADE. CHAPTER. CIRCA. *CLUB*. COLD.
CONSERVATIVE. CUBA (*car plate*). ABOUT. *KEY*; *NOTE*.
100, ONE HUNDRED; MANY. SQ NO ($10 \times 10 = 100 = C$).

C3.3 OSCAR WILDE (prison number).

CA ABOUT, CIRCA. CHARTERED ACCOUNTANT.
CALIFORNIA (US *state*). CALCIUM (*chem*).

CABINET MAKER PRIME MINISTER, PM. ADAM,
CHANNON, CHIPPENDALE, HEPPLEWHITE, *KENT*,
SHERATON.

CABLE WIRE; MESSAGE, TELEGRAM. 200 YARDS, CCYD,
MEASURE (naut).

CACUS Rom myth s of *Vulcan*, who *robbed Hercules* of some of his
cattle and was slain.

CAD *BOUNDER*, BRUTE, LOUT, SCOUNDREL, *SWINE*.

CADETS ATC, *BB*, JTC, OTC; BOYS BRIGADE, SCOUTS.
YOUNGER SONS.

CADMIUM *METAL*; CD (*chem*). *COLOUR* (orange).

CAESAR 1. AUTOCRAT, CZAR, DICTATOR, EMPEROR,
KAISER, TSAR; **celeb**: AUGUSTUS, CALIGULA,
CLAUDIUS, NERO or, specifically, GAIUS JULIUS,
102–44 B.C., s of Caesar and Aurelia; mar (1) Cossutia (div,
unconsummated), (2) Cornelia, d of Cinna (died; one d: Julia), (3)
Pompeia, d of Pompeius Rufus (div for adultery), and (4)
Calpurnia, d of Piso. Brilliant general, orator and writer, he was
ass Ides (15) Mar 44 B.C. by *conspiracy* of Brutus, Casca, Cassius
etc. [Invasion of Britain, Rubicon (crossed to Italy and civil war),
veni, vidi, vici (Pharnaces at Zela), leap year (introduced), *July*,
Cleopatra (one s: Caesarion), Mark *Antony*, *Pompey*, et tu Brute!
Conspirators. Appeared as *ghost* to *Brutus* before the battle of
Philippi. *Shak* (A and C; Caesar)]. 2. Implies put into Latin, e.g.
Seen (or conquered) by Caesar (4) = VIDI (or VICI).

CAIN (s/l *cane*). ADAMSON, FIRST BORN, FIRST ISSUE
[murderer]. **Comp** = *Abel*.

~ & ABEL *TABLE* (*rh sl*).

CAKE SWEETBREAD; **celeb**: *Angel*, banana, cherry, chocolate,
Christmas, coffee, Dundee, éclair, *fairy*, gâteau, Madeira, marble,
Parkin ~ (Guy Fawkes; ginger), plum, *Sally Lunn*, seed ~, tipsy ~
etc. OATBREAD (Sc). CONGLOMERATE, WAD. *COAT*,
COVER. BENEFITS, NATIONAL OUTPUT, PROFITS.

CALCULATOR ABACUS, *ADDER*, COMPUTER, *SUMMER*.
GOLD DIGGER.

CALENDAR (s/l *calender*). CHRONOLOGICAL LIST, DATING
SYSTEM, DIARY (*Chinese* ~; *French Revolution*; Julius *Caesar*).
LIST, REGISTER, SCHEDULE, *TABLE*.

CALF BACK OF LEG, LEG MUSCLE. SMALL ICEBERG.

ISLAND. Offspring of *cow*, *elephant*, walrus, *whale*; BOBBY.

CALIGULA Rom *emperor* and *tyrant*, an illness rendered him *mad* and savagely cruel. He declared himself a god, made his horse Incitatus a consul, caused men and women to be tortured to d at his meals, threw part of the audience to the wild beasts at the *circus*, and gave a banquet on a bridge then threw guests into the water. He was ass in A.D. 41.

CALL 1. PHONE, *RING*, TELEPHONE; *PAGE*, SHOUT: HI, HEY, HO etc. CHRISTEN, NAME, NOMINATE. BECK, SIGNAL. 2. *Pronounce as* . . . sound like. **Comp** = *beck*.

~ GIRL TELEPHONIST. PROSTITUTE.

CALLIOPE One of the nine Gk *MUSES* (epic *poetry*).

CALL SYSTEM DIAL, PAGING, PUBLIC ADDRESS, STD, TANNOY®, TOCSIN.

CAMBRIDGE C, CANTAB; LIGHT BLUES; *UNIVERSITY* [cantabrigian]. DUROLIPONS (*Roman*).

CAMEL RUMINANT; OONT, SHIP OF THE DESERT [*llama*]; **breeds**: ARABIAN, DOOD, DROMEDARY (one hump), BACTRIAN (two humps). CIGARETTE (US). *COLOUR* (fawn). SPONSON. *AIRCRAFT* (fighter). RIVER (Eng).

CAMELOT Site of *King Arthur's* court: CADBURY CASTLE, CAMELFORD or TINTAGEL [round table].

CAMEO BROOCH, RELIEF WORK (**opp** = intaglio). THUMB-NAIL SKETCH.

CAMP *BASE* (mil), FORT, SETTLEMENT; CASTRA (Rom). TENTS (gipsies, guides, holiday-makers, scouts etc); LODGE. ADHERENTS, FOLLOWERS. DAVID (US). AFFECTED, BIZARRE, DRAG, EFFEMINATE, EPICENE, EXAGGERATED, HOMOSEXUAL, TRANSVESTITE.

CAMPTOWN *RACETRACK*. ALDERSHOT, CHESTER, LARKHILL, TIDWORTH. [*Roman place name*].

CAN *TIN*; PRESERVE. IS ABLE. *GAOL* (sl). RIVER (Eng). **Pl** = HEADPHONES (sl).

Can Canada, ~ian.

CANADA CDN (*car plate*). [Canuck. Maple leaves].

CANARD *HOAX*. *DUCK* (Fr). CONTROL SURFACE (aero).

CANDY SWEETMEAT; CRYSTALLIZE, PRESERVE. *Anniversary* (6th). GIRL. Old Man (Steinbeck).

CANE (s/l *Cain*). *BEAT*, CHASTISE, *TAN*, THRASH; BIRCH, ROD, *SWITCH*, MALACCA, STICK. SUGAR.

CANNED DRUNK (sl). PRESERVED; TINNED, hence word in

'can' or 'tin', e.g. **Skirt canned Egyptian god** (5) = T*RA*IN.

CANNON (s/l *canon*). GUN, ORDNANCE, PIECE, *WEAPON*;
RA. COLLIDE, STRIKE; KISS (billiards).

CANON (s/l *cannon*). CHURCH DECREE, PAPAL LAW;
CRITERION, PRINCIPLE. CATHEDRAL OFFICIAL,
CHURCHMAN. TYPEFACE.

CANT CANNOT, UNABLE (**opp** = *may*). CATCH PHRASE,
JARGON; HYPOCRISY. BEVEL, SLOPE, *TILT*; *LEAN*,
SLEW, SWING, *TIP*. CANTICLES.

CANTAB Of C University.

CANTABRIGIAN Member of C or of Harvard University.

CANTERBURY 1. MUSIC HOLDER (furniture). *UNIVERSITY*
(NZ). DUROVERNUM (*Rom*). 2. **Episcopal sig** = CANTUAR.
3. ~ Tales (*Chaucer*).

CANTON DIVISION ON SHIELD (*herald*). SUB-DIVISION OF
COUNTRY (see *Swiss* ~ for list). TOWN (Ch).

CAP *HAT*, HEADGEAR. CAPITAL. CHAPTER. COMMON
AGRICULTURAL POLICY (European farming). COVER,
TOP. **Comp** = gown.

CAPE HEADLAND, NESS, *POINT*, PROMONTORY. CLOAK,
TALMA, TIPPET. APPLE.

CAPER FRISK, LARK, LEAP. *SPICE*. BOER, S AFRICAN
(crypt).

CAPITAL AI, FIRST RATE; VITAL. CORNICE (*architecture*).
CHIEF, HEAD, LEADING, IMPORTANT, PRINCIPAL. UC,
UPPER CASE (**opp** = lower case). First letter, first city, seat of
government e.g.:

Country	Capital
Abyssinia (now Ethiopia)	ADDIS ABABA
Aden (now S Yemen)	ADEN
Afghanistan	KABUL
Albania	TIRANA
Algeria	EL DJEZAIR
	(was ALGIERS)
Andorra	LA VIEJA
Angola	LUANDA
(was Port W Africa)	
Antigua Is	ST JOHN'S
Argentina	BUENOS AIRES
Ascension Is	GEORGETOWN

Australia	CANBERRA
Austria	VIENNA
Bahamas	NASSAU
Bahrain	MANAMAH
Balearic Is	PALMA
Bangladesh	DACCA
Barbados	BRIDGETOWN
Basutoland (now Lesotho)	MASERU
Bechuanaland (now Botswana)	MAFEKING
Belgian Congo (now Zaire)	LEOPOLDVILLE
Belgium	BRUSSELS
Belize (was Br Honduras)	BELMOPAN
Benin (was part Fr W Africa, then Dahomey)	PORTO NOVO
Bermuda	HAMILTON
Bhutan	THIMBU
Bolivia	SUCRE
Botswana (was Bechuanaland)	GABORONE
Burkina Faso (was Upper Volta)	OUAGADOUGOU
Brazil	BRASILIA (was RIO DE JANEIRO)
Br Honduras (now Belize)	BELIZE
Bulgaria	SOFIA
Cambodia (was part Fr Indo-China, now Kampuchea)	PHNOM PENH
Cameroon	YAOUNDE
Canada	OTTAWA
Canary Is	LAS PALMAS
Cape Verde Is	SAO THIAGO
Central African Republic (was part Fr Eq Africa)	BANGUI
Ceylon (now Sri Lanka)	COLOMBO
Chad (was part Fr Eq Africa)	NDJAMENE (was FORT LAMY)
Chile	SANTIAGO
China	PEKING (was XIAN)
Colombia	BOGOTA
Corsica	AJACCIO

Costa Rica	SAN JOSE
Crete	CANEA
Cuba	HAVANA
Cyclades Is	HERMOUPOLIS
Cyprus	NICOSIA
Czechoslovakia	PRAGUE
Dahomey (now Benin)	PORTO NOVO
Denmark	COPENHAGEN
Djibouti (was Fr Somaliland)	DJIBOUTI
Dominica Is	ROSEAU
Dominican Republic	SANTO DOMINGO
Dutch East Indies (now Indonesia)	BATAVIA (now JAKARTA)
Dutch Guiana (now Surinam)	PARAMARIBO
Ecuador	QUITO
Egypt	CAIRO (was MEMPHIS)
Eire	DUBLIN
Elba Is	PORTO FERRAIO
El Salvador	SAN SALVADOR
England	LONDON
Eq Guinea (was Sp Guinea)	MALABO (was SANTA ISABEL)
Eritrea (now part Ethiopia)	ASMARA
Est(h)onia	TALLINN
Ethiopia (was Abyssinia)	ADDIS ABABA
Faeroe Is	THORSHAVN
Falkland Is	PORT STANLEY
Fiji Is	SUVA
Finland	HELSINKI
Formosa (now Taiwan)	TAIPEH
France	PARIS
Fr Eq Africa (now Cameroon, Central Af Republic, Chad, Congo and Gabon)	BRAZZAVILLE
Fr Guiana	CAYENNE
Fr Indo-China (now Cambodia, Laos and Vietnam)	SAIGON (now HO CHI MINH CITY)
Fr Somaliland (now Djibouti)	JIBUTI

Fr W Africa (now Benin, Guinea, Ivory Coast, Mauritania and Senegal)	DAKAR
Friendly Is (Tonga)	NUKUALOFA or TONJOTABU
Gabon (was part Fr Eq Africa)	LIBREVILLE
Gambia	BANJUL (was BATHURST)
Germany, East	BERLIN
Germany, West	BONN
Ghana	ACCRA
Granada (ancient kingdom)	GRANADA
Greece	ATHENS
Greenland	GODTHAB
Grenada Is	ST GEORGE'S
Guadeloupe	BASSE-TERRE
Guatemala	GUATEMALA
Guinea (was part Fr W Africa)	CONAKRY
Guinea Bissau (was Port Guinea)	BISSAU
Guyana	GEORGETOWN
Haiti	PORT AU PRINCE
Holland	THE HAGUE
Honduras	TEGUCIGALPA
Hong Kong	VICTORIA
Hungary	BUDAPEST
Iceland	REYKJAVIK
India	DELHI
Indonesia (was NL E Indies)	JAKARTA (was BATAVIA)
Iran (was Persia)	TEH(E)RAN
Iraq (was Mesopotamia)	BAGHDAD
Ireland, North	BELFAST
Ireland, Rep of	DUBLIN
Israel (disputed)	JERUSALEM
Italy	ROME
Ivory Coast (was part Fr W Africa)	ABIDJAN

Jamaica	KINGSTON
Japan	TOKYO (was EDO, YEDDO)
Jordan	AMMAN
Kampuchea (was Cambodia)	PHNOM PENH
Kenya	NAIROBI
Kiribati (was Gilbert Is)	JARAWA
Korea, North	PYONGYANG
Korea, South	SEOUL
Kuwait	KUWAIT
Laos (was part Fr Indo-China)	VIENTIANE
Latvia	RIGA
Lebanon	BEIRUT
Leeward Is	ST JOHN
Lesotho (was Basutoland)	MASERU
Liberia	MONROVIA
Libya	TRIPOLI
Liechtenstein	VADUZ
Lithuania	VILNA
Luxembourg	LUXEMBOURG
Madagascar (now Malagasy Rep)	ANTANANARIVO
Malagasy Rep (was Madagascar)	TANANARIVE
Malawi (was Nyasaland)	LILONGWE
Malaysia (was Fed Malay States)	KUALA LUMPUR
Mali (was Fr Sudan, Fr W Af)	BAMAKO
Malta	VALETTA
Manoa (myth)	EL DORADO (myth)
Martinique Is	FORT DE FRANCE
Mauritania (was part Fr West Africa)	NOUAKCHOTT
Mauritius	PORT LOUIS
Mesopotamia (now Iraq)	BAGHDAD
Mexico	MEXICO CITY
Moçambique (was Port E Africa)	MAPUTO (was LOURENÇO MARQUES)
Monaco	MONACO

Mongolia	ULAN BATOR (was URGA)
Montenegro	CETINJE
Morocco	RABAT
Muscat & Oman (now Oman)	MUSCAT
Namibia (was S W Africa)	WINDHOEK
Nepal	KAT(H)MANDU
Netherlands	THE HAGUE
New Zealand	WELLINGTON
Nicaragua	MANAGUA
Niger (was part Fr W Africa)	NIAMEY
Nigeria	ABOUGA (was LAGOS)
North Vietnam	HANOI
Norway	OSLO
Nyasaland (now Malawi)	ZOMBA
Oman (was Muscat & Oman)	MUSCAT
Pakistan	ISLAMABAD (was KARACHI)
Palestine (disputed)	JERUSALEM
Panama	PANAMA
Papua New Guinea	PORT MORESBY
Paraguay	ASUNCION
Patagonia (now Argentina & Chile)	PUNTA ARENAS
Persia (now Iran)	TEH(E)RAN
Peru	LIMA
Philippines	QUEZON CITY
Poland	WARSAW (was CRACOW)
Portugal	LISBON
Port E Africa (now Moçambique)	LOURENÇO MARQUES
Port Guinea (now Guinea Bissau)	BISSAU (was BOLAMA)
Port W Africa (now Angola)	LUANDA
Puerto Rico	SAN JUAN
Qatar	DOHA
Rhodesia (now Zambia and Zimbabwe)	SALISBURY

Romania	BUCHAREST
Ruritania (fict)	STRELSAU (fict)
Russia	MOSCOW
Rwanda	KIGALI
Sabah (was N Borneo)	KOTA KINABALU
St Helena Is	JAMESTOWN
St Kitts-Nevis Is	BASSETERRE
St Lucia Is	CASTRIES
St Vincent Is	KINGSTOWN
Samoa	PAGO PAGO
San Marino	SAN MARINO
Sarawak	KUCHING
Sardinia	CAGLIARI
Saudi Arabia	RIYADH (was MECCA)
Scotland	EDINBURGH
Senegal (was part Fr W Africa)	DAKAR
Seychelles	VICTORIA
Siam (now Thailand)	BANGKOK
Sicily	PALERMO
Sierra Leone	FREETOWN
Sikkim (now part India)	GANGTOK
Singapore Is	SINGAPORE
Solomon Is	HONIARA
Somali (was Br and It East Africa)	MOGADISHU
Somaliland, Br (now part Somali)	HARGEISA
Somaliland, Fr (now Djibouti)	JIBUTI
Somaliland, It (now part Somali)	MOGADISHU
South Africa	PRETORIA
South Yemen (was Aden Protectorate)	MADINAT ASH SHAB
Spain	MADRID
Sp Guinea (now Eq Guinea)	SANTA ISABEL
Sp Sahara (now Saharan Arab Dem Rep)	VILLA CISNEROS
Sri Lanka (was Ceylon)	COLOMBO
Sudan	KHARTOUM
Surinam (was NL Guiana)	PARAMARIBO
Swaziland	MBABANE
Sweden	STOCKHOLM

Switzerland	BERNE
Syria	DAMASCUS
Taiwan (was Formosa)	TAIPEH
Tanganyika (now Tanzania)	DAR ES SALAAM
Tanzania (was Tanganyika)	DODOMA
Thailand (was Siam)	BANGKOK
Tibet	LHASA
Togo	LOME
Tonga (Friendly Is)	NUKUALOFA or TONJOTABU
Transylvania (was part Hungary, now part Romania)	CLUJ
Trinidad & Tobago	PORT OF SPAIN
Tristan da Cunha	EDINBURGH
Tunisia	TUNIS
Turkey	ANKARA
Tuvalu (was Ellice Is)	FUNAFUTI
Uganda	KAMPALA
Upper Volta	OUAGADOUGOU
Uruguay	MONTEVIDEO
USA	WASHINGTON
USSR	MOSCOW
Utopia (fict)	AMAUROTE (fict)
Vanuatu (was Espiritu Santo)	VILA
Venezuela	CARACAS
Vietnam (was part Fr Indo-China)	HANOI
Virgin Is, Br	ROADTOWN
Virgin Is, US	CHARLOTTE AMALIE˙
Wales	CARDIFF
West Irian (was NL New Guinea/Irian Jaya)	JAYAPURA
Windward Is	ST GEORGE
Yemen, North	SANA
Yemen, South (was Aden Protectorate)	MADINAT ASH SHAB (Aden)
Yugoslavia	BELGRADE

Zaire (was Belgian Congo)   KINSHASA
Zambia (was N Rhodesia)   LUSAKA
Zimbabwe (was S Rhodesia)   HARARE

CAPPED (s/l *capt*). CHOSEN, PICKED, SELECTED; awarded cap/colours for club/county/country. COVERED, PROTECTED, SHEATHED. FOLLOWED/IMPROVED (story, yarn).
CAPT (s/l *capped*). CAPTAIN, *OFFICER*. HEAD BOY/GIRL, *LEADER*, MASTER; **celeb**: ABSOLUTE (Rivals, Sheridan); *AHAB* (Moby Dick); NOLL BLUFF (Congreve); BOBADIL (*coward*, Jonson); BUOTH (Fielding); *CAT* (Mrs Dale's Diary, radio); CUTTLE (Dombey, *Dickens*); *DOG* (Archers, radio); FLINT (*parrot*, Treasure Island); GADSBY (*Kipling*); GULLIVER (*Swift*); HOOK (*Barrie*); HORNBLOWER (Forester); *JEHU* (bibl); *JOAB* (bibl); KETTLE (Hyne); NAAMAN (bibl); OSBORNE (Thackeray); *SENTRY* (Addison); DISCO TROOP (*Kipling*); EDWARD WAVERLEY (*Scott*).
CAPTURE *CATCH*, *COP*, *TRAPPED*; TAKING.
CAR AUTO, VEHICLE; **types (all ®)**: AUSTIN, BENTLEY, *BL*, BUICK, CADILLAC, CHEVROLET, *DODGE*, FIAT, *FORD*, GENERAL MOTORS, MERCEDES, *MG*, *MINI*, MODEL T, MORRIS, ROLLS, ROVER, SUNBEAM, *T*, TRIUMPH, VAUXHALL, VOLKSWAGEN etc. *CARRIAGE*, CHARIOT, NACELLE, GONDOLA (aero).
CARBON *MINERAL*; C (*chem*).
CAR CLUB *AA*, RAC.
CARD CAUTION, *CASE*, CHARACTER, WAG. CARDINAL. *TAROT*; CLUB, DIAMOND, HEART, SPADE; TRUMP; (*Alice*); **coll** = cartophilist; **games**:

3-letters	SKAT	POKER
GIN	*SNAP*	RUMMY
LOO	SOLO	SPOOF
NAP	*STOP*	*WHIST*
PIT		

	5-letters	**6-letters**
	BUNKO	BOSTON
4-letters	*DEMON*	*BRIDGE*
BRAG	MONTE	ECARTE
CRIB	OMBRE	EUCHRE
GRAB	PITCH	FAN-TAN
FARO		

PIQUET
RED DOG
SPIDER

7-letters
BEZIQUE
CANASTA
CARLTON
THE STAR
STREETS

8-letters
ALL FOURS
BACCARAT

CANFIELD
THE CLOCK
CRIBBAGE
GIN RUMMY
KLONDYKE
NAPOLEON
PATIENCE
PINOCHLE

9+ letters
AUNT AGATHA
BEGGAR-MY-
  NEIGHBOUR
BLACKJACK

FOUR SEASONS
GERMAN FLEET
HAPPY FAMILIES
MISS MILLIGAN
ONE FOUNDATION
RACING DEMON
THE REGIMENT
ROUGE ET NOIR
TRENTE ET
  QUARANTE
TWENTY-ONE
VINGT-ET-UN

CARDIGAN *JERSEY*, PULLOVER, SWEATER, WOOLLY.
  EARL (Balaclava). *CASTLE.*
CARDINAL FUNDAMENTAL, IMPORTANT. *CHURCHMAN*
  [eminence, HE]. SONGBIRD (US). CLOAK. E, N, S, W
  (naut).
CARE ATTENTION, CAUTION, PAINS, TROUBLE. *CHARGE*,
  LOOK AFTER, PROTECT(ION). ANXIETY, WORRY;
  CONCERN, REGARD, *SORROW*. AFFECTION, LIKING,
  LOVE. [~ of = CO].
CARMELITE MENDICANT *FRIAR*, WHITE *FRIAR* [Berthold].
CARNATION *FLOWER*. BUTTONHOLE. MOTOR-RACE
  (crypt).
CARP *FISH*, *ID*, *ROACH*. CRITICIZE, FIND FAULT [captious].
CARPENTER *CABINET-MAKER*, JOINER, WOODWORKER
  [*Company* (livery)]; **celeb**: ADAM BEDE (Eliot), *JESUS*,
  JOSEPH, QUINCE, SNUG (MND, *Shak*), MUDDLE (Marryat);
  [*Alice*; *Chaucer*].
CARPET DRUGGET, PILE, RUG [Axminster, Persian, Wilton].
  REPRIMAND, REPROVE, *ROCKET*, TELL OFF (sl).
CAR PLATE REGISTRATION. **Int identification:**

Country	Letters	Country	Letters
Albania	AL	**Australia**	AUS
Alderney	GBA	**Austria**	A
Algeria	DZ	**Bahamas**	BS
Argentina	RA	**Belgium**	B

Country	Letters	Country	Letters
Brazil	BR	Jersey	GBJ
Bulgaria	BG	Luxembourg	L
Canada	CDN	Malta	M
Colombia	CO	Morocco	MA
Costa Rica	CR	Monaco	MC
Cuba	C	Netherlands	NL
Cyprus	CY	New Zealand	NZ
Czechoslovakia	CS	Norway	N
Denmark	DK	Panama	PA
Egypt	ET	Peru	PE
Finland	SF	Poland	PL
France	F	Portugal	P
Germany, East	DDR	Romania	R
Germany, West	D	South Africa	ZA
Great Britain	GB	Spain	E
Guernsey	GBG	Sweden	S
Hong Kong	HK	Switzerland	CH
Hungary	H	Turkey	TR
Iceland	IS	UK	GB
India	IND	USA	USA
Iran	IR	USSR	SU
Ireland	IRL	Vatican City	V
Isle of Man	GBM	Vietnam	VN
Israel	IL	Yugoslavia	YU
Italy	I	Zaire	ZR
Jamaica	JA	Zambia	Z
Japan	J		

CARRIAGE *DELIVERY*, FREIGHT. *BEARING*, GAIT. PRAM,
PUSH-CHAIR. HORSE-DRAWN VEHICLE [dalmatian];
types:

3-letters	EKKA	GARRY
CAB	SHAY	*STAGE*
FLY	TRAP	*SULKY*
GIG		TONGA

	5-letters	
4-letters	*BRAKE*	**6-letters**
BIGA	BUGGY	BERLIN
DRAY	*COACH*	CALASH

CHAISE
GHARRI, -Y
HANSOM
JINGLE
LANDAU
RANDEM
SURREY
SPIDER
TANDEM
TELAGA
TROIKA
WHISKY

7-letters
CAROCHE
CHARIOT
DROSHKY

GROWLER
HACKERY
HACKNEY
PHAETON
RATTLER
TILBURY
VIS-A-VIS

8-letters
BAROUCHE
BROUGHAM
CARRIOLE
CLARENCE
CURRICLE
DEARBORN
QUADRIGA
SOCIABLE

STANHOPE
VICTORIA

9+ letters
BONESHAKER
CABRIOLET
CURRICULUM
DILIGENCE
FOUR-IN-HAND
KITTEREEN
LANDAULET
OPPENHEIMER
POST-CHAISE
STAGE COACH
TARANTASS
WAGONETTE

CARRY *BEAR*, SUPPORT, TOTE. BE PREGNANT.
~ **ON** CONTINUE. FLIRT. EMBARK, LOAD.
CARTOONIST ARTIST, CARICATURIST, DRAWER; **celeb**:
ARNO, Peter (US); BAIRNSFATHER, Bruce (Old Bill, Eng);
BATEMAN, H. M. (Eng); BIRD, Kenneth (Fougasse, Eng);
BROWNE, H. K. (Phiz, *Dickens*); CRUICKSHANK, George
(*Dickens*); HEATH-ROBINSON, William (Eng); KEENE,
Charles Samuel (Punch, Eng); LANCASTER, David (Maudie
Littlehampton, Eng); LANGDON, David (Eng); *LOW*, Sir David
(Col Blimp, NZ); PHIZ (*Browne, Dickens*); SEARLE, Ronald (St
Trinian's, Eng); SHEPARD, Ernest H. (*Milne*, Eng); *SPY* (*Ward*);
TENNIEL, Sir John (*Alice*); THELWELL (ponies, Eng); *WARD*,
Sir Leslie (*Spy*, Eng); *WREN*, Chris (aircraft, Eng).
CASE 1. *BAGGAGE*, BOX, GRIP. COVER, ENCLOSE.
CAUSE, EVENT, SUIT (leg). CIRCUMSTANCE, INSTANCE,
POSITION. CONDITION (med). NOUN FORM (gram):
ABLATIVE, ACCUSATIVE, DATIVE, NOMINATIVE,
POSSESSIVE. UPPER/LOWER TYPEFACE. *CARD*,
CAUTION, *CHARACTER*, COMEDIAN, *COMIC*, RIGHT
ONE, WAG. 2. **In** ~: IF, LEST. CRATED, ENCASED (crypt).
Put designated word round another as a ~ or enclosure, e.g. **In his
case, biscuit without it is a plant** (8) = HI(BISCU**)S, or else **Refusal
in any case is to give offence** (5) = AN(NO)Y.

CASH *MONEY*, READY; *COIN* (Ch and Ind); CENT, DOLLAR, PENNY, POUND etc [*currencies*, q.v. for list]. DRAW OUT, PLAY WINNER (cards).

CASHIER ACCOUNTANT, BANK CLERK, TELLER. DISCHARGE, DISMISS (mil).

CASSANDRA 1. Gk myth d of *Priam* and *Hecuba*. *Apollo* gave her the ability to prophesy, but always unheeded. She was killed by *Clytemnestra*. [T and C (*Shak*)]. 2. A minor *PLANET*.

CASSOWARY Flightless bird (Aus) [Dinornis (ex, NZ), Emu, Moa, Nandoo, Ostrich].

CAST (s/l *caste*). PITCH, *SHED*, *SHY*, THROW. *FORM*, FOUND, MOLD (US), MOULD, SHAPE. ACTORS, DRAMATIS PERSONAE, PLAYERS, THESPIANS. WORM MOUND. TWIST; SQUINT. SHADE, TINGE. QUALITY, TYPE. *Assembly* of hawks.

CASTE (s/l *cast*). CLASS (Hind).

CASTLE *CHESSPIECE*, *ROOK*. WICKET (cricket sl). CITADEL, FORT(RESS), STRONGHOLD [**arch**: bailey (courtyard), ballistraria (arrow slot), barbican (outwork), bartizan (overhanging turret), bastion (rampart), battlement (indented parapet), crenel (embrasure), donjon (keep), drawbridge (lifting access), embrasure (battlement niche), keep (inner fort), merlon (battlement upright), moat (ditch), motte (fortified mound), oilette (missile slot), parapet (low projecting wall), portcullis (drop gate), postern (private entrance), rampart (defensive wall), turret (tower)]. **Examples in UK**:

3-letters	DORE (Eng)	ROCH (Wal)
HAY (Wal)	DOTE (Eng)	*STAR* (Wal)
MAY (Sc)	DRUM (Sc)	UDNY (Sc)
MEY (Sc)	DUNS (Sc)	*YORK* (Eng)
MOY (Sc)	*FAST* (Eng)	
ODO (Wal)	HOLT (Wal)	**5-letters**
OER (Sc)	LEOD (Sc)	BLAIR (Sc)
RED (Sc)	MAOL (Sc)	BORVE (Sc)
	MAUD (Sc)	BOYNE (Sc)
4-letters	PIEL (Eng)	BURGH (Eng)
ACRE (Eng)	POOL (Wal)	CAREW (Wal)
BERE (Wal)	RABY (Eng)	CHIRK (Wal)
DEAL (Eng)	RAIT (Sc)	CLARE (Eng)
DOON (Sc)	*RING* (Eng)	COITY (Eng)

CORFE (Eng)
COWES (Eng)
CROFT (Eng)
CUTRA (Ire)
DONNE (Sc)
DOVER (Eng)
DROGO (Eng)
DUART (Sc)
ELCHO (Sc)
EWLOE (Wal)
FLINT (Wal)
FYVIE (Sc)
GYLEN (Sc)
HAWEN (Ire)
HEVER (Eng)
HURST (Eng)
KEISS (Sc)
KELDY (Eng)
KNOCK (Sc)
LEEDS (Eng)
LEWES (Eng)
LYMNE (Eng)
MYLOR (Eng)
POWIS (Wal)
RIBER (Eng)
SLANE (Ire)
SWEEN (Sc)
TENBY (Wal)
ZENDA (fict, *Hope*)

6-letters
ABOYNE (Sc)
AIRLIE (Sc)
AUCHEN (Sc)
BODIAM (Eng)
BOLTON (Eng)
BRODIE (Sc)
BROUGH (Eng)
BUILTH (Wal)
CAWDOR (Sc)
CONWAY (Wal)

CORNET (CI)
DUDLEY (Eng)
DUFFUS (Eng)
DUNDEE (Sc)
DUNURE (Sc)
DURHAM (Eng)
EDZELL (Sc)
FLOORS (Sc)
FORTER (Sc)
FRASER (Sc)
GLAMIS (Sc)
GORDON (Sc)
GWRYCH (Wal)
GWYDIR (Wal)
HAILES (Sc)
HODDOM (Sc)
HOWARD (Eng)
HUNTLY (Sc)
KENDAL (Eng)
LUDLOW (Eng)
MAIDEN (Eng)
MIDMAR (Sc)
MILLOM (Eng)
MORTON (Sc)
NEWARK (Eng)
NUNNEY (Eng)
OGMORE (Wal)
OXFORD (Eng)
PICTON (Wal)
RAGLAN (Eng)
RAHEEN (Ire)
ROWTON (Eng)
SPYNIE (Sc)
STRAME (Sc)
WALMER (Eng)
WALTON (Eng)
YESTER (Sc)

7-letters
ADAMANT (*G and S*)
AFFLECK (Sc)

ALNWICK (Eng)
APPLEBY (Eng)
ARDROSS (Sc)
ARUNDEL (Eng)
BALLOCH (Sc)
BARHOLM (Sc)
BEESTON (Eng)
BELVOIR (Eng)
BLARNEY (Ire)
BRAEMAR (Sc)
BRAMBER (Eng)
BRATTON (Eng)
BRODICK (Sc)
CADBURY (Eng)
CAISTER (Eng)
CARDIFF (Wal)
CHESTER (Eng)
COOLING (Eng)
COWDRAY (Eng)
CRATHES (Sc)
CULZEAN (Sc)
DENBIGH (Wal)
DOUGLAS (Sc)
DUNLUCE (Ire)
DUNSKEY (Sc)
DUNSTER (Eng)
DUNTULM (Sc)
DYNEVOR (Wal)
FINAVON (Sc)
GUTHRIE (Sc)
HARLECH (Wal)
HUNTLEY (Sc)
KANTURK (Ire)
KENNEDY (Sc)
KIELDER (Eng)
KILMORY (Sc)
KINKELL (Sc)
LOCHNAW (Sc)
LOWTHER (Sc)
MINGARY (Sc)
NAWORTH (Eng)

NEWPORT (Wal)
NORWICH (Eng)
PENRHYN (Wal)
PENRICE (Wal)
PENRITH (Eng)
RATTRAY (Sc)
RUTHVEN (Sc)
SADDELL (Sc)
ST DENIS (Wal)
ST MAWES (Eng)
SEAGATE (Sc)
SIZERGH (Eng)
SKIPTON (Eng)
STALKER (Sc)
SUDELEY (Eng)
SWANSEA (Wal)
TAUNTON (Eng)
THREAVE (Sc)
TILBURY (Eng)
TUTBURY (Eng)
UISDEIN (Sc)
WARWICK (Eng)
WIGMORE (Eng)
WINDSOR (Eng)
WRESSLE (Eng)

8-letters
ABERDOUR (Sc)
AMBERLEY (Eng)
ARDMADDY (Sc)
BALMORAL (Sc)
BALVENIE (Sc)
BAMBURGH (Eng)
BERKELEY (Eng)
BROUGHAM (Eng)
BRUCKLEY (Sc)
BURLEIGH (Sc)
CAMPBELL (Sc)
CARDIGAN (Wal)
CARLISLE (Eng)
CARSLUTH (Sc)

CHEPSTOW (Wal)
CIGERRAN (Wal)
CORGARFF (Sc)
CRAWFORD (Sc)
CRICHTON (Sc)
DARNAWAY (Sc)
DEGANWY (Wal)
DELGATIE (Sc)
DIRLETON (Sc)
DOUBTING
   (Pilgrim's Progress)
DRYSLWYN (Wal)
DRUMMOND (Sc)
DUNOTTAR (Sc)
DUNTRUNE (Sc)
DUNVEGAN (Sc)
FINLARIG (Eng)
GOODRICH (Eng)
HELMSLEY (Eng)
HERTFORD (Eng)
KIDWELLY (Wal)
KILCHURN (Sc)
LANGWELL (Sc)
MAXSTOKE (Eng)
MOUNTJOY (Ire)
MUCHALLS (Sc)
NEIDPATH (Sc)
NOTTLAND (Sc)
PEMBROKE (Wal)
PEVENSEY (Eng)
PITCAPLE (Sc)
PITSLIGO (Sc)
PITTULIE (Sc)
PLYMOUTH (Eng)
RHUDDLAN (Wal)
RICHMOND (Eng)
ROTHESAY (Sc)
ST DONATS (Wal)
SANDWICH (Eng)
SOUTHSEA (Eng)
STIRLING (Sc)

STOKESAY (Eng)
STORMONT (Ire)
SYCHARTH (Wal)
TAMWORTH (Eng)
THETFORD (Eng)
TINTAGEL (Eng)
URQUHART (Sc)
WALWORTH (Eng)
YARNBURY (Eng)

9-letters
ALLINGTON (Eng)
BEAUMARIS (Wal)
BLACKNESS (Sc)
BORTHWICK (Sc)
CARDONESS (Sc)
CARLSWITH (Sc)
CAULFIELD (Ire)
CILGERRAN (Wal)
CLAYPOTTS (Sc)
CLITHEROE (Eng)
COMLONGON (Sc)
CRAIGNISH (Sc)
CRICCIETH (Wal)
CROOKSTON (Sc)
DALHOUSIE (Sc)
DALNAGLAR (Sc)
DINAS BRAN (Wal)
DONNAMORE (Ire)
DRUMMINOR (Sc)
DUMBARTON (Sc)
DUNDONALD (Sc)
EARLSHALL (Sc)
EAST COWES (Eng)
EDINBURGH (Sc)
FINDLATER (Sc)
FINDOCHTEY (Sc)
GLASCLUNE (Sc)
GREYSTOKE (Eng)
HAVERFORD (Wal)
HEDINGHAM (Eng)

HERMITAGE (Sc)
KIESSIMUL (Sc)
KILDRUMMY (Sc)
KILKERRAN (Sc)
KILLOCHAN (Sc)
KILRACOCK (Sc)
KIMBOLTON (Eng)
LANCASTER (Eng)
MANORBIER (Wal)
MIDDLEHAM (Eng)
MUNCASTER (Eng)
NEWCASTLE (Eng)
OLD SLAINS (Sc)
PEMBRIDGE (Eng)
PENDENNIS (Eng)
PICKERING (Eng)
POWDERHAM (Eng)
RESTORMEL (Eng)
ROCHESTER (Eng)
ST ANDREWS (Sc)
SAN SIMEON (US)
SCALLOWAY (Sc)
SKENFRITH (Wal)
TANTALLON (Sc)
TREGENNIS (Eng)
ULZIESIDE (Sc)
WARKWORTH (Eng)

10+ letters
ABERYSTWYTH (Wal)
ARMATHWAITE (Eng)
ASHBY DE LA ZOUCH (Eng)
AUCHINDOWN (Sc)
AUGHENTAINE (Ire)
BERRY POMEROY (Eng)
CAERLAVEROCK (Sc)
CAERNARFON (Wal)
CAERPHILLY (Wal)
CARISBROOKE (Eng)
CARMARTHEN (Wal)
CARNASSERIE (Sc)

CARREG CENNEN (Wal)
CASTELL Y BERE (Wal)
CASTLECRAIG (Sc)
CHILLINGHAM (Eng)
CHRISTCHURCH (Eng)
COCKERMOUTH (Eng)
COLCHESTER (Eng)
CONISBROUGH (Eng)
CRAIGIEVAR (Sc)
CRAIGNETHAN (Sc)
DOLWYDDELAN (Wal)
DONNINGTON (Eng)
DUNSTANBURGH (Eng)
EILEAN DONNAN (Sc)
FORT GEORGE (Sc)
FORT WILLIAM (Sc)
FOTHERINGHAY (Eng)
FRAMLINGHAM (Eng)
FRAOCH EILEAN (Sc)
HARRY AVERY'S (Ire)
HERSTMONCEUX (Eng)
INVERALLOCHY (Sc)
INVERLOCHY (Sc)
KAIM OF MATHERS (Sc)

KENILWORTH (Eng)
KINLOCHALINE (Sc)
KIRKCUDBRIGHT (Sc)
LAUNCESTON (Eng)
LINDISFARNE (Eng)
LINLITHGOW (Sc)
LLANSTEPHAN (Wal)
LOCHINDORE (Sc)
LOUGH CUTRA (Ire)
OKEHAMPTON (Eng)
PAINSCASTLE (Wal)
PONTEFRACT (Eng)
POR(T)CHESTER (Eng)
PORTSMOUTH (Eng)
RAVENSBURGH (Eng)
RAVENSCRAIG (Sc)
ROCKINGHAM (Eng)
ST BRIAVELS (Eng)
SCARBOROUGH (Eng)
SMAITHAM TOWER (Sc)
SUTHERLAND (Eng)
TATTERSHALL (Eng)
TOWER OF LONDON (Eng)
WINCHESTER (Eng)

[~s in the Downs = DEAL, *SANDWICH*, WALMER]. **Comp** = *Elephant*.

CASTOR (s/l caster). 1. (SWIVEL) WHEEL. BEAVER EXTRACT. OIL. *HAT* (sl). 2. Gk myth *twin* of *Pollux*. A horse tamer and patron of seamen. One of the *ARGONAUTS*. With Pollux, two stars: Dioscuri.

CAT 1. RAISE/WEIGH ANCHOR (naut). BURGLAR, *ROBBER*. JAZZ ENTHUSIAST. LASH, SCOURGE, *WHIP*, [~ o' nine tails]. *FAMILIAR*, GRIMALKIN [*witch*]. MALICIOUS WOMAN. VOMIT (sl). 2. Feline animal. KITTY, MOGGIE, PUSS(Y), TOM; MARMALADE, TABBY, TORTOISESHELL [T. S. Eliot; Bast (Egy *god*); *Freya*; *Lear*; 9 lives]; **breeds:** ABYSSINIAN (swims), AFGHAN, BLOTCHED, BLUE RUSSIAN, BURMESE, CHARTREUSE, KILKENNY (fighting), MALTESE, MANX (tailless), PERSIAN, SIAMESE; **male** = TOM, **fem** = QUEEN, **offspring** = KITTEN; **assembly** = cluster (but kindle of kittens); **comp** = mouse; ~ **family**: BOBCAT, CARACAL, CHEETAH, CIVET, COUGAR, EYRA, GENET, JAGUAR, (SNOW) LEOPARD, *LION, LYNX*, MARGAY, NANDINE, OCELOT, *OUNCE*, PUMA, RASSE, SERVAL, *TIGER*, TIGON [feral; *weasel*]; **celeb**: BAGHEERA (*Kipling*), CAPTAIN (Mrs Dale, radio), CHESHIRE (*Alice*), DINAH (*Alice*), FELIX (Sullivan cartoon), MITTENS, MOPPET (*Potter*), ORLANDO (Marmalade ~), SHERE KHAN (*Kipling*), SILVESTER (Tweetie Pie cartoon), SIMKIN (*Potter*). TABITHA TWITCHIT (Beatrix *Potter*), ~ that walked by himself (Just So Stories, *Kipling*), TOM (~ and Jerry cartoon), TOM KITTEN (Beatrix *Potter*) and, all from T. S. Eliot: BUSTOPHER JONES (~ about Town, *club*), OLD DEUTERONOMY (*long life*), GROWLTIGER (bargee, GRIDDLEBONE), GUS (theatre), JELLICLE ~s (*dancing*), JENNYANYDOTS (Gumbie), MACAVITY (*Napoleon* of crime, *unseen*), MR MISTOFFELEES (conjuror), MORGAN (*pirate*, commissionaire), MUNGOJERRIE and RUMPLETEAZER (*robbers*), RUMPUSCAT (fierce), RUM TUM TUGGER (curious), SKIMBLESHANKS (*railway*). [Dick Whittington; Puss in Boots].

CATCH ARREST, CAPTURE, LAND, SNARE, *TRAP. INCUR*, RECEIVE. AIR, DITTY, *SONG*. HIT. BAG (fishing, shooting). DISMISS (*cricket*). COUP, GOOD MATCH.

CATHAY CHINA (arch).

CATHEDRAL CHURCH (diocesan) [*bishop; episcopal sig; see*]. **Parts**: aisle, altar, aumbry, chancel, chapterhouse, choirschool, clerestory, crypt, faldstool, Lady chapel, lectern, lich/lych (corpse) gate, muniment room, nave, organ loft, presbytery, reredos, rood screen, sanctuary, side chapel, tabernacle, triforium, vestry (and see *Architecture; Window*). **Celeb**: Aberdeen, Bath, Bristol, Canterbury, Chester, Chichester, Coventry, Durham, Edinburgh, Ely, Exeter, Glasgow, Gloucester, Guildford, Lichfield, Lincoln, Norwich, Oxford, Peterborough, Rochester, St Albans, St Pauls, Salisbury, Tewkesbury, Truro, Wells, Winchester, Worcester, York Minster.

CATO 1. Rom statesman/general (234–149 B.C.). Consul and *censor*, he disliked Carthage. 2. Descendant of (1), *Stoic philosopher* who lived 95–46 B.C., and was enemy of *Caesar*. 3. ~ Street, the site of an unsuccessful plot to murder Castlereagh in 1820.

CATTLE COW(S), KINE, LIVESTOCK, NEAT, *OX(EN)*, STOCK; LOWER (crypt); **assembly** = drove, herd, **male** =

BULL, **fem** = *COW*, **offspring** = *CALF*; **breeds**: ABERDEEN ANGUS, AYRSHIRE, CAT(T)ALO, CHAROLAIS, *DEXTER*, FRIESIAN, *GUERNSEY*, HEREFORD, HIGHLAND, *JERSEY*, KERRY, KYLOE, REDPOLL, SHORTHORN, SOUTH DEVON, WELSH BLACK.

CAUCASIAN *WHITE*.

CAUGHT (s/l *court*). C, CT, DISMISSED (*cricket*). SNAGGED, SNARED, TRAPPED.

CAURUS Rom myth NW *WIND* (**Gk** = SKIRON).

CAUTION PRUDENCE; WARNING. *CASE*, CHARACTER, WAG.

CAVE CELLAR, ROCK DWELLING, POTHOLE [*Aeolus*; *study*]. *FORE*, LOOK-OUT (Lat). COLLAPSE, SUBSIDE.

CAVEMAN *HERMIT*, TROGLODYTE; CELLIST (crypt). LOOK-OUT, SENTRY (crypt). POTHOLER.

CB COMPANION (Order of the Bath), *ORDER*. RADIO.

CBE COMPANION (Order of the Br Empire), *MEDAL*.

CBI BOSSES, EMPLOYERS (Confederation of Br Industry).

CBS *BROADCASTING* (US).

CC CUBIC CENTIMETRES. TWO HUNDRED.

CD CADMIUM (*chem*). CIVIL DEFENCE. CORPS DIPLOMATIQUE.

CDR COMMANDER, OFFICER.

CE CERIUM (*chem*). CHURCH (OF ENGLAND). CIVIL ENGINEER.

CEASEFIRE Stop shooting, hence CUT (crypt).

CEDILLA *ACCENT* (ç = sibilant).

CELEBRATED EXTOLLED, FAMOUS, PRAISED, WELL-KNOWN, HONOURED, OBSERVED, OFFICIATED, PERFORMED, SUNG.

CELEBRITY BIG-WIG, *LION*, *STAR*, VIP.

CELLIST *BOWMAN* (crypt); FIDDLER. CAVEDWELLER, *HERMIT*, PRISONER, RECLUSE (crypt). *GAOLER*, JAILER, WARDER (crypt).

CELSIUS C (centigrade temperature).

CENSORSHIP CUTTING, FAULT-FINDING, PRUNING, SCREENING [*Cato*]; **film categories**: A (adults only; advisory), AA (over 15, was over 14), G (general audience — US), H (horrific; over 16), PG (parental guidance), R (clubs; and restricted — US), U (universal), X (sexy — over 18).

CENT (s/l *scent*, sent). CENTURY. *COIN*.

CENTAUR 1. Myth horse with human head (thus with man's head, M*ORSE); *CHIRON*, NESSUS (*Hercules*), PHOLUS.
2. *CONSTELLATION*.

CENTIGRADE C [Celsius; temperature].

CENTRE MIDDLE. Centre of word or phrase, e.g. **Civic centre** = v, or **Town centre** = ow (crypt).

CERAMICS *CHINA*, EARTHENWARE, PORCELAIN, POTTERY; **types**:

BOW	LOWESTOFT
BRISTOL	MASON
CAUGHLEY®	MEISSEN (Ger)
CHELSEA	MING (Ch)
COALPORT®	MINTON®
COPELAND®	NEW HALL
DAVENPORT	ROCKINGHAM
DELFT (NL)	SEVRES (Fr)
DERBY	SPODE®
DOULTON®	STAFFORDSHIRE
DRESDEN (Ger)	TANG (Ch)
DUX	*WORCESTER*

CERBERUS Gk myth three-headed dog, guarding *Hades* on the banks of the *Styx*.

CERCYON Gk myth *bully*, who wrestled strangers to death; k by *Theseus*.

CERES (s/l *series*). 1. Rom goddess of *NATURE*; EARTH MOTHER; m of *Acheron*. **Gk** = *DEMETER*. 2. Largest of the minor *PLANETS*, with orbit between *Mars* and *Jupiter*.

CERTAIN *BOUND*, SPECIFIC, SURE.

CESTR *Episcopal sig* of *CHESTER*.

CETACEA AQUATIC MAMMAL: *DOLPHIN*, *PORPOISE*, *WHALE*.

CEZAR *AWARD*® (films, Fr).

CF COMPARE. CONFER. CARRY FORWARD (comm).

CH CHAPTER. CHILD. CHINA. CHURCH. (*COMPANION* OF) HONOUR. SWITZERLAND (*car plate*).

Ch China, ~ese.

CHAFF BADINAGE, BANTER, *TEASING*. HUSKS. ANTI-RADAR FOIL; WINDOW (mil code name).

CHAIR FASTENING, RAILHOLDER, SOCKET (rly).

PROFESSORSHIP. ~MAN, PRESIDENT; CONTROL, PRESIDE. THE ELECTRIC ~. SEAT, STOOL; and see *FURNITURE* for list.

CHAIRED CONTROLLED, TOOK THE CHAIR. CARRIED SHOULDER-HIGH. SEATED, UPHOLSTERED (crypt). Railway lines (crypt).

CHAIRMAN *MC*, PRESIDENT. SEDAN-BEARER (arch). Cabinet/furniture maker, upholsterer (crypt) e.g. ADAM, CHIPPENDALE, HEPPLEWHITE, SHERATON.

CHALCEDONY *GEM*, SEMI-PRECIOUS STONE; *AGATE*, *BLOODSTONE*, CHRYSOPRASE, *CORNELIAN*, *ONYX*, *SARD*, SARDONYX.

CHAMPION ACE, RECORD HOLDER. *COMIC*. WONDER *HORSE*.

CHANGE *Anag*. 1. ALTER, EXCHANGE, SUBSTITUTE, SWITCH, VARIETY. REDRESS (crypt). LOOSE COINS, MONEY: CENTS, PENCE etc. 2. Appearing as part of the answer, *anags* its fellow word, e.g. **Rove, for instance, the switch** (10) = CHANGEOVER.

CHANGE SIDES 1. CROSS THE FLOOR, DEFECT, SWITCH ALLEGIANCE, TURNCOAT. 2. *Anag* of 'sides', e.g. SISED, DISES etc (crypt).

CHAOS 1. CONFUSION, PANDEMONIUM, UPROAR (**opp** = *order*). FORMLESS SPACE, PRIMORDIAL DEEP, VOID. 2. Gk *goddess* of vacant space which existed before the Creation, m of Erebus and *Nyx*, and the oldest of the gods. **Egy** = *Nun*.

CHAPERONE DUENNA; GUARD OF HONOUR, NEAR MISS (crypt).

CHAPMAN COMMERCIAL TRAVELLER, DRUMMER, PEDLAR, *REP*. *WRITER*. COWBOY (crypt).

CHAPTER C, CH. ACT, STATUTE. ORDER. SECTION.

CHAR BURN, SCORCH. CLEAN(ER), DAILY, DO, DOMESTIC, MRS MOPP, TREASURE, WASHER-WOMAN. TEA (sl); **comp** = wad. *FISH*, TROUT.

CHARACTER IDENTITY, PERSONALITY, TRAIT; TYPE (*study*). ATTRIBUTE, PROPERTY, QUALITY. LETTERS. *CASE*, COMEDIAN.

CHARGE CARE; *MINOR*, *WARD*. ASSAULT, ATTACK, ONSLAUGHT, RUSH. BOOST, ENERGIZE, REVITALIZE. PAYMENT, PRICE.

CHARIOT HORSE-DRAWN *CARRIAGE*, CURRICULUM (race

~), *JUGGERNAUT*, QUADRIGA (mil) [*Aurora, Boadicea,*
Elijah, *Freya, Jehu, Medea, Phaeton*; *constellation*]. (*tarot*).

CHARM ATTRACTION, BEWITCH, DELIGHT, ENTICE,
ENTRANCE, FASCINATE, TEMPT. *GRACE*, IT, *SA*.
AMULET, FETISH, MASCOT, TALISMAN; CANTRIP,
INCANTATION, SPELL. *Assembly* of FINCHES.

CHARON Gk myth s of Erebus and *Nyx*. FERRYMAN of the dead
over the rivers *Acheron* and *Styx* [*Cocytus, Lethe, Periphlegethon*],
past the dog *Cerberus*; his fee was the Obolus.

CHART DIRECT, *PLOT*, RECORD. MAP, PLAN, SEA-MAP.
Pl = RATING [top ten etc].

CHARTER *DEED*, GRANT. HIRE. *RIGHTS*. NAVIGATOR
(crypt).

CHARY *SHY*, WARY.

CHARYBDIS A whirlpool which, with the rock *Scylla*, formed a
hazard to seafarers in the Straits of Messina; now called Galofaro.

CHAUCER GEOFFREY (c 1340–1400); s of Agnes and John ~
vintner, mar Philippa and f of Lewis. *Page* to wife of Edward III's
son and a court diplomat. Father of English poetry. **His works
include**: Consolations of Philosophy (trans of treatise on the
astrolabe), Romance of the Rose (trans), The Book of the
Duchess, The House of Fame, The Legend of Good Women, The
Parliament of Fowls, Troilus and Cressida, and The Canterbury
Tales with its Prologue, whose **characters** assembled at the Tabard
Inn, Southwark, **include**: the Canon's Yeoman, the *Cook*, the
Doctor of Medicine (Physician), the Franklin, the *Friar* (a Limiter),
Host (Harry Bailey), the *Knight*, the Lady Prioress (Madam
Eglantine), the Manciple, Milibeus, the Merchant, the Miller (a
wrestler), the *Monk*, the *Nun's* Priest, the Pardoner, the *Parson*
and his br the Ploughman, the *Reeve*, the *Scholar* (Clerk), the Sea
Captain, *Sailor* or Shipman (his boat, the Magdalen), the Second
Nun, the *Sergeant-at-Law* (Man of Law), Sir *Topaz*, the Squire (s
of the Knight), the Summoner and the Wife of Bath (gap-toothed);
also travelling, but without a recorded tale, were the *Carpenter*, the
Dyer, the Haberdasher, the Ploughman, the Tapestry Maker, the
Weaver and the Yeoman.

CHCH CHRISTCHURCH.

CHE GUEVARA, REVOLUTIONARY.

CHEAT CON, COZEN, DECEIVE(R), FIDDLE, FRAUD,
SWINDLE(R), TRICK(STER).

CHECK DAM, HOLD IN, IMPEDE, PAUSE, SLOW, *STEM*.

CONTROL, MAKE SURE, *MARK*, *TICK*. REBUFF,
REBUKE, RESTRAIN(T). THREATEN (chess). *BILL*,
CHEQUE, DRAFT, LETTER OF CREDIT (US). HATCH,
PLAID, SQUARED, *TARTAN*.

CHEESE MALLOW FRUIT. SKITTLES DISC. VIP (sl).
Decorative coil of rope (naut). [camera, smile]. PRESSED
CURDS; **comp** = *bread*;

types (all®):	8+ letters
under 8-letters	BRICKBAT
BLUE	CAMEMBERT
BOURSIN	CHESHIRE
BRIE	COTSWOLD
CHEDDAR	GAMBOZOLA
COTTAGE	GLOUCESTER
CREAM	GORGONZOLA
DUTCH	JARLSBERG
EDAM	LYMESWOLD
GOUDA	PARMESAN
GRUYERE	PECORINO
MYCELLA	PORT SALUT
SAGE	ROQUEFORT
STILTON	TILSITER
SWISS	WENSLEYDALE
	WESTMINSTER BLUE

Chem Chemistry.
CHEMICAL ELEMENT BASIC SUBSTANCE,
    IRRESOLVABLE; e.g.:

Actinium	= *AC*	**Fluoride**	= *F*
Aluminium	= *AL*	**Gold**	= *AU*
Argon	=*A*	**Helium**	=*HE*
Arsenic	=*AS*	**Hydrogen**	=*H*
Barium	= *BA*	**Iodine**	= I
Boron	= *B*	**Iridium**	= IR
Cadmium	= *CD*	**Iron**	= FE
Carbon	= *C*	**Krypton**	= KR
Chromium	= *CR*	**Lead**	= PB
Cobalt	= *CO*	**Magnesium**	= *MG*
Copper	= *CU*	**Mercury**	= HG

Neon	= NE	**Silver**	= *AG*
Nickel	= *NI*	**Sodium**	= *NA*
Nitrogen	= *N*	**Sulphur**	= *S*
Oxygen	= *O*	**Tin**	= SN
Palladium	= *PD*	**Titanium**	= TI
Phosphorus	= *P*	**Uranium**	= *U*
Platinum	= *PT*	**Wolfram**	= *W*
Potassium	= *K*	**Xenon**	= XE
Silicon	= *SI*	**Zinc**	= ZN

A	= ARGON	**K**	= POTASSIUM
AC	= ACTINIUM	**KR**	= KRYPTON
AG	= *SILVER*	**MG**	= MAGNESIUM
AL	= ALUMINIUM	**N**	= NITROGEN
AS	= ARSENIC	**NA**	= *SODIUM*
AU	= *GOLD*	**NE**	= NEON
B	= BORON	**NI**	= *NICKEL*
BA	= BARIUM	**O**	= OXYGEN
C	= CARBON	**P**	= PHOSPHORUS
CD	= CADMIUM	**PB**	= *LEAD*
CO	= COBALT	**PD**	= PALLADIUM
CR	= CHROMIUM	**PT**	= *PLATINUM*
CU	= *COPPER*	**S**	= SULPHUR
F	= FLUORINE	**SI**	= SILICON
FE	= *IRON*	**SN**	= *TIN*
H	= HYDROGEN	**TI**	= TITANIUM
HE	= HELIUM	**U**	= URANIUM
HG	= *MERCURY*	**W**	= WOLFRAM
I	= IODINE	**XE**	= XENON
IR	= IRIDIUM	**ZN**	= ZINC

CHEMIST DISPENSER. MPS.

CHESSPIECE BISHOP, *CASTLE*, *KING*, *KNIGHT*, PAWN, *QUEEN*, *ROOK*. BOARDMAN (crypt).

CHEST BREAST, BUST, FRONT TORSO, THORAX [pectoral]. FUND. COLLECTOR, CONTAINER, RESERVOIR (tech). *BOX*, STORAGE CONTAINER; and see *FURNITURE* for list.

CHESTER 1. DEVA (*Rom*). *CASTLE*. *RACETRACK* (horses). 2. **Episcopal sig** = CESTR. 3. *Herald*.

CHESTERTON 1. Gilbert Keith, *poet* and *writer*; **books**: The *Club* of *Queer* Trades, Father Brown *detective stories*, The Man who was

Thursday, The *Napoleon* of Notting Hill. 2. DURNOVARIA (*Rom*).

CHIC A LA MODE, FASHIONABLE, IN, SMART.

CHICHESTER 1. *WORLD-GIRDLER*. NOVIOMAGUS (*Rom*). 2. **Episcopal sig** = CICESTR.

CHICKEN AFRAID. YOUNG WOMAN. BIDDY, HEN, POULTRY (*male* and *female*).

CHIEF GOD **Gk** = *ZEUS*, **Rom** = JOVE, *JUPITER*, **A-Sax** = *WODEN*, **Bab** = ANU, BEL/BELUS, **Ch** = XANGTI, **Egy** = *OSIRIS*, TEMU, **Ind** = BRAHMA, SHIVA, **Nor** = *ODIN*, **Phoen** = *BAAL*.

CHIEF GODDESS **Gk** = *HERA*, **Rom** = *JUNO*, **Egy** = *ISIS*, **Ind** = *DEVI*, **Bab** = BELIT/BELTIS.

CHILD 1. CH, ISSUE. TOT. Human *offspring*. [*Dickens*; *Moloch*; *patron saint*]. 2. Monday's ~ is fair of *face*; Tuesday's ~ is full of *grace*; Wednesday's ~ is full of woe; Thursday's ~ has far to go; Friday's ~ is *loving* and giving; Saturday's ~ works hard for its *living*; but the ~ that is born on a Sabbath day is bonny and blithe, and *good* and gay.

CHILDBIRTH 1. BEARING, DELIVERY, LABOUR. 2. **Goddess:** **Gk** = *HERA*, **Rom** = *JUNO*.

CHIM(A)ERA Gk myth firebreathing *MONSTER* (front lion, middle goat, back dragon), slain by *Bellerophon*. VOLCANO. [*Typhon*].

CHINA Ch. CATHAY [mandarins, *study*]. *CERAMICS*; DISHES, PLATES, SERVICE. 20th *anniversary*.

CHINAMAN *BOXER*, CHINK, MANDARIN. *BOSIE*, GOOGLY (*cricket*).

CHINESE CALENDAR In order to get to know the animals better, Buddha called them to him, and promised to reward all who came. Only twelve turned up, so he dedicated a year to each in order of arrival.

Goat	1931	'43	'55	'67	'79	*Buffalo*	1937	'49	'61	'73	'85
Monkey	1932	'44	'56	'68	'80	*Tiger*	1938	'50	'62	'74	'86
Cock	1933	'45	'57	'69	'81	*Rabbit*	1939	'51	'63	'75	'87
Dog	1934	'46	'58	'70	'82	*Dragon*	1940	'52	'64	'76	'88
Pig	1935	'47	'59	'71	'83	*Snake*	1941	'53	'65	'77	'89
Rat	1936	'48	'60	'72	'84	*Horse*	1942	'54	'66	'78	'90

(The Year of the Monkey always exactly divides by 12)

CHINESE DYNASTY *Noble* house (or *royal family*) of Ch; in order: HSIA *c.*2205–1750 B.C.; SHANG *c.*1750–1127 B.C.; CHOU *c.*1127–225 B.C. (Confucius); QING 225–206 B.C. (Great Wall); HAN 206 B.C.–A.D. 220; Three Kingdoms A.D. 220–265; Six Dynasties A.D. 265–588; SUI A.D. 589–618 (*Huns*, Attila, Hsiung-Nu); TANG A.D. 618–906; Five Dynasties A.D. 906–959; SUNG 960–1260; YUAN 1260–1368 (Mongols, Genghis Khan, Kublai Khan, Marco Polo); MING 1368–1644; MANCHU or CHIN 1644–1911.

CHIRON 1. Gk myth wise CENTAUR, teacher of *Achilles*, Diomedes and *Jason* in gymnastics, hunting, medicine, music and prophecy. 2. A minor *PLANET* orbiting the *Sun* between *Saturn* and *Venus*.

CHLORIS Gk *goddess* of *FLOWERS*. **Rom** = *FLORA*.

CHOICE PREFERENCE, SELECTION. APPROPRIATE, ELITE, EXQUISITE, *FLOWER*, SELECT. ALTERNATIVE [Devil and deep blue sea; Hobson's ~; Scylla and *Charybdis*].

CHOPSTICKS CLEAVE/SPLIT FIREWOOD. PIANO TUNE. EATING TOOLS, KHAI-ZI (Ch).

CHORIAMB *FOOT*.

CHRISTCHURCH CHCH. (*University*) COLLEGE. *CASTLE*.

CHRISTMAS NATIVITY. PRESENT DAY (crypt) [Santa Claus]. ~ box, ~ cake, ~ card, ~ present, ~ stocking, ~ tree, ~ *song*:

(12) *Lords* a-leaping	(6) *Geese* a-laying
(11) Ladies *dancing*	(5) Golden *rings*
(10) *Pipers* piping	(4) Calling *birds*
(9) *Drummers* drumming	(3) French *hens*
(8) *Maids* a-milking	(2) Turtle *doves*
(7) Swans a-swimming	A *partridge* in a pear-tree.

CHRISTOPHER *KIT*, TRAVELLER. *PATRON SAINT* (wayfarers).

CHROMATIC INTERVAL, SCALE (mus). BRIGHT-COLOURED.

CHROMIUM CR (*chem*).

CHRYSOBERYL *GEM* (green/yellow).

CHRYSOLITE *GEM*, PRECIOUS STONE; OLIVINE, PERIDOT. *Birthstone* (September).

CHRYSOPRASE *GEM*, SEMI-PRECIOUS STONE; CHALCEDONY (green).

CHURCH CH. CE, RC. HOUSE OF WORSHIP. ESTABLISHMENT.

CHURCH DRESS Headgear: BIRETTA (RC), CALOT(T)E (RC), HOOD (friar), MITRE (abbot, bishop), SHOVEL HAT (clergy), TIARA (pope). **Vestments**: ALB (clergy), AMICE (shoulders), APRON (bishop), CANONICALS (clergy), CASSOCK (clergy), CHASUBLE (clergy), CHIMERE (bishop), COPE (processional cloak), DALMATIC (bishop, deacon), DOMINO (cloak), EPHOD (Jewish), GREMIAL (bishop's apron), MANIPLE (eucharistic napkin), MORSE (cope fastening), ORPHREY (embroidered scarf), ROCHET (surplice), SCAPULAR, ~Y (monk), SOUTANE (RC), STOLE (scarf), SURPLICE (clergy), TIPPET (cloth band), TUNICLE (bishop), VEXILLUM (crosier cloth).

CHURCHMAN WREN (crypt). CLERGY, DD, *FATHER*, PRELATE, PRIEST, REVEREND, RR, e.g.:

4-letters
ABBE (RC)
CURE (RC)
DEAN
GURU (Ind)
IMAM (Mos)
LAMA (Bud)
MONK
POPE (Gk; RC)
YOGI (Ind)

5-letters
ABBOT
CANON
DRUID (Wal)
FAKIR (Mos)
FRIAR
HADJI (Mos)
MUFTI (Mos)
PADRE
PRIOR
VICAR

6-letters
BEADLE

BISHOP
CLERIC
CURATE
DEACON
MULLAH (Mos)
PARSON
PASTOR
RECTOR
SCRIBE (Heb)
SEXTON
VERGER

7-letters
ACOLYTE
BRAHMIN (Ind)
BROTHER
MUEZZIN (Mos)
PONTIFF (RC)
PRELATE
PRIMATE

8+ letters
ARCHBISHOP
ARCHDEACON

AYATOLLAH (Mos)   MINISTER
CARDINAL (RC)   MISSIONARY
CHAPLAIN   PATRIARCH (Gk)
CHURCHWARDEN   PREBENDARY
ECCLESIASTIC   PRECENTOR
GODBOTHERER (sl)   PRESBYTER
METROPOLITAN (Gk)   SKYPILOT (sl)

CHURCHWOMAN ABBESS, CANONESS, MOTHER SUPERIOR, NOVICE, NUN, POSTULANT, PRIORESS, *SISTER*.

CI CHANNEL ISLANDS. CIRRUS. (Order of the) CROWN OF INDIA.

CIA CENTRAL INTELLIGENCE AGENCY.

CICERO 1. DRUM *HORSE*. *TYPEFACE*. 2. TULLY, Rom ORATOR, 104–43 B.C.; mar (1) Terentia (one d Tullia, one s Marcus), (2) Publilia. Ass by Mark *Antony* 43 B.C.. Writings include: De Oratore, De Republica, De Legibus, De Officiis, De Finibus etc.

CICESTR *Episcopal sig* of CHICHESTER.

CIGARETTE CANCER STICK, CIG(GY), COFFIN NAIL, DOG END, FAG END, GASPER, JOINT, *REEFER* (drugged), SMOKE, SNOUT, WEED (all sl); **brands** (most ®): ARDATH, *CAMEL* (US), DE RESKE, GAULOIS (Fr), KENSITAS, LUCKY STRIKE (US), MARLBORO, PASSING CLOUD (Turk), *PLAYERS* (Please), STUYVESANT, V, *VICTORY*, *WEIGHTS*, *WILLS*, WOODBINE.

CINQUE PORTS DOVER, HASTINGS, HYTHE, ROMNEY, *SANDWICH* (+ *RYE* and WINCHELSEA) [Lord Warden. Walmer *Castle*]. Vessel (*Crusoe*).

CIPANGU *JAPAN*.

CIRCA *ABOUT*, *C*, *CA*.

CIRCLE O, *RING*, ROUNDEL, *ZERO* [*Pi*].

CIRCUMFLEX BENDING, CURVED. *ACCENT* (^).

CIRCUMNAVIGATORS EXPLORERS, *WORLD-GIRDLERS*.

CIRCUS 1. Convergence of streets, e.g. Oxford ~, Piccadilly ~. 2. AMPHITHEATRE, STADIUM; ARENA (~ Maximus, Rom) [*Caligula*]. 3. Travelling company of barnstormers (flying ~) or acrobats, animals, *clowns*, jugglers and trapeze artists, working in a tent or big top; **celeb**: ASTLEY'S, BARNUM & BAILEY, BERTRAM MILLS, CHIPPERFIELD, HENGLER, Rolf KNIE

(Swi), PINDER (Fr), RINGLING (US), SANGER.

CIRRUS *CI*, *CLOUD*, MACKEREL SKY.

CISTERCIAN *MONK*; BENEDICTINE, *TRAPPIST*.

CITY 1. Large municipality, normally with a *bishop*; style granted in the UK by the *monarch*; **comp** = town. 2. Financial centre of *London*; SQUARE MILE [*company*]. 3. Abbr for certain *football* teams, e.g. Bristol ~, Leicester ~, Manchester ~.

CIVIL SERVICE CS (**Unions** = NALGO, NUPE) [Bumble (Oliver, *Dickens*); Dogberry (Much Ado, *Shak*); mandarin]. REGISTRY OFFICE WEDDING (crypt). POLITE WAITER (crypt).

CLASS *FORM*, *REMOVE*, SCHOOL. TYPE, RANK. STYLE, TONE, *U* (and crypt, e.g. **Quietly classy** = U*P).

CLASSED DESIGNATED, RANKED, REGISTERED. AT SCHOOL, IN FORM, LEARNING (crypt).

CLASSIC 1. A.1, FIRST CLASS, STANDARD. 2. Five specific horse races (One Thousand Guineas, Two ~, Derby, Oaks, St Leger). 3. A word or phrase based on Lat or Gk, hence implies put into Lat or Gk, e.g. **Classically where . . .** = UBI . . .

CLAUDIUS Rom s of Drusus and Antonia (the d of Mark *Antony*), he was made *emperor* by the soldiers in A.D. 41. Weak, with a stammer, ~ mar four times, incl (3) Valeria Messalina (1 s Britannicus) and (4) Agrippina (~'s niece), who had *Nero*, her s by a previous mar, declared successor instead of Britannicus; Agrippina then had ~ k A.D. 54.

CLAUSTROPHOBIA *Aversion* to enclosed spaces.

CLEAN SHEET FRESH START. UNWRITTEN, VIRGIN PAPER. NEW BEDLINEN.

CLEF BASS, TREBLE; *KEY*.

CLEOPATRA 1. QUEEN OF EGYPT (68–30 B.C.); d of *Ptolemy* Anletes, mar her br Ptolemy; was lover (1) Julius *Caesar* (one s, Caesarion) and (2) *Antony*. Caused Antony to lose the sea battle of Actium by withdrawing her fleet, then spread the rumour that she had died. Antony stabbed himself, whereupon she also killed herself, with an asp [beauty; billiards (A & C, *Shak*); snake]. 2. Minor *PLANET*. 3. *Shak* (A and C). *Shaw* (Caesar and ~).

CLERGY *CHURCHMEN*.

CLERK CLERGYMAN, LAY OFFICER (~ of Oxenford, *Chaucer*). HOTEL/SHOP ASSISTANT (US). AGENT, COURT OFFICIAL, RECORDER. OVERSEER. BANK/OFFICE WORKER; **celeb** (all *Dickens*): BOB CRATCHIT (Scrooge's in Xmas Carol); URIAH HEEP ('umble to Wickfield in Copperfield);

TIM LINKINWATER (Cheerybles' in Nich Nick); NEWMAN
NOGGS (Ralph Nickleby's in Nich Nick); JOHN WEMMICK
(Jaggers' in Great Ex).

CLIFFHANGER TENSE SITUATION, THRILLER. NEST (crypt).
ROCKY PLANT e.g. IVY, MESA VERDE, SAMPHIRE (crypt).

CLIMBER ALPINIST, MOUNTAINEER. IVY, *PLANT*, LIANA,
MESA VERDE, SAMPHIRE, STEPHANOTIS. SOCIAL
SNOB, PUSHER.

CLIMBING 1. MOUNTAINEERING, MOUNTING, SCALING.
PUSHING. 2. Word reads upwards (dn) e.g. **Climbing weed** =
DEEW (crypt, dn).

CLIMBING FRAME LADDER (crypt). EMARF (dn, crypt).

CLINK *GAOL* (sl). CLANK, *RING*.

CLIO One of the nine Gk *MUSES* (myth).

CLIPJOINT DIVE, NIGHTCLUB, SPEAKEASY. STAPLE,
PAPER-CLIP (crypt). BARBERSHOP, HAIRDRESSER
(crypt).

CLIPPER *BOAT*, SAILING SHIP. SCISSORS, SHEARS,
SNIPPERS; HEDGE-TRIMMER. BARBER (crypt).

CLOAK CONCEAL. DISGUISE, MASK. GARMENT; CLOKE
(arch); **types**: BURNOUS (Arab), DOLMAN (Turk), KIRTLE
(arch), PALETOT (19th cent), PALLIUM (Gk), *TABARD*
(herald, knight), TOGA (Rom). [*Penelope*]; **comp** = dagger.

CLOCK TIME-KEEPER, TIME-PIECE, *WATCH*; TICKER;
GRANDFATHER [*Company* (livery); Knibb, Tompion]. FACE
(sl). And see *furniture* for types.

CLOSE *NEAR*, NIGH. MEAN, MISERLY, NIGGARDLY,
STINGY, TIGHT. *END*, FINISH; *SEAL*, SHUT. PRIVATE,
QUIET [oyster]. MUGGY, OPPRESSIVE, *SULTRY*, WARM
(**opp** = *cold*). COURTYARD, QUAD.

CLOTH FABRIC, *MATERIAL*, RAG [*Company* (livery); *measure*].
DUSTER. *CLERGY*.

CLOTHES CLOBBER, *DRESS(ES)*, DUDS, GEAR, GLAD
RAGS, RIG. BEDECKS. [Hans *Andersen*].

CLOUD BEFOG, OBFUSCATE. WATER-VAPOUR e.g. *CI*,
CIRRUS, *CU*, CUMULUS, NIMBUS, STRATUS.

CLOWN RUSTIC (arch). BERGOMASK, *FOOL*, *JESTER* (q.v.);
PAGLIACCIO, RIGOLETTO (Verdi; *hunchback*).

CLUB 1. COSH, CUDGEL, NIGHTSTICK, TRUNCHEON,
WEAPON [*Periphites*]. GOLF STICK; **types**: BLASTER,
BRASSIE, CLEEK, *DRIVER*, *IRON*, MASHIE, NIBLICK,

PUTTER, SANDWEDGE, *SPOON*, *WEDGE*, *WOOD*. **Pl** =
CARDS, *SUIT*; SOLDIERS (*Alice*). 2. C; ASSOCIATION,
SOCIETY [*Cat*; *Chesterton*]; **celeb London ~s**:

Alpine	Junior Naval & Military
Army & Navy (the Rag)	Junior Carlton
Athenaeum	Kit-Cat
Bachelors	Lyceum
Badminton	Marlborough
Bath	National Sporting
Bellona (Sayers)	Naval & Military (In and Out)
Boodle's	Portland
Brooks's	Pratt's
Buck's	Public Schools
Carlton	Reform
Cavalry	Royal Air Force
Cavendish	Royal Automobile
Conservative	Royal Thames Yacht
Constitutional	St James's
Diogenes (*Holmes*)	Savage
Drones (*Wodehouse*)	Savile
Eccentric	Travellers'
Garrick	United Services
Guards	White's

CLUBLAND ST JAMES. GOLF COURSE (crypt).
CLUBMAN ROTARIAN. GOLFER (crypt). COSHER, THUG
   [*Periphites*].
CLYTEMNESTRA 1. Gk myth sis of *Castor*, *Pollux* and *twin* of
   Helen; mar *Agamemnon* (one s *Orestes*, three d *Electra*,
   Chrysothermis and Iphigenia), whom she k in his *bath*; k by her s
   Orestès for adultery with Aegisthus while Agamemnon was fighting
   at *Troy*. 2. A minor *PLANET*.
CO CARE OF. COBALT (*chem*). (COMMANDING) OFFICER.
   COLORADO (US *state*). COLOMBIA (*car plate*). *COMPANY*,
   FIRM.
COACH BUS, *CARRIAGE*, CHARABANC, TRANSPORT.
   CRAMMER, INSTRUCT(OR), TEACH(ER), TRAIN(ER),
   TUTOR. **Comp** = *horses*.
COATED 1. CAKED. PAINTED. DRESSED (crypt). 2. Word
   outside another e.g. **Beaten egg is sent back coated with mud** (6) =
   MU*GGE*D.

COATING COVERAGE, LAYER. JACKET, OVERCOAT, REEFER.

COB *BOAT*. BREAD, LOAF. CLAY BRICK. COAL. GULL (dial). *HORSE*. NUT, PIPE. *SPIDER*. SWAN (*male*).

COBALT *METAL*; CO (*chem*).

COBBLER CORDWAINER, SHOEMAKER, SNOB [*last*, Manette (*Dickens*)]. *DRINK*. **Pl** = BALLS (*rh sl*). NORTHAMPTON (*football* team).

COCAINE *DRUG*, SNOW; NUMBER (crypt). [*Holmes*].

COCKTAIL *Anag*. *DRINK*: JOHN COLLINS, HIGHBALL, MARTINI®, SCREWDRIVER, SIDECAR etc. AMALGAM, MIX(TURE). FEATHER (crypt). K (crypt).

COCYTUS Gk myth tributary of the river *Acheron* [*Underworld*].

COD *FISH*. CASH ON DELIVERY.

CODE LAWS, RULES, STATUTES. ETHIC, STANDARD. CRYPTOGRAM, CYPHER (mil). *MORSE*, SEMAPHORE, W/T. STD.

COIGN (s/l *coin*). CORNER, VANTAGE POINT.

COIN (s/l *coign*). 1. INVENT, MAKE; UTTER. Put CO* in word (crypt), e.g. **Coin sop ladle** (5) = S*CO*OP; **vague inherent coin** (5) = IN*CO*HERENT. 2. *CURRENCY* (q.v.), MONEY, SPECIE, SMALL CHANGE (hence MALLS; crypt); C, D, P, S. **Types (OE gold)**: JOANNES (36s 0d), MOIDORE (27s 0d), JACOBUS or UNITE (25s 0d), CAROLUS (23s 0d), *GUINEA* (21s 0d), *MARK* (13s 4d), *ANGEL* (10s 0d), NOBLE (6s 8d), *DOLLAR* (4s 6d); **(OE silver)**: *TESTER* (6d), GROAT (4d). **Old Scots**: BODLE (2d), PLACK or GROAT (4d), BAWBEE (6d), SHILLING (12d), *POUND* (20s), MERK (13s 4d). **Others**:

2-letters	
AS (Rom)	*MARK* (Eng, Fin, Ger)
	MITE (bibl)
3-letters	PEAG (Ind)
BOB (UK)	REAL (Sp)
ECU (Fr)	
SOU (Fr)	**5-letters**
	CROWN (Eng, Scand)
4-letters	DUCAT (Eur)
ANNA (Ind)	FRANC (Fr)
CASH (Ch, Ind)	*FRANK* (Eur)
CENT (US etc)	OBANG (Jap)

(first column also:) DIME (US)

PENNY (UK)   ZECHIN (Hebr)
POUND (UK)
ROYAL (Eng)   **7+ letters**
                             CAROLIN (Ger)
6-letters   DENARIUS (Rom)
DOLLAR (US et al)   DOUBLOON (Sp)
GUINEA (UK)   FARTHING (UK)
NICKEL (US)   KRUGERRAND (SA)
PESETA (Sp)   MARAVEDI (Sp)
ROUBLE (USSR)   MARIA THERESA DOLLAR (A)
SHEKEL (Hebr)   PIECE OF EIGHT (Sp)
STATER (Gk)   PRINDLE (Sc)
STIVER (sl)   QUARTER (US)
TALENT (bibl)   SOLIDUS (Rom)
TANNER (UK)   SOVEREIGN (UK)
TESTER (Eng)

Coll = numismatist. And see *currency*.
COL *COLONEL, SOLDIER. COLUMN. DEPRESSION, LOW.
DEFILE, PASS, SADDLE.*
COLCHESTER 1. *CASTLE.* NATIVE, *OYSTER* [Whitstable].
2. Scene of battle by *Boadicea.* CAMULODUNUM (Rom).
COLD C, CHILLY, NIPPY, FRIGID, ICY (**opp** = *close, heat*).
CORYZA, SNIFFLES [catarrh]. **Comp** = *hot*.
COLLECTION ACCUMULATION, *ASSEMBLY*, GATHERING,
GROUP. CALLING FOR, FETCHING; REMOVAL (postal)
[*COD*]. OFFERING [eccles]. CONCENTRATION,
RECOVERING (senses).
COLLECTOR ADMINISTRATOR (Ind). ACCUMULATOR,
ASSEMBLER, GATHERER, HOBBYIST, *MAGPIE* (sl),
SQUIRREL (sl). In the list which follows, some words have been
coined by enthusiasts to describe their own hobby; a few of these
creations have been accepted into the dictionaries (deltiologist,
phillumenist); some have encountered opposition (arcturologist,
tegestologist); some are admittedly rather far-fetched, but have
been included in this first-ever collection of collectors because they
are used by aficionados of the subject concerned (buttonier,
programmaniac). Other hobbyists have adopted existing words
which have had their original meaning extended to cover collection,
as well as a love or knowledge of the subject (bibliophile,
horologist, gemmologist — but see my remarks below, regarding

the difference between the Greek word 'logos' and the Latin
'legere'). Somewhat surprisingly, however, the most popular kind
of collector has no generic noun known to this lexicographer, who
has been unable to resist the temptation to suggest a word for a
collector of autographs. The first candidate was sigillarist, deriving
from sigillary (in most dictionaries as the adjectival form of sigil, a
seal or signet). This was discarded in favour of signaturist, largely
because Dr Johnson includes it as 'One who holds the doctrine of
signatures; a word rarely used.' It would have been nice to revive a
word already going out of use in 1757, but it has a suspect pedigree
for our usage, so the impeccable Latin ancestry of signalegist was
finally preferred (signum, a sign + legere to collect), much as
florilegist comes from florilegium (which finds a place in the Collins
English Dictionary).

   Amateur lexicologists should note that -logy derives from the
Greek 'logos' meaning a word or reasoning, and implies the study
of a subject, and that the Latin verb 'legere' means to collect; thus
the suffix -logist = expert, while -legist = collector (not always the
same thing). There are therefore grounds for using gemmolegist,
horolegist and even ichthyolegist when meaning collectors (rather
than devotees) of gems, clocks or fishes. **Examples:**

antiques	ANTIQUARY
archaic words	ARCHAIST
autographs	SIGNALEGIST
bank notes	NOTAPHILIST
beer mats	TEGESTOLOGIST
beetles	COLEOPTERIST
birds' eggs	OOLOGIST
books	BIBLIOPHILE
butterflies	LEPIDOPTERIST
buttonhooks	BUTTONIER
certificates	SCRIPOPHILIST
cheese labels	FROMOLOGIST
cigarette cards	CARTOPHILIST
clocks	HOROLOGIST
coins	NUMISMATIST
ephemeral trivia	EPHEMERIST
fishes	ICHTHYOLOGIST
flowers	FLORILEGIST
gramophone records	DISCOPHILE

Greek philosophy	DOXOGRAPHER
herbs (med)	HERBALIST
husbands	POLYANDRIST
insects	ENTOMOLOGIST
languages	GLOSSOLOGIST
literary excerpts	CHRESTOMATHIST
matchboxes	PHILLUMENIST
medals	NUMISMATIST
moths	LEPIDOPTERIST
postcards	DELTIOLOGIST
precious stones	GEM(M)OLOGIST
programmes	PROGRAMMANIAC
proper names	ONOMASIOLOGIST
quotations	COLLECTANEIST
shells	CONCHOLOGIST
stamps	PHILATELIST
teddy bears	ARCTUROLOGIST
walking sticks	RABDOPHILIST
wives	POLYGAMIST

COLLEGE *ETON*. [*universities*].

COLONEL (s/l *kernel*). CO, *COL*, OFFICER; REGIMENTED (crypt); **celeb**: BLIMP (Low, *cartoonist*); BOGEY (Sousa, *composer*); BLOOD (*Scott*); DIRKOVITCH (*Kipling*); NEWCOMBE ('Adsum', Thackeray).

COLOUR INFLUENCE; INTEREST. BLUSH, FLUSH, REDDEN. PAINT; HUE e.g.:

Blacks	BERYL
COAL	BICE
DUSKY	*CAMBRIDGE*
EBON(Y)	CERULEAN
JET(TY)	*COBALT*
PITCH	*ELECTRIC*
SABLE (*herald*)	INDIGO
SOOT	LAPIS LAZULI
SWART	*NAVY*
	OXFORD
Blues	PERSE
AQUAMARINE	*ROYAL*
AZURE (*herald*)	SAPPHIRE

SEA
SKY
SMALT
TURQUOISE
ULTRAMARINE
WATCHET

Browns
AUBURN
BAY
BISTRE
CAMEL
ECRU
FAWN
HAZEL
HENNA
KHAKI
OCHRE
PUCE
RUSSET
SARD
SEPIA
SORREL
TAN
TAWNY
TENNY (*herald*)
VANDYKE

Greens
BERYL
BICE
EMERALD
JADE
OLIVE
RESEDA
TURQUOISE
VERDIGRIS
VERT (*herald*)

Oranges
BRASS

CADMIUM
COPPER
FLAME
OCHRE
SARD

Purples
AMETHYST
INDIGO
LAVENDER
LILAC
MAUVE
PLUM
PUCE
PURPURE (*herald*)
VIOLET

Reds
BURGUNDY
CARMINE
CERISE
CINNABAR
CRIMSON
GULES (*herald*)
MAGENTA
MINIUM
MODENA
PILLAR-BOX
RUBY
RUST
SARD
SCARLET
VERMILION

Whites
BLANCH
BLEACH
CHALKY
CREAMY
IVORY
LILY

MILK
PEARL

Yellows
AMBER
AUREATE
BUFF
CREAM
FALLOW
GAMBOGE

GILDED
GILT
GOLD
LEMON
PRIMROSE
SAFFRON
SULPHUR
TOPAZ
XANTHIC

Heraldic colours: black = *SABLE*, **blue** = *AZURE*, **brown** = TENNE/TENNY, **green** = VERT, **gold** = OR, **purple** = PURPURE, **red** = GULES, **silver** = ARGENT. **Primary colours:** *GREEN*, *RED*, VIOLET. **Primary colours (painting):** *BLUE*, *RED*, *YELLOW*. **Rainbow colours** (from outside to in): *RED*, *ORANGE*, *YELLOW*, *GREEN*, *BLUE*, INDIGO, VIOLET.

COLT 1. GREENHORN, TYRO. AUTOMATIC, *WEAPON*®. 2. *Offspring* of camel or horse. **Pl** = JUNIOR TEAM. *Football team* (US).

COLUMN COL. FILE, TROOPS. VERTICAL CYLINDER/DIVISION/JET, PILLAR (and see *architecture*). ARTICLE, REPORTING.

COMBER BREAKER, FOAM, SURF, WAVE. HAIRDRESSER (crypt) [curry ~]. *BEE* (crypt). FISH.

COMEBACK 1. ENCORE, RETURN, REVIVAL. EMOC (crypt). 2. Word written backwards, e.g. **Elba's comeback looks gloomy** (5) = SABLE.

COMEDOWN ANTICLIMAX. ALIGHT, *LAND* (crypt).

COMET 1. TAILED STAR, SUN SATELLITE (Biela, Ericke, Halley). AIRCRAFT. *REINDEER*. 2. First Br passenger (paddle) steamer.

COMFORTER DUMMY. SCARF. HOLY SPIRIT. One who eases pain or affliction; **opp** = *Job's* ~.

COMIC AMUSING, BURLESQUE, FACETIOUS, *FUNNY*, HUMOROUS, LAUGHABLE, RIDICULOUS, RISIBLE, WITTY; *CASE*, COMEDIAN. Children's periodical, **names** (all ®): BEANO, BOP, BOY'S OWN PAPER, *BULLSEYE*, *CHAMPION*, *DANDY*, *EAGLE*, HOTSPUR, MAGNET, ROVER, TIGER TIM, *WIZARD*.

COMING TO One word precedes another, e.g. **Commie coming**

Companion 139

to see · · · (3, 4) = RED SPOT.

COMMANDER AOC, CINC, FOC, GOC (mil), [SEAC]. *TARTAN* (bibl). WOODEN MALLET.

COMMANDING DIGNIFIED, IMPRESSIVE. OVERLOOKING. CO, *COMMANDER*, IC, IN CHARGE.

COMMANDMENT DIVINE COMMAND, *TEN* ~s (q.v.) [Moses, Mt Sinai]. Ten in *song*.

COMMON(LY) 1. PUBLIC, SHARED. VILLAGE GREEN. ORDINARY, REGULAR, USUAL; **comp** = *garden*. NOUS, SENSE (sl). **Pl** = FOOD, RATIONS. *HOUSE, LEGISLATIVE ASSEMBLY*. 2. INFERIOR, PLEBEIAN, *SLANG* (q.v.), VULGAR (**opp** = *noble*, *U*); NON-U (sl), hence (crypt) remove letter U from clue-word, e.g. **An example of common cause** (4) = CA*SE; or else **Commonly laud the boy** (3) = LA*D. 3. Employ slang in the answer, e.g. **Son is not commonly a good man** (5) = S*AINT.

COMMONSENSE NOUS.

COMMONWEALTH GOVERNMENT (Cromwell). STATE. **British members**: Australia, Bahamas, Bangladesh, Barbados, Bermuda (colony), Botswana, Brunei, Canada, Cyprus, East Caribbean States, Fiji, Gambia, Ghana, Grenada, Guyana, India, Jamaica, Kenya, Lesotho, Malawi, Malaysia, Malta, Mauritius, Nauru, New Zealand, Nigeria, Papua New Guinea, Sierra Leone, Singapore, Sri Lanka, Swaziland, Tanzania, Tongo, Trinidad and Tobago, Uganda, United Kingdom, Western Samoa, Zambia.

COMMUNIST COMMIE, RED, *TROT*; IVAN.

COMMUNITY BODY, FELLOWSHIP. EEC (Treaty of Rome).

Comp Abbr for *COMPANION*; esp in this book means any word commonly associated with the entry word, e.g. bill/coo, coach/horses.

COMPANION 1. DECKHOUSE, HATCHWAY, hence ACCESS STEPS (naut). ASSOCIATE, BROTHER IN ARMS, FELLOW, FRIEND, *MATE*, OPPO (sl), PAL. AU PAIR, HOUSEKEEPER, LIVER-IN. *REFERENCE WORK*. *CH* (crypt). 2. Word commonly associated with another (crypt), e.g. **Bill's** ~ = COO; **Cop's** ~ = PROP; **Jeff's** ~ = MUTT; **celeb** ~s: AENEAS/ACHATES, BIRDS/BEES, BOSWELL/JOHNSON, CASTOR/POLLUX, DAMON/PHINTIAS (not Pythias), DANTE/BEATRICE, DARBY/JOAN, DAVID/JONATHAN, EURALUS/NISUS, FORTNUM/MASON, GIN/TONIC, MASON/DIXON, MOHAMMED/MOUNTAIN, ORESTES/PYLADES, PETRARCH/LAURA, PUNCH/JUDY,

ROLAND/OLIVER, ROMEO/JULIET, SOHRAB/RUSTAM
(-EM, -UM), SNAKES/LADDERS, SWAN/EDGAR,
WHISKY/SODA or SPLASH, WILL/WAY (see also *model* and
lovers).

COMPANY *ASSEMBLY*, *COMPANIONS*, GUESTS, *PARTY*,
VISITORS. ACTORS, CAST [touring ~]. CREW (naut).
BODY OF MEN, *SOLDIERS*, TROOPS. BUSINESS, *CO*,
CONCERN, CORPORATION, *COY*, *FIRM*, GUILD, PLC; **City
livery ~s:**

APOTHECARIES
BAKERS
BARBERS
BASKET MAKERS
BLACKSMITHS
BREWERS
BUTCHERS
CARPENTERS
CLOCKMAKERS
CLOTHWORKERS
COACH & COACH HARNESS MAKERS
COOPERS
CORDWAINERS
CURRIERS
CUTLERS
DISTILLERS
DRAPERS
DYERS
FANMAKERS
FARRIERS
FELTMAKERS
FISHMONGERS
FLETCHERS
FOUNDERS or COPPERSMITHS
FRAMEWORK KNITTERS or STOCKING WEAVERS
FRUITERERS
GIRDLERS
GLASS SELLERS
GLAZIERS
GOLD & SILVER WYRE DRAWERS
GOLDSMITHS

GROCERS
HABERDASHERS
INNHOLDERS
IRONMONGERS
LEATHER SELLERS
MASONS
MERCERS
MERCHANT TAYLORS
PAINTERS or PAINTER STAINERS
PATTEN MAKERS
PEWTERERS
PLAISTERERS or PARGETTORS
PLAYING CARD MAKERS
PLUMBERS
POULTERS
SADDLERS
SALTERS
SCRIVENERS
SHIPWRIGHTS
SKINNERS
SPECTACLE MAKERS
STATIONERS
TALLOW CHANDLERS
TIN PLATE WORKERS
TURNERS
TYLERS & BRICKLAYERS
VINTNERS
WAX CHANDLERS
WEAVERS
WHEELWRIGHTS

COMPARE (s/l compère). *CF*, LIKEN. *MEASURE*.
COMPASS *BOUNDARY*, CIRCUMFERENCE, LIMIT [*Joshua* (Jericho)]; EXTENT, RANGE, SCOPE. LODESTONE, PELORUS (naut). INSTRUMENT, SCRIBER [dividers].
COMPLAINT AILMENT: CHICKENPOX, DIPHTHERIA, FEVER, MALARIA, MEASLES, MUMPS, POX, TYPHOID etc. ACCUSATION, CASE, GRIEVANCE.
COMPOSED OF *Anag.* COMPRISING, MADE OF.
COMPOSER CONSTRUCTOR. PEACE-MAKER, *SETTLER*. ARRANGER, MUSICAL AUTHOR; **celeb**:

3-letters
BAX, Sir Arnold Edward Trevor (Eng)
CUI, Cesar (Fr/USSR)
IVE, Simon (Eng)
MAW, Nicholas (Eng)

4-letters
ARNE, Thomas Augustine (Eng)
BACH, Johann Sebastian (Ger)
BERG, Alban (A)
BLOW, John (Eng)
BYRD, William (Eng)
HART, Lorenz (US)
IVES, Charles (US)
KERN, Jerome (US)
LOWE, Frederick (US)
LOWE, Karl (Ger)
NERI, St Philip (It)
ORFF, Carl (Ger)
PERI, Jacopo (It)
RICE, Tim (Eng)
WOLF, Hugo (A)

5-letters
BALFE, Michael William (Ire)
BIZET, Georges (Fr)
BLISS, Sir Arthur (Eng)
CESTI, Marcantonio (It)
ELGAR, Sir Edward (Eng)
FAURE, Gabriel Urbain (Fr)
GLUCK, Christoph von (Ger)
GRIEG, Edvard Hagerup (Nor)
GROFE, Ferdie (US)

HANDY, William Christopher (US)
HAYDN, Franz Joseph (A)
HOLST, Gustav (Eng)
LISZT, Franz (Hung)
LOEWE (see *LOWE*)
RAVEL, Maurice (Fr)
SOUSA, John Philip (US)
SUPPE, Franz von (A)
VERDI, Giuseppe (It)
WEBER, Carl Maria von (Ger)
WEILL, Kurt (Ger/US)

6-letters
ARNOLD, Matthew (Eng)
BARTOK, Bela (Hung)
BERLIN, Irving (Israel Baline) (USSR/US)
BOULEZ, Pierre (Fr)
BRAHMS, Johannes (Ger)
CHOPIN, Frederic François (Pol)
COWARD, Sir Noel (Eng)
DELIUS, Frederick (Eng)
DVORAK, Antonin (Cz)
FLOTOW, Friedrich von (Ger)
FOSTER, Stephen (US)
FRANCK, Cesar Auguste (Belg)
GLINKA, Michael (USSR)
GOUNOD, Charles (Fr)
LERNER, Alan (US)
HANDEL, George Fredk (Ger/Eng)
HARRIS, Roy (US)
LANNER, Joseph Franz Karl (A)
LENNON, John (Eng)
LERNER, Alan Jay (US)

MAHLER, Gustav (A)
MOZART, Wolfgang
  Amadeus (A)
PORTER, Cole (US)
RIDLEY, Arnold (Eng)
SEARLE, Humphrey (Eng)
STRAUS, Oscar (A)
WAGNER, Richard (Ger)
WALTON, Sir Wm Turner
  (Eng)

SMETANA, Bedrich (Cz)
STAINER, John (Eng)
STRAUSS, Eduard (A)
STRAUSS, Johann I, II &
  III (A)
STRAUSS, Joseph (A)
STRAUSS, Richard (Ger)
TIPPETT, Sir Michael
  (Eng)
VIVALDI, Antonio (It)

7-letters
ARENSKY, Anton (USSR)
BELLINI, Vicenzo (It)
BENNETT, Sir William
  Sterndale (Eng)
BERLIOZ, Hector (Fr)
BORODIN, Alexander
  (USSR)
BRITTEN, Edward
  Benjamin (Eng)
COPLAND, Aaron (US)
DEBUSSY, Claude Achille
  (Fr)
GIBBONS, Orlando (Eng)
HERBERT, Victor (US)
IRELAND, John (Eng)
JANACEK, Leos (A/Cz)
LAMBERT, Constant
  (Eng)
LUTYENS, Elizabeth
  (Eng)
NOVELLO, Ivor (Eng)
POULENC, Francis (Fr)
PUCCINI, Giacomo (It)
PURCELL, Henry (Eng)
RODGERS, Richard (US)
ROMBERG, Sigmund
  (Hung)
ROSSINI, Gioacchino
  Antonio (It)

8-letters
BENEDICT, Julius (Ger)
BRUCKNER, Anton (A)
CLEMENTI, Muzio (It)
COUPERIN, François (Fr)
GERSHWIN, George (US)
KREISLER, Fritz (A)
MASSENET, Jules Emile
  (Fr)
PAGANINI, Nicolo (It)
SCHUBERT, Franz Peter
  (A)
SCHUMANN, Robert
  Alexander (Ger)
SIBELIUS, Jean (Fin)
SKRYABIN (SCRIABIN),
  Alexander (USSR)
SONDHEIM, Stephen
  Joshua (US)
SPONTINI, Gasparo Luigi
  (It)
SULLIVAN, Sir Arthur
  Seymour (Eng)
WHITEMAN, Paul (US)
ZARENSKI (Pol)

9+ letters
BEETHOVEN, Ludwig van
  (Ger)
DONIZETTI, Gaetano (It)

GRUENBERG, Louis (USSR/US)
HAMMERSTEIN, Oscar (US)
HUMPERDINCK, Engelbert (Ger)
LLOYD-WEBBER, Andrew (Eng)
McCARTNEY, Paul (Eng)
MENDELSSOHN, Felix (Ger)
MEYERBEER, Giacomo (Ger)
MONTEVERDI, Claudio (It)
MUSSORGSKY, Modeste (USSR)
OFFENBACH, Jacques (Ger/Fr)
PROKOFIEV, Sergei (USSR)
RACHMANINOV, Sergei (USSR/US)
RIMSKY-KORSAKOV, Nikolai (USSR)
SAINT-SAENS, Charles Camille (Fr)
SCARLATTI, Alessandro (It)
SCARLATTI, Domenico (It)
SCHO(E)NBERG, Arnold (A)
SHOSTAKOVICH, Dmitri (USSR)
STOCKHAUSEN, Karlheinz (Ger)
STRAVINSKY, Igor (USSR)
TCHAIKOVSKY, Peter Ilyich (USSR)
VAUGHAN WILLIAMS, Ralph (Eng)
XANARCHIS (Gk)

COMPUTER CALCULATOR, MICRO-PROCESSOR [bits, bytes, ERNIE, memory, retrieval bank, VDU].

CON CHEAT, DIDDLE, *DO*. *AGAINST* (**opp** = *pro*). *LOOK*, *STUDY*. NAVIGATE, PILOT, *SAIL*, *STEER*. **Comp** = *pro*.

CONCEAL Hidden word. *HIDE*, *SCREEN*, SECRETE.

CONCERN WORRY. *FIRM*, *COMPANY*. AFFECT.

CONCERNING *ABOUT*, ANENT, *OVER*, RE.

CONCERTINA ACCORDION; PRESS-BOX (crypt). COLLAPSE, COMPRESS, *FOLD*, PLEAT.

CONCLUSION 1. DECISION, REALIZATION. *END*. [*Theseus*].
2. Last letter of word concerned, e.g. **Bob's conclusion is encored** (3) = B*IS.

CONDITION *STATE*. *TERM*.

CONDUCTOR 1. GUARD, TICKET COLLECTOR. DRAGOMAN, GUIDE; *SHOWMAN* (crypt). *EARTH* (elect). **Myth**: *ANUBIS*, *CHARON*. 2. BAND-LEADER, MAESTRO, MD (mus); **celeb**: BARBIROLLI, Sir John (Brit); BEECHAM, Sir Thomas (Eng); BERNSTEIN, Leonard (US); *BLACK*, Stanley

(Eng); BOULEZ, Pierre (Fr); BOULT, Sir Adrian (Eng);
COSTA, Sir Michael (It/Brit); DAVIES, Andrew (Eng); DAVIS,
Sir Colin (Eng); DEL MAR, Norman (Eng); DORATI, Antal
(Hung); ELDER, Mark (Eng); FURTWANGLER, Wilhelm
(Ger); GIBSON, Sir Alexander (Sc); GLOVER, Jane (UK);
GROVE, Sir Charles (Eng); HAITINK, Bernard (NL); HALLE,
Sir Charles (Ger/UK); HARTY, Hamilton (Ire); INGLIS,
Anthony (Eng); KEMPE, Rudolf (Ger); KLEMPERER, Otto
(Ger); LAMBERT, Constant (Eng); MACKERRAS, Sir Charles
(Aus); MAHLER, Gustav (A); MARRINER, Sir Neville (Eng);
MEHTA, Zubin (Isr); *POTTER*, Cipriani (Eng); PREVIN, Andre
(Ger/US); PRITCHARD, Sir John (Eng); RATTLE, Simon
(Eng); RICHTER, Hans (Ger); SAFONOV, Vasily (Russ; 1st);
SARGENT, Sir Malcolm (Eng); SINNOPOLI, Giuseppi (It);
SOLTI, Sir Georg (Hung/Brit); STOKOWSKI, Leopold (Eng/US);
STRAUSS, Richard (Ger); TAUSKY, Vilem (A); TOSCANINI,
Arturo (It); VON BULOW, Hans (Ger); WALTER, Bruno (Ger);
WEINGARTNER, Felix (Y); *WOOD*, Sir Henry (Eng);
YANSONS, Mariss (USSR).

CONFINING 1. BORDERING, ENCLOSING, LIMITING,
RESTRICTING; *GAOLING*. BEDDING, LABOURING
[childbirth]. 2. Word round another, e.g. **He's confining publicity,
and it's Hell** (5) = H*AD*ES.

CONFUSED *Anag.* BEWILDERED, MUDDLED.

CONNECTION 1. AFFILIATION, ASSOCIATION; DEALINGS.
JOINERY, UNITY (crypt). TRANSFER (rly). EARTH, ON
MAINS (elect). 2. Join two words, e.g. **See the connection bubble
up** (4) = SEE*THE = BOIL.

CONQUEROR *VICTOR*, VIC. WILLIAM.

Cons Conservative.

CONSCIENTIOUS PUNCTILIOUS, SCRUPULOUS,
THOROUGH. HAMLET (crypt).

CONSPIRATOR PLOTTER; **celeb**: MARCUS BRUTUS, DECIUS
BRUTUS, CASCA, CASSIUS, METELLUS CIMBER, CINNA,
LIGARIUS, TREBONIUS (*Shak*, Caesar); GUY FAWKES.

CONSTABLE ARTIST, *PAINTER*, RA. *POLICEMAN*. HEAD
OF HOUSEHOLD (hence H, crypt). MAJOR DOMO,
SENESCHAL; **celeb** (all *Shak*): DULL (LLL), ELBOW (Meas for
Meas), MALVOLIO (12th Night), VERGES and DOGBERRY
(Much Ado).

CONSTELLATION *STAR* CLUSTER/GROUP/OUTLINE; **celeb**:

3-letters
ARA
LEO (Zod) (lion)

4-letters
CRUX (southern cross)
GRUS
LYRA (lyre)

5-letters
ARIES (Zod) (ram)
CETUS (sea monster)
DRACO (dragon)
HYDRA
INDUS
LEPUS
LIBRA (Zod) (scales)
LUPUS (wolf)
MUSCA
ORION (hunter)
VIRGO (Zod) (virgin)

6-letters
AQUILA (eagle)
AURIGA (charioteer)
BOOTES (herdsman)
CANCER (Zod) (crab)
CARINA (keel)
CORVUS (crow)
CRATER
CYGNUS (swan)
DORADO
FORNAX
GEMINI (Zod) (twins)
HYDRUS
PISCES (Zod) (fishes)

PUPPIS
TAURUS (Zod) (bull)
TUCANA

7-letters
CEPHEUS (myth king)
COLUMBA (dove)
PEGASUS (winged horse)
PERSEUS
PHOENIX
SCORPIO (Zod) (scorpion)
SERPENS (serpent)

8+ letters
ANDROMEDA
AQUARIUS (Zod)
(water carrier)
CANES VENATICI
CANIS MAJOR (great dog)
CANIS MINOR (little dog)
CAPRICORNUS (Zod)
(sea-goat)
CASSIOPOEIA (myth queen)
CENTAURUS
CORONA BOREALIS
(northern crown)
DELPHINUS (dolphin)
ERIDANUS
HERCULES
OPHIUCHUS (serpent bearer)
PISCIS AUSTRALIS
SAGITTARIUS (Zod) (archer)
TRIANGULUM
TRIANGULUM AUSTRALE
URSA MAJOR (great bear)
URSA MINOR (little bear)

CONSUMER DRINKER, EATER; PURCHASER, USER.
SPENDER, WASTER. MOUTH (crypt).
CONTAINS 1. HOLDS, KEEPS IN. 2. Hidden word; one word in
another.

CONTEND CLAIM, MAINTAIN. VIE, WAR.

CONTINENT LAND MASS: PANGAEA (pre-hist supercontinent); GONDWANA, LAURASIA (first split); AFRICA, AMERICA, ANTARCTICA, ASIA, AUSTRALASIA, EUROPE. CHASTE, CONTROLLED, TEMPERATE.

CONTINUOUS 1. ENDLESS, UNBROKEN, UNENDING, UNINTERRUPTED. 2. Join two or more words in clue, e.g. **Heat her continuously for another girl** (5) = HEAT*HER = ERICA.

CONTRACT AGREEMENT. JOB. SHORTEN, SHRINK, TIGHTEN. *BRIDGE* (cards).

CONTRIVED *Anag.* FABRICATED, INVENTED. MANAGED (**opp** = *automatic*).

CONTROL (GEAR) LEVER, THROTTLE, JOY-STICK, RUDDER; *REIN*. DIRECT, MONITOR, ORGANIZE. DISCIPLINE. [AWACS (av)].

CONVERSE 1. CHAT, SPEAK WITH, TALK. OPPOSITE. 2. Word reversed, e.g. **Rat's converse shines brightly** (4) = STAR.

CONVICT ADJUDGE, DECLARE GUILTY [belief, convince, persuade]. CRIMINAL, *GAOL*-BIRD, LAG, *PRISONER*; (**celebrated**): Magwitch (Great Ex, *Dickens*).

COOK *Anag.* CHEF, GALLEY SLAVE; MRS BEETON, BETTY CROCKER, FANNY FARMER (books); KITCHENER (crypt). CONCOCT, PREPARE FOOD. BAKE, BOIL, FRY, GRILL, ROAST, SEETHE, SIMMER, STEW. *FIDDLE*, FIX. *STRAIT*. *EXPLORER*. *Chaucer* character.

COOKED *Anag* DONE (**opp** = *raw*). *FIDDLED*, FIXED, FORGED.

COOKER BURNER, GRILL, HOB, OVEN, STOVE. VOLCANO (crypt). FORGER (crypt). And see *Cook*.

COOLER *GAOL* (sl). AIR CONDITIONER, *BREEZE*, DRAFT, DRAUGHT, *FAN*, JALOUSIE, SHADE; LESS HOT, NOT SO HOT (**opp** = *warmer*). DEEP FREEZE, FRIDGE.

COP *POLICEMAN*. ATTRACT, CAPTURE. HA'PENNY (crypt: half cop*per). SPOOL [prop and ~].

COPPER *METAL*; CU (*chem*). *POLICEMAN*. PENNY, D. WASH-BOILER. *COLOUR* (orange). *AGE*. *Anniversary* (7th). **Pl** = CHANGE; POLICE; MPS.

COPY CARBON, CRIB (sl), DOUBLE, DUPLICATE, IMITATION, REPRODUCTION, RINGER; FACSIMILE (any craftsman), REPLICA (original craftsman); TRANSCRIBE. ADVERTISING TEXT; PRINTER'S TEXT. *BORROW*.

CORA *PERSEPHONE*.

CORAL Calcareous secretion of marine polyps; REEF. COLOUR (pink). LOBSTER ROE. *SEA* [*battle*]. *SNAKE*. *Anniversary* (35th).

CORALLINE *SEAWEED*. CORAL-RED.

CORDIAL FRIENDLY. *DRINK*.

CORE (s/l caw). 1. CENTRE, KERNEL, MIDDLE. 2. Use middle letter(s), e.g. **Apple core** = P.

CORNELIAN *GEM*, SEMI-PRECIOUS STONE, CHALCEDONY: AGATE (red). *Birthstone* (July).

CORNWALL SW. *WRITER* (Le Carre).

CORPORAL CPL, NCO; **celeb:** HITLER, ~ JOHN (Marlborough), NAPOLEON, NYM (*Shak*), TRIM (Tristram Shandy, Sterne). BODILY. CLOTH, *MATERIAL* (eccles).

CORPORATION TOWN COUNCIL. FATNESS, OBESITY.

CORSAIR *AIRCRAFT*. *PIRATE*.

CORYBANTES PRIESTS of *Cybele*, frenzied and noisy dancers.

COS BECAUSE (sl). COSINE. *ISLAND*. LETTUCE.

COSH MUG; CUDGEL, CLUB, *WEAPON*; NIGHTCLUB (crypt).

COTTON CLOTH, *MATERIAL*, THREAD. ADMIRE, LIKE, TAKE TO, UNDERSTAND. 2nd *anniversary*.

COUGH *HAWK*, *HEM*. CONFESS (sl). PAY-UP (sl).

COULD BE *Anag*. MAYBE.

COUNT (E)NUMERATE, *NUMBER*, RECKON, *TELL*, *TOT*. EARL, *NOBLE*; *DRACULA*.

COUNTER AGAINST, OPPOSITE; CONTRADICT, OPPOSE, RIPOSTE. DUPLICATE. CHIP, TALLY, TOKEN. ADDER, CALCULATOR, CASHIER, COMPUTER, *SUMMER* (crypt), TELLER. BAR, TABLE. HORSE'S NECK. SHIP'S STERN. SHOE'S HEEL. SKATING FIGURE.

COUNTRY FATHERLAND, LAND, MOTHERLAND, NATION, REGION, TERRITORY. RURAL AREA. And see *capital cities*.

COUNTRY HOUSE MANSION, PLACE, SEAT, *STATELY HOME* (q.v. for **celeb, fact**). CHESHIRE HOME, SWISS COTTAGE (crypt); **celeb, fiction:**

> BARCHESTER TOWERS (~, Trollope)
> BARTON PARK (Sense and Sensibility, *Austen*)
> BLANDINGS CASTLE (Lord Emsworth, *Wodehouse*)
> BLEAK HOUSE (~, *Dickens*)

BRIDESHEAD (CASTLE) (~ Revisited, *Waugh*)
CASTLEWOOD (The Virginians, Thackeray)
DONNELL ABBEY (Emma, *Austen*)
DORINCOURT (Little Lord Fauntleroy, Burnett)
DORLCOTE MILL (Mill on the Floss, Eliot)
ELSINORE CASTLE (Hamlet, *Shak*)
ENSCOMBE (Emma, *Austen*)
HARTFIELD (Emma, *Austen*)
HEARTBREAK HOUSE (~, *Shaw*)
KELLYNCH HALL (Persuasion, *Austen*)
LOCKSLEY HALL (~, Tennyson)
LONGBOURNE (Pride and Prejudice, *Austen*)
MANDERLEY (Rebecca, du Maurier)
MANSFIELD PARK (~, *Austen*)
NAVRON HOUSE (Frenchman's Creek, du Maurier)
NETHERFIELD PARK (Pride and Prejudice, *Austen*)
NORLAND PARK (Sense and Sensibility, *Austen*)
NORTHANGER ABBEY (~, *Austen*)
OVERCOMBE MILL (Trumpet Major, Hardy)
SATIS HOUSE (Great Ex, *Dickens*)
TARA (Gone With the Wind, Mitchell)
THORNFIELD HALL (Jane Eyre, C. *Brontë*)
USHER (The House of ~, E. A. Poe)
WHITE LADIES (Berry & Co, Dornford Yates)
WILDFELL HALL (Tenant of ~, A. *Brontë*)
WUTHERING HEIGHTS (~, E. *Brontë*)

COUNTY 1. ARISTOCRATIC, LAH-DI-DAH, *U*, WELL-BRED. CO. 2. ~ of the UK, see *DIVISION*.
COURSE E, N, S, W, NE, SE etc. DIRECTION, LINE. *RACETRACK*; *LINKS*. CURRENT, RIVER BED. PURSUE, RUN. *SAIL*. LECTURE SERIES. CAREER. *LAYER*, STRATUM. *MEAL*: AFTERS, DESSERT, ENTREE, ENTREMETS, HORS D'OEUVRE, MEAT, PUDDING, SAVOURY, SOUP, *STARTER*, SWEET.
COURT (s/l *caught*). WOO. HALL OF JUSTICE, TRIBUNAL. PLAYING AREA (squash, *tennis* etc). ROYAL ENTOURAGE. CT, QUAD(RANGLE), YARD.
COURTED WOOED. JUDGED, SUED (crypt). WIMBLEDON, *TENNIS VENUE* (crypt).
COURTESAN ADVENTURESS, CONCUBINE,

DEMI-MONDAINE, *ENCHANTRESS*, FAVOURITE, FEMME FATALE, HETAERA (Gk), MISTRESS, PARAMOUR, SEDUCTRESS, *SIREN*. **Celeb**: ASPASIA (Gk); BARRY, Comtesse du (Jeanne Becu; Louis XV); CAMPASPE (*Alexander*); LADY CHATTERLEY (Connie Reid/Mellors; D. H. Lawrence); DELILAH (*Samson*); FITZHERBERT, Maria Anne (George IV); MATA HARI (*spy*); FANNY HILL (John Cleland); JEZEBEL (*Ahab*); LAIS (Gk); LILY LANGTRY (theat, Edward VII); MAINTENON, Marquise de (Françoise d'Aubigne; Louis XIV); NELL GWYNN (Charles II); PHRYNE (Gk); POMPADOUR, Marquise de (Jeanne Poisson; Louis XV); RACAMIER (*Napoleon*); THAIS (Gk); VIOLETTA (La Traviata, Verdi).

COURT EXPERT BARRISTER, JUDGE, *LAW PRACTITIONER*, LAWYER. SEED (tennis, crypt).

COURTING WOOING. ACTION, DEFENDING, PLEADING, PROSECUTING, SUITING (crypt). SERVING, *TENNIS* (crypt). ROYAL HOUSEHOLD (crypt).

COVEN *Assembly* of *witches*.

COVER 1. ALTER EGO, DISGUISE, NOM DE PLUME, PSEUDONYM. ASSURANCE, INSURANCE. CAP, COWL, *HAT*, HOOD, LID. *CLOAK*, DRESS, SHROUD. ENVELOPE, WRAP(PING). FRONT PAGE, JACKET. *CRICKETER*, FIELDER. 2. Enclose word in another, e.g. **He covers the order to get a house** (4) = H*OM*E.

COVERING LID, CAP, *HAT*. *DRESSING*.

COVER STORY BLUFF, FALSE BACKGROUND, LIE. LEADER, LEADING ARTICLE (crypt).

COVER UP DRESS. CONCEAL(MENT). REVOC (dn).

COVEY *Assembly* of partridges [*Christmas song*].

COW DOMINATE. *CASTLE* (arch). *CATTLE*, KINE, NEAT, STEER; LOWER (crypt); *female* cattle, walrus etc (**offspring** = calf, **yak/cow** = dzho, dzo). [*Io*].

COWARDLY 1. AFRAID, FRIGHTENED, SCARED, YELLOW (**saying**); [Bob Acres (The Rivals, Sheridan); Bardolph, Nym, Pistol (H.v., Merry Wives); Capt Bobadil (Ben Jonson); Braggadochio (Faerie Queene, Spenser); lion (Wizard of Oz); Parolles (All's Well, *Shak*); Conscience (Hamlet, *Shak*)]. 2. Written by Noel Coward (crypt) hence MASTERLY (from nickname).

COWBOY GAUCHO, HERDSMAN, VAQUERO; STEERSMAN (crypt); **celebrated**: GENE AUTRY (singing), HOPALONG

CASSIDY, WILLIAM S. HART, TOM MIX, AUDIE
MURPHY, ROY ROGERS (horse Trigger), JOHN WAYNE.
[Wells Fargo; *outlaw*]. CHAPMAN (crypt). **Pl** = *football* team
(US).

COWGIRL Fem *cowboy*; DAIRYMAID, MILKMAID; **celeb**:
ANNIE OAKLEY (US); CALAMITY JANE (US); *IO* (myth,
crypt); PATIENCE (*G and S*); MAIDEN (all forlorn); My pretty
maid (trad) [and see *shepherdess*].

COY *ARCH*, BASHFUL, DIFFIDENT, *SHY*. COMPANY.

CPL *CORPORAL*.

CR CHROMIUM (*chem*). COSTA RICA (*car plate*). CREDIT.

CRAB 1. CRITICIZE, SPOIL. *APPLE*. SOUR PERSON.
HOIST, LIFT (mech). GO/WALK SIDEWAYS.
CRUSTACEAN (Brachyura). 2. *Constellation* (Cancer); (4th)
sign of *Zodiac*.

CRACKED *Anag*. BROKEN, CHIPPED, *SPLIT*, BEATEN,
OVERCOME. *CRAZY*.

CRAFT ABILITY, *ART*, SKILL, TRADE. FREEMASONRY.
CUNNING, DECEIT, GUILE. *BOAT(S)* (q.v. for **types**),
SHIP(S), *VESSEL(S)* (q.v. for **celeb**). AEROPLANE(S),
AIRCRAFT (q.v. for **types**), *SPACECRAFT* (q.v. for **celeb**).

CRAFTSMAN ARTISAN, SKILLED WORKER. TRICKSTER
(crypt). CREWMAN, *SAILOR* (crypt).

CRANE DERRICK, HOIST, JIB. CAMERA PLATFORM,
DOLLY. *BIRD*. PEER, STRETCH.

CRAZY *Anag*. CRACKED, DERANGED, LUNATIC, *MAD*.
RANDOM, SCATTERED (paving).

CREATOR 1. FABRICATOR, MAKER, MANUFACTURER,
ORIGINATOR, PRODUCER. FUSSPOT, GRUMBLER. 2.
Gods: Gk = ZEUS, **Rom** = JOVE, *JUPITER*, **A-Sax** = *WODEN*,
Bab = BEL/BELUS, **Egy** = *OSIRIS*, TEMU, **Ind** = BRAHMA,
SHIVA, **Nor** = *ODIN*, **Phoen** = *BAAL*.

CREDIT CR. BALANCE. *TICK*. ASCRIBE, BELIEF,
BELIEVE, TRUST; ACKNOWLEDGEMENT; MERIT,
REPUTATION.

CREEK *RIVER*. *AMERICAN INDIAN*.

CREEP CRAWL, *INCH*; INSINUATE, SNEAK. TOADY. LOW
ARCH. MOVEMENT. **Pl** = SHIVERS (fear).

CREEPER *BIRD*. IVY, CLIMBING PLANT. *INSECT*.

CRESTA RACE, *RUN* [toboggan].

CREW EIGHT, EQUIPE, FOUR, *TEAM*. DECKHAND, *MAN*,

SAILOR. BOASTED, EXULTED.

CRIB *CHEAT*, COPY, EMULATE. COT, CRADLE. *CARD GAME*.

CRICKET BAT AND BALL, *GAME*; TEST [Thomas *Lord*]. *INSECT*. [~ on the Hearth (*Dickens*)].

CRICKETER PLAYER (FLANNELLED FOOL), DRY-*BOB*; TESTER (crypt). *BATSMAN*: BAT, OPENER, INNER (crypt), INSIDER (crypt); *FIELDER*: *BOWLER*, CATCHER, *COVER*, FINE-LEG, GULLY, KEEPER, LONG-OFF, LONG-ON, LONG-STOP, MID-OFF, MID-ON, MID-WICKET, OUTSIDER (crypt), *POINT*, SHORT-LEG, SILLY-POINT, SLIP, THIRD-MAN; **celeb**: GRACE, W. G.; RAFFLES, A. J.

CRICKET GROUND PLAYING FIELD, TEST ZONE, TESTING GROUND; **celeb**: EDGBASTON (Birmingham), FENNERS (C), GRACE ROAD (Leicester), THE HILL (Sydney), HEADINGLEY (Leeds), LORD'S (MCC), OLD TRAFFORD (Manchester), THE *OUTER* (Melbourne), THE OVAL (Adelaide, Kennington), THE PARKS (O), TRENT BRIDGE (Nottingham), WACA (Perth), (WOOLLOON)GABBA (Brisbane).

CRIPPLED *Anag.* DEFORMED, *GAME*, HALT, *LAME*. [*patron saint*].

CROCODILE REPTILE (saurian): ALLIGATOR (Amer, Ch), CAYMAN (S Amer), GHARIAL (Ind), MUGGER (Ind) [~ tears]; Capt Hook (*Barrie*); Punch & Judy show]. Schoolchildren in line.

CROESUS KING OF LYDIA, RICH MAN [Dives, *Midas*].

CRONOS Gk *god* of AGRICULTURE (**Rom** = *SATURN*). s of *Uranus* and *Ge*; f by *Rhea* of *Demeter*, *Hades*, *Hera*, *Poseidon* and *Zeus*.

CROONER BING; *SINGER*.

CROSS 1. X; CRUCIFIX, MARK, ROOD, SALTIRE. ANGRY, ANNOYED, *MAD*. FRUSTRATE, THWART. HALF-CASTE, HYBRID. 2. *Constellation* (Crux).

CROSSBOW-MAN *CELLIST*, FIDDLER, VIOLINIST (crypt). *ARCHER* [*weapon*].

CROSS DECISION ELECTION, VOTE (crypt).

CROSSING *BRIDGE*, FERRY, *FORD*, TRAVERSING. BELISHA, PELICAN, ZEBRA. KISS (crypt). VOTING, POLL (crypt).

CROSSPATCH GROUCH, GRUMPY PERSON, SCOLD. PEDESTRIAN *CROSSING* (crypt).

CROSSWORD PUZZLE. ~ **solver** = cruciverbalist; **lover of** ~ = cruciverbophile; **aversion to** ~ = cruciverbophobia (myth). **Pl** = ARGUMENT. *ROW* (crypt).

CROW *BIRD* (corvidae); CARRION ~, CHOUGH, DRONGO, GREY, HOODED ~, JACKDAW, JAY, MAGPIE, RAVEN, *ROOK*, ROYSTON ~ (*assembly*, *constellation*). BUTTERFLY (*lepidoptera*). *CRY*, EXULT, TRIUMPH (past tense = *crew*). *AMERICAN INDIAN*.

CROWD ATTENDANCE, AUDIENCE, *GATE*, SPECTATORS; **celebrated**: THE HILL (Sydney cricket), THE KOP (Liverpool football), THE *OUTER* (Melbourne cricket), THE SHED (Chelsea football), THE TAVERN (Lord's cricket).

CROWN 1. CORONET, DIADEM; **comp** = anchor; *rose*. 'STEPHEN'. *WREATH*. *COIN*. TOP (of anchor/arch/head/hill). CAP, PROTECTION. 2. *Constellation* (Corona Borealis).

CRUSE (s/l *crews*, cruise). BOWL, VESSEL [widow (*Elijah*)].

CRUSOE Robinson ~. Book by Defoe *modelled* on adventures of Alexander Selkirk, stranded from the galley *Cinque Ports* on Juan Fernandez island, 1704–9.

CRY *CALL*, EXCLAIM, SHOUT, YELL, YELP: HI, OUCH, OW [~ Wolf]. APPEAL, ENTREATY. RUMOUR. BEWAIL, BLUB, *GREET*, *KEEN*, LAMENT, SHED TEARS, WAIL, WEEP [*Niobe*, *Ruth*]. *BARK*, *HAWK*, PEDDLE, TOUT.

CRYSTAL MINERAL. GLASS. *PALACE*. *BALL* [forecasting, prophecy; clarity]. *Anniversary* (15th).

CS CAESIUM (*chem*). *CIVIL SERVICE*.

CT *CAUGHT*. *COURT*.

CU *COPPER* (*chem*). CUBE, ~IC. CUMULUS.

CUB YOUNG SCOUT. YOUNG REPORTER. *OFFSPRING* (bear, etc).

CUBE CU. BOX. EIGHT (crypt).

CUBIST PAINTER. DICE PLAYER (crypt).

CUDGEL CLUB, STICK, *WEAPON*. RACK, WORRY (brains).

CUER (s/l *queuer*). BILLIARD/POOL/SNOOKER PLAYER.

CULTURE CIVILIZATION [*study*]. FARMING, TILLING (crypt).

CUMBERLAND A *division* of England. *BUTCHER* (mil).

CUMBRIA NW.

CUPBEARER 1. CHAMPION, TROPHY WINNER. 2. WINE-SERVER; NEHEMIAH (to King Artaxerxes); SAKI (Rubaiyat, Omar Khayyam). **Gk god** = GANYMEDE; **Gk goddess** = *HEBE*, **Rom** = *JUVENTAS*.

CUPID Rom *god* of *LOVE*; also AMOR (**Gk** = EROS). Son of
Venus and *Jupiter* (some say *Mars* or *Mercury*); an *archer*; fell in
love with *Psyche* (q.v.). 2. *REINDEER*.

CURE HEAL, MEND; REMEDY, RESTORATIVE
TREATMENT [*spa*]. *DRY*, HARDEN, MATURE,
PRESERVE, SMOKE. *CHURCHMAN*, PRIEST (Fr).

CURRANT (s/l *current*). RIBES; DRIED GRAPE. FRUIT
(black~, red~, white~).

CURRENCY FLUENCY, REPUTATION. RIVER,
WATERFLOW (crypt). AC, DC, ELECTRICITY (crypt).
COINAGE, **celeb** (worldwide):

Country	Currency
Albania	LEK
Algeria	DINAR
American Ind	WAMPUM
Argentina	PESO
Australia	DOLLAR
Austria	SCHILLING
Belgium	FRANC
Bolivia	PESO
Brazil	CRUCADOS
Bulgaria	LEV
Burma	KYAT
Canada	DOLLAR
Chile	PESO
China	YUAN
Colombia	PESO
Costa Rica	COLON
Cuba	PESO
Cyprus	MIL
Czechoslovakia	KORUNA
Denmark .	KRONE
Ecuador	SUCRE
Egypt	*POUND*
El Salvador	COLON
Ethiopia	DOLLAR
Finland	MARKKA
France	FRANC
Germany, E.	MARK
Germany, W.	DEUTSCHMARK

Greece	DRACHMA
Guatemala	QUETZAL
Hungary	FORINT
Iceland	KRONA
India	RUPEE
Iran	RIAL
Iraq	DINAR
Ireland	PUNT
Israel	SHEKEL
Italy	LIRA
Japan	YEN
Kenya	*SHILLING*
Korea	WHAN
Lebanon	*POUND*
Libya	DINAR
Malawi	KWACHA
Mexico	PESO
Netherlands	GUILDER
New Zealand	DOLLAR
Nigeria	NAIRE
Norway	KRONE
Pakistan	RUPEE
Peru	SOL
Poland	ZLOTY
Portugal	ESCUDO
Rumania	LEU
Russia	ROUBLE
South Africa	RAND
Spain	PESETA
Sweden	KRONA
Switzerland	FRANC
Syria	*POUND*
Thailand	BAHT
Tunisia	DINAR
Turkey	LIRA
UK	*POUND*
USA	DOLLAR
USSR	ROUBLE
Uruguay	PESO
Venezuela	BOLIVAR
Vietnam	DONG

Yemen	RIYAL
Yugoslavia	DINAR
Zambia	KWACHA

Currency	Country
Baht	THAILAND
Bolivar	VENEZUELA
Colon	COSTA RICA, EL SALVADOR
Crucados	BRAZIL
Deutschmark	WEST GERMANY
Dinar	ALGERIA, IRAQ, LIBYA, TUNISIA, YUGOSLAVIA
Dollar	AUSTRALIA, CANADA, ETHIOPIA, NEW ZEALAND, USA
Dong	VIETNAM
Drachma	GREECE
Escudo	PORTUGAL
Forint	HUNGARY
Franc	BELGIUM, FRANCE, SWITZERLAND
Guilder	NETHERLANDS
Koruna	CZECHOSLOVAKIA
Krona	ICELAND, SWEDEN
Krone	DENMARK, NORWAY
Kwacha	MALAWI, ZAMBIA
Kyat	BURMA
Lek	ALBANIA
Leu	RUMANIA
Lev	BULGARIA
Lira	ITALY, TURKEY
Mark	EAST GERMANY
Markka	FINLAND
Mil	CYPRUS
Naire	NIGERIA
Peseta	SPAIN
Peso	ARGENTINA, BOLIVIA, CHILE, COLOMBIA, CUBA, MEXICO, URUGUAY
Pound	EGYPT, LEBANON, SYRIA, UK
Punt	EIRE, *IRELAND*
Quetzal	GUATEMALA
Rand	SOUTH AFRICA

Rial	IRAN
Riyal	YEMEN
Rouble	USSR
Rupee	INDIA, PAKISTAN
Schilling	AUSTRIA
Shekel	ISRAEL
Shilling	KENYA
Sol	PERU
Sucre	ECUADOR
Wampum	N. *AMERICAN INDIAN*
Whan	KOREA
Yen	JAPAN
Yuan	*CHINA*
Zloty	POLAND

CURRENT (s/l *currant*). EXISTING. COURSE, FLUID, RUNNING, STREAM, TIDE, UNDERTOW [river]. AMP, ELECTRICITY; AC, DC.

CURTAIL 1. DOCK, SHORTEN. 2. Omit last letter, e.g. **Some curtailed party** (4) = PART.

CURTAIN BARRIER, DRAPE, SCREEN. **Pl** = TABS (theat). *DEATH*, FINISH, THE END.

CUSTOM *HABIT*, PRACTICE, PRAXIS, TRADITION, USAGE, USE, WONT. **Pl** = DUTY, PREVENTIVE MEN, LEVY [*smuggle, tax*]. MORES [O tempora, O mores! (Cicero)].

CUT 1. LANCE, PARE, SEVER, SLICE. STOP FILMING. EDIT(ED); CENSORED. IGNORE, *OMIT*, SEND TO COVENTRY, SHUN, SNUB. STROKE (*cricket*). 2. Shortened form of . . . e.g. **Defence cut** (3) = DEF. **Comp** = thrust.

~ **DOWN** CHOP(PED), FELL(ED). REDUCE(D).

~ **UP** *Anag.* CHOP(PED), DICE(D), FELL(ED), SLICE(D). DISTRESSED, HURT, PAINED. TUC (dn).

CWT HUNDREDWEIGHT, *MEASURE*.

CYBELE 1. RHEA. Gk *goddess* of *FERTILITY*, whose priests were the *Corybantes* (**Rom** = *CERES*). 2. A minor *PLANET*.

CYCLOPES Gk myth one-eyed *monsters*: ACAMUS, ARGES, BRONTES, POLYPHEMUS, PYRACMON, STEROPES.

CYNIC 1. One who is contemptuous of honest morality. PESSIMIST; SARCASTIC. 2. Gk sect which scorned worldly goods and advocated self-control (see also *Stoic*). **Celeb**: ANISTHENES, CHRYSIPPUS, *DIOGENES* [Spartans].

CYNOPHILE *Lover of dogs*.
CYNOPHOBIA *Aversion to dogs*.
Cz Czechoslovakia.

D DAUGHTER. DAY. DELTA. DENARIUS. DEUTERIUM
(*chem*). *DIED*. *DIRECTOR*, ~ED. *DOWN*. GERMANY (*car plate*). *KEY*; *NOTE*. PENNY. 500.
d daughter. died.
DACTYL 1. FOOT (_..). FINGER. 2. **Pl** = GIANTS [discovered
iron; served *Rhea*].
DAD *FATHER*. FIRST IN DIVINITY (crypt: D*A*D).
DAEDALUS Gk myth sculptor, who built the labyrinth to house the
Minotaur at Cnossos in Crete for King *Minos*. Imprisoned, he
made wings for himself and Icarus (his s) and flew to Sicily; the wax
securing Icarus' wings melted, and he fell into the sea and was
drowned.
DAILY *CHAR*. EACH DAY. JOURNAL, *NEWSPAPER*,
PAPER, QUOTIDIAN; EXPRESS, MAIL, MIRROR,
OBSERVER, SUN, TELEGRAPH, TIMES etc (all ®).
~ **LEADER** D (crypt). ED, EDITOR. COVER STORY.
~ **WORKER** (NEWS)PAPER. HAND. *CHAR*.
DAMAGE(D) *Anag*. RUIN(ED), SPOIL(ED). **Pl** =
COMPENSATION.
DANAE 1. Gk myth *goddess* of *FERTILITY*. m of *Perseus* by *Zeus*,
who came to her in a *shower* of gold. **Rom** = *CERES*, *DIANA*.
2. A minor *PLANET*.
DANCE *BALL*, *BALLET* (q.v.), *BOB*, CAPER, *FOOT*, HOP,
JIVE, *MEASURE*, PAS, *SET*, *STEP*, TOE. [*cat*; Hans *Andersen*,
Salome]. **Gk goddess** = TERPSICHORE (*Muse*) [*Corybantes*].
Celeb:

3-letters		5-letters
JIG	FOLK	BELLY
PAS	GO-GO	CONGA
SUN ~	HAKA	FLING
WAR ~	HORA	GALOP
	HULA	GIGUE
4-letters	*REEL*	GO-PAK
BARN	ROCK	LIMBO
CLOG	SHAG	*MAMBA*

PAVAN	*SQUARE*	HULA-HULA
POLKA		RIGADOON
RUMBA	**7-letters**	SARABAND
SAMBA	CZARDAS	
SWORD	FOXTROT	**9+ letters**
TANGO	GAVOTTE	ALLEMANDE
TWIST	HOE-DOWN	BLACK BOTTOM
VOLTA	LANCERS	BUMPS-A-DAISY
WALTZ	MAZURKA	CHA-CHA-CHA
	MUSETTE	CHARLESTON
6-letters	ONE-STEP	CORROBOREE
BALLET	TWO-STEP	EIGHTSOME
BOLERO		FARANDOLE
CHA-CHA	**8-letters**	LAMBETH WALK
FLORAL	BIG APPLE	POLONAISE
MINUET	BUNNY-HUG	ROCK 'N' ROLL
MORRIS	CAKEWALK	QUADRILLE
NEWALA	COTILLON	QUICKSTEP
PAVANE	FANDANGO	STRATHSPEY
POW-WOW	FOURSOME	SCHOTTISCHE
RHUMBA	GALLIARD	TARANTELLA
SHIMMY	HORNPIPE	TURKEY-TROT

DANCE CENTRE BALLET SCHOOL. MAYPOLE (crypt). N (crypt).

DANDY BLOOD, FOP, *RIP*. *GOOD*, EXCELLENT, FINE. *COMIC*.

DANIEL Noble bibl youth, with reputation for *wisdom*. Served first *Belshazzar* then Darius, who was tricked into casting ~ into a den of *lions*, but ~ was miraculously preserved; d 536 B.C.

DAPHNE 1. Gk myth d of a river god, she was changed into a laurel tree to escape the pursuit of *Apollo*, and it became his favourite tree. 2. A minor *PLANET*. 3. Flowering shrub.

DARBY (s/l *Derby*). Husband of *Joan*. **Pl** = HANDCUFFS.

DARDANELLES HELLESPONT [*Helle*. Gallipoli].

DARKNESS GLOOM, NIGHT, OBSCURITY, STARLESSNESS; WICKEDNESS. **Egy god** = *SET*; **Gk goddess** = *HECATE*.

DARLING ACUSHLA (Ire), DEAREST, FAVOURITE, *PET*, SWEETHEART. *GRACE* ~ (lighthouse-keeper's d; rescuer). *WENDY* (Peter Pan). RIVER (Aus).

DART *DASH*. *ARROW*, FLECHETTE. GUSSET (seam). *RIVER*. **Pl** = ARROWS, *GAME*.

DASH *DART*, FALL. ADVANCE, MOVE, ONSET, RUSH,
 SPEED; *WHIP*. BOTTLE (sl), DRIVE, ELAN; *DOG* (Queen
 Victoria's). CONFOUND, DAUNT, DISCOURAGE,
 FRUSTRATE, SHATTER. *CAST*, FLING, HURL, KNOCK,
 THROW, THRUST. DILUTE, DROP, INFUSION, SPLASH,
 SPOT. DAMN, DARN (swear). SCRIBBLE. PARENTHESIS;
 MACRON, TILDE (accent ~). LONG SIGN (morse; **opp** = *dot*).
DATA GEN, INFORMATION, PARAMETERS, QUANTITIES
 (math), TABLE [problem].
DATE ESTABLISHED PERIOD; *TIME*; IDES, NONES (Rom).
 APPOINTMENT, MEETING, TRYST; ESCORT, TAKE'OUT.
 PALM-BERRY, *PHOENIX*, ~ FRUIT; *TREE*.
DATED AG(E)ING, OLD-FASHIONED, *SQUARE*. *FRANKED*,
 STAMPED. ESCORTED, SQUIRED, TAKEN OUT, TOOK
 OUT.
DAUGHTER D; *OFFSPRING*, PROGENY (fem); GIRL.
DAVID 1. *Patron saint* (Wal; 1st Mar), s of Non, uncle of *King
 Arthur*. 2. King of Sc, s of Robert Bruce. 3. Bibl youngest s of
 Jesse, mar Michal and f of *Absolom*, Adonijah and Amnon
 (*c.* 1045–975 B.C.). With his sling, ~ the *shepherd* boy k the giant
 Philistine Goliath, and his rise to favour was rapid. ~ was a *poet*,
 harpist and psalmist, and was made court musician, soon becoming
 armour-bearer to *Saul*, king of Judea, with whose s Jonathan ~
 formed one of the great friendships of history, and whose d Michal
 he mar. On Saul becoming too despotic, ~ was chosen by *Samuel*
 as successor, but had to flee; his w Michal was taken from him and
 he mar *Abigail* and then had these children by the following wives
 and concubines: Amnon (s) by Ahinoam, Chileab (s) by *Abigail*
 (w), *Absolom* (s) and Tamar (d) by Maacah, Adonijah (s; see
 Solomon) by Haggith, Shepatiah (s) by Abital, and Ithream (s) by
 Eglah (w). When Saul was defeated at Gilboa, ~ returned to
 become an all-conquering king. He coveted Bathsheba, w of Uriah
 the Hittite, and caused *Joab*, his nephew and mil captain, to
 contrive Uriah's d in battle, and Bathsheba later bore him a s
 Solomon. *Absolom* (q.v.) led a revolt but was k, and ~ was
 succeeded by Solomon. In his old age ~ mar Abishag. 4. Jacques
 Louis ~, Fr court *PAINTER* to *Napoleon*.
DAVIDSON ABSALOM.
DAWN 1. AUBADE, MORNING, SUNRISE. COME TO,
 REALIZE. 2. **Goddess:** Gk = EOS, **Rom** = AURORA.
DAY D. *SUNDAY*, *MONDAY*, *TUES* etc; S, M, T etc (**opp** =

night). DAYLIGHT. DATE, PERIOD; **comp** = ever; night.
VICTORY. [Policeman ~ (*Kipling*)].

DB DECIBEL (noise).

DC DIRECT CURRENT; *CURRENCY* (crypt, elect); **comp** = AC.
DISTRICT COMMISSIONER. DISTRICT OF COLUMBIA.

DD DIVINE, DOCTOR OF DIVINITY; *CHURCHMAN*.
DAUGHTERS.

DDR EAST GERMANY (and *car plate*).

DEAD D, DEFUNCT, EX, EXPIRED, LATE, PASSED
ON/OVER (**opp** = live). FINISHED, OVER. UNCHARGED.
SEA.

DEAR (s/l *deer*). *DARLING*, DUCK, HONEY, LIEF, *LOVE*,
LUV, SWEETIE. A LOT, COSTLY, EXPENSIVE, PRICEY.

DEATH 1. EXPIRATION, FATHER TIME, FINIS, REAPER,
THE END; [*Charon*; 'this fell sergeant ~' (Hamlet, *Shak*)]. 13
(*tarot*). 2. **God: Gk** = THANATOS, **Rom** = MORS, **Egy** =
ANUBIS/OSIRIS, **Ind** = SHIVA.

DEB L, BEGINNER, DEBUTANTE, TYRO [come out]. BACK
SEAT (crypt).

DEBT IN THE RED, IOU, MARKER [bankruptcy]. See *IN* ~ (2).

DEBTOR BANKRUPT, *DR*, OWER.

DEC DECLARED, INNINGS CLOSED. DECEASED.
DECEMBER.

DECEMBER (12th) MONTH, M, DEC (Rom 10th month, until
Julius *Caesar* reorganized the calendar). **Birthstone** = Turquoise.

DECIBEL DB, NOISE-LEVEL.

DECK ADORN, BEDECK, DRESS, GARLAND, ORNAMENT.
BRIDGE, LEVEL (naut). GROUND (sl). PACK (*cards*).

DECLARE AFFIRM, ASSERT, *AVER*, SAY, STATE. CLOSE
INNINGS, DEC (*cricket*).

DECLINE *REFUSE*, REJECT. DESCENT, DOWNWARD
PATH/SLOPE, SETTING, STEP DOWN. DECAY, DROOP,
FALL (OFF). INFLECT (gram).

DECORATION *MEDAL*: VC, GC, DSO, GM, DSC, MC, DFC,
DCM, MM, DFM; RIBBON, *STAR*, GONG (sl); IRON CROSS
etc. ADORNMENT, APPEARANCE, PAINTWORK;
FILIGREE.

DECREASE DIMINISH, LESSEN. *IRON*, PRESS (crypt).

DEED ACT, FACT, PERFORMANCE. CHARTER,
DISPOSITION, INSTRUMENT, PROOF OF TITLE.

DEER (s/l *dear*). RUMINANT QUADRUPED (Cervidae); **breeds**:

AXIS, BARKING, CARIBOU, CHITAL, ELK, FALLOW, HIND, IZARD, MOOSE, MUNTJAK, MUSK, NUR, *RED*, *REINDEER*, ROE, RUSA, SAMBUR, SIKA, *SKIPPER*, WAPITI. **Assembly** = herd; **male** = *buck*, hart, *stag*; **fem** = doe, hind; **offspring** = *fawn* [*antelope*, Bambi, *goat*, venison].

DEERSTALKER GHILLIE, KEEPER. *HAT* [*Holmes*].

DEFEAT BEAT, OVERCOME, WORST.

DEFECT FAULT, FLAW. ABANDON, CHANGE SIDES, CROSS THE FLOOR, RENEGE, SWITCH ALLEGIANCE, TURNCOAT.

DEFILE GORGE, PASS. MARCH IN FILE. BEFOUL, CORRUPT, DESECRATE, PROFANE, RUIN, SPOIL.

DEFORMED *Anag.* CRIPPLED. MISSHAPEN, TWISTED.

DEGREE GRADE, LEVEL, SCALE, STANDARD, STEP [hot, cold]. ANGLE, MEASUREMENT (naut; math) [latitude, longitude]. CLASS, CONDITION, PROFICIENCY, RANK, STATUS; BA, MA [*university*].

DEL DELINEAVIT, DREW. LED BACK (crypt).

DELETED 1. ERASED, REMOVED. 2. Delete letter 'd' from clue, e.g. **Drink deleted is iced** (4) = *RINK.

DELIBERATE EXPRESS, ON PURPOSE, PURPOSEFUL, STUDIED. CONSIDER, DISCUSS. IMPRISON (crypt).

DELIVERY *BALL*. *CARRIAGE*, FREIGHT. *CHILDBIRTH*. *POST*. TRANSFER. RESCUE, SALVATION. *SPEECH*.

~ **MAN** *BOWLER*, *PITCHER*. ROUNDSMAN. TRADESMAN. DOCTOR, MALE NURSE (crypt).

DELPHI Town in Phocis on Parnassus, with *Oracle*; now Kastri.

DELTA D; 4th Gk letter. RIVER MOUTH.

Dem Democrat [elephant].

DEMAND ASK, REQUEST. MARKET; **comp** = supply.

DEMETER Gk *goddess* of NATURE, d of *Cronos* and *Rhea*. Her d *Persephone* (Proserpine) by *Zeus* was seized by *Pluto*, and *Hermes* brought her back. **Rom** = *CERES*.

DEMIJOHN LARGE *BOTTLE*.

DEMOCRAT PARTY (polit; anti-Rep) [elephant].

DEMON CRUEL BEING, GHOUL. AFREET, AFRIT (Mos), EVIL *SPIRIT*. *CARD GAME*.

DEMONSTRATE PROVE, SHOW. PARADE, RALLY.

DEN STUDY, WORKROOM. *HABITATION*, LAIR. DENIER (cloth count).

DENARIUS D, COIN (penny). [L, S, D].

DENMARK DK (*car plate*). *STRAIT*. [*Hamlet*].

DENTIST BDS, *DRAWER*, EXTRACTOR, ORTHODONTIST, PULLER; FANG-PRANGER (sl). PANEL-BEATER (crypt).

DEPARTED GONE, *LEFT*, WENT. *DEAD*, EX, LATE.

DEPLOYED 1. *Anag.* ARRANGED, SET OUT. 2. Remove letters PLOY from word(s).

DEPOSIT *LODGE*. ASH, SILT.

DEPRESSION *BLUES*, DUMPS. DENT, DIP, HOLLOW; GLEN, VALE, VALLEY. *COL*, CYCLONE, *LOW* (met).

DERANGED *Anag.* CRAZY. DISTURBED.

DERBY (s/l *Darby*). BOWLER, *HAT*. *CLASSIC*. LORD. *CERAMICS*®. CITY (Baseball ground, *football*).

DESCRIBE 1. ABOUT, ANENT, RE. *DRAW*, ENCIRCLE, MARK OUT. EXPLAIN, QUALIFY, RECITE DETAILS OF. 2. Word round another, e.g. **On foot, she describes a circle** (4) = $\acute{S}$H*O*E.

DESERT (s/l *dessert*). 1. *LEAVE*, RAT, RUNAWAY [*turncoat*]. ASSEMBLY OF LAPWINGS. (SANDY) WASTELAND; **celebrated**: ARABIAN (Af), ANATOLIAN (Turk), AN NAFUD (Arab), ATACAMA (Chile), AUSTRALIAN (Aus), BARREN (Pers), BLACK SAND (USSR), COLORADO (US), DAHNA (Arab), DASHT-E-LUT (Iran), DEATH VALLEY (US), EASTERN (Af), GIBSON (Aus), GILA (US), GOBI (Ch), GREAT SANDY (Arab; Aus), GREAT SALT (Pers; US), GREAT VICTORIAN (Aus), KALAHARI (Af), KARA (USSR), KAVIR (Pers), KYZYL (USSR), LIBYAN (Af), LUT (Pers), MARGO (Afghan), MOHAVE (US), MONGOLIAN (Ch), NAFUD (Arab), NAMIB (Af), NAZCA (Peru), NEGEV (Israel), NUBIAN (Af), QARA QUM (USSR), SAHARA (Af), SECHURA (Peru), SHAMIYA (Arab), SINAI (Egy), SOMALI (Som), SONORAN (Mex/US), SYRIAN (Arab), TAKLA MAKAN (Ch), THAR (Ind), TURKESTAN (Asia), ZIRREH (Afghan). **Pl** = *FATE*, MERITS, REWARDS. 2. Remove letter(s) indicated, e.g. **Trust gunners to desert rarely** (4) = **RELY.

DESIGN AIM, END, INTENT. DRAWING, PLAN, PATTERN [archit].

DESIRE LONGING, WISH, *MANIA*.

DESK COUNTER, SERVERY. BOOK REST, LECTERN, SUPPORT: MUSIC STAND. EDITORIAL DEPARTMENT. BUREAU, WRITING TABLE; and see *furniture* for types.

DESSERT (s/l *desert*). AFTERS, PUDDING, SWEET: *COURSE* (FRUIT, NUTS).

DESTROY *Anag.* ANNIHILATE, *BREAK*, CRUSH, FINISH.
DETAIL 1. ITEMIZE, ORDER, TELL OFF, LIST. MINOR
   PARTICULAR. DETACHMENT (mil). DOCK (crypt).
   2. Remove last letter(s), e.g. **Fine detail at the end** (3) = FIN*.
DETECTIVE *POLICEMAN*; DICK, FBI, G-MAN, GUMSHOE
   (sl), INVESTIGATOR, PRIVATE EYE, SCOTLAND YARD,
   TEC [*AGENT*]. **Pl** = YARDMEN (crypt). **Celeb** (fiction):

BERGERAC	(TV)
FATHER BROWN	(*Chesterton*)
BUCKET	(*Dickens*)
FRANK CANNON	(TV)
NICK CARTER	(Hammett)
LEMMY CAUTION	(Films)
CHARLIE CHAN	(Films; Biggers)
COLUMBO	(TV)
DUPIN, AUGUSTE	(Rue Morgue, Poe; 1st fict)
GREGSON	(*Holmes*)
INSP FRENCH	(Allingham)
HARRY O	(TV)
HART & HART	(TV)
KOJAK	(TV; Mann)
LESTRADE	(*Holmes*)
MAIGRET	(Simenon)
PHILIP MARLOW	(Chandler)
MISS MARPLE	(Christie)
PERRY MASON	(Gardner)
McCLOUD	(TV)
McMILLAN & WIFE	(TV)
HERCULE POIROT	(Christie)
TOM SAWYER	(Mark *Twain*)
EDDIE SHOESTRING	(TV)
SAM SPADE	(Hammett)
SHERLOCK *HOLMES*	(Conan Doyle)
TENAFLY	(TV)
LORD PETER WIMSEY	(Sayers)

Pl = FBI, *Pinkerton* Agency, Scotland Yard.

DETOUR *Anag.* 1. DEVIATION, DIGRESSION. 2. Remove
   letters TOUR (or synonym) from clue, e.g. **Detour along the coast is
   a fiddle** (3) = CON****.

DEUCALION Gk myth, s of *Prometheus* and Clymene, and
  progenitor of Gk race. With his w Pyrrha, ~ built a boat to escape
  the flood sent by Zeus; it came to rest on Mt Parnassus (c.f. *Noah*).
  They then threw stones over their shoulders to repopulate the earth
  [*Python*].
DEUTERIUM D (*chem*); HYDROGEN ISOTOPE.
DEVELOP *Anag.* PROCESS, TREAT (photo). REVEAL,
  UNFOLD; ELABORATE. CONVERT LAND. PROGRESS.
DEVI Chief Ind *goddess*, wife of Shiva. Depicted with *many arms*;
  personification of destruction.
DEVIL DEMON, EVIL, IMP, TEMPTER; ABADDON (Hebr),
  APOLLYON (bibl), BELIAL (Hebr), DEUCE, *DICKENS, DIS,
  HADES* (Gk), LUCIFER (Lat), MEPHISTOPHELES (Ger),
  (OLD) NICK, OLD *SCRATCH*, PLUTO, SATAN (bibl, lit =
  accuser). 15 (*tarot*). ERRAND BOY (printer's); JUNIOR (leg);
  RESEARCH, SORT.
DEVISE 1. CONTRIVE, INVENT, PLAN, PLOT, SCHEME.
  ASSIGN, BEQUEATH, WILL [testament, testify]. 2. Remove
  letters 'vise' from word or sentence, e.g. **Derv is eating devised for
  removal of household tariffs** (8) = DER****ATING.
DEVOUT PI, PIOUS, RELIGIOUS, REVERENTIAL.
  EARNEST, GENUINE, HEARTY.
DEXTER RIGHT (*herald*). *CATTLE* (Ire).
DEXTERITY ADROITNESS. ON THE RIGHT,
  RIGHT-HANDEDNESS.
DEXTEROUS ADROIT, HANDY, SKILFUL. RIGHT-HANDED.
DG DEI GRATIE, BY GOD'S GRACE. DIRECTOR GENERAL.
DI *DIANA.* DOUBLE . . . **PI** = *PLUTO.*
DIA DIAMETER. ACROSS . . ., APART . . ., THROUGH . . .
DIAERESIS *ACCENT* (ë pronounced separately), UMLAUT.
DIAL FACE (sl). CALL, RING [STD]. INSTRUMENT.
DIAMOND *GEM*, PRECIOUS STONE; RHINESTONE;
  CARBON, ICE (sl), ROCKS (sl) [girl's best friend]. *DOG*
  (Newton). LOZENGE, RHOMB. BASEBALL FIELD (US).
  Anniversary (60th or 75th). *Birthstone* (April). *TYPEFACE.*
  PI = SUIT (*cards*). COURTIERS (*Alice*).
DIANA 1. DELIA, DI; HORSEWOMAN, HUNTRESS. 2. Rom
  goddess of HUNTING, MOON and FERTILITY; d of *Jupiter*; her
  temple at Ephesus was one of the *Seven Wonders of the World.*
  Gk = *ARTEMIS/HECATE.* [*Actaeon; Shak*].
DIARIST LOGGER, RECORDER; **celeb**: FANNY BURNEY, SIR

SIMON D'EWES, JOHN EVELYN, ANNE FRANK (NL), ADRIAN *MOLE* (fict, Sue Townsend), SAMUEL PEPYS, SAMUEL SEWALL (US).

DICE Pl of DIE: BONES, CRAPS, LIAR ~, POKER ~. CHECKER (US), CHEQUER, CHOP INTO CUBES, CUT UP.

DICER CRAPS PLAYER/SHOOTER [sharpshooter]. CHOPPER, CUBIST (crypt).

DICKENS 1. *DEVIL*, DEUCE. 2. Monica ~, fem Eng writer. 3. Charles (John Huffam), writer 1812–70; mar Catherine Hogarth 1836, separated 1858. BOZ, QUIZ. **Illustrators**: Hablot Knight Browne (Phiz), George Cruickshank. **Novels: Barnaby Rudge** (abbr: Rudge). Against a background of the Gordon Riots, family enmity is transcended by the love of Edwin Chester for Emma Haredale. Barnaby Rudge and his pet raven *Grip* carry messages; **Bleak House** (abbr: Bleak Ho). Richard Carstone secretly weds his cousin Ada Clare while they are wards of John Jarndyce. Esther Summerson is shown to be the love child of Lady Dedlock. The *lawyers* devour the fortune in the endless case in Chancery of Jarndyce v Jarndyce; **The Christmas Books** (abbr: Xmas books). A series dealing with Christmas and, often, the supernatural: The Battle of Life, The Chimes, A Christmas Carol, The *Cricket* on the Hearth, and The Haunted Man; **David Copperfield** (abbr: Copperfield). Raised by his wicked step-f Murdstone, ~ finds friendship from the Peggottys, incl his *nurse* Clara (whom 'Barkis is willin' ' to mar), and their niece Little Em'ly. After unhappy schooling at Mr Creakle's Salem House, ~ is lodged with the Micawbers and works in Murdstone's warehouse; he runs away to his aunt Betsy Trotwood, who adopts him, and he lodges with her lawyer Wickfield and his charming d Agnes; Uriah Heep is the 'umble clerk. ~ is articled to Spenlow and Jorkins and mar the d Dora as a child bride, who d after a few years. Steerforth, an old school friend, seduces Little Em'ly but is drowned. Uriah Heep's plans to control Wickfield are foiled by Micawber and ~, who finally mar Agnes and finds success as a writer. Largely autobiographical, it also *models* Micawber on the author's f John; **Dombey & Son, Dealings With the Firm of** (abbr: Dombey). Paul ~ is a cold egoist who puts his business standing before all else. His s Paul dies and d Florence is estranged. She eventually mar Walter Gray and forgives her f; **Great Expectations** (abbr: Great Ex). *Recluse* Miss Havisham, who was jilted on her wedding day, lets Pip — Philip Pirrip — believe that he owes his fortune to her, but it comes from the *convict* Magwitch, whom he helped at one time. Estella, whom he loves vainly, is shown to be Magwitch's d, brought up by Miss Havisham to spurn men; **Hard Times, For these Times** (abbr: Hard Times). Josiah Bounderby, a self-made oafish banker, mar young Louisa Gradgrind who, with her br Tom, has been raised by her f in Coketown to acknowledge hard facts. Strife and strikes occur among the workers, and Tom is shown to be a thief; Louisa runs back to her f; **Little Dorrit** (abbr: Dorrit). Amy Dorrit, d of William ~, spends her childhood unsullied by the corrosive atmosphere of the Marshalsea debtors' *prison*. Father and daughter inherit money and are released, while their friend Arthur Clenham is sentenced in his turn. Intrigue and theft form a damning social comment on complacent bureaucracy; **Martin Chuzzlewit** (abbr: Chuzzle). Young Martin ~ is sacked at his grandfather's behest by Pecksniff, and seeks his fortune in America. He returns to make peace with the old man; his uncle Jonas ~ commits murder and suicide. Sarah Gamp, coarse midwife and *nurse* 'dispoged' to gin, converses with her non-existent and *unseen* friend Mrs *Harris*; **The Mystery of Edwin Drood** (abbr: Drood). Edwin ~ breaks off betrothal to Rosa Bud, ward of Mr Grewgious and music pupil of John Jasper, who lusts after her. Neville Landless has to flee when Edwin disappears, and the odious Jasper fosters the suspicion which falls on him. The novel is unfinished; **Nicholas Nickleby** (abbr: Nich Nick). Ralph ~ places his nephew Nicholas with Wackford Squeers, *schoolmaster* of Dotheboys Hall; and his niece Kate with Madame Mantalini, a dressmaker. Squeers ill-treats all his boys, especially Smike, who dies and turns out to have been Ralph ~'s s. All is eventually put right by the *twin* bros Cheeryble; **The Old Curiosity Shop** (abbr: OC Shop). Nell Trant's grandfather is proprietor of the shop, and he gets into debt to Daniel Quilp, an evil *dwarf* with designs on Little Nell. They have to flee when the grandfather cannot pay. Quilp victimises several people who try to help, and eventually all three die; **Oliver Twist, or The Parish Boy's Progress** (abbr: Oliver). Oliver ~ grows up in the workhouse. He runs away and is picked up by Jack Dawkins (twice) who is one of Fagin's young thieves and known as the Artful Dodger. Bill Sikes murders Nancy when she tries to help Oliver, whose genteel background is finally revealed by Mr Brownlow; **Our Mutual Friend** (abbr: Mutual F). The body of John Harmon is found in the Thames, and papers show that his fortune should go to Nicodemus *Boffin*, a dustman. Mistaken identity, blackmail and greed abound

along the river, as Bella Wilfer rejects intrigue and is united with the real John Harmon. The deformed Jenny Wren has to work as a doll's dressmaker to keep her drunken f; **The Pickwick Papers, or the Posthumous Papers of the Pickwick Club** (abbr: Pickwick). Adventures of the four members of the Corresponding Society of the Pickwick Club: Samuel Pickwick, Augustus Snodgrass, Tracy Tupman and Nathaniel Winkle. Mr Pickwick, supported by his manservant Samuel Weller, also has to fight a breach of promise case brought by Mrs Bardell; **A Tale of Two Cities** (abbr: 2 Cities). Dr Manette is released from the Bastille after 18 years as a *prisoner* in Cell 105, North Tower, the Bastille, and eventually becomes *mad*; his d Lucie mar Charles Darnay, nephew of the Marquis de St Evremonde. Sidney Carton adores Lucie and eventually substitutes himself for her jailed husband, and goes to the guillotine in his stead: 'It is a far, far better thing . . . than I have ever done'.
Characters: Artful Dodger (*robber*; Oliver); Bagstock, Major (JB, Josh, Old Joe; Dombey); Bardell, Mrs (Pickwick); Barkis (a carrier; '~ is willin' '; Copperfield); *Boffin*, Nicodemus (Mutual F); Brass, Sampson & Sally (solicitors; OC Shop); Brownlow, Mr (Oliver); Bucket (*detective*; Bleak Ho); Bumble (petty official; Oliver); Buzfuz, Serjeant (advocate, Pickwick); Carker, James (office manager; Dombey); Carton, Sidney (2 Cities); Cheeryble bros (*twins*; Nich Nick); Codlin & Short (travelling showmen; OC Shop); Copperfield, David (Trot, ~); Corney, Mrs (workhouse matron; Oliver); Cratchit (*clerk*; Xmas Carol); Cuttle, Capt (*sailor*; Dombey); Darnay, Charles (2 Cities); Defarge, Mme (knits; 2 Cities); Dodson and Fogg (*lawyers*; Pickwick); Fagin (*robber*; Oliver); Fang (*magistrate*; Oliver); Fips (legal agent; Chuzzle); Flite, Miss (pesters Chancery; Bleak Ho); Gamp, Sarah (*nurse*; Chuzzle); Gargery, Joe (*blacksmith*; Great Ex); Gradgrind (*schoolmaster*, 'facts'; Hard Times); Grimwig ('eat my head'; Oliver); Guster (*maid*; Bleak Ho); Havisham, Miss (*recluse*; Great Ex); Heep, Uriah ('umble lawyer's *clerk*; Copperfield); Jaggers (advocate; Great Ex); Jingle, Alfred (swindling actor; Pickwick); Jo (poor outcast; Bleak Ho); Jorkins (*lawyer*; Copperfield); Jupe (*jester*; Hard Times); Krook (rag and boneman; Bleak Ho); La Creevy, Miss (talkative *painter*; Nich Nick); Little Dorrit (*child* of Marshalsea debtors' prison; Dorrit); Little Em'ly (vain; Copperfield); Little Nell (tragic death; OC Shop); Lorry (banker; 2 Cities); Manette, Dr and Lucie (2 Cities); Mantalini (milliner; Nich Nick); Marchioness, the (*nursed* and mar Dick Swiveller; OC Shop); Micawber ('something will turn up'; Copperfield); Miggs,

Miss (*maid*; Rudge); Mould (*undertaker*; Chuzzle); Moucher, Miss
(*hairdresser*; Copperfield); Nancy (murdered by Sikes; Oliver);
Nipper, Susan (Dombey); Noggs, Newman (*clerk*; Nich Nick);
Omer (*undertaker*; Copperfield); Pecksniff, Seth (hypocrite;
Chuzzle); Peggotty, Clara (*maid* who mar Barkis; Copperfield);
Pickwick, Samuel (benevolence; Pickwick); Pinch, Tom (drudge;
Chuzzle); Pip (sis mar Gargery; Great Ex); Pipchin, Mrs
(*landlady*; Dombey); Plummer, Caleb (*toymaker*; Cricket on the
Hearth); Prig, Betsy (*nurse*; Chuzzle); Pross, Miss (*governess*; 2
Cities); Quilp (*dwarf*; OC Shop); Sawyer, Bob (surgeon;
Pickwick); Scrooge, Ebenezer (converted miserly killjoy; Xmas
Carol); Sikes, Bill (murdering *robber*; Oliver); Sleary (circus
owner; Hard Times); Smike (s of Ralph Nickleby; Nich Nick);
Snagsby (Peffer and ~, law stationers; Bleak Ho); Snodgrass,
Augustus (Pickwick); Spenlow, Dora (child wife of D Copperfield);
Spenlow & Jorkins (*lawyers*; Copperfield); Squeers (*schoolmaster*,
Dotheboys Hall; Nich Nick); St Evremonde, Marquis de (2 Cities);
Steerforth, James (rake; Copperfield); Swiveller, Dick (debtor; OC
Shop); Tapley, Mark (cheerful *servant*; Chuzzle); Tiny Tim (lame
boy; Xmas Carol); Toots, Mr P ('It's of no consequence';
Dombey); Traddles, Thomas (sad boy at Salem House;
Copperfield); Trotter, Job (Jingle's servant; Pickwick); Trotwood,
Betsy ('Janet! Donkeys!'; Copperfield); Tulkinghorn, Mr (*lawyer*;
Bleak Ho); Tupman, Mr Tracy (lady's man; Pickwick); Twist,
Oliver ('more please'; Oliver); Varden, Dolly (locksmith's
daughter; Rudge); Verisopht, Lord (spineless sycophant; Nich
Nick); Weller, Sam (Pickwick's *servant*; Pickwick); Wemmick,
John (*clerk* to Jaggers; Great Ex); Wickfield, Agnes (*lawyer's* d,
mar Copperfield); Wilfer (*clerk*; Mutual F); Winkle (Pickwick);
Wren, Jenny (deformed child; Mutual F).

DICKY *Anag*. RICHARD, BOY. ILL, SHAKY, UNSOUND,
UNWELL. BIRD. DONKEY. SHIRTFRONT. BACKSEAT.
RUMBLE-SEAT.

DICTIONARY LEXICON, WORD-BOOK; CHAMBERS®,
COLLINS®, OED®, WEBSTER®; DR JOHNSON;
[encyclop(a)edia, thesaurus].

DIDO 1. ANTIC, CAPER, PRANK. DID NOTHING (crypt). 2.
Princess of Tyre, sis of *Pygmalion*. Real name ELISSA (not
Astarte). Founded Carthage. Stabbed herself on a funeral pyre
rather than marry Iarbas [*Aeneas*]. 3. A minor *PLANET*.

DIED (s/l *dyed*). D, EXPIRED, OBIIT, *OSP* (without issue),
PEGGED OUT.

DIET BANT, SLIM; REGIME. *LEGISLATIVE ASSEMBLY*.

DIFFERENTLY *Anag*. DISSIMILARLY, DISTINCTLY.

DIFFIDENT MODEST, RETIRING, SHY, UNCONFIDENT.

DIG EXCAVATE, FORK OVER, UNEARTH. APPROVE, UNDERSTAND (sl). **Pl** = LODGINGS.

DIGEST ASSIMILATE. ABSTRACT, PRECIS, RESUME, SUMMARY, SYNOPSIS. HEAT (*chem*). ENDURE.

DIGGER MINER, PITMAN. EXCAVATOR. AUSTRALIAN.

DILIGENCE INDUSTRY, PERSISTENCE. *CARRIAGE*.

DIN *ROW*. DRUM (into), REPEAT. German standard (photo).

DINNER LUNCH, MEAL, SUPPER. NOISE-MAKER. PERCUSSIONIST (crypt).

DINOSAUR REPTILE (ex); **herbivores**: ATLANTOSAURUS, BRONTOSAURUS, CETIOSAURUS, DIPLODOCUS, GUANODON, STEGOSAURUS, TRICERATOPS; **carnivores**: MEGALOSAURUS, TYRANNOSAURUS.

DIOGENES 1. Gk cynic *PHILOSOPHER* who lived in a *tub*. 2. London Club of Mycroft *Holmes*.

DIONYSUS Gk equivalent of *BACCHUS*.

DIPLOMATIC CORPS CD [Court of St James].

DIRAE *FURIES*.

DIRECT *CONTROL*, INSTRUCT, ORGANIZE. ROUTE, STEER. STRAIGHT.

DIRECTION E, N, S, W, NE, SE etc; ROUTE, WAY. *CONTROL*, INSTRUCTION.

DIRECTOR ARROW, SIGN, SIGNBOARD. RUDDER, STEERING. CONTROLLER, MANAGER; **Pl** = BOARD.

DIS = *ORCUS*, *PLUTO*. Rom *god* of the *Underworld* (**Gk** = *HADES*).

DISARMING DEFUSING. DISBANDING, DEPRIVING OF WEAPONS. PACIFYING. AMPUTATING [Venus de Milo].

DISCHARGE BOOT, CASHIER, CANCEL, DISMISS, FIRE, RELEASE, SACK. CARRY OUT, PERFORM. LIQUIDATE, *PAY*. *SHOOT*. ASSOIL, UNLOAD.

DISCIPLE FOLLOWER (especially the 12 *apostles*).

DISCOVERER *EXPLORER*; *INVENTOR*. DISCLOSER, EXHIBITOR, FINDER. BETRAYER (arch). *SPACECRAFT*.

DISCOVERY 1. DISCLOSURE, REVEALING; *INVENTION*; **celebrated**: DISPLACEMENT, LEVER (3rd cent B.C. *Archimedes*); BLOOD CIRCULATION (1628 Harvey);

GRAVITY (1689 Newton); VACCINATION (1798 Jenner);
ELECTRICAL INDUCTION (1830 Faraday); ANTISEPSIS (1864
Lister); INOCULATION (1886 Pasteur); ELECTRON (1897
Thomson); RADIUM (1903 Curies); RELATIVITY (1905
Einstein); NUCLEAR PHYSICS (1913 Rutherford and Bohr);
PENICILLIN (1928 Fleming); NEUTRON (1932 Chadwick).
2. SHIP (Baffin, Cook, Scott; *explorers*).

DISPLEASURE *ANGER*, DISAPPROVE, DISSATISFACTION.
HUNTING (crypt).

DISTEMPER *ANGER*, DERANGE, UPSET; DISORDER.
DISEASE (dogs). WALL PAINT.

DISTRESS *Anag.* 1. ANGUISH, PAIN, SORROW, STRAITS,
VEX. MAYDAY, SOS. BREATHLESSNESS,
EXHAUST(ION). CUT HAIR, SHEAR, SCALP (crypt). 2.
Remove synonym for hair from clue, e.g. **Distressed warlock in a
fight** (3) = WAR****.

DISTRIBUTION *Anag.* APPORTIONMENT, ARRANGEMENT,
CLASSIFICATION, DISPERSAL, SCATTER, SHARING.

DISTRICT AREA, COUNTY, CANTON, *DIVISION*, REGION,
SHIRE, STATE, TERRITORY, TRACT, *WARD*.

DITTO *DO*, DUPLICATE, SAME [*copy*].

div divorced.

DIVERSION *Anag.* DETOUR, DEVIATION. DISTRACTION,
FEINT. *GAME*, PASTIME.

DIVE 1. DELVE, PENETRATE, SEARCH. HEADER,
PLUNGE, PLUMMET, SUBMERGE, SWIM UNDERWATER;
positions: *pike*, straight, tuck; **types**: armstand, back ~, forward ~,
inward ~, reverse ~, somersault, swallow ~, twist (bellyflop)
[aqualung, snorkel, skindiving, subaqua]; and see *swimming*.
2. *BAR*, HIDING PLACE, *NIGHTCLUB*, SPEAKEASY (US).
Pl = RICH MAN (St Luke) [Croesus, *Midas*].

DIVIDER SEPARATOR, SCREEN; NET (tennis, crypt). **Pl** =
COMPASSES.

DIVINE DD, *CHURCHMAN*, PRIEST. GODLIKE;
BEAUTIFUL, DELIGHTFUL, EXCELLENT, GIFTED.
CONJECTURE, FORESEE, GUESS, PREDICT.

DIVISION DISTRIBUTION, SHARING. DISAGREEMENT,
DISCORD, SEVERANCE. CLASSIFICATION, GRADE.
FUNCTION, PROCESS (math). NET (tennis). VOTE (polit).
BOUNDARY, *DISTRICT*, PARISH, PART, SECTION, SEE,

ZONE; **specifically** COUNTY, REGION, SHIRE; ~ **of England**:

AVON	
BEDFORDSHIRE	*BEDS*
BERKSHIRE	BERKS
BUCKINGHAMSHIRE	*BUCKS*
CAMBRIDGESHIRE	CAMBS
CHESHIRE	CHES
CLEVELAND	CLEV
CORNWALL	(SW)
CUMBERLAND (ex)	CUMB
CUMBRIA	CUMB
DERBYSHIRE	DERBYS
DEVONSHIRE	DEVON
DORSETSHIRE	DORSET
DURHAM	DUR
ESSEX	ESX
GLOUCESTERSHIRE	GLOS
GREATER LONDON	
GREATER MANCHESTER	
HAMPSHIRE	HANTS
HEREFORD (ex)	
HEREFORD & WORCESTER	H & W
HERTFORDSHIRE	HERTS
HUMBERSIDE	
HUNTINGDONSHIRE (ex)	HUNTS
ISLE OF WIGHT	IOW
KENT	(SE)
LANCASHIRE	LANCS
LEICESTERSHIRE	LEICS
LINCOLNSHIRE	LINCS
LONDON (ex)	
MERSEYSIDE	MERS
MIDDLESEX (ex)	MIDDX
NORFOLK	
NORTHAMPTONSHIRE	NORTHANTS
NORTHUMBERLAND	
NOTTINGHAMSHIRE	NOTTS
OXFORDSHIRE	*OXON*
RUTLAND (ex)	
SHROPSHIRE	SALOP

SOMERSET	SOM
STAFFORDSHIRE	STAFFS
SUFFOLK	
SURREY	
SUSSEX (E & W)	E/W SSX
TYNE & WEAR	T & W (NE)
WARWICKSHIRE	WARKS
WEST MIDLANDS	W MIDS
WESTMORLAND (ex)	
WILTSHIRE	WILTS
WORCESTERSHIRE (ex)	WORCS
YORKSHIRE (N, S & W)	N/S/W YORKS

Subdivisions: hundred (all counties pre-Conquest), lathes (Kent), rapes (Sussex), ridings (Yorks), wapentakes (Lincs, Notts, Yorks), wards (Cumb, Dur, Northumberland, Westmorland).

~ of Scotland
(Regions & Island Areas)

BORDER	DUNBARTONSHIRE
CENTRAL	DUMFRIESSHIRE
DUMFRIES &	EAST LOTHIAN
GALLOWAY	FIFESHIRE
FIFE	INVERNESS-SHIRE
GRAMPIAN	KINCARDINE
HIGHLAND	KINROSS
LOTHIAN	KIRKCUDBRIGHTSHIRE
ORKNEY	LANARKSHIRE
SHETLAND	MIDLOTHIAN
STRATHCLYDE	MORAYSHIRE
TAYSIDE	NAIRN
WESTERN ISLES	PEEBLES
	PERTHSHIRE
(ex Counties of Scotland)	RENFREWSHIRE
ABERDEENSHIRE	ROSS & CROMARTY
ANGUS	ROXBURGH
ARGYLLSHIRE	SELKIRK
BANFF	STIRLINGSHIRE
BERWICKSHIRE	SUTHERLAND
CAITHNESS	WEST LOTHIAN
CLACKMANNANSHIRE	WIGTOWN

~ of Wales
(Counties)
CLWYD
DYFED
GLAMORGAN,
    MID/SOUTH/WEST
GWENT
GWYNEDD
POWYS

(ex Counties of Wales)
ANGLESEY
BRECKNOCK
CAERNARVON
CARDIGAN
CARMARTHEN
DENBIGH
FLINT
GLAMORGAN
MERIONETH
MONMOUTH
MONTGOMERY
PEMBROKE
RADNOR

~ of Northern Ireland
(Counties)
ANTRIM
ARMAGH
BELFAST
DOWN
FERMANAGH
LONDONDERRY
TYRONE

~ of Eire
(Counties)
CARLOW
CAVAN
CLARE
CONNAUGHT
CORK
DONEGAL (Tirconnel)
    ex ULSTER
DUBLIN
GALWAY
KERRY
KILDARE
KILKENNY
KING'S COUNTY
    (now OFFALY)
LAOIS (LEIX)
    (ex QUEEN'S COUNTY)
LEINSTER
LEITRIM
LIMERICK
LONGFORD
LOUTH
MAYO
MEATH
MONAGHAN
MUNSTER
OFFALY
    (ex KING'S COUNTY)
QUEEN'S COUNTY
    (now LAOIS)
ROSCOMMON
SLIGO
TIPPERARY
WATERFORD
WESTMEATH
WEXFORD
WICKLOW

DIY HOME HELP, SELF-HELP [handyman].
dn Down clues only.

DNA GENES. AND BACK (crypt).
DO ACCOMPLISH, ACHIEVE, ACT, CARRY OUT, EXECUTE,
PERFORM, REALIZE, *SHIFT*. *PLAY* (theat).
CELEBRATION, FESTIVITY, FIESTA, JOLLIFICATION,
PARTY, RECEPTION, TREAT. DITTO. *CHAR*, CLEAN.
KILL. CHEAT, CON, COZEN, DEFRAUD, DIDDLE,
SWINDLE, TRICK. NOTE (mus; also DOH). **Pl** = *DEER*,
HARES (*fem*).
DOC (s/l *dock*). DOCTOR. *DWARF* (Snow White).
DOCH AN DORIS STIRRUP CUP (drink at the door).
DOCK (s/l *doc*). CURTAIL, CUT, LESSEN, LOP. BASIN,
JETTY, QUAY, TERMINAL, WHARF. WEED. CRUPPER.
ENCLOSURE (leg).
DOCTOR ADULTERATE, FIDDLE, FIX. *WIND* (cricket). DD
(eccles); DR, GP, MB, MD, MO (med) [*patron saint*, vet]; B MUS
(mus); **celeb**: AMBROSE, AUGUSTINE, GREGORY and
JEROME (4 bibl ~s); CAIUS (*Shak*); COL BLOOD (crown
jewels); CRIPPEN (Edwardian murderer); DOLITTLE (*Lofting*);
FAUST/US (necromancy; Goethe, Marlowe); *GRACE* (*cricketer*);
GULLIVER (*Swift*); HAKIM (Saladin disguised, Talisman, Scott);
HIPPOCRATES (s of HERACLIDES, f of DRACON and
THESSALUS, and f-in-law of POLYBUS, all ~s); JEKYLL
(*Hyde*); JOHNSON (dict); LIVESEY (Treasure Island, Defoe);
LIVINGSTONE (explorer); LUKE (bibl); MANETTE (*Dickens*);
MELAMPOS (*prophet* Gk myth, 1st ~); NO (Bond);
SCHWEIZER (missionary, *philosopher*); SLOP (Tristram Shandy,
Sterne); STRANGELOVE (film); SYN (Russell Thorndike);
SYNTAX (William Combe); WATSON (*Holmes*); WHO (TV);
ZHIVAGO (Pasternak); *Chaucer* character [*Asclepius*].
DODGE AVOID, *DUCK*, ELUDE, SHUFFLE. ARTIFICE,
EXPEDIENT, *SHIFT*, TRICK. RACKET. CAR®. CITY (US).
DOE JOHN (average man). DEER (*fem*), HARE (*fem*). **Pl** =
ACTS, PERFORMS (see *DO*).
DOG 1. FOLLOW, PURSUE, TAIL, TRACK. LOCK; BAR,
GRIP, PAWL. **Pl** = *ISLAND*. 2. *Male* canine (**fem** = bitch;
offspring = puppy); **breeds**:

Hounds	BLOODHOUND
AFGHAN	BORZOI
BASSET	DACHSHUND
BEAGLE	DEERHOUND

ELKHOUND
FOXHOUND
GREYHOUND
HARRIER
IRISH WOLFHOUND
OTTERHOUND
SALUKI
WHIPPET

Terriers
AIREDALE
BEDLINGTON
BULL TERRIER
CAIRN
DANDIE DINMONT
FOX TERRIER
IRISH TERRIER
KERRY BLUE
SCOTTISH TERRIER
SEALYHAM
SKYE TERRIER
STAFFORDSHIRE
   TERRIER
WELSH TERRIER

Non-sporting
ALSATIAN
BOSTON
BOXER
BULLDOG
BULL MASTIFF
CHOW
COLLIE
CORGI
DALMATIAN

DOBERMAN PINSCHER
GREAT DANE
MASTIFF
NEWFOUNDLAND
POODLE
PYRENEAN
   MOUNTAIN DOG
ST BERNARD
SAMOYED
SCHNAUZER
SHEEPDOG

Gundogs
CLUMBER SPANIEL
COCKER
LABRADOR
POINTER
RETREIVER
SETTER
SPANIEL
SPRINGER
WEIMARANER

Toy
CHIHUAHUA
GRIFFON
KING CHARLES SPANIEL
PAPILLON
PEKIN(G)ESE
POMERANIAN
PUG
SPITZ
TOY POODLE
YORKSHIRE TERRIER

Celeb: ARGUS (*Ulysses*); ASTA (Thin Man); BLUEBELL,
JESSIE, PITCHER (Animal Farm, *Orwell*), BOATSWAIN
(Byron), *BUCK* (Call of the Wild, London), *BULLSEYE* (Oliver,
Dickens), *CAPTAIN* (Archers, radio), CAVALL (King Arthur),
CERBERUS (*Charon*), *DASH* (Queen Victoria), DIAMOND (Sir

Isaac Newton), DIGBY (Biggest in world), DOG OF FO (Ch lion dog), *FIDO* (acronym), FLUSH (Barretts of Wimpole Street), FURY (*Alice*), GYPSY and ROGUE (Charles I), HOUND OF THE BASKERVILLES (Sherlock *Holmes*), JIP (Copperfield, *Dickens*; and Dr Dolittle, *Lofting*), KEP (*Potter*), KRATIM (Seven Sleepers), LAIKA (First *space traveller*), LASSIE (films), MICK THE MILLER (greyhound), MONTMORENCY (*Three* Men in a Boat, Jerome), NANA (Peter Pan), NIPPER (HMV/RCA/Victor), ORTHRUS (Gk myth, *many-headed*), OWD BOB (Edinburgh), PILOT (Jane Eyre, C. *Brontë*), *PLUTO* (acronym and Disney), RIN-TIN-TIN (films), SIRIUS (Dogstar), SNOOPY (Peanuts), TIMMY (Famous Five), TOBY (Punch & Judy), TOTO (Wizard of Oz), TRAY (Struwwelpeter), TRUMP (Hogarth), and (all John Peel) BELLMAN, RANTER, RINGMAN, RUBY, *TRUE*. *Constellations*. [*Ch calendar*; Hans *Andersen*].

DOLE GRIEF, MISERY, DISTRIBUTION, UNEMPLOYMENT BENEFIT/PAY, JAM ROLL (*rh sl*) [job centre].

DOLLAR (s/l *dolour*). *BUCK*, *COIN*, *CURRENCY*, GREENBACK, MONEY, S.

DOLOUR (s/l *dollar*). GRIEF (**opp** = *joy*).

DOLPHIN *CETACEAN* MAMMAL, GRAMPUS; BOTTLE-NOSE, WHITE-BACKED, WHITE-SIDED; KILLER *WHALE* [Pelorus Jack]; *Constellation*. BEACON, STAKE (naut). **Pl** = *FOOTBALL* TEAM (US).

DOMESTIC *CHAR*. HOMELOVING. HOME MADE, *NATIVE*; TAME.

DOMINICANS BLACKFRIARS, PREACHING *FRIARS*.

DON FELLOW, TUTOR. NOBLEMAN (Sp). ASSUME, PUT ON. BRADMAN (*cricket*). RIVER (Eng; Sc; USSR). GOD (Celt). **Pl** = ABERDEEN; WIMBLEDON (both *football* teams).

DONE (s/l dun). *Anag*. ACCEPTABLE, MANNERS, U. COMPLETED, *ENDED*, FINISHED. TIRED. COOKED (**opp** = *raw*). **Comp** = *said*.

DONKEY *ASS*, BURRO (US), MOKE; NEDDY. [Republican, *Silenus*, hinny, *mule*]; **breed**: ONAGER; [*male/female*]. EEYORE (*Milne*). DULLARD, FOOL. **Pl** = [Trotwood, *Dickens*].

DOODLEBUG BUZZBOMB, DIVER (code name), FLYING BOMB, VI; *MISSILE*.

DOOLITTLE 1. *DUSTMAN*, Eliza's f in Pygmalion, My Fair Lady (*Shaw*). 2. Hilda ~, US poetess (known as HD). 3. Gen,

USAAF. 4. See *Lofting* for Dr Dolittle.

DOORWAY 1. ENTRANCE, OPENING. 2. **God: Gk** = HORUS, **Rom** = JANUS, **Egy** = HOR, SET. 3. Five *symbols* at ~ in *song*.

DOPE *DRUG. INFORMATION*.

DOPEY DRUGGED, SLEEPY. *DWARF* (Snow White).

DOR (s/l door). *BEETLE*. TOWN (*bibl*).

DORADO FISH. EL ~ (*lost city* of gold). *Constellation*.

DORIS 1. GIRL. [*Doch an* ~]. 2. Gk myth d of Oceanus and Tethys; mar her br *Nereus* and m of the Nereides, hence the SEA. Also an area in Greece. [Order (Gk archit)].

DORY *BOAT. FISH. Alice* character.

DOT *MARK*, SPECK, SPOT. DECIMAL POINT. DOWRY. HIT, STRIKE (sl). SHORT SIGN (*morse*; **opp** = *dash*).

DOUBLE 1. DEAD SPIT, DOPPELGANGER, LOOKALIKE, IMAGE, *TWIN* [*Hope* (2); Prince & Pauper (*Twain*)]. TWOFOLD, TWICE. RUN. ROUND, TURN; FOLD, LOOP. 2. Repeat any following letter(s), e.g. **Doubles** = ss.

DOUBLE ENTENDRE AMBIGUITY. *ECHO* (crypt). PORTMANTEAU WORD (crypt).

DOUBLET BODYGARMENT, LEOTARD. TT (crypt).

DOUBLETON TWO *CARDS*. 200. CC (crypt).

DOVE *BIRD*, PIGEON (*Constellation*) [*Noah*]. PEACELOVER (**opp** = *hawk*). HOLY SPIRIT. DIVED. 'JEMIMA'. RIVER (Eng).

DOWN *D*, DN. FROM ABOVE; ALIGHTED. FEATHERS, FLUFF, PLUMAGE. *BLUE*, DEPRESSED, DISPIRITED, LOW. HILLS, OPEN LAND. *DRINK*, SWALLOW. *Division* of N Ire. **Comp** = *out*. *Assembly* of hares. **Pl** = SEA (N Dover Straits) [**castles in the** ~**s** = Deal, *Sandwich*, Walmer].

DP DISPLACED PERSONS; hence PRONES, SPERON etc (anag).

DR *DEBTOR. DOCTOR.* DRACHM (*measure*). DESPATCH RIDER (mil). TOM (crypt: dr = ½ drum = ½ tom-tom).

DRACULA Blood-sucking *monster* from Bram Stoker's novel, *modelled* on Prince Vlad of Wallachia in Rumania.

DRAGOMAN *CONDUCTOR*, GUIDE, INTERPRETER.

DRAGON BAT, CRONE, SCOLD, *SHREW*, TERMAGANT. *MONSTER*, WYVERN (*Constellation*; *herald*; *Medea*). BEN-ALI (*pirate, Lofting*). CONTINUE, DRAW OUT, PROLONG (all crypt). [*Ch calendar*; ~fly; *insect*; *Python*].

DRAIN 1. DRAW OFF, EBB, *EMPTY*; TRICKLE. *DRINK*. CONDUIT, PIPE, TUBE (med); *SEWER*. DEMAND,

EXPENDITURE, WITHDRAWAL; SAP. 2. Waterloo & City
Line (sl; rly). 3. Put letters DRA in word(s), e.g. **Drain UN ft for
rehash** (7) = UN*DRA*FT.

DRAKE *DUCK* (*male*) [*Potter*]. *MILITARY LEADER*, PIRATE;
BOWLER (crypt) [Armada (*battle*)]. MAYFLY. **Pl** = ISLAND.

DRAMA PLAY; *THEATRE*. [Aeschylus, Euripides, Sophocles;
Shakespeare].

DRAW DESIGN, DEPICT, PEN, SKETCH [artist].
ATTRACT(ION), EXTRACT, MOVE, PULL, TOW, TUG.
SHARE, TIE. ELONGATE. LOTTERY. SMOKE (crypt).

DRAWBACK CON, DISADVANTAGE (**opp** = *pro*).
DEDUCTION, REMITTED TAX. WARD (crypt).

DRAWER ARTIST, RA. DENTIST (crypt). PUBLICAN,
TAPSTER. *TOWER*, TUG. SLIDING RECEPTACLE
(*furniture*). *SMOKER* (crypt). **Pl** = BLOOMERS, KNICKERS,
PANTIES.

DRAY *CARRIAGE*, CART. *Habitation* (squirrels).

DREAM 1. BROWN STUDY, FANCY, REVERIE, VISION;
BEAUTY. 2. **God: Rom** = MORPHEUS, **Egy** = SERAPIS, **Gk**
= HERMES.

DRESS *Anag.* BANDAGE. BEDECK, BEFLAG, *COVER*,
DECK; GARNISH, PIPE. CLOTHE (**opp** = *strip*); ATTIRE,
FROCK, *HABIT*, OUTFIT, RIG, ROBE [*suit*]. ALIGN,
RANGE, SIZE. PREPARE (cook).

DRESSING CLOTHING, COVERING, DONNING (CLOTHES),
ROBING. ALIGNMENT, *ROW* (mil). MAYONNAISE.
BANDAGE, PLASTER.

DREW DEL, DELINEAVIT, SKETCHED. ATTRACTED,
PULLED. SHARED, TIED.

DRIER AIRER, SPINNER, TOWEL; LESS WET. OAST HOUSE.

DRILL COACH, PARADE; *TRAIN*. AUGER, AWL, *BORE*,
GIMLET. BABOON, *MONKEY*. CLOTH, *MATERIAL*.
FURROW, ROW.

DRINK DITCH, OGGIN, SEA (all sl). ABSORB, DRAIN, LAP,
QUAFF, SIP, SWALLOW, TOPE; (BOTTLE/CUP/GLASS OF)
LIQUID, LIQUOR; and see *spirit*. **Types** (many ®):

3-letters		**4-letters**
ALE	RUM	ARAK
GIN	RYE	*BEER*
POP	*TEA*	*CHAR*

COLA
FLIP
MEAD
MILD
MILK
OUZO
PORT
SAKE, -I
SODA
TENT (arch)
WINE

5-letters
BUMBO
COCOA
GLOGG
HOOCH
KVASS
LAGER
NEGUS
PIMMS®
SHRUB
SIROP
SLING
TONIC
VODKA

6-letters
BITTER
BRANDY
COFFEE
COGNAC
EGG-NOG
GENEVA
GRAPPA
KIRSCH
KÜMMEL®
PORTER
RED-EYE

SCOTCH
SHERRY
SPIRIT
SQUASH
WHISKY (Sc)

7-letters
AQUAVIT
BOURBON
CAMPARI®
CINZANO®
COBBLER
COLLINS
CORDIAL
CURAÇAO
KOUMISS
LIQUEUR
MADEIRA
MARTINI®
MINERAL
OENOMEL
SHERBET
STENGAH
STINGER
WHISKEY (Ire)

8+ letters
ABSINTHE
BENEDICTINE®
CHOCOLATE
COCKTAIL
COINTREAU®
DRAMBUIE®
DUBONNET®
GINGER
    ALE/BEER
GLUHWEIN
GRAND MARNIER
HIGHBALL

HOLLANDS
HORSE'S NECK
JOHN COLLINS
LEMONADE
LIMEJUICE
MANHATTAN
OLD FASHIONED
ORANGEADE
SCHIEDAM
SCHNAPPS
SCREWDRIVER
SUNDOWNER
TIA MARIA®
TOM COLLINS
WHITE LADY

Measures
CUP
NIP
DRAM
PINT
SHOT
SLUG
FIFTH
GLASS
SNORT
FINGER
NOGGIN
SPLASH
TIPPLE
DOCH AN DORIS
NIGHTCAP
ONE FOR
    THE ROAD
OTHER HALF
QUICKIE
QUICK ONE
STIRRUP-CUP

DRIVE ENTHUSIASM, GO, IMPULSE. CONDUCT, STEER; OUTING. HIT, TEE OFF; STROKE (*cricket, golf*). FORCE, IMPEL. ENTRANCE, PRIVATE ROAD.

DRIVER 1. *CLUB*, WOOD (**opp** = iron); GOLFER. CHAUFFEUR, CAR-MAN, L. MARTINET. RAILWAYMAN. COWBOY, HERDSMAN (drover). 2. **Celeb**: *FREYA*, *PHAETON* (myth), TOAD (*Grahame*), *JEHU* (bibl).

DROP 1. LET FALL, RELEASE. FALL, LOWER. OMIT, *SHED*. EARRING, PENDANT. CASCADE, SPLASH, WATERFALL. LOZENGE, SWEET. PARACHUTE. 2. Leave off letter/word, e.g. **Alfred drops the gangster and is a different man** (4) = **FRED.

DROP-OUT 1. HIPPIE, LAYABOUT. HERMIT, MONK, RECLUSE. PARACHUTIST (crypt). 2. Leave out letter concerned, e.g. **Alice, a drop-out, evinces parasites** (4) = *LICE.

DRUG ANAESTHETIC. MEDICAMENT. HALLUCINOGEN, NARCOTIC, OPIATE, STIMULANT; **types**: BHANG, CANNABIS, COCAINE, DOPE, GRASS, HASHISH, HEMP, HERB, HEROIN, LSD, MARIJUANA, POT, SNOW, SPEED, WEED [gone, high, mainline, spaced-out, trip]. UNSALEABLE.

DRUM TUB, VAT, BARREL, CYLINDER, SHAFT. BEAT, RESONATE, SUMMON, TAP, THRUM, THUMP. DRIVE, INJECT, PLAY. *INSTRUMENT* (mus), TRAP. MOUND. VOID.

DRUMMER 1. BANDSMAN; BEATER, SKINNER, TAPPER. CHAPMAN, COMMERCIAL TRAVELLER, PEDLAR, REP. *BIRD*, BITTERN, SNIPE. *FISH*. TEAPARTY. *EAR* (crypt). 2. Ninth day of *Christmas* in *song*.

DRUNK CONSUMED, DOWNED, SWALLOWED. HIGH, INEBRIATED, LIT, SMASHED, SOUSED, TIDDLY, TIGHT (**opp** = sober; *abstainer*).

DRY ARID, PARCHED, THIRSTY. MILKLESS, TT, WATERLESS. ALCOHOL-FREE. BARE, BITTER, COLD, IMPASSIVE, MEAGRE, SOLID, STERILE. SEC (Fr). CURE, SMOKE. SUNNY. DRAIN, SPIN, TOWEL, WIPE; **comp** = *home*.

DUCK O, LOVE, NIL, NOUGHT, NO SCORE, ZERO. *BOB*, CURTSEY. (NOSE)*DIVE*, PLUNGE. *DODGE*. *DEAR*, LUV. CANVAS. **Pl** = PANTS, SHORTS, TROUSERS. [~s and drakes; richochet, skim. Bombay ~ (fish)]. *BIRD* of genus Anatidae; **breeds**:

AYLESBURY	*MANDARIN*
CANVAS BACKED	MERGANSER
EIDER	SCAUP
GADWALL	SCOTER
GOLDENEYE	SHELDRAKE
MALLARD	SHOVELLER
MUSCOVY	*SMEE*
PINTADO	SMEW
PINTAIL	TEAL
POCHARD	WI(D)GEON

[**assembly** = flight, flock; **male** = *drake*; **fem** = duck; **offspring** = duckling]. **Celeb**: DAB-DAB (*Lofting*), DAFFY, DONALD (cartoon film), JEMIMA PUDDLEDUCK (Beatrix *Potter*), *Alice* character. [Hans *Andersen*; *Lear*].

DUD BAD, DEFECTIVE. BAD CHEQUE. **Pl** = *CLOTHES*.

DUN (s/l *done*). IMPORTUNE, PESTER. GREY-BROWN (*colour*).

DUNELM *Episcopal sig* of DURHAM.

DURHAM 1. *CASTLE. GAOL. UNIVERSITY*. 2. **Episcopal sig** = DUNELM.

DUSTMAN REFUSE COLLECTOR: NICODEMUS *BOFFIN* (Mutual F, *Dickens*), ALFRED DOOLITTLE (Pygmalion, G. B. *Shaw*). SANDMAN.

DUTCH SHARING PAYMENT. *WIFE. CHEESE. HOLLAND*, NETHERLANDS. [courage = *bottle* (crypt)].

DV DEO VOLENTE, GOD WILLING.

DWARF OVERAWE, TOWER OVER. MINI(ATURE), PUNY, STUNTED; ELF, GNOME, MIDGET, PYGMY, RUNT, TROLL (**opp** = *giant*); **celeb**: ALBERICH, MIME (Wagner's Ring [Nibelheim]); BASHFUL, DOC, DOPEY, GRUMPY, HAPPY, SLEEPY, SNEEZY (Snow White); CERCOPES (Gk myth); SIR GEOFFREY HUDSON (Scott); LILLIPUTIANS (*Swift*); MISS MOWCHER (Copperfield, *Dickens*); MUNCHKIN (Wizard of Oz, Frank Baum); QUILP (OC Shop, *Dickens*); RUMPELSTILTSKIN (Grimm); TOM THUMB (US and Perrault); VAMANA (Hindu incarnation). ~ **god** = Bes (Egy).

DYED (s/l *died*). COLOURED, TINTED (blue rinse, highlights, peroxide). [Idmon].

E 1. *EAST. ENERGY.* ENGLISH. *BRIDGE PLAYER. KEY*;
NOTE. POINT. SPAIN (*car plate*). 2. Second class at *Lloyd's*.

EA EACH. EAST AFRICA. EAST ANGLIA. RIVER. Bab Jew
god (wisdom).

EAGLE 1. *BIRD* (**habitation** = eyrie; **offspring** = eaglet); **breeds**:
bald ∼, crowned ∼, erne, golden ∼, hawk ∼, sea ∼, white-tailed
∼ [∼ owl; *Ganymede*]. ENSIGN, *STANDARD. ISLAND.*
COMIC. $10. LINEAGE (crypt: L*IN*EAG()E). **Pl** = *Football
team* (US). 2. Two under par on *golf course*. 3. *Constellation*.

EAR HEAD, SPIKE (corn). HANDLE, LUG. ATTENTION,
LISTENING; APPRECIATION. AUDITOR (crypt),
HEARING ORGAN; **parts, inner**: cochlea, labyrinth; **middle**:
anvil, eustachian tube, incus, malleus (hammer), ossicle; syrinx,
tympanum (eardrum, membrane), vestibule; **outer**: concha, helix,
pinna, scapha; **disorders**: barotrauma, deafness, mastoiditis,
Ménière's, otitis media [cauliflower ∼].

EARLY 1. BEFORE TIME, PREMATURE (**opp** = *late*);
FORWARD. ARISTOCRATIC, *NOBLE* (crypt). 2. Use first
letter(s), e.g. **Early afternoon** = A or AF; or, more cryptically, **Early
speech** = DIAL(ect).

EARTH 1. LAND, MOULD, SOIL (Fuller's). WORLD, PLANET
[*study*]. HABITATION (*badger, fox*). CONDUCTOR,
CONNECTION, GROUND (elect). 2. **Goddess: Gk** = *CERES*,
GAEA/GE; **Rom** = LUA, MAIA, TELLUS, TERRA.

EARTHQUAKE *QUAKER*, TREMBLER [epicentre; Richter;
seismograph]; GROUNDRENT (crypt). HARTE, HEART,
RATHE etc. (anag; crypt).

EASE (s/l eee). FACILITY. RELIEVE, LOOSEN, SLACKEN.
REST.

EASTERN OFFICIAL BEY, CADI, DEWAN, NABOB, NAWAB,
SAHIB, SATRAP, SULTAN, TUAN [*Turkish official*].

EAST KENT SE. **Pl** = BUFFS (mil).

EASY FACILE, SIMPLE; **comp** = *free*. SITTER. [Midshipman ∼].

EAT OUT BARBECUE, PICNIC [al fresco]. ATE, TEA (anag;
crypt).

EAVESDROPPER BUG, LISTENER. ICICLE (crypt).

EBB DRAIN. DECLINE, DECAY. FLOW BACK, hence WOLF
(crypt). RECEDE; **comp** = *flow*.

EBBTIDE DRAIN. DECLINE, DECAY. OUTFLOW (hence
WOLF: crypt); EDIT (crypt).

EBOR *Episcopal sig* of *YORK*. RETIRING GOWN (crypt).

EC EAST CENTRAL, EAST END; CITY.

ECCENTRIC *Anag*. IRREGULAR, *ODD*, OFF-BEAT, WHIMSICAL. OFF-CENTRE, CAM. *CARD*.

Eccles Ecclesiastic. *Church*.

ECHO 1. *COPY*, IMITATION, REPEAT, REPETITION, RESOUND. *SPACECRAFT*. 2. Gk myth mountain *nymph*, made speechless by *Hera*, so that she could only repeat the last word of others. Loved *Narcissus* vainly, and pined away. 3. A minor *PLANET*.

ECONOMIZE BE FRUGAL, DO WITHOUT (hence D.....O; crypt, e.g. **Do without one race, all the same** (5) = D*ITT*O). SAVE, SPARE. USELESS (crypt).

EDDY 1. ROTARY MOTION, DUST DEVIL, SWIRL, VORTEX, WHIRLPOOL, WHIRLWIND; *CHARYBDIS* (myth, Sicily [*Scylla*]); MAELSTROM (Lofoten Is, Nor). COUNTER CURRENT. DEVIATION, DISTURBANCE (life, thought). 2. EDWARD (abbr). 3. Mary Baker ~, founder of Christian Science.

EDENBURG *Episcopal sig* of EDINBURGH.

EDINBURGH *Capital* of Scotland. *CASTLE*. **Episcopal sig** = EDENBURG. *RACETRACK* (horses). *UNIVERSITY*.

EDIT *Anag*. ARRANGE, CUT; COOK, GARBLE. PREPARE (MS). EBBTIDE (crypt).

EDITION VERSION. BOOK, TOME, VOLUME.

EDMUND IRONSIDE. ED.

EDWARD ED, NED, TED. BEAR (*Milne*). LEAR. R. POTATO. HYDE [Henry Jekyll; R. L. Stevenson].

EEC (COMMON) MARKET, COMMUNITY, EUROPE (treaty of Rome).

EEL FISH [**offspring** = elver; slippery].

EFGHIJKLMN *ETON* (crypt).

EG EXEMPLA GRATIA, FOR EXAMPLE/INSTANCE.

EGG ENCOURAGE, EXHORT, SPUR, STIMULATE, *URGE*. OVUM; O. BOMB. PERSON (sl). *ZERO*. **Pl** = OO, OVA, ROE, SPAWN. **Pl comp** = bacon; *ham*.

EGGER *MOTH*. SPUR, STIMULATOR. HEN (crypt).

EGYPTIAN GOD *ANUBIS*, HOR, MAAT, *OSIRIS*, *RA*, SEB, SERAPIS, *SET*, *TEMU*.

EIGHT 1. See *number*. OCTAD, VIII. BLUE, ROWING CREW; **Reserve** ~s: GOLDIE (C), *ISIS* (O). 2. Bold *rangers* (*song*). *Maids* a-milking (*Christmas* song). [Pieces of ~ (parrot, Treasure Island, *Stevenson*)].

ELBOW HINGE (crypt); JOINT. NUDGE, PUSH. *Shak* character (M for M).

EL DORADO *Lost city* of gold. **Capital** = Manoa.

ELECTRA 1. Gk myth d of *Agamemnon*, sis of Iphigenia and *Orestes*, with whom she avenged the murder of her f by her m. 2. A minor *PLANET*. *TYPEFACE*. 3. Complex of d on f (**opp** = *Oedipus*).

ELECTRICITY AC, AMPS, DC, VOLTS; CURRENCY (crypt) [BEAB].

ELEGANT CHIC, *FASHIONABLE*, IN, MODISH, STYLISH.

ELEMENT 1. AIR, *EARTH*, *FIRE*, *WATER*. COMPONENT, FACTOR, RUDIMENT. RESISTANCE WIRE. 2. Hidden word, e.g. **An element of beach air is relaxing** = CH*AIR.

ELEPHANT ELP, MAMMOTH (ex), PACHYDERM [Democrat; roc]; **celebrated**: BABAR, CELESTE, DUMBO, HEFFALUMP, JUMBO, KALAWAG, NELLIE [**assembly** = herd, **fem** = *cow*, **male** = *bull*, **offspring** = *calf*]. *MEASURE* (paper). **Comp** = *castle*.

ELEVEN 1. See *number*. HENDECA, II, IX; SIDE, SQUAD, TEAM. IMPAIRED (crypt). **Pl** = SNACK. 2. Went to *Heaven* (*song*). Ladies *dancing* (*Christmas* song).

ELI Bibl high priest and *judge* of Israel. *Samuel* was a boy in his house. Hophni and Phineas were the two s of ~, and news of their d caused ~ to fall down d (*c.* 1000 B.C.).

ELIA ESSAYIST; LAMB; *WRITER*. **Pl** = *ELIJAH*, PROPHET.

ELIJAH The Tishbite (Elias). 9th cent B.C. bibl prophet who was a *hermit* until emerging to rail against *Baal*-worship. Outlawed for denouncing *Ahab* and Jezebel, ~ spent most of his life on the run (he was fed by *ravens* and the widow's inexhaustible barrel of meat and *cruse* of oil). Only ~ was able to call down to Mt Carmel fire from Heaven. He finally ascended to Heaven in a fiery chariot.

ELIMINATE 1. DEFEAT. REMOVE, GET RID OF. 2. Remove word(s)/letter(s) indicated, e.g. **A to-do to eliminate to-do** (3) = A*DO.

ELISHA 9th cent bibl disciple of *Elijah*. Said to have been *bald*, ~ once made an axe-head float; he also sent *bears* to destroy children who has been teasing him.

ELISSA *DIDO*.

ELIZABETH 1. ASTRAEA, BELPHOEBE, GLORIANA, MERCILLA (Faerie Queene, Spenser). ER; QUEEN. 2. St ~ of Hungary (bread *transformed* into *roses*). 3. [German *Garden*].

ELL LENGTH, *MEASURE* (cloth).
ELYSIUM 1. ELYSIAN FIELDS, *HEAVEN*. 2. Gk myth place
where souls of the good dwelt after death [*Valhalla*].
EM THEM (abbr). GAUGE (model rly). *MEASURE* (printing).
Pl = RIVER (Ger). EUROPEAN MONETARY SYSTEM
(SNAKE). MINES (crypt, M*in*ES).
EMBARRASSED *Anag.* ASHAMED, AWKWARD;
PERPLEXED. COMPLICATED. ENCUMBERED,
IMPEDED.
EMBRACE 1. CLASP, COMPRISE, ENCLOSE, HUG,
INCLUDE. ACCEPT, TAKE IN. 2. Hidden word; word
contains another, e.g. **He embraces a foreign engineer and swings
for it** (5) = H*ING*E.
EMERALD 1. GEM: BERYL. GREEN. 2. *Anniversary* (55th).
Birthstone (May).
EMINENCE *HILL*, MOUND, MOUNT, TOR. *CARDINAL*, HE.
~ **GRISE** RICHELIEU'S SECRETARY (PERE JOSEPH).
MANIPULATOR, *UNSEEN* INFLUENCE; ROYAL
ENGINEER (crypt).
EMIT GIVE OUT, ISSUE, SEND FORTH, TRANSMIT. TIME
OUT, TIME-WARP, WRONG ITEM (anags; crypt).
EMMY *AWARD* (TV).
EMPEROR 1. BUTTERFLY (purple ~); MOTH (*lepidoptera*).
MEASURE (paper). PENGUIN. *TAROT* (4). 2. SOVEREIGN
of empire [*Andersen* (writer); *Caesar*; *Ch dynasty*; czar, khan;
mikado; *monarch*; O'Neill (writer); *Ptolemy*; shah; tsar]; **abbr** =
IMP (Lat); **fem** = *empress*. **Celeb**:

ALEXANDER (Macedon; Russ)	GENGHIS KHAN (Mongol)
AUGUSTUS (*Caesar*; 1st Rom)	HAILE SELASSIE (Ethiopia)
BOKASSA (Cent Af)	HIROHITO (Jap)
CALIGULA (Rom)	IVAN (Russ)
CHARLEMAGNE (H Rom)	JOSEF (H Rom)
CHARLES V (H Rom)	KUBLAI KHAN (Mongol)
CHI'EN LUNG (Ch)	MONTEZUMA (Aztec)
CONSTANTINE (E Rom)	*NAPOLEON* (Fr)
DARIUS (Pers)	*NERO* (Rom)
FRANZ JOSEF (A)	NICHOLAS (Russ)
FREDERICK (Ger)	OTTO (H Rom)
FREDERICK BARBAROSSA	PAUL (Russ)
(H Rom)	*PETER* (Russ)

PHARAOH (Egy)	TAISHO (Jap)
PTOLEMY (Egy)	WILLIAM (Ger)
SIGISMUND (H Rom)	*XERXES* (Pers)

EMPLOY 1. USE. OCCUPY. HIRE. 2. Hidden word, e.g. **Mad American employs a gardener** (4) = AD*AM.
EMPRESS Fem *emperor* [czarina; *monarch*; tsarina]. *TAROT* (3). **Celeb**:

CATHERINE (Russ)	MARIA THERESA (A)
CLEOPATRA (Egy)	MARIE LOUISE (Fr)
EUGENIE (Fr)	TZU HSI (Ch)
IRENE (E Rom)	VICTORIA (Brit)

EMPTY 1. HOLLOW, VACANT, VACATE. 2. Remove middle letter(s) from word, e.g. **Empty threat** (4) = TH**AT. 3. Insert O in word, e.g. **Empty cup** (4) = C*O*UP.
EMU FLIGHTLESS *BIRD* (Aus) [cassowary, dinornis (ex, NZ), moa, nandoo, ostrich].
EN 1. Put word in another, e.g. **Enlist Z** (5) = LIS*Z*T. 2. *MEASURE* (printing).
ENCHANT CHARM, DELIGHT, *ENTRANCE*, SPELLBIND, TRANSPORT (**opp** = *bore*).
ENCOMPASS CONTAIN, SURROUND. NORTH ORIENTATE; relate to magnetic compass, e.g. **Tidings encompassed** (4) = NEWS.
ENCOURAGE ABET, AID, EGG, *URGE*. GO.
END 1. *AIM*, DESIGN, GOAL, PURPOSE. *CLOSE*, CONCLUSION, FINISH (**opp** = *start*). SESSION (bowls). 2. Last letter of word, e.g. **Southend** = H. **Pl** = letters at each end of word(s), e.g. **Dead ends** = D**D; **Ends of the earth** = E***H.
ENDANGER JEOPARDIZE, PUT AT RISK. MAKE PEACE, MAKE UP (crypt).
ENDING 1. CLOSURE. 2. Last letter (see *END* above).
ENDLESS 1. CEASELESS, PERPETUAL, UNCEASING. CIRCLE, RING, O. AIMLESS, POINTLESS; TIPOFF (crypt). 2. No first (or last) letter, e.g. **Endless hate** (3) = HAT.
ENERGY FORCE, POTENTIAL, POWER, VIGOUR. E, ERG, ERGON.
ENG ENGLISH [*patron saint*].
Eng England, English. Engineer.
ENGAGED AFFIANCED, BETROTHED, MATCHED,

PROMISED. *BOOKED*, BUSY, OCCUPIED, RESERVED, TIED UP (**opp** = *free*). HIRED, TOOK ON.

ENGAGEMENT AFFRAY, *BATTLE*, SKIRMISH. BETROTHAL, MATCH. OCCUPATION. APPOINTMENT, DATE.

ENGINE MACHINERY, POWER SOURCE; INSTRUMENT, MEANS. WAR MACHINE; CATAPULTA, TESTUDO (Rom).

ENGINEER ARRANGE, CONTRIVE, FIX, MANAGE, ORGANIZE. CE, DESIGNER (mech), ENG. WORKER (elect, mech [**union** = AUEW], rly [**unions** = ASLEF, NUR]). BRIDGEBUILDER. RE, SAPPER.

ENGLISH E, ENG. SIDE, SPIN (ballgames — US). *TYPEFACE*.

ENGRAVE CARVE, ETCH, INSCRIBE, PRINT; FIX, IMPRINT. BURY, *INTER* (crypt).

ENGROSS ABSORB, ENRAPTURE, OCCUPY. DRAW UP, EXPRESS, PREPARE (leg). CORNER, MONOPOLIZE (arch).

ENIGMATIC *Anag*. BEWILDERING, PERPLEXING, PUZZLING.

ENLARGE EXPAND, EXPATIATE. DILATE, MAGNIFY. FREE, LIBERATE (arch).

ENLIST 1. ENGAGE, ENROL(L), JOIN COLOURS. 2. Word contained in another, especially in 'list' or 'roster', e.g. **Enlist one to revel** (7) = RO*I*STER.

ENOCH 1. Eldest s of *Cain*; founded the first city. 2. Seventh in descent from *Adam*; s of Jared and f of *Methuselah*; a prophet who did not d, but 'walked with God.' 3. Grand-s of *Abraham*. 4. A s of Reuben, and thus a grand-s of *Jacob*.

ENOUGH AMPLE, ENOW, SUFFICIENT.

ENTANGLEMENT *Anag*. 1. AFFAIR, INVOLVEMENT, LIAISON. 2. Caught in barbed wire, brambles, net, etc; **celeb**: *Absolom* (oak tree); fly (spider's web or 'parlour'); *Merlin* (rose bush); Peter Rabbit (Mr MacGregor's gooseberry net, *Potter*); Pooh (Rabbit's front door, *Milne*).

ENTER GO IN (**opp** = *leave*). LOG, *RECORD*, WRITE. BIND (contract, treaty). JOIN (church, forces; **opp** = *desert*).

ENTHUSIAST *FAN*.

ENTITLED 1. CALLED. ALLOWED, PERMITTED, RIGHTFUL. 2. With a title, e.g. Count, Dame, Sir etc.

ENTRANCE *DOOR(WAY)*, GATE, PASSAGE. ARRIVAL, ENTRY. ADMISSION FEE. *ENCHANT*.

ENVIRONMENT 1. MILIEU, SURROUNDINGS. 2. Word round

another, e.g. **Or the environment** = O*THE*R (or TH*OR*E).

EOLITHIC *AGE*.

EOS 1. Gk *goddess* of DAWN (**Rom** = *AURORA*). 2. A minor *PLANET*.

EPICUREAN HEDONISTIC. Follower of Epicurus (Gk), and devoted to sensual pleasure; **celeb**: LUCULLUS (Rom), PHAEDRUS (Gk); **opp** = *Stoic*.

EPISCOPAL SIGNATURE Initials or name of bishop, followed by archaic name for his see, e.g.

ABERDON	(Aberdeen)
ALBAN	(St Albans)
CANTUAR	(Canterbury)
CESTR	(Chester)
CICESTR	(Chichester)
DUNELM	(Durham)
EBOR	(York)
EDENBURG	(Edinburgh)
EXON	(Exeter)
NORVIC	(Norwich)
OXON	(Oxford)
PETRIBURG	(Peterborough)
ROFFEN	(Rochester)
SARUM	(Salisbury)
TRURON	(Truro)
VIGORN	(Worcester)
WINTON	(Winchester)

Eq Equatorial. Equals.

EQUAL EVEN, LEVEL, LIKE, PAR, SAME; MATCH. PEER; BROTHER.

~ **WINNER** *TIER*; DEAD-HEATER; DRAWER (crypt).

ERASED 1. DELETED, ERADICATED, REMOVED, RUBBED OUT. 2. Delete D from clue, e.g. **Draft erased is logged** (4) = *RAFT.

ERATO 1. Gk myth; one of the nine *Muses* (Love songs and erotic *poetry*). 2. A minor *PLANET*.

ERG ENERGY UNIT [dyne]. SAHARA DUNES [*desert*].

ERIC LITTLE BY LITTLE (Farrar). (THE) RED.

ERICA *HEATH(ER)*. GIRL.

ERIE (s/l eyrie). *AMERICAN INDIAN. LAKE*.

ERINYES *FURIES* (Gk).

ERIS Gk *goddess* of DISCORD, sis of *Ares* (**Rom** = DISCORDIA). Angry at not being invited to the wedding of Peleus and Thetis, she threw among the guests a golden *apple* inscribed 'To the fairest'. *Aphrodite*, *Athene* and *Hera* all claimed it, and the judgement of *Paris* was that it be awarded to Aphrodite; this indirectly caused the Siege of *Troy*.

ERMINE STOAT [weasel]. FUR [judges, peers, *herald*].

EROS Gk *god* of *LOVE* (**Rom** = AMOR, CUPID), depicted as an *archer*; s of *Aphrodite* by *Zeus* (some say by *Ares* or Hermes); **opp** = Anteros [Piccadilly Circus].

ERRATIC *Anag.* WAYWARD, WILD. *ODD.* IRREGULAR, UNCERTAIN.

ERROR *BLOOMER*, BISH, DEVIATION, FAULT, INFRINGEMENT, MISTAKE, SIN, WRONG.

ERUPTION *Anag.* BREAK-OUT, BURST, OUTBREAK; RASH.

ESAU Bibl s of *Isaac* and Rebecca, elder twin br of *Jacob* and known as EDOM (the Red) or the HAIRY ONE. A cunning *HUNTER*, ~ was tricked by Jacob to exchange his inheritance or birthright for 'a mess of pottage' (lentils), when ~ was hungry from the chase; ~ was similarly tricked by his br from the blessing of Isaac due by custom to the first born.

ESCAPOLOGIST HOUDINI. JACK SHEPHERD. ESCAPER.

ESSAY (s/l s,a). ATTEMPT, EFFORT, TEST, TRY. ARTICLE. COMPOSITION [*Elia*: Lamb].

ESSAYIST TRIER. *WRITER*: ELIA, LAMB.

ESTABLISHMENT AUTHORITY, ORGANIZATION, THEY [Civil Service (**union** = NALGO)]. GROUP, SET, SETTLEMENT, STAFF, VERIFICATION; AUTHORIZED HOLDING/MANNING. THE CHURCH.

ESTATE CLASS, ORDER. CONDITION. LAND, PROPERTY. VEHICLE (hatchback, shooting brake). [*three* ~s; fourth ~].

ETA ARRIVAL TIME, EXPECTED TIME OF ARRIVAL (**opp** = ETD).

ET AL AND OTHERS.

ETC ETCETERA, AND SO ON.

ETERNAL FLOWER ASPHODEL. ARTESIAN WELL, SPRING (crypt).

ETHIOPIAN KING RA.

ETON 1. COLLEGE, *PUBLIC SCHOOL* [*Pop*]. E—N (crypt). 2. Returned note (crypt).

EUMINIDES *FURIES* (Gk).

EUROPA Gk myth d of Agenor and m of *Minos* by *Zeus* (who took the form of a bull). 2. A satellite of the *planet* Jupiter.

EUROPE EEC [Common Market. Treaty of Rome]. *CONTINENT*.

EUROS Gk myth SE *WIND* (**Rom** = VOLTURNUS).

EURYDICE 1. Gk myth d of *Nereus* and *Doris*, who mar *Orpheus*. When she died of a snake bite, Orpheus brought her back from *Hades* by magic, but lost her again by *looking back* for her. 2. A minor *PLANET*.

EUTERPE 1. Gk myth; one of the nine *Muses* (lyric *poetry*). 2. A minor *PLANET*.

EVA EXTRA-VEHICULAR ACTIVITY, SPACE-WALK. GIRL, SPACE-GIRL. PERON. 'LIFE'.

EVE (s/l eave). 1. EVENING, VIGIL. *ISLAND*. 'LIFE'. 2. Mother of Cain, Abel and Seth; wife of Adam. FIRST LADY. SECOND PERSON [apple; Eden; rib]. **Comp** = *Adam*.

EVELYN *DIARIST*. JOHN; *WRITER* [Pepys].

EVEN LEVEL, *SMOOTH*, UNIFORM. NOT ODD. *JUST*, QUITE, SIMPLY, STILL. EVENING. EQUABLE, UNRUFFLED. BALANCED, EQUAL. **Pl** = EQUAL STAKES [odds]. *IRONS*, SMOOTHS (crypt).

EVENING *PM*. IRONING, SMOOTHING (crypt).

EVENING STAR *VENUS/HESPERUS* (Gk/Rom); **opp** = *Lucifer* (Venus)/*Phosphorus*.

EVER ALWAYS, EER. STILL. **Comp** = *anon*; *day*.

EVERGREEN BAY, CEDAR, FIR, LAUREL etc.

EVERLASTING ENDLESS, ETERNAL, NEVERENDING.

EVERMORE ALWAYS. NEVERTHELESS (crypt).

EWE (s/l you, *U*). *SHEEP* (*fem*). *ISLAND*.

EWER CROCK, JUG, PITCHER, POT, URN, *VESSEL*. SHEPHERD (crypt).

EX (s/l X). *DEAD*, LATE, FORMER. OUT OF, *OUTSIDE*, WITHOUT.

Ex No longer extant.

EXALTATION 1. ELATION, *ENCHANTMENT*, RAPTURE, REJOICING. 2. *Assembly* (larks).

EXAM GREATS (O), LITTLE-GO (C); ORAL, VIVA VOCE, WRITTEN TEST [sit]. REGARD.

EXCELLENT AI, FIRST CLASS, *NOBLE*, PREEMINENT, VERY GOOD.

EXCEPT *BUT*, NOT INCLUDING; UNLESS. EXCLUDE, LEAVE OUT.

EXCERPT 1. EXTRACT, QUOTE. 2. Hidden word, e.g. **An excerpt from Milton's 'Il Penseroso' is throaty stuff** (6) = TONS*IL.

EXCHANGE *Anag.* CHANGE, INTERCHANGE, SWAP, SWOP, SWITCH. CURRENCY, MONEY CHANGING. BOURSE (Fr), COUNTING HOUSE; COMMERCIAL TRANSACTIONS. PBX, SWITCHBOARD, TELEPHONE CENTRE.

EXCLUSIVENESS 1. HIGH-CLASS. SELECTIVITY. 2. Delete 'ness' from clue, e.g. **Exclusiveness makes the prince's address exalted** (4) = HIGH(ness).

EXECUTE CARRY OUT, *DO*, PERFORM. VALIDATE. ASSASSINATE, BEHEAD, DECAPITATE, DISPATCH, EXTERMINATE, FINISH, GAS, GUILLOTINE, *HANG*, KILL, MURDER, PUT TO DEATH, SHOOT, SLAUGHTER, SLAY, WASTE, *TOP*.

EXERCISE PE, PT; DRILL, EXERTION, TRAINING (gym). PERPLEX, WORRY. DISCHARGE (duty). EMPLOYMENT, PRACTICE. TASK. COMPOSITION. MANOEUVRE (mil).

EXETER 1. ISCA DUMNUNIORUM (*Roman town*). *UNIVERSITY*; *UNIVERSITY COLLEGE*. 2. **Episcopal sig** = EXON.

EXHAUST FATIGUE, TIRE; BEGGAR, FINISH. OUTLET, PORT (tech).

EXHORT *URGE*.

EXIST AM, ARE, BE.

EXIT 1. DEPARTURE, DEATH. WAY OUT. 2. Stage direction to leave the scene; '~, pursued by a bear' (W Tale, *Shak*).

EXON *Episcopal sig* of EXETER.

EXPEL 1. CAST AWAY/OUT, EJECT, TURN OUT. 2. Remove letter(s) indicated, e.g. **I am expelled from Sofia for a rest** (4) = SOF*A.

EXPERIENCED ACQUAINTED; FELT, UNDERWENT. SKILLED, TRIED (opp = *green*, tyro).

EXPERT *ACE*, DAB (HAND), PRO(FESSIONAL) (opp = *learner*). ABLE, CAPABLE. (opp = *fool*).

EXPLORER EXAMINER, INVESTIGATOR. *SPACECRAFT*, *SPACE TRAVELLER*. *DISCOVERER*, TRAVELLER; **celebrated**: AMUNDSEN ('Gjoa', 'Maud'), BYRD (North Pole), CABOT ('Mathew'), COLUMBUS ('Nina', 'Pinta', 'Santa Maria'),

COOK ('Discovery', 'Endeavour', 'Resolution'), DARWIN ('Beagle'), DRAKE ('Pelican', 'Golden Hind'), FROBISHER ('Gabriel'), HILARY (Everest), HUNT (Everest, South Pole), *MAGELLAN* ('Trinidad', 'Vittoria'), NANSEN ('Fram'), SCOTT ('Discovery', 'Terra Nova'), SHACKLETON ('Endurance'), VASCO DA GAMA (Cathay), ZHENG HE (Ch).

EXPLOSION *Anag.* BURST, OUTBREAK. BANG, LOUD NOISE.

EXPRESS FORMULATE, SAY, STATE. EXPEDITE, FAST, SPEEDY. NEWSPAPER®. TRAIN (rly).

EXTRA ODD, OVER, SPARE, SUPERNUMERARY; EXCESS; FURTHER. GRACE NOTE (mus). BIT PLAYER, CROWD (film). PS. BYE, LEG BYE, NO BALL, RUN, WIDE (cricket).

EXTRACTOR DRAWER, PULLER. FAN, VENTILATOR. COPIER (crypt). DENTIST (crypt).

EXTRA LARGE OS, OUTSIZE, X.

EXTREME 1. FARTHEST, FURTHEST, OUTERMOST, UTTERMOST. SEVERE, STRINGENT. 2. **Pl** = use letters/words at each end, e.g. **Extremes of valour** = VR.

EXTREMELY 1. HIGHLY; SEVERELY, VERY, UNCO (Sc). 2. Use letters/words at each end, e.g. **Extremely kind** = KD.

EYE (s/l Aye, I). EXAMINE, INSPECT, LOOK, REGARD. SIGHT. OPTIC; **parts**: *ball*, cornea, *iris*, lens, orbit, *pupil*, retina, rods, sclerotic, white; **disorders**: astigmatism, blindness, cast, cataract, conjunctivitis, glaucoma, iritis, myopia, myosin, myosis, myotic, nystagmus, squint, stye, tunnel vision.

EYESORE FRIGHT, HIDEOSITY, UGLY, OBJECT. *EYE DISORDER* (crypt).

F FAHRENHEIT. *FELLOW*. *FEMININE*. FLUORINE (*chem*). FOLIO, PAGE. FORTE. FRANCE (*car plate*). FRENCH. FRIDAY. *KEY*; *NOTE*. LOUD.

FA NOTE (mus; also FAH). FANNY ADAMS, NOTHING (sl). FOOTBALL ASSOCIATION.

FABRIC *MATERIAL* (felt, knit or weave). TEXTURE, TISSUE. BUILDING, EDIFICE, FRAME, STRUCTURE.

FACE CLOCK, DIAL, *MUG*, *PAN*, VISAGE [Monday's *child*]. CONFRONT, OPPOSE; LOOK TOWARDS. *OBVERSE* (**opp** = *reverse*). *TYPEFACE*.

FACTOR AGENT. ELEMENT.

FACTORY MILL, *PLANT*, WORKS.

FACULTY APTITUDE, COMPETENCE, e.g. HEARING,
MEMORY, REASONING, SIGHT and esp the Four ~s: ARTS,
LAW, SCIENCE, THEOLOGY. AUTHORIZATION,
LICENCE. SCHOLASTIC DEPARTMENT; TEACHING
STAFF.

FAHRENHEIT F.

FAIL BREAK. FLUNK, PIP, PLOUGH, PLOW (US).

FAIR (s/l *fare*). EVEN HANDED, UNBIASED. BLOND(E).
ISLAND. *STRAWBERRY, WIDDICOMBE*. BEAUTIFUL
[Monday's *child*].

FAIRY HOMO, QUEER; CAMP, GAY. (HOB)GOBLIN, IMP,
SPRITE; **celebrated**: TITANIA (queen), OBERON (king),
COBWEB, MOTH, MUSTARDSEED, PEASBLOSSOM, and
PUCK/ROBIN GOODFELLOW (all MND), ARIEL (Tempest),
TINKERBELL (Peter Pan), TRIPSITINKA (Queen, *Lofting*).
[*Barrie*, Grimm; Iolanthe (*G & S*). MND (*Shak*)].

FALL CROPPER, *DECLINE*, DESCEND, DROP, SLIP.
WATERFALL (q.v.). RAIN. ROPE (naut). AUTUMN,
SEASON (US). *Assembly* (woodcock).

~ **OUT** HAPPEN. DISAGREE. NUCLEAR DEBRIS/DUST;
SIDE-EFFECTS. DISMISS, LEAVE RANKS (mil).

FALSE *Anag*. ARTIFICIAL, COUNTERFEIT, DECEITFUL,
DUMMY, FICTITIOUS, FRAUDULENT, ILLEGAL,
PHON(E)Y, SHAM, SPURIOUS, WRONG (**opp** = correct).
UNFAITHFUL (**opp** = *true*).

~ **REPORT** CANARD, HOAX, LIE. PORTER, PERROT etc
(anag, crypt).

FAMILIAR COMMON, CURRENT, FRIENDLY, INTIMATE,
USUAL, WELL-KNOWN. CASUAL, INFORMAL,
UNCEREMONIOUS. *CAT*, DEMON, *SPIRIT* (*witch*).
SECRETARY, SERVANT (of pope, RC *bishop*).

FAMILY CHILDREN, DESCENDANTS, HOUSE, KIN, KITH,
LINEAGE. COMMON STOCK, GENUS, RACE.

FAMOUS FIVE ANNE, DICK, GEORGE, JULIAN, TIMMY (dog)
[Enid Blyton]. JOHNNIE BULL, BOB CHERRY, FRANK
NUGENT, RAM JAM SINGH, HARRY WHARTON [*Bunter*,
Greyfriars] (Frank Richards).

FAN WAFT, WINNOW; *COOLER*; (Lady Windermere's ~,
Wilde). PROPELLER (av), SCREW (naut). *SAIL* (windmill).

SPREAD OUT. ADMIRER, ENTHUSIAST, FOLLOWER, SUPPORTER.

FANG 1. *TOOTH* (dog, snake, wolf). PRONG. 2. Character in *Dickens* and *Shak*.

FANNY ADAMS FA, NOTHING (murder victim). CANNED MEAT (naut).

FARE (s/l *fair*). *FOOD. PASSAGE* MONEY. *GO*, JOURNEY, TRAVEL. HAPPEN, TURN OUT.

FAREWELL ALOHA, AVE, BYE BYE, GOODBYE, TA-TA, VALE (**opp** = *greeting*).

FARM HOLDING, RANCH; CULTIVATE, TILL [*husbandry*]. HIRE OUT, SPREAD.

FARO (s/l *pharaoh*). *CARD GAME*.

FAR SIDE 1. BEYOND. 2. Second part of word, e.g. **Far side of the Moon** = ON.

FASHION MODE, TON, HAUTE COUTURE. CONSTRUCT, MAKE, *SHAPE*.

FASHIONABLE A LA MODE, CHIC, *IN*, IN THE SWIM, MODISH, NEAT, SMART, UNSQUARE. MALLEABLE, WORKABLE.

FAST *FLEET*, QUICK, SPEEDY; **comp** = furious; loose. ABSTAIN, *LENT*; RAMADAN (Mos). *FIRM, SET. CASTLE.*

FATE 1. DESERTS, DESTINY, LOT; KISMET. PREORDAIN. 2. **Pl** = *GODS*, WEIRD SISTERS. Three *goddesses* of DESTINY: **Gk** = MORAI: CLOTHO (thread of life), LACHESIS (quality and length), ATROPOS (severance); **Rom** = PARCAE; **Nor** = NORN.

FATHEAD CLOT, DUNCE, FOOL. F (crypt).

FATHER (s/l farther). ABBOT, *CHURCHMAN*, FR, *FRIAR*. DAD, GENERATOR, GOVERNOR, GUVNOR, OLD MAN, PA, PATER (FAMILIAS), POP; PROCREATE, SIRE, SPAWN (~'s **delight** = *Abigail*). [~ Brown, *Chesterton*; Old ~ William (*Alice*); Old ~ Thames; ~ Time].

FATHERLAND *COUNTRY. GERMANY.*

FATHERLESS 1. ORPHAN. *Nyx* (q.v.) had several children without benefit of husband. 2. Remove DAD, PA, POP from clue-word (crypt), e.g. ~ **patron saint shows success as a bridger** (5) = (pa)TRICK.

FAUN (s/l *fawn*). Rom eq of Gk *SATYR*.

FAUNUS Rom *god* of *herds*; s of Picus. Also INUUS, LUPERCUS. **Gk** = *PAN*.

FAVONIUS Rom myth WEST *WIND* (**Gk** = ZEPHYRUS).

FAVOUR BOON, *GRACE*, KINDNESS; **comp** = *fear*; *grace*. PREFER. BUTTONHOLE, ROSETTE.

FAVOURITE PET, PREFERRED (**opp** = bête noire). MISTRESS.

FAWN (s/l *faun*). CRINGE, GROVEL; LICK-SPITTLE, TOADY, SYCOPHANT. *COLOUR* (PALE BROWN). *OFFSPRING* (DEER).

FBI *DETECTIVES*, FEDS, G-MEN.

FDR ROOSEVELT. WEST GERMANY.

FE *IRON* (*chem*). *SMITH* (Lord Birkenhead).

FEAR ALARM, APPREHENSION, *AVERSION*, DREAD, FRIGHT, PANIC, PHOBIA, SHRINK, TERROR. COWARDICE, FRIGHT, FUNK [yellow]. **Comp** = *favour*.

FEATHER 1. DOWN, PLUME, QUILL. 2. *Anniversary* (3rd).

FEATURE PORTRAY, *STAR*. LANDMARK. CHIN, EAR, EYE, MOUTH, NOSE etc.

FEBRUARY (2nd) MONTH, M, FEB (Lat februar = purification feast). **Birthstone** = *Amethyst*.

FED UP GORGED, SATED. BORED, BROWNED OFF, TIRED (**opp** = *enchanted*). DEF (dn; crypt).

FEET 1. Pl of *FOOT*; *MEASURE*. 2. Metric rhythm or scanning of verse; see *FOOT*.

FELL COLLAPSED, TRIPPED. AXE, CUT DOWN. HIDE, *SKIN*. *HILL*, MOUNTAIN. FIERCE, RUTHLESS ['this ~ sergeant, *death*' (Hamlet)].

FELLOW F. CHAP, COVE, DON, GENT, GUY, HE, MAN. CO-, PEER.

~ TRAVELLER COMMIE, RED. BACK-SEAT DRIVER, CREW MEMBER, OBSERVER (av), NAVIGATOR (av), PILLION PASSENGER.

FEMALE fem; FEMININE, (CHILD)BEARER. GIRL, WOMAN. For animal genders, see *Male and Female*.

FEMININE F. FEMALE, WOMANLY.

FENCE BANK, BULWARK, ENCLOSE, FORTIFY, HEDGE, PALISADE, PROTECT, RAILING, SCREEN, SHIELD, WALL. GAUGE, GUARD, GUIDE (mech). RECEIVER [*robber*]. PARRY, WORD PLAY. SWORDPLAY [lunge, parry, riposte; prime, seconde, tierce, quart, quinte, sixte, septime, octave].

FENCER DUELLIST, SWORDSMAN. STEEPLECHASER (crypt). BOUNDARY LAYER, FRONTIERSMAN (crypt).

FERRET SCOUT-CAR (mil). HUNT, SEARCH (hence
DETECTIVE). *WEASEL* (**fem** = gill).
FERRY CONVEY, CROSS, TRANSPORT. TENDER,
WORKBOAT. [*Acheron, Anubis, Charon, Lethe, Styx*].
FERTILITY 1. ABUNDANCE, FECUNDITY, FRUITFULNESS.
2. **Gods: Gk** = *DIONYSUS*, HYMEN; **Rom** = *BACCHUS*,
GENIUS, LIBER; **Egy** = OSIRIS; **Ind** = KRISHNA; **Nor** =
FREY. **Goddesses: Gk** = CYBELE, *DANAE*, RHEA; **Rom** =
CERES, DIANA, OPS; Other = FRIGG (**Nor**); BELIT, INNIN,
ISHTAR (**Bab**); ATERGATIS (**Syrian**); EOSTRE (**A-Sax**; easter).
FF FOLIOS, PAGES. FORTISSIMO, VERY LOUD.
FIDDLE BOW, PLAY, SCRAPE, VIOLIN. FIDGET.
ARRANGE, *CHEAT*, COOK, FIX, MANIPULATE.
FIDO *DOG*. Acronym (Fog Investigation Dispersal Operation, av).
FIELDING CAMPAIGNING. GRAZING, PLOUGHING (crypt).
WRITER. AREA, PANORAMA, SPHERE. BOWLING, NOT
IN (*cricket*). [Bow Street *Policeman*].
FIELDSMAN CATCHER, *CRICKETER*; OUTSIDER (crypt).
[MCC]. FARMER, *SHEPHERD* (crypt). GATHERER.
SCARECROW (crypt).
FIFTEEN See *number*. XV, SIDE, TEAM [rugby].
FIFTH 1. AMENDMENT. *DRINK, MEASURE*. VTH. G (mus).
2. Beethoven's ~ = H (crypt).
~ **MAN** GUY FAWKES (crypt) [Robert Catesby, Thomas Percy,
Gunpowder Plot].
FIFTY See *number*. L. HALF TON.
FIGHT *BATTLE*, COMBAT, DING DONG, QUARREL, SCRAP,
SCRIMMAGE, SET-TO, WAR.
FIGHTER COMBATANT, WARRIOR. *AIRCRAFT*; *WEAPON*.
BOXER, PUGILIST.
FIGURE THINK, WORK OUT. INTEGER. CONE, TRIANGLE
etc. APPEAR, FEATURE. *FORM*, LINE, *SHAPE* [vital
statistics]. PERSON. DIAGRAM, DRAWING,
ILLUSTRATION; IMAGE LIKENESS, REPRESENTATION.
EMBLEM, SIMILE, TYPE.
FILLING REPLENISHMENT, TOP-UP. APPLE, FRUIT, JAM,
MINCE, PUREE etc (cook). STOPPING (dental).
SATISFYING. OCCUPYING.
FILM COATING, *LAYER*, MEMBRANE, PLATE, SKIN.
MOVIE; *SHOOT*. CASSETTE, REEL (photo). **Pl** = CINEMA,
FLICKS.

FILM CATEGORY A, AA, G (US), H, PG, R, U, X [*censorship*].
~ **PART** REEL. ROLE, STAR. FI, FIL, ILM etc (crypt).
~ **STUDIO** Room or premises of film company; by association,
name of such a company; **celeb**: Allied Artists, Br Lion, Cannon,
Columbia, Ealing, Epic (Ind), Fox, Gainsborough, Gaumont,
Mancunian, Merton Park, MGM, Monogram, Nettlefold,
Paramount, Pathe, PRC, Rank, Republic, RKO, Twentieth
Century, United Artists, Universal, Walt Disney, Warner.
FINN FINLAND. ~ MacCool (f of Ossian, Ire legend); Huckleberry
~ (*Twain*).
FINAL 1. *LAST*, ULTIMATE, Z, OMEGA. CONCLUSIVE,
DEFINITE. LATEST EDITION/NEWS. **Pl** = LAST EXAMS,
DECIDER (games). 2. Use last letter of word indicated, e.g. **Final
destination** = N; **Your final . . .** = R. 3. AFL (crypt: F*in*AL).
FINALE 1. CONCLUSION, *END*, ENDING. 2. Add letter E at
end of word indicated, e.g. **Artist finale** (7) = ARTISTE.
3. AFLE/ALFE (crypt: F*in*ALE).
FINCH BIRD (**assembly** = *charm*).
FINISH (s/l Finnish). 1. CEASE, COMPLETE, *END* (**opp** = *start*).
ANNIHILATE, DESTROY, DISPATCH, KILL, OVERCOME.
PERFECT; POLISH, SHEEN. 2. Last letter(s) of word, e.g.
Quick finish = K.
FIRE 1. BLAZE, BRAND, FLAME, INFERNO, SPARK. *LIGHT*
[*St Elmo's* ~]; **comp** = brimstone, *water*. BOOT, *DISCHARGE*,
DISMISS, SACK. SHOOT. BAKE, GLAZE. 2. **Gods: Gk** =
HEPHAESTUS; **Rom** = VULCAN; **Nor** = *LOKI*; **Jew** =
MOLOCH.
FIREMAN ARSONIST, BLAZER. EXTINGUISHER. GUNNER,
MARKSMAN, RA, SNIPER [*patron saint*]. FOOTPLATE-MAN
(**Union** = ASLEF, NUR).
FIRE-RAISER ARSONIST. MATCH. ERIF (dn; crypt).
FIREWORK *BANGER*, ROCKET, SQUIB, WHIZZBANG; **Pl** =
ROW, RUCTION. CHARCOAL BURNING (crypt).
GUNNERY (crypt).
FIRM COMPACT, FIXED, RIGID, *SET*, SOLID, *SOUND*,
STABLE, *STAUNCH*, STEADY. BUSINESS, CO, LTD, PLC,
WORKS. SIGNATURE, STYLE. CONSTANT, RESOLUTE,
STEADFAST, UNFLINCHING. 'CONSTANTINE'.
FIRST 1. A, I, IST, NO I. ALPHA, BEFORE(HAND).
EARLIEST, FOREMOST, FORMER (of two), LEADING,
PRIME, PRIMUS, TOP, WINNER. GOLD MEDALLIST.

2. Use first letters of word(s) indicated, e.g. **First-aid man** = AM;
First of all prehensiles everywhere (3) = APE. 3. Put letter or word
in front, e.g. **Try at first to give evidence** (6) = AT*TEST.

FIRST BORN B. CAIN. ELDEST [Herod].

~ **CLASS** C. AI. KINDERGARTEN, NURSERY SCHOOL
(crypt).

~ **FALLER** F. *ADAM*.

~ **ISSUE** I. CAIN. ELDEST.

~ **LADY** L. EVE. PRESIDENT'S WIFE (US). *PANDORA*.

~ **OFFENDER** EVE.

~ **OF MONTH** M. J, JAN, JANI; F, FEB, FEBI etc.

~ **PERSON** P. *ADAM*. I, WE.

FISH 1. LOOK FOR (compliment). JOIN/MEND A SPAR (naut).
2. ANGLE, CATCH; TRAWL, TROLL. COLD-BLOODED
MARINE ANIMAL; BOMBAY DUCK; **assembly** = school,
shoal; **offspring** = fry; **types**:

2-letters	BRET	LUMP
ID	BRIT	OPAH
	BURT	(ORCA)
3-letters	BUTT	ORFE
BIB	*CARP*	PARR
COD	CHAD	*PIKE*
DAB	CHAR	*POUT*
DAR	CHUB	RUDD
DOG	CLAM	*RUFF*
EEL	CUSK	SCUP
EFY	DACE	*SEER*
GAR	DORY	SHAD
GED	ESOX	*SOLE*
IDE	FAAP	TOPE
(ORC)	GEDD	TUNA
RAY	GOBY	TUSK
TAI	HAKE	
	HUSS	**5-letters**
4-letters	KELT	ABLEN
AMIA	KETA	ABLET
BASS	LING	ALLIS
BIRT	LIPP	ALOSE
BLAY	LOMP	*ANGEL*
BLEY	LUCE	ASKER

BANNY	QUARL	BELUGA
BASSE	ROACH	BLENNY
BERYX	ROKER	BONITO
BINNY	SARDA	BOUNCE
BLEAK	SAURY	BOWFIN
BLECK	SCROD	BRAIZE
BONGO	SEPIA	BRASSE
(BOOPS)	SEWEN	BUCKIE
BREAM	SEWIN	BURBOT
BRILL	*SHARK* (q.v.)	CAPLIN
CAPON	*SKATE*	CARANX
CHARR	SKEET	CARVEL
CISCO	*SMELT*	CEPOLA
CNIDA	SMOLT	CLIONE
COLEY	SMOUT	CLUPEA
DANIO	SNOEK	COCKLE
DOREE	SNOOK	CONGER
DORSE	SOLEN	CUTTLE
ELOPS	SPRAG	CYPRIS
ELVER	SPRAT	DENTEX
FLECK	SPROD	DERBIO
GIBEL	SQUID	DIODON
GUPPY	SUDAK	DIPNOI
JULIS	SWORD	DOCTOR
KNOUD	TENCH	DORADO
LOACH	TOGUE	(DUGONG)
LOCHE	TORSK	ELLECK
LOGGE	TROUT	FINNAN
LYTHE	TUNNY	FINNER
MANTA	TWAIT	FINNOC
MARAY	UMBRE	FLYING ~
MORAY	(*WHALE*)	GARDON
MUGIL		GERVIE
MURAY	**6-letters**	GILPIN
MURRY	ACEDIA	GORAMY
MYXON	ALEVIN	GRILSE
POGGE	ALLICE	GUNNEL
PERCH	ANABAS	GURNET
PORGY	BAGGIT	HALION
PRAWN	BARBEL	HAUTIN
PRILL	BELONE	HILSAH

INKBAG
INKSAC
IVIGAR
KIPPER
LAITHE
LAUNCE
LIMPET
LOLIGO
– LOUVAR
MAHSIR
MARGOT
MATIES
MEAKER
MEDUSA
MENNAD
MILTER
MINNOW
MORGAY
MULLET
MUSSEL
MYXINE
(NARWAL)
NERITE
OSTREA
OYSTER
PARTAN
PECTEN
PETREL
PHINOC
PHOLAS
PLAICE
PLAISE
POLLAN
PORGIE
POULPE
PUFFER
RED-EYE
REMORA
RIGGLE
ROBALO
ROCCUS

ROCHET
ROMERO
RUFFIN
SABALO
SADINA
SAITHE
SALMON
SALTIE
SAMLET
SARDEL
SARGUS
SARSIA
SAUGER
SAUREL
SAURUS
SAYSAY
SCARUS
SEA-BAT
SEA-BUN
SEA-CAT
SEA-COW
SEA-DOG
SEA-EEL
SEA-EGG
SEA-FOX
SEA-HOG
SEA-ORB
SEA-OWL
SEA-PAD
SEA-PIG
SEA-RAT
SEPHEN
SHANNY
SHIPOV
SHRIMP
SILURE
SNACOT
SOOSOO
SUCKER
TAMBOR
TARPON

TARPUM
TAUTOG
TINKER
TITLER
TOMCOD
TOMPOT
TRITON
TRYGON
TURBOT
(TURTLE)
TWAITE
URCHIN
(WALRUS)
WAPPER
WEEVER
WINKLE
WRASSE
ZANDER
ZINGLE

7-letters
ACALEPH
ACTINIA
ALE-WIFE
ANCHOVY
ANEMONE
ANODONT
ASCIDIA
ASTERID
BARNAGH
BERGYLT
BIVALVE
BLOATER
BOCKING
BONETTA
BRASSIE
BRIABOT
CALAMAR
CAPELIN
CATFISH
(CETACEA)

CICHLID	*MEDUSA*	SAWFISH
CIDARIS	MERLING	SCALLOP
CODFISH	MOLLUSC	SCHELLY
CODLING	MONODON	SCOLLOP
CROAKER	MOONEYE	SCOMBER
CROWGER	MORRHUA	SEA-BASS
CRUCIAN	MUDFISH	SEA-COCK
CRUSIAN	(NARWHAL)	SEA-DACE
(DOLPHIN)	NAUTILI	SEA-FISH
ECHINUS	OARFISH	SEA-LILY
ETHERIA	OCTOPUS	SEA-LUCE
FINBACK	OPHIURA	SEA-MINK
FINFISH	PATELLA	SEA-PERT
FINNACK	*PEGASUS*	SEA-PIKE
FINNOCK	PELAMID	SEA-ROSE
GARFISH	PENFISH	SEA-RUFF
GARPIKE	PETEREL	SEA-SLUG
GARVOCK	PIDDOCK	SEA-WIFE
GIRROCK	PILTOCK	SEA-WOLF
GLADIUS	PINCHER	SELACHE
GALUCUS	PIN-FISH	SERIOLA
GOSNICK	POLLACK	SEVRUGA
GOURAMI	POLLOCK	SHADINE
GOURNET	POLYPUS	SHALLOW
(GRAMPUS)	POLYZOA	SILLAGO
GRUNDEL	POMFRET	SILURUS
GRUNTER	QUAHAUG	*SKIPPER*
GUDGEON	QUINNAT	SKULPIN
GURNARD	RED-BASS	SNAPPER
GWINIAD	RED-DRUM	SNEDDEN
HADDOCK	RED-FISH	SOCKEYE
HAGFISH	RHYTINA	SPUR-DOG
HALIBUT	RIPSACK	STERLET
HERLING	RONCHIL	SUNFISH
HERRING	RONQUIL	TORPEDO
KEELING	(RORQUAL)	TREPANG
LAMPERN	ROTCHET	TRIGGER ~
LAMPREY	SAND-DAB	TUBFISH
LOBSTER	SAND-EEL	VENDACE
MAHSEER	SARDINE	VESTLET
(MANATEE)	SARGINA	WHIP-RAY

WHITING
XIPHIAS
ZIPHIAS
ZYGAENA

8-letters
ACALEPHA
ACEPHALA
ALBACORE
BILLFISH
BLUEFISH
BOARFISH
BRISLING
BUMMALOE
(CACHALOT)
(CETACEAN)
COALFISH
CRAYFISH
DRAGONET
EAR-SHELL
ESCALLOP
(FIN-WHALE)
FLATFISH
FLOUNDER
FORKTAIL
FROGFISH
GILT-HEAD
GOLDFISH
GRAYLING
(HUMPBACK)
LUMPFISH
LUNGFISH
MACKEREL
MONKFISH
NAUTILUS
PICKEREL
PILCHARD
(PORPOISE)

ROCKFISH
SAIL-FISH
SALMONET
SANDFISH
SEA-ADDER
SEA-BREAM
SEA-DEVIL
SEA-PERCH
SEA-ROBIN
SEA-SHARK
SEA-SNAIL
SEA-SQUID
SEA-TENCH
SEA-TROUT
SOLASTER
SPARLING
STARFISH
STINGRAY
STURGEON
THRASHER
UNIVALVE
ZOANTHUS

9+ letters
AMBERJACK
ANGELFISH
ANGELSHARK
ANGLERFISH
ARCHERFISH
BALLOON FISH
BARRACUDA
BARRAMUNDI
BASKING SHARK
BLACKFISH
BLUE SHARK
BROWN TROUT
BULLTROUT
BUTTERFISH

CANDLEFISH
CARPSUCKER
COELACANTH
CONGER EEL
CUTTLEFISH
DEMOISELLE
DEVILFISH
DOLLY VARDEN
DRAGONFISH
FINGERLING
FLYING-FISH
GLOBE FISH
GUITAR FISH
HAMMERHEAD
HIPPOCAMPUS
JELLYFISH
NEEDLEFISH
PADDLEFISH
PARROTFISH
PERIWINKLE
PILOT FISH
PORBEAGLE
RAINBOW TROUT
SANDHOPPER
SPEARFISH
SPOONBILL
STARGAZER
STICKLEBACK
STOCKFISH
STONEFISH
SUCKERFISH
SWORDFISH
THRESHER *SHARK*
TIGER *SHARK*
TRIGGER FISH
WHITEFISH
WOBBEGONG
ZEBRA SHARK

3. *Constellation* (Pisces); (12th) sign of *Zodiac*.
FISHERMAN ANCHOR. BEND, *KNOT*. BOAT. EVANGELIST

(fig, Matt iv, 19). ANGLER, CATCHER, TRAWLER(MAN), TROLLER; BANKER (crypt); **celeb**: ANDREW; PETER, Simon; JAMES (s of Zebedee); JOHN; all *apostles* of *Jesus*; Isaak WALTON (The Compleat Angler). GANNET, KINGFISHER (birds).

FIT HALE, IN FORM, *SOUND*, *WELL*. SEIZURE, SPASM. CORRESPOND, FILL UP, MATCH, RIGHT SIZE. ADAPT, COMPETENT, PROPER, RIGHT, SUITED. EQUIP, MEASURE, TRY ON (clothes).

FIVE 1. See *number*. PENTAD, V. BLUE BALL (snooker). *FAMOUS* ~. [*Holmes case*]. 2. *Symbols* at your *door* (*song*); gold *rings* (*Christmas* song). **Pl** = GAME.

~ CLASSIC ORDERS COMPOSITE, CORINTHIAN, DORIC, IONIC, TUSCAN.

500 See *number*. D.

£500 DL, LD, MONKEY.

FIVE TOWNS BURSLEM, FENTON, HANLEY, LONGTON, STOKE (potteries).

FIX DILEMMA, QUANDARY. ARRANGE, *FIDDLE*, JOIN. BOLT, FASTEN, *NAIL*, *SCREW*, SECURE. *DRUG*, INJECTION, SHOT. ESTABLISH POSITION (naut); DETERMINE, SPECIFY.

FLAG BUNTING, ENSIGN, FLIER, PENNANT, STANDARD. PIN. *IRIS*, PLANT. DROOP, FADE, FAIL, FALTER. (PAVING) STONE. QUILL FEATHER.

FLAK AA. CRITICISM.

FLAPPER YOUNG THING. FIN, FLIPPER. BIRD. PANICKER.

FLAT APARTMENT, PENTHOUSE. EVEN, LEVEL, SMOOTH. RUN DOWN, UNCHARGED (elect). PUNCTURE (US).

FLATTER BUTTER UP, FAWN, PRAISE. BECOME, SUIT. MORE EVEN, SMOOTHER, IRONER, LAUNDRYMAID (crypt).

FLEET *FAST*, QUICK, RAPID. RN, SHIPS, USN, TASK FORCE. *GAOL*. *ISLAND*, *RIVER*. [~ Street].

FLIER *FLAG*. AVIATOR, PILOT. *BIRD*. *DAEDALUS*, *ICARUS*.

FLIGHT 1. STAIRS, *STEPS*. ARROW. ESCAPE, EVASION. FLYING, TRAJECTORY. FLOCK. VOLLEY. 2. *Assembly* (*ducks*).

FLOCK 1. WOOL, TUFT. CONGREGATION, *FOLD*. TROOP.
2. *Assembly* (*geese, sheep*).

FLORA 1. *FLOWERS*, *PLANTS* [fauna]. ~ MACDONALD
[Bonnie Prince Charlie]. 2. Rom *goddess* of *FLOWERS* (**Gk** =
CHLORIS). 3. A minor *PLANET*.

FLORENCE *NIGHTINGALE*. FIRENZE (old *capital* city of Italy
in Tuscany).

FLOUNDERING *Anag.* WALLOWING. FISHING (crypt).

FLOW CIRCULATE, GLIDE, MOVE(MENT) [fluent, smoothly].
GUSH, *RUN*, SPRING, WELL UP. STREAM. RISE (tide);
comp = *ebb*. UNDULATE (dress, figure). BELLY, CAMBER,
DRAFT (sails).

FLOWER 1. CHOICE, CREAM, ESSENCE, PICK. CURRENT,
RIVER (q.v.), SPRING, TIDE, WELL (all crypt). BLOOD
(crypt). ICHOR (crypt). 2. ANNUAL, *BLOOMER*,
PERENNIAL. **Pl** = BOUQUET, BUNCH, NOSEGAY,
GARLAND, LEI, SPRAY; **goddess: Gk** = CHLORIS, **Rom** =
FLORA; *anniversary* (4th). [Ikebana (*Jap*)]. **Types**:

3-letters	DAISY	BIZARD
LIS (herald)	DILLY	BOODLE
MAY	GOWAN	CALTHA
	LILAC	CAMASS
4-letters	LOTUS	CISTUS
ARUM	LUPIN	CLOVER
DISA	OX-EYE	CROCUS
FAAM	OXLIP	CYPHEL
FLAG	PANSY	DAHLIA
FLAX	PEONY	FUNKIA
IRIS	PHLOX	JASMIN
LILY	POPPY	KERRIA
MUSK	*STOCK*	KOWHAI
PINK	TULIP	MARIET
ROSE	VINCA	MIMOSA
	YUCCA	MOUTAN
5-letters	YULAN	MUGGET
ASPIC		NERINE
ASTER	6-letters	NERIUM
BRIAR	*ADONIS*	NUPHAR
BROOM	AZALEA	ORCHID
CALLA	BELLIS	ROSULA

SCILLA
SHASTA
SQUILL
TAGETE
THRIFT
VIOLET
YARROW
ZINNIA

7-letters
ACONITE
ALTHAEA
ANEMONE
BANKSIA
BEGONIA
CAMPION
COWSLIP
CUP-ROSE
DOG-ROSE
FREESIA
FUCHSIA
GLADWYN
GODETIA
HONESTY
JASMINE
JONQUIL
KINGCUP
LOBELIA
NELUMBO
NIGELLA
PETUNIA
PICOTEE
PRIMULA
RAMBLER
SERINGA
SHIRLEY
SYRINGA
TEA-ROSE
TRIPOLY
TRITOMA
VANILLA

VERBENA

8-letters
AGRIMONY
AMARANTH
ASPHODEL
AURICULA
BLUEBELL
BUDDLEIA
CAMELLIA
CLEMATIS
CYCLAMEN
DAFFODIL
DIANTHUS
DOG-BRIER
FOXGLOVE
GARDENIA
GERANIUM
GILLENIA
GIRASOLE
GLOXINIA
GOLD-LILY
HAREBELL
HAWTHORN
HIBISCUS
HOTTONIA
HYACINTH
JAPONICA
LARKSPUR
LAVENDER
LENT-LILY
MAGNOLIA
MARIGOLD
MYOSOTIS
NOISETTE
OLEANDER
PLUMBAGO
PRIMROSE
SNOWDROP
SWEET-PEA
TUBEROSE

TURNSOLE
WISTARIA
WOODBINE

9-letters
BUSY LIZZY
BUTTERCUP
CAMPANULA
CANDYTUFT
CARNATION
CINERARIA
COLUMBINE
DANDELION
EDELWEISS
EGLANTINE
FORSYTHIA
GLADIOLUS
GOLDENROD
HYDRANGEA
NARCISSUS
SPEEDWELL
SUNFLOWER

10+ letters
ANTIRRHINUM
BUSY LIZZIE
CANTERBURY BELL
CHRYSANTHEMUM
CORNFLOWER
DELPHINIUM
FORGET ME NOT
FRANGIPANI
GUERNSEY LILY
GYPSOPHILA
HONEYSUCKLE
LADY'S MANTLE
LOVE IN A MIST
MORNING GLORY
NASTURTIUM
PERIWINKLE
POINSETTIA

RED HOT POKER   SNAPDRAGON   SWEET WILLIAM
RHODODENDRON   STEPHANOTIS   WALLFLOWER

FLUORINE F (*chem*) [halogen].

FLUSH BLUSH, *COLOUR*, REDDEN. POKER HAND; SUITED
(crypt). RICH, WELL OFF. PUT UP (game bird). *Assembly*
(mallards). *DOG* (celeb).

FLUTER PHIL; INSTRUMENTALIST, WHISTLER. REBATE
PLANE.

FLY DESERT, FLEE, RUN AWAY, TURN TAIL. AVIATE,
PILOT; SCRAMBLE (code word). *INSECT*. AWARE,
KNOWING. *BOAT*. BUTTON. *CARRIAGE*. *RIVER*.

FLYING BOMB BUZZBOMB, DOODLEBUG, DIVER (code
name), *ROCKET*, VI.

FLYING FORTRESS *AIRCRAFT* (bomber), B17, BXVII,
BOEING: CASTLE IN THE AIR (crypt).

FO FOLIO. FOREIGN OFFICE. BACK OF (crypt, e.g. **Back of
Whitehall** = FO).

FOC ADMIRAL, FLAG OFFICER COMMANDING.

FOG BRUME, FRET, HAZE, MIST [FIDO]. CLOUD (photo).
BEWILDER, OBFUSCATE, PERPLEX. AFTERMATH,
LONG WINTER *GRASS*.

FOLD (s/l foaled). ENCLOSE, *PEN*, POUND. CHURCH,
CONGREGATION, *FLOCK*. BEND, *CONCERTINA*,
DOUBLE. CLASP, EMBRACE, ENVELOP, *WIND*.

FOLLOWER 1. *DISCIPLE*, FAN, SUPPORTER; ADHERENT.
2. Next letter in alphabet, e.g. **A follower** = B; **Paul's last
follower** = M.

FOOD BOARD, COMMONS, EDIBLES, FARE, GRUB, KEEP,
MEALS, MESS, NOURISHMENT, NUTRIMENT,
PROVISIONS, RATIONS, SCOFF, *TABLE*, VICTUALS.
Comp = *drink*.

FOOL ASS, BUFFOON, CLOT, DUPE, GOOSE, IDIOT,
JUGGINS, TWIT (**saying**; opp = *expert*). CLOWN, *JESTER*.
0 (*tarot*). DECEIVE. PLAY, TINKER. FRUIT CRUSH,
PUDDING, SWEET. TRINCULO (Tempest; *Shak*).

FOOT 1. DISTANCE, *MEASURE*, 12 INCHES. *DANCE*, PACE,
STEP, TREAD. *BASE*, BOTTOM, PEDESTAL, ROOT.
LIMB, MEMBER (*bone*). LEGEND (crypt). SUPPORT,
UNDERSTANDING (crypt). 2. Stress on syllable in metre of a
verse: AMPHIBRACH (·—·), ANAPEST (··—), CHORIAMB

(—·—), DACTYL (—··), IAMBUS (·—), MOLUSSUS
(— — —), PYRRHIC (··), SPONDEE (— —), TRIBRACH (···),
TROCHEE (—·).

FOOTBALL BALL GAME; AMERICAN ~, ASSOCIATION ~,
RUGBY ~, RUGGER, SOCCER [FA, FIFA, UEFA, World Cup
(Rimet Trophy); League, Rugby ~]. **Celeb teams (US):**

Home	Name
Atlanta	FALCONS
Baltimore	*COLTS*
Buffalo	*BILLS*
Chicago	*BEARS*
Cincinnati	BENGALS
Cleveland	*BROWNS*
Dallas	*COWBOYS*
Denver	BRONCOS
Detroit	*LIONS*
Green Bay	PACKERS
Houston	*OILERS*
Kansas City	CHIEFS
Los Angeles	RAIDERS
Los Angeles	*RAMS*
Miami	DOLPHINS
Minnesota	VIKINGS
New England	PATRIOTS
New Orleans	*SAINTS*
New York	GIANTS
New York	JETS
Philadelphia	*EAGLES*
Pittsburgh	STEELERS
St Louis	CARDINALS
San Diego	CHARGERS
San Francisco	49-ERS
Seattle	SEAHAWKS
Washington	*REDSKINS*

competition: Superbowl; **venue:** Rose Bowl

Celebrated teams (UK):

Team	Nickname	Ground
Aberdeen	*Dons*	Pittodrie Park
Arsenal	*Gunners*	Highbury

Bournemouth	Cherries	Dean Court
Brighton	Seagulls	Goldstone
Bristol City	*Robins*	Ashton Gate
Cardiff City	Bluebirds	Ninian Park
Chelsea	*Pensioners*	Stamford Bridge
Coventry City	Sky Blues	Highfield Park
Crystal Palace	Glaziers	Selhurst Park
Derby County	*Rams*	Baseball Ground
England		Wembley
Everton	Toffees	Goodison Park
Glasgow Rangers	Light Blues	Ibrox Park
Huddersfield	*Terriers*	Leeds Road
Hull City	*Tigers*	Boothferry Park
Ireland		Lansdowne Road
Liverpool	*Reds*	Anfield
Manchester United	Red Devils	Old Trafford
Mansfield Town	*Stags*	Field Mill
Middlesbrough	Boro'	Ayresome Park
Northampton	*Cobblers*	County Ground
Norwich	Canaries	Carrow Road
Notts County	*Magpies*	Meadow Lane
Portsmouth	Pompey	Fratton Park
Scotland		Hampden Park
Sheffield Wednesday	*Owls*	Hillsborough
Southampton	*Saints*	The Dell
Torquay	*Gulls*	Plainmoor
Tottenham Hotspur	*Spurs*	White Hart Lane
Wales		Cardiff Arms Park
West Ham United	*Hammers*	Upton Park
Wolverhampton Wanderers	*Wolves*	Molineux

FOOTBALLER PLAYER; BACK, CENTRE-BACK, FORWARD, FULL-BACK, GOALIE, GOALKEEPER, HALF-BACK, INSIDE, KEEPER, OUTSIDE, STRIKER, SWEEPER, WINGER.

FOOTMAN BUTLER, *WAITER*. GI, INFANTRY, PBI (crypt). HIKER, PACER, RAMBLER, RUNNER, WALKER. TRIVET. *BUTTERFLY*.

FOOTWEAR BOOT, CLOG, GUMBOOT, GYMSHOE, MOCCASIN, MULE, PUMP, SABOT, SANDAL, *SHOE*, SLIPPER, SOCK, STOCKING, WELLINGTON BOOT.

FOR (s/l *fore*, *four*). FAVOURING, IN FAVOUR, PRO (**opp** = *con*). BECAUSE.

FORBIDDEN BANNED, BARRED, EXCLUDED, PREVENTED, TABOO, TABU.

FORCE COERCE, CRAM, DRIVE, LEVER, PRISE, PROPEL, PUSH, SHOVE. IMPOSE, *PRESS*. *POLICE*; TROOPS. EFFORT, IMPETUS, POWER, STRENGTH, VIOLENCE; DYNE, ERG (eng). COMPEL, RAVISH; CAPTURE, OVERPOWER.

FORCED SEED HOTHOUSE PLANT. RAPE (crypt).

FORD WADE; CROSSING. *CAR*®, T. *GAOL*. *PRESIDENT* (US). Mistress ~ (Merry Wives, *Shak*).

FORE (s/l *for*, *four*). *BOW* (naut). FRONT. *CAVE*, (golf).

FOREGROUND FRONT, NEAR PLAN. *GOLF COURSE* (crypt).

FOREIGN 1. ABROAD. STRANGE, UNCO (Sc). 2. Translate, e.g. **He's foreign** = IL (Fr), ER (Ger) etc.

~ OFFICE FO. BUREAU (crypt, Fr), AMT (crypt, Ger).

FOREST [Football team]. TREES, WOODLAND; TAIGA (USSR) [**opp** = Savannah (tropics), Steppe (USSR), Tundra (Arctic), *desert*, *plain*]; **celeb (UK)**:

2-letters	5-letters	EPPING (Eng)
AE (Sc)	ARDEN (Eng)	FINDON (Sc)
	CRAIK (Sc)	LAGGAN (Sc)
	DREVA (Sc)	LENNOX (Sc)
3-letters	GAICK (Sc)	LOSSIE (Sc)
BIN (Sc)	ORKEL (Sc)	MIDMAR (Sc)
MOY (Sc)	SALEN (Sc)	MINARD (Sc)
NEW (Eng)	STRUY (Sc)	OGMORE (Wal)
		QUEENS (Sc)
4-letters	6-letters	RADNOR (Wal)
AMAT (Sc)	ACHRAY (Sc)	RHEOLA (Wal)
BERE (Eng)	ATHOLL (Sc)	SALCEY (Eng)
DEAN (Eng)	ATTRIC (Sc)	
PLYM (Eng)	BORGIE (Sc)	7-letters
TOWY (Wal)	CLUNES (Sc)	ARDROSS (Sc)
WARK (Eng)	COULIN (Sc)	ASHDOWN (Eng)
WYRE (Eng)	CULBIN (Sc)	BENMORE (Sc)

BOWLAND (Sc)
BOWMONT (Sc)
CARRICK (Sc)
CHANGUE (Sc)
CRYCHAN (Wal)
CULACHY (Sc)
DEVILLA (Sc)
EREDINE (Sc)
FIUNARY (Sc)
GLENGAP (Sc)
GLEN LOY (Sc)
HARWOOD (Eng)
KIELDER (Eng)
LOCH ARD (Sc)
LOCH ECK (Sc)
LYMINGE (Eng)
MAMLORN (Sc)
MILBURN (Eng)
NEWTYLE (Sc)
ROSARIE (Sc)
SKIDDAW (Eng)
TRAWDEN (Eng)
WAREHAM (Eng)
WINDSOR (Eng)

8-letters
ATTADALE (Sc)
BALMORAL (Sc)
BEINNEUN (Sc)
BEN DAMPH (Sc)
BOBLAINY (Sc)
BORROBOL (Sc)
BRAEMORE (Sc)
CALLODEN (Sc)
CARDRONA (Sc)
DELAMERE (Eng)
DUNDEUGH (Sc)
DUNLOINN (Sc)
ERCHLESS (Sc)
FEARNOCH (Sc)
GLENISLA (Sc)

HAREWOOD (Eng)
KERSHOPE (Eng)
KINFAUNS (Sc)
KNAPDALE (Sc)
LEITHOPE (Sc)
MORANGIE (Sc)
NEEDWOOD (Eng)
QUANTOCK (Eng)
RINGWOOD (Eng)
ROTHBURY (Eng)
ST GWYNNO (Wal)
SHERWOOD (Eng)
SHOTOVER (Eng)
TORRIDON (Sc)
TUNSTALL (Eng)
WAUCHOPE (Sc)
WYCHWOOD (Eng)
YAIR HILL (Sc)

9-letters
ABERNETHY (Sc)
ALICE HOLT (Eng)
BEDGEBURY (Eng)
BLAIRADAM (Sc)
CLOCAENOG (Wal)
CORLARACH (Sc)
EAST MONAR (Sc)
FASNAKYLE (Sc)
GLENCOICH (Sc)
GLENDEVON (Sc)
GLENDUROR (Sc)
GLENGARRY (Sc)
GLENLIVET (Sc)
GLENTRESS (Sc)
GLENTROOL (Sc)
GRISEDALE (Eng)
GUISACHAN (Sc)
INVERINEN (Sc)
INVERTAEL (Sc)
INVERWICK (Sc)
LAURISTON (Sc)

LEANACHAN (Sc)
LETTEREWE (Sc)
MONAUGHTY (Sc)
PARKHURST (IofW)
PITFICHIE (Sc)
PORTCLAIR (Sc)
REDESDALE (Eng)
SAVERNAKE (Eng)
SCOOTMORE (Sc)
SPEYMOUTH (Sc)
STRATHYRE (Sc)
TEINDLAND (Sc)
TENTSMUIR (Sc)

DRUMTOCHTY (Sc)
DUNDREGGAN (Sc)
FETTERESSO (Sc)
FISHERFIELD (Sc)
GLAS FYNYDD (Wal)
GLENARTNEY (Sc)
GLENBRANTER (Sc)
GLENCARRON (Sc)
GLENFESHIE (Sc)
HAMSTERLEY (Eng)
INVERMONSTON (Sc)
KILDERMOIRE (Sc)
KILMICHAEL (Sc)
MICHELDEVER (Eng)
MONTREATHMONT (Sc)

10+ letters
ACHAGLACHGACH (Sc)
APPLECROSS (Sc)
BALLOCHBUIE (Sc)
BARCALDINE (Sc)
BRIGHTSTONE (IofW)
CAIRN EDWARD (Sc)
CARRON VALLEY (Sc)
CAENNACROC (Sc)
CLASHINDARROCH (Sc)
COIGNAFEARN (Sc)
COIRRIEYAIRACK (Sc)
CORRIEHALLIE (Sc)
DAILNAMAIN (Sc)
DALBEATTIE (Sc)

PENNINGHAME (Sc)
RENDLESHAM (Eng)
RHIDORROCH (Sc)
ROCKINGHAM (Eng)
ROSSENDALE (Eng)
ROWARDENNAN (Sc)
ST LEONARDS (Eng)
STRATHCONON (Sc)
STRATHDEARN (Sc)
STRATHLACHLAN (Sc)
STRATHNAIRN (Sc)
TOLLOMUICK (Sc)
WHITEHAUGH (Sc)

FOR EXAMPLE 1. EG, (FOR) INSTANCE, SAY. 2. Shows word
starting IM (I am), e.g. **Bristol for example** (6) = IM*PORT. 3.
Answer describes word indicated, e.g. **I, for example, accumulated
wealth** (7) = CAPITAL.

FORFEND AVERT, KEEP OFF.

FORGER COPIER, COUNTERFEITER, FABRICATOR,
INVENTOR; COMPEYSON (Great Ex, *Dickens*).
BLACKSMITH, *SMITH* (crypt). ADVANCER, PROGRESSER
(crypt).

FORGET 1. NEGLECT, OMIT: DISREGARD, SLIGHT. 2. Omit
letter(s) indicated, e.g. **Don't forget the duck** = D*NT.

FOR INSTANCE 1. EG, FOR EXAMPLE, SAY. 2. Shows word
starting IM (I am), e.g. **Rose, for instance** (7) = IM*PLANT.

FORM BENCH. CONDITION, *FIGURE*, SCHEDULE. *CLASS*.
CAST, MOULD, *PATTERN*, *SHAPE*. TRACK RECORD.
Habitation (hare).

FORMER 1. ERSTWHILE, *EX*, *LATE*, OLD. FIRST (of two).
CASTER, MOULDER, POTTER (crypt). PUPIL,
SCHOOLBOY/GIRL (crypt). 2. Indicates use of old-fashioned
word(s), e.g. **The former** (2) = YE; **was formerly** (4) = WERT.

FORM OF *Anag*.

FORTE (s/l *forty*). F, LOUD. SWORD BLADE, STRONG
POINT. RESTAURANT®, SERVICE STATION®.

FORTH (s/l fourth). INTO VIEW, OUT; FORWARD. *RIVER*
(Sc).

FORTISSIMO FF, VERY LOUD; NOISY (**opp** = pianissimo,
piano).

FORTUNE 1. CHANCE, DESTINY, LUCK [*tarot*]. *THEATRE*.
PROSPERITY, RICHES, WEALTH; **comp** = fame. HAP,
HAPPEN, OCCUR. 2. **Goddesses: Gk** = TYCHE, **Rom** =
FORTUNA.

FORTY (s/l *forte*). See *number*. XL. *TOPS* (darts). L (crypt; life
begins at ~).

FORWARD ADVANCED, AHEAD, ON. PERT,
PRECOCIOUS. PROMOTE. CENTRE, INSIDE, OUTSIDE,
STRIKER (*football*, hockey). **Pl** = SCRUM (rugby).

FOUL (s/l *fowl*). CONTRAVENTION, ERROR, FAULT,
INFRINGEMENT. BAD, EVIL, LOATHSOME, STINKING.

FOUND DISCLOSED, DISCOVERED, REVEALED; **comp** =
lost. ESTABLISH, ORIGINATE, SET UP. *CAST*, FUSE,
MELT, MOULD.

FOUNDATION *AUC*, ESTABLISHMENT. BASE, GROUND,
PRINCIPLE. [corset]. **Pl** = BASE, UNDERPINNING (archit).

FOUR (s/l *for*, fore). 1. See *number*. IV, QUARTET, TETRAD.
BOUNDARY (*cricket*). BROWN BALL (snooker). TEAM
(horses, card players). POMPEY (*rh sl*). **Pl** = RACE (rowing).
GLOVES, SHOES (size). 2. *Gospel*-makers (*song*); calling birds
(*Christmas* song). [*Holmes* case].

~ **POINT** IVE, IVS etc (crypt). NEWS (crypt). SQUARE.

FOURTH (s/l *forth*). QUARTER, QUARTUS. TOP (mech gear).
F, HARMONIC, INTERVAL (mus). INDEPENDENCE DAY
(US).

FOURTH ESTATE THE PRESS.

~ MAN SETH.

FOX DISSEMBLE, FOOL, OUTWIT. FUR. *AMERICAN INDIAN*. QUADRUPED; FENNEC, REYNARD, RUSSEL, VOLPONE (Ben Jonson); **comp** = *hounds*; **assembly** = skulk; **habitation** = *earth*; **male** = dog; **fem** = vixen; **offspring** = cub [cunning; uneatable (Wilde)]. **Celeb**: BASIL BRUSH (TV), BRER ~ (Uncle Remus, Tar-baby; Harris), CHARLES JAMES ~ (polit), GEORGE ~ (*Quakers*).

FR FATHER. FRANCE, FRENCH [*patron saint*]. FRANCIUM (*chem*). **Pl** = Fellow of the Royal Society; SAVANT.

FRANCISCAN *GREYFRIAR*; MENDICANT FRIAR; BUNGIEBIRD. CAPUCHIN.

FRANK (s/l franc). 1. CANDID, *FREE*, OPEN, OVERT. CANCEL, STAMP. *BIRD. COIN. DIARIST*. 2. Free men of lower Rhine, who warred with the Romans and settled in Gaul under Clovis in A.D. 496.

FRATERNITY BROTHERHOOD, ASSOCIATION; **celeb**: BUFFALOES (RAOB), FREEMASONS, ODDFELLOWS, PROBUS, ROTARY, ROUND TABLE.

FREE FOR NOTHING, GRATIS, UNCHARGED. ENLARGE, LIBERATE, RID; LIBERAL, LOOSE (**opp** = *limited*); **comp** = *easy*. *FRANK*, OPEN. UNOCCUPIED, VACANT (**opp** = *engaged*). 'FRANCIS'.

FRENCH 1. F, FR. DRINK, VERMOUTH; **comp** = *gin*. 2. Translate, e.g. **A (or the) French . . .** = UN/UNE or LA/LE/LES.

~ MAN M, MONS.

~ ONE UN, UNE.

~ REVOLUTIONARY CALENDAR Revised calendar of France, 1789. Months (with starting dates) were:

VENDEMIAIRE (22 Sept)	GERMINAL (21 Mar)
BRUMAIRE (22 Oct)	FLOREAL (20 Apr)
FRIMAIRE (21 Nov)	PRAIRIAL (20 May)
NIVOSE (21 Dec)	MESSIDOR (19 June)
PLUVIOSE (20 Jan)	THERMIDOR (19 Jul)
VENTOSE (19 Feb)	FRUCTIDOR (18 Aug)

FRESH *Anag. NEW*; *GREEN*, YOUNG (**opp** = old, stale). CHEEKY, FORWARD, IMPERTINENT.

FRESHER NEWER, MORE FORWARD. COLLEGE STUDENT (1st year), UNDERGRADUATE.

FRESH START CARTE BLANCHE, CLEAN SHEET. TARTS, RATTS (crypt, *anag*).

FRET ADORN, CHEQUER, PATTERN (saw). CHAFE, CONSUME, CORRODE, GNAW, RUST. ANNOY, DISTRESS, IMPATIENCE, IRRITATE, RUFFLE, WORRY. SEA-MIST. BAR, RIDGE (mus).

FREY(R) Nor *god* of fertility and sunshine; s of Njord, and br of *Freya*; k when he gave away his magic sword to win the love of Gerda.

FREYA Nor *goddess* of love. Second wife of *Odin*, d of Njord and sis of *Frey*; travelled in chariot drawn by two cats. Received the souls of those slain in battle. Her prized possession was the necklace Brisingamen, guarded by Heimdal, *watchman* of the gods.

FRIAR (s/l fryer). *FATHER*, RC MENDICANT, *Chaucer* character. AUGUSTINIAN (Austin Friar, *hermit*), CARMELITE (White Friar), DOMINICAN (Blackfriar, Friars Major), FRANCISCAN (Bungiebird, Capuchin, *Greyfriar*, Friars Minor, Minorite) [Trinity/Red Friar and Crutched/Crossed Friar = Canons Regular. Monks are not friars].

FRIDAY 1. F. MAN ~ (Robinson Crusoe). 2. Day of *Frigg*. ~'s **child** = loving & giving. [Solomon *Grundy*].

FRIEND ALLY, *COMPANION*, MATE, OPPO (sl), PAL (**opp** = foe). *QUAKER*.

FRIEZE (s/l frees, freeze). RELIEF WORK (sculpture). CLOTH.

FRIGG(A) 1. Nor *goddess* of fertility; mar *Odin*, m of *Balder* [*Friday*]. 2. A minor *PLANET*.

FRINGE BORDER, EDGE, SURROUND. *BANG*, HAIRSTYLE.

FROG BUTTONING. SWORD STRAP. FASTENING (rly). FRENCHMAN (sl). HORN (horse's foot). AMPHIBIAN, ANGLER ~, ANOURA, PADDOCK (*offspring*). TOAD; JUMPER (crypt). **Celeb**: DAN'L WEBSTER (The Celeb Jumping ~ of Calaveras County; M. *Twain*), JEREMY FISHER (Beatrix *Potter*), KERMIT (TV), MOWGLI (Jungle Book), TOAD (~ of Toad Hall; *Grahame*).

FROM 1. EX, OUT OF. ORIGIN, STARTING POINT. 2. Hidden word, e.g. **Two from a group Air Show** (4) = P*AIR. 3. Indicates *anag*, e.g. **Queen is from army** (4) = MARY.

FROWN DISAPPROVE, FURROW, KNIT BROWS. HEADLINES (crypt).

FRUIT 1. PRODUCT, REVENUE. *OFFSPRING* (bibl). **Pl** = CONSEQUENCE, ISSUE, RESULT. 2. Edible seed; **types**:

3-letters
FIG
HAW
HIP
NUT

4-letters
CRAB
DATE
DIKA
DOUM
EJOO
GEAN
KAKI
KIWI
LIME
PEAR
PLUM
SKEG
SLOE
TUNA
UGLI

5-letters
ABHAL
ACORN
ANANA
APPLE
BERRY
GOBBO
GRAPE
GUAVA
JUMBO
LEMON
LOGAN
MANGO
MELON
MOREL
MORUS
OLIVE
PAPAW

PEACH
RHEIC
RHEUM
RIBES
WHORT

6-letters
BANANA
BURREL
CHERRY
CITRON
CITRUL
CODLIN
COLMAR
DAMSON
DRUPEL
DURIAN
DURION
EGROIT
GROSER
LITCHI
LOQUAT
LUCAMA
LYCHEE
MAMMEE
MEDLAR
MUSCAT
ORANGE
PAPAYA
PAW-PAW
PIPPIN
PISANG
POMELO
PUMELO
PUNICA
QUINCE
RAISIN
RAMOON
RENNET
RUDDOC
RUSSET

SHARON
TAMPOE
TOMATO
WAMPEE

7-letters
ACHAENE
APRICOT
AVOCADO
BOUCHET
BULLACE
BURLACE
CANDOCK
CODLING
COSTARD
CUMQUAT
CURRANT
DEUTZIA
ETAERIO
GENIPAP
GOLDING
KARATAS
KUMQUAT
LEECHEE
MORELLA
MORELLO
PASSION
POMELOE
POMEROY
POMPION
POMPIRE
PUMPKIN
(RHUBARB)
RIBSTON
ROSE-HIP
RUDDOCK
SAFFRON
SATSUMA
SHALLON
SOROSIS
SULTANA

SYRINGA
WINESAP

8-letters
ABDALAVI
BERGAMOT
BILBERRY
BLENHEIM
BROMELIA
BURGAMOT
CADILLAC
CLEMATIS
FAEBERRY

FENBERRY
JAPONICA
MANDARIN
MARIGOLD
MULBERRY
MUSCATEL
MYOSOTIS
PEARMAIN
PLANTAIN
PRUNELLO
SHADDOCK
XYLOCARP

9+ letters
BLACKBERRY
BLACKCURRANT
GOOSEBERRY
LOGANBERRY
NECTARINE
PINEAPPLE
RASPBERRY
REDCURRANT
STRAWBERRY
TANGERINE
WHITECURRANT

FRY 1. QUAKER (*Fox*). *COOK. PAINTER. WRITER*. 2. *Offspring* of *FISH*.

FUEL ALCOHOL, AVGAS, BUTANE, CALOR®, CHARCOAL, COAL, COKE, DERV, DIESEL, GAS(OLINE), KEROSENE, METHANE, METHS, OIL, PARAFFIN, PETROL, PROPANE, WOOD; [*Pluto*]. FEED FIRE, STOKE.

FULLER EARTH; CLOTH CLEANER. MORE REPLETE. GROOVED TOOL. *POET*.

FUNNY COMICAL, HUMOROUS [peculiar/ha-ha]. *BOAT*.

FURIAE *FURIES* (Rom).

FURNITURE *HARNESS*, TRAPPINGS. STUMPS, WICKET (cricket sl). CONTENTS, thus ~ of pocket = money, ~ of mind = knowledge, ~ of shelves = books, and esp the ~ of house = chairs, tables, etc. [*Adam*, Chippendale, Hepplewhite, Sheraton], e.g.

    beds: angel ~, bunk ~, camp ~, couch, divan, four-poster ~, hospital ~, litter (and see *bed*).

    chairs: arm ~, backstool, Bath ~, balloon-back ~, bentwood ~, berbice ~, bergere, cabriole, campaign ~, cane ~, carver, chaise-longue, cockfighting ~, comb ~, conversation ~, court-cupboard ~, easy ~, faldstool, farthingale, fiddle-back, hall ~, hoop-back ~, joint-stool, kitchen ~, ladder-backed ~, library ~, Morris ~, prie-dieu, ribband-backed ~, rocking ~, Sedan ~, shield-back ~, smoker's ~, spindle-back ~, spoon-back ~, stool, tabouret, tub ~, wheel-back ~, Windsor ~, wing ~ (and see *chair*).

    chests: Armada ~, bible box, camphor-wood ~, coffer, Hope ~, nonsuch, ~ of drawers.

clocks: bracket ~, carriage ~, coaching inn ~, grandfather ~, grandmother ~, (half) hunter, lantern, long case ~, turnip, wristwatch (and see *clock*) [Knibb, Tompion].

desks: ambo, bureau, Davenport, escritoire, fall-front ~, knee-hole ~, office ~, reed-top ~, roll-top ~, school ~, secretaire, tambour ~ (and see *desk*).

tables: architect's ~, butterfly ~, card ~, coach ~, coffee ~, console, dining ~, draw ~, dressing ~, dumb-waiter, games ~, gate ~, gate-leg ~, Kent ~, loo ~, nest of ~s, omnium, opium ~, Pembroke ~, pie-crust ~, pier ~, quartetto ~, refectory ~, Rudd's ~, secretaire, shovel-board ~, side ~, sofa ~, spider ~, Sutherland ~, tea ~, teapoy, trestle ~, tripod ~, what-not, writing ~ (and see *table*).

other: almirah, canterbury, cellaret, chesterfield, cheval mirror, commode, cupboard, dresser, jardiniere, peer-glass, settee, settle, sociable, sofa, spinning-wheel, tall-boy, tea-caddy, wardrobe, wine-cooler.

terms: acanthus, apron, astragal, banding, bead, boule, cabriole, cartouche, claw and ball, console, cornice, dentil, diaper, endive, escutcheon, finial, gadroon, intaglio, marquetry, ogee, ormulu, patina, pie-crust, plinth, serpentine, spandrel, spindle, splat, swag.

FURY 1. ANGER, PASSION, RAGE. VIOLENCE (met). *DOG* (*Alice*). 2. VIRAGO, *SHREW*. **Pl** = avenging minor *goddesses* with snakes for hair, sent from Tartarus to punish crimes of perjury, murder etc; hence any avenging spirit. **Gk** = ERINYES/EUMENIDES (ALECTO, MEGAERA, TISIPHONE); **Rom** = DIRAE/FURIAE.

FUSE AMALGAMATE, BLEND, MELD. DETONATE, IGNITER (impact ~, magnetic ~, time ~, vibratory ~). BLOW-OUT, SAFETY LINK; MELT, SHORT-CIRCUIT; UNEARTH (crypt).

FUSTIAN *MATERIAL*. BOMBAST, TURGID SPEECH.

G GENERAL AUDIENCE (film *censorship*, US). *GERMAN(Y)*. GIGA (*int unit*). GRAMS. *GRAND*. GRAVITY. GREAT. GREEK. *KEY*; *NOTE*. ~STRING. THOUSAND (sl).

GAEA *GE*.

GALAHAD Kt of the *Round Table*, s of *Lancelot* and Elaine [*Camelot*. Holy Grail. Purity, virtue].

GALATEA 1. Gk myth ivory statue, who came to life and was mar by *Pygmalion*. [Hermione, W. Tale (*Shak*)]. 2. Gk myth sea *nymph*, d of *Nereus* and *Doris*. 3. A minor *PLANET*.

GALL (s/l *Gaul*). ANNOY; NERVE. CLUBROOT, HYPERTROPHY. *FLY*. LIVERBILE. HORSE-SORE.

GALLERY BALCONY, *GODS*. COLONNADE, PORTICO. PLATFORM. CORRIDOR, PASSAGE. EXHIBITION; TATE.

GALLEY SLAVE *PRISONER*, *ROWER*. CHEF, *COOK*, PANTRY BOY, PROOFREADER, SCULLERY MAID (all crypt).

GALLOPHILE *Lover* of French ways.

GALLOPHOBIA *Aversion* to French ways.

GALOFARO *CHARYBDIS*.

GAMBLE (s/l *gambol*). *BET*, SPEC(ULATE), WAGER.

GAMBOL (s/l *gamble*). FROLIC, PLAY [*lamb*].

GAME 1. *BRAVE*, COURAGEOUS, PREPARED, WILLING; opp = reluctant, *shy*. CRIPPLED, HALT, LAME. 2. WILD LIFE e.g. *ANTELOPE*, *DEER*, GROUSE, HARE, PARTRIDGE, PHEASANT, WOODCOCK (see also *big game* for bush and jungle dwellers). 3. *MATCH*, PARTIE, PASTIME, RECREATION, *SPORT* (q.v.); **types (indoors)**: *BOARD* ~ (q.v.), *CARD* ~ (q.v.), BADMINTON, *BILLIARDS*, BINGO (HOUSEY-HOUSEY, KENO, LOTTO, TOMBOLA), BOWLING, CHARADES, CONSEQUENCES, CRAMBO, CRAPS (US), *DARTS*, DIABOLO, *DICE*, DOMINOES, DUMB CRAMBO, *FIVES*, GRANDMOTHER'S FOOTSTEPS, HANDBALL, HIDE AND SEEK, I SPY, JACKSTRAWS (US), MAH-JONGG, *MARBLES*, MURDER, NETBALL, NIM, NINEPINS, PING-PONG, POOL (US), POSTMAN'S KNOCK, *RACKETS*, ROULETTE, RUBIK CUBE, *SARDINES*, SHOVE HA'PENNY, SKITTLES, *SNOOKER*, SOFTBALL, SPILLIKINS, SQUASH, *TENNIS*, TEN-PIN BOWLING, TIDDLY-WINKS, TWO-UP (Aus), UP JENKINS, VOLLEY-BALL; **types (outdoors)**: BADMINTON, *BASEBALL*, BOULE, *BOWLS*, *CRICKET*, CROQUET, CURLING, *FOOTBALL* (Association ~, Am ~, Aus Rules ~, *Rugby* ~, Rugby League ~), FRENCH & ENGLISH, *GOLF*, HIDE AND SEEK, HOCKEY, HOP-SCOTCH, HURLING, KICK THE CAN, LACROSSE, PALL-MALL, PELOTA, PETANQUE, POLO, QUOITS,

ROUNDERS, RUGGER, *SAILING*, SHINTY, SOFTBALL, *SWIMMING*, *TENNIS* (deck ~, lawn ~, padder ~, real/royal ~, table ~), WATER POLO, WINTER *SPORTS* (q.v.); and see *SPORT*. **Pl** = Asian ~, *Commonwealth* ~, *Olympic* ~, Pan-American ~, *Pythian* ~.

G & S Gilbert and Sullivan. **Operas**:

Title	Alternative	Detail
The Gondoliers	The King of Barataria	Venice. Duke of Plaza Toro
The Grand Duke	The Statutory Duel	Grand Duchy of Pfennig Halbpfennig, Rudolph, Ernest Dummkopf, Ludwig
Iolanthe	The *Peer* and the *Peri*	*Parliament*, *Fairies*, Lord Chancellor
Mikado	The Town of Titipu	*Japan*. Nanki-Poo, Yum-Yum, Ko-Ko, Pooh-Bah, Pitti-Sing, Wandering *Minstrel*, Lord High Executioner
Patience	Bunthorne's Bride	Dragoons, Raffle, Capt Reece, Mantelpiece
HMS Pinafore (abbr: Pinafore)	The Lass that Loved a *Sailor*	Dick Deadeye, Buttercup
Pirates of Penzance (abbr: Pirates)	The Slave of Duty	Cornwall. Frederic (*pirate*), *Ruth* (*maid*, *nurse*)
Princess Ida (abbr: Ida)	Castle Adamant	King Hildebrand, Gama (*monster*), Hilarion, *women warriors*
Ruddigore	The Witch's Curse	*Cornwall*. *Ghosts*, Mad Margaret, Sir Ruthven Murgatroyd

Sorcerer	—	Country house. John Wellington Wells
Trial by Jury (abbr: Trial)	—	Law courts. Angelina, Edwin
Utopia Limited (abbr: Utopia)	—	King Paramount I, Scaphio, Phantis, Tarara, Princess Zara
Yeoman of the Guard (abbr: Yeoman)	The Merryman and his *Maid*	Tower of London. Wilfred Shadbolt (*gaoler*), Col Fairfax, Meryll, Jack Point (*jester*)

GANGSTER GODFATHER, GUNMAN, HOOD(LUM), MAFIA BOSS, MOBSTER, VILLAIN; **notorious**: AL CAPONE, BONNIE & CLYDE, PRETTY BOY FLOYD, LUCKY LUCIANO, BUGSY MALONE, DUTCH SCHULTZ, BUGSY SIEGEL.

GANYMEDE 1. Gk myth youth, celeb for his beauty, abducted by *Zeus* (who *transformed* himself into an *eagle*) as his *cupbearer* on Mount *Olympus*. 2. A satellite of the *planet Jupiter*.

GAOL *BRIG* (naut), CAN, CELL, CHOKEY, CLINK, COOLER, GLASSHOUSE (mil), INSIDE, JAIL (US), JUG, *NICK*, PETER, PRISON, QUOD, SLAM(MER), STIR [porridge. Fry, Howard; M for M (*Shak*)]; **celeb**:

ALBANY	(Eng)	DARTMOOR	(Eng)
ALCATRAZ	(US, ex)	DEVIL'S ISLAND	(Fr, ex)
ARMLEY	(Eng)	*DURHAM*	(Eng)
BARLINNIE	(Sc)	*FLEET*	(Eng, ex)
BASTILLE	(Fr)	*FORD*	(Eng)
BORSTAL	(Eng, jun)	FRESNES	(Fr)
BOTANY BAY	(Aus, hist)	HOLLOWAY	(Eng, fem)
BRIDEWELL	(Eng, ex)	HULL	(Eng)
BRIXTON	(Eng)	KINGSTON	(Eng)
BROADMOOR	(Eng, med)	LONG MARTIN	(Eng)
		LEEDS	(Eng)
CAMP HILL	(Eng)	MARSHALSEA	(Eng, ex)
COOKHAM WOOD	(Eng)	THE MAZE	(Ire)

MILLBANK	(Eng, ex)	THE SCRUBS	(Eng)
THE *MOOR*	(Eng)	SING SING	(US, ex)
NEWGATE	(Eng, ex)	STYAL	(Eng)
NORFOLK IS	(Aus, ex)	VERNE	(Eng)
NORTHEYE	(Eng)	WAKEFIELD	(Eng)
OSSINING	(US)	WALTON	(Eng)
PARKHURST	(Eng)	WINSOM GREEN	(Eng)
PENTONVILLE	(Eng)	WINCHESTER	(Eng)
PORTLAND	(Eng)	WORMWOOD	
RAMPTON	(Eng, med)	SCRUBS	(Eng)
RISLEY	(Eng)		

Fictional: Chateau d'If (Dumas), Zenda (*Hope*).

GAOLER JAILER (US), KEY-HOLDER (crypt), KEY MAN
(crypt), PRISON OFFICER, SCREW (sl), TURNKEY (arch),
WARDER. WILLIAM SHADBOLT (*G & S*).

GARBLED *Anag.* MUDDLED, *SCRAMBLED.*

GARDEN CULTIVATION, *PLOT*; **comp** = *common.* BABYLON,
EDEN, KEW [Elizabeth and her Ger Garden (Beau champ)].

GARDENER CULTIVATOR. *ADAM* (crypt). 'CAPABILITY'
BROWN; ANDRE LENOTRE (Fr); ANDREW FAIRSERVICE
(Rob Roy, Scott). ELIZABETH, INIGO JONES, MR
MCGREGOR (*Potter*). **Pl** = SPADES (*Alice*).

GARLAND ADORN, BEDECK, *DECK*, LEI; FLOWERS. JUDY
(films).

GARNET *MINERAL*; GEM (red). *Birthstone* (January).

GARTER *HERALD* [Black Rod]. KNIGHTHOOD [Honi soit qui
mal y pense; stocking]. BAND, STRAP.

GATE (s/l gait). 1. ACCESS, BARRIER, CLOSURE,
ENTRANCE, EXIT, *OPENING*, POSTERN, WICKET.
SHUTTER (mech). ATTENDANCE, CROWD, SPECTATORS;
TAKE, TAKINGS. MOUTH (sl). 2. ~s of **London**:
ALDERSGATE, ALDGATE, BISHOPSGATE, BRIDESGATE,
CRIPPLEGATE, DOWGATE, LUDGATE, MOORGATE,
NEWGATE, POSTERN, PRAETORIAN WAY.

GATHERING *ASSEMBLY*, MEETING. COLLECTING,
CULLING. BOIL, SWELLING, TUMOUR.

GAUGE *EM*, *TT*, *Z*. CAPACITY, EXTENT, *MEASURE*, SCOPE,
STANDARD, WIDTH, *TRACK*. INSTRUMENT. ASSESS,
CALCULATE, ESTIMATE.

GAUL (s/l *gall*). GALLIA, ROMAN FRANCE (cisalpine, transalpine).

GB GREAT BRITAIN (*car plate*).

GBA ALDERNEY (*car plate*).

GBG GUERNSEY (*car plate*).

GBJ JERSEY (*car plate*).

GBM ISLE OF MAN (*car plate*).

GE = GAEA. Gk *goddess* of the EARTH. Mother (by Uranus) of the *Titans* (**Rom** = TELLUS, TERRA). GERMANIUM (*chem*).

GEAR *CLOTHES*, GOODS, KIT, RIG. APPARATUS, EQUIPMENT, FITTINGS, HARNESS, KIT, TACKLE. MESHING COGS (mech).

GEESE Pl of *Goose*.

GEHENNA HELL (bibl), PLACE OF BURNING.

GEM BEST/CHOICEST PART. *TYPEFACE*. JEWEL, PRECIOUS STONE, ENGRAVED SEMI-PRECIOUS STONE: *AGATE*, *AMETHYST*, *AQUAMARINE*, *BERYL*, *BLOODSTONE*, *CHALCEDONY*, *CHRYSOBERYL*, *CHRYSOLITE*, *CHRYSOPRASE*, *CORAL*, *CORNELIAN*, *DIAMOND*, *EMERALD*, *GARNET*, *JADE*, *LAPIS LAZULI*, *ONYX*, *OPAL*, *PEARL*, PERIDOT, PYROPE, *RUBY*, *SAPPHIRE*, *SARD*, SARDIUS (bibl), *SARDONYX*, *TURQUOISE*, *ZIRCON* [*anniversary*, *birthstone*].

GEMINI 1. *TWINS*; DIOSCURI (Castor and Pollux). 2. *Constellation*; (3rd) sign of *Zodiac*. 3. *SPACECRAFT*.

GEN *GENERAL* (mil). *INFORMATION*.

GENERAL G (film *censorship*, US). GEN, *TARTAN* (bibl); OFFICER: LEE, SMUTS, SLIM (and see *military leaders*). IMPARTIAL, MAIN, UNIVERSAL (**opp** = particular).

GENES (s/l jeans). CHROMOSOMES, *DNA* (heredity).

GENIE GOBLIN, IMP, *SPIRIT* [Aladdin's lamp].

GENIUS 1. ABILITY, BRILLIANCE. 2. Rom myth *god* of fertility and marriage (**Gk** = *HYMEN*).

GENOPHILE *Lover* of people.

GENOPHOBIA *Aversion* to people.

GEORGE PATRON SAINT (Eng; Port; armourers) [dragon, order of garter, 23 April]; 'A RUSTIC'. *WRITER*. [*Three* Men in a Boat]. KING (Eng/Hanover; *mad*).

GERMAN 1. G. HEINIE, HEINZ, JERRY, FRITZ, KRAUT, *HUN*. D, DDR (*car plate*). 2. Translate, e.g. **The German** = DAS, DER, DIE; **German song** = LIED.

GERMANY DDR, *FDR*, REICH, FATHERLAND, WEIMAR.

GET ON *AGREE*. *BOARD*, EMBARK. *AGE*.

GET OUT EMERGE, FLEE, *LEAVE*. BOWL, CATCH, RUN OUT, STUMP (*cricket*).

GET UP STYLE (clothes). *DRESS*, MAKE TOILET, RISE. *MOUNT* (horse). Write upwards (dn). BECOME VIOLENT, WORK UP (sea, temper). ORGANIZE. TEG (dn; crypt).

GHOST DOUBLE IMAGE, OUTLINE, SEMBLANCE. (HACK) WRITER. APPARITION, MANES, PHANTOM, *SHADE*, SOUL, SPECTRE, *SPIRIT*, POLTERGEIST; HAUNT, PROWL; **celeb**: BANQUO (Macbeth), CAESAR (to *Brutus*, before battle of Philippi), CANTERVILLE (Wilde), CLAUDIUS (Hamlet's father), ELVIRA (Blithe Spirit, Coward), MISS JESSEL and QUINT (*governess* and valet; The Turning of the Screw, James), JACOB MARLEY (Xmas Carol, *Dickens*), PHANTOM (of the Opera, Leroux) [Ruddigore (*G and S*); *lemur*].

GI SOLDIER, PFC, PRIVATE (US).

GIANT 1. LARGE, MONSTROUS, SUPERHUMAN, TITANIC (**opp** = *dwarf*). **Pl** = New York baseball team. 2. Myth *MONSTER*: *DACTYLS*, *GIGANTES*, GOG, MAGOG, ORGOGLIO (Faerie Queene, Spenser), GARGANTUA & PANTAGRUEL (Rabelais), GOLIATH (bibl), NEPHILIM (bibl), *PERIPHITES* (Gk myth) [Brobdingnag (*Swift*)].

GIBRALTAR ROCK. *STRAIT*. [pillars of *Hercules*].

GIGANTES Gk myth *monsters* (not to be confused with the *Titans*); ALCYONEUS, ENCELADUS, EPHIALTES, MIMAS, PALLAS, PHRYTOS, PORPHYRION, RHOETUS. They had wings, and snakes for feet.

GILBERT 1. Sir William Schwenck ~, Eng *writer* and librettist; with *Sullivan* wrote operettas (for details, see *G and S*). 2. Sir Humphrey ~, navigator. *PAINTER*. Unit of force (elect).

GILL (s/l Jill). GIRL. *MEASURE*, ¼ PINT, hence P, I, N or T. DEWLAP, WATTLE (poultry). *BREATHER* (*fish*). RAVINE. SAIL IDLY. YOUNG WOMAN. FERRET, POLECAT (fem).

GIN (s/l djinn, ginn). *DRINK*, GENEVA, HOLLANDS, SCHIEDAM; **comp** = *Fr*; *It*; *tonic*. *NET*, SNARE, TRAP. CRANE, WINDLASS. COTTON MAKER. *CARD GAME*.

GIRDLE BELT, CORD, CORSET. RING, SURROUND. GRILL. [labour of *Hercules*].

GIRL HER, SHE. DAMOSEL, DAMSEL, GAL, LASS, MISS, WENCH. ANN, DORA, ENID, SUE etc [~ **and boy** = pigeon pair].

GIVE AWAY DONATE. *BETRAY*, SHOP.

Gk Greece, Greek.
GLASS 1. BAROMETER. MIRROR. MAGNIFIER.
MICROSCOPE. GLAZING, QUARREL, WINDOW,
TRANSPARENCY. DRINKING VESSEL: BUMPER,
COPITA, POKAL, PONY, SCHOONER, TANKARD,
TUMBLER; BRANDY ~, LIQUEUR ~, PORT ~, SHERRY
~, WINE ~. LORGNETTE, MONOCLE, QUIZZING ~. **Pl** =
BINOCULARS, BIN(N)S (sl), SPECTACLES. 2. Mixture of
sand and potash (*chem*), hence by *anag* (crypt) A SHOP STAND,
or PASS TO HAND etc.
GLEE PART-SONG. DELIGHT, MERRIMENT, MIRTH.
GO ANIMATION, DRIVE, *PEP*, VIGOUR, ZIP. DEPART,
FARE, OFF, PART, *REPAIR*, START. ATTEMPT, SHOT,
TRY, TURN. BOARD-GAME (Jap). [Little ~ (exam C)].
GOAT 1. SILLY FOOL. ATTACK, SHOT*AT, TRY*AT (crypt).
ISLAND. 2. Ruminant, genus CAPRA; BUTTER (crypt).
MURIEL (*Orwell*). **Breeds**: BAGOT, CHAMOIS, IBEX,
IZARD (Sp), MARKHOR, TAHR (see also *antelope*, *deer*).
Assembly = *flock*, herd; **offspring** = *kid*; **male** = BILLY; **fem** =
NANNY [*Ch calendar*; Vidar (Nor)]. 3. *Constellation* (Capricorn);
(10th) sign of *Zodiac*.
GOBLIN BROWNIE, ELF, GENIE, IMP, *SPIRIT*, SPRITE.
GOBY *FISH*. PASS (crypt). TRAVEL*BY/IN (crypt).
GOC GENERAL OFFICER COMMANDING, OFFICER (mil).
GOD 1. ADORED/INFLUENTIAL MAN. DEITY, ADONAI
(Heb), ALLAH (Arab), ELOHIM (Heb), JAHBULON
(*Masonic*), JEHOVA, YAHVEH (Heb), OBJECT OF
WORSHIP: IDEA, IDOL, IMAGE, SUPERHUMAN (MALE)
BEING; [ambrosia, nectar, trinity]. EXCLAMATION: GOLLY,
GOSH. **Pl** = GALLERY (theat); **opp** = parterre, stalls. 2. Gods
and *goddesses* figured largely in the lives of the ancient world. Most
of the seasons, ideas and natural events such as love, war, hunting
and the harvest (with earth, sun and moon) which influenced life
were personified by early peoples such as the Egyptians,
Phoenicians, Indians and Norsemen; those of Greece and Rome
were particularly literate, so their deities are well documented. In
the lists which follow, the alert reader will note that interesting
qualities such as fertility rate no less than ten Greek and Roman
gods and goddesses (not to mention another dozen Nordic and
eastern equivalents), while dull old virginity has only one deity
from among all the nations (and even that one is also the goddess

of Nature, so there is hope for her yet). Greece was responsible for much of the lore and mythology which grew up, and much of this was handed on to the Romans; in general terms, there were six principal Greek gods and six principal goddesses, who all lived on Mount *Olympus*: *APOLLO, ARES, HEPHAESTUS, HERMES, POSEIDON* and *ZEUS*; *Aphrodite, Artemis, Athene, Demeter, Hera* and *Hestia*. **Celeb** gods and minor gods include **Greek**:

ABRAXAS	divine emanations
AEOLUS	*winds*
AGATHODAEMON	prosperity
ALASTOR	fate
APELIOTES	east *wind*
APOLLO	beauty, healing, music, oracles, plagues, prophecy, sun
ARES	war
ASCLEPIUS	medicine
BOREAS	north *wind*
CRONOS	harvest
DIONYSUS	fertility, wine
ERIS	discord
EROS	love
EUROS	SE *wind*
GANYMEDE	cup-bearer
HADES	*underworld*
HELIOS	sun
HEPHAESTUS	fire
HERMES	dreams, messenger, *robbers*
HORUS	doorway
HYMEN	fertility, marriage
HYPNOS	sleep
KAIKAS	NE *wind*
LIPS	SW *wind*
MOMOS	ridicule
NEREUS	sea
NOTOS	south *wind*
OCEANUS	river
PAN	herds, hunting, shepherds
PLUTO	*underworld*
PLUTUS	wealth
POSEIDON	sea, *horses*

SKIRON	NW *wind*
THANATOS	*death*
URANUS	heaven
ZEPHYRUS	west *wind*
ZEUS	chief ~, king

Roman:

AESCULAPIUS	medicine
AFRICUS	SW *wind*
AMOR	love
APOLLO	beauty, healing, music, oracles, plagues, prophecy, sun
AQUILO	NE *wind*
ATLAS	world
AUSTER	south *wind*
BACCHUS	fertility, wine
CAURUS	NW *wind*
COMUS	revelry
CUPID	love
DIS	*underworld*
DISCORDIA	discord
FAUNUS	herds
FAVONIUS	west *wind*
FULGURATOR	storms
FULMINATOR	lightning
GENIUS	fertility, marriage, prosperity
IACCHUS	= *BACCHUS*
INUUS	= *FAUNUS*
JANUS	doorway
JOVE	chief ~, king, thunder
JUPITER	chief ~, thunder
LAR(ES)	household
LIBER	= *BACCHUS*
LUPERCUS	= *FAUNUS*
MARS	husbandry, war
MERCURY	messenger
MORPHEUS	dreams
MORS	*death*
NEPTUNE	sea, *horses*
ORCUS	*underworld*
PENATES	household

PHOEBUS	sun
PLUTO	*underworld*
PLUVIUS	rain
SATURNUS	harvest
SEPTENTRIO	north *wind*
SILVANUS	*trees*
SOL	sun
SUBSOLANUS	east *wind*
TERMINUS	boundaries
TONANS	thunder
VOLTURNUS	SE *wind*
VULCAN	fire

~s (not Gk or Rom)

AAH (Egy)	moon
AEGIR (Nor)	chief
AGNI (Ind)	fire
AMEN-RA (Egy)	chief, harvest
ANU (Bab)	chief
ANUBIS (Egy)	death
APIS (Egy)	sun
BAAL (Phoen)	chief, sun
BALDER (Nor)	sun
BEL(US) (Bab)	chief
BES (Egy)	music, revelry
BRAG (Nor)	poetry
BRAHMA (Ind)	chief
CHAC (Mex)	rain
DAGAN (Bab)	earth
DAGON (Phil)	chief
DON (Celt)	heavens
DONAR (Ger)	thunder
EA (Bab)	wisdom
FREY (Nor)	fertility, sun
GEB (Egy)	earth
HEIMDAL (Nor)	watchman
HOR (Egy)	doorway
HORUS (Egy)	sun
INDRA (Ind)	rain
INTI (Inca)	sun
KON-TIKI (Inca)	sun
KAMA (Ind)	love

KRISHNA (Ind)	fertility
LOKI (Nor)	fire
MAIT (Egy)	truth
MARDUK (Bab)	healing
MITHRA (Pers)	sun
MOLOCH (Jew)	fire
MORRIGAN (Ire)	war
NABU (Bab)	wisdom
NIORDHR (Nor)	sea
NJORD (Nor)	sea
NQA, NQING, NQONG (Aus)	chief (*Kipling*)
NUN (Egy)	chaos
ODIN (Nor)	chief
OG (Celt)	chief, death, fertility
OSIRIS (Egy)	rain, underworld
PTAH (Egy)	arts, magic, death
RA/RE (Egy)	sun
RAIDEN (Jap)	thunder
SEB (Egy)	agriculture
SERAPIS (Egy)	dreams, underworld
SET (Egy)	night
SHAMASH (Bab)	sun
S(H)IVA (Ind)	chief, death
SHU (Egy)	air
TAMMUZ (Syrian)	sun
TEMU (Egy)	chief
THOR (Nor)	thunder
THOTH (Egy)	wisdom
TIW (Ger)	war
VIDAR (Nor)	silence
VISHNU (Ind)	healing
WODEN (A-Sax)	chief
WOTAN (Ger)	chief
XANGTI (Ch)	chief
YAMA (Ind)	death

Equivalent gods include:

Agriculture: Gk *CRONOS*; **Roman** *SATURNUS*; **Other** SEB (Egy) [*fertility, harvest*]

Beauty: Gk *APOLLO*; **Roman** *APOLLO*

Boundaries: Roman TERMINUS

Chief: Gk *ZEUS*; **Roman** *JOVE, JUPITER*; **Other** WODEN (A-Sax), ANU, BEL/BELUS (Bab), OG (Celt), XANGTI (Ch), AMEN-RA, OSIRIS, TEMU (Egy), WOTAN (Ger), BRAHMA, SHIVA, VISHNU (Ind), ODIN (Nor), DAGON (Phil), *BAAL* (Phoen), NQA, NQING, NQONG (Aus, *Kipling*)

Death: Gk THANATOS; **Roman** MORS; **Other** ANUBIS/*OSIRIS*, PTAH (Egy), SHIVA, YAMA (Ind)

Discord: Gk *ERIS*; **Roman** DISCORDIA

Doorway: Gk *HORUS*; **Roman** *JANUS*; **Other** HOR (Egy)

Dreams: Gk *HERMES*; **Roman** *MORPHEUS*; **Other** SERAPIS (Egy)

Fate: Gk ALASTOR

Fertility: Gk *DIONYSUS, HYMEN*; **Roman** *BACCHUS, GENIUS*; **Other** OG (Celt), *OSIRIS* (Egy), KRISHNA (Ind), *FREY* (Nor) [*agriculture, harvest*]

Fire: Gk *HEPHAESTUS*; **Roman** *VULCAN*; **Other** *LOKI* (Nor), AGNI (Ind)

Harvest: Gk CRONOS; **Roman** SATURNUS; **Other** AMEN-RA, SEB (Egy) [*agriculture, fertility*]

Healing: Gk *APOLLO*; **Roman** *APOLLO*; **Other** MARDUK (Bab), VISHNU (Ind) [*medicine*]

Heaven: Gk *URANUS*; **Other** ANU (Bab), VALHALLA (Nor)

Herds: Gk *PAN*; **Roman** *FAUNUS*, INUUS, LUPERCUS

Household: Roman *LAR(ES)*, PENATES

Hunting: Gk *PAN*

Husbandry: Roman *MARS*; **Other** DAGAN (Bab)

Lightning: Gk *ZEUS*; **Roman** FULMINATOR

Love: Gk *EROS*; **Roman** *AMOR, CUPID*; **Other** KAMA (Ind)

Marriage: Gk *HYMEN*; **Roman** *GENIUS*

Medicine: Gk *ASCLEPIUS*; **Roman** AESCULAPIUS [*healing*]

Messenger: Gk *HERMES*; **Roman** *MERCURY*

Moon: Other AAH (Egy)

Night: Other *SET* (Egy)

Oracles: Gk *APOLLO*; **Roman** *APOLLO*

Plagues: Gk *APOLLO*; **Roman** *APOLLO*

Prophecy: Gk *APOLLO*; **Roman** *APOLLO*

Prosperity: Gk AGATHODAEMON; **Roman** *GENIUS*

Rain: Gk *ZEUS*; **Roman** *JUPITER*, *PLUVIUS*; **Other** *OSIRIS* (Egy), INDRA (Ind), CHAC (Mex)

Revelry: Roman COMUS; **Other** BES (Egy)

Ridicule: Gk MOMOS

River: Gk *OCEANUS*

Robbery: Gk *HERMES*

Sea: Gk *NEREUS*, *POSEIDON*; **Roman** *NEPTUNE*; **Other** AEGIR, NIORDHR, NJORD (Nor)

Shepherds: Gk *PAN*

Storms: Gk *ZEUS*; **Roman** FULGURATOR

Sun: Gk *APOLLO*, *HELIOS*; **Roman** *PHOEBUS*, *SOL*; **Other** APIS, *HORUS*, PTAH, RA/RE (Egy), INTI, KON-TIKI (Inca), *BALDER*, *FREY* (Nor), *MITHRA* (Pers), *BAAL* (Phoen), TAMMUZ (Syrian)

Thunder: Gk *ZEUS*; **Roman** *JOVE*, *JUPITER*, *TONANS*; **Other** DONAR (Ger), RAIDEN (Jap), *THOR* (Nor)

Truth: Other MAAT (Egy)

Underworld: Gk *HADES*; **Roman** *DIS*, *ORCUS*, *PLUTO*; **Other** *OSIRIS*, SERAPIS (Egy)

War: Gk *ARES*; **Roman** *MARS*; **Other** TIW (Ger), MORRIGAN (Ire)

Watchman: Other HEIMDAL (Nor)

Wealth: Gk *PLUTUS*

Winds: Gk *AEOLUS* (see *winds*); **Rom** (see *winds*); **Other**
VAYU (Pers)

Wine: Gk *DIONYSUS*; **Roman** BACCHUS, LIBER [revelry]

Wisdom: Other EA, ENKI, NABU (Bab), THOTH (Egy)

World: Roman *ATLAS*.

GODDESS 1. ADORED/INFLUENTIAL WOMAN. DEITY,
OBJECT OF WORSHIP: IDEA, IDOL, IMAGE, (FEMALE)
SUPERHUMAN BEING [ambrosia, nectar]. LOVED ONE. 2.
See *gods* for brief description of the deity ethos of ancient peoples.
The Greeks had six principal *gods* and goddesses, who all lived on
Mouth *Olympus*: *Apollo*, *Ares*, *Hephaestus*, *Hermes*, *Poseidon* and
Zeus; *APHRODITE*, *ARTEMIS*, *ATHENE*, *DEMETER*, *HERA*
and *HESTIA*. **Celeb** goddesses and minor goddesses include,
Greek:

AMPHITRITE	sea
APHRODITE	beauty, love
ARTEMIS	hunting, messenger, nature
ATE	infatuation, retribution
ATHENE	arts, war, wisdom
CHAOS	primordial space
CHLORIS	flowers
CYBELE	fertility
DANAE	fertility
DEMETER	nature
ENYO	war
EOS	dawn
ERINYES	*furies*
EUMENIDES	*furies*
GAEA/GE	earth
HEBE	cup-bearer, youth
HERA	childbirth, queen ~
HECATE	night, underworld, witchcraft
HESTIA	hearth
HYGIEA	health
IRENE	peace
IRIS	rainbow

MAIA	eldest of the *Pleiades*
MOIRAI	*fates*
NEMESIS	retribution
NIKE	victory
NYX	night
PERSEPHONE	underworld
PLEIADES	rain
RHEA	fertility
SELENE	moon
TERPSICHORE	dance, song
TYCHE	fortune
UPIS	childbirth

Roman

AURORA	dawn
BELLONA	*war*
CERES	earth, fertility, nature
DIANA	fertility, nature, hunting, moon
FAUNA	earth
FLORA	flowers
FORTUNA	fortune
FURIAE	*furies*
JUNO	queen ~, childbirth, moon
JUVENTAS	youth
LIBERA	= *PROSERPINE*
LUNA	moon
MAIA	oracles
MINERVA	arts, invention, war, wisdom
NOX	night
OPS	earth, nature
PARCAE	*fates*
PAX	peace
PROSERPINE	underworld
SALUS	health
TELLUS/TERRA	earth
VENUS	beauty, love
VESTA	hearth
VICTORIA	victory

~s (not Gk or Rom)

ASTARTE (Phoen)	love

ATERGATIS (Syrian)	fertility
BAST (Egy)	pleasure
BELIT/BELTIS (Bab)	chief, fertility
BENDIS (Thrace)	hunting, moon
BRUNHILDA (Nor)	war
DEVI (Ind)	destruction
EOSTRE (A-Sax)	fertility (Easter)
FREYA (Nor)	love
FRIGG(A) (Nor)	fertility
GULI (Bab)	healing
HATHOR (Egy)	love
HEL (Nor)	destruction, night
HOLDA (Ger)	nature
INNIN (Bab)	fertility
ISHTAR (Bab)	fertility, love
ISIS (Egy)	chief, love, nature
KALI (Ind)	destruction
LUA (It)	earth
MENI (Bab)	retribution
NEPHTHYS (Egy)	funerals
NERIO (Sabine)	war
NUT (Egy)	mother earth
SULIS (Celt)	wisdom
TEFNUT (Egy)	sea
TIAMIT (Bab)	chaos
UPIS (Egy)	chief, nature
UZUME (Jap)	mirth

Equivalent goddesses include:

Arts: Gk *ATHENE*; **Roman** *MINERVA*

Beauty: Gk *APHRODITE, ARTEMIS*; **Roman** *DIANA, VENUS*

Chaos: Gk *CHAOS*; **Other** TIAMIT (Bab)

Chief: Gk *HERA*; **Roman** *JUNO*; **Other** *ISIS, UPIS* (Egy), *DEVI* (Ind), BELIT/BELTIS (Bab)

Childbirth: Gk *HERA*; **Roman** *JUNO*

Cup-bearer: Gk *HEBE*; **Roman** *JUVENTAS*

Dance: Gk *TERPSICHORE*

Dawn: Gk *EOS*; **Roman** *AURORA*

Destruction: Other DEVI, *KALI* (Ind), *HEL* (Nor)

Earth: Gk *GAEA/GE*; **Roman** *CERES, FAUNA, MAIA, TELLUS/TERRA*; **Other** LUA (It) [*fertility, nature*]

Fates: Gk *MOIRAI*; **Roman** *PARCAE*

Fertility: Gk *CYBELE, DANAE, RHEA*; **Roman** *CERES, DIANA, OPS*; **Other** *FRIGG* (Nor), BELIT, INNIN, ISHTAR (Bab), ATERGATIS (Syrian), EOSTRE (A-Sax [Easter]) [*earth, nature*]

Flowers: Gk *CHLORIS*; **Roman** *FLORA*

Fortune: Gk TYCHE; **Roman** FORTUNA

Furies: Gk *ERINYES*, EUMENIDES; **Roman** *FURIAE*

Health: Gk *HYGIEA*; **Roman** SALUS

Hearth: Gk *HESTIA*; **Roman** *VESTA*

Hunting: Gk *ARTEMIS*; **Roman** *DIANA*; **Other** BENDIS (Thrace)

Infatuation: Gk *ATE*

Invention: Roman *MINERVA*

Lightning: Roman *MINERVA*

Love: Gk *APHRODITE*; **Roman** *VENUS*; **Other** *ISHTAR* (Bab), *ISIS* (Egy), *FREYA* (Nor), *ASTARTE* (Phoen)

Messenger: Gk *ARTEMIS*

Moon: Gk *ARTEMIS, SELENE*; **Roman** *DIANA, JUNO, LUNA*; **Other** BENDIS (Thrace)

Nature: Gk *ARTEMIS, DEMETER*; **Roman** *CERES, DIANA, OPS*; **Other** *ISIS, UPIS* (Egy), HOLDA (Ger)

Night: Gk *HECATE, NYX*; **Rom** Nox; **Other** *HEL* (Nor)

Oracles: Roman *MAIA*

Peace: Gk *IRENE*; **Roman** *PAX*

Pleasure: Other BAST (Egy), UZUME (Jap)

Rainbow: Gk *IRIS*

Retribution: Gk *ATE, NEMESIS*; **Other** MENI (Bab)

Sea: Gk *AMPHITRITE*; **Other** TEFNUT (Egy)

Song: Gk *TERPSICHORE*

Space: Gk CHAOS

Truth: Other MA, MAAT (Egy)

Underworld: Gk *HECATE, PERSEPHONE*; **Roman** *LIBERA, PROSERPINE*; **Other** *HEL* (Nor)

Victory: Gk *NIKE*; **Roman** *VICTORIA*

Virginity: Gk *ARTEMIS*

War: Gk *ATHENE*, ENYO; **Roman** BELLONA, *MINERVA*; **Other** *BRUNHILDA* (Nor), NERIO (Sabine)

Wisdom: Gk *ATHENE*; **Roman** *MINERVA*; **Other** SULIS (Celt)

Witchcraft: Gk *HECATE*

Youth: Gk *HEBE*; **Roman** *JUVENTAS*

GOD'S BLOOD ICHOR.
GOD WILLING DG, DV.
GO IN(TO/SIDE) 1. ENTER, PENETRATE. 2. Hidden word, e.g. **Miss Theresa Wayman goes in with a will** (6, 1, 3) = THERE'S A WAY. 3. Word or letter goes into another, e.g. **To serve, I have to go into the water** (6) = WA*I*TER.
GOLD *METAL*; AU (*chem*). OR (*herald*). BULLSEYE (archery). OLYMPIC WINNER. YELLOW *COLOUR*. *Anniversary* (50th). [**fool's gold** = pyrites. *Company* (livery); *Danae*].
~ **DIGGER** FORTY-NINER, PANNER, PROSPECTOR. LEECH, TRAMP, VAMPIRE.
GOLDEN FLEECE Skin of fabled golden ram which rescued *Helle* and her br Phrixus. It was hung in the temple of Ares until brought back by *Jason* and the *Argonauts*.
GOLF CLUB BLASTER, BRASSIE, CLEEK, *DRIVER*, *IRON*, MASHIE, NIBLICK, *PUTTER*, SAND-WEDGE, *SPOON*, *WEDGE*, *WOOD*. PGA, R AND A, USGA. HOYLAKE, PORTLAND, ST ANDREWS.
GOLF COURSE LINKS; FOREGROUND (crypt). BIRKDALE, HOYLAKE, MUIRFIELD, PORTLAND, ST ANDREWS, *SANDWICH*, SUNNINGDALE, TROON. [par, bogey (evens), *birdie* (1 under), *eagle* (2 under), *albatross* (3 under)].

GOLLY DOLL. GOSH, MY.

GOOD ADEQUATE, EFFICIENT, GENUINE, RIGHT,
SATISFACTORY, SOUND, VALID. AGREEABLE,
BENEVOLENT, COMMENDABLE, EXCELLENT,
FAVOURABLE, KIND, UNTAINTED, VIRTUOUS,
WHOLESOME [Sabbath/Sunday's *child*]; (**opp** = evil).
OBEDIENT, PROPER, WELL-BEHAVED/MANNERED (**opp**
= *bad*). **Pl** = FREIGHT, LINE, MERCHANDISE, WARES.
THE REAL THING.

GOODFELLOW SOCIABLE PERSON. ROBIN; *FAIRY*. SAINT,
ST (crypt).

GOODMAN FATHER, HUSBAND. SAINT, ST (crypt).

GOON DOLT, FOOL. GUARD (mil sl). HEAVY, THUG.
CONTINUE, PROCEED (crypt go*on).

GOOSE 1. SILLY CREATURE, SIMPLETON. IRON (tailor's).
POKE. 2. *BIRD* of genus ANSER: BARNACLE, BEAN,
BRENT, CANADA, GREYLAG, PINKFOOTED, SOLAN
(gannet), WHITEFRONTED. **Assembly** = flock, gaggle, skein;
male = GANDER; **fem** = GOOSE; **offspring** = gosling. Sixth day
of *Christmas* song.

GORGON Gk myth winged fem *monsters*, with snakes for hair:
EURYALE (the Leaper), *MEDUSA* (the Ruler), STHENO (the
Strong).

GOSPEL DOCTRINE, GLAD TIDINGS; CHRIST'S
BIOGRAPHY [Matthew, Mark, Luke, John]. Four gospelmakers
in *song*. BASIC TEACHING/TRUTH.

GOVERNESS Privately employed fem teacher, NANNY; **celeb**: Alice
(*Milne*); Anna Leon-Owens (Anna & the King of Siam, Margaret
Landon); Jane Eyre (~, C. *Brontë*); Henriette Desportes (All This
and Heaven Too, Rachel Field); Miss Madrigal (The Chalk
Garden, Enid Bagnold); Maria (von Trapp, the Sound of Music);
Mary Poppins (~, P. L. Travers); Miss Jessel (*ghost*, The Turn of
the Screw, Henry James); Nana (*dog* in Peter Pan, J. M. *Barrie*);
Miss Prism (The Importance of Being Earnest, Wilde); Miss Pross
(2 Cities, *Dickens*); The Storyteller (~ to Flora and Miles; The
Turn of the Screw, Henry James).

GOVERNOR 1. BEY (Turk). HE. CONTROLLER (mech).
FATHER. 2. RULER, usually mil and often on behalf of some
other person or authority; COMMISSIONER, TETRARCH,
VICEROY; **celeb**: CLIVE (Ind); FELIX (Rom); WARREN
HASTINGS (Brit); PONTIUS PILATE (Rom).

GO WRONG *Anag.* ERR, SIN. GET LOST. OG (crypt).

GP *DOCTOR. GROUP.*

GR GRAND, GREAT. GREECE. GRAIN. GRAM(ME).

GRACE 1. ADORN, *HONOUR*, *SET OFF*. CHARM,
ELEGANCE, REFINEMENT [Tuesday's *child*]. FAVOUR,
LIKING, BOON, CONCESSION, PRIVILEGE. CLEMENCY,
MERCY. PRAYERS, THANKSGIVING. ADDRESS (form of,
for Archbishop, Duchess, Duke). EXTRA NOTE (mus).
BATSMAN, CRICKETER, EM, GF, WG. *DARLING*.
'HANNAH'. 2. Gk *goddess* daughters of Zeus, bestowers of
beauty, charm and mirth: AGLAIA, EUPHROYSNE and
THALIA. CHARITES (Gk); GRATIAE (Rom).

~ **ROAD** TEST GROUND (*cricket*).

GRADUATION MARKING, *MEASUREMENT*, SCALE;
VERNIER. ACADEMIC DEGREE, PASS, QUALIFICATION.

GRAEAE The PHORCYDES, Gk myth old women, sis to *Gorgons*:
DINO, ENYO and PEPHREDRO. Had the bodies of *swans*, only
one tooth and one eye between them; consulted by *Perseus* in his
quest for *Medusa*.

GRAHAME KENNETH, *WRITER* (Wind in the Willows; Toad of
Toad Hall; *Badger*, *Mole*, Ratty, *Toad*).

GRAND G, GR. CHIEF, HIGHEST RANK. DISTINGUISHED,
FINE, GRANDIOSE, GREAT, MAGNIFICENT, *NOBLE*,
SPLENDID. PIANO. RIVER (Can). WATERFALL. $1,000;
£1,000; THOUSAND, hence M or K. *THEATRE*.

GRASS 1. *BETRAY*, NARK, SNEAK. *SNAKE*. *DRUG*, HERB,
POT. FELL, KNOCK DOWN (sl). 2. *PLANT*. GRAZING,
HERBAGE, LAWN, PASTURE, *PLAIN*, SWARD, TURF;
FODDER. ASPARAGUS (sl) [aftermath; hay, ted]. And see
PLAIN for geog grasslands. **Types:**

3-letters	COIX	TORE
ERS	DISS	
FOG	DOUB	**5-letters**
RYE	DURA	*ARROW*
	KANS	BRIZA
4-letters	LYME	BUNCH
AIRA	REED	COUCH
ALFA	RUSA	CUTCH
BENT	TARE	DURRA
BLUE	TEFF	GRAMA

HALFA
HAULM
MELIC
ORYZA
PANIC
QUAKE
SEDGE
SPEAR
VETCH

MEDICK
NARDUS
PAMPAS
PHLEUM
QUITCH
REDTOP
RUPPIA
TWITCH
UNIOLA

SORGHUM
SQUITCH
TIMOTHY
VETIVER
WAGWANT
WHANGEE
ZIZANIA

8+ letters
CITRONELLA
CLEAVERS
DOG-GRASS
DOG-WHEAT
ELEUSINE
GYNERIUM
JOB'S TEARS
PUSS-TAIL

6-letters
BAJREE
BARCOO
CACTUS
DARNEL
FESCUE
FIORIN
LOLIUM
MARRAM

7-letters
ALFALFA
CLIVERS
ESPARTO
EULALIA
FESTUCA
FOGGAGE
FOXTAIL
LUCERNE

GRASSHOPPER CICADA, *CRICKET*, GRIG, KATYDID; *INSECT*; JUMPER (crypt).

GRATE (s/l *great*). FIREPLACE [Adam]. GRIND, IRRITATE, RASP, RUB. GRATING, GRILLE. GRATITUDE (arch).

GRAVE TOMB, TRENCH. CARVE, ENGRAVE, ETCH, SCULPT. IMPORTANT, SERIOUS, WEIGHTY; DIGNIFIED, PLAIN, SOLEMN, SOMBRE. CLEAN, SCRAPE, SCRUB (naut). ACCENT (`). 'TRISTRAM'. Pl = *POET*.

GRAVITY G. MASS, WEIGHT. SERIOUSNESS.

GRAYS INN LAW SOCIETY [benchers, call to the bar, griffin].

GREAT (s/l *grate*). ABLE, IMPORTANT, PRE-EMINENT; G, BIG, LARGE. Pl = Final exam in classics/philosophy (O). [Alexander the ~ (Gk), Alfred the ~ (Eng), Catherine the ~ (Russ), Frederick the ~ (Prussia), Peter the ~ (Russ)].

GREAT LAKES Group of *lakes* in Canada and US: **in both**: ERIE, HURON, ONTARIO, SUPERIOR (biggest); **in US only**: MICHIGAN.

GREED(Y) AVARICIOUS, CUPIDITY, GLUTTONY, PIGGY (sl), VORACIOUS [*Bunter*, Fat Boy (Pickwick), Phaeax, Mammon, *Seven Deadly Sins*].

GREEK G, Gk. CUNNING PERSON, SHARPER. DOUBLE

DUTCH, INCOMPREHENSIBLE.

GREEK GOD See *GOD*.

~ GODDESS See *GODDESS*.

GREEN *COLOUR*, VERT (*herald*). IN LEAF, VERDANT,
VITAL. FRESH, UNRIPE. ISLAND. DEB, GULLIBLE,
IMMATURE, INEXPERIENCED, MILD, *RAW*, TYRO,
YOUNG, *VIRGIN* (**opp** = *experienced*). COMMON LAND.
PUTTING AREA (golf). RIVER (US). **Pl** = VEGETABLES.

GREENBACK BUCK, DOLLAR (sl). NEERG (crypt).

GREEN RUSHES See *song*.

GREET ACCOST, HAIL, *SALUTE*; AVE, HI, WELCOME.
CRY, WEEP (Sc).

GREETING AVE, HEY, HI, HO; *SALUTE*. HALLO, HELLO,
HILLO, HOLLO, HULLO (**opp** = farewell). CRYING,
WEEPING (Sc).

GREGORY APERIENT, POWDER. PECK (film). POPE.

GREY *COLOUR*. WHIG. DEPRESSING, DISMAL. RIVER
(NZ). ANONYMOUS, INDETERMINATE,
UNIDENTIFIABLE. ANCIENT, EXPERIENCED,
IMMEMORIAL. BERYL ~ (theat). LADY JANE ~. **Pl** = 2nd
DRAGOONS (mil).

GREYFRIAR FRANCISCAN, *FRIAR*. **Pl** = *SCHOOL* [*Bunter*,
Famous Five].

GRIEF DOLE, DOLOUR, MISERY, REGRET, SORROW,
TROUBLE. DISASTER.

GRILSE *FISH*. *Offspring* of *salmon*.

GRIP *BITE*, CLASP, NIP, *PINCH*, SQUEEZE. *BAGGAGE*.
RAVEN (Barnaby Rudge, *Dickens*).

GROOM FIANCE, HUSBAND, MATE. OSTLER; BRUSH,
CURRYCOMB, TIDY.

GROUND EARTH (elect). EDUCATE, TEACH, TRAIN.
PREVENT FLYING, KEEP OUT OF THE AIR. HONED,
POLISHED, POWDERED. BOTTOM, SEABED; SOLID.
BASE, FOUNDATION, SUBSTRATUM; SURFACE. AREA,
EARTH, LAND, TERRITORY; STREET-LEVEL. PLAYING
FIELD (*cricket* ~, *football* ~, *golf course*, *racetrack*, *rugby* ~,
tennis court). **Pl** = BELIEF, PRINCIPLE, REASONS.
GRANULES, POWDER. PREMISES, PROPERTY.

GROUND RENT HIRE CHARGE, LEASE. CANYON,
CREVASSE, FISSURE, RAVINE (crypt); EARTHQUAKE
(crypt).

GROUNDS FOR 1. AUTHORITY, FOUNDATION, REASON TO BELIEVE. 2. See *cricket*, *football*, *golf*, *racetrack*, *rugby*, *tennis*.

GROUP GP. CLIQUE, CLUSTER, KNOT. *SET*. CLASSIFY.

GROUSE *BIRD*, GAMEBIRD, CAPERCAILLIE, MOOR FOWL, PTARMIGAN, RED ~ (**assembly** = pack; **male red** ~ = GORLOCK). COMPLAIN, GRUMBLE, *TICK*.

GRUB STREET THE *PRESS*. HACK WRITERS (now Milton Street).

GRUMPY BEARISH, ILL-TEMPERED, SURLY. *DWARF* (Snow White).

GRUNDY 1. Solomon ~ (b on Monday, christened on Tuesday, mar on Wednesday, took ill on Thursday, got worse on Friday, d on Saturday and was buried on Sunday). 2. Mrs ~; personification of prudery (*unseen* neighbour of Mrs Ashfield in Tom Morton's Speed the Plough).

GUARD PROTECT, SENTRY, *WATCH*, VIGIL; CAVEMAN (crypt) [~ **of honour** = *chaperone*]. *CONDUCTOR* (rly), RAILWAYMAN. **Pl** = COLDSTREAM, FOOT, GRENADIER, HORSE, IRISH, LIFE, SCOTS, WELSH; BLUES, ROYALS [*household* ~]. OLD ~, PRAETORIAN ~, PRUSSIAN ~, YEOMAN, YOUNG ~.

GUERNSEY SWEATER, WOOLLY (jersey). *CATTLE*. *ISLAND* (CI). GBG (*car plate*). *LILY*.

GUEVARA CHE.

GUIDE ASSIST, LEAD, SHOW; ADVISER, CICERONE, SCOUT. *CONDUCTOR*, DRAGOMAN, INTERPRETER, PILOT. INSTINCT. MANUAL. STANDARD. CHANNEL. GUARD, *RAIL*, ROD (mech).

GUIDED MISSILE ARROW, DART. *WEAPON* (and see *MISSILE*).

GUINEA *COUNTRY* (ex Fr W Af). GOLD *COIN*, 21 SHILLINGS. (PROFESSIONAL) FEE.

~ **BISSAU** *COUNTRY* (ex Port Guinea).

~ **FOWL** *BIRD*.

~ **PIG** PET, RODENT. TEST CASE. Pl (crypt).

GUINEVERE The queen of *King Arthur*, her infidelity with *Lancelot* led to the break-up of the *Round Table*. [*Camelot*, Mordred].

GULES RED (*herald*).

GULF ABYSS, CHASM, DEPTH, GAP. LARGE INLET/BAY (geog); **celebrated**:

ADEN (Af/Arab)
ALASKA (US)
ANTALYA (Turk)
AQABA (Isr)
BOTHNIA (Fin/Swe)
CALIFORNIA (Mex)
CAMBAY (Ind)
CARPENTARIA (Aus)
CHIHLI (Ch)
CORINTH (Gk)
FINLAND (~)
GAETA (It)
GASCONY (Fr)
GENOA (It)
GIZHIGA (USSR)
GUINEA (NW Af)
HONDURAS (~)
ISKENDERUN (Turk)
IZMIR (Turk)
KUTCH (Ind)
LAKONIA (Gk)
LIONS (Fr)
MARTABAN (Bur)
MESSINA (Gk)
MEXICO (~/US)

MOSQUITOS (Panama)
OB (USSR)
OMAN (Arab/Pers)
ORISTANO (It)
PANAMA (~)
PAPUA (New Guinea)
PATRAS (Gk)
PERSIAN (Arab/~)
RIGA (USSR)
ST LAWRENCE (Can)
ST MALO (Fr)
SALERNO (It)
SAN JORGE (Arg; Sp)
SAN MATIAS (Arg)
SIAM (~ etc)
SIDRA/SIRTE (Libya)
SPENCER (Aus)
SUEZ (Egy)
TARANTO (It)
TARTARY (USSR)
TONA (USSR)
TONKING (Ch)
VALENCIA (Sp)
VENICE (It)

GULL DUPE, FOOL. SEABIRD; **breeds**: BLACK-BACKED ~,
COB, COMMON ~, FULMAR, HERRING ~, KITTIWAKE,
MEW ~, TERN. **Pl** = TORQUAY (*football* team).
GUN ARM, FIREARM, GAT, ROD, ORDNANCE, *WEAPON*.
SHOOT. **Celebrated**: BIG BERTHA, THE KING'S
DAUGHTER (H.v.), THE LONDON (H.v.), THE
MESSENGER (H.v.), MONS MEG, ZAM-ZAMMAH (Kim,
Kipling). **Pl** = RA (battery).
GUNMAN GANGSTER, MOBSTER. RA (crypt). STARTER.
GUNNEL *BUTTERFISH*. GUNWALE (boat's side).
GUNNER *GUNMAN* (q.v.). RIFLEMAN. [*patron saint*]. RA. **Pl**
= ARSENAL (*football*).
GUTTER PRESS NEWSPAPER, RAG.
GUY CHAP, FELLOW. FAWKES [Robert Catesby, Thomas Percy,
Parkin Cake]. ROPE, STAY.

GYGES Gk myth *MONSTER* (Uranid), s of *Uranus* and *Ge*, with 100 arms and 50 heads.

GYM LESSONS PE, PT; EXERCISES.

GYNOPHOBIA *Aversion* to women.

H 1. HARD. HORRIFIC (film *censorship*). HOSPITAL. HOT. HOTEL. HOUR. HUNGARY (*car plate*). HYDROGEN (*chem*). 2. Dropping the letter H is indicated by an apostrophe in the clue, e.g. **Little brother makes money with 'is loaf** (5) = BR*EAD (**loaf** = head; **money** = bread).

h Husband of.

HA HAHNIUM (*chem*). HORSE ARTILLERY. HALF-LAUGH (crypt).

HABIT *CUSTOM*, WONT. *DRESS*.

HABITATION ABODE, *HOME*, *HOUSE*, LIVING QUARTERS; **specifically**:

Animal	Habitation
Badger	*EARTH*, SET(T)
Beaver	*LODGE*
Bee	HIVE
Bird	NEST
Cattle	MANGER, MIDDEN
Eagle	EYRIE
Fox	BURROW, *EARTH*
Hare	*FORM*
Heron	COLONY
Horse	*STABLE*
Insect eggs	NIDUS
Otter	*HOLT, LODGE*
Penguin	*ROOKERY*
Pig	*STY*
Rabbit	*BURROW*, WARREN
Rook	*ROOKERY*
Seal	*ROOKERY*
Sparrow	COLONY
Squirrel	*DRAY*, DREY
Swan	COLONY
Wild beast	*DEN*, LAIR

Habitation	Animal
Burrow	*FOX, RABBIT*
Colony	HERON, SPARROW, *SWAN*
Den	WILD ANIMAL
Dray, Drey	SQUIRREL
Earth	*BADGER, FOX*
Eyrie	*EAGLE*
Form	HARE
Hive	*BEE*
Holt	OTTER
Lair	WILD ANIMAL
Lodge	*BEAVER*, OTTER
Manger	*CATTLE*
Midden	*CATTLE*
Nest	*BIRD*
Nidus	INSECT EGGS
Rookery	PENGUIN, *ROOK*, SEAL
Set(t)	*BADGER*
Stable	*HORSE*
Sty	PIG
Warren	*RABBIT*

HADES Gk *god* of the *UNDERWORLD*, s of *Cronos* and *Rhea*, br of
Poseidon and *Zeus*, mar to *Persephone* (**Rom** = *DIS*, ORCUS,
PLUTO). By association, *HELL* itself; ABADDON (Heb),
EREBUS (Gk), GEHENNA (bibl), INFERNO (Dante), SHEOL
(Heb), TARTARUS (Gk myth), VALHALLA (Nor); [*Cerberus*,
Charon, *Hecate*, *Styx*].
HAGGARD 1. DRAWN, WILD LOOKING. UNTAMED HAWK.
2. (Sir Henry) RIDER ~ (writer; **books**: Ayesha, Dawn, King
Solomon's Mines, Jess, She; Allan Quartermain).
HAIL (s/l *hale*). ALOHA, AVE; SALUTE. FROZEN RAIN.
HAIR FILAMENT. CURL, LOCK, TRESS [*Absolom*; *Esau*, Nisus,
Samson; hirsute]; BARNET (*rh sl*).
HAIRDRESSER BARBER, COIFFEUR, WAVER; **celeb**: MISS
MOUCHER (Copperfield, *Dickens*); MR PARTRIDGE (Tom
Jones, Fielding); PAUL SWEEDLEPIPE (Chuzzle, *Dickens*);
FIGARO (Barber of Seville, Rossini); SWEENEY TODD.
BRUSH, COMB, CURLER, *GRIP*, SLIDE (crypt).
HAL HENRY.
HALE (s/l *hail*). FIT, WELL. ORIGINATE. HAUL.

HALF 1. DEMI, SEMI; SPLIT. 2. Half of preceding or next word, e.g. **Half bottle** = BOT or TLE. 3. As, **Not** ~, remove half of word, e.g. **Mrs Mopp's charming, not half!** (4) = CHAR(ming).

~ **BACK** *FOOTBALLER*. IMED, IMES (crypt). BA or CK (crypt).

~ **DAY** EARLY CLOSING. AM, PM (crypt).

~ **HEARTED** 1. LUKEWARM, UNENTHUSIASTIC. 2. Remove one of two identical letters in middle of word indicated, e.g. **Half hearted rabble** = RABLE.

~ **HUNTER** WATCH. HUN or TER (crypt).

~ **SOVEREIGN** TEN SHILLINGS, XS. WILLIAM or MARY (crypt).

HALT STOP (**opp** = *go on*). CRIPPLED, LAME, LIMP.

HAM Bibl s of *Noah*. BUTTOCK, THIGH. SALT PIG; **comp** = *eggs*. AMATEUR RADIO OPERATOR, BREAKER (sl), CB ENTHUSIAST. ACT BADLY (hence CAT — crypt), CABOTIN, POOR PERFORMER.

HAMBLEDON *CRICKET* GROUND.

HAMLET VILLAGE. GREAT DANE, PRINCE OF DENMARK (*Shakespeare*). PIGLET, PORKER (crypt).

HAMMER NAILER, TOOL; BIRMINGHAM SPANNER (sl); STRIKE. EDWARD, [Wallace (hist)]. PIGFARMER (crypt). **Pl** = WEST HAM (*football team*).

~ **THROWER** THOR (Nor myth).

HAMPDEN PARK *FOOTBALL* GROUND (Sc).

HAMPER BASKET [Fortnums; picnic]. HINDER, LET (**opp** = *help*).

HAND MITT, PALM, PAW (*bone*; *Belshazzar*; *Jeroboam*). HELP; PASS. HOLDING (cards). CREWMAN, SEAMAN (naut). BUNCH (bananas). JOINT (pork). POINTER (clock). 4 INS (horse).

HANDLE FEEL, TOUCH. *GRIP*, HOLDER. MANAGE, TREAT. DEAL IN. ADDRESS, TITLE (sl).

HANGMAN EXECUTIONER; TOPPER (crypt) [*tarot*]; **celeb**: PETIT ANDRE (Quentin Durward, Scott), DENNIS (Rudge, *Dickens*), DERRICK, KETCH, PIERREPOINT. GALLERY DIRECTOR (crypt).

HAPPY CONTENTED. *DWARF* (Snow White).

HARD H; DURABLE, TOUGH. RELENTLESS.

~ **LINES** TOUGH LUCK. BR, *RAILWAY* TRACK, RLY (crypt).

HARNESS EQUIP(MENT), FASTEN(ING), LIGAMENT,

STRAP. HORSE TRAPPINGS: BIT, BRIDLE, BRIDOON, CURB, HACKAMORE, HEADSTALL, MARTINGALE, PELHAM, REINS, RESTRAINT, SNAFFLE, TRACE [loriner]. HOOK UP, UTILIZE. DEFENSIVE ARMOUR.

HARP NAG. PLUCK; *INSTRUMENT* (mus), LYRE [*Aeolus*].

HARPY 1. HARRIDAN, *SHREW*, TERMAGANT. LYRICAL (crypt). 2. Malignant monsters with woman's head and vulture's body, capable of defiling all they touched: AELLO, CELAENO, OCYPETE, PODARGE. **Pl** = storm *winds* in the form of the dd of *Electra* and Thaumas. 3. *Ship* (Mr Midshipman Easy, Marryat).

HARRIER *BIRD*, HAWK. HUNTING *DOG*. COUNTRY RUNNER (hare and hounds). *AIRCRAFT®*: FIGHTER, JUMP JET, VTO. HARASSER, MOLESTER.

HARRIS *MATERIAL*, TWEED. [*Three* Men in a Boat; *unseen* in Chuzzle (*Dickens*)].

HARROW BREAKER, DRAG (farm). LACERATE, WOUND. HARRY, ROB. WRACK. *PUBLIC SCHOOL*.

HARRY HAL, HENRY; 'HOME RULER'. TATE. HARASS, MOLEST, WORRY. (Old ~ = devil).

HARVARD UNIVERSITY (US) [Cantabrigian]. AIRCRAFT (trainer).

HARVEST 1. CROP, GATHER. PRODUCE, YIELD. REAP. HUSBAND, LAY UP. 2. **God: Gk** = CRONOS, **Rom** = SATURNUS.

HAT HEAD COVERING: BEARSKIN, BERET, BILLYCOCK, BONNET, BOWLER, BUSBY, CAP, COVER, DERBY (US), EASTER BONNET, FEDORA (US), FLAT ~, GIBUS, HOMBERG, KEPI, LID, MITRE, OPERA ~, PEAKED ~, PETASUS (Gk), PORKPIE, SHAKO, SOMBRERO, STETSON, STOVEPIPE ~, TEN-GALLON ~, TILE, TITFER (*rh sl*), TOP ~, TOPEE, TOP GEAR (crypt), TOPI, TOPPER, TRILBY, WIDEAWAKE, PANAMA, LEGHORN.

HATRED 1. *AVERSION*, DISLIKE, ABHORRENCE (**opp** = *love*). MILITARY POLICE, MP (crypt). STAFF OFFICER (crypt). 2. Prefix miso- as misogamy (marriage), misogyny (women), misology (reason), misoneism (novelty).

HAVISHAM *RECLUSE* (Gt Ex, *Dickens*). *LAWYER* (Little Lord Fauntleroy, Burnett).

HAWK BIRD OF PREY; **breeds**: BUZZARD, CARACARA, *EAGLE*, FALCON, GOSHAWK, GYRFALCON, HOBBY ~, KESTREL, LANNER, *MERLIN*, MUSKET, OSPREY,

PEREGRINE, RAPTOR, SPARROW ~, VULTURE; **assembly**
= *cast*, **offspring** = bowet [falconer; ostringer]. AIRCRAFT.
COUGH, SPIT. PEDDLE. PLASTERER'S BOARD.
WARMONGER (**opp** = dove).

HAWKER *AIRCRAFT*. FALCONER [hood, jess, lure].
CHEAPJACK, PEDLAR, TINKER.

HAY DRIED GRASS [*measure*; ted]. *CASTLE*. DANCE
FIGURE. *RIVER* (Aus, Can).

HE HELIUM (*chem*). HIS EMINENCE. HIS EXCELLENCY;
GOVERNOR. HIGH EXPLOSIVE. MAN, MALE.

HEAD 1. BEAN, LOAF (*rh sl*), NAPPER, NOD, NODDLE,
NOGGIN, NOODLE, ONION, PATE, POLL, SWEDE; **comp** =
shoulders [*bone*]. CHIEF, MASTER, TOP. CAPE, NESS
(geog). FACE, OBVERSE (coin; **opp** = reverse, tail). 2. Use
first letter, e.g. **Spithead** = s.

HEADGEAR *HAT* [*Church dress*]. PIT WINDING.

HEADINGLEY TEST(ING) GROUND (*cricket*).

HEADLINE BANNER, LEADER, STREAMER. PROFILE,
SILHOUETTE. **Pl** = FROWN (crypt).

HEAD OFF 1. EXECUTE, GUILLOTINE. INTERCEPT. 2. Drop
first letter, e.g. **Head off Jack's partner, and she's not very well** (3)
= (J)ILL.

HEAD OF MI.5 M; Q.

HEADQUARTERS CENTRAL OFFICE, HQ. H, E, A or D
(crypt). Q (crypt). N, E, S, W (crypt).

HEAL (s/l *heel*). GET BETTER, MEND (**opp** = wound).

HEALING 1. MENDING, RECOVERING. 2. **God: Gk and Rom** =
APOLLO; **Ind** = VISHNU.

HEALTH 1. FITNESS, SOUNDNESS, WELFARE, WELLBEING
(**Unions** = COHSE, NUPE). TOAST (drink). 2. **Goddesses: Gk**
= HYGIEA, **Rom** = SALUS.

HEAR (s/l *here*). 1. HARK, LIST(EN), PERCEIVE. 2. *Sounds
like*, often given as 'we hear', e.g. **We hear you when the cuppa's
downed** (5, 3) = AFTER TEA (after T in the alphabet, comes U).

HEARD (s/l *herd*). 1. HARKENED, LISTENED, PERCEIVED.
2. *Sounds like*, e.g. **Elk are heard in loving talk** = DEAR.

HEARER AUDITOR, LISTENER. EAR (crypt).

HEART (s/l hart). 1. CENTRE, CORE, MIDDLE. COURAGE,
WILL; BREAST, LOVE, MIND, SOUL, INTELLECT.
ORGAN (med, *study*), PUMP (sl); **comp** = soul. BRAVE
FELLOW. **Pl** = CARDS, SUIT (*Alice*). 2. Middle of word, e.g.

heartbreak = E; **lighthearted** = G. 3. Put word in another, e.g. **A man little by little at heart in the New World** (8) = A*M*ERIC*AN.

HEARTH 1. FIREPLACE. 2. **Goddesses: Gk** = *HESTIA*, **Rom** = VESTA.

HEARTLESS 1. CRUEL, PITILESS, MERCILESS. 2. Omit middle letters, e.g. **Heartless maple** = MALE.

HEAT ANGER, INFLAME. HOT WEATHER, WARMTH (**opp** = cold). ELIMINATOR, SINGLE RACE.

HEATHER CALLUNA, ERICA, LING. WARM HER (crypt).

HEAVEN 1. FIRMAMENT, SKY, VAULT. EMPYREAN, GOD'S ABODE, PROMISED LAND; ASGARD, VALHALLA (Nor); ASSAMA (Islam); ELYSIAN FIELDS, ELYSIUM, *OLYMPUS* (Gk myth); NIRVANA (Ind); ZION (Christ). 2. **Gk god** = *URANUS, ZEUS*; **opp** = *underworld*.

HEAVENLY 1. ATTRACTIVE, DIVINE, EXCELLENT. 2. Of or in the sky, thus **Heavenly pub** (6) = SK*INN*Y.

~ **BODY** MOON, ORB, *PLANET*, STAR, SUN. BATHING BEAUTY, MISS WORLD®.

HEBE 1. Gk *goddess* of YOUTH; cup-bearer to the gods; d of *Zeus* and *Hera*; mar *Hercules*. DIA. **Rom** = JUVENTAS. 2. A minor *PLANET*. 3. SHRUB (evergreen).

HECATE 1. Gk *goddess* of night, witchcraft and the *underworld* [*Nyx, Persephone*, Proserpine]. 2. A minor *PLANET*.

HECTOR *BULLY, HARROW*, HARRY, INTIMIDATE. 2. Gk myth s of *Priam* and *Hecuba*; mar Andromache; k by *Achilles* at *Troy*. One of the *Nine Worthies*. [T and C (*Shak*)].

HECUBA 1. Gk myth wife of *Priam* (king of *Troy*), m of *Cassandra, Hector* and *Paris*. 2. A minor *PLANET*.

HEEL (s/l *heal*). BASE OF MAST. PART OF FOOT [*Achilles; bone*]. CAD, SCAMP. LEAN, LIST, TILT.

HEL (s/l *hell*). Nor *goddess* who received those who died of misery and darkness; d of *Loki* and Angurboda.

HELD 1. DETAINED, GRASPED, GRIPPED, KEPT, RESTRICTED. OCCUPIED, OWNED, POSSESSED. SUPPORTED. CELEBRATED, OBSERVED (*custom*). CONTINUED. 2. Hidden word, or word in another, e.g. **Wolfishly upheld by a thread** (6) = L*UP*INE.

~ **BACK** 1. RESTRAINED. HESITATED, IMPEDED, REFRAINED. 2. Hidden word backwards, e.g. **Held back by Sir, approaching the Capital** (5) = PA*RIS. 3. Word reversed in another, e.g. **It's held back by row over a joint** (7) = BA*STI*NG.

HELEN 1. GIRL. 'FIREBRAND'. 2. Gk myth d of *Leda* and *Zeus*, the *twin* of *Clytemnestra*; mar Menelaus, king of Sparta, whence *Paris* carried her off, thus starting the war at *Troy*. Renowned for her *beauty* [T and C (*Shak*)]. 3. A minor *PLANET*.

HELENUS Gk myth s of *Priam*.

HELIOS Gk *god* of the SUN. Son of Hyperion and The(i)a; br of *Eos* (**Rom** = Aurora) and *Selene* (**Rom** = Luna). **Rom** = SOL.

HELIUM HE (*chem*).

HELL (s/l Hel). *HADES*, HECK, INFERNO, PIT, *UNDERWORLD* (q.v.); **opp** = *heaven*. HE WILL (crypt).

HELLE Gk myth d of Athamas and Nephele. She and her br Phrixus were rescued by Nephele from sacrifice by Ino; they flew away on a golden ram (origin of the *golden fleece*), but Helle was drowned when she fell into the sea, which was thereafter called the *Hellespont*.

HELLESPONT DARDANELLES. Strait between Asias Major and Minor, named after *Helle*. [*Hero*, *Leander*].

HELP AID, ASSIST, HAND (**opp** = *hamper*); REMEDY. AVOID, ESCAPE. *CHAR*.

HELPLESS 1. LACKING ASSISTANCE. 2. Remove letters AID or HELP from word indicated, e.g. **Helpless maid** = M or, more cryptically, **Helpless first aid man** (4) = first*man = ADAM.

HEM BORDER, EDGE, TURN-UP. HESITATION. *COUGH*, HAWK.

HEN-HOUSE BATTERY, COOP.

HENRY HAL, HARRY. MEASURE (elect). DR JEKYLL [Edward *Hyde*].

~ VIII's WIVES in order: CATHERINE OF SPAIN (div), ANNE BOLEYN or BULLEN (beheaded), JANE SEYMOUR (d), ANNE OF CLEVES (div), CATHERINE HOWARD (beheaded), CATHERINE PARR (survived).

HEPHAESTUS Gk *god* of *FIRE*, s of *Zeus* and *Hera*. **Rom** = *VULCAN*.

HERA Queen of Gk *goddesses* (and of childbirth); d of *Cronos* and *Rhea*; sis of and mar to *Zeus*; m of Ares (**Rom** = *Mars*), *Hebe* (**Rom** = Juventas) and Hephaestus (**Rom** = *Vulcan*). **Rom** = JUNO.

HERACLES Gk myth s of Zeus and Alcmene; mar to Megara; an *Argonaut*. Maddened by *Hera*, he killed his children, and the Delphic *oracle* made him perform twelve labours; see Rom equivalent *HERCULES* for details.

HERALD FORESHADOW, FORETELL, *PROPHESY*.
MESSENGER, TRUMPETER, USHER (~ **of the gods** =
HERMES). COURT OFFICIAL, OFFICER OF STATE
(armorial bearings, pedigree, precedence): BATH,
CLARENC(I)EUX, *GARTER*, LORD LYON, NORROY,
ULSTER (all kings of arms); and *CHESTER*, LANCASTER,
RICHMOND, SOMERSET, WINDSOR, *YORK*. *MONTJOY*
(*Shak*); STENTOR (*Troy*). **Heraldic colours: black** = sable, **blue**
= azure, **brown** = tenne or tenny, **green** = vert, **gold** = or, **orange**
= tenny, **purple** = purpure, **red** = gules, **silver** = argent. **Heraldic
terms**: accosted (side by side), achievement (shield), addorsed
(back to back), cabossed (head cut at the neck), *canton* (a corner),
couchant (beast lying with head up), crined (bearing a mane),
dexter (right hand side), disclosed, displayed (wings spread),
dormant (beast lying with head down), embowed (bent), estoile
(star), fess (horizontal band), gardant (beast looking outward),
gorged (beast with crown round the neck), hauriant (fish with head
up), in pride (peacock with tail spread), jessed (with thongs),
lymphad (ship with oars), naiant (fish swimming), passant (beast
walking), rampant (beast upright on hind legs), regardant (beast
looking over its shoulder), sinister (left hand side), *wyvern* (winged
serpent).

HERB HERBERT (abbr). ANNUAL PLANT, BANE, WORT.
SIMPLE. [flavour; *spice*]; **types of ~s and spices** (includes carrots,
parsnips, turnips etc):

3-letters	AMENT	TANSY
BAY	AVENS	THYME
RUE	BASIL	
	CAPER	**6-letters**
4-letters	CHILI	BENNET
ALOE	CHIVE	BORAGE
DILL	CLARY	CATNIP
GEUM	CLOVE	CHILLI
MACE	CUMIN	CUMMIN
MINT	CURRY	ENDIVE
MOLY (myth)	INULA	FENNEL
RACE	MOULI	FERULA
SAGE	MUDAR	GARLIC
5-letters	ORVAL	GINGER
AGAVE	SPIKE	HARMEL

HERBAR	HARMALA	CHARLOCK
HYSSOP	KEDLACK	CINNAMON
LOVAGE	MUSTARD	COSTMARY
NUTMEG	OREGANO	MARJORAM
ORIGAN	PAPRIKA	ROSEMARY
PEPPER	PARSLEY	SAMPHIRE
RATTLE	PIMENTA	TARRAGON
SAVORY	PIMENTO	TRUE-LOVE
SESAME	RUE-WORT	TURMERIC
	SAFFRON	WOODRUFF
7-letters	SINAPIS	
ACONITE	WITLOOF	**9+ letters**
CARAWAY		ARTEMISIA
CAYENNE	**8-letters**	CORIANDER
CHERVIL	ALLSPICE	GILLYFLOWER
CHICORY	BRASSOCK	HOREHOUND
GINSENG	CAPSICUM	MONKSHOOD
		WOLFSBANE

HERCULES 1. *Constellation*. *HORSE*. 2. Latinised name of
HERACLES, also known as ALCIDES. The s of *Zeus* and
Alcmene, and half-br of Iphicles, ~ mar (1) Megara, (2) Deianira
and (3) *Hebe* (after he had been made immortal). Sentenced by the
Delphic *oracle* to perform 12 labours for Eurystheus as follows:

(1) Fight with Nemean *lion*.

(2) Killing the *hydra* at Lerna.

(3) Capture of the Arcadian *stag*.

(4) Destruction of the Erymanthian *boar*.

(5) Cleansing of the stable of *Augeas*.

(6) Destruction of the cannibal birds of Lake Stymphalis.

(7) Capture of the Cretan *bull*.

(8) Capture of the *mares* of Diomedes.

(9) Seizure of the *girdle* of Queen *Hippolyte*.

(10) Capture of the *monster* Geryon's *oxen* in Erythia.

(11) Fetching the golden *apples* of the *Hesperides*.

(12) Bringing *Cerberus* from *Hades*.

~ d when wife (2) steeped his cloak in the blood of the *centaur*
Nessus (who had been k by ~ with a poisoned arrow) so that the
poison transferred to ~ and k him. [*pillars of ~*].

HERD (s/l *heard*). 1. Noun of *assembly* (buffalo, cattle, elephants
etc); [*shepherd*]. **God: Gk** = *PAN*, **Rom** = *FAUNUS*, INUUS,

LUPERCUS. 2. *Constellation*.

HERE (s/l *hear*). 1. HAS ARRIVED. IN THIS PLACE. 2. Means 'in this answer', e.g. **Here I have shot at Shakespeare's villain** (4) = I*A*GO.

HEREWARD THE WAKE. HITHER (crypt).

HERMES 1. Gk myth s of *Zeus*, *HERALD* and MESSENGER of the *gods*; he is said to have invented the *lyre* by putting strings across the shell of a tortoise. (**Rom** = MERCURY) [caduceus; *robbers*]. 2. A minor *PLANET*.

HERMIT ANCHORITE, ASCETIC, *CAVEMAN*, CELLIST, C(O)ENOBITE, EREMITE, LONER, MONK, *RECLUSE* (q.v.), STYLITE; 9 (*tarot*); **celeb**: *ELIJAH* (bibl); PETER the ~ (Fr monk); SIMON STYLITES; TIMON (of Athens); patron St Alexis. CRAB.

HERO 1. Gk myth priestess of *Aphrodite* at Seston on the *Hellespont*. Her lover Leander used to swim across from Abydos to see her, and was drowned when the lighthouse failed one night. 2. IDOL. CHIEF CHARACTER, MALE LEAD (theat). BRAVE SOLDIER, SUPERMAN (**opp** = *coward*); **celeb** (**male**): *ACHILLES*, *ACTAEON*, *ADONIS*, *AENEAS*, *AGAMEMNON*, *AUTOLYCUS*, *BELLEREPHON*, *CASTOR*, *DAEDALUS*, *GANYMEDE*, *HECTOR*, *HERACLES*, *HERCULES*, *ICARUS*, *JASON*, *LAERTES*, *LEANDER*, LYSANDER, *ODYSSEUS*, *OEDIPUS*, *ORESTES*, ORION, *ORPHEUS*, *PARIS*, *PERSEUS*, POLLUX, *PRIAM*, *PYGMALION*, *NARCISSUS*, *SISYPHUS*, *TANTALUS*, *THESEUS*, *ULYSSES*; **celeb** (**fem**): *ANDROMEDA*, *ARACHNE*, *ATALANTA*, *CASSANDRA*, *CLYTEMNESTRA*, *DAPHNE*, *DIDO*, *DORIS*, *ELECTRA*, *ELISSA*, *EUROPA*, EURYDICE, *GALATEA*, IPHIGENIA, *HELEN*, *HELLE*, *HIPPOLYTE*, *JOCASTA*, *NIOBE*, *PANDORA*, *PENELOPE*.

HEROD 1. ~ the Great (b 73 B.C.); bibl king who mar Mariamne and was grand-f of Herodias [*Salome*]. His massacre of the innocents to avoid the rivalry of *Jesus* is now questioned. 2. ~ Antipas, s of (1), he mar Herodias (his own niece and w of his br) who was m of *Salome* by his br. ~ ordered the d of John the Baptist, when Herodias persuaded Salome to ask for it as payment for dancing (the seven veils) before him. 3. ~ Agrippa, two bibl kings, one of whom (grand-s of (1) and br-in-law of (2)) k James br of John, and the other (s of (3)) tried St Paul.

HERRING *FISH*: ALLICE, BLOATER (dried), KIPPER (smoked),

SHAD, TWAIT [~ bone, ~ gull, ~ pond].

HESITATION DELAY, ER, UM. STAMMERING, STUTTERING.

HESPERIDES Gk myth maidens (AEGLE, ERYTHEIA and HESPERUS), who guarded the golden apples given by *Ge* to *Hera* when she mar *Zeus*. [*Hercules*].

HESPERUS 1. One of the *Hesperides*; Gk and Rom name for *VENUS* as the EVENING STAR; **opp** = *Lucifer* (Rom). *Phosphorus* (Gk). 2. SCHOONER (Longfellow).

HESTIA 1. Gk myth *goddess* of the *HEARTH*; d of Cronos and Rhea (**Rom** = VESTA). 2. A minor *PLANET*.

HE WILL *HELL*.

HE WOULD HED.

HG MERCURY (*chem*).

HIAWATHA *Modelled* on HAIOHRATHA, a Mohawk chief, Longfellow's poetic hero is an Ojibway grand-s of Nokomis (d of the Moon), raised on the shores of Gitche-Gumee, Big-Sea-Water (Lake Superior); he had magical moccasins (mile-long strides) and mittens (to crush rocks). He fought his f (West Wind) over wrongs done to his m (Wenonah); he defeated the Corn Spirit; he mar Minnehaha (Laughing Water), and thus made peace with the Dakota tribe. His friends were Chibiabos (*musician*) and Kwasind (*strength*); when they d, ~ k Pau-Puk-Keewis over an insult. ~ foresaw the coming of the White Man, which was heralded by a swarm of golden bees.

HIDDEN CACHED, CONCEALED, DOGGO, ESOTERIC, *SECRET*.

Hidden word There are not as many ways of conveying that the answer is hidden somewhere in the clue, as there are of implying that an anagram is intended. Nevertheless, words such as 'found in . . .', '. . . we see', 'from', 'part of . . .', 'reads', 'reveals', 'some of . . .' and 'taken from . . .', all suggest that the word lies somewhere written before your eyes (see HELD/*HOLD BACK* for a hidden word reading backwards). The answer may also be revealed if you take note and respond sensibly to undue awkwardness in phraseology (this sentence has been included not only to warn the puzzler to be on the look-out for stilted sentence construction, which may betray the fact that the puzzle setter has been trying to work the answer into the clue, but also as an example itself. It starts by telling us that 'the answer may be revealed'; it goes on to instruct that a note — A, B, C, D, E, F, G or H — should be taken away somewhere from what follows. Thus, if we remove the letter D from 'respond sensibly' we find that we are left with RESPON*SE(nsibly) — which is another word for 'answer'.) So the clue may have to be added to or shortened, or even read in reverse, to find the hidden word; but the instruction will be there somewhere, together with an indication of the meaning of the answer itself — in the example above, it was the phrase 'the answer may also be revealed'.

HIDE (s/l hied, *hyde*). *FELL*, PELT, *SKIN*.

HIDE (s/l hied, *hyde*). *FELL*, PELT, *SKIN*. CONCEAL(MENT). HARBOUR, *SCREEN* (**opp** = reveal, *unearth*).

HIDING CANING, THRASHING, WHIPPING. CONCEALMENT.

HIGHBALL DRINK. LOB (crypt).

HIGH CLASS AI. U. FLYING SCHOOL (crypt).

HIGHLY 1. EXTREMELY, VERY. 2. High in the body, building etc, e.g. **Highly painful** (8) = HEADACHE, MIGRAINE.

HIGH POST TOP JOB. AIR MAIL (crypt).

HIGH STANDING TALL; ON STILTS, hence STILTED (crypt).

HIGHWAYMAN ROAD MENDER (crypt). BANDOLERO, FOOTPAD, ROBBER OF THE ROAD; **celeb**: PAUL CLIFFORD (Bulwer-Lytton), CLAUDE DUVAL, TOM FAGGUS (Lorna Doone, Blackmore), CAPT MACHEATH and JEREMY TWITCHER (Beggar's Opera, Gay), DICK TURPIN.

HIJKLMNO WATER (H to O, hence H_2O — crypt).

HILL *BANK*, BUTTE, *DOWN*, DUN, EMINENCE, HEAP, INCLINE, MOUND, MOUNT, SLOPE, TOR (**opp** = *vale*). SYDNEY *CRICKET* GROUND. *POET*. [Roland ~; postage, *stamp*].

HINDER DETER, HAMPER, IMPEDE, *LET*, MAR, OBSTRUCT, PREVENT, *STOP* (**opp** = *abet*). REARMOST. DEERSTALKER (crypt).

HINGE JOINT, SWING. ANKLE, ELBOW, KNEE, KNUCKLE, SHOULDER. GHE (crypt: H*in*GE).

HINNY STALLION/ASS *offspring*. NHY (crypt: H*in*NY).

HINT INDICATION, *TIP*, WRINKLE.

HIPPOCRATES Celebrated Gk *doctor*, b Cos *c.* 460 B.C., d Thessaly 357 B.C. [doctor's oath].

HIPPOLYTE Gk myth d of *Ares*; Queen of the Amazons. She wore a girdle, the object of one of *Hercules'* 12 labours.

HIPPOPHILE *Lover* of horses.

HIPPOPHOBIA *Aversion* to horses.
HISTORY 1. ANNALS, CAREER, RECORD, SAGA.
AUTOBIOGRAPHY (crypt). [Herodotus; Pliny; *Tacitus*]. 2. **Gk muse** = *CLIO*.
HIT *Anag*. CUFF, PUNCH, SLAP, STRIKE; **comp** = run.
SUCCESS (**opp** = *miss*).
HM ER, HER/HIS MAJESTY, KING, QUEEN.
HARBOURMASTER.
HO HOLMIUM (*chem*). HOME OFFICE. HOUSE. HALLO,
HELLO, HILLO, HOLLO, HULLO.
HOAX CANARD, FALSE REPORT; JAPE, PRACTICAL JOKE.
HOCUS.
HOD 1. Shoulder CARRIER, TRAY (bricks, mortar). SCUTTLE
(coal). HACK (literary). 2. Br of *Balder* (Nor myth).
HOIST JACK (UP). RAISE(D) (**opp** = *lower*). ELEVATOR,
LIFT (mech). FLAG SIGNAL (naut). PULLEY, *WHIP* (naut).
HOLD CATCH, CLASP, GET, GRAB, GRASP, *GRIP*, KEEP.
DETAIN, RESIST. CONTAIN, RESTRICT. OWN, POSSESS.
THREAT. BELIEVE, CONSIDER, THINK. CARGO
COMPARTMENT. **Pl** = Hidden word (see *HELD*), or word
round another, e.g. **He holds order in the house** (4) = H*OM*E.
~ **BACK** 1. IMPEDE, RESTRICT, RESTRAIN. 2. Hidden word
backwards, e.g. **The Royal Aero Club holds back the money —
quite right, it's Spanish** = REA*L.
HOLDING FARM, TENURE. PORTFOLIO. FISTFUL,
HANDFUL.
HOLD UP 1. DETAIN. PROP, SUPPORT. RAID, STICK UP. 2.
Word backwards in another (dn) clue, e.g. **The subject is: he holds
me up after the car goes over us both** (5) = T*H*EM*E.
HOLLAND NL, NETHERLANDS. LINEN, *MATERIAL*. **Pl** =
DUTCH, GIN.
HOLMES (s/l *homes*). *DETECTIVE*, SHERLOCK. Created by Sir
Arthur Conan Doyle and *modelled* on Dr Joseph *Bell*; lived first in
Montague Street and then at 221B Baker Street, London. Stamford
introduced him to Dr John H. Watson, ex-Indian Army, wounded
Afghanistan in the leg/shoulder (some confusion) and saved by
Murray his orderly. Holmes played the *violin*, took *cocaine*, kept
his tobacco in a Persian slipper, had a gasogene for soda water,
used the door as a target for revolver practice, and wore a
deerstalker hat; his br Mycroft was a Civil Servant and a member of
the *Diogenes* Club; his housekeeper was Mrs Hudson, his pageboy

Billy, his young helpers the Baker Street Irregulars (leader: Wiggins); Scotland Yard detectives were Gregson and Lestrade; principal adversaries were Irene Adler ('the' Woman), Col Sebastian Moran, and Professor James Moriarty ('the Napoleon of Crime') who was killed — supposedly with Holmes — at the Reichenbach Falls in Switzerland. **Celeb cases**:

A Study in Scarlet
The Sign of Four
A Scandal in Bohemia
The Red-headed League
A Case of Identity
The Boscombe Valley Mystery
The Five Orange Pips
The Man with the Twisted Lip
The 'Gloria Scott'
The Musgrave Ritual
The Reigate Puzzle
The Crooked Man
The Resident Patient
The Greek Interpreter
The Naval Treaty
The Final Problem
The Hound of the Baskervilles
The Valley of Fear
His Last Bow
The Adventure of:
~ the Blue Carbuncle
~ the Speckled Band
~ the Engineer's Thumb
~ the Noble Bachelor
~ the Beryl Coronet
~ the Copper Beeches
~ the Empty House
~ the Norwood Builder
~ the Dancing Men
~ the Solitary Cyclist
~ the Priory School
~ Black Peter
~ Charles Augustus Milverton
~ the Six Napoleons

~ the Three Students
~ the Golden Pince-Nez
~ the Missing Three-Quarter
~ the Abbey Grange
~ the Second Stain
~ Wisteria Lodge
~ the Cardboard Box
~ the Red Circle
~ the Bruce-Partington Plans
~ the Dying Detective
~ the Devil's Foot
~ the Illustrious Client
~ the Blanched Soldier
~ the Mazarin Stone
~ the Three Gables
~ the Sussex Vampire
~ the Three Garridebs
~ the Creeping Man
~ the Lion's Mane
~ the Veiled Lodger
~ Shoscombe Old Place
~ the Retired Colourman

HOLT COPSE, WOOD. *HABITATION*, LAIR (otter). *CASTLE*.

HOLY (s/l wholly). SAINTLY; GOOD. *ISLAND*. HOLED (crypt).

~ **GRAIL** CHRIST'S CUP [*Galahad*; *Round Table*].

HOME COUNTRY, DWELLING, LAND, REFUGE, VILLA; **comp** = *dry*. FIND, LOCATE (radio). OWN GROUND (*cricket*, *football*, *rugby*); **opp** = away. *PRIME MINISTER*.

~ **COUNTIES** SE (geog, crypt).

~ **HELP** *CHAR*. DIY.

~ **OFFICE** HO.

HOMER 1. Gk *poet* b *c.* 1000 B.C. **Works** (not all authenticated): Iliad (War of *Troy*); Odyssey (based on legends of Odysseus/Ulysses after Troy); Homeric Hymns (to *Aphrodite*, *Demeter*, *Hermes*, Delian and Pythian *Apollo*). 2. RUN (baseball). *PIGEON* (crypt).

HONEY DARLING, DEAR, PET, SWEETHEART. NECTAR, SWEETNESS [mead].

HONOUR 1. CBE, CH, KBE, MBE, OBE, OM etc. AWARD,

KNIGHTHOOD. GRACE, RECOGNIZE. VIRTUE [**guard of**
~ = *chaperone*]. ACE, KING, QUEEN, JACK/KNAVE (cards).
2. TITLE which goes with some high honours, e.g. **Man of honour**
(3) or (6) = SIR or KNIGHT.

HONOURED 1. ACCEPTED, PAID. CBE, CH, KBE etc (see
HONOUR). DIGNIFIED, ENRICHED. ENTITLED. 2.
TITLE which often goes with an honour or ennoblement, e.g.
Honoured lady (4) = DAME.

HOOCH *DRINK*. *AMERICAN INDIAN*.

HOOD BONNET, COWL; CANOPY, COVER. GANGSTER,
GUNMAN, HOODLUM, THUG; MAFIA. ROBIN, RICHARD
LOCKSLEY *modelled* on Robert FitzOoth of Locksley [Friar
Tuck, Little *John*, *Maid* Marion, Nottingham Sheriff, Sherwood
Forest, Will Scarlet]. RED RIDING ~. *POET*.

HOOK CATCH, SNARE, TRAP. ANGLED WIRE,
ATTACHMENT, CROOK. CURVED BLADE. BEND.
HEEL (rugby). PULL, STROKE (*cricket*, golf). BLOW, HIT,
PUNCH (boxing). *PIRATE*.

HOOKER FORWARD (rugby). PROSTITUTE (US sl). *BOAT*,
SHIP (sl). ANGLER, FISHERMAN (crypt).

HOOKY TRUANCY (US). ANGULAR; ANGLING, FISHING
(crypt).

HOPE 1. ASPIRATION, DESIRE, EXPECT, WISH.
PROBABILITY, PROMISE. BOB ~ (theat). 2. Sir Anthony ~
(Hawkins), b 1863, d 1933. Barrister and *writer*, his most famous
books being The Prisoner of Zenda, and its sequel Rupert of
Hentzau. They relate how a *double* secured the Ruritanian *royal
family* of Strelsau Palace against a would-be usurper from Castle
Zenda. **Characters: (the good guys)** Rudolf Rassendyll (red-
headed), King Rudolf Elphberg (his double), Princess Flavia
(Elphberg), Col Sapt, Fritz von Tarlenheim; and **(the baddies)**
Duke Michael (Elphberg) of Strelsau, Rupert of Hentzau, Bauer
and Antoinette de Mauban.

HOPPER *BOUNDER*; CRICKET, FLEA, FROG, *KANGAROO*.
CONTAINER. HOP-PICKER; OAST HOUSE.

HORACE Flaccus; Rom *poet* (65–8 B.C.) b Apulia. His patron (with
Virgil) was Maecenas. Was on losing side at Battle of Philippi.
Works: Book of Satires; Epistles; Epodes; Odes; and, principally,
Ars Poetica.

HORAE (s/l hoary). Gk goddesses of the seasons (especially *rain*)
and order (especially *justice* and *peace*). Known in Athens as

AUXO, CARPO and THALLO, but named by Hesiod as DIKE
(justice), EUNOMIA (good order) and *IRENE* (peace), the three
dd of Themis and *Zeus*.
HORRIFIC H (film *censorship*). FRIGHTFUL, SCANDALOUS,
SHOCKING.
HORSE (s/l hoarse). CLOTHES DRIER, TRESTLE. *DRUG*,
HEROIN. *ISLAND*. *LARK*, *PLAY*. MAINSHEET SPAN
(naut). OBSTRUCTION (mining). BUCK, VAULTING
BLOCK. QUADRUPED of genus equus; DOBBIN, GG, NAG
(all sl); ROCKING; BAY, CHESTNUT, DAPPLED, GREY,
PIEBALD, ROAN, SKEWBALD; PONY, STEED; KELPIE (Sc
myth); **types**: CARTHORSE, CIRCUS ~, *COB*, *RACEHORSE*,
SCREW, SHOW ~, (STEEPLE)CHASER, *THOROUGHBRED*,
TROTTER; **breeds**: ARABIAN, CASPIAN, CONNEMARA,
CLYDESDALE, DARTMOOR, HANOVARIAN,
LIPPIZANER, NEW FOREST, PALOMINO, PRZEWALSKI'S
~ (wild), QUARTER ~, SHETLAND, SHIRE, TARPAN,
WELSH. **Assembly** = *herd*; **habitation** = stable; **male** = stallion
(colt), stud ~; **fem** = mare (filly); **offspring** = foal (colt, filly).
Celeb: ARION (talking ~, offspring of *Poseidon* and *Demeter*),
ARKLE (steeplechaser), BLACK BEAUTY (Anna Sewell),
BLACK BESS (Dick Turpin), BOXER (*Orwell*), BORAK
(*Mohammed*), BUCEPHALUS (*Alexander* the Great),
CHAMPION (Wonder ~), CICERO (drum ~, mil),
COPENHAGEN (*Wellington*), GOLDEN MILLER
(steeplechaser), GRANE (Brunhilda, Wagner's Ring);
HERCULES (Jorrocks, Soapey Sponge. Steptoe & Son),
INCITATUS (Caligula's consul), LAMRI (King Arthur),
MARENGO (*Napoleon*), MARSALA (Garibaldi), *PEGASUS*
(winged ~ of *Bellerophon*; *constellation*), RED RUM® (Grand
National), REKSH (Rustam), RONALD (Lord Cardington's,
Charge of the Light Brigade), ROSINANTE (Don Quixote),
SCOUT (Tonto [Lone Ranger]), *SILVER* (Lone Ranger [Tonto]),
SLEIPNER (eight-legged of *Odin*), SORREL (William III),
TRIGGER (Roy Rogers), TUC ~ (*Low*), VELVET (Enid
Bagnold), VOLONEL (Field Marshal Earl Roberts VC), WHITE
SURREY (Richard III), Wooden ~ of *Troy*; XANTHUS and
BALIUS (*Achilles*; offspring of Zephyrus and the *Harpy* Podarge)
[*centaur*; *Ch calendar*; ~ power, Munnings (*painter*); Prince
Monolulu ('I got a ~'); *racetrack*; stalking ~; Thelwell (*cartoonist*);
unicorn]. **Pl** = HOUYHNHMS (*Swift*). **Gods: Gk** = *Poseidon*;

Rom = *Neptune* [white ~s; wild ~s]; **Comp** = *coach, hounds*.
HORSEGUARDS BLUES, *ROYALS*. PARADE GROUND.
HORSEPOWER HP (550 ft/lb/sec).
HORUS Gk form of Egy *god* of the SUN; s of *Isis*. God of doorways.
HOSPITAL H. *NURSERY* (crypt), SANATORIUM, SICKROOM.
HOST ARMY, COMPANY (arch). GREAT NUMBER, LOTS.
INNKEEPER, *LANDLORD*, *Chaucer* character (Harry Bailey).
ENTERTAINER, PARTY-GIVER, WELCOMER;
AMPHITRYON (Molière). RECEIVER, RECEPTACLE (of
commensal, parasite, transplant). CONSECRATED BREAD
(eccles). **Pl** = ANGELS, STARS.
HOT H; CLOSE, NEAR, OPPRESSIVE, SULTRY,
SWELTERING, TORRID, WARM (**opp** = *cold*). STOLEN (sl).
~ **SPOT** TROPICS; SAHARA. OVEN. VOLCANO.
HOUND HARRY, PURSUE, WORRY. BOUNDER, CAD. *DOG*
(**assembly** = kennel, pack, **male** = dog, **fem** = bitch, **offspring** =
puppy) [Baskervilles; hunting]. **Pl comp** = *fox*; horse.
HOUR (s/l our). H, HR. **Pl** = *HORAE*, the Gk seasons (q.v.).
HOUSE HO. MPS, COMMONS, *LEGISLATIVE ASSEMBLY*,
LORDS, WESTMINSTER. BINGO®, FULL CARD, LOTTO®.
BUNGALOW, COTTAGE, *HOME*, PREMISES, SEMI; and see
COUNTRY ~ for **celeb fict**, and *STATELY HOME* for **celeb fact**.
CHINESE DYNASTY, *ROYAL FAMILY* (q.v. for lists).
AUDIENCE (theat). BUSINESS, *COMPANY*, FIRM;
TELLSON'S BANK (2 Cities, *Dickens*).
HOUSEHOLD CAVALRY BLUES, ROYALS.
HOUSEHOLDER OWNER-OCCUPIER, HEAD OF HOUSE
(hence H). FRANCHISEE (arch). *LAR* (crypt). POKER
PLAYER (crypt). SNAIL, WHELK (crypt). **Pl** = *GUARDS*;
BLUES, ROYALS (crypt). *LARES*, PENATES (Rom, crypt).
HOUSEHOLD GODS *LARES*, PENATES (Rom).
HOUSE OF COMMONS DEBATING CHAMBER, *LEGISLATIVE*
ASSEMBLY, MPS.
HOUSE OF LORDS UPPER HOUSE, OTHER PLACE.
STATELY HOME. TAVERN (crypt, cricket).
HOUSEPARTY BINGO®, LOTTO®.
HOY CALL, HAIL. *BOAT*. *ISLAND*.
HP HOUSE OF PARLIAMENT, MPS, WESTMINSTER.
HORSEPOWER. SAUCE®.
HQ HEADQUARTERS; hence H, E, A or D (crypt).
HR HOUR.

HST HIGH SPEED TRAIN.
HUMANIST ERASMUS (NL).
HUN ATTILA (*Ch dynasty*). GERMAN, NOMAD, PRUSSIAN.
   HALF-HUNTER (crypt).
HUNCHBACK CROOKBACK, HUMPBACK [*camel, whale*];
   celebrated (fact): Alexander Pope, Richard III; **(fiction):** ~ of Notre
   Dame, Quasimodo (Hugo), Punch, Rigoletto (*jester*, Verdi),
   Rumpelstiltskin (Grimm).
HUNDRED See *number*. C, CENTURY, TON. 100 [~ days
   (*Napoleon*); ~ years war]. LAND AREA.
HUNDREDWEIGHT CWT, *MEASURE*.
Hung Hungary, ~ian.
HUNGRY (s/l Hungary). 1. AVID, KEEN, STARVING. 2. Word
   with O added in it, e.g. **Joan is no longer hungry, and is quite a**
   different girl (3) = J*AN.
HUNTER 1. *HORSE*, HUNTSMAN: JOHN PEEL, JORROCKS
   (HERCULES), UNSPEAKABLE (Wilde). CHASER, SEEKER,
   ESAU (bibl), *NIMROD* (bibl) [*patron saint*]. *AIRCRAFT*.
   (COVERED) WATCH. 2. **Myth:** *ACTAEON, ARTEMIS,*
   DIANA, HECATE, MELEAGER, *ORION*, UPIS.
   3. *Constellation* (Orion).
HUNTING 1. CHASING, SEEKING (fox); SHOOTING (big
   game). OSCILLATING, PULSATING, WAVERING. 2. **God:**
   Gk = *PAN*; **goddess:** Gk = *ARTEMIS*, **Rom** = *DIANA*.
HURRIED UP HASTENED. DECAR, NAR (dn; crypt).
HUSBAND CONSORT, MAN, MATE, OLD MAN, PARTNER,
   POT AND PAN (*rh sl*) [Darby and Joan]. CONSERVE,
   GUARD.
HUSBANDRY 1. *FARMING*. ACCOUNTING, MANAGEMENT.
   MARRIAGE (crypt). 2. **Rom god** = MARS.
HUSSY *BAGGAGE*, HUZZY, JADE, MINX.
HYADES Gk myth maidens guarding *Dionysus*, now a group of *seven*
   stars (in Taurus, near *Pleiades*; rain).
HYBRID CROSSBRE(E)D. *MULE*. HINNY.
HYDE (s/l *hide*, hied). HEATH, PARK. EDWARD ~ [Dr Henry
   Jekyll; R. L. *Stevenson*].
HYDRA 1. Gk myth nine-headed *monster*, destroyed by *Hercules* at
   Lerna. 2. *Constellation*.
HYDROGEN H (*chem*).
HYDROPHOBIA *Aversion* to water [rabies].
HYENA TASMANIAN WOLF. QUADRUPED (order Hyaenidae)

[laughing; *Anubis*; jackal].

HYGEIA 1. Gk myth *goddess* of HEALTH, d of *Asclepius*. 2. A
minor *PLANET*.

HYMEN 1. MEMBRANE, VIRGINITY. 2. Gk myth *god* of
fruitfulness and marriage; s of *Dionysus* (**Rom** = *Bacchus*) and
Aphrodite (**Rom** = *Venus*). Also marriage song.

HYMN 1. SONG OF PRAISE. 2. **Gk myth muse** =
POLYHYMNIA/POLYMNIA.

HYPERION A *Titan*, s of *Uranus* and *Ge*, f of *Eos*, *Helios* and
Selene.

HYPNOS Gk myth *goddess* of SLEEP, d of *Nyx* without benefit of
father [*Morpheus*].

I ACE. IODINE (*chem*). ISLAND. ITALY (*car plate*). ME,
NUMBER ONE, PERSONAL PRONOUN.

IACCHUS = *BACCHUS*.

IAMBUS *FOOT*.

IAPETUS 1. Gk myth *TITAN*. All men are reputed to be descended
from him. 2. A satellite of the *planet* Saturn.

IB(ID) IN THE SAME PLACE (**opp** = *alibi*).

IBA INDEPENDENT *BROADCASTING* AUTHORITY, LOCAL
RADIO, TV.

IC IN CHARGE.

ICARUS 1. Gk myth s of *Daedalus*, who flew too near the sun and
fell, when the wax securing his wings was melted [mausoleum].
2. A minor *PLANET*.

ICE HARD WATER. DIAMONDS. CHOC ~, CORNET,
DAIRY CREAM ~, KNICKERBOCKER GLORY, SORBET,
VANILLA, WHIP. GROWLER, ~BERG, PACK ~.

ICED CHILLED, FROZEN. RINK (crypt).

ICENI Tribe of Ancient Britons in East Anglia [*Boadicea*].

ID I WOULD. THE SAME. *CARP*, *FISH*. INSTINCT.

IDLE INEFFECTIVE, VAIN, WORTHLESS. TICK OVER.
INDOLENT, LAZY, UNOCCUPIED, USELESS.

IE ID EST, THAT IS.

IF PROVIDED, ~ING, SUPPOSING, AN (arch). WHENEVER.
INTERMEDIATE FREQUENCY. POEM (*Kipling*). *GAOL*
(Dumas). **Pl comp** = *buts*.

IGNIS FATUUS FRIAR'S LANTERN, JACK O' LANTERN, WILL O' THE WISP; MARSH GAS [c.f. St Elmo's Fire (which is chem different); methane; *mirage*].

II ELEVEN; TWO. SIDE, TEAM.

IL THE ITALIAN. ISRAEL (*car plate*). ILLINOIS (US *state*).

ILL NOT WELL, SICK. I WILL (crypt). ILLUSTRATED. ILLINOIS (US *state*).

IM 1. INTRA MUSCULAR. I AM. HALF-TIME (crypt). 2. Used in a clue at the start of a word to describe the solution, e.g. **'Imperfect' he could have said** (7) = GALAHAD; or may be included in the answer with the same effect, e.g. **Said by reporter to cut a figure** (7) = IM*PRESS. As 'im in the clue, implies omission of H from clue or answer, e.g. **Speech from 'im who held the bridge to the north** (7) = (H)ORATIO*N; may also in the answer be written as 'him commonly', e.g. **Years to him commonly give appearance** (5) = (h)IM*AGE.

IMITATE *APE*, COPY, MIMIC. *BORROW*.

IMP AFREET, AFRIT, *DEVIL*, *PERI*, EVIL *SPIRIT*. *EMPEROR*, IMPERATOR; IMPERIAL. IMPORTANT.

IMPAIRED DAMAGED, WEAKENED. II (crypt); AYE-AYE (crypt). TWINNED (crypt).

IMPOSING 1. *GRAND*, *NOBLE*. PRESUMING. LAYING ON (hands, eccl). LAYING OUT (print). 2. Read as: 'I am acting/modelling/pretending . . .' (crypt).

IMPRESS CONSCRIBE, CONSCRIPT, ENFORCE, *PRESS GANG*, SEIZE, SHANGHAI. DENT, EMBOSS, SEAL, STAMP, STRIKE. CUT A FIGURE, INFLUENCE. [*im*].

IMPRESSIONIST 1. IMITATOR, MIMIC. *PRESS GANG* (crypt). CARVER, ETCHER (crypt). INFLUENTIAL (crypt). 2. School of modern painting; **celeb**: BOUDIN, CEZANNE, DEGAS, MANET, MONET, PISSARO.

IN 1. AT HOME, INSIDE, NOT OUT. *BATTING*. ESOTERIC. *FASHIONABLE*. INDIANA (US *state*). INDIUM (*chem*). 2. One word in another, e.g. **An intent to be a leaseholder** (6) = TEN*AN*T, or **Four indulge to reveal** (7) = D*IV*ULGE.

INCENSE *ANGER*, ENRAGE. HOLY SMOKE, SPICE. PRAISE.

INCH IN. *MEASURE*, PART OF FOOT. *CREEP*. *ISLAND*.

IN CHARGE 1. IC, OVER. 2. By inference, word in synonym for charge, e.g. **The cadets and I are in charge — nonsense** (7) = RU*BB*I*SH.

264 *Incitatus*

INCITATUS *Horse* which belonged to the mad Rom emperor *Caligula* (A.D. 12–41), whose reign was characterized by orgies of cruelty and debauchery; he made ~ a Consul.

INCLINED ANGLED, BIASED, LEANING [Pisa], SLOPED, SLOPING, TILTED; BENT. HALF A MIND (hence MI or ND — crypt). READY, TENDED, TENDING.

INCLUDE 1. COMPREHEND, COMPRISE, CONTAIN, EMBRACE, ENCLOSE. 2. The clue contains a *hidden word* as answer, e.g. **The king is included in his will, I am quite sure** (7) = WILL*I*AM.

INCOMPLETE 1. EMBRYO, IMMATURE, PART MADE, UNFINISHED. 2. Part of sentence, as a hidden word, e.g. **Spread an incomplete topic, nicely prepared** (6) = PIC*NIC.

IN DEBT 1. IN THE RED, OVERDRAWN, OWING. 2. Place word indicated into DEBT, e.g. **First appearance of society in debt** (5) = DEB*U*T. 3. Similarly place word in RED, e.g. **Fish in debt was pulled in** (6) = R*EEL*ED. 4. May also have IOUS added, e.g. **Officer in debt takes exception** (8) = CAPT*IOUS.

INDEED 1. CERTAINLY, REALLY, YEA, YES. 2. Word placed in DEED, e.g. **Bit indeed would go against one** (7) = DE*BIT*ED.

INDIA 1. Subcontinent in Asia. IND (*car plate*). *ANTELOPE*. HINDU (and see *Religion*). **Provinces**: Andhra Pradesh, Arunnchal Pradesh, Assam, Bengal, Bihar, Gujarat, Haryana, Mimachal Pradesh, Jamm, Kashmir, Karnatak, Kerala, Madhya Pradesh, Maharashtra, Manipur, Meghalaya, Nagaland, Orissa, Punjab, Rajasthan, Sikkim, Tamil Nadu, Tripura, Uttar Pradesh (UP), West Bengal [*American* ~n (Red ~n); ~n ink; ~ paper; ~ rubber; ~ tea]. 2. INACT(ION), INDO (crypt).

INDIAN 1. Native product of ~. 2. *American* ~ (q.v. for tribes).

INDIVIDUAL EGO, I, ONE, SELF. CHARACTERISTIC, PARTICULAR, *SINGLE*, SPECIAL.

INDRA Ind *god* of *RAIN*.

INDUCED 1. BROUGHT ABOUT/ON, CAUSED. INFERRED, PERSUADED, PREVAILED ON. 2. Letter or word put into another, e.g. **Politician, nothing induced to clean** (3) = M*O*P. 3. Word placed into letters DUCED, e.g. **King induced a wetting** (6) = DUC*K*ED.

INDUS *RIVER*. *CONSTELLATION*.

INDUSTRY BUSINESS, FACTORY, MANUFACTURING, WORKS; CBI. APPLICATION, HARD WORK.

IN ERROR *Anag.* 1. OUT, WRONG, MISTAKENLY (**opp =**

right). 2. Word placed in synonym for error, e.g. **Draw off wine in error; it is salty** = B*RACK*ISH.

INEXPERIENCED DEB, *GREEN*, IMMATURE, TYRO, VIRGIN, *YOUNG* (**opp** = *expert*).

INFATUATION 1. CRUSH, LOVESICKNESS. 2. **Goddess** = ATE (Gk).

INFERIOR LESSER, LOWER, SUBORDINATE, UNDER. NON-U.

INFORMATION DATE, *DOPE*, *GEN*, GRIFF, INFO, *INTELLIGENCE*, KNOW-HOW, LOW-DOWN. TABLES, TIDINGS. [COI]. FLIGHT, SQUADRON, VEE (all crypt).

INIGO 1. JONES; *ARCHITECT*. 2. Place letter I in word indicated, e.g. **Inigo cons money from it** (5) = CO*I*NS.

INITIALLY 1. AT FIRST, STARTING. 2. Use the first letters of words indicated, e.g. **He is trying initially to make a success** (3) = H*I*T.

INLAY 1. EMBED, FILLING, INSERT; ORNAMENT; **types**: BOULE, BUHL, FILIGREE, MARQUETRY, OYSTER VENEER, PARQUETRY, PIQUE, POSE D'OR, TUNBRIDGE WARE. 2. Letter(s) or word(s) placed in letters LAY, e.g. **Final inlay is idle** (4) = LA*Z*Y.

INN *BAR*, PH (abbr), PUB, REFUGE, TAVERN.

INNER INTERIOR, INTERNAL. (Second) TARGET RING [*bullseye*, *magpie*, *outer*]. BATSMAN (crypt). PUBCRAWLER, *LANDLORD*, PUBLICAN (crypt).

INNER TEMPLE LAW SOCIETY, *INN OF COURT*.

INNS OF COURT GRAY'S INN, INNER TEMPLE, LINCOLN'S INN, MIDDLE TEMPLE [benchers; call to the bar].

IN ORDER 1. ALL RIGHT, ALLOWED, OK, PERMITTED. BY ROTA, ON ROSTER, SERIATIM. SERVICEABLE, WORKING. **Pl** = *CHURCHMAN*, ORDAINED. 2. Word placed in *decoration* or order, e.g. **Latin in order like earth** (6) = OB*LAT*E.

IN RUINS *Anag*. 1. BROKEN, COLLAPSED. 2. Word in RUINS, e.g. **Briefly equal in ruins for French sharks** (7) = R*EQ*UINS.

INSECT 1. CREATURE, INVERTEBRATE (genus insecta), *LEPIDOPTERA*; SIX-FOOTER (crypt) [arachnid: mite, scorpion, *spider*, tick]. **Celeb**: *ALEXANDER* (*Milne*). **Types**:

3-letters		4-letters
ANT	*DOR*	FLEA
BEE	*FLY*	GNAT

MITE
MOTH
WASP

5-letters
APHID
APHIS
EMMET
LOUSE
MIDGE

6-letters
BEETLE
CADDIS
CICADA

EARWIG
HORNET
LOCUST
MANTIS
MAYFLY
SAWFLY
SCARAB

7-letters
BLOWFLY
CRICKET
CREEPER
DAMOSEL

8+ letters
ALDERFLY

BLUEBOTTLE
BUTTERFLY
CADDIS FLY
COCKROACH
DRAGONFLY
GRASSHOPPER
HORSEFLY
HOUSEFLY
LEPIDOPTERA
POND SKATER
ROVE BEETLE
WATER BOATMAN
WATER SCORPION
WHIRLIGIG BEETLE

2. Put letter(s) or word(s) into SECT, e.g. **Reticent about insect** (6) = SEC*RE*T, or **The Spanish insect is choice** (6) = S*EL*ECT.

INSIDE 1. CONTAINED. *GAOL*. FOOTBALLER: FORWARD, STRIKER. 2. Word in another, hidden word, e.g. **It's all go, inside any pain** (5) = A*GO*NY.

INSPIRATION ANIMATION, INTUITION, *MUSE*, PROMPTING, THOUGHT; **celeb**: BEATRICE (Dante); DARK LADY (sonnets, *Shak*); LAURA (Petrarch); WH (Onlie Begetter, sonnets, *Shak*) [Enigma Variations (Elgar); see also *companions*, *lovers*; *model* (q.v. for fict characters modelled on real life)]. BREATHING, INHALATION (crypt).

INSTALL(ED) 1. PUT IN, FITTED; STABLED (crypt). 2. Word placed in another, e.g. **Bed with girl installed is forbidden** (6) = B*ANN*ED.

INSTEAD 1. ALTERNATIVE, IN LIEU, SUBSTITUTE. 2. Word placed in letters STEAD, e.g. **Cooked me instead** (7) = STEA*ME*D.

INSTITUTE ORIGINATE, START, *FOUND*. *ORGANIZATION*, SOCIETY (tech); MIT.

INSTRUMENT 1. IMPLEMENT, TOOL. DIAL, MEASURING DEVICE, POSITION FINDER (aero, naut). ARRANGER, CHANNEL, PERFORMER. FORMAL/LEGAL DOCUMENT. 2. MUSICAL DEVICE, SOUND PRODUCER; **types**:

(strings, blown): *AEOLIAN* HARP; **(strings, bowed)**: ARPEGGIONE, CELLO, CRWTH (no *vowel*), DOUBLE BASS,

GAMBA, HURDY-GURDY, JAPANESE FIDDLE, REBEC,
TROMBA MARINA, VIOL, VIOLA, *VIOLIN*; **(strings,
hammered)**: CLAVICHORD, CLAVIER/KLAVIER,
DULCIMER, PANTALEON, *PIANO*(FORTE),
SCHLAGZITHER, ZIMBALON; **(strings, plucked)**:
BALALAIKA, BANJO, BARREL ORGAN, BELL HARP,
CEMBALO, CITHERA, CITHER(N), CITTERN, CLARSACH,
DITAL HARP, GITTERN, GUITAR, *HARP*, HARPSICHORD,
HURDY GURDY, KITHERA, LUTE, *LYRE*, MANDOLA,
MANDOLIN, MANDORA, PSALTERY, SITAR, UD (Arab),
UKULELE, VICTALELE, VIHUELA, VINA (Ind),
VIRGINAL, ZITHER; **(wind, brass)**: ALPHORN, BUCCINA
(Rom), BUGELHORN (Ger), BUGLE, CORNET,
FLUGELHORN (Ger), FRENCH HORN, OLIPHANT,
POSTHORN, SAXHORN, *SERPENT*, TROMBONE,
TRUMPET, TUBA, VAMPHORN; **(wind, reed)**: ACCORDION,
BAGPIPES, BASSOON, BOMBARD, CHENG (Ch),
CLARINET, COR ANGLAIS, HARMONICA, HORNPIPE,
MOUTHORGAN, OBOE, PIBCORN, PIBROCH (Sc), *QUAIL*,
REGAL, SAXOPHONE, SHAWM, STOCK HORN; **(wind,
tube)**: BARREL ORGAN, BIGOPHONE, BIN (Ind), FIFE,
FLAGEOLET, *FLUTE*, GALOUBET, HURDY GURDY,
KAZOO, MIRLITON, *NIGHTINGALE*, *ORGAN*, PANPIPES,
PENNY WHISTLE, PIPE, *RECORDER*, TIN WHISTLE,
WHIFFLE; **(percussion)**: *ANVIL*, *BELL*, *BONES*, CASTANET,
CELESTA, CHANG (Ch), CRESCENT, CYMBALS,
DEAGAN, *DRUM*, DULCIMER, DULCITONE,
GLOCKENSPIEL, GONG, JEWS HARP, KETTLEDRUM,
MARIMBA, MARROWBONES, RATTLE, SALT BOX,
SANTIR (Pers), SISTRUM (Egy), SNARE DRUM, TABLA
(Ind), TABOR, TAMBOURINE, TARBOUKA, TIMPANI,
TRAPS, *TRIANGLE*, WOOD BLOCKS, XYLOPHONE.

INTELLIGENCE BRAINS, NOUS, IQ (**opp** = *stupidity*). *GEN*,
CIA, MIV, SOE [espionage; *agent*].
INTENT 1. BENT. MEANING. 2. Word in the letters TENT, e.g.
An intent leases = TEN*AN*T.
INTER AMONG, BETWEEN. BURY, ENTOMB.
INTERMINABLE 1. ENDLESS, PERPETUAL [eternity]. 2. Omit
last letter(s), e.g. **Interminable hate on one's head** (3) = HAT*.
INTERNATIONAL UNITS PEACEKEEPING FORCE, UN

PATROLS. MEASUREMENT SYSTEM, SI; **prefixes (multiples)**:

Factor	Prefix	Symbol
10^{12}	tera-	T
10^9	giga-	G
10^6	mega-	M
10^3	kilo-	k
10^2	hecto-	h
10	deca-	da
10^{-1}	deci-	d
10^{-2}	centi-	c
10^{-3}	milli-	m
10^{-6}	micro-	μ
10^{-9}	nano-	n
10^{-12}	pico-	p
10^{-15}	femto-	f
10^{-18}	atto-	a

INTERVAL INTERMISSION, HALF-TIME (hence TI or ME), PAUSE. OCTAVE; SECOND, SEVENTH etc (mus).

INTRIGUE FASCINATE. CABAL, *PLOT*.

INUUS Rom god of *herds*. **Gk** = *PAN*.

INVENTION 1. BRAINCHILD, *DISCOVERY*, IDEA [patent]; **celeb**:

GUNPOWDER	(1320 Schwarz)
TELESCOPE	(1607 Galileo)
PIANOFORTE	(1710 Cristofalli)
MERCURY THERMOMETER	(1721 Fahrenheit)
SPINNING JENNY	(1763 Hargreaves)
STEAM ENGINE	(1764 Watt)
HOT AIR BALLOON	(1783 Montgolfier)
MINER'S SAFETY LAMP	(1815 Davy)
SEWING MACHINE	(1841 Howe)
STEEL	(1856 Bessemer)
DYNAMITE	(1868 Nobel)
TORPEDO	(1868 Whitehead)
TELEPHONE	(1876 Bell)
PHONOGRAPH	(1877 Edison)

WIRELESS	(1898 Marconi)
TANK	(1899 Simms)
AEROPLANE	(1903 Wright)
RADAR	(1935 Watson-Watt)
JET ENGINE	(1939 Heinkel)
POLYESTER	(1941 Whinfield & Dixon)
ROCKET WEAPON	(1944 von Braun)
ATOMIC BOMB	(1945 USA team)

2. **Goddess** = *MINERA* (Rom).

INVERSE CAPSIZE, INVERT, UPEND. OPPOSITE. POETIC, RHYMING (crypt).

INVEST 1. BESTOW, CLOTHE, ENDOW. BESIÉGE. PLOY, PUT MONEY IN, SPEND. 2. Place synonym for money in word or letters indicated, e.g. **Invested in bed, and lost everything?** (4) = B*L*ED. 3. Any word placed round another, e.g. **Medical man investing in a foreign currency** (5) = D*INA*R.

INVOLVED *Anag.* COMPLICATED, CONVOLUTED, ENTANGLED, INTRICATE (**opp** = *simple*). ENTAILED, IMPLICATED. CONCERNED, IN QUESTION.

IN WRITING 1. IN LONGHAND, WRITTEN [libel]. 2. Put MS round word or letters indicated, e.g. **Put a small amount of money in writing atlases** (4) = M*AP*S.

IO 1. Gk minor *goddess*, d of King Inachus of Argos. Turned by *Zeus* into a heifer (hence *COWGIRL*, crypt); guarded by *Argus*. Escaped, and swam to Asia Minor (whence Bosphorus = Ox-ford), before reaching Egypt and human form again. 2. A satellite of the *planet* Jupiter.

IODINE I (*chem*) [antiseptic].

ION (s/l *iron*). 1. PARTICLE [atom]. 2. Gk myth s of *Apollo*, who founded the Ionian race.

IOU *DEBT*, MARKER (US), PROOF OF DEBT, OWING.

IQ INTELLIGENCE QUOTIENT.

IR IRAN (*car plate*). IRIDIUM (*chem*).

IRE *ANGER*. IRELAND (*car plate* = IRL).

IRELAND Ire. IRL (*car plate*). EIRE, ERIN; EMERALD ISLE; HIBERNIA; for counties of ~, see *divisions* [*patron saint*]. *COMPOSER*. (*Shak* forger).

IRENE Gk *goddess* of PEACE, d of Themis and *Zeus*; one of the *Horae*. **Rom** = PAX.

IRIDIUM IR (*chem*).

IRIS 1. *EYE*. *FLAG*, *FLOWER*, *LILY*, ORRIS. 2. Gk *goddess* of rainbow, d of *Electra* by Thaumas [*Harpies*], mar to *Zephyrus*. 3. A minor *PLANET*.

IRISH MICK, PADDY, PAT etc [*RM*]. *SEA*. CONTRADICTORY. ERSE, HIBERNIAN (for ~ counties, see *divisions*).

IRON (s/l *ion*). *METAL*, FE (*chem*). FERROUS [blacksmith; *Dactyls*]. *AGE*. *CLUB*; **opp** = *driver* (*golf*). *PRESS*, *SMOOTH(ER)*; *DECREASE*, *EVENING* (crypt). **Pl** = CUTLERY (mil sl); CHAINS, HANDCUFFS.

IRRITATE *Anag*. ANNOY, BOTHER, IRK, VEX. EXCITE. DEFEAT, NULLIFY.

IS EXISTS. *ISLAND*. ISLES OF SCILLY. ICELAND (*car plate*). ~ **DOUBLE** *ISIS* (crypt).

ISAAC Bibl s of *Abraham* and *Sarah*; mar his cousin Rebecca and f of twins *Esau* and *Jacob*. When ~ became blind, he was tricked into giving Jacob the inheritance and blessing which were Esau's right as the first-born; ~ felt the former's hands and neck which had been covered with goatskins to imitate the hairiness of Esau, and said 'The voice is Jacob's voice, but the hands are the hands of Esau.'

ISHTAR *Goddess* of *LOVE* (Bab).

ISIS 1. THAMES (at Oxford). Reserve *eight* (O). IS DOUBLE (crypt). 2. Egy *goddess* of *LOVE*, motherhood and Nature, m of *Horus*. 3. A minor *PLANET*.

ISLAM PREACHER IMAM, MUEZZIN, MULLAH.

ISLAND REFUGE. I, IS, AIT, AYOT, EYOT, *INCH*, ISLE, ISLET. **Celebrated (fict)**: BARATARIA (Gondoliers, *G and S*), BENSALEM (Bacon), GLUBBDUBRIB (Sorcerers, *Swift*), LAPUTA (flying ~, *Swift*), LILLIPUT (*dwarfs*, *Swift*), SPIDERMONKEY (Lofting), TREASURE ~ (Defoe), UTOPIA (More). **~s of Britain and Ireland** (* = non-island):

3-letters

ELY*	(Eng)	RAT	(Eng, Wal)
EVE	(Ire)	*RED*	(Ire)
EWE	(Sc)	ROA	(Eng)
HOY	(Ork)	*RUM*	(Sc)
MAN	(Eng)		
MEW	(Ire)	**4-letters**	
NEB	(Eng, IOM)	*ADAM*	(Ire)

ARAN	(Ire)	BURNT	(Sc)
BEAR	(Ire)	CAPEL	(Ire)
BIRD	(Ire)	CARNA	(Sc)
BUTE	(Sc)	CLARE	(Ire)
CALF	(IOM, Ire)	CLEAR	(Ire)
COLL	(Sc)	CONEY	(Ire)
*DOGS**	(Eng)	DANNA	(Sc)
EDAY	(Ork)	*EAGLE*	(Ire)
EIGG	(Sc)	EORSA	(Sc)
FAIR	(Sc)	FARNE	(Eng)
GOAT	(Ire)	*FLEET*	(Sc)
GUGH	(IS)	FOULA	(Sh)
HERM	(CI)	*GRAIN**	(Eng)
HOLY	(Eng, Sc, Wal)	*GREEN*	(Ire)
JURA	(Sc)	HANDA	(Sc)
LONG	(Eng, Ire)	*HORSE*	(Ire)
MUCK	(Ire, Sc)	ISLAY	(Sc)
MULL	(Sc)	KEDGE	(Ire)
NOSS	(Sc)	*LAMBS*	(Wal)
OMEY	(Ire)	LEWIS	(Sc, Wal)
OSEA	(Eng)	LUING	(Sc)
PIEL	(Eng)	LUNDY	(Eng)
RHUM	(Sc)	MAGEE	(Ire)
RONA	(Sc)	*SHEEP*	(Eng, Wal)
SALT	(Wal)	SHELL	(Wal)
SARK	(CI)	SHUNA	(Sc)
SKYE	(Sc)	SPIKE	(Ire)
SUNK	(Eng)	STERT	(Eng)
SWAN	(Ire)	SULLY	(Wal)
TORY	(Eng)	TIREE	(Sc)
UIST	(Sc)	*WHALE**	(Eng)
ULVA	(Sc)	*WHITE*	(IS)
UNST	(Sh)	WIGHT	(Eng)
YELL	(Sh)		

6-letters

5-letters

		ACHILL	(Ire)
ANNET	(IS)	*BADGER*	(Ire)
ARRAN	(Sc)	*BOTTLE*	(Sc)
BARRA	(Sc)	*BURROW*	(Eng)
BARRY	(Wal)	CALDY	(Wal)
BURGH	(Eng)	CANVEY**	(Eng)

COQUET	(Eng)	GOMETRA	(Sc)
DRAKES	(Eng)	GORUMNA	(Ire)
DURSEY	(Ire)	HAYLING	(Eng)
FETLAR	(Sh)	ISLEHAM	(Eng)
FLOTTA	(Ork)	KEERAGH	(Ire)
JERSEY	(CI)	KERRERA	(Sc)
JETHOU	(CI)	LISMORE	(Sc)
HARRIS	(Sc)	OWENBOY	(Sc)
HESTAN	(Sc)	PORTSEA	(Eng)
HILBRE	(Eng)	PURBECK*	(Eng)
HORSEA	(Eng)	RATHLIN	(Ire)
LAMBAY	(Ire)	ROCKALL	(Sc)
MAIDEN	(Ire)	ST AGNES	(IS)
MERSEA	(Eng)	ST MARYS	(IS, Sc)
OLDANY	(Sc)	SCARIFF	(Ire)
POTTON	(Eng)	SHEPPEY*	(Eng)
PRIEST	(Sc)	SHERKIN	(Ire)
PUFFIN	(Wal)	THORNEY*	(Eng)
RAASAY	(Sc)	WESTRAY	(Ork)
RABBIT	(Ire)	WHALSAY	(Sh)
RAMSEY	(Wal)		
ROUSAY	(Ork)	**8-letters**	
SAMSON	(IS)	ALDERMAN	(Ire)
SANDAY	(Ork)	ALDERNEY	(CI)
SCARBA	(Sc)	ANGLESEY	(Wal)
SKIDDY	(Ire)	BIRNBECK	(Eng)
SKOMER	(Sc, Wal)	BROWNSEA	(Eng)
STAFFA	(Sc)	CARDIGAN	(Wal)
STROMA	(Ork)	COLONSAY	(Sc)
THANET	(Eng)	COPELAND	(Ire)
TRESCO	(IS)	FLAT HOLM	(Wal)
UTOPIA	(fict)	FOULNESS	(Eng)
WALNEY	(Eng)	GATEHOLM	(Wal)
WHIDDY	(Ire)	GRAEMSAY	(Ork)
		GRUINARD	(Sc)
7-letters		*GUERNSEY*	(CI)
BARDSEY	(Wal)	MAINLAND	(Ork, Sh)
BRESSAY	(Sc)	MINGULAY	(Sc)
CORKBEG	(Ire)	PORTLAND*	(Eng)
CUMBRAE	(Sc)	ST HELENS	(IS)
FOULNEY	(Eng)	ST TUDWAL	(Wal)

SHETLAND	(Sh)	ISLEWORTH*	(Eng)
SKOKHOLM	(Wal)	LITTLE CUMBRAE	(Sc)
STRONSAY	(Ork)	LITTLE ROSS	(Sc)
VALENCIA	(Ire)	LLANDDWYN	(Wal)
VATERSAY	(Sc)	MIDDLE MOUSE	(Wal)
		MUCKLE ROE	(Sh)
9+ letters		N RONALDSAY	(Ork)
BALLYCOTTON	(Ire)	NORTH UIST	(Sc)
BENBECULA	(Sc)	PAPA STOUR	(Sh)
BURNTISLAND	(Sc)	PAPA WESTRAY	(Ork)
CALF OF MAN	(IOM)	RONALDSAY	(Ork)
EAST MOUSE	(Wal)	ST MICHAELS	(IOM)
GREAT CUMBRAE	(Sc)	SHAPINSAY	(Ork)
ISLEABBOTTS	(Eng)	S RONALDSAY	(Ork)
ISLE OF BREWERS	(Eng)	SOUTH UIST	(Sc)
ISLE OF LEWIS	(Sc)	STEEP HOLM	(Wal)
ISLE OF MAN	(Eng)	WEST MOUSE	(Wal)
ISLE OF WIGHT	(Eng)	WHITEHORN	(Sc)
ISLEORNSAY	(Sc)		

ISLAND AREAS See *Divisions*.
~ **GIRL** MIRANDA (The Tempest, *Shakespeare*). FLORA.
~ **RACE** BRITONS, IRISH. (MANX) TT.
ISLE OF MAN IOM; GBM (*car plate*). MONAVIA INSULA
 (Rom). MONA (also Anglesey). MANX.
ISLE OF WIGHT IOW. VECTIS INSULA (Rom).
ISRAEL JACOB. JEWISH STATE; **12 tribes**: ASHER,
 BENJAMIN, DAN, EPHRAIM, GAD, ISSACHAR, JUDAH,
 MANASSEH, NAPHTALI, REUBEN, SIMEON, ZEBULEN.
IS SORRY APOLOGIZES, CARES, REGRETS, RUES.
ISSUE CHILD, *OFFSPRING*, LITTER, PROGENY [*assembly*].
 DISCHARGE, *EMIT*, OUTFLOW, OUTLET. COME OUT,
 EMERGE. OUTCOME, PROCEED, RESULT. POINT,
 TOPIC. PUBLISH; *BOOK*, EDITION, *VOLUME*.
IT ITEM, THING. SA, CHARM, SEX APPEAL. ITALIAN,
 VERMOUTH. **Comp** = *gin*.
It Italy, ~ian.
ITA *BROADCASTING*, COMMERCIAL TV.
ITALIAN 1. IT, VERMOUTH. 2. Trans, e.g. **With Italian** = CON.
ITALY I (*car plate*).
ITEM ARTICLE, ENTRY, THING, UNIT. ALSO, LIKEWISE.

TIME-OUT, TIME-WARP (crypt).

ITV *BROADCASTING*, COMMERCIAL TV.

IVORY *COLOUR* (white). TOOTH, TUSK; *anniversary* (14th).
Pl = KEYBOARD (piano).

~ **GATE** Myth gate of sleep, transmission of false hopes from the
lower world.

IVY LEAGUE BROWN, CORNELL, COLUMBIA,
DARTMOUTH, HARVARD, PENNSYLVANIA,
PRINCETON, YALE (American college *football*).

I WILL ILL.

I WOULD ID.

IXION Gk myth king, tied by *Zeus* to an evermoving *wheel*.

J *JACK*. JAPAN (*car plate*). JOULE. *JUDGE*. [*Three* Men in a
Boat].

JACK 1. AB, *SAILOR*, TAR. (COURT) *CARD*, KNAVE. LIFT,
HOIST (car). TURNSPIT (cook; hence TIPS, crypt). JOHN;
comp = Jill (*Gill*). TARGET BALL (bowls). *FISH*, PIKE.
MONEY (sl). *FLAG* (naut). TUNIC. INDIAN FRUIT.
[~ CADE. ~ FROST. ~ O' LANTERN (*ignis fatuus*).
~ SPRAT]. 2. Male animal, e.g. ass.

JACOB Bibl s of *Isaac* and Rebecca; young twin br of *Esau*. Went to
his uncle Laban in Egy and there mar his cousins Leah and Rachel
(the former was covertly substituted for the more beautiful latter);
f by Leah of Reuben, Simeon, Levi (grand-f of *Moses*), Judah,
Issachar, Zebulon and Dinah, and by Rachel of *Joseph* and
Benjamin. Had dreams, among them of a ladder to heaven. With
his m's help, he cheated Esau out of his birthright (for a 'mess of
pottage', i.e. lentils) and of the blessing due from *Isaac* to Esau as
the first-born.

JADE *MINX*. *GEM*. *COLOUR* (green). NAG, SCREW (*horse*).

JAILER US for *GAOLER*.

JANUARY (1st) MONTH, M, JAN (**Rom** = *Janus*). **Birthstone** =
garnet.

JANUS Rom *god* of the doorway; facing front and rear. **Gk** =
HORUS, **Egy** = HOR.

JAPAN 1. LACQUER, PAINT, VARNISH. SEA. 2. J (*car plate*).
CIPANGU, NIPPON (country), Jap (abbr); **islands**: Honshu
(biggest), Hokkaido, Kyushu, Shikoku. **Words**: aikido (self-

defence), bugeikan (karate), bushido (mil honour code), daimyo
(noble), dan (judo), *Go* (*board-game*), hara-kiri (ritual suicide),
ikebana (flower arrangement), jujitsu (unarmed self-defence), kami
(divine spirit), kami-kaze ('divine wind', mil suicide), karate
(martial art), kendo (cross-staff fencing), kung-fu (Ch karate),
netsuke (pouch toggle), *No* (classic drama), obang (gold coin), obi
(sash), origami (paper folding), seppuku (mil suicide), shinto
(religion), shogun (hereditary mil ruler), te (karate), Tora-Tora
(Pearl Harbor *battlecry*; tiger-tiger) [Mikado, *G and S*].

JAR JERK, JOG, NUDGE. *EWER*. GRATING SOUND,
SHOCK. DISAGREEMENT, QUARREL.

JASON Gk myth hero, mar to *Medea*. Sent (to get him out of the
way) by his half br Pelias at the head of the *Argonauts* to get the
golden fleece, where he was sure to be killed. He returned with it
and killed Pelias.

JEANS (s/l genes). DENIM TROUSERS.

JEHU Bibl s of Nimshi, who brought about the death of Jehoram and
Jezebel, and was cruel towards their relations. Renowned for
furious chariot driving. Successor to *Ahab* [*Phaeton*].

JEKYLL Dr in *Stevenson's* book, who *transformed* himself by chem
experiment into the evil Mr *Hyde*.

JENNY 1. LOCOMOTIVE CRANE. JANET; GIRL; LEE; LIND.
SPINNER. 2. *Female* donkey or mule; assess (crypt).

JEROBOAM 1. LARGE *BOTTLE* (4 times normal). 2. Son of
Nabat, king of Israel; set up golden calves at Dan and Bethel.

JERSEY PULLOVER, SWEATER [*cardigan*, Guernsey];
KNITWEAR. *CATTLE*. *ISLAND* (CI). GBJ (*car plate*).

JESTER CLOWN, COURT COMEDIAN, FOOL; **celeb (fact)**:
AUGUSTE (Fr), COCO (circus), GRIMALDI (Joseph, 18th
cent), GROCK (Swi); WILL KEMP (Shakespeare's company);
celeb (fiction): COSTARD (LLL); 'SIR' DAGONET (Idylls);
FESTE (12th Night); GOBBO (Merchant of Venice); JUPE (Hard
Times, *Dickens*); LAUNCE (Two Gentlemen of Verona);
LAVACHE (All's Well); JACK POINT (Yeoman of the Guard);
POMPEY (M for M); PUCK (MND); SPEED (Two Gentlemen of
Verona); TOUCHSTONE (AYLI); TRINCULO (Tempest);
WAMBA (Ivanhoe); YORICK (Hamlet) and, all MND:
BOTTOM (weaver), FLUTE (bellowsmender), QUINCE
(carpenter), SNOUT (tinker), SNUG (joiner), STARVELING
(tailor) [bauble, motley]. 0 (*tarot*). PAGLIACCIO.

JESUS 1. Author of Book of Ecclesiasticus, *c.* 180 B.C. 2. A Christian

who was with St Paul in Rome *c.* A.D. 67. 3. CHRIST, SON OF
GOD, SAVIOUR; b at Nazareth or at Bethlehem (*c.* 4 B.C.), s of
Joseph and Mary, and br of James, Joses, Simon and *Judas*
(Matthew 13). Escaped the massacre of the innocents (*Herod*), and
was raised at Nazareth as a *carpenter*, like his f. His Ministry lasted
from age 30–33, and **His life incl**: genealogy and birth (Matthew
1–2; Luke 2–3); massacre of the innocents (Matthew 2); baptism
(Matthew 3; Mark 1; Luke 3); temptation in the wilderness
(Matthew 4; Mark 1–3); first miracle (water into wine; John 2);
cleansing the temple (Mark 11); selection of the 12 *apostles*
(Matthew 10; Mark 1); sermon on the mount (Matthew 4); feeding
the 5,000 (Matthew 14; Mark 6; John 6); walking on water (Mark
6; John 6); transfiguration (Matthew 17; Mark 9; Luke 9); raising
of Lazarus (John 11); the last supper, betrayal by *Judas* and denial
by Peter (Matthew 26; Mark 14; Luke 22; John 18; Acts 1);
Gethsemane (Matthew 26–7; Mark 14); trial before *Pilate* and
crucifixion between 2 *robbers* (Matthew 27; Mark 15; Luke 23;
John 18–19); resurrection and ascension (Matthew 28; Mark 16;
Luke 24; John 20; Acts 1).

JETTY KEY, QUAY, MOLE, PIER, WHARF. BLACK.

JEW HEBREW, ISRAELI, SEMITE; MISER, USURER; **celeb**:
ESTHER (bibl); FAGIN (*Dickens*); ISAAC (of York, *Scott*);
JACOB (bibl); *JESUS* (bibl); ~ of Malta (Marlowe); *JOSEPH*
(bibl); *JUDAS* (bibl); MORDECAI (bibl); NATHAN DE WEISE
(Lessing); REBECCA (bibl, and Ivanhoe, *Scott*); SHYLOCK
(*Shak*); SVENGALI (du Maurier); WANDERING ~ (trad).

JEWEL THIEF *MAGPIE*. CAPT BLOOD (crown jewels, Tower of
London).

JM BARRIE (Admirable Crichton. Peter Pan).

JOAB Bibl s of Zerniah and nephew of *David*, *c.* 650 B.C. A great mil
capt of David, ~ defeated *Absolom* at Gilboa, and caused the d of
Uriah the Hittite (see *David*). When David d, ~ fled to sanctuary
where he was found and k on *Solomon's* orders.

JOAN 1. ~ OF ARC, LA PUCELLE, THE *MAID* (of Orleans);
Shak character (H.vi). Book by Mark *Twain*. 2. Wife of John
Darby (Darby and ~).

JOB 1. DUTY, OCCUPATION, RESPONSIBILITY, TASK,
WORK. BURGLARY, CRIME, ROBBERY (sl). BUY/SELL
(as middleman). 2. Patient Jewish bibl patriarch, who maintained
his faith under test, despite so-called ~'s comforters who merely
added to his distress [~'s Tears, *grass*].

JOCASTA Mother and wife of *Oedipus*.

JOG *TROT*. REMIND. *JAR*, NUDGE.

JOHN BOY. DOE. PRESTER. LITTLE ~ (Robin *Hood*).
LONG ~ SILVER (*Stevenson*). LOO.

JOINT FORK, HINGE, JUNCTION, SEAM, T(EE), TENON.
BARON, LEG, SIDE (beef, lamb etc). DIVE, NIGHTCLUB.
CIGARETTE, *REEFER* (*drug*). ANKLE, ELBOW, FINGER,
HIP, KNEE, KNUCKLE, SHOULDER, TOE, WRIST.
COMBINED.

JOKER WILD CARD. *JESTER*, WAG.

JOLLIFICATION *DO*, FIESTA, PARTY.

JOLLY HAPPY, LIVELY. MARINE, RM.

JOLT *Anag*. JERK, SHAKE, SHOCK, SURPRISE.

JONES *INIGO* (*archit*). PAUL (US Navy).

JONSON BEN (The Alchemist, Epicoene, Volpone).

Jor Jordan.

JOSEPH 1. Bibl s of *Jacob* and Rachel, who made him a 'coat of
many colours'. ~ was sold into slavery in Egy, but rose to be chief
minister and mar Osnath (d of Potiphar, a priest of *On*). 2. A
carpenter of Nazareth, s of Heli; mar to Mary who was m of *Jesus*;
~ was also f of James, Joses, Simon and *Judas*, either by Mary
after Jesus was born, or by a previous mar. 3. ~ of Arimathea;
bibl Jew who went to *Pilate* after the d of Jesus and begged for his
body, which he laid in a tomb.

JOSHUA Bibl s of Nun, ~ was the lieutenant of *Moses* who took
Jericho by '*compassing*' the city seven times and blowing on seven
rams' horns; ~ eventually took the whole Promised Land.

JOURNALIST *REPORTER* (**Union** = NUJ).

JOURNEY *TRIP*.

JOVE = *JUPITER*, Rom chief *god* (**Gk** = *Zeus*).

JOY DELIGHT, GLEE, PLEASURE; SATISFACTION (**opp** =
dolour). GIRL.

JP JUSTICE OF THE PEACE, MAGISTRATE.

JUDAS 1. ~ Maccabaeus; the eldest s of Mattathias who d 161 B.C. 2.
~ Iscariot (A.D. 30). *Apostle* (treasurer) who betrayed *Jesus* for '30
pieces of silver', which were later used to buy the *Potter's* Field, a
plot of land known as Aceldama, which became the burial ground
for Jews who did not live in the city. 3. Thaddeus (A.D. 30).
Another *Apostle*, possibly the author of the Epistle of Jude. 4. Br
of *Jesus*, another possible author of Jude's Epistle. 5. *WINDOW*.

JUDGE J. ARBITER, ASSESS, *LAW* OFFICER. CENSURE,

CONSIDER, CRITICIZE, DECIDE, DECREE, SENTENCE, SUPPOSE, TRY. *DANIEL, ELI, SAMUEL.*

JUDGEMENT MISFORTUNE, SENTENCE. ASSESSMENT, DISCERNMENT, ESTIMATE, OPINION. 20 (*tarot*).

JUG *GAOL. EWER. NIGHTINGALE* SONG.

JUGGERNAUT 1. Krishna idol (Ind), wheeled in procession on *chariot*; frenzied devotees threw themselves under the wheels. Any destroying force. 2. HGV, *LORRY*, TRUCK (comm).

JULY (7th) MONTH, M, JUL (Julius *Caesar*). **Birthstone** = *cornelian.*

JUMPER CARDIGAN, GUERNSEY, JERSEY, PULLOVER. **Animal ~s:** *ANTELOPE*, CICADA, *CRICKET*, FLEA, *FROG*, *GRASSHOPPER*, KANGAROO. (STEEPLE)CHASER. PARA(CHUTIST). *BOUNCER, BOUNDER,* LEAPER [*Gorgon*].

JUNCTION *JOINT.*

JUNE 1. GIRL. 2. (6th) MONTH, M, JUN (Juno). **Birthstone** = *agate.*

JUNK *DRUG. BOAT* (Ch), LORCHA. SALT MEAT (naut). RUBBISH.

JUNO 1. BEAUTIFUL/STATUESQUE WOMAN. 2. Rom myth Queen of the *gods* and of marriage; w of *Jupiter.* **Gk** = *HERA.*

JUPITER 1. Rom myth King of the *gods*; also JOVE, PLUVIUS (rain) or TONANS (thunder). Son of *Saturn* and Ops, he mar his sis *Juno.* **Gk** = *ZEUS.* 2. Largest of the sun's *planets.*

JUST DESERVED, EQUITABLE, FAIR, WELL-GROUNDED. BARELY. EVEN, EXACTLY, PRECISELY, QUITE, RECENTLY. Also = JOUST.

JUSTICE JP; SHALLOW, SILENCE (*Shak*). THE LAW. FAIR TREATMENT. 8 (*tarot*). Fifth age (*Shak's seven ages*; AYLI).

JUST SO SIC. STORIES (*Kipling*).

JUVENTAS Rom *goddess* of YOUTH. **Gk** = *HEBE.*

K KELVIN. KILO(METRE). KING. KOCHEL (mus). POTASSIUM (*chem*). 1,000 (hence M).

k Killed. *Int unit.*

KAIKAS Gk myth NE *WIND* (**Rom** = AQUILO).

KALI Ind *goddess* of destruction, to whom practising *Thugs* sacrificed their victims; she is the consort of Shiva, and is depicted with many arms.

KANGAROO 1. *MARSUPIAL*, Macropus genus: BRUSH ~,
GREAT GREY ~, POTOROO, QUOKKA, RAT ~, ROCK ~,
TREE ~, WALLABY. **Assembly** = *mob*; **male** = BOOMER.
[*Kipling, Lear*, pouch]. HOPPER, *JUMPER* (crypt). 2. ~ **court**
= lynch mob, rough justice.

KC KILOCYCLE. KING'S COUNSEL.

KEEN *ACUTE*, SHARP, STRONG, VIVID. EAGER, WILLING;
DETERMINED, SET UPON. *CRY*, DIRGE, FUNERAL
SONG, WAIL (Sc).

KEEN-EYED SHARP-EYED, FAR-SIGHTED, GIMLET,
X-RAY. **Celeb**: *ARGUS*, LYNCEUS (Gk myth); *CAT*, *EAGLE*,
HAWK, *LYNX*, *OWL*.

KEEP INNER FORT, STRONGHOLD, TOWER (*castle*).
CONFINE, DEFEND, DETAIN, GUARD, HOLD, POSSESS,
RETAIN, STOCK, STORE. LOOK AFTER, MAINTAIN (dog;
mistress). PRESERVE, RESERVE, WITHHOLD (judgement).
ASSOCIATE (~ company). OBSERVE (Christmas, Ramadan).
REMAIN, STAY IN/ON (place, seat). (TAKE) CARE,
CHARGE, WATCH. BOARD, LIVING, LODGE, LODGING,
MAINTENANCE, SUPPORT.

KEEP OFF AVERT, FORFEND, WARD OFF. STAY CLEAR.

KELVIN K.

KENT *Division* of UK, SE, GARDEN (of Eng); UNIVERSITY.
CABINET-MAKER. CLARK ~ (SUPERMAN® [*Krypton*; Lois
Lane]). *PAINTER*. **Pl** = *BUFFS* (mil).

KERNEL (s/l *colonel*). NUT CENTRE (hence U) [shelling].

KETCH EXECUTIONER, HANGMAN. (SAIL)BOAT.

KEY (s/l *quay*). A, B, C, D, E, F or G (mus). CLEF, CLEVIS,
MAJOR, MINOR, NOTE; TONIC (mus). CLUE, SOLUTION.
HYPE. IMPORTANT, CENTRAL. TAP. *WARD*; *LOCKER*
(crypt). **Pl** = *LEGISLATIVE ASSEMBLY*.

KEYHOLDER *GAOLER*.

KG KNIGHT OF THE GARTER [Edward III, Countess of
Salisbury, Honi soit qui mal y pense].

KHAN CARAVANSERAI (Arab), INN, WAYPOST. RULER
(Ch, Mong, Turk); **celebrated**: AGA ~, BATU, GENGHIS ~,
HULEGU, KUBLAI ~, MONGKE, OGEDEI.

KICK *PUNT*, HACK (with foot) [*Sciron*]. RESILIENCE,
STIMULUS, THRILL. RECOIL. DENT IN BOTTLE.

KID DUPE, FOOL, HOAX, HUMBUG. TUB. LEATHER.
CHILD, TOT. *Offspring* of goat.

KIDDED FOOLED, HOAXED. GAVE BIRTH, PARENTHOOD (crypt).

KILL CULL, DEADEN, DESTROY, DISPATCH, EXTERMINATE, FINISH, WASTE (sl). BAG (game).

KILO K (*int units*).

KIND OF *Anag.* KIDNEY, SORT, TYPE. AMIABLE OF, GENEROUS OF.

KINEMOPHILE *Lover* of the cinema.

KING 1. (COURT) *CARD. CHESSPIECE. SNAKE.* **Pl** = RIVER (Ire). 2. HM, K, R, REX; male *MONARCH* (q.v. for ~s of UK), SOVEREIGN, e.g. CR (Charles), GR (George), etc. CLARK GABLE (~ of Hollywood) [and see *emperor, pharaoh*]; **celeb (bibl)**: AGAG, AGRIPPA, *AHAB*, AHAZ, AMON, ARTAXERXES, ASA, BAASHA, BALAK, *BELSHAZZAR*, BERA, CYRUS, DARIUS, *DAVID*, EGLON, ELAH, EVI, GOG, HADAD, *HEROD*, HEZEKIAH, HIRAM, HOHAM, HORAM, HOSEA, HUR, JABIN, JAPHIA, JEHORAM, JEHOSHAPHAT, *JEHU, JEROBOAM, JESUS*, JORAM, JOSIAH, JUDAH, LEMUEL, MAGOG, MANASSEH, MELCHIZEDEK, NABAT, *NEBUCHADNEZZAR, OG*, OMRI, *PHARAOH*, PIRAM, *PTOLEMY*, PUL, *REHOBOAM*, REZIN, *SALMANAZAR*, SARGON, *SAUL*, SENNACHERIB, *SO, SOLOMON*, TOI, TRYPHON, UZZIAH, *XERXES*, ZACHARIAH, ZEBAR, ZEDEKIAH, ZIMRI; **celeb (fict)**: ~ of Barataria (LUIZ, Gondoliers, *G and S*), ~ of Hearts (*Alice*), HILDEBRAND (Ida, *G and S*), LEAR (*Shak*), OBERON (MND, *Shak*), PANDION (Ode, Barnfield), PARAMOUNT (Utopia, *G and S*), Red and White ~s (*Alice*); **celeb (early Eur)**: ALFRED, ARTHUR, ATHELSTAN, CANUTE/CNUT/KNUT, CARA(C)TACUS, CHARLEMAGNE, CHARLES the Bald, ~ the Bold, ~ the Fat, *DAVID*, EADRID, EADWIG, E(C)GFRITH, EDGAR, EDMUND (Ironside), EDWARD (the Confessor), EDWIN, EGBERT, (A)ETHELBALD, (A)ETHELBERT, (A)ETHELRED (the Unready), (A)ETHELWULF, GODWIN, GUTHRUM, HARALD (Barefoot; Hardrada), MALCOLM, OFFA, OLAF, OLEG, SWEIN/SWEYN. **Celeb, various**: CROESUS (~ of Lydia; rich); CROSBY (~ of swing; film); GABLE (~ of Hollywood; film); MIDAS (Gk myth ~ of Phrygia; gold); PRESLEY (~ of rock 'n' roll; theat); CETEWAYO (Zulus).

~ **ARTHUR** King of Silures in Ancient Britain. Son of Uther

Pendragon (br of Morgana), mar *Guinevere*. Wounded fighting Mordred (his nephew) at Camlan in Cornwall, and d Isle of Avalon [*Camelot, Round Table*].

KING EDWARD POTATO. ED, RED, REXED, RTED, KTED (crypt).

~ OF ARMS CHIEF HERALD: BATH, *GARTER*, LORD LYON, *ULSTER* (St Patrick), CLARENCIEUX (thistle), NORROY.

~'s COUNSEL KC. RICHELIEU.

~s of UK See *MONARCHS* for list.

KINGSWAY REGALLY, ROYALLY (crypt).

KIPLING Rudyard, writer; b Bombay 1865, d 1936 [Nobel (lit)]. **Works**: Actions and Reactions; Barrack Room Ballads; A Book of Words; The City of Dreadful Night; The Day's Work; Debits and Credits; Departmental Ditties; A Diversity of Creatures; The Five Nations; Gunga Din (watercarrier); If; The Jungle Book (animals); The Just So Stories [The Alphabet; Armadilloes; *Butterfly*; *Camel* (hump); The *Cat* that Walked by Himself; *Crab*; The Elephant's Child ('satiable curiosity; trunk); The First Letter; The Kangaroo (Yellow-Dog Dingo); The Leopard (spots); The Rhinoceros (skin); The *Whale* (throat)]; Kim (Anglo-Indian orphan); The Light that Failed; The Phantom Rickshaw; Plain Tales from the Hills; Puck of Pook's Hill; Rewards and Fairies; Schoolboy Lyrics; The Seven Seas; Soldiers Three; Stalky & Co (schoolboys); The Story of the Gadsbys; Traffics and Discoveries; Under the Deodars; Wee Willie Winkie; The Years Between.

KIPPER SALMON, SMOKED HERRING. SLEEPER (sl).

KISS BUSS, OSCULATE, *SALUTE*, X; **comp** = *tell*. BRUSH, TOUCH. CANNON (billiards). [Blarney Stone].

KIT *BAGGAGE*, EQUIPMENT, GEAR, RIG. CHRISTOPHER. KITCHENETTE, SMALL KITCHEN (crypt).

KITCHENER C IN C, EARL, GENERAL. CHEF, COOK, GALLEY SLAVE (crypt).

KITTY FUND, POOL. *CAT*, PUSS(Y). GIRL.

KLEPTOMANIA *Obsession* with stealing.

KNAP (s/l *nap*). CHIP, WORK FLINT.

KNIGHT (s/l *night*). 1. BART, BT, CHEVALIER, KG, KT, SIR; PALADIN. *Chaucer* character. [Round Table]. *CHESSPIECE*. *PAINTER*. 2. **Orders of knighthood, with motto**:

THE GARTER (KG)	Honi soit qui mal y pense
THE THISTLE (KT)	Nemo me impune lacessit

ST PATRICK (KP)	Quis separabit?
THE BATH (KB)	Tria juncta in uno
THE STAR OF INDIA (ex)	Heavens light our guide
ST MICHAEL & ST GEORGE (KMG)	Auspicium melioris aevi
THE INDIAN EMPIRE (ex)	Imperatricis auspiciis
ROYAL VICTORIAN ORDER	Victoria
THE BRITISH EMPIRE	For God and the Empire

KNIT (s/l nit). ENTANGLE, *KNOT*. CROCHET, PURL, PLAIN, STITCH [*jersey*; Mme Defarge, 2 Cities, *Dickens*].

KNOCK RAP, *STRIKE*. CRITICIZE. ASTONISH. INNINGS. *CASTLE*.

KNOCKOUT *Anag*. KO. EMPTY (pipe). KONCK, NOCKK etc (crypt).

KNOCK UP WAKEN. SLEEP WITH (US). PAR (dn, crypt).

KNOT (s/l *not*). KT, *MEASURE* (naut), NMPH, RATE, SPEED (naut). *BIRD*, DUNLIN. PROBLEM. CLUSTER, GROUP. BEND, HITCH, LOOP: BECKET, *BOW*, BOWLINE, CLOVE HITCH, *FISHERMAN'S* BEND, GRANNY, HALF HITCH, REEF ~, SHEEPSHANK, SHEET BEND, STOPPER ~, TIMBER HITCH. SPLICE: *CROWN*, MATTHEW WALKER, MONKEY'S FIST, TURK'S HEAD, WALL ~. TIE; KNIT.

KNOW (s/l *no*). BE AWARE, RECOGNIZE. SLEEP WITH (bibl). **Pl** = (s/l noes, *nose*); REALIZES, *UNDERSTANDS*.

KOCHEL K, SCORE (mus) [Mozart].

KOP (s/l *cop*). *FOOTBALL* GROUND (Anfield, Liverpool).

KR KRYPTON (*chem*).

KRAKEN Nor myth sea *monster*.

KRISHNA Ind *god* of *fertility*. **Idol** = *juggernaut* chariot.

KRYPTON KR (*chem*). GASEOUS ELEMENT. PLANET (fict; Superman).

KT *KNIGHT* OF THE THISTLE [James II, St Andrew, Queen Anne, Nemo me impune lacessit]. *KNOT* (naut).

L *LAKE*. LARGE. LATIN. *LEARNER*. LEFT. *LIBERAL*. LIRA. LITTLE. *LONG*. LOVE. LUXEMBOURG (*car plate*). FIFTY. POUND.

£1,050 CLASSIC, ONE THOUSAND GUINEAS.

£2,100 CLASSIC, TWO THOUSAND GUINEAS.

LA *LAKE*. LANTHANUM (*chem*). LOS ANGELES. LOUISIANA. NOTE (mus; also LAH).

LAB LABORATORY. LABOUR.

LABOUR LAB. CHILDBIRTH. ELABORATE. EXERTION, TRAVAIL, TOIL, WORK [*Hercules*]. JOB CENTRE.

LABYRINTH 1. Complicated irregular structure in Gk myth, designed by *Daedalus* to house the *Minotaur* at King *Minos'* palace in Cnossos, hence any MAZE. 2. INNER *EAR*.

LACE CORD, TIE. BEAT, DEFEAT, LASH, WHIP. FLAVOUR, SPIKE. FINE FABRIC, *MATERIAL*, ORRIS; *anniversary* (13th).

LACKING 1. WITHOUT, UN-. 2. Put letters NO or UN (or similar) in front of word indicated, e.g. **Corner lacking approval** (4) = NO*OK. 3. Delete *ing* from clue-word, e.g. **Ingrate lacking speed** (4) = ***RATE. Note that this clue could also imply that a synonym for **speed** should be dropped, i.e. omit **rate** = ING****.

LADDER STEPS; CLIMBING FRAME. PATH, ROUTE. RUN (*tights*). **Pl comp** = *snakes*.

LADY WOMAN. Title (dame; d of earl; w of lord etc).

LADYBIRD Coleopterous insect of genus coccinella. LADYBUG (US), LADYCOW, LADYFLY (Bishop Barnaby, Cushcow Lady; nickname, e.g. Lucie (to Miss Pross, 2 Cities, *Dickens*); Mrs L. B. Johnson (to h, President ~). Also (crypt) any female bird, e.g. hen, pen, reeve (see *Male & Female*) ['~, ~ fly away home . . .' (trad)].

LADY OF THE LAKE 1. ELAINE (*Lancelot*). 2. NIMIANE, NIMUE, VIVIEN, VIVIENNE [*Merlin*]. 3. ELLEN DOUGLAS (~, Sir Walter Scott). 4. LADY WINDERMERE (crypt).

LAERTES 1. Father of *Ulysses* [see *Penelope*]. 2. Son of Polonius (Hamlet, *Shak*).

LAID UP ABED, ILL, SICK. HAULED OUT, WINTERING (naut). DIAL (dn, crypt).

LAKE L, LA, LOCH, LOUGH, TARN. PIGMENT; *COLOUR* (red). INLAND WATER [*Great ~s*]; **world's principal large** ~s:

2-letters
NO (Af)

3-letters
XAU (Af)
ZUG (Swi)

4-letters
ARAL (salt) (USSR)
CHAD (Nig)
ERIE (Can/US)
EYRE (salt) (Aus)

NESS (Sc)
TANA (Ethiopia)

5-letters
ABAYA (Ethiopia)
FROME (salt) (Aus)
HURON (Can/US)
LEMAN (Swi)
MWERU (Zam)
ONEGA (USSR)
POOPO (Bol)
RUKWA (Tanz)
TAUPO (NZ)
VOLTA (Ghana)

6-letters
BAIKAL (USSR; deepest)
GENEVA (Swi)
KARIBA (Zimbabwe)
LADOGA (USSR)
MALAWI (Mal)
MOBUTU (Ug/Zaire)
NASSER (Egy)
RUDOLF (salt) (Ken)

7-letters
AGASSIS (N Am, primeval)
CASPIAN (Pers/USSR; largest salt)

ICHKEUL (Af)
KOKO-NOR (salt) (Ch)
LUCERNE (Swi)
ONTARIO (Can/US)
TORRENS (salt) (Aus)
TURKANA (salt) (E Af)

8-letters
BALKHASH (USSR)
CONISTON (Eng)
ISSYK-KUL (USSR)
MICHIGAN (US)
REINDEER (Can)
SUPERIOR (Can/US;
  largest fresh)
TITICACA (Peru/Bol)
VICTORIA (Ken/Tan/Ug)
WINNIPEG (Can)

9+ letters
ATHABASCA (Can)
GITCHE-GUMEE (*Hiawatha*)
GREAT BEAR (Can)
GREAT SLAVE (Can)
MARACAIBO (Venez)
NICARAGUA (Nic)
TANGANYIKA (Tan/Zam/Z)
WINDERMERE (Eng)

LAMB (s/l lam). *JOINT*, MEAT; **comp** = mint (sauce). *Offspring*
of sheep. SKIPPER (crypt). YEAN. *ISLAND*. INNOCENT.
ELIA, ESSAYIST, *WRITER*. 'AGNES'.
LAMBETH *PALACE* (eccles). *THAMES BRIDGE*.
LAME *CRIPPLED*, DISABLED, HALT. IMPERFECT,
UNCONVINCING. GOLD/SILVER-THREADED
MATERIAL, ORRIS.
LANCELOT Kt of the *Round Table*; mar Elaine (*Lady of the Lake*),
f of *Galahad*. Seduced *Guinevere*. [*Camelot, King Arthur*].
LANCING CUTTING, PIERCING, PRICKING. DANCING
(quadrille). *PUBLIC SCHOOL*.
LAND *COUNTRY*, EARTH; ACRES, SPACE [*measure*].

ALIGHT, COME DOWN, PITCH, SETTLE [Huma, myth bird which never ~s]. SET DOWN. GET, OBTAIN (job).

LANDING ALIGHTING, PANCAKE (av sl), SETTLEMENT (crypt) [*Fido*]. PLATFORM, PONTOON. BETWEEN FLIGHTS (crypt).

LANDLADY Keeper of boarding-house, inn, lodgings; **celeb**: MRS BOUNCE (Box and Cox, Morton), MRS CRUPP (Copperfield, *Dickens*), MRS MACSTINGER (Dombey, *Dickens*), MRS PIPCHIN (Dombey, *Dickens*), MISTRESS QUICKLY (Boar's Head, H.iv, H.v, *Shak*), MRS TODGERS (Chuzzle, *Dickens*).

LANDLORD LESSER, LETTER; **comp** = *tenant*. *HOST*, INN-KEEPER, PUBLICAN; **celeb**: HARRY BAILEY (The Tabard, Canterbury Tales, *Chaucer*), BENDIT (La Bohème, Puccini), BONIFACE (Beaux' Stratagem, Farquhar), JOHN WILLET (The Maypole, Rudge, *Dickens*).

LAND'S END D or S (crypt). Tip of Cornwall. SW.

LANSDOWNE ROAD *FOOTBALL/RUGBY* GROUND.

LAPIS LAZULI GEM (blue). *COLOUR* (blue).

LARES Rom HOUSEHOLD *gods*; **comp** = penates. GIBBON, *MONKEY*.

LARGE M, L. BIG, GRAND, GREAT. BROAD, FREE, SWEEPING. **Comp** = *by*.

LARK GAME, HORSEPLAY; HOAX, JAPE, JOKE. *BIRD*. **assembly** = bevy, exaltation [singing].

LASER (s/l *lazer*). RADIATION, RAY.

LASS GAL, *GIRL*, MISS.

LAST 1. OMEGA, Z, ZED, ZEE (US). ENDURE, END, FINAL, FINALLY, LATEST, LOWEST (**opp** = *first*). [*Holmes* case]. MATRIX, SHOE MOULD. *MEASURE* (wool). 2. Last letter of word(s) concerned, e.g. **Last will and testament** = LDT.

~ **MONTH** DECEMBER; ULT. H (crypt). Any abbreviation for the current previous month.

~ **VEHICLE** E (crypt). HEARSE (crypt).

~ **WORDS** EPITAPH, OBITUARY. AMEN. PS, YOURS (FAITHFULLY/SINCERELY/TRULY). COBBLER, SHOE, UPPER, WELT etc (crypt).

LAT LATIN. *LATITUDE* [navigation].

LATE D, DEAD, EX, FORMER. RECENT. BACKWARD, OVERDUE, TARDY. EVENING, SMALL HOURS.

~ **NEWS** EPITAPH, OBIT(UARY).

LATIN 1. L, LAT [school]. 2. Put word(s) indicated into Latin, e.g.

I am Latin in total (3) = SUM.

LATITUDE MOVEMENT, *PLAY*, SCOPE. CLIME, REGION, TROPIC [parallel]. BREADTH, LEEWAY, ROOM.

LAUGH BE AMUSED, CHORTLE, CHUCKLE, GIGGLE, GRIN, SMILE; HA-HA [*funny*, ludicrous, risible]. RIDICULE, SCORN. [donkey, hyena, jackass (~ penguin), Kookaburra, laughing jackass, mockingbird].

LAUNCHER ROCKET PAD, *WEAPON* FIRER. ORIGINATOR, STARTER. COXSWAIN (naut).

LAUREL 1. *TREE*; BAY. **Comp**: Hardy. 2. In Gk myth, *DAPHNE* was changed into a laurel to escape *Apollo*.

LAVA *AA*, IGNEOUS ROCK, MAGMA, TUFA, TUFF.

LAW REGULATION, RULE; INJUNCTION. JUDICIAL REMEDY, LITIGATION. **Comp** = *order*. LEGAL KNOWLEDGE/PROFESSION; **celeb practitioners**: Aedile (Rom); Sampson and Sally Brass (OC Shop, *Dickens*); Sgt Buzfuz (Pickwick, *Dickens*); Dodson and Fogg (Pickwick, *Dickens*); Draco (Gk); Fang (magistrate, Oliver, *Dickens*); Fips (legal agent, Chuzzle, *Dickens*); Miss Flite (Bleak Ho, *Dickens*); Fury (dog, *Alice*); Jaggers (advocate, Great Ex, *Dickens*); Portia (M of V, *Shak*); Reeve (*Chaucer*); Serjeant of Law (*Chaucer*); Justice Shallow (H.iv and Merry Wives, *Shak*); Justice Silence (H.iv, *Shak*); Snagsby (Bleak Ho, *Dickens*); Spenlow and Jorkins (proctors, Copperfield, *Dickens*); Tulkinghorn (lawyer, Bleak Ho, *Dickens*); George Warrington (barrister, Pendennis, Thackeray); Mr Whymper (Animal Farm, *Orwell*); Mr Wickfield (lawyer, Copperfield, *Dickens*).

LAWFUL APPOINTED, PERMITTED, QUALIFIED, RECOGNIZED. LEGAL, LICIT.

LAX LOOSE, REMISS, SLACK. LACROSSE (sl).

LAY AMATEUR, NON-PROFESSIONAL. NON-CLERICAL, NOT IN ORDERS (hence UNORDERED — crypt). DEPOSIT, PLACE, PUT DOWN; ARRANGE, DISPOSE, PREPARE. PRODUCE (egg). LIE, TWIST (rope). POEM, *SONG*. COPULATE WITH, BED (US).

LAYER COATING, FILM; *COURSE*, STRATUM. *BIRD*, HEN (crypt).

LAYMAN AMATEUR, NON-EXPERT, UNPROFESSIONAL. NON-CLERICAL; UNORDERED (crypt). EGG-PRODUCER, CHICKEN FARMER (crypt). CROONER, SINGER (crypt).

LAZER (s/l *laser*). *LOAFER*, IDLER.

LB *MEASURE*, POUND WEIGHT.

LEAD *METAL*; PB (*chem*), BASE METAL. DEPTH SOUNDER (naut). CHANNEL, CONDUCT, *DIRECT*, GUIDE; DIRECTION, GUIDANCE. PASS, SPEND. OPEN; PLAY CARD. STARRING ROLE. GO FIRST; VAN. WATERCOURSE.

LEADER (s/l *lieder*). 1. DUCE, FUHRER. CO. DIRECTOR, GUIDE, TOP PERSON [*military* ~]. COVER STORY, LEADING ARTICLE. 2. First letter of word(s) indicated, e.g. **Military leader** = M.

LEAGUE ASSOCIATION, CLIQUE. THREE MILES (arch).

LEAN *BANK*, BEND, INCLINE, LIST, *TILT*. FAT-FREE, SLENDER, SLIM (**opp** = fat, obese) [diet. Jack Sprat].

LEANDER 1. Gk myth lover of *Hero*, drowned when the lighthouse failed as he was swimming the *Hellespont* from Abydos to visit her at Sestos. 2. Rowing club.

LEANING ASLANT, LISTING, OBLIQUE, *TILTED* (**opp** = *upright*). BENT, INCLINATION, WISH.

LEAR 1. *MAD KING* (3 d: Cordelia, Goneril, Regan [*Shak*]). 2. Edward ~, writer. **Books/rhymes**: The Book of Nonsense, More Nonsense Rhymes, Laughable Lyrics; The Dong with the Luminous Nose, The Duck and the Kangaroo, The Jumblies, The Owl and the Pussycat, The Pobble Who Has No Toes, The Quangle-Wangle's Hat, The Two Old Bachelors, The Akond of Swat, The Pelican Chorus, Mr & Mrs Discobbolos. 3. Aircraft company.

LEARNER L, PUPIL; APPRENTICE, BEGINNER. TIRO, TYRO (**opp** = expert).

LEARNING KNOWLEDGE, LORE. FINDING OUT. EDUCATION.

LEATHERNECK JOLLY, MARINE, RM.

LEAVE ABANDON, *DESERT*, GET OUT, PART, QUIT (**opp** = enter). MAKE *WILL*, TESTIFY. EXEAT, FURLOUGH, HOLIDAY [AWOL]. **Pl** = FOLIAGE. FF, FOLIOS, SHEETS.

LEAVING 1. Indicates word or letter(s) removed from clue, e.g. **Ship leaving Moscow** = MO; or **Animal doctors leaving Moscow** (3) = COW. 2. **Pl** = DREGS, LEES, ORT, REMAINS.

LECTURE *LESSON*, READING, TALK. TAKE TO TASK, TALKING TO.

LEDA (s/l *leader*, *lieder*). Queen of Sparta, m of *Helen*, *Clytemnestra*, Castor, Pollux by *Zeus* (who *transformed* himself into a *swan* to seduce her).

LEE SHELTER (**opp** = *open*, windward). *MILITARY LEADER* (US). **Pl** = DREGS, *LEAVINGS*, ORT, REFUSE, REMAINS, SEDIMENT.

LEFT L, P; LARBOARD, PORT (naut), *RED*, *SINISTER*. NOT RIGHT. ABANDONED, OVER, REMAINING. DEPARTED, GONE, WENT. COMMUNIST, LABOUR.

LEG CRUS (**Pl** = Crura). LIMB, MEMBER [*bone*]. PROP, SUPPORT; UNDERSTANDING (crypt). WALK, HOP, LENGTH, RUN, SECTION, SPAN, STAGE, TACK. ON (*cricket*; **opp** = *off*).

LEGISLATIVE ASSEMBLY *BOARD*, *CABINET*, COUNCIL, DEBATING CHAMBER, FORUM, *HOUSE*, SENATE, e.g. BUNDESTAG (W Ger), CONGRESS (House of Representatives, Senate, US), CORTES (Port, Sp), DAIL (Seanad, Eire), DIET (Holy Roman Empire), DUMA (Russia), FOLKETING (Denmark), FORUM (Senate, Rom), *HOUSES* OF PARLIAMENT (*Commons*, *Lords*, UK), REICHSRAT (A-Hung), REICHSTAG (Ger), RIKSDAG (Swe), STORMONT CASTLE (N Ire), STORTHING (Nor), THING (ON), TYN(E)WALD (House of Keys, IOM), WITANAGEMOT (Sax). [Iolanthe (*G & S*)].

LEMON *FRUIT*. *TREE*. *COLOUR* (yellow). ANSWER (crypt).

LEMUR Nocturnal mammal; **types**: BABAKATO, BROWN ~, BUSHBABY, COLUGO (flying ~), GALAGO, (WOOLLY) INDRI(S), KINKAJOU, KUKANG, LEPI, LORIS, MAKI, MALMAG, MOUSE ~, POTTO, QUANACO, RACOON, RINGTAIL ~, SIFAKA, *SLOTH*, TANA, TARSIER [Madagascar, *monkey*; *ghost*].

LENGTH *MEASURE*. ELL, PERCH, POLE, ROD. FOOT, FT, IN, INCH, YARD, YD etc. LEAGUE, METRE, VERST.

LENT (s/l leant). ABSTAIN, FAST TIME [Easter]. ADVANCED, LOANED (**opp** = borrowed).

LEOTARD DOUBLET (hence TT, crypt), TIGHTS [*ballet*].

LEPIDOPTERA WINGED *INSECTS*; BUTTERFLIES, MOTHS, BUGS; **breeds (butterflies)**: Birdwing, Blue Crow, Brimstone, Cabbage White, Comma, Common Blue, Common White, *Copper*, Crow ~, Diadem, *Emperor*, *Footman*, Fritillary, Green-veined White, Hairstreak, Heliconid, Large Skipper, Large White, Leaf ~, Meadow Brown, *Monarch*, Orange Tip, Owl ~, Painted Lady, Peacock, Pearl Bordered Fritillary, Red Admiral, Ringlet, *Skipper*, Small Copper, Small Heath, *Tiger*, Tortoiseshell, Wall Brown,

Woodnymph, Yellow Brimstone; **breeds (moths)**: Buff Tip, Burnet,
Cinnabar, Drinker, Eggar, Elephant Hawkmoth, *Emperor*, Eyed
Hawkmoth, Hawkmoth, Hummingbird Hawkmoth, Kentish Glory,
Lackey, *Magpie*, *Psyche*, Pussmoth, Silver Y, Six-spot Burnet,
Tigermoth, Vapourer, White Ermine, Yellowtail, Yellow
Underwing.

LES LESLIE. THE FRENCH.

LESSEN (s/l *lesson*). 1. *DECREASE*, DIMINISH, REDUCE. 2.
Delete letters EN, e.g. **If you lessen Penates, on your heads be it** (4)
= P**ATES.

LESSER 1. MINOR, SMALLER. *LANDLORD*. 2. Delete letters
ER, e.g. **Lesser copper ice-wood** (7) = COPP**ICE.

LESSON (s/l *lessen*). 1. INSTRUCTION, TEACHING [*study*].
READING, SCRIPTURE. ADMONISH, EXAMPLE,
OCCURRENCE, PUNISHMENT, REBUKE. 2. Delete ON from
clue, e.g. **Mutton lesson is stupid** (4) = MUTT**.

LESS THAN 1. UNDER. NOT SO MUCH. 2. Drop one or two
letters from word indicated, e.g. **Inside is less than an evening meal**
(5) = *INNER.

LET LEASE, RENT. *ALLOW*, PERMIT (**opp** = *hinder*).
HINDER, PREVENT (arch; **opp** = *allow*).

LETHE Gk myth personification of oblivion; the *underworld* river
from which souls of the departed drank and thereby forgot
everything of the upper world [*Styx*].

LETTER MAIL, MESSAGE, MISSIVE, POST. CHARACTER:
A, B, C etc. *LANDLORD*. HINDRANCE, PREVENTER
(arch).

~ **OPENER** L (crypt). KNIFE. DEAR MADAM/SIR (crypt).

~ **SENDER** CORRESPONDENT, WRITER, POSTER. YOURS
FAITHFULLY/SINCERELY/TRULY (crypt).

LEVEL *EVEN*, HORIZONTAL. DRAWN, EQUAL, TIED.
STRAIGHT. HEIGHT.

LEVY *COLLECT*, EXTORT, IMPOSE, RAISE; DUTY, RATE,
SCOT, TAX, TOLL. CONSCRIBE, *ENLIST*, ENROL;
CONSCRIPT, PRESSED MAN.

LIAR (s/l *lyre*). FIBBER, STORY TELLER. **Celeb**: ANANIAS
(bibl); DE TOTT (Baron); MATILDA (Belloc); MUNCHAUSEN
(Baron); OBLOMOV (Gonchorov).

LIB LIBERAL. LIBERATION.

LIBER = *BACCHUS*.

LIBERA = *PROSERPINE*.

LIBERAL L, LIB; POLITICIAN. ABUNDANT, AMPLE (**opp** = *mean*), CANDID, *FREE*, GENEROUS, OPENHANDED.

LICK TASTE [tongue]; **comp** = promise. *BEAT* (sl). *SPEED* (sl).

LID *HAT. COVER.*

LIED FIBBED, TOLD STORY. *SONG* (Ger).

LIEDER (s/l *leader*). *SONGS* (Ger).

LIFE PAYMENT RANSOM. PENSION. CAPITAL PUNISHMENT.

LIFT RAISE, TAKE UP (**opp** = *lower*) [hitch hike]. ELEVATOR, PATERNOSTER [Otis, inventor]. CHARGE, EXHILARATION, KICK. *STEAL* [*robber*].

LIGHT NOT DARK, BLOND(E), PALE. NOT HEAVY, UNLADEN; TRIVIAL. *BEAM*, FLOOD ~, *RAY*, SPOT ~, LAMP; ILLUMINE. 'PHOEBE'. *FIRE, MATCH.* GIDDY, NIMBLE, *NIPPY.* CLUE, PRINCIPLE, TENET. PORTHOLE, WINDOW (naut). EYE (poet). SHORT, UNDERSUBSCRIBED. **Pl** = INNARDS, KIDNEYS, LIVER, LUNGS, OFFAL.

LIGHTER MATCH, SPILL. PALER. LESS BURDENED. BARGE. GLAZIER (crypt). LAMP, SUN (crypt).

LIGHTNING 1. DISCHARGE (met); **comp** = *thunder*. SPEEDY. *AIRCRAFT.* 2. **God: Rom** = FULMINATOR; **goddess: Rom** = *MINERVA.*

LIKE *AS*, EQUAL, SIMILAR. CONSENT. FIND AGREEABLE.

LIKING FANCY, FONDNESS, REGARD, TASTE (**opp** = *aversion*). See also *Lover of.*

LILY *FLOWER* of genus LILIUM: ARUM, BELLADONNA, CALLA, *GUERNSEY, IRIS*, LENT, MADONNA, RED-HOT POKER, TORCH ~, TRITOMA, WATER ~, WHITE ~. 'SUSAN'. [~ Langtry (Jersey ~); ~ Marlene (song)]. **Pl** = ROYAL ARMS (Fr Bourbon).

LIMIT *BOUNDARY.* CONTROL. END, TERMINUS. MAXIMUM SPEED.

LIMITED LTD, PLC. RESTRICTED (**opp** = *free*).

~ **FRENCH** SA.

~ **GERMAN** AG, GMBH.

LINCOLN 1. ABE. *AIRCRAFT.* GREEN. *PIG. RACETRACK* (horses). *UNIVERSITY COLLEGE.* USS ~ (Mme *Butterfly*). 2. LINDUM (Rom). US *state* capital.

LINCOLN'S INN *INN OF COURT*, LAW SOCIETY.

LINE FILE, *ROW*, TIER. LETTER. BOAST. RAILWAY: GWR, LMS, LNER, SR etc (often as 'old ~'). FISHING TACKLE, GUT, PATERNOSTER; **comp** = *rod*. FIGURE. **Pl** = BR, RLY, RY. ODE, POEM, POETRY, VERSE. IMPOT (sl), PUNISHMENT.

LINER 1. *BOAT*, SHIP, *STEAMER*. PROTECTION, SLEEVE. COTTON, LINEN, LINING, SILESIA. ARTIST, CARTOONIST, DRAUGHTSMAN, DRAWER (all crypt). ACTOR, PLAYWRIGHT (crypt). RULER (crypt). 2. Put word inside another, e.g. **Bag with thin liner is popular in the sea** (7) = BA*THIN*G.

LINESMAN FOOTBALL OFFICIAL, TOUCHJUDGE. SOLDIER (crypt). CONDUCTOR, ENGINE DRIVER, GUARD, RAILWAYMAN, TRAIN DRIVER (all crypt). AUTHOR, POET, WRITER (all crypt). ELSMAN (crypt: L*in*ESMAN).

LINE UP ALIGN, DRESS. PARADE. REPRESENTATIVES, TEAM. ENIL (dn, crypt).

LING *FISH*. *HEATHER*.

LINKS (s/l *lynx*). CONNECTIONS, TIES. CUFF BUTTONS. *GOLF COURSE*. KLS (crypt: L*in*KS).

LION 1. BIG *CAT*, KING OF BEASTS, LEO; **assembly** = pride, **offspring** = cub, lioncel (*herald*); **comp** = unicorn. [Alfred (Stanley Holloway); Androcles (Rom slave); *Daniel* (bibl); *Holmes* case]. 2. BRAVE PERSON, HERO. CELEBRITY, STAR, VIP. **Pl** = *Football* team (US). *RUGBY PLAYERS*. 3. One of the labours of *Hercules*. 4. *Constellation*; (5th) sign of the *Zodiac* (Leo). 5. Character in *Alice* and in *The Wizard of Oz*.

LIONHEART COEUR DE LION, RICHARD [Blondel, Durnstein castle]. *IO* (crypt).

LIP CHEEK, IMPUDENCE, INSOLENCE. EDGE, RIM, TIP. **Pl** = 1. MOUTH; SPEAKERS. 2. Gk myth SW *wind* (**Rom** = AFRICUS).

LIQUEUR ALCOHOL, AFTER-DINNER DRINK; **types** (all ®): ABSINTHE (wormwood), BENEDICTINE (brandy), COINTREAU (orange), CREME DE MENTHE (mint), CURAÇAO (orange), DRAMBUIE (whisky), KIRSCH (cherry), KUMMEL (caraway), GRAND MARNIER (brandy/orange), MARASCHINO (cherry), NOYAU (fruit kernels), TIA MARIA (coffee).

LIRA L.

LIST *BOOK*, CATALOGUE, INDEX, ROLL, *TABLE*. HEEL,

LEAN, TILT. BORDER, EDGE, HEM. ATTENTION, HARK, HEED, LISTEN. **Pl** = TILTING GROUND (jousting).

LISTENER AUDITOR, HEARER; *EAR* (crypt). **Pl** = AUDIENCE.

LIT ILLUMINATED, ILLUMINED, LIGHTED. DRUNK. STRUCK; SET FIRE TO.

LITTER BROOD [*offspring*]. RUSHES, STRAW. RUBBISH. BED, BIER, HURDLE, STRETCHER; PALANQUIN (Ind) [Sedan chair].

LITTLE 1. L; DIMINUTIVE, *DWARF*, MINI, PYGMY, SMALL, WEE (**opp** = *big*). *THEATRE*. 2. Use abbreviated or shortened version, e.g. **Each little** = EA. 3. **Celeb (fict)**: ~ Billee (Trilby, du Maurier); Bingo ~ (*Wodehouse*); ~ Bo-peep (trad); ~ Boy Blue (trad); ~ Dorrit (*Dickens*); ~ Em'ly (Copperfield, *Dickens*); Eric or ~ by ~ (Farrar); ~ Foxes (Hellman); ~ Jack Horner (trad); ~ John (Robin *Hood*); ~ Lord Fauntleroy (Burnett); ~ Men (Alcott); ~ Mildred (*Kipling*); ~ Nell (OC Shop, *Dickens*); ~ Princess (Burnett); ~ Red Riding *Hood* (trad); ~ Tim (Xmas Carol, *Dickens*); ~ Women (Alcott).

~ **BOY** 1. LAD, YOUNGSTER. 2. Use abbreviated or familiar version of boy's name, e.g. **A little boy is a handsome youth** (6) = A*DON*IS.

~ **BY** ~ ERIC (Farrar). LL (crypt).

~ **GIRL** 1. LASS, YOUNGSTER. 2. Use short or familiar form of girl's name, e.g. **Laughing little girl joins the monarch** (6) = JO*KING.

~ **MAN** 1. *DWARF*, MIDGET. 2. Use abbreviated form of name, e.g. **Little man joins little particle to make lots** (7) = BILL*ION.

~ **MONEY** C, D, P etc. CENT, PENNY. SMALL CHANGE.

~ **TIME** HR, MIN, MO, SEC, TICK, TIM (crypt).

~ **WOMAN** 1. *DWARF*, MIDGET. *WIFE*. 2. Use abbreviated form of name, e.g. **The little woman puts on weight and becomes huge** (7) = MEG*A*TON. 3. AMY, BETH, JO, MEG (Louisa May Alcott).

LIVE EXIST. DOSS, HANG OUT, INHABIT. QUICK (**opp** = *dead*). INSTANT; SPONTANEOUS, UNRECORDED. CHARGED, ON, SHOCKING (elect). **Pl** = EXISTS, IS.

LIVER SURVIVOR. ORGAN, OFFAL [*Prometheus*]; **comp** = bacon.

LIVING ALIVE, EXISTING, QUICK (**opp** = *dead*). EXISTENCE, LIVELIHOOD [Saturday's *child*]; CAREER. BENEFICE, PARISH (eccles).

LIZARD REPTILE (*dinosaur*, lacertilia); AGAMA, ANOLIS, BASILISK, BEADED MONSTER, BLIND WORM, CHAMELEON, GECKO, GILA, GREEN ~, HATTERIA (NZ), IGUANA, MOLOCH (Aus), *MONITOR*, OLM, SALAMANDER, SAND ~, SEPS, SKINK, SWIFT ~, TUATERA (NZ), UTA, WORREL, ZONURE [loses tail; newt]. **Celeb**: BILL (*Alice*).

LLAMA (s/l lama). Domesticated ruminant 2-toed quadruped (S Am); **breeds**: ALPACA, GUANACO, HUANACO, PACO, VICU(G)NA [*camel*].

LLOYDS *BANK®*. INSURERS, MARINE UNDERWRITERS [coffee house; Lutine bell]. SHIP SURVEYORS; REGISTER [A1; yachts]. *REFERENCE WORK* (ships).

LO BEHOLD, LOOK, SEE.

LOAF IDLE, SLACK (**opp** = *beaver*). BREAD, *COB*, COTTAGE. HEAD (*rh sl*).

LOAFER IDLER, *LAZER*, SLACKER. *BAKER* (crypt).

LOBSTER CRUSTACEAN (10-footed); CRAWFISH, CRAYFISH [langouste, langoustine, prawn, shrimp; quadrille (*Alice*)]. UNDERARM BOWLER (*cricket*). BRITISH SOLDIER (arch).

LOCAL BELONGING TO, PECULIAR TO; NEAR BY, NEIGHBOURING, VICINITY. PARTLY, RESTRICTED. *PUB. TRAIN. ANAESTHETIC.*

LOCH L, LAKE, LOUGH (Ire); NESS.

LOCK BOLT, KEY, WARD. CURL, *HAIR*, TRESS.

LOCKER CUPBOARD. CHEST, COMPARTMENT (naut). *KEY*; *GAOLER*, TURNKEY, WARDER (crypt). BARBER, *HAIRDRESSER* (crypt).

LOCK-KEEPER CANAL GATE OPERATOR. COMB, HAIR-GRIP, HAIRPIN, SLIDE (all crypt). *HAIRDRESSER* (crypt).

LOCO-MEN RAILWAY MEN (**Unions** = ASLEF, NUR). CRANKS, IDIOTS, MADMEN, NUTTERS.

LODGE DEPOSIT, LAY DOWN. PUT UP, RESIDE, STAY. *Habitation* (*beaver*, otter). BRANCH MEMBERS. COTTAGE, DWELLING.

LOFTING 1. LOBBING (sport). STORING, WAREHOUSING (comm). 2. Laying-out full-scale lines of a hull (naut). 3. Hugh ~, WRITER. **Books**: Dr Dolittle's Caravan, ~'s Circus, ~'s Garden, ~'s Post Office, ~'s Zoo, Story of ~, Voyages of ~, Story of Mrs Tubbs, Porridge Poetry. **Characters**: Dr John Dolittle (talked with animals), Barbary *Dragon*, Ben-Ali (*pirate*), Chee-Chee (*monkey*),

Dab-Dab (*duck*), Gub-Gub (*pig*), Jabizri (*beetle*), Jip (*dog*), Jolliginki (*African tribe*, Queen Ermintrude, Prince Bumpo), Polynesia (*parrot*), Pushmipullyu (2-headed animal), Tommy (*cobbler's* son), Too-Too (*owl*), Tripsitinka (*Fairy* Queen); Spidermonkey Island. See also *Doolittle*.

LOG ENTER, *RECORD*, REGISTER; *LIST*. LOGARITHM [Napier]. BILLET (wood).

LOGGER LUMBERJACK, SAWYER. DIARIST, RECORDER (crypt).

LOKI Nor *god* of FIRE; m Angurboda; f of Fenris (*wolf*), *Hel* and Midgard (*serpent*).

LONDON 1. CAPITAL, SMOKE [*Gates. Thames bridges*]. *BOXER. UNIVERSITY. WRITER.* 2. LONDINIUM (*Rom*).

LONDON DISTRICT EC, SW, WC etc; hence N*ONE, W*EIGHT (i.e. N1, W8 — crypt).

LONG L; ENDURING, LENGTHY (**opp** = *short*). CRAVE, LANGUISH, PANT, *PINE*, YEARN. LONGITUDE [meridian, navigation]. ISLAND (Eng, Ire, US).

LONGING CRAVING, YEARNING, YEN. BELONGING TO (arch).

LONG LIFE UHT. OCTOGENARIAN; METHUSELAH. [*cat*].

LONG PANTS SLACKS, TROUSERS, COMBS, ~ JOHNS. *LONGING* (crypt).

LOOK *CON*, GLANCE, LEER, LO, *PEER*, PRY, REGARD, SEE, STARE, SURVEY; BUTCHERS (*rh sl*); DEKKO (sl). AIR, ASPECT, *BEARING*, MIEN.

~ **BACK** 1. REFLECT, REMINISCE. TURN HEAD, TURN ROUND [*Eurydice, Lot, Orpheus*]. 2. Word reads backwards, e.g. **Royal looks back for his beer** (5) = LAGER.

~ **FOR** SEARCH, SEEK; *FISH*.

~ **OUT** *CAVE* (hence CAVEMAN — crypt), FORE, TAKE CARE, WARE. OBSERVER, *SENTRY, WATCHER* [crow's nest].

LOON *BIRD*, DIVER, GREBE. IDLER, SCAMP. DOLT, IMBECILE, LUNATIC.

LORD *NOBLE*, PEER. DOMINATE, DOMINEER. Thomas ~ (cricket). **Pl** = *LEGISLATIVE ASSEMBLY*, ANOTHER PLACE. PEERAGE. *CRICKET* GROUND; TEST(ING) GROUND (crypt). 12th day of *Christmas* in song.

LORRY (s/l Laurie). 1. FLAT CAR, FLOAT, *JUGGERNAUT*, PANTECHNICON, (MOTOR) TRUCK, VAN, WAG(G)ON. 2. BANKER (2 Cities, *Dickens*).

LOSE 1. GET RID OF, MISLAY, MISPLACE (**opp** = *discover*).
BE/GET DEFEATED (**opp** = *beat*); SURRENDER. BECOME
SLOW. IMMERSE. 2. Delete letter(s) indicated, e.g. **Encourage
to lose no ace (4)** = ****UR*GE.

~ **HEART** 1. DESPAIR. ADORE, FALL IN LOVE. 2. Omit
middle letter(s), e.g. **Peter loses heart, the noble fellow** = PE*ER.

LOSING ONE Omit letter I, e.g. **I'm a rat, losing one French
Revolutionist (5)** = *M*A*RAT.

LOST CITY ATLANTIS, *EL DORADO*, LYONESSE, SHANGRI-
LA. [Mu (Continent)].

LOT 1. HIGH NUMBER, LASHINGS, MANY hence C, D, M.
SALE ITEM. CHANCE, DRAW, FATE, SORT, STRAW.
PLOT. TAX DUE. DEPARTMENT, *RIVER* (Fr). *AIRLINE*
(Pol). 2. Abraham's nephew, s of Haran. His wife was turned into
a pillar of salt, on *looking back* as she fled from the destruction of
Sodom and Gomorrah.

LOUD F, FF; DIN, NOISE, *ROW* (**opp** = *quiet*).

LOUGH L, IRISH LAKE.

LOVE 1. L, O, DUCK, EGG, NIL, ZERO, ZILCH. ADORE,
DEAR, HONEY; ALOHA. 'Charity'. [Friday's *child*]. 2. **Gods:**
Gk = EROS, **Rom** = AMOR, *CUPID*; **goddesses: Gk** =
APHRODITE, **Rom** = VENUS, **Bab** = ISHTAR, **Egy** = *ISIS*,
Nor = *FREYA*, **Phoen** = ASTARTE.

~ **APPLE** TOMATO.

LOVER 1. AMANT, AMOUR, GIRL/BOY FRIEND,
INAMORATA, SWEETHEART; [*companion*; *inspiration*; *patron
saint*; *seven ages (Shak)*]; **Pl** = 6 (*tarot*); **celeb:** CASANOVA (It);
DON JUAN (~, Byron); LOCHINVAR (Marmion, Scott);
LOTHARIO (The Fair Penitent, Rowe); TOM JONES
(~, Fielding). **Pl** = ABELARD/HELOISE (Fr);
ANTONY/CLEOPATRA (Rom/Egy and *Shak*);
CELADON/AMELIA (The Seasons, Thomson);
CHOPIN/GEORGE SAND; DARBY/JOAN (trad ballad);
HENRY II/FAIR ROSAMOND (Talisman, Scott);
LEANDER/HERO (Gk myth); NAPOLEON/JOSEPHINE (Fr);
NELSON/EMMA (UK); PYRAMUS/THISBE (Bab myth and
MND *Shak*); ROMEO/JULIET (~, *Shak*). 2. One who is keen on
a subject (**opp** = one who has an *aversion* to a subject), e.g.

Books	BIBLIOPHILE
Cinema	KINEMOPHILE

Death	NECROPHILE
Dogs	CYNOPHILE
English ways	ANGLOPHILE
Feet	PODOPHILE
Foreigners	XENOPHILE
French ways	FRANCOPHILE
God	THEOPHILE
Horses	HIPPOPHILE
Learning	PHILOMATH
Pain	ALGOPHILE
People	GENOPHILE
Russian ways	RUSSOPHILE
Wine	OENOPHILE
Women	PHILOGYNIST

3. In dn clue, put L before (or 'over') word indicated, e.g. **Oaf-lover sounds needed** (4) = L*OAF.

LOVE-SICK AMOROUS; LOST HEART, hence (crypt) omit middle letter(s) as in *LOSE HEART* above.

LOW ABJECT, *BASE*, DEJECTED, DISPIRITED, DOWN, HUMBLE (**opp** = high). COARSE, DEGRADED, MEAN, VULGAR (**opp** = U). QUIET. COL, CYCLONE, DEPRESSION (met). BELLOW, MOO. *CARTOONIST* (Blimp, TUC horse).

LOW CREATURE *BULL*, *COW*, *OX* (crypt). SNAKE. TUC HORSE (crypt).

LOWER DEBASE, DEGRADE, DIMINISH, DISGRACE; BENEATH, NETHER. DESCEND, LET DOWN, SINK (**opp** = *hoist*, *lift*). FROWN, LOUR. BOVINE, *COW*, *OX*, NEAT etc (crypt).

LOW-LYING DEPRESSED. IN HIDING (crypt).

LP RECORD.

LSD (OLD) MONEY. *DRUG*.

LUCIFER 1. *MATCH* (arch). *DEVIL*. 2. Rom name for *VENUS* as the MORNING STAR; **Gk** = PHOSPHORUS (**opp** = *Hesperus*).

LUG PULL. PAWL. EAR.

LUGGAGE *BAGGAGE*.

LUNA (s/l *lunar*). Rom myth *goddess* of the *MOON* (**Gk** = *SELENE*).

LUNAR (s/l *luna*). MONTHLY. *MOON*. MOONIE (crypt).

LUNATIC *FOOL*, IDIOT, MADMAN, *NUTCASE*.

LYDIA 1. GIRL. 2. Part of Asia Minor, MAEONIA (**King** = *Croesus*).

LYNX (s/l *links*). *CAT*. HELICOPTER.

LYON (s/l *lion*). *HERALD*. RIVER (Sc). TOWN (Fr). **Pl** = CAFE (*Nippy*).

LYRE (s/l *liar*). 1. *BIRD*. INSTRUMENT (mus) [*Hermes*, *Orpheus*]. 2. *Constellation* (Lyra).

M *MAIDEN*. MALTA (*car plate*). *MARK*. *MARRIED*. *MALE*, MASCULINE. MEDIUM. MEGA (*Int unit*). *MEMBER*. MERIDIEM, NOON. METRE. MILLION. MONDAY. MONSIEUR. *MOTHER*. Head of MI5. THOUSAND.

MA MASTER OF ARTS; DEGREE. *MOTHER*, MUM. MASSACHUSETTS (US *state*). MOROCCO (*car plate*). *Goddess* of Truth (Egy).

MACBETH THANE; THE SCOTTISH PLAY [damned spot; *Shak*].

MACE NUTMEG, *SPICE*. SPIKED CLUB, *WEAPON*. STAFF OF OFFICE [House of Commons; Speaker].

MACRON ACCENT (ā = long sound).

MAD *Anag.* BATS, CRAZY, DOTTY, IDIOTIC, LUNATIC, *NUTTY*; **celeb**: Bertha *Mason* (Jane Eyre, *Brontë*); *Caligula* (Incitatus); Mr Dick (Copperfield, *Dickens*); Giselle (*Adam*); Hamlet (*Shak*); ~ Hatter (*Alice*); Landseer (*painter*); Dr Manette (2 Cities, *Dickens*); Mignon (Goethe); Nijinski (ballet); Ophelia (Hamlet, *Shak*); *Saul* (2); Schumann (*composer*); van Gogh (*painter*); and see *Mad King*. ANGRY, ANNOYED, *CROSS*.

MADE (s/l *maid*). BUILT, CONSTRUCTED, CREATED, *FASHIONED* (**opp** = *broke*, destroyed). ARRIVED, REACHED.

MAD KING CHARLES VI (Fr), GEORGE III (Eng), LEAR (*Shak*), LUDWIG (Bavaria), *SAUL* (bibl).

MADMAN IDIOT, LUNATIC, *NUTCASE*.

MAGELLAN *EXPLORER*. *STRAIT*.

MAGI Bibl wise men of Chaldaea, ASTROLOGERS, MAGICIANS, PRIESTS (Zoroastra), especially the three ~ of the Nativity: *Balthazar*, Caspar and Melchior.

MAGICIAN CONJUROR, GRAMMARIAN, NECROMANCER, WIZARD; SORCERER, WARLOCK. **Celeb (fact)**: HOUDINI, MASKELYNE AND DEVANT; **(fiction)**: FAUST (Goethe;

Marlowe), MANDRAKE (bot, legend), *MEDEA* (Gk myth),
MEPHISTOPHELES (Goethe; Marlowe), MERLIN (*King Arthur*), PROSPERO (Tempest, *Shak*).

MAGISTRATE (A)EDILE (Rom), JP, *LAW PRACTITIONER*,
STIPENDIARY. **Celeb**: DRACO (Gk); FANG (*Dickens*).

MAGNESIUM *METAL*; MG (*chem*).

MAGNUM *BOTTLE* (double size).

MAGPIE TARGET RING (penultimate). CHATTERER,
GOSSIP. COLLECTOR, *KLEPTOMANIAC*. *LEPIDOPTERA*
(moth). *BIRD* (pica pica or crow family); (1) sorrow, (2) joy, (3)
girl, (4) boy, (5) letter, (6) something better, (7) greeting, (8) wish,
(9) kiss, (10) meeting; [bad luck, stealing; Thieving ~ (mus)]. **Pl** =
NOTTS COUNTY (*football* team).

MAIA 1. Gk myth d of *Atlas* and Pleione; eldest of the *Pleiades*; m by
Zeus of *Hermes*. 2. Rom myth *goddess* of Earth; the first fruits
were offered in *May*.

MAID (s/l *made*). DAMOSEL, DAMSEL, *GIRL*, LASS;
SPINSTER, UNWED. SERVANT, SERVING GIRL, WENCH,
TWEENY. **Celeb**: ABIGAIL (The Scornful Lady, Beaumont and
Fletcher), FAIR ~ (of Kent), *JOAN* (of Arc), KEZIA (Mill on the
Floss), MARIA (12th N, *Shak*), MISS MIGGS (Rudge, *Dickens*),
CLARA PEGGOTTY (Copperfield, *Dickens*), GUSTER (Bleak
Ho, *Dickens*), ~ MARION (Robin *Hood*), NERISSA (M of V,
Shak), RUTH (Pirates, *G & S*), SUZUKI (Madam *Butterfly*)
[Yeoman, Mikado (3 pretty ~s) *G & S*].

MAIDEN M, UNMATED, UNWED, VIRGIN; [~ over, *cricket*].
FIRST. GUILLOTINE (hist Sc). 'CORA'. *CASTLE*.
MALCOLM (Sc king).

MAIL (s/l *male*). LETTERS, POST. ARMOUR. NEWSPAPER®.

MAIN (s/l *mane*). CHIEF, PRINCIPAL; **comp** = *might*. SUPPLY
(drains, electricity, gas, water). *SEA*.

MAIN COURSE SHIP'S HEADING. PRINCIPAL DISH (*course*).
SEAFOOD (crypt).

MAJOR PRINCIPAL (**opp** = *minor*). PITCH, SCALE (mus).
MAJ, OFFICER, SOLDIER (crowned — crypt); **celeb**:
BAGSTOCK (Dombey, *Dickens*); BRIDGENORTH (*Scott*);
PENDENNIS (Thackeray); PENTO (Thackeray); PIG (*Orwell*).

MAKE *Anag*. BUILD, CONSTRUCT, FABRICATE, FASHION.
COMPEL, FORCE, IMPEL(L). SUCCEED; **comp** = break.
BRAND, MARQUE, MODEL, TYPE. CONSORT, PEER
(arch).

MAKER *Anag.* *GOD*. FABRICATOR, MANUFACTURER.
MAKE UP *Anag.* IMAGINE, INVENT. CONCOCT, COMPOSE.
COMPENSATE; COMPLETE. RECONCILE, *SETTLE*.
CHARACTER, TEMPERAMENT. COSMETICS;
WAR-PAINT (sl). EKAM (dn, crypt).
MALE MASCULINE; STAG. INTERNAL FITTING (mech).
~ AND FEMALE There are many special words for denoting male or
female genders for various animals. These are sometimes used
misleadingly, to lure the solver into an incorrect train of thought,
e.g. **Pen, pot and pan is nutty** (3) = COB ('pot and pan' being
rhyming slang for 'old man', or husband; the husband of a pen
(swan) is a 'cob', which also means a nut). Therefore particular
note should be taken of those genders which offer a second
meaning or cryptic clue, such as **tup** (put back), **queen** (*monarch*),
drake (*military leader*), **doe** (pl = does), **ewe** (you sound . . .) and
so on. **Genders include**:

Genus	Male	Female
Ass	JACKASS	*JENNY*
Bird	COCK	HEN
Bovine	*BULL*	*COW*
Canine	*DOG*	BITCH
Cat	*TOM*	QUEEN
Cattle	*BULL*	*COW*
Chicken	COCK	HEN
Child	BOY	GIRL
Crab	COCK	HEN
Deer	BUCK, HART, STAG	DOE, HIND
Donkey	*JACK*	*JENNY*
Duck	*DRAKE*	*DUCK*
Elephant	*BULL*	*COW*
Ferret	*BUCK*	*DOE*, GILL
Fox	*DOG*	VIXEN
Goat	BILLY	*NANNY*
Goose	GANDER	*GOOSE*
Hare	*BUCK*	*DOE*
Hawk	T(I)ERCEL	
Horse	STALLION	MARE
Human	MAN	WOMAN
Hunting dog	*HOUND*	BRACH

Lobster	COCK	HEN
Monarch	*KING*	*QUEEN*
Monastic	ABBOT,	ABBESS,
recluse	*MONK*	NUN
Ox	*BULL*	*COW*
Pig	BOAR	SOW
Rabbit	*BUCK*	*DOE*
Rat	*BUCK*	*DOE*
Ruff	RUFF	REEVE
Salmon	COCK	HEN
Sandpiper	RUFF	REEVE
Sheep	RAM, TUP	*EWE*
Sovereign	*KING*	*QUEEN*
Swan	*COB*	*PEN*
Walrus	*BULL*	*COW*
Turkey	COCK, *STAG*	HEN

Male	Genus
Abbot	MONASTIC RECLUSE
Billy	*GOAT*
Boar	*PIG*
Boy	CHILD
Buck	CATTLE, *DEER*, *RABBIT*, RAT
Bull	BOVINE, CATTLE, ELEPHANT, OX, WALRUS
Cob	*SWAN*
Cock	*BIRD*, *CHICKEN*, CRAB, LOBSTER, SALMON, TURKEY
Dog	CANINE, *FOX*
Drake	*DUCK*
Gander	*GOOSE*
Hart	*DEER*
Hound	HUNTING DOG
Jack	*DONKEY*
Jackass	ASS
King	MONARCH, SOVEREIGN
Man	HUMAN
Monk	MONASTIC RECLUSE
Ram	*SHEEP*
Ruff	SANDPIPER (RUFF)
Stag	*DEER*, TURKEY

Stallion	*HORSE*
T(i)ercel	*HAWK*
Tom	*CAT*
Tup	*SHEEP*

Female	**Genus**
Abbess	CONVENT/MONASTIC RECLUSE
Bitch	CANINE
Brach	HUNTING DOG
Cow	BOVINE, CATTLE, ELEPHANT, *WALRUS*
Doe	*DEER*, FERRET, HARE, *RABBIT*, RAT
Duck	*DUCK*
Ewe	*SHEEP*
Gill	FERRET, POLECAT
Girl	CHILD
Goose	*GOOSE*
Hen	*BIRD*, *CHICKEN*, CRAB, LOBSTER, SALMON
Hind	*DEER*
Jenny	ASS, *DONKEY*
Mare	*HORSE*
Nanny	*GOAT*
Nun	CONVENT/MONASTIC RECLUSE
Pen	*SWAN*
Queen	*CAT*, *MONARCH*, SOVEREIGN
Reeve	RUFF (SANDPIPER)
Sow	*PIG*
Vixen	FOX
Woman	HUMAN

MALLARD *DUCK*; **assembly** = flock, flush.
MAMBA *DANCE*. *SNAKE*.
MAN HE, HOMO SAPIENS, HUMANITY [Heidelberg ~, Java ~, Peking ~, Piltdown ~]; ONE, PERSON. *MALE*, MASCULINE GENDER. HUSBAND. BOB, TOM, WILL etc. *CREW*, *SAILOR*. FILL, FURNISH. SOLDIER. *CHESS*/GAMES PIECE. IOM, *ISLAND*. MANITOBA (*Province*, Can).
MANAGE ORGANIZE, *RUN*. *HANDLE*.
MANAGING DIRECTOR MD (**Union** = ASTMS).
MANDARIN OFFICIAL (Ch). BUREAUCRAT,

ESTABLISHMENT FIGURE, GURU, PARTY LEADER (hence P — crypt). CHINESE LANGUAGE. *DUCK*. CITRUS *FRUIT*.

MANGANESE *METAL*; MN (*chem*). HARD METAL.

MANIA CRAZE, EAGER PURSUIT, EXCESSIVE ENTHUSIASM, *OBSESSION*.

MANLY BUTCH, MASCULINE, VIRILE (crypt).

MANOEUVRE *Anag.* MANEUVER (US). EXERCISE, PLAN (mil). FIGURE, MOVEMENT. HANDLE, MOVE, STEER, TURN (aero; naut).

MAN WOULD HED.

MANX CAT *CAT* (breed); it has no tail, hence CA (crypt).

MANX RACE TT, BIKE RACE. DOUBLET (crypt).

MANY LOTS, hence C, D, M.

MANY-ARMED ARMY, WELL-ARMED (crypt). **Celeb**: *DEVI*; ENCELADUS; *GY(G)ES*; *KALI*; STARKADDER (Nor myth); *URANIDS*.

MANY-DAUGHTERS Celeb: DANAUS, *NEREUS*.

MANY-EYED *Keen-eyed*. **Celeb**: *ARGUS*; DRAGONFLY; LYNCEUS.

MANY-HEADED MIRV (mil *missile*). **Celeb**: *CERBERUS* (dog); CRATAEIS; GERYON (*Hercules*); *GY(G)ES*; *HYDRA*; ORTHRUS (dog); *SCYLLA*; *TYPHON*; *URANIDS*.

MANY-LEGGED Insect. **Celeb**: CRATAEIS; SLEIPNIR (*horse*).

MANY-LOVERS/WIVES Polygamist. **Celeb**: CASANOVA; *DAVID*; DON JUAN; LOTHARIO; *SOLOMON*; ZEUS.

MANY-SONS Celeb: AEGYPTUS, *PRIAM*.

MAR (s/l *ma*). DISFIGURE, *HINDER*, *IMPAIR*, *RUIN*, *SPOIL*. *MARRIED*. *MARCH*. **Pl** = Rom *god* of war.

MARBLE LIMESTONE, POLISHED STONE. **Pl** = BRAINS (sl). GAME; *AGATE*, ALLY, *TAW*.

MARCH 1. MEASURED TREAD, PARADE, *STEP*, *TRAMP*, TRUDGE, WALK. DISTANCE, PROGRESS. BORDER, *BOUNDARY*, FRONTIER; TERRITORY. 2. (3rd) MONTH, M, MAR (*Mars*). **Birthstone** = *bloodstone*.

MARE *HORSE* (fem) [labour of *Hercules*]. SEA (Lat); CRATER (moon).

MARGIN BORDER, BRIM, EDGE. ROOM, SPACE. CLEARANCE. LEEWAY.

MARINE JOLLY, LEATHERNECK, RM. MARITIME, NAUTICAL, SEA.

MARK BLAZE, DENT, IMPRESS, SCRATCH, SOIL, SPOT, STAIN. BRAND, *CROSS*. PUNTER, SUCKER (sl). TARGET. *COIN. ANTONY*; TWAIN. **Pl comp** = Spencer.

MARKER CHALKER, SCORER. PYLON, SIGNPOST. IOU (US sl).

MARKET DEMAND. BARTER, BUY, SELL. EXCHANGE, SALES/TRADE PLACE; **London** ~s: BILLINGSGATE (fish); COVENT GARDEN (fruit, vegetables, flowers); LEADENHALL (meat); NINE ELMS (fruit, vegetables, flowers); SMITHFIELD (cattle); PETTICOAT LANE (street ~); PORTOBELLO ROAD (antiques). FLEA ~ (Paris), SOUK (Arab).

MARRIAGE 1. MATRIMONY, WEDDING; SPLICING, *UNION* [Darby and *Joan*]. 2. **Gods: Gk** = *HYMEN*, **Rom** = GENIUS.

~ **LICENCE** MATE'S TICKET; UNION CARD (crypt).

MARRIED M, *MAR*. COUPLED, HITCHED, JOINED, MATED, PAIRED, SPLICED, *WED*(DED).

MARRY COUPLE, HITCH, JOIN, MATE, PAIR, SPLICE, TAKE THE PLUNGE, WED. CORRELATE, UNITE. GOLLY, GOSH, GRACIOUS (arch).

MARS 1. Rom *god* of WAR; mar Bellona (**Gk** = Enyo); f by *Rhea* (Silvia) of *Romulus* and Remus [*March*]. **Gk** = ARES. 2. RED *PLANET. SPACECRAFT*.

MARSUPIAL POUCHED MAMMAL: BANDICOOT, GLIDER, KANGAROO, KOALA, OPOSSUM, PHALANGER, TASMANIAN DEVIL, WALLABY, WOMBAT.

MARXIST COMMIE, RED. KARL [Highgate cemetery]. CHICO, HARPO, GROUCHO, GUMMO, ZEPPO (all crypt).

MASCOT *PET*, TOTEM.

MASCULINE M; BUTCH, MANLY, VIRILE (and see *male and female*).

MASON 1. STONEWORKER. 2. Member of fraternity of Free and Accepted ~s [Grand Master, lodge, ritual]. 3. Bertha ~, *mad* w of Mr Rochester (Jane Eyre, *Brontë*).

MASS CONVOCATION, LITURGY, (MUSICAL) *SERVICE*. AGGREGATION, AMOUNT, EXPANSE; MATTER. MASSACHUSETTS (*State* of US).

~ **MEETING** CONVOCATION, RALLY, SYMPOSIUM, TEACH-IN. CHURCH SERVICE (crypt).

MASTER MA. MFH. DOMINIE, MR CHIPS, MONITOR, *SCHOOLMASTER*, TEACHER, TUTOR (**Union** = NUT). DOMINATE, DEFEAT, OVERCOME. CAPTAIN, *SKIPPER*

(naut). EMPLOYER; SAHIB, TUAN. HEAD OF HOUSE.
CRAFTSMAN, *PAINTER*. MATRIX.

MATCH CONGREVE, FUSEE, LUCIFER, STRIKER, VESTA®.
COMPARE, COPY, EQUAL, MATE, PAIR, TALLY.
CONTEST, FRIENDLY, GAME, *TEST*. ENGAGEMENT,
MARRIAGE, UNION, WEDDING.

MATCHBOX CONTAINER; **coll** = phillumenist. BOTTOM
DRAWER, WEDDING PRESENT (crypt).

MATCHED ENGAGED, MARRIED, *WED*. FITTED, TONED.
CONTESTED, PLAYED. *FIRED*, LIT (crypt).

MATCHLESS INCOMPARABLE, PEERLESS. BACHELOR,
SPINSTER, UNWED (crypt).

MATE HUSBAND, *MATCH*, PAIR, WIFE. JOIN. ALLY,
COMPANION.

MATERIAL 1. CLOTH, COTTON, DRAB, FABRIC, FLAX,
KNITWEAR, POLYESTER, STUFF, WEAVE, WOOL
[*measure*]. **Types** (most ®): ACRILAN, BARATHEA,
BAYADERE, BROCADE, BURLAP, CALICO, CHIFFON,
CORDUROY, CORPORAL (eccles), DACRON, DAMASK,
DIMITY, DRILL, FELT, GABARDINE, HARRIS, HESSIAN,
JUTE, LAME, LAWN, LUSTRE, MOREEN, MUNGO,
MUSLIN, NAINSOOK, NANKEEN, NET, NYLON,
ORGANDIE, ORGANZA, ORGANZINE, ORRIS,
PARRAMATTA, PLAID, REP, SAMITE, SATIN, SHODDY,
SILK, TERYLENE, TULLE, TWEED, VELVET, WORSTED.
2. ELEMENTS. CORPOREAL, IMPORTANT. JOKES,
LINES (theat).

MAUSOLEUM TOMB, especially that one designed by *Daedalus* for
Artemisia in memory of King Mausolus. One of the *Seven
Wonders of the World*.

MAXWELL GAUSS, MAGNETIC FLUX.

MAY 1. IS ALLOWED, CAN, MIGHT, PERMITTED (**opp** =
cant). HAWTHORN. *CASTLE*. **Pl** = EXAMS (C); BOAT
RACES. 2. GIRL. 3. (5th) MONTH, M (Rom *Maia*); **birthstone**
= *emerald*.

MAYA *Am Ind* tribe inhabiting Yucatan, with cities Merida (capital),
Chichen Itza and Uxmal. Ancient culture incl human sacrifice, and
gods Chac (rain), Quetzalcoatl (feathered serpent).

MAYBE *Anag.* 1. MYTHICAL, PERHAPS. 2. Sounds like, e.g.
Massage may be wanted (5) = KNEAD.

MAYFAIR WEST END. WI.

MB BACHELOR OF MEDICINE, DOCTOR.
MBE *DECORATION*, MEDAL.
MC MASTER OF CEREMONIES. MILITARY CROSS;
DECORATION, MEDAL. MONACO (*car plate*).
MD DOCTOR (OF MEDICINE). MANAGING DIRECTOR.
MENDELEVIUM (*chem*). MUSICAL DIRECTOR,
CONDUCTOR. MARYLAND (US *state*). 1,500.
ME I, NUMBER ONE, PERSONAL PRONOUN, SELF. MAINE
(US *state*). MIDDLE EAST. MIDDLE ENGLISH. AIRCRAFT
(Ger); MESSERSCHMITT. HALF TIME (crypt). NOTE (mus;
also MI).
MEAL FEAST, PICNIC, REPAST, SPREAD: BREAKFAST,
BRUNCH, *DINNER*, LUNCH, SUPPER, TEA. GRAIN,
MAIZE, PULSE. **Pl** = *BOARD*, KEEP.
MEAN (s/l *mien*). INTEND, IMPLY. AVERAGE, *PAR*. NEAR,
MISERLY, NIGGARDLY, PARSIMONIOUS, STINGY (**opp** =
liberal). **Pl** = FACILITIES, WHEREWITHAL.
MEANING DRIFT, EXPLANATION, INTENTION,
SIGNIFICANCE. EXPRESSIVE.
MEASURE 1. *DANCE*. ACTION, LAW, LEGISLATION.
COMPARE, EVALUATE, ESTIMATE, *GAUGE*. *DEGREE*,
EXTENT; *STANDARD*; TRAVERSE. *ROD*, TAPE. MARK
OFF; QUANTITY, SIZE. CC, CM, FT, IN, LB, MM etc;
CUBIT; DRAM, FIFTH, FINGER, SLUG, TOT. *FOOT*,
METRE, RHYTHM. 2. In the following lists of types of measure,
the figures in parentheses between different units of measurement
represent the quantity of the first unit which is required to make up
one of the second:
Area: SQ IN (144) SQ FT (9) SQ YD (30¼) SQ
ROD/POLE/PERCH (40) ROOD (4) ACRE (640) SQ MILE
[SQ CHAIN, HECTARE].
Capacity: GILL or *NOGGIN* (4) PINT (2) QUART (4)
GALLON (2) *PECK* (4) BUSHEL (8) *QUARTER* (4½)
CHALDRON.
Beer: GILL (4) PINT (2) QUART (4) GALLON (4½) PIN (2)
FIRKIN (2) KILDERKIN (2) BARREL (1½) HOGSHEAD
(2) BUTT or *PIPE* (2) TUN [PUNCHEON, TIERCE].
Fish: BARREL, QUINTAL, *BOX*, WARP.
Timber: LOAD, STACK, CORD.
Wine: SPLIT (2) PINT (2) *BOTTLE* (2) MAGNUM (2)
JEROBOAM (1½) REHOBOAM (1⅓) METHUSELAH

(1½) SALMANAZAR (1⅓) BALTHAZAR (1¼)
NEBUCHADNEZZAR (= 20 bots).

Weight:

Avoirdupois: DRAM (16) OUNCE/OZ (16) POUND/LB (14) *STONE* (2) *QUARTER* (4) HUNDREDWEIGHT/CWT (20) TON [GRAINS (7,000 = 1 LB)].

Apothecaries: GRAIN (20) SCRUPLE (3) DRACHM (8) OUNCE/OZ (12) POUND.

Troy: GRAIN (24) PENNYWEIGHT/DWT (20) OUNCE/OZ (12) *POUND*/LB.

Hay: LB (56) TRUSS (36) LOAD.

Wool: LB (7) CLOVE (2) *STONE* (2) TOD (6½) WEY (2) SACK (12) *LAST*.

Length: NAIL (2¼) *INCH*/IN (12) *FOOT*/FT (3) YARD/YD (22) CHAIN (10) FURLONG (8) MILE.

Cloth: *INCH*/IN (2¼) NAIL (4) QUARTER (5) *ELL*.

Land: LINK (25) *ROD/POLE/PERCH* (4) CHAIN (80) MILE.

Naut: *FOOT*/FT (6) FATHOM (100) CABLE (10) NAUTICAL MILE [degree; knot].

Paper size: FOLIO (F), QUARTO (4to), OCTAVO (8vo), DUODECIMO (12mo). CROWN, DEMY, ELEPHANT, FOOLSCAP, IMPERIAL, LARGE POST, MEDIUM, *POST*, *ROYAL*.

Paper qty: SHEET (24) QUIRE (20) REAM (2) BUNDLE (5) *BALE*.

Biblical: DIGIT (4) PALM (3) SPAN (2) CUBIT (4) FATHOM (2) ARABIAN POLE (10) MEASURING LINE (3) STADIUM (5) SABBATH JOURNEY (2) EASTERN MILE (24) DAY'S JOURNEY.

Foreign: PICUL (Ch weight); LI (Ch mile); VERST (Russ mile).

MED MEDICAL, MEDICINE. MEDITERRANEAN. MEDIUM.

MEDAL VC, GC, GM, DSO, DSC, MC, DFC, DSM, MM, DFM, TD etc. GONG (sl). **Coll** = numismatist.

MEDEA Gk myth magician who mar *Jason*. She killed their children when he remarried, and then also slew the new wife.

MEDIA COUNTRY (Pers). VEIN (insect). CONSONANT (phonetics). *PRESS* (q.v.), NEWSAGENCIES, RADIO, TV. And see *MEDIUM*.

MEDICAL *MO*.

MEDICINE 1. DOCTORING, HEALING, MEDICAL ART.

ELIXIR, NOSTRUM, PILL, POTION. CHARM, FETISH, INCANTATION, SPELL. 2. **Gods: Gk** = *ASCLEPIUS*; **Rom** = AESCULAPIUS.

MEDIUM M, MED, MIDDLE QUALITY. CONDITIONS, ENVIRONMENT. AGENCY, MEANS. SPIRITUALIST, MADAME ARCATI (Blithe Spirit, Coward). NEWS SYSTEM. **Pl** (media) = *PRESS*, *RADIO*, *TV*, *WIRELESS*. COUNTRY (Pers).

MEDUSA 1. 'The Ruler'. In Gk myth, one of the *Gorgons*, m of Chrysaor and *Pegasus* by *Poseidon*. Anyone who looked at her head, even after it was cut off by *Perseus*, was turned to stone [*Andromeda*, *Athene*, *Atlas*]. 2. JELLYFISH (Port man o' war; sea nettle).

MEDWAY TOWNS CHATHAM, GILLINGHAM, *ROCHESTER*.

MEET (s/l *meat*, mete). ENCOUNTER. FITTING, PROPER, SUITABLE. HUNT, RACE DAY [*fox*, *hounds*].

MEGA M (*int units*).

MEGAERA *FURY* (myth).

MEGALOMANIA *Obsession* with grandiose ideas.

MELPOMENE Gk myth; one of the nine *Muses* (Tragedy).

MEMBER M, MEP, MBE, MP. ARM, FINGER, HAND, LEG.

MEMORY RECALL, RECOLLECTION, REMEMBRANCE [Munin (*raven*)]; REPUTATION [rosemary]. ACCUMULATOR, COMPUTER CELL, RETRIEVAL BANK, STORAGE.

MENDER *Anag.* REPAIRER, RESTORER.

MEPHISTOPHELES *DEVIL* (Goethe). SORCERER (Marlowe).

MERCILESS *IRON*, PITILESS, RUTHLESS, UNPITYING.

MERCURY 1. *METAL*; HG (*chem*). LIQUID METAL, QUICKSILVER. 2. Rom *messenger* of the *gods*, s of *Jupiter* and *Maia*; he wore a winged cap (petasus) and winged sandals, and carried the caduceus. **Gk** = HERMES. 3. A *PLANET*. 4. *SPACECRAFT*.

MERCY COMPASSION, FORBEARANCE, PITY, QUARTER, RUTH [*sisters of* ~].

MERE *LAKE*. *SIMPLE*. MAORI WAR-CLUB, *WEAPON*.

MERIT DESERVE, EARN. OM.

MERLIN *BIRD*. AIRCRAFT ENGINE. *MAGICIAN* [*King Arthur*].

MERMAID 1. Myth sea creature, half-woman, half-fish, possibly inspired by the *manatee* [dugong, halicore, sea-cow; *Miranda*]. 2. *TAVERN* at Cheapside, burned in the Great Fire of London. *THEATRE*.

MERMAN Male counterpart of *mermaid*; **celeb**: TRITON (s of *Poseidon* and *Amphitrite*).

MESH *NET*, WEAVE. [gears].

MESOLITHIC *AGE*.

MESS *Anag.* MIX-UP, MUDDLE. POTTER. *FOOD*, *MEAL* [*Esau*; *Jacob*; officers].

MESSAGE *CABLE*, *LETTER*, *NOTE*. MEANING, SIGNIFICANCE.

MESSENGER 1. FORERUNNER, *HERALD*: HAIGHA, HATTA (*Alice*). 2. **Gods: Gk** = HERMES; **Rom** = *MERCURY*. **Goddess: Gk** = ARTEMIS.

METAL QUALITY, WORTH. RAILS (rly); TARMAC (roads). BROADSIDE (mil); HEAVY ~; ARMOUR, TANKS (mil). ELEMENT (*chem*); ALLOY, GLASS, ORE (and see *mineral*) e.g.

3-letters
TIN (SN)

4-letters
GOLD (AU)
IRON (FE)
LEAD (PB)
ZINC (ZN)

5-letters
CUPRO- (CU)
FERRO- (FE)
PLUMB (PB)

6-letters
BARIUM (BA)
COBALT (CO)
COPPER (CU)
NICKEL (NI)
RADIUM (RA)
SILVER (AG)
SODIUM (NA)

7-letters
ARGENTO- (AG)

BISMUTH (BI)
CADMIUM (CD)
CALCIUM (CA)
GALLIUM (GA)
IRIDIUM (IR)
LITHIUM (LI)
MERCURY (HG)
THORIUM (TH)
URANIUM (U)
WOLFRAM (W)

8-letters
ANTIMONY (SB)
CHROMIUM (CR)
PLATINUM (PT)
THALLIUM (TL)
TITANIUM (TI)
TUNGSTEN (W)
VANADIUM (V)

9+ letters
ALUMINIUM (AL)
BERYLLIUM (BE)
MAGNESIUM (MG)
MANGANESE (MN)

MOLYBDENUM (MO)   STRONTIUM (SR)
PALLADIUM (PD)   YTTERBIUM (YB)
PHOSPHORUS (P)   ZIRCONIUM (ZR)
POTASSIUM (K)

METHUSELAH 1. *BOTTLE* (wine) = 8 normal ~s. 2. The s of *Enoch* and Lamech, a bibl *wise man* who is said to have lived for 969 years; f of *Noah*.

METRE DISTANCE, *MEASURE*. *BEAT*. *FOOT*.

METRIC PREFIX See *International Units*.

METROPOLITAN *CAPITAL*, CENTRAL; HOME COUNTRY. *CHURCHMAN* (Gk). *THEATRE*.

Mex MEXICO.

MG MAGNESIUM (*chem*). *CAR*, MORRIS GARAGE.

MID 1. AMID; CENTRAL, MIDDLE. 2. Use middle letter(s), e.g. **Mid Sussex** = SS.

MIDAS 1. Gk myth king of Phrygia. All he touched turned to *gold*, even his food. He gained relief by bathing in the river Pactolus [Croesus, Dives]. 2. *SPACECRAFT*.

MIDDAY 1. NOON. TWELVE. A (crypt). 2. Put letter or word into synonym for day, e.g. **Airs nitrogen midday** (5) = TU*N*ES.

MIDDLE COURT *INN OF COURT*, LAW SOCIETY. U (crypt).

MIDNIGHT 0000. TWELVE. DARKNESS. G (crypt).

MIDSHIPMAN P (crypt). BRASS-BOUNDER (merchant navy), ENSIGN (US), MIDDY (sl), SNOTTY (sl); EASY (Marryat), MIDSHIPMITE (Nancy Bell, *G & S*). *FISH*.

MIEN (s/l *mean*). APPEARANCE, *BEARING*, *LOOK*.

MIGHT COULD, MAY. *MAIN*, POWER, STRENGTH.

MIL *CURRENCY* (Cyprus). MILITARY (abbr). 1/1000th part (abbr).

MILANION Gk myth m of *Atalanta* [*apples*].

MILITARY CROSS *DECORATION*, MC, MEDAL.

MILITARY LEADERS Celebrated soldiers, sailors and airmen, e.g.

Air
BADER, G/C Sir D.
BALBO, Gen (It)
BALL, Capt Albert VC
BISHOP, Col VC
CHESHIRE, G/C VC
DOOLITTLE, Gen J.

DOWDING, A/M Lord
GALLAND, Gen Adolf
GIBSON, W/C Guy VC
GOERING, F/M Hermann
MANNOCK, Major VC
RICHTOFEN, Baron von
RICKENBACKER, Capt

SPAATZ, Gen Carl
TEDDER, MRAF Lord
TRENCHARD, MRAF Lord
Land
ALEXANDER, q.v.
ANTIPATER, Macedon
CAESAR, Julius
CUSTER, Gen George
EISENHOWER, Gen
GENGHIS KHAN
HANNIBAL
JACKSON, Gen
KESSELRING, F/M
LEE, Gen Robert E.
MACARTHUR, Gen
MONTGOMERY, F/M Lord
NAPOLEON
PATTON, Gen George
ROMMEL, F/M Erwin

SLIM, F/M Lord
WELLINGTON, Duke of
Sea
BLIGH, Capt Wm.
DOENITZ, Gd Adm Karl
DRAKE, Sir Francis
HALSEY, Adm William
HAWKINS, Sir John
JONES, Capt John Paul
MOUNTBATTEN, Adm Lord
NELSON, Adm Lord
NIMITZ, Adm Chester
POUND, Adm Sir Dudley
RALEIGH, Sir Walter
RAEDER, Gd Adm
RODNEY, Adm Lord
SHOVEL, Adm Sir C.
SPRUANCE, Adm
YAMAMOTO, Adm

MILITARY POLICE MP, SP, REDCAP (hence R, crypt).
MILK NOURISHMENT, PAP [Poppaea (asses' ~)]; **comp** = sugar. EXTRACT. *COLOUR* (white). RIVER (US).
MILLION M.
MILNE A. A., *WRITER* (*Alexander* Beetle, Edward Bear, Christopher *Robin*, Eeyore, Heffalump, Kanga, Piglet, Pooh, Roo, *Rabbit*, Rabbit's Friends and Relations, Winnie the Pooh, Wol, Tigger).
MINCE (s/l *mints*). MINCED MEAT; SWEETMEAT (~ pie). CUT SMALL; RESTRAIN. WAGGLE, WALK AFFECTEDLY. **Pl** = EYES (*rh sl*).
MIND (s/l *mined*). ATTENTION, FEELING, THINKING. NURSE, TAKE CARE. BRAIN, INTELLECT, SOUL [*study*]. OPINION; CONCERN, TAKE NOTE. MEMORY, REMEMBRANCE. FUSS, OBJECT, WORRY.
MINE EXCAVATION, PIT, SAP; *BURROW*, DIG, UNDERMINE. POSSESSIVE (**opp** = theirs, yours). *BANGER*, EXPLOSIVE, *WEAPON*.
MINER (s/l *minor*). COLLIER (**Union** = NUM), *PITMAN* (crypt). *WORKER*. *DIGGER*, FORTYNINER, PROSPECTOR.
MINERAL 1. WATER naturally impregnated with ~, or artificially

carbonated; MIXER, SODA, TONIC. 2. Inorganic matter, especially crystalline; extracted or mined *ORE* (**comp** = animal, vegetable, abstract) e.g.

3-letters	QUARTZ	GRAPHITE
JET	SILICA	OBSIDIAN
ORE	SPINEL	PYROZENE
		SIDERITE
4-letters	**7-letters**	SILICATE
CLAY	*ARSENIC* (AS)	TINSTONE
COAL	ASPHALT	
COKE	AZURITE	**9-letters**
LIME	BAUXITE	ALABASTER
MARL	BITUMEN	BRIMSTONE
MICA	LIGNITE	FLUORSPAR
PEAT	OLIVINE	FOOL'S GOLD
SALT	PERLITE	IRONSTONE
SPAR	PYRITES	LIMESTONE
TALC	REALGAR	LODESTONE
	SILICON	MALACHITE
5-letters	TRIPOLI	MARCASITE
BORON (B)	ZEOLITE	WULFENITE
EMERY		
	8-letters	**10+ letters**
6-letters	ANTIMONY (SB)	CHALCEDONY
BARITE	ASBESTOS	IRON PYRITES
CARBON (C)	CHROMITE	MEERSCHAUM
GARNET	CINNABAR	MOLYBDENITE
GYPSUM	CORUNDUM	*PHOSPHORUS* (P)
IOLITE	CRYOLITE	PITCHBLENDE
PUMICE	FELDSPAR	
PYRITE	FLUORITE	

MINERVA 1. Rom myth *goddess* of Invention, Wisdom and the Arts (**Gk** = PALLAS *ATHENE*), and later of War. 2. A minor *PLANET*.

MINI *LITTLE*, SMALL (**opp** = mega). SKIRT. *CAR*.

~ **STATES Celeb**: ANDORRA, LIECHTENSTEIN, LUXEMBOURG, MONACO, MONTENEGRO (ex), SAN MARINO, TONGA.

MINOR (s/l *miner*). 1. *CHARGE*, INFANT, JUNIOR, WARD;

UNDER 18/21. THE YOUNGER. PITCH, *SCALE* (mus).
INFERIOR, LESSER (**opp** = *major*). 2. Use diminutive,
abbreviation, e.g. **Minor operation** = OP.

MINOS Gk myth king of Crete. Son of *Zeus* and *Europa*, he mar
Pasiphae. His palace at Cnossos contained the *labyrinth*, where the
Minotaur was kept until killed by *Theseus*.

MINOTAUR Gk myth Cretan *monster* (half man, half bull) of *Minos*.
Kept in the *labyrinth*, which was designed by *Daedalus*, it was fed
on human flesh in the form of seven youths and seven maidens sent
yearly as tribute from Athens, until *Theseus* volunteered to be
included and he killed it.

MINSTREL ENTERTAINER, MUSICIAN, SINGER; LAYMAN
(crypt) [Blondel (*Lionheart*). Mikado (*G & S*)]. **Pl** = NEGRO
SINGERS.

MINT AROMATIC HERB; **comp** = *lamb*. CANDY, SWEET.
COIN, MAKE MONEY, UTTER. LOT OF MONEY.

MINX *BAGGAGE*, HUSSY, JADE.

MIRAGE ILLUSION, REFLECTION, REFRACTION; **celebrated**:
BROCKEN (Harz Mt, Ger); DELIBAB (Hung); FATA
MORGANA (Messina, It) [*ignis fatuus*. Desert, water].
AIRCRAFT (Fr).

MIRANDA 1. Girl's name, especially the d of Prospero (Temp,
Shak). 2. *Mermaid* (theat). 3. Satellite of *planet* Uranus. 4.
Carmen ~, film star (Port).

MIRROR NEWSPAPER®. 1. LOOKING GLASS, POLISHED
SURFACE; REFLECT, REVERSE IMAGE, hence read
backwards, or sometimes form a palindrome, e.g. **Midday mirror**
(4) = NOON. 2. Used by *Perseus* so as not to look directly at
Medusa when he slew her.

MIS- Added as prefix to mean 'amiss', 'badly' or 'wrongly'. In
crosswords, is often used to mean *anag.*, e.g. **Mistake** (4) = KATE
or TEAK. It can also be included into the answer, e.g. **Lure** (7) =
MISRULE.

MISER *BORE* (tech). HOARDER; NIGGARD, STINGY
PERSON; **celeb**: GRANDET (Balzac), HARPAGON (Molière),
SCROOGE (*Dickens*), SHYLOCK (M of V, *Shak*).

MISO- *HATRED* OF —

MISS (s/l *mis-*). *GIRL*, MAIDEN. [**near** ~ = *chaperone* (crypt)].
SCHOOLMISTRESS. Any girl's name. AVOID, DODGE,
FAIL (**opp** = *hit*) [mile]. MISSISSIPPI (US *state*).

~ FRENCH MLLE.

MISSILE *ARROW*, BULLET, DART, FLECHETTE, ROCKET,
SLINGSHOT; WEAPON. **Celeb**: CRUISE, ICBM, MIRV,
PERSHING, POLARIS, MX, SAM, SS 10, SS 20, TRIDENT, *VI*.
MIST (s/l missed). FRET, HAZE, VAPOUR. DIM, FILM, FOG.
MISTAKEN 1. *Anag.* IN ERROR, AT FAULT; GAFFED (crypt).
ROB, STEAL, THIEVE (crypt). 2. Take 'mis' as indicated, e.g.
remove the letters 'mis', as in: **Lock the mistaken courtesan** (5) =
***TRESS.
MISTER ADDRESS, TITLE; MASTER, MR, SIR; BWANA (Af),
EFFENDI (Turk), HERR (Ger), MASTER (Ch), MIJNHEER
(NL), MIRZA (Pers), *MONSIEUR* (Fr), SAHIB (Arab, Ind),
SARDAR (Sikh), SENHOR (Port), SENOR (Sp), SIGNOR (It),
TUAN (Malay).
MISUSE *Anag.* ABUSE, ILL-TREAT. SUE (crypt).
MITHRA *God* of the SUN (Pers).
MIX *Anag.* COMBINE, JOIN, MINGLE, SCRAMBLE. FIX.
1009 (crypt, Lat).
MIXER *Anag.* BITTER LEMON, SODA, TONIC; *DRINK*.
BEATER, FOOD PROCESSOR, WHISK.
MIXTURE *Anag.* MEDICINE. AMALGAMATION,
COMBINATION.
MIX-UP *Anag.* CONFUSION, INVOLVEMENT. XIM (dn, crypt).
MLLE MADEMOISELLE; MISS FRENCH; FRENCH GIRL.
MM FRENCHMEN, MESSIEURS. MILITARY MEDAL.
MILLIMETRE. 2,000.
MME MADAME; MRS FRENCH.
MNEMOSYNE 1. Mother by *Zeus* of the nine Gk *Muses* [memory].
2. A minor *PLANET*.
MO MEDICAL OFFICER. MODUS OPERANDI.
MOLYBDENUM (*chem*). MOMENT. *DOCTOR*. MISSOURI
(US *state*).
MOA *BIRD* (ex; flightless; NZ) [cassowary, dinornis (NZ, ex), emu,
nandoo, ostrich].
MOB GANG, RABBLE. ATTACK, MOLEST. CAP, *HAT*.
Assembly of *kangaroos*.
MOBY DICK *WHALE* [Ahab, Herman Melville. Vessel: *Pequod*].
MODEL FIGURE, PUPPET, REPRESENTATION. CARVE,
FASHION, *FORM*, SHAPE. MANNEQUIN, POSER. NORM,
PAR, *STANDARD*. *DESIGN*, MARK, MARQUE, MATRIX,
PATTERN, STYLE, TEMPLET, TYPE; real life persons
reportedly used as ~s for fict characters:

Alice (Carroll) modelled on	Alice Lidell
Alice (nanny, *Milne*)	Olive Brockwell
Anna (and the King of Siam)	Anna Leonowens
Beatrice (Dante)	Bice Portinari
William Boot (Scoop, Waugh)	Lord Deedes
Father Brown (*Chesterton*)	Father O'Connor
Buggins (~ turn)	Admiral Fisher (coined)
Bulldog Drummond (Sapper)	Gerard Fairley
David Copperfield (*Dickens*)	Charles Dickens himself
Dotheboys Hall (*Dickens*)	Bowes Hall
Drones Club (*Wodehouse*)	Pelican Club
Hiawatha (Longfellow)	Haiohratha (Mohawk chief)
Robin *Hood* (trad)	Robert FitzOoth of Locksley
Robinson *Crusoe* (Defoe)	Alexander Selkirk
Dracula (Bram Stoker)	Prince Vlad of Wallachia
Sherlock *Holmes* (Conan Doyle)	Dr Joseph *Bell*
Humpty Dumpty	Duke of Gloucester (1640)
Jack (and the beanstalk)	Tom Hickathrift (of Ely)
King of Siam (Anna and ~)	King Maha Mungkut
Laura (Petrarch)	Laure de Noves
Mr Micawber (*Dickens*)	John Dickens (f of Charles ~)
Stalky (~ & Co, *Kipling*)	Rudyard Kipling himself
Toby Jug	Harry Elwes
Winnie the Pooh (*Milne*)	Sir Owen Seaman
Mrs Worthington's d (Coward)	Angela Fox (née Lonsdale)

MODEST *BASHFUL*, COY, DIFFIDENT, HUMBLE, RETIRING, SELF-EFFACING (**opp** = *bragging*). CHASTE, DECOROUS (**opp** = *arch*). RESTRICTED, SMALL.

MOHAMMED MOHAMET, MUHAMID, MUHAMMED etc. Founder of Islam, mar Ayesha; 1 d Fatima. Qur'an (Koran) tells of Allah, Adam, Abraham, Gabriel, Isaac, Jesus, Moses, Noah. **Priests**: Ayatollah, Muezzin, Mufti; **caliphs**: Abu Bekr, Omar, Ali; **sects**: Shiite, Sunni. Pilgrimage (haj) to Mecca; holy war (jehad); heretics, Druses (**opp** = Moronites). Leader Aga (Khan); M (crypt). **Comp**: mountain.

MOIRAI Gk *goddesses* of the three *FATES*. **Rom** = PARCAE.

MOLE BREAKWATER, JETTY, QUAY. *AGENT*, SPY. *DIARIST*. BURROWING RODENT [*Grahame*]. BLEMISH, *SPOT*

MOLOCH Fire-god (Jew) to whom children were sacrificed. *LIZARD* (Aus).

MOLYBDENUM *METAL*; MO (*chem*).
MOMENT MO. INSTANT, MINUTE. IMPORTANT.
MONACO MC (*car plate*). *RACETRACK* (cars).
MONARCH 1. BUTTERFLY (*lepidoptera*). 2. EMPEROR,
  EMPRESS, KING, RULER, QUEEN, SOVEREIGN [*governor*;
  regent; viceroy]. ~s of England and Britain:

England
Saxons and Danes

Egbert	827– 839
Ethelwulf	839– 858
Ethelbald	858– 860
Ethelbert	860– 865
Ethelred	865– 871
Alfred the Great	871– 899
Edward the Elder	899– 924
Athelstan	924– 939
Edmund	939– 946
Edred	946– 955
Edwig	955– 959
Edgar	959– 975
Edward the Martyr	975– 978
Ethelred the Unready	978–1016
Edmund Ironside	1016–1016
Canute (Knut)	1017–1035
Harold I	1035–1040
Hardicanute	1040–1042
Edward the Confessor	1042–1066
Harold II	1066–1066

Normans

William I	1066–1087
William II	1087–1100
Henry I	1100–1135
Stephen	1135–1154

Plantagenets

Henry II	1154–1189
Richard I	1189–1199
John	1199–1216
Henry III	1216–1272

Edward I	1272–1307
Edward II	1307–1327 (deposed)
Edward III	1327–1377
Richard II	1377–1399 (deposed)
Henry IV ⎤	1399–1413
Henry V ⎬ **Lancaster**	1413–1422
Henry VI ⎦	1422–1461 (deposed)
Edward IV ⎤	1461–1483
Edward V ⎬ **York**	1483–1483
Richard III ⎦	1483–1485

Tudors

Henry VII	1485–1509
Henry VIII	1509–1547
Edward VI	1547–1553
Jane (9 days)	1553–1553
Mary	1553–1558
Elizabeth I	1558–1603

Britain
Stuarts

James I (VI of Scotland)	1603–1625
Charles I	1625–1649 (beheaded)

Commonwealth

Oliver Cromwell	1649–1658
Richard Cromwell	1658–1659

Stuarts

Charles II	1660–1685
James II (VII of Scotland)	1685–1688 (deposed)
William and Mary	1689–1702
Anne	1702–1714

Hanovers

George I	1714–1727
George II	1727–1760
George III	1760–1820
George IV	1820–1830
William IV	1830–1837
Victoria	1837–1901

Windsors

Edward VII	1901–1910
George V	1910–1936
Edward VIII	1936–1936 (abdicated)
George VI	1936–1952
Elizabeth II	1952–

Celeb monarchies: Bhutan, Cook Is, Denmark, Liechtenstein
(Principality), Luxembourg (Grand Duchy), Nepal, Norway,
Monaco (Principality), Spain, Swaziland, Sweden, Tonga, United
Kingdom. **Recently extinct**: Afghanistan, Albania, Bulgaria,
Egypt, Ethiopia, Germany, Greece, Hungary, Iraq, Italy, Iran,
Rumania, Russia, Siam (Thailand) and various Indian States.

MONDAY MON. DAY OF THE MOON. ~s child = fair of face.
[Solomon *Grundy*].

MONEY C, D, L, P, S; CENTS, DOLLARS, POUNDS,
SHILLINGS. BRASS, CASH, *COIN*, *CURRENCY* (q.v.),
LOOT, PELF, READY, RHINO, TIN. RESOURCES,
SHINERS, MINT. BEES AND (*rh sl*). [~ *spider*].

MONGREL *Anag.* CROSSBREED, IMPURE, MIXED [heinz].

MONITOR LIZARD. PREFECT. GUNSHIP, WARSHIP,
WEAPON. *CONTROL*, EAVESDROP, TAP.

MONK MONASTIC RECLUSE (male), HERMIT; *Chaucer*
character. CELLIST (crypt). BENEDICTINE, BUDDHIST,
CARTHUSIAN, CISTERCIAN, ESSENE, TRAPPIST (silence);
[*friar* (mendicant)]. Monks are not *friars*.

MONKEY 1. FIDDLE, INTERFERE, PLAY. £500. MACHINE
HAMMER. WATER VESSEL. APE, MIMIC, MOCK. 2.
MAMMAL, *PRIMATE*; APE; **breeds**: BABOON (Af, Arab),
BARBARY (Gibraltar), BOONDER (Rhesus), BUSHBABY
(Af), CAPUCHIN (Af), CEBUS (S Am), CHACMA (Af),
CHIMPANZEE (Af), COAITA (S Am), COLOBUS (Af),
DRILL (Af), ENTELLUS (Ind), GALAGO (Af), GIBBON
(Asia), GORILLA (Af), GRIVET (Ethiopia), GUENON (Af),
HANUMAN (Ind), HOWLER (S Am), LANGUR (Asia),
LAR(ES) (Asia), LEAF ~ (Asia), *LEMUR* (Madagascar),
MACAQUE (Asia), MACQUES (Af), MAGOT (Af),
MANDRILL (Af), MARMOSET (Am), MURIQUI (Braz),
ORAN(G)-OUTAN(G) (SE Asia), *OWL* ~ (S Am), PONGO
(Af), PROBOSCIS ~ (S Am), RHESUS ~ (Asia), SAI (Braz),
SAKI (S Am), SAGOIN(-UIN) (S Am), SAPAJOU (Am),

SIAMANG (Malay), SIMPAI (Sumatra), *SPHINX* ~ (Af),
SPIDER ~ (S Am), SQUIRREL ~ (S Am), TAMARIN (S Am),
TEE-TEE, TITI (S Am), VARI (Madagascar), VERVET (Af),
WEEPER; **celeb**: BANDERLOG (*Kipling*), CHEE-CHEE
(*Lofting*), CHETA (*Tarzan*), KING KONG (Edgar Wallace) [*Ch
calendar*; PG Tips].

MONOMANIA *Obsession* with one idea.

MONSIEUR M; MR FRENCH (crypt).

MONSTER 1. ENORMOUS, HUGE. CRUEL, WICKED.
ABORTION, MIS-SHAPEN. 2. IMAGINARY ANIMAL
(incongruous, deformed or large);

celebrated monsters:

ABOMINABLE SNOWMAN/YETI	(Himalayas)
ARGUS	(100 eyes)
BIGFOOT/SASQUATCH	(N American Yeti)
BUNYIP	(Aus)
CENTAUR	(head human, body horse)
CHIM(A)ERA	(head lion, body goat, legs dragon)
CRATAEIS	(12 feet, 6 heads; barked)
CYCLOPES	(one eye)
DRACULA	(Bram Stoker)
DRAGON	(fire-breathing)
FRANKENSTEIN'S CREATION	(manufactured humanoid)
GAMA	(Ida, *G & S*)
GERYON	(Labours of *Hercules*)
GIGANTES	(winged; legs ending in snakes)
GOG & MAGOG	(British giants)
GOLIATH	(bibl)
GORGONS	(winged; snakes for hair)
GRIFFIN/GRYPHON	(winged; head eagle, body lion)
HARPY	(head woman, body vulture)
HYDRA	(nine heads)
IDRIS	(Welsh mountain giant)
KRAKEN	(Nor sea monster)
MAGOG	(See GOG above)
MINOTAUR	(Head bull, body man)
NESSIE	(Loch Ness, Sc)

ODIN	(Nor; one eye)
PAN	(head and body man, legs goat)
POLYPHEMUS	(one eye)
PYTHON	(serpent)
SASQUATCH/BIGFOOT	(N American Yeti)
SCYLLA & CHARYBDIS	(six-headed sea monsters)
SPHINX	(head human, body lion)
TYPHON	(100 heads; fire-breathing)
URANIDS	(100 arms, 50 heads)
WODEN	(A-Sax; one eye)
WYVERN	(*herald*)
YAMINSKAY	(S Andes Yeti)
YETI/ABOMINABLE SNOWMAN	(Himalayas)
YMIR	(frost, Nor)

MONTH *Calendar* ~: JAN, FEB, MAR etc; *lunar* ~: 4 WEEKS, 28 DAYS; *TIME*. LIKING, INCLINATION (arch).

MONUMENT COMMEMORATION, MEMORIAL, (TOMB)STONE; **celeb**: ALBERT MEMORIAL (Prince Albert), ARC DE TRIOMPHE (French Army), BRANDENBURG GATE (Berlin), CENOTAPH (World Wars dead; Lutyens), CLEOPATRA'S NEEDLE (Embankment; Heliopolis), INVALIDES (Napoleon), MENIN GATE (Ypres), THE MONUMENT (Great Fire, London), PYRAMIDS (Gizeh; sacred rites), NELSON'S COLUMN (Trafalgar), QUEEN VICTORIA (The Mall, Brock), RUNNYMEDE (Commonwealth Air Forces), SOMME (Lutyens), UNKNOWN WARRIOR (Westminster Abbey/UK; Arc de Triomphe/Fr; Santa Maria degli Angeli/It; Arlington Cemetery/USA).

MOON 1. *MOPE*. EARTH SATELLITE, LUNAR BODY [Nokomis (d of the ~) *Hiawatha*]. 18 (*tarot*). [Monday; over the ~ = delighted (**opp** = sick as a *parrot*)]. 2. **Goddesses: Gk** = *ARTEMIS*, *PHOSPHORUS*, SELENE; **Rom** = *DIANA*, JUNO, LUNA.

MOOR FEN, HEATHLAND, OPEN LAND; MARSH. MAKE FAST, TIE UP (naut). *GAOL*. BACKROOM (crypt). BLACK MAN; **celeb**: AARON (Titus Andronicus), OTHELLO (*Shak*), LAILA (Southey).

MOPED WAS BORED, DEPRESSED, LISTLESS, MOONED. (MOTOR) SCOOTER.

MORE WORK UTOPIA (crypt).

MORNING (s/l mourning). 1. AM, FORENOON. 2. ~ **star** =
Lucifer (Rom), *Phosphorus* (Gk); **opp** = *Hesperus*.

MORPHEUS Rom myth s of Sleep and *god* of Dreams. [Hypnos].

MORSE *WALRUS*. CLASP. ALPHABET CODE, SIGNAL (dot,
dash).

MOSES 1. Bibl lawgiver; s of Amram and Jochebed, br of *Aaron* and
Miriam (*c.* 15th cent B.C.). At ~'s birth, *Pharaoh* ordered all
infants to be k. Jochebed hid ~ in some reeds (or bullrushes),
watched over by Miriam, and he was found by Pharaoh's d
(possibly Merrhis); Miriam suggested Jochebed as a nurse. He grew
up in the royal house and became a *shepherd*; mar Zipporah and
was f of Gershom and Eliezer. When cast down before *Pharaoh*,
his rod was transformed into a *serpent*. Despite a rebellion by his br
Aaron, ~ led the Israelites out of Egy with *Joshua* as his
lieutenant, across the Red Sea to the Promised Land. Because of
disobedience to divine command, he was not vouchsafed entry to
the Promised Land, but he saw it before he d on Mt Pisgah.
2. *PAINTER* ('Grandma' ~).

MOSQUITO ANOPHELES, CULEX. GNAT, *INSECT*;
BLOODSUCKER. *AIRCRAFT*. **Pl** = GULF.

MOSTLY 1. MAINLY, PRINCIPALLY. 2. Nearly an anagram, e.g.
Material which is mostly a masked product (6) = DAMASK (the E is
omitted from **a masked**).

MOTH *INSECT*, *LEPIDOPTERA* (q.v.). **Coll** = lepidopterist.
RIVER (NZ).

MOTHER ABBESS. MA, MATER, MATERNAL PARENT,
MUM; OLD LADY (sl); BEARER (crypt); **celeb**: ~ Goose,
~ Hubbard, ~ Riley, ~ Shipton. *ISIS* (Egy myth). VINEGAR
PRODUCT. HYSTERIA. BUG HUNTER, LEPIDOPTERIST
(crypt).

MOTOR RACE GRAND PRIX; TT. CAR*NATION (crypt).
For ~ **tracks**, see *Racetrack*.

MOTORWAY MI, MIV, MV etc.

MOULD DECAY, MILDEW, ROT. *CAST*, *FORM*, MATRIX,
PATTERN, SHAPE, TEMPLET.

MOUNT ASCEND, CLIMB. EMINENCE, HILL, MOUND,
TOR. GET ON; SADDLE. STEED. CARD, MARGIN;
DISPLAY, SET OFF. STAMP HINGE. ARRANGE,
PRODUCE, STAGE (theat).

MOUNTAIN HEAP, PILE. ELEVATION, HILL, *MOUNT*;

pl = range; **celeb**: ALASKA RANGE (US), ANDES (S Am),
ALPS (Eur), APENNINES (It), APPALACHIANS (US), ATLAS
(N Af), BLUE RIDGE (US), BROOKS RANGE (US),
ETHIOPIAN HIGHLANDS (E Af), FLINDERS RANGE (Aus),
GREAT DIVIDING RANGE (Aus), HAMMERSLEY RANGE
(Aus), HINDU KUSH (Asia), HIMALAYAS (Asia), KUN LUN
SHAN (Ch), LOMONDSOV RIDGE (Arctica), MACDONNEL
RANGE (Aus), PAROPAMISUS (Asia), ROCKY ~s (Can/US),
SIERRA MADRE (Mex), SIERRA NEVADA (N Am), TIBESTI
(N Af), TIEN SHAN (Asia), TRANSANTARCTIC ~s
(Antarctica), URALS (USSR), VINSON PLATEAU
(Antarctica). **Comp** = *Mohammed*.
MOUNTED ASCENDED, CLIMBED. ASTRIDE, HORSED,
RIDING, SADDLED, UP. HILLY (crypt). CARDED,
DISPLAYED, SET OFF. PRODUCED, STAGED (theat).
MOUNT OLYMPUS DIVINE ABODE, HEAVEN. See
OLYMPUS.
MOUTH FACE, GOB, KISSER, LIPS, NORTH AND SOUTH (*rh
sl*), TRAP (sl). CHATTER; CHEEK, IMPUDENCE.
OPENING. RANT, RAVE, SPEAK, UTTER. GRIMACE.
MOUTHORGAN HARMONICA, *INSTRUMENT* (mus).
TONGUE (crypt).
MOVING *Anag.* EMOTIONAL, TENDER. AFOOT, AGATE,
MOBILE (**opp** = *still*). SHIFTING; CHANGING HOUSES.
MP MEMBER OF PARLIAMENT, REPRESENTATIVE.
MILITARY POLICE, REDCAP. **Pl** = *MEMBERS*; *POLICE*;
CHEMIST.
MR 1. MISTER. 2. *Male* of species named, e.g. **Mr Swan** = COB.
MRS 1. MISTRESS, MISSUS, WIFE. 2. *Female* of species named,
e.g. **Mrs Fox** = VIXEN.
~ FRENCH MADAME, MME.
MUFTI CHURCHMAN (Mos). CIVILIAN CLOTHES, CIVVIES
(*mil*; **opp** = *uniform*).
MUG BEAT UP (hence TAEB, dn crypt), COSH [GBH]. CUP,
TROPHY. *FACE*, *MOUTH*. FOOL. CRAM, SWOT.
MULE HYBRID; *offspring* of donkey and horse, hence DON or
KEY (crypt); [*Absolom*; *Silenus*]; **celeb**: MUFFIN.
OBSTINATE. DOLT, *FOOL*. MACHINE, SPINNER. *SHOE*,
SLIPPER.
MULL CONSIDER, PONDER, THINK. HUMUS. MESS,
MUDDLE. *MATERIAL*, MUSLIN. *ISLAND*. MAKE

PUNCH, DRINK. PROMONTORY (Sc). SNUFFBOX.

MURMURATION *Assembly* of starlings.

MURPHY POTATO, SPUD, TUBER.

MURRAYFIELD *RUGBY* GROUND.

MUSE (s/l mews). 1. PONDER, THINK. POET. 2. Gk myth (**Rom** = CAMENAE) nine *goddesses* of song, who presided over the arts, sciences and poetry. They were d's of *Zeus* and *Mnemosyne*, and lived on Parnassus, being the companions of *Apollo*: CALLIOPE (epic poetry), CLIO (history), ERATO (love songs), EUTERPE (lyric poetry), MELPOMENE (tragedy), POLYHYMNIA/POLYMNIA (singing), TERPSICHORE (choral dance), THALIA (comedy) and URANIA (astronomy). [*theat*].

MUSEUM BM.

MUSIC 1. SONG. NOTES, SCORE, SHEETS [*instrument*; *patron saint*; *tempo*]; **comp** = words. 2. **Gods, Gk** = *Apollo* [*Muses*]; **other** = Bes (Egy). 3. ~ **terms; notes** (each is twice as long as its successor): breve, semi-breve, minim, crotchet, quaver, semi-quaver, demi-semi-quaver, hemi-demi-semi-quaver; **opus**: cantata, concerto, fugue, nocturne, oratorio, scherzo, sonata, suite, symphony, toccata; **tempi**: adagietto, adagio, allegretto, allegro, animato, comodo, largamente, largo, lento, maestoso, pressando, prestissimo, presto, rallentando, rubato, stringendo, vivace; **voices**: alto, bass, basso profundo, contralto, counter tenor, mezzo-soprano, soprano, tenor, treble; **all terms** (incl inflexion, intensity and marks):

1-letter
f
p

2-letters
ff
fz
mf
mp
pp

3-letters
bis
rit

4-letters
alto (voice)
bass (voice)
brio
capo
flat

5-letters
breve (note)
forte
fugue (opus)
largo (tempo)
lento (tempo)
minim (note)
mosso

piano
sharp
suite (opus)
tacet
tenor (voice)

6-letters
adagio (tempo)
comodo (tempo)
de capo
legato
presto (tempo)
quaver (note)
rubato (tempo)
sonata (opus)

suivez
treble (voice)
vivace (tempo)

7-letters
agitato
allegro (tempo)
amoroso
andante (tempo)
animato
cadenza
calando
cantata (opus)
con brio
forzato
morendo
natural
soprano (voice)
toccata (opus)
tremolo
vibrato

8-letters
animando
arpeggio
calcando
castrato (voice)
concerto (opus)
con mosso
crotchet (note)
falsetto (voice)
maestoso (tempo)
nocturne (opus)
obligato
oratorio (opus)
ritenuto
staccato

symphony (opus)

9-letters
a capella
adagietto (tempo)
cantabile
contralto (voice)
crescendo
glissando
obbligato
pizzicato
pressando (tempo)
semi-breve (note)
sostenuto
sotto voce

10+ letters
accelerando
allargando
allegretto (tempo)
counter-tenor (voice)
decrescendo
demi-semi-quaver (note)
diminuendo
fortissimo
largamente (tempo)
mezzo-forte
mezzo-piano
mezzo-soprano (voice)
mezzo-staccato
pianissimo
prestissimo (tempo)
rallentando (tempo)
ritardando
semi-quaver (note)
stringendo (tempo)

MUSICIAN B MUS; BANDSMAN, *INSTRUMENTALIST*,
PLAYER; **celeb**: APOLLO (Gk); ASAPH (bibl); CHIBIABOS
(*Hiawatha*); *DAVID* (bibl); TERPANDER (Gk) [*composer*;

conductor; *instrument*; *Muses*; *music* (q.v.)].

MUST HAVE TO. NEW WINE. MOULD. FRENZY.

MUSTANG *AIRCRAFT. HORSE.*

MUSTER GATHERING (mil). LIST, ROLL (mil). ENROL. SUMMON. *ASSEMBLY* (peacocks).

MYTH Mythology, especially the legends which grew up in Greece and Rome, played a large part in the lives of the ancients. Various poets and writers wove stories to account for natural phenomena such as volcanoes, whirlpools, cloud-capped mountains etc; they also sought to explain the Creation itself and some of the everyday events of life such as love, childbirth and the harvest, through personification in the form of *gods* and *goddesses* (q.v.). Most ancient civilizations and peoples developed their own folklore and mythology.

N NAME(D). NAPOLEON. NEUTER. NITROGEN (*chem*). NOON. NORWAY (*car plate*). NORTH; POINT. NOUN. BRIDGE PLAYER.

NA *SODIUM* (*chem*).

NAG *HORSE*, PONY, SCREW. HARP, SCOLD.

NAIAD *NYMPH.*

NAIL FINGER-TIP, TOE-TIP; HORN; CLAW, TALON; **comp** = *tooth*. [fingerplate]. FASTENING, SPIKE: BRAD, HOB, OVAL. CATCH, ENGAGE, FASTEN, FIX, SECURE. *MEASURE* (cloth).

NAKED NUDE.

NAME N. CALL, CHRISTEN. REPUTATION, REPUTE; **saying**. N*OR*M (catechism — crypt).

NANDOO BIRD (S American) [cassowary, dinornis (NZ, ex), emu, moa (ex), ostrich].

NANNY *GOVERNESS* (q.v. for **celeb**), NURSE. GRANNY (sl). Fem *goat*; *BUTTRESS* (crypt).

NAP (s/l *knap*). NAPOLEON; BONEY. DOZE, KIP, *SLEEP*. PILE. *CARD GAME*. CERT, SURE THING.

NAPOLEON N, NAP, BONEY. *CARD GAME*. GOLD PIECE (Fr). PIG (Animal Farm, Orwell). [*Bellerophon, Corporal, Emperor*, First Consul. *Chesterton*. Macavity (*cat*, Eliot). Moriarty (*Holmes*)].

NARCISSUS 1. *FLOWER*. 2. Gk myth youth, for whom *Echo* bore unrequited love, so that she pined away. He fell in love with his own reflection and also pined away, so that he turned into the flower which bears his name. [self-admiration].

NATIVE ABORIGINE; BORN, INDIGENOUS. BIVALVE, *OYSTER*. DOMESTIC. WILD MAN, SAVAGE. ~ **of Australia** = ABORIGINE, *EMU*; ~ **of Britain** = CELT; ~ **of Ireland** = PICT, CELT; ~ **of N Britain** = PICT, CELT; ~ **of NZ** = KIWI, MAORI; ~ **of USA** = *REDSKIN*; ~ **of Wales** = CELT.

NATURE 1. CHARACTER, INCLINATION. MOTHER EARTH. 2. **Goddesses: Gk** = *ARTEMIS*, *DEMETER*; **Rom** = *CERES*, *DIANA*, OPS; **Egy** = *ISIS*, UPIS. [*Pleiades*].

NAUT NAUTICAL, NAVAL, MARITIME. [*measure*].

NAVIGATE CON, *SAIL*, STEER [Henry. *Pytheas*].

NAVY *FLEET*, MARINE, NAUTICAL, RN, TARS, USN. *COLOUR* (blue).

NAY (s/l *neigh*). CONTRADICTION, DENIAL, NO, REFUSAL. AND MORE, EVEN, MOREOVER, RATHER, WELL, WHY.

NB NORTH BRITAIN. NOTA BENE, TAKE NOTE. NEW BRUNSWICK (*Province*, Can). NIOBIUM (*chem*).

NCO CPL, RSM, SGT.

ND NO DATE, UNDATED. NEODYMIUM (*chem*).

NE *NEON* (*chem*). NEAR EAST. NORTH-EAST (i.e. Tyneside etc).

NEAR BY; *CLOSE*. MEAN, *STINGY*.

NEARLY 1. ALMOST, NIGH. 2. Word less one or two letters, e.g. **The cricketer is nearly done** (3) = DON (Bradman).

NEAR MISS CLOSE THING, NARROW SHAVE. CHAPERONE, DUENNA, HONOUR GUARD (crypt).

NEAT UNDILUTED. ORDERED, TIDY; *CHIC*, DEFT, ELEGANT, SMART. *CATTLE*, OX(EN); LOWER (crypt).

NEB NATIONAL ENTERPRISE BOARD. *BEAK* (Sc). HILL-CLIMB (dn, crypt).

NEBUCHADNEZZAR 1. LARGE *BOTTLE*. 2. King of Babylon who carried the Jews to Chaldea.

NECESSITY COMPULSION, CONSTRAINT, INDISPENSABILITY, NEED.

NEEDLE IRRITATE, PROVOKE. KNIT, *SEW*. Pl = ROCKS (geog, IOW).

NEEDLER IRRITANT. ANAESTHETIST, ACUPUNCTURIST; NUMBER (crypt). SEAMSTRESS, *SEWER* (crypt). TATTOOIST.

NEEDLEWORK IRRITATION, PROVOCATION.
  ACUPUNCTURE; ANAESTHETICS, DEADENING,
  NUMBING (crypt). *TATTOO. KNITTING*, *SEWING*.
NEGLIGÉE NIGHTIE, PEIGNOIR, UNDRESS.
NEIGH (s/l *nay*). WHINNY (*horse*).
NEMESIS 1. Gk *goddess* of retribution (similar to *Ate*); d of *Nyx*
  without benefit of a father. 2. A minor *PLANET*.
NEOLITHIC *AGE*.
NEON NE (*chem*).
NEPTUNE Rom *god* of the SEA (**Gk** = *POSEIDON*). On the
  overthrow of *Saturn*, his realm was divided: the heavens to *Jupiter*,
  the underworld to *Pluto* and the seas to Neptune.
NEREID 1. Gk myth sea-nymph (as opposed to fresh water nymphs),
  d's of *Nereus* and *Doris*. Propitious to sailors (especially to the
  Argonauts), one of them was Thetis, m of *Achilles* [*Andromeda*].
  2. A satellite of the *planet Neptune*.
NEREUS Gk myth *god* of the sea, s of Pontus and *Ge*, he had 50 d's
  by *Doris*, who were the *Nereids*. Also *POSEIDON*. **Rom** =
  NEPTUNE, OCEANUS.
NERO The last Rom *Caesar* (A.D. 54–68) and *Emperor* of Rome, he
  mar (1) Octavia (div and later ass by ~), (2) Poppaea (d as the
  result of a kick from ~), and (3) Statilia Messalina. In a reign of
  terror he ass his adopted br Britannicus, his m Agrippina, and two
  of his wives. The burning of Rome, at which he is said to have
  'fiddled' (idled), he blamed on the Christians, and he massacred
  thousands. Piso's conspiracy was put down with brutality, but
  eventually ~ committed sui to escape from Galba.
NESS CAPE, *HEAD*, POINT. LOCH [*monster*].
NET *GIN*, MESH, SNARE, *TRAP*, WEB. CLEAN, CLEAR; **opp**
  = *gross*. *BARRIER*, DIVIDER (*tennis*). PRACTICE AREA
  (*cricket*).
NETHERLANDS NL (*car plate*).
NETTLE ANNOY, *BOTHER*, IRK, IRRITATE, WORRY. *WILD
  PLANT*, *STING*.
NEUTER 1. N. ASEXUAL, NO SEX, CASTRATE. 2. Remove
  letters 'sex' from clue, e.g. **Neuter Middlesex** = MIDDLE.
NEVER-ENDING 1. CONTINUOUS, ENDLESS. CIRCLE,
  RING. 2. Word with last letter(s) removed, e.g. **Disapproval of the
  never-ending book** (3) = BOO(k).
NEVER NEVER EASY TERMS, HIRE PURCHASE. PAN
  COUNTRY (*Barrie*; crypt).

NEVERTHELESS DESPITE THAT, *NOTWITHSTANDING*. EVERMORE (crypt).

NEW (s/l knew). *Anag.* CHANGED, DIFFERENT, FRESH, FURTHER, NOVEL, RECENT (**opp** = old). *DISCOVERED*, *INVENTED*. *FOREST*. *THEATRE*. **Pl** = INFORMATION, TIDINGS [*media*]. ALL POINTS, ALL QUARTERS, FOUR QUARTERS (crypt).

NEWSPAPER *DAILY*, JOURNAL, *PRESS*, RAG, SHEET, TABLOID, WEEKLY [Fleet Street].

NEW TESTAMENT NT (**opp** = OT).

NEXT MONTH PROX, PROXIMO; name of the current next month.

NI NICKEL (*chem*). NORTHERN IRELAND.

NICK *GAOL*. ARREST, DETAIN. *STEAL*. NOTCH, *SCORE*. THE *DEVIL*. NICHOLAS (abbr), SMALL BOY.

NICKEL *METAL*; NI (*chem*). *COIN* (US).

NICKNAME 1. *PRISON* (crypt). 2. Abbreviated or familiar name given to anyone, often associated with their surname or occupation, e.g.

American	= YANK
Arab	= WOG
Australian	= DIGGER
Englishman	= BRIT, GRINGO (S Am), LIMEY (US), POM (Aus), WHITEY
Frenchman	= FROG
German	= FRITZ, HUN, KRAUT
Irishman	= PADDY
Italian	= WOP
Scot	= JOCK
Welshman	= TAFFY
Bell	= DINGER
Clark	= NOBBY
Dean	= DIXIE
Grey	= DOLLY
Lane	= SHADY
Miller	= DUSTY
Smith	= SMUDGER
White	= CHALKY
Wilson	= TUG

NIGHT (s/l *knight*). 1. Darkness (**opp** = *day*). 2. **Gk goddess** =
HECATE, *NYX*. **Rom** = NOX.

NIGHTCLUB CLIPJOINT, *DIVE*, SPEAKEASY. COSH,
TRUNCHEON (crypt).

NIGHTFLIER BAT, MOTH, OWL.

NIGHTINGALE *BIRD*; SINGER [Hans *Andersen*; jug]. JENNY
LIND (Swe). INSTRUMENT (mus). FLORENCE ~, LADY
OF THE LAMP, *NURSE*, SANTA FILOMENA (Longfellow).

NIKE Gk *goddess* of VICTORY (**Rom** = VICTORIA); d of *Pallas*
and *Styx*.

NIL O, *DUCK*, *LOVE*, ZERO.

NIMROD 1. Bibl s of Cush and descended from *Noah* (grand-s of
Ham); 'a mighty hunter.' 2. Maritime aircraft based on the de
Havilland Comet.

NINE See *number*. IX; ONE OVER THE EIGHT. *MUSES*.
DAYS WONDER. ~ GODS (Lars Porsena, Macaulay).
~ LIVES (*cat*). ~ Drummers drumming in *Christmas* song;
~ Bright Shiners in *song*. ~ of diamonds = curse of Scotland.
Pl = ELABORATELY, TO PERFECTION (dress).

~ **ANGELIC ORDERS** *ANGELS*, ARCHANGELS, CHERUBIM,
DOMINATIONS, *POWERS*, PRINCIPALITIES, SERAPHIM,
THRONES, VIRTUES.

~ **WORTHIES** MEDIAEVAL HEROES: JOSHUA, DAVID,
JUDAS MACCABAEUS, *HECTOR*, *ALEXANDER* THE
GREAT, JULIUS *CAESAR*, *KING ARTHUR*,
CHARLEMAGNE, GEOFFREY OF BOUILLON.

NIOBE 1. Gk myth d of Tantalus, w of the King of Thebes. She
turned to stone at the death of her children and shed incessant
tears. 2. A minor *PLANET*.

NIPPY BITING, COLD, CHILLY, PARKY. AGILE. WAITRESS
(Lyons).

NITROGEN N (*chem*).

NL NETHERLANDS, HOLLAND (and *car plate*).

NO (s/l *know*). 1. NAY, NEGATIVE; REFUSAL; O, LOVE, NIL.
Nobelium (*chem*). NORTH. NOT OUT (*cricket*). LAKE (Af).
Classic drama (*Jap*). NUMBER, NUMERO. NEIN (Ger), NIET
(USSR), NON (Fr); **opp** = *yes*. 2. Omit letter or word indicated,
e.g. **No right turn for VAT** (3) = TU*N. 3. Opposite of word
indicated, e.g. **No matter** (4) = MIND. 4. Reflection on . . . (crypt
= NO).

~ **BETTER** NOT WORSE, STATIC, THE SAME. *WINNER*

(crypt). ANTI-GAMBLING (crypt).

NO CHARGE *FREE*, GRATIS. *FLAT*, RUN DOWN (elect).
DEFENDING, NO ATTACK.

NOAH Bibl grand-s of *Methuselah* and s of Lamech; and f of Shem,
Ham, (grand-f of *Nimrod*) and Japeth; ~ built the ark to escape
the flood. Towards the end, he sent out a *raven* (which did not
return), and then a dove (twice), which came back the second time
with an olive leaf; the ark then came to rest on Mt Ararat (c.f.
Deucalion). Another legend makes ~ the first vintner.

NOBLE 1. GOLD COIN (OE). FALCON. VILLAIN (Dornford
Yates). DIGNIFIED, *EXCELLENT*, *GRAND*, *IMPOSING*;
opp = ignoble. 2. Resistant to oxydization (*chem*).
3. ARISTOCRAT, ARMIGER, *PEER* [*emperor, monarch*];
UK = DUKE/DUCHESS, EARL/COUNTESS, LORD/LADY,
MARQUIS/MARCHIONESS, VISCOUNT/VISCOUNTESS,
BARON/BARONESS [*knight*, baronet]; **others** = AG(H)A
(Turk); ATHELINE (A-Sax); BEG, BEY (Turk); BEGUM (Ind);
BOYAR (Russ); COMTE/-ESSE (Fr); CONTE/-ESSA (It);
COUNT/-ESS (Eur); DAIMYO (Jap); DATO (Malay; DAUPHIN/
-E (Fr); EMIR (Islam); GRAF/-INE (Ger, Swe); GRANDEE (Sp);
HIDALGO (Sp); INFANTE/-A (Port, Sp); KHAN (Ch, Turk);
KHEDIVE (Egy); LANDGRAF/-GRAVE (Ger); MAHARAJA/
-RANI (Ind); MARGRAF/-GRAVINE (Ger); MIRZA (Pers);
NABOB (Ind); NAWAB (Ind); PALSGRAVE/-GRAVINE (Ger);
PASHA (Turk); RAJAH/RANEE (Ind, Malay); SEIGNEUR (Fr);
SEIGNIOR (OE); SHEIK(H) (Arab); VICOMTE/-ESSE (Fr);
WALDGRAVE/-GRAVINE (Ger).

NODDY SIMPLETON. SEA-BIRD. [Toyland].

NOGGIN *HEAD*. *DRINK*. *MEASURE*: GILL, ¼ PINT hence
P, I, N or T.

NO GOOD 1. *BAD*, DUFF, DUD. NE'ER-DO-WELL, RAKE. 2.
Delete any reference to 'good' or its synonym from the clue, e.g.
No-good racecourse (4) = ****WOOD.

NOISELESS QUIET, SILENT, SOUNDLESS. *ODIN* (crypt).

NOISY F, FF. ROWDY [DB] (**opp** = *quiet*).

NO LONGER EX, LATE, WAS. SHORTER.

NONCONFORMIST *Anag*. DISSENTING, FREE CHURCH.

NONPLUS AMAZE, ASTOUND. MINUS (crypt).

NON-U 1. *COMMON*. 2. Delete letter 'U' from clue, e.g. **Non-U guy**
= G*Y.

NOON 1. N; MERIDIEM, MIDDAY, M. 2. Delete letters 'On',

e.g. **Noon Monday** = M**DAY.

NO-ONE 1. NOBODY. NOI (crypt). 2. Delete letter 'I' from clue, e.g. **Landlords no-one hoists** (5) = HO*STS.

NO QUARTER 1. *MERCILESS*, PITILESS. 2. Delete letters E, N, S and W from clue, e.g. **No quarter for Wales man in battle** (4) = *AL**MA*.

Nor Norse, Norway.

NO RIGHT 1. NO ENTITLEMENT. *LEFT*. NOR (crypt). 2. Delete letters 'R' or 'RT' from clue, e.g. **Reward no right party** (3) = PA**Y.

NORM ACCEPTED STANDARD, *PAR*; AVERAGE. NORMAN, NAME (catechism, crypt).

NORMAN BOY, MAN. INVADER, NORTH FRENCH (hence NORD, crypt). [*stone*].

NORTH 1. N; POINT; *BRIDGE PLAYER*. POLE. *SEA*. 2. Reads upwards (dn).

~ **AND SOUTH** NS, NANDS. MOUTH (*rh sl*). BRIDGING TEAM (crypt).

~ **WIND Gk** = BOREAS, **Rom** = SEPTENTRIO.

NORVIC *Episcopal sig* of NORWICH.

NORWAY N (*car plate*). *WRITER*; NEVIL SHUTE.

NORWICH Episcopal sig = NORVIC.

NOSE (s/l *knows*, noes). FEATURE; BREATHER, HOOTER, SCHNOZZLE (sl). *AIRPORT*, AIRWAY (crypt). AROMA, BOUQUET; SENSE OF SMELL.

NOT (s/l *knot*). 1. NEGATIVE. 2. Omit word referred to, e.g. **Hire character is not billed** (7) = CHAR**TER.

NOTABLE WELL KNOWN. EMINENT, REMARKABLE, STRIKING. BUSTLING, CAPABLE, HOUSEWIFELY (arch). INCAPABLE (crypt). MUSICAL (crypt).

NOTE *NOTICE*. *CASH*, MONEY [*currencies*]: *BUCK*, FIVER, ONCER, *QUID*, TENNER. *KEY*, PITCH, SOUND, TONE, *TONIC*: FLAT, NATURAL, SHARP; A, B, C, D, E, F, G; DO/DOH, RAY/RE, ME/MI, FA/FAH, SO/SOH, LA/LAH, TE/TI; BREVE = 2 SEMI-BREVES = 4 MINIMS = 8 CROTCHETS = 16 QUAVERS. COMPOSE (crypt, e.g. **He noted** = name of any composer).

NOTED 1. FELT, NOTICED, REGISTERED, REMARKED, SEEN. KEYBOARD; MUSICAL; SCORE (crypt). 2. Remove letters ED or TED from clue, e.g. **Noted Te Deum** = T**EUM or ***EUM. 3. Add any note to word indicated, e.g. **Is hesitantly noted**

before = ER*E, or **Anger is noted for giving illusion** = MI*RAGE. 4.
COMPOSER (crypt: 'he noted').

NOT EVEN NOT ONLY. *ODD*.

NOTHING *LOVE*, O, NIL, ZERO, e.g. **Is nothing to me** = IS*O*ME.
~ **LESS** 1. AT LEAST, IN TRUTH. 2. Omit synonym for nothing
from clue, e.g. **Shocking Olive, nothing less** (4) = *LIVE.

NOTICE *AD*, POSTER, PROCLAMATION. REMARK, *SEE*,
SPOT. MELTED, WARM (crypt).

NOTOS Gk myth SOUTH WIND (**Rom** = AUSTER).

NOT OUT AT HOME, *IN*. BATTING (*cricket*). BLACKLEG.

NOT RIGHT INCORRECT. LEFT. WRONG. See also *NO
RIGHT* (2).

NOTWITHSTANDING ALL THE SAME, ALTHOUGH,
NEVERTHELESS. SEATED, SITTING, LYING (crypt).
GIVING WAY, YIELDING (crypt).

NOUN N.

NOVEMBER (11th) MONTH, M, NOV (Rom ninth month until
Caesar reorganized the calendar). **Birthstone** = *topaz*.

NOWADAYS AT PRESENT. AD.

NT NEW TESTAMENT (**opp** = OT); BIBLE.

NUDE 1. NAKED (**opp** = *dressed*). [Hans *Andersen*]. 2. Remove
synonym for clothes from clue, e.g. **Nude lawsuit** = LAW or, more
cryptically, **Nude Ursula** = AN(dress).

NUMBER AGGREGATE, *NO*, QUANTITY, SUM; *COUNT*,
RECKON, TELL. *ANAESTHETIC*, DEADENING, *DRUG*,
NEEDLE (all crypt). V = 5, X = 10, L = 50, C = 100, B = 300,
D = 500, M = 1,000. **Pl** = BOOK (bibl, OT). **Specific ~s:**
  0 = CYPHER, DUCK, EGG, LOVE, NIL, NIX, NOTHING,
  ROUND, ZERO, ZILCH; A- [calm (Beaufort scale), fool
  (*tarot*)].
  1 = A, I; *FIRST*, MONAD, ONCE(-R), *ONE*, ONLY, SELF,
  SINGLE, SOLO, UNITY; EIN (Ger), UN, -E (Fr); MONO-
  [paper (*anniversary*), sorrow (*magpie*), red ball (*snooker*), all
  alone (*song*), partridge (*song*), juggler (*tarot*), First Letter
  (*Kipling*)].
  2 = II; BIS (Fr), DEUCE, DUET, DUO, DYAD, ENCORE,
  SECOND, *TWICE*, *TWO*; DEUX (Fr), ZWEI (Ger); BI-
  [cotton (*anniversary*), cannon (*billiards*), joy (*magpies*),
  conversion (*rugby*), yellow ball (*snooker*), lilywhite boys (*song*),
  turtledoves (*song*), female pope (*tarot*), ~ bits].
  3 = III; TER, *THIRD*, *THREE*, THRICE, TRIAD, TRIO;

DREI (Ger), TROIS (Fr); TRI- [feather (*anniversary*), red ball
(*billiards*), gables (*Holmes*), Garridebs (*Holmes*), ~ quarters
(*Holmes*), students (*Holmes*), Soldiers ~ (*Kipling*), girl
(*magpie*), try (*rugby*), green ball (*snooker*), French hens (*song*),
rivals (*song*), empress (*tarot*), ~ estates]. **Quotes**: 'There are ~
kinds of lies: lies, damned lies and statistics' (Disraeli); '~ little
maids from school' (Mikado, *G & S*); 'Come the ~ corners of
the world in arms, and we shall shock them' (John, *Shak*);
'~ ravens sat on a tree' (ballad).
4 = IV; *FOUR(TH)*, QUARTET, TETRAD; VIER (Ger);
QUAD(R)- [flower (*anniversary*), boundary (*cricket*), Sign of
~ (*Holmes*), boy (*magpie*), brown ball (*snooker*), calling birds
(*song*), gospel makers (*song*), emperor (*tarot*); bissextile (leap
year)]. **Quotes**: '~ essential human freedoms . . . speech . . .
worship . . . from want . . . from fear' *FDR* Jan 41).
5 = V; *FIFTH*, *FIVE*, PENTA, PENTAD, QUINQUE,
QUINTET; **Pl** = ballgame [wood (*anniversary*), orange pips
(*Holmes*), Nations (*Kipling*), letter (*magpie*), lustrum,
quinquennium (period), ~ *towns* (potteries), gold rings (*song*),
symbols (*song*), pope (*tarot*), ~ *classic orders*. **Quote**: 'Full
fathom ~ thy father lies' (Temp, *Shak*).
6 = VI; HEXAD, SEXTET, SICE, *SIX*(TH); SEX- [~ *nations*
(*American Indians*), candy (*anniversary*), boundary (*cricket*),
~ Napoleons (*Holmes*), ~ honest serving men (*Kipling*),
something better (*magpie*), pink ball (*snooker*), geese a-laying
(*song*), proud walkers (*song*), lovers (*tarot*)]. **Quote**: '~ days
shalt thou labour' (Exodus).
7 = VII; HEPTAD, SEPTAD, *SEVEN*(TH); SEPTO-; **Pl** =
rugby [copper or wool (*anniversary*), near gale (Beaufort scale),
~ Seas (*Kipling*), greeting (*magpie*), septenary (period), ~ hills
(Rom), black ball (*snooker*), stars in the sky (*song*), swans a-
swimming (*song*), chariot (*tarot*), ~ *ages* (*Shak*), ~ *deadly sins*,
~ *hills*, ~ *sages*, ~ *sisters*, ~ *wonders of the world*]. **Quotes**: 'If
~ maids with ~ mops swept for half a year' (*Alice* thro' the
Looking-Glass); 'His acts being ~ ages' (AYLI, *Shak*).
8 = VIII; EIGHT(H), OCTAD, OCTET; OCTO-; ROWING
CREW, BLUE, GOLDIE (C reserve ~), ISIS (O reserve ~)
[bronze (*anniversary*), gale (Beaufort scale), wish (*magpie*),
maids a-milking (*song*), bold rangers (*song*), justice (*tarot*)].
Quote: 'Pieces of ~' (parrot, *Stevenson*).
9 = IX; *NINE*, NINTH, NONAD, NONET; NONA-, NOV-.

Pl = ELABORATELY, TO PERFECTION (dress) [pottery
(*anniversary*), kiss (*magpie*), bright shiners (*song*), drummers
drumming (*song*), ~ of diamonds (curse of Scotland), hermit
(*tarot*), ~ *Muses*, ~ points of the law, ~ *angelic orders*]. **Quote**:
'~ bean rows will I have there' (Innisfree, Yeats).

10 = X; DECIMAL, TEN(TH), DECA- [tin (*anniversary*),
storm (Beaufort scale), decade (period), *commandments* (*song*),
green bottles (*song*), pipers piping (*song*), wheel of *fortune*
(*tarot*)].

11 = II, XI; ELEVEN(TH); HENDECA-; IMPAIRED (crypt);
Pl = SNACK [steel (*anniversary*), side/team (cricket, rugby etc),
ladies dancing (*song*), ~ who went to Heaven (*song*), strength
(*tarot*)].

12 = XII; DOZEN, DUODECIMAL, TWELFTH, TWELVE;
DODECA- [silk (*anniversary*), hurricane (Beaufort scale),
apostles (*song*), lords a-leaping (*song*), *hanged* man (*tarot*),
glorious ~th (grouse shooting), ~th Night (*Shak*)].

13 = XIII; BAKER'S DOZEN, THIRTEEN(TH), UNLUCKY
[lace (*anniversary*), side/team (rugby league), *death* (*tarot*)].

14 = XIV; FOURTEEN(TH) [ivory (*anniversary*), temperance
(*tarot*)].

15 = XV; FIFTEEN(TH) [crystal (*anniversary*), side/team
(rugby union), *devil* (*tarot*), rebellion (Old Pretender)].

16 = XVI; SIXTEEN [*tower* (*tarot*)].

17 = XVII; SEVENTEEN [*star* (*tarot*)].

18 = XVIII; EIGHTEEN [*moon* (*tarot*)].

19 = XIX; NINETEEN [*sun* (*tarot*)].

20 = XX; JACKSON (sl), *SCORE*, TWENTY [china
(*anniversary*), TOPS (darts), day of *judgement* (*tarot*)]. **Quote**:
'~ love-sick maidens we' (Patience, *G & S*).

21 = XXI; MAJORITY, VINGT-ET-UN (Fr) [world (*tarot*)].

25 = XXV; PONY (sl), QUARTER CENTURY [*silver*
(*anniversary*)].

30 = XXX; THIRTY; 2nd XV (rugby) [*pearl* (*anniversary*),
~ Years' War]. **Quote**: 'And they covenanted with him for
~ pieces of silver' (St Matthew).

35 = XXXV [*coral* (*anniversary*)].

40 = XL: FORTY [ruby (*anniversary*), roaring ~s (*winds*),
~ winks (sleep)].

45 = XLV [sapphire (*anniversary*), rebellion (Young
Pretender)].

50 = L; HALF CENTURY, HALF TON (sl) [gold (*anniversary*), bullseye (darts)].

52 = LII; PACK (cards).

55 = LV [*emerald* (*anniversary*)].

60 = LX [*diamond* (*anniversary*), ~ glorious years]. **Quote**: 'If you can fill the unforgiving minute with ~ seconds worth of distance run' (If, *Kipling*).

70 = LXX [*platinum* (*anniversary*)].

75 = LXXV [diamond (*anniversary*)].

76 = TROMBONES (song).

78 = TAROC, *TAROT* (pack).

100 = C; CENTURY, *HUNDRED*, TON (sl); HECTO- [Old ~th (All people that on earth do dwell; psalm 100); Chiltern ~s (stewardship, MP's resignation)].

101 = DALMATIANS (Disney film).

105 = NORTH TOWER (2 Cities, *Dickens*).

144 = GROSS.

180 = MAXIMUM (darts).

200 = CC; DOUBLE CENTURY, TWO TON (sl).

300 = B (Rom).

500 = D; *MONKEY* (sl).

600 = DC [Balaclava, Cardigan, Light Brigade]. **Quote**: 'Into the valley of death rode the ~' (Charge of the Light Brigade, Tennyson).

1,000 = K, M; *GRAND* (sl), MIL (meas); KILO- [chiliad, millennium (period), ~ Guineas (*classic* horserace)].

1,009 = M*IX, AD*M*IX (crypt).

1,500 = *MD*.

1,760 = MILE (yards).

1,976 = ASCOT MILE (yards).

2,000 = KK, MM [~ Guineas (*classic* horserace)].

6,100 = VI*C (crypt).

6,350 = VI*TRIO*L (crypt).

6,500 = PENNSYLVANIA (*song*, Glen Miller).

NUMBER OF PLAYERS DUET, OCTET, QUARTET etc. ELEVEN, FIFTEEN, *SIDE*, TEAM.

~ **ONE** *ME*, I, SELF; NO*I.

NUN (s/l none). *CHURCHWOMAN*; CONVENT GIRL, *SISTER*; *Chaucer* character. *BIRD*: BLUE TIT, *PIGEON*, SMEW. The f of *Joshua*. CHAOS (Egy god).

NURSE DEVELOP, FOSTER, HARBOUR. WORKER (insect).
FISH, *SHARK*. CARE, COSSET, LOOK AFTER, TEND;
SUCKLE. AMAH (Asia), AYAH (Ind), NANNY, *SISTER*, SRN
(**Union** = COHSE); **celeb (fiction)**: SARAH GAMP (Chuzzle,
Dickens); MARCHIONESS (OC Shop, *Dickens*); MRS POOLE
(Jane Eyre, C. *Brontë*); BETSY PRIG (Chuzzle, *Dickens*); MISS
PROSS (2 Cities, *Dickens*); RUTH (Pirates, *G & S*); TILLY
SLOWBOY (Cricket on the Hearth, *Dickens*); **celeb (fact)**: EDITH
CAVELL, FLORENCE *NIGHTINGALE*.

NURSERY HOTHOUSE, PROPAGATION PLOT. HOSPITAL,
WARD (crypt). CHILD'S BEDROOM; ROCKERY (crypt).

NURSERYMAN MARKET GARDENER. BOY BLUE, JACK
HORNER, SIMPLE SIMON etc (crypt, from ~ rhymes).

NUT FASTENING [bolt]. ENTHUSIAST, FAN; FOOL. Egy
goddess. HEAD (sl). COAL LUMP. FRUIT (shell [kernel])
types: ACORN, ALMOND, BRAZIL, CASHEW, FILBERT,
GROUNDNUT, HAZEL, PEANUT, PECAN, PISTACHIO,
WALNUT. TEACHERS (*union*). **Pl** = *MAD*. **Pl comp** = bolts.

NUT-CASE LUNATIC, MADMAN. *SHELL* (crypt).

NYM CORPORAL, SOLDIER (*Shak*).

NYMPH 1. *INSECT* (immature), PUPA: DAMSELFLY,
DRAGONFLY. GIRL, HOURI (Mos). YOUNG WOMAN. 2.
Gk myth Naiad, one of the fresh water maidens (as opp to the salt
water *Nereids*, or the Oceanides of the great oceans). Nymphs are
distinct from *goddesses*, in that they belong to one particular spot,
as opp to the goddesses' overall domain. **Mountain nymphs** =
OREADS; **tree nymphs** = DRYADS and HAMADRYADS;
nymphs of the groves and glens = NAPAEAE.

NYMPHOMANIA Obsession (in women) with sex.

NYX Gk *goddess* of NIGHT (**Rom** = NOX); d of *Chaos* and m,
without benefit of husband, of many *gods* and *goddesses*, including
the *HESPERIDES*, *HYPNOS*, *MOIRAE*, MOMOS,
THANATOS and *NEMESIS*, also by Erebus of *Charon*.

NZ NEW ZEALAND (and *car plate*).

O OHIO. OXFORD. OXYGEN (*chem*). DUCK, LOVE, NIL,
ROUND, ZERO. CRY, EXCLAMATION.

OAK *TREE* [*Absolom*; Charles I]. **Pl** = *CLASSIC*.

OAR (s/l *or*, ore). GALLEY SLAVE, *ROWER*. PADDLE.

OARSMAN *ROWER*: *BOW*, *STROKE*. *CHARON*.

OAST HOUSE DRIER, HOP DRIER, *HOPPER*.

OATH APPEAL, ASSERT, PROMISE, SWEAR [*Hippocrates*, Witness]. CURSE, PROFANITY: BLAST, BLOW, BOTHER, DAMN, DASH, DRAT etc.

OB *DIED*, OBIT. ALUMNUS, OLD BOY [Tom Brown's Schooldays, T. Hughes' pseudonym]. OUTSIDE BROADCAST.

OBJECT 1. *AIM*, *END*, *POINT*. THING. *BAR*, COMPLAIN, DISAPPROVE. 2. Accusative case, e.g. **I object** = ME.

OBSERVE *NOTE*, *SEE*, *WATCH*.

OBSESSION EAGER PURSUIT, EXCESSIVE ENTHUSIASM, MANIA e.g.:

ANGLOMANIA	= **English customs**
BIBLIOMANIA	= **books**
EROTOMANIA	= **sexual passion**
KLEPTOMANIA	= **stealing**
MEGALOMANIA	= **grand ideas**
MONOMANIA	= **one idea**
NECROMANIA	= **death**
NYMPHOMANIA	= **sexual desire (in women)**
PYROMANIA	= **fire-raising**

OBTAINABLE *Anag.* e.g. **Camp follower obtainable from Ulster** (6) = SUTLER. ACQUIRABLE; AVAILABLE, ESTABLISHED, PREVALENT.

OBVERSE FACE, FRONT; HEAD (*coin*; **opp** = reverse). COUNTERPART.

OC ONLY CHILD. OFFICER COMMANDING.

OCCIDENT(AL) W, WESTERN (**opp** = oriental).

OCEAN One of the main areas of sea water: ARCTIC, ANTARCTIC, ATLANTIC, INDIAN, PACIFIC [*Pluto* (acronym); seven seas].

OCEANIDES Gk myth *NYMPHS* of the great oceans.

OCEANUS Gk myth river flowing round the (supposedly circular flat) earth, and also the associated *god*, mar to Tethys; later came to mean the Atlantic (i.e. the water beyond the known Mediterranean sea).

OCTOBER 1. BEER. 2. (10th) MONTH, M; OCT (8th Rom month, before *Caesar* reorganized the calendar). **Birthstone** = *opal*.

ODD *Anag.* e.g. **How odd** = WHO. 1. UNEVEN. CASTING, *EXTRA*, OVER. REMAINING, ADDITIONAL, CASUAL,

UNCONNECTED. *ECCENTRIC*, EXTRAORDINARY,
QUEER, REMARKABLE, SINGULAR, STRANGE, UNCO
(Sc). 2. **Pl** = ADVANTAGE, BALANCE, CHANCES,
HANDICAP, PROBABILITIES, SP (betting). REMNANTS.
DIFFERENCE, INEQUALITIES, STRIFE, VARIANCE.

ODIN 1. Nor myth chief warrior *god* (br of Ve), who mar (1) *Frigg*
(s = *Balder*) and (2) *Freya* (s = Tyr). One-eyed, he lived in
Valhalla; his horse Sleipner had eight legs; his two *ravens* Hugin
(*reflection*) and Munin (*memory*) conveyed news of the outside
world. (**Gk** = *ZEUS*, **Rom** = *JUPITER*, **A-Sax** =
WODEN/WOTAN). 2. NOISELESS, QUIET (crypt).

ODYSSEUS = *ULYSSES*.

OEDIPUS Gk myth s of King Laius and Queen Jocasta of Thebes.
Banished as a baby because an oracle prophesied that Laius would
be killed by his own son, who would then marry his mother.
Returning, Oedipus fulfilled the prophecy by slaying his
unrecognized father on the way. He then relieved the Thebans by
solving the riddle of the *Sphinx*, so that he was made king 'and mar
his own mother. When the facts were revealed, Jocasta killed
herself and Oedipus blinded himself. [~ complex; **opp** = *Electra*].

OF OLD FRENCH. FROM.

~ COURSE NATURALLY, OBVIOUSLY. [crypt = *golfing*; *meals*;
racing].

OFF *Anag.* 1. APART, AWAY. NOT ON. *GO*, START.
LOOSE, SEPARATE. CANCELLED. *BAD*, MOULDY. THE
COVERS (*cricket*; **opp** = *on*, *leg*). ASLEEP (crypt). 2. Delete
word or letters indicated, e.g. **Hit it off** = H(it).

OFFHAND CASUAL, INFORMAL. DIGITAL (crypt).

OFFICE BUREAU, QUARTERS. APPOINTMENT, DUTY,
JOB, POSITION, POST, TASK. ATTENTION, KINDNESS,
SERVICE. WORSHIP.

OFFICER FUNCTIONARY, MINISTER, SERVANT: BAILIFF,
CHAIRMAN, CONSTABLE, HERALD, PRESIDENT,
SECRETARY, TREASURER. Commissioned rank in mil
services: CAPT, CDR, *CO*, *COL*, LT, PO etc; ENSIGN,
GENERAL, SUBALTERN etc. **Comp** = gentleman.

OFFING DISTANCE. TOPPLING, UNSEATING, UPSETTING
(crypt).

OFFSPRING DIVE (crypt). BROOD, CHILD(REN),
DESCENDANT, PROGENY, LITTER, YOUNG, **specifically**:

Adult	Young
Ass/mare	MULE
Bear	*CUB*
Bird	CHICK
Camel	*COLT*
Cat	KITTEN
Cow	*CALF*
Deer	*FAWN*
Dog	PUP
Duck	DUCKLING
Eagle	EAGLET
Eel	ELVER
Elephant	*CALF*
Fish	*FRY*
Fox	*CUB*
Frog	TADPOLE
Goat	*KID*
Goose	GOSLING
Hare	LEVERET
Hawk	BOWET, EYAS, NYAS
Hen	CHICK
Heron	CHICK
Horse	COLT (m), FILLY (f), FOAL
Human	BABY, CHILD
Lion	*CUB*
Pig	PIGLET, SHOAT
Salmon	PEAL, GRILSE, SMOLT
Sheep	*LAMB*
Stallion/Ass	HINNY
Swan	CYGNET
Tiger	*CUB*
Turkey	POULT
Walrus	*CALF*
Whale	*CALF*
Wild boar	GRICE
Wolf	*CUB*
Yak/Cow	DZHO, DZO

Young	Adult
Baby	HUMAN
Bowet	*HAWK*

Calf	*COW, ELEPHANT, WALRUS, WHALE*
Chick	*BIRD*, HEN, HERON
Child	HUMAN
Colt	*CAMEL, HORSE* (m)
Cub	*BEAR, FOX, LION, TIGER, WOLF*
Cygnet	*SWAN*
Duckling	*DUCK*
Dzho, dzo	YAK/COW
Elver	*EEL*
Eaglet	*EAGLE*
Fawn	*DEER*
Filly	*HORSE* (f)
Foal	*HORSE*
Fry	*FISH*
Gosling	*GOOSE*
Grice	WILD BOAR
Grilse	*SALMON*
Hinny	STALLION/*ASS*
Kid	*GOAT*
Kitten	*CAT*
Lamb	*SHEEP*
Leveret	HARE
Mule	*ASS*/MARE
Peal	*SALMON*
Piglet	*PIG*
Poult	TURKEY
Pup	*DOG*
Shoat	*PIG*
Smolt	*SALMON*
Tadpole	*FROG*

OG OLD GERMAN. GO BACK (crypt). KING (bibl). ORIGINAL GUM (stamps). OWN GOAL. GOD (Celt; chief, death, fertility).

OH CALL, *CRY*. OHIO (US *state*).

OILER GREASER, MECHANIC. BRIBER. **Pl** = TEAM (US *football*). OPEC (crypt).

OLD 1. ANCIENT, EX, FORMER, ONCE (**opp** = *new*). AGED, GREY [*study*]. **Comp** = *young*. 2. Use old form of word indicated, e.g. **Old enough** = ENOW; **the old** = YE. 3. Use Roman name, e.g. **Old Exeter** = ISCA.

OLD BOY ALUMNUS, *OB* (author of Tom Brown's Schooldays).
~ FASHIONED *DATED*, OUT OF DATE, SQUARE (**opp** = *in*);
use arch words, e.g. **Are** ~ = ART; **If** ~ = AN. COCKTAIL,
DRINK.
~ FLAME EX, PAST LOVE. ASH, EMBER (crypt).
~ FRENCH OF. VIEUX (trans).
~ GERMAN OG. ALT (trans).
~ LADY *MOTHER*. CRONE.
~ MAN *HUSBAND*; POT AND PAN (*rh sl*). GAFFER.
~ RAILWAY GWR, LMS, LNER, SR etc.
~ STYLE *OS*.
~ TESTAMENT OT.
~ TRAFFORD *CRICKET GROUND*, TESTING GROUND.
~ WOMAN *WIFE*.
OLIVER NOLL. CROMWELL. *PAINTER*. ~ TWIST ('more').
Comp = Roland.
OLYMPIC 1. GAMES. MAGNIFICENT, SUPERIOR. 2. Of
Olympus, hence relating to Gk myth *gods* and *goddesses*.
OLYMPUS Thessalian mountain, dwelling place of *Zeus* and the
principal Gk *gods* and *goddesses*. [*Seven Wonders*].
OM ORDER OF MERIT.
OMAR KHAYYAM, TENT MAKER [astronomy, maths, poetry].
OMIT 1. *CUT*, FAIL, LEAVE OUT, NEGLECT. 2. Omit letter(s)
or word(s) from clue as indicated, e.g. **Lord Peter omits tea
apparently** (4) = PE*ER.
ON *BET*, WAGERED. AHEAD. POSSIBLE. *CONNECTED*.
CITY, HELIOPOLIS (Egy). LEG (*cricket*; **opp** = *off*). *OVER*.
No reflexion . . . (crypt = ON).
~ BOARD 1. EMBARKED, LOADED, SHIPPED; NAUTICAL.
FOOD, ON THE TABLE. SURFER (crypt). 2. Put letter(s) or
word(s) into synonym for boat or ship (often into letters s...s), e.g.
Pool on board rolls (6) = S*POOL*S. 3. Any object which is
normally used on a board, e.g. **Food on board** = CHEESE; **piece on
board** = CASTLE, PAWN, ROOK etc, and (crypt) DRAUGHTSMAN; also
any *boardgame* (q.v. for types).
ONCE 1. ARCHAIC, EX. ONE TIME. 2. Put into Lat or old Gk,
e.g. **But** ~ = SED.
ONE 1. See *number*. A, ACE, I, MONAD, UNIT. RED BALL
(snooker). 2. All *alone* in *song*; *partridge* in a peartree (*Christmas
song*).
ONE-ARMED Single-handed (crypt). **Celeb**: BANDIT (slot

machine); NELSON (*mil leader*); CAPT HOOK (Peter Pan, *Barrie*).

ONE BY ONE IN ORDER, SERIATIM, SINGLY. ELEVEN, II (crypt).

~ **CARD** *ACE*.

ONE-EYED INEFFICIENT (sl). Singularly observant (crypt). **Celeb**: *CYCLOPES* (*monsters*); *GRAEAE*; ARIMASPASIANS; HORATIUS; NELSON (*mil leader*); *ODIN*; POLYPHEMUS; PHILIP (of Macedon, f of *Alexander*); POPEYE (Disney); SQUEERS (*schoolmaster*, *Dickens*); *WODEN*; WOTAN (and see *blind*) ['~ man is king' (Country of the Blind, H. G. Wells)].

ONE-LEGGED One-sided, unequal (sl). **Celeb**: Capt *AHAB* (Melville); BERCHTA (Ger myth); LONG JOHN SILVER (*Stevenson*).

~ **THOUSAND GUINEAS** CLASSIC.

ON SHOW 1. DEMONSTRATED, EXHIBITED, EXPOSED. 2. Hidden word, e.g. **Fit for a king on show at the picture gallery** (5) = RE*GAL.

ONWARD FORWARD, FURTHER ON, PROGRESSING. IN HOSPITAL (crypt).

ONYX *GEM*, SEMI-PRECIOUS STONE; *CHALCEDONY*; *AGATE*.

OO EXCLAMATION, OH. BIRD (Hawaiian). *DUCKS*, EGGS, *LOVES*, OVA (all crypt). PAIR (cricket).

OOH EXCLAMATION, OH. BACKWATER (H_2O backwards, crypt — but *chem* inaccurate).

OP OBSERVATION POST. MINOR OPERATION, OPERATION. OPUS, WORK. OPPOSITE PROMPT, STAGE RIGHT (theat). ORDER OF PREACHERS (DOMINICANS). OUT OF PRINT. OPTICAL. **Pl** = Rom *goddess* of *NATURE*.

OPAL *GEM*, PRECIOUS STONE. *Birthstone* (October). SILICA QUARTZ.

OPEN OVERT. WINDWARD, WINDY (**opp** = *lee*). CRACK, UNDO, UNWRAP; **comp** = shut. TAKE STRIKE (*cricket*). *UNIVERSITY*. GOLF CHAMPIONSHIP, TOURNAMENT; PRO-AM (crypt).

~ **AIR** AL FRESCO, OUTSIDE. CANDOUR.

OPENER 1. DOOR, GATE. *KEY*. (FIRST) BAT (*cricket*). TIN OPENER. **Pl** = QUALIFYING HOLDING (cards). 2. First letter, e.g. **Letter opener** = L.

OPENING 1. CRACK, FISSURE, GAP, HOLE [Sesame].

OVERTURE. GAMBIT. 2. First letter, e.g. **Clever opening** = c.

OPERATING THEATRE SURGERY. WORK ROOM. WORKSHOP.

OPERATION MANIPULATION, WORKING. OP. SURGERY. *BATTLE*; ACTION, ENGAGEMENT (mil).

OPERATOR MANIPULATOR, WORKER. SURGEON (crypt).

OPPORTUNITY CHANCE. PAT, TIMELY.

OPPOSITE ANTONYM. CONTRAST; FACING. [~ **sides** = EW, HC, LR (crypt)]. **Pl** = BACK/FRONT, CHALK/CHEESE, IN/OUT, ON/OFF.

OPS 1. WORKS. 2. Rom *goddess* of *NATURE*.

OPTION CHOICE; REFUSAL.

OR (s/l *oar*, ore). *GOLD* (*herald*). BEFORE, ERE (arch). EITHER (arch). ALTERNATIVE.

ORACLE 1. ADVISER, AUTHORITY, DIVINE INSPIRATION, JUDGEMENT. *PROPHET*. TELETEXT (ITV); **opp** = Ceefax (BBC). 2. Sacred place of divine response, given by a priest or priestess to enquiry by a votary. Often with a carefully worded double meaning. Two celebrated oracles were at Delphi (*Apollo*) and Dodona (*Zeus*); others were at Branchidae and Patara [*Sibyl*]. 3. **God: Gk/Rom** = *APOLLO*; **goddess: Rom** = *MAIA*.

ORAL (s/l *aural*). EXAM(INATION), VIVE VOCE. SAID, SPOKEN, VERBAL. BY MOUTH.

ORANGE *COLOUR*. FRUIT, *TREE* [*Holmes* case]; **Pl comp** = *lemons*. *RIVER* (SA). TOWN (Fr). ROYAL FAMILY (NL).

ORCUS Rom equivalent of *HADES*. Synonymous with *PLUTO* (q.v.).

ORDER ASSOCIATION, *CLUB*, FRATERNITY, MOVEMENT. CLASS, KIND, RANK, SORT. DECREE, EDICT; BULL (papal), UKASE (Russ). **Comp** = *law*. ADJUST, ARRANGE, TIDY; ARRANGEMENT, *ROW*, SEQUENCE, SUCCESSION. DECORUM (**opp** = *chaos*) [*Speaker*]. NEATNESS, *SERIES*. COMMISSION, INDENT, SEND FOR. COMMAND, DO, INSTRUCT. AWARD, DECORATION, HONOUR: CBE, DSO, KBE, MBE, OBE, OM etc. **Pl** = CLERICAL STATUS, ORDINATION. [*five* classical ~s; *nine* angelic ~s].

ORDERED *Anag*. ARRANGED, TIDIED. SENT FOR. COMMANDED, INSTRUCTED. *CHURCHMAN* (crypt). Also CBE, DSO etc as *ORDER* (crypt).

ORDER OF MERIT OM. MITRE, TIMER etc (crypt).

ORDNANCE MOUNTED CANNON/GUNS, *WEAPONS*; **types**:

BASILISK, BASSE, CANNON DOUBLE, CANNON ROYAL, CARRONADE, CULVERIN, DEMI-CANNON, DEMI-CULVERIN, DEMI-SLING, FALCON, FIELD-GUN, HOWITZER, MINION, MORTAR, SAKER, SLING, STERN-CHASER. *WEAPON*.

ORE (s/l *oar*, *or*). CURRENCY (Dan, Nor, Swe). *MINERAL* (q.v. for types).

OREAD *NYMPH* (mountain).

ORESTES Gk myth s of *Agamemnon* and *Clytemnestra*. With his sis *Electra*, he killed his adulterous mother. [**Companion**: Pylades].

ORGAN 1. PART OF BODY (hence B, O, D or Y — crypt), e.g. APPENDIX, COLON, also *mouthorgan* = TONGUE (crypt). MAGAZINE, MEDIUM, MOUTHPIECE, NEWSPAPER. 2. HARMONIUM, MUSICAL INSTRUMENT; **parts**: backfall, bellows, diapason, feeder, keyboard, pallet, pipe, slider, sticker, stop, swell-box, tracker, wind-chest; **stops**: bourdon, diapason, flue, gamba, mixture, musette, mutation, reed, string-toned, tremulant.

ORGANIZATION *Anag.* ASSOCIATION, CLUB, FRATERNITY, MANAGEMENT, MOVEMENT, SCHEME, SET-UP.

ORIENT(AL) E, *EAST*, EASTERN (**opp** = occidental).

ORIGINAL 1. EARLIEST, FUNDAMENTAL, INITIAL, INNATE, PRIMITIVE, PRIMORDIAL. MATRIX, PATTERN. CREATIVE, INVENTIVE. 2. First letter, e.g. **Original sin** = s.

ORION Gk myth *HUNTER*. When killed in Crete with *Artemis*, he became a *constellation* [belt; sword; *dog*; Sirius].

Ork Orkneys.

ORPHEUS Gk myth poet, who charmed all Nature with his *lyre*; he accompanied the *Argonauts* [*siren*]. He mar *Eurydice* and, when she died, followed her to *Hades* and won her back with his music; but when he *looked back* to see if she was following, she was taken back again. His grief angered the Thracian women, who tore him to pieces, and his lyre was placed among the stars as a *constellation* (Lyra).

ORT LEAVING, *REFUSE*, *SCRAP*.

ORWELL 1. RIVER (Eng). 2. GEORGE (Eric Blair), writer. Animal Farm **characters**: dogs = Bluebell, Jessie, *Pitcher*; donkey = Benjamin; farmer = Mr Jones; goat = Muriel; horses = *Boxer*, Clover, Mollie; pigs = *Major*, Minimus, *Napoleon*, Snowball, *Squealer*; raven = Moses; solicitor = Mr Whymper. 1984

characters: Big Brother (BB), Julia, O'Brien, Parsons, Syme,
Winston Smith; **words**: Airstrip One, doublethink, Ingsoc, Miniluv,
Minipax, Miniplenty, Minitrue, newspeak, prole, thought police,
unperson, Eastasia, Eurasia, Oceania.

OS OSMIUM (*chem*). OLD STYLE. BIG, LARGE, OUTSIZE.

OSCAR *AWARD*® (US film; the original statuette reminded a
secretary 'of her uncle Oscar').

OSIRIS Gk form of Egy *god* of death and eternal life. Mar *Isis*, br of
Set.

OSP OBIIT SINE PROLAE (d without issue).

OSTRICH BIRD genus RATITAE STRUTHIO (Af; flightless; head
in sand) [aepyornis (ex), cassowary, dinornis (NZ ex), emu, moa,
mooruk, nandoo, rhea].

OT OLD TESTAMENT (**opp** = NT); BIBLE.

OTHELLO MOOR (*Shak*).

OTHERS ET AL, REST.

OTTER ~ BOARD (fishing). Aquatic musteline animal of *weasel*
family; **celeb**: MIJ (Ring of Bright Water, Maxwell), TARKA.

OUNCE *CAT*. *MEASURE*, OZ.

OUR TIME AD, NOWADAYS.

OUT *Anag*; e.g. **Eats out** = TEAS, or **outpost** = STOP. 1. NOT AT
HOME, NOT IN. READY (e.g. **pan out** = READY TO COOK). AT
FAULT, IN ERROR. FINISHED; **comp** = *down*. BLOOMING,
FLOWERING. B, CT, LBW (*cricket*). EMERGED,
HATCHED, e.g. **Chickened out?** (7) = HATCHED. 2. Word outside
another, e.g. **Directed me to help out** (5) = AI*ME*D. 3. Letter or
word omitted, e.g. **Criminal, caught out, fleeced** (6) = (C)ROOKED.
4. Decide against, e.g. **No holidays under canvas** (7, 3) = CAMPING
OUT.

OUTDOORS AL FRESCO. EXITS (crypt).

OUTER EXTERNAL. OBJECTIVE. BOWLER (crypt).
CRICKET GROUND (Melbourne). TARGET RING [*bullseye*,
inner, *magpie*].

OUTING EXPEDITION, TRIP. BOWLING, WICKET TAKING
(*cricket*, crypt). BLOOMING, FLOWERING (crypt).

OUTLANDISH ODD. ABROAD, FOREIGN (crypt). Trans
(crypt).

OUTLAW DISQUALIFY, FORBID, PROHIBIT. BADDIE,
BADMAN, LAW-BREAKER (crypt **opp** = in-law); **celeb**: BILLY
THE KID, THE CISCO KID, THE CLANCEYS, THE
DALTONS, DOC HOLLIDAY, THE DOONES, JESSE JAMES,

NED KELLY (Aus) [*cowboy, highwayman, robber*]. (JUST) WILLIAM (BROWN), DOUGLAS, GINGER, HENRY [Violet Elizabeth]; Richmal Crompton.

OUT OF 1. EX. FOALED BY (mare). 2. Hidden word, e.g. **Horses out of form are stabled** (5) = M*ARE*S. 3. One word or letter placed outside another, e.g. **He is out of work with optimism** (4) = H*OP*E.

OUTPOST *SETTLEMENT*.

OUTRIGHT 1. ALTOGETHER, ENTIRELY, OPENLY. DIRECT, DOWNRIGHT, THOROUGH. 2. Remove letters RIGHT, RT or R from word, e.g. **Print outright for a drink** (4) = P*INT.

OUTSIDE 1. EXTERIOR, FIELDER (*cricket*, crypt). WINGER (*football*). 2. Word placed round another, e.g. **When in, he is outside the order** (4) = H*OM*E.

~ **BROADCAST** OB.

OUTSIDER 1. *BOUNDER*, CAD. FIELDER (*cricket*, crypt). 2. **Pl** = first and last letters, e.g. **Complete outsiders** = C*E.

OUTSIZE BIG, OS.

OUTSTANDING CONSPICUOUS, EMINENT, REMARKABLE, SIGNAL. *OVERDUE*, UNPAID, UNSETTLED. GROYNE, JETTY, PIER (crypt). *CAMEO*, FRIEZE, TRIGLYPH (crypt).

OUTWARDLY 1. APPARENTLY, EXTERNALLY, VISIBLY. 2. One word round another, e.g. **He is outwardly feline, the deceiver** (5) = C*HE*AT.

OVA (s/l *over*). EGG, O.

OVAL EGG-SHAPED, ELLIPTICAL. *CRICKET GROUND*, TESTING GROUND. *NAIL*.

OVER (s/l *ova*). 1. ABOVE [~ the *moon* = delighted (**opp** = sick as a *parrot*)]. ENDED; LEFT, REMAINING. *CONCERNING*. REVERSED. SIX BALLS/DELIVERIES (*cricket*). ON. 2. In down clue, word preceding another, e.g. **Residuum form of rise overdue** (7) = RESI*DUE.

OVERDRAWN OD, IN THE RED, hence word in RED, e.g. **Overdrawn State stayed behind** (8) = RE*MAINE*D.

OVERDRESS FLAMBOYANCY [Beau Brummel]. APRON, *PINAFORE* (crypt).

OVERDUE LATE. *OUTSTANDING*, UNPAID, UNSETTLED.

OVERHAUL OVERTAKE, *PASS*. EXAMINE, PATCH, REPAIR, *SERVICE*.

OVERHEAD FIXED COST, STANDING CHARGE. HAT (crypt);

ROOF (crypt); UMBRELLA (crypt). **Opp** = under foot,
understanding (crypt).

OVERLOOK FORGET, TAKE NO NOTICE. OVERSEE,
SUPERINTEND. GIVE ONTO, HIGHER THAN. BEWITCH.

OVERMAN *BOSS*, FOREMAN, MANAGER,
SUPERINTENDENT. BOWLER (crypt).

OVERSIGHT OMISSION. EYEBROW, EYELASH, FOREHEAD
(crypt).

OVERTURE 1. OPENING (mus). FEELER, PROPOSAL. 2. First
letter, e.g. **Handel's overture** = H.

OVERWEIGHT 1. FAT, OBESE. 2. In down clue, word preceding,
or over, synonym for weight, e.g. **Foolish Herb is overweight** (9) =
SIMPLE*TON.

OWE (s/l O, *Oh*). DEBT, DUE, *OVERDRAW*.

OWL BIRD; NIGHT-FLYER; **breeds**: BARN ~, BUBO, EAGLE
~, FISH ~ (Jap), (GREAT) GREY ~, HAWK ~, LONG-
EARED ~, MOPOKE, MOREPORK (Aus, NZ), SAWWHET
(Arcadia), SHORT-EARED ~, SNOWY ~, TAWNY ~
[eyesight, wisdom]; **comp** = nightingale (OE, de Guildford);
pussycat (*Lear*). **Celeb**: TOO-TOO (*Lofting*), *BUNTER*, OLD
BROWN ~ (*Potter*), ASCALAPHUS (myth), WOL (*Milne*).
BUTTERFLY (lepidoptera). **Pl** = football team.

OWN POSSESS. *ADMIT*, CONFESS. ALONE, INDEPENDENT,
PERSONALLY, UNRIVALLED; TOD SLOAN (*rh sl*).

OX BOVINE ANIMAL (genus Bos): AUROCHS (ex, and =
URUS), BISON, BUFFALO, GAYAL (Ind), KOUPREY (SE
Asia), MITHAN (Ind), MUSK-OX, SELADANG (Malay),
TAKIN (Asia), UNICORN (myth), WISENT, YAK, ZEBU.

OXFORD **Episcopal sig** = OXON. *UNIVERSITY* (q.v.); **comp** =
Cambridge. *CASTLE*. *COLOUR* (dark blue). *SHOE*.
BOSPHORUS.

OXON *Episcopal sig* of OXFORD. *UNIVERSITY*.

OXYGEN O (*chem*).

OYSTER BIVALVE, *NATIVE* [*Colchester*, Whitstable]; *SHELL*
(*close*, *silent*). *Alice* character.

OZ *OUNCE* [*measure*]. *WIZARD*. *Aus* (sl).

P PAGE. PARK(ING). PENNY. PHOSPHORUS (*chem*).
PIANO, QUIET, SUBDUED. PORT. PORTUGAL (*car plate*).

PRESIDENT. **Pl** = PP, PS.

PA (s/l *par*). *FATHER.* PANAMA (*car plate*). PROTACTINIUM (*chem*). PENNSYLVANIA (US *state*).

PACK 1. BUNDLE, KNAPSACK, *MEASURE*, PACKET, RUCKSACK; LOT, SET (cards). BAG, BOX, *COVER*, WRAP. CROWD, CRUSH, FILL. CARRY (gun). STACK (jury). *ICE.* CAKE (cosmetics, *medicine*). 2. *Assembly* of *brownies*, *cards*, *cubs*, *grouse*, *hounds*, *hyenas*, Rugby forwards, submarines, wolves.

PACKMAN PEDLAR (arch); BOB JAKIN (Mill on the Floss, Eliot). JACK, KING, KNAVE; DEALER (cards, crypt).

PAGE ATTENDANT, BUTTONS, BELL-BOY, BELL-HOP; (*Chaucer*). CALL, SUMMON. P, FOLIO, LEAF, RECTO, (RE)VERSO, VO. BOOKMAKER (crypt). Mistress ~ (Merry Wives, *Shak*). **Pl** = FF, PP.

PAIN (s/l *pane*). AGONY, HURT; STITCH. **Aversion to** ~ = ALGOPHOBIA; **lover of** = ALGOPHILE. FRENCH BREAD (trans, crypt).

PAINTED *MADE UP.* *COATED*, COLOURED, PIGMENTED; PINXIT. [La Creevy, *Dickens*].

PAINTER MOORING LINE/ROPE; BOW-TIE (crypt). BEAUTICIAN, COSMETICIAN, MAKE-UP ARTIST (crypt). DECORATOR; HITLER. RA; *ARTIST*, MASTER; CUBIST, EXPRESSIONIST, FAUVE, IMPRESSIONIST, LANDSCAPE ~, MINIATURE ~, MODERNIST, PORTRAIT ~, RENAISSANCE ~, STILL-LIFE ~, SURREALIST; CANVASSER, EXHIBITIONIST (crypt). **Goddess, Gk** = *Athene*, **Rom** = *Minerva*. In classic Gk times (*c.* 400 B.C.), Zeuxis and Parrhasius competed for superiority in still-life painting. The former painted a bunch of grapes which deceived the birds, who tried to eat them; he then called upon the latter to unveil his painting so it could be judged — but the curtain covering it was the painting, which won because it had deceived a fellow artist [*Athene*, Minerva, fine arts, *Company* (livery)]; **celeb**:

3-letters

COX, David	Eng
DOU, Gerard	NL
FRY, Roger	Eng

4-letters

BELL, Robert Anning	Eng

BONE, Sir Michael	Eng
COPE, Sir Arthur	Eng
CUYP, Albert	NL
DALI, Salvador	Sp
DORE, (Paul) Gustave	Fr
DUFY, Raoul	Fr

DYCK, Anthony van NL
ETTY, William Eng
EYCK, Hubert van NL
GOGH, Vincent van NL
GOYA, Francisco de Sp
GRIS, Juan Sp
HALS, Frans NL
HEEM, David van NL
HUNT, William
  Holman Eng
JOHN, Augustus
  Edwin Eng
KENT, William Eng
KLEE, Paul Swi
LELY, Sir Peter Eng
LENS, Bernard Eng
MAES, Nicholas NL
MARC, Franz Ger
MIRO, Joan Sp
NASH, Paul Eng
RENI, Guido It
RITT, Augustus Russ
ROSA, Salvator It
SHEE, Sir Martin
  Archer Ire
WEST, Benjamin US
WINT, Peter de Eng
WOOD, Christopher UK
ZORN, Anders
  Leonhard Swe

5-letters
BACON, Francis Ire
BAYEU, Francisco Sp
BLAKE, William Eng
BROWN, Ford Madox Eng
COROT, Jean-Baptiste Fr
CUNEO, Terence
  Tenison Eng
DANBY, Frances Eng
DAVID, Jacques Fr

DAYES, Edward Eng
DEGAS, Hilaire Germain
  Edgar Fr
DULAC, Edmond Fr
DURER, Albrecht Ger
ENSOR, James Belg
ERNST, Max Ger
FRITH, William Powell Eng
GOYEN, David van NL
GRECO, el Gk
GROSZ, George Ger
HOOCH, Pieter de NL
JACON, Max Fr
JONES, George Eng
KLIMT, Gustav A
KLINE, Franz US
LEGER, Fernand Fr
LEWIS, Wyndham US
LIPPI, Fra Filippo It
LOWRY, Lawrence
  Stephen Eng
MANET, Edouard Fr
MARIN, John US
MARIS, Jacob NL
MONET, Claude Fr
MOSES, Anna
  'Grandma' US
MUNCH, Edvard Nor
NOLDE, Emil Ger
ORPEN, Sir William Ire
REDON, Odilon Fr
ROCHE, Hippolyte (Paul)
  de la Fr
ROSSI, Giovanni It
SCOTT, Sir Peter Eng
SMART, John Eng
SPEAR, Ruskin Eng
STEEN, Jan It
TOBEY, Mark US
VELDE, Jan & William van
  de NL

VINCI, Leonardo da It
WATTS, George
  Frederick Eng

6-letters
ANCHER, Michael Dan
ARCHER, James
  Wykeham Eng
BODINI, Giambattista It
BRAQUE, Georges Fr
BUFFET, Bernard Fr
CLAUDE, Lorrain
  (Gelee) Fr
COOPER, Alexander &
  Samuel Eng
COPLEY, John US
COSWAY, Richard Eng
COTMAN, John Sell Eng
COZENS, John Robert Eng
DERAIN, Andre Fr
DE WINT, Peter Eng
EVENOR Ancient Gk
FOSTER, Miles Eng
GIBSON, Charles Dana US
GIBSON, Richard Eng
GIOTTO (di Bondone) It
GIRTON, Thomas Eng
GREUZE, Jean-Baptiste Fr
HAYDON, Benjamin
  Robert Eng
HEARNE, Thomas Eng
HUYSUM, Jan van NL
INGRES, Jean Fr
KNIGHT, Dame Laura Eng
KROYER Dan
LASZLO, Philip de Hung
LAVERY, Sir John Ire
LEBRUN, Marie Fr
MABUSE, Jan de NL
MCEVOY, Ambrose Eng
MATSYS, Quentin NL

MILLET, Jean Francois Fr
OLIVER, Isaac &
  Peter Eng
OROZCO, Jose Mex
PLIMER, Andrew &
  Nathaniel Eng
RENOIR,
  Pierre-Auguste Fr
RIVERA, Diego Mex
ROMNEY, George Eng
ROTHKO, Mark US
RUBENS, Peter Paul NL
SEURAT, Georges
  Pierre Fr
SIGNAC, Paul Fr
SISLEY, Alfred Fr
TITIAN (Tiziano
  Vecello) It
TURNER, Joseph Malord
  Wm Eng
VARLEY, John Eng
VERNET, Claude Fr
WARHOL, Andy US
WEYLER, Jean-Baptiste Fr
WILKIE, Sir David Sc
WILSON, Richard Wal
WYLLIE, William
  Lionel UK
ZEUXIS Ancient Gk

7-letters
APELLES Ancient Gk
BARTOLI, Taddeo It
BELLINI, Gentile &
  Giovanni It
BONNARD, Pierre Fr
BORDONE, Paris It
BOUCHER, Francois Fr
BRUEGEL, Jan
  (Velvet) NL
CASSATT, Mary US

CEZANNE, Paul Fr
CHAGALL, Marc Russ/Fr
CHARDIN, Jean-Baptiste
Simeon Fr
CHIRICO, Giorgio
de Gk/It
COLLIER, John Eng
COURBET, Gustave Fr
DAUMIER, Honore Fr
DA VINCI, Leonardo It
DE HOOCH, Pieter NL
EL GRECO Gk
FRANCIA, Francesco It
GAUGUIN, Paul Fr
GILBERT, Sir John Eng
GUTHRIE, Sir James Sc
HOBBEMA, Meindert NL
HOGARTH, William Eng
HOKUSAI, Katsushuka Jap
HOLBEIN, Hans Ger
HOPPNER, John Eng
HOSKINS, John Eng
JANSSEN, Cornelius Ger
KNELLER, Sir
Godfrey Eng
KOONING, William
de NL/US
LARSSON, Carl Swe
LAUTREC, Henri de
Toulouse Fr
LEONARD, Michael Eng
LIEVENS, Jan NL
LINNELL, John Eng
LORRAIN, Gelee
(Claude) Fr
MALBONE, E. G. US
MATISSE, Henri Fr
MILLAIS, Sir John Eng
MORISOT, Berthe Fr
MURILLO, Bartolome Sp
NASMYTH, Alexander Sc

PICASSO, Pablo (Ruiz) Sp
POLLOCK, Jackson US
POUSSIN, Nicholas Fr
RAEBURN, Sir Henry Sc
RAPHAEL (Sanzio) It
ROBERTS, William Eng
ROUAULT, Georges Fr
SARGENT, John
Singer Eng
SICKERT, Walter Eng
SINGRAY,
Jean-Baptiste Fr
SOLOMON, Solomon
Joseph UK
SOUTINE, Chaim Fr
SPENCER, Sir
Stanley Eng
TENIERS, David NL
TENNANT, Stephen James
Napier Eng
THAULOW, Frits Nor
UCCELLO, Paolo It
UTRILLO, Maurice Fr
VAN DYCK, Anthony NL
VAN EYCK, Hubert NL
VAN GOGH, Vincent NL
VAN HEEM, David NL
VERMEER, Jan NL
WATTEAU, Antoine Fr
WOOTTON, Frank Eng
ZOFFANY, John Eng

8-letters

ANGELICO, Fra Guido It
ANNIGONI, Pietro It
BOCCIONE, Umberto It
BOUGHTON, George
Henry Eng
BRUEGHEL, Pieter
(*Hell*) NL
CARRIERA, Rosalta It

DE LASZLO, Philip Hung
DELAUNAY, Robert Fr
DE MABUSE, Jan NL
HILLIARD, Nicholas &
Laurence Eng
JAMESONE, George Sc
KOLLWITZ, Kathe Ger
LANDSEER, Sir Edwin
Henry Eng
LAWRENCE, A. K. Eng
LAWRENCE, Sir
Thomas Eng
LEIGHTON, Lord
Frederick Eng
MANTEGNA, Andrea It
MASACCIO (Tommaso
Guido) It
MEEGEREN, Hans van
(forger) NL
MONDRIAN, Piet NL
MULREADY, William Ire
MUNNINGS, Sir
Alfred Eng
PISSARRO, Camille Fr
PERUGINO (Pietro
Vannucci) It
REYNOLDS, Sir
Joshua Eng
RICHMOND, Sir William
Blake Eng
RICKETTS, Charles Eng
ROSSETTI, Dante
Gabriel Eng
ROUSSEAU, Henri Fr
RUYSDAEL, Jakob
van NL
SALBREUX, Louis Lie
Perin Fr
SOHLBERG, Harald Nor
STOTHARD, Thomas Eng
VAN GOYEN, David NL

VERONESE, Paola It
VLAMINCK, Maurice
de Fr
VUILLARD,
Jean-Edouard Fr
ZURBARAN, Francisco
de Sp

9-letters
CANALETTO,
Michelangelo da It
CHURCHILL, Sir
Winston Eng
CONSTABLE, John Eng
CORREGGIO, Antonio
da It
DE CHIRICO,
Giorgio Gk/It
DE KOONING,
William NL/US
DELACROIX, Eugene Fr
DE LA ROCHE, Hippolyte
(Paul) Fr
DONATELLO, Donato It
EDELFELDT, Albert Finn
FEININGER, Lyonel US
FRAGONARD, Jean Fr
GIORGIONE, Giorgio It
GREENAWAY, Kate Eng
HONTHORST, Gerhard
van NL
KANDINSKY, Vasili Russ
KAUFFMANN,
Angelica Swi
KOKOSCHKA, Oskar A
LAVREINCE,
Nicholas Swe
LLEWELLYN, Sir
William Eng
MCTAGGART, William Sc

REMBRANDT (van
  Rijn)   NL
SANSOVINO, Andrea   It
SIQUEIROS, David
  Alfaro   Mex
VAN HUYSUM, Jan   NL
VELASQUEZ, Diego   Sp
or
VELAZQUEZ, Diego   Sp

10+ letters
ARCHER-SHEE, Sir
  Martin   Ire
BARTOLOMMEO, Fra   It
BOTTICELLI, Sandro   It
BUONARROTI
  (Michelangelo)   It
CARAVAGGIO,
  Michelangelo da   It
DA CORREG(G)IO,
  Antonio   It
DE ZURBARAN,
  Francisco   Sp
GAINSBOROUGH,
  Thomas   Eng

GHIRLANDAIO bros   It
GIACOMETTI,
  Alberto   Swi
MACWHIRTER, John Sc
MICHELANGELO
  (Buonarroti)   It
MODIGLIANI, Amedeo It
PARRHASIUS Ancient Gk
ROTHENSTEIN, Sir
  William   Eng
SUTHERLAND,
  Graham   Eng
TINTORETTO (Jacopo
  Robusti)   It
TOULOUSE-LAUTREC,
  Henri de   Fr
VAN DE VELDE, Jan &
  William   NL
VAN HONTHORST,
  Gerard   NL
VAN MEEGEREN, Hans
  (Vermeer forger) NL
VAN RUYSDAEL,
  Jakob   NL

PAIR (s/l *pear*, *pare*). PR. OO (cricket sl). BRACE, COUPLE, TWO (**pigeon** ~ = one of each sex); **comp** = *carriage*. AFFIANCE, *ENGAGE*, MARRY, MATE, *WED*.
Pak Pakistan.
PALACE BISHOP'S/PRESIDENT'S/SOVEREIGN'S RESIDENCE. Any grand building, *THEATRE* etc, such as:

ALEXANDRA (Eng)
BILSKIRNIR (Nor myth)
BUCKINGHAM (Eng)
CAESAR'S (US)
CNOSSOS (*Minos*)
CRYSTAL (Eng)
DOGE'S (It)
ELYSEE (Fr)

HAMPTON COURT (Eng)
HATFIELD (Eng)
HOLYROOD (Sc)
KENSINGTON (Eng)
LAMBETH (Eng)
NONSUCH (Eng)
PINK (Arg)
ST JAMES'S (Eng)

STRELSAU (fict, *Hope*) VICTORIA (Eng)
ST STEPHEN'S (Eng) WESTMINSTER (Eng)
TOWER OF LONDON (Eng) WHITEHALL (Eng)
VERSAILLES (Fr) WINDSOR (Eng)

PALAEOLITHIC *AGE*.

PALATIAL GRAND, SPLENDID; like a *palace*.

PALLADIUM 1. *METAL*; PD (*chem*). *THEATRE*. 2. Any image of Pallas Athene, conferring safety on the town which possessed it, but especially that held at *Troy* until it was removed by *Odysseus* and Diomedes.

PALLAS 1. = *ATHENE* [*Palladium*]. 2. A *TITAN*, s of Orius and Eurybia, mar *Styx* and f of *Nike*. 3. A minor *PLANET*.

PALM 1. *HAND*. CONCEAL. LAUREL, VICTORY GARLAND. 2. TREE; **types**: ARECA, ARENG, BACTRIS, BAMBOO ~, CALUMNUS, CARNAUBA, COCO(A)NUT, COHUNE, COKERNUT, CURYPHA, DATE ~, DOUM, EJOO, ELAEIS, FAN ~, GOMUTI, -O, GRU-GRU, JUPATI, KITOOL, -TUL, MORICHE, NARGIL, NIPA, OIL ~, PALMETTO, PALMYRA, PAXIUBA, *PHOENIX*, PIASSABA, -VA, RAPHIA ~, RATTAN ~, RHAPSIS, SAGO ~, TALIPAT, -ET, -OT, -UT, TUCUM, WAX ~, WINE, ZALACCA, ZAMIA [frond, raffia].

~ **OIL** FAT, GREASE (candles, soap). BRIBE (crypt).

PAN 1. DISH, POT. BERATE, CRITICIZE. WASH *GOLD* [*digger*]. SWING (photo). PETER [*Barrie*; Never Never *Land*]. 2. Gk *god* of *shepherds*; chief *satyr*. 3. With hyphen = all-embracing, universal, e.g. pan-American.

PANDORA 1. STRINGED INSTRUMENT. 2. Gk myth first woman on earth. She opened the box containing all human ills, and only Hope remained inside. 3. A minor *PLANET*.

PANE (s/l *pain*). *SHEET*. HAMMERHEAD (hence H), PEEN.

PANIC ALARM, *FEAR*, FRIGHT, TERROR. *GRASS*.

PAPER PRESS, RAG **names** (all ®): HERALD, MIRROR, STAR, SUN, TELEGRAPH, TIMES, TRIBUNE etc. DECORATE. BUMF, DOCUMENT, RECORD. WRAPPER. PAPYRUS [*measure*, origami (*Jap*)]; *anniversary* (1st).

PAPERWORK ADMINISTRATION, ARCHIVES, BUMF (sl), RECORDS, RED TAPE, ORIGAMI (Jap, crypt).

PAR (s/l *pa*). *EQUAL*, *EVEN*, LEVEL. *AVERAGE*, *MEAN*. BOGEY, NORM, STANDARD (*golf*).

PARADISE EDEN, ELYSIUM, *HEAVEN*, UTOPIA, *VALHALLA* [Asphodel meadows].

PARASITE Animal or plant living on another [host, commensal], e.g. **bot**: DODDER, EPIPHYTE, FUNGUS, GALL-NUT, MISTLETOE, SAPROPHYTE, YEAST; **zool**: ACARNO, BACTERIUM, FLEA, GUINEA-WORM, ICHNEUMON FLY, LEECH, LOUSE, TAPE-WORM, TRICHINA; hence HANGER-ON, TOADY. DROPPING-ZONE (mil, crypt).

PARCAE Rom *goddesses* of the three *FATES*. **Gk** = MOIRAI.

PARE (s/l *pair*, *pear*). *CUT*, *PEEL*, SHAVE, *TRIM*, WHITTLE.

PARENTAL GUIDANCE A, *CENSORSHIP* (film).

PARIS 1. *Capital* of France, hence (crypt) F. PLASTER. 2. Gk myth s of *Priam*. He judged *Aphrodite* the fairest against *Athene* and *Hera* for a coveted golden apple. Loved Oenone before he ran off with *Helen*, who was mar to Menelaus, and thus started the war of *Troy*. He killed Achilles by shooting him in the heel. 3. *Shak* character(s).

PARKING P. [Mansfield Park, *Austen* (crypt)].

PARLIAMENT COUNCIL, DEBATING CHAMBER, *LEGISLATIVE ASSEMBLY* [Commons, Lords, the House].

PARNASSUS Gk myth mountain home of the *Muses*.

PARROT COPY, MIMIC, REPEAT. RIVER. *BIRD* (Psittaciformes). **Types**: BUDGERIGAR, BUDGIE, COCKATIEL, COCKATOO, CONURE, CORELLA, KAKA (NZ), KAKAPO (NZ), KEA (NZ), LORIKEET, LORY, MACAW, NESTOR, PAR(R)AKEET, PAROQUET, ROSELLA, ZATI. **Celeb**: Capt Flint (*Stevenson*), POLYNESIA (*Lofting*). [Sick as a ~ = disappointed, *upset* (**opp** = over the *moon*)]. **Sea** ~ = puffin.

PARSON 1. *CHURCHMAN*, INCUMBENT, PADRE (mil), RECTOR, VICAR; GOD-BOTHERER, SKY-PILOT (sl); **celeb** (**fict**): ~ Adams (Fielding); Amos Barraclough (*Kipling*); Boanerges (Mrs Oliphant); Brocklehurst (Jane Eyre, *Brontë*); Father Brown (*Chesterton*); Vicar of Bray (18th-cent song); Caponsacchi (Browning); Chadband (Bleak Ho, *Dickens*); Elmer Gantry (Sinclair Lewis); Archdeacon Grantly (Trollope); Harding (Trollope); Charles Honeyman (Thackeray); Friar John (Rabelais); Dr Middleton (Meredith); Primrose (Goldsmith); Quiverful (Trollope); Dominie Samson (*Scott*); ~ Samson (Thackeray); Obadiah Slope (Trollope); Shepherd Stiggins (Pickwick, *Dickens*); Dr Syntax (Coombe); Friar Tuck (Ivanhoe, *Scott*); Vicar of

Wakefield (Goldsmith); and character in *Chaucer*. 2. BIRD, TUI
[~'s nose].

PART 1. *Anag. GO, LEAVE,* QUIT. ROLE. PIECE, SOME (**opp**
= *all*). COMPONENT, SPARE. **Comp** = parcel. SPLIT HAIRS
(crypt). 2. Hidden word, e.g. **Love is part of Much Ado re Nothing**
(5) = ADO*RE. 3. **Pl** = word split, e.g. **Romantic in parts about
Talia** (7) = I*TALIA*N.

PARTNER ASSOCIATE, *COMPANION,* FELLOW, OPPO.
WIFE/HUSBAND. **Pl** = EW, NS, HC, RL. MAST GATE
(naut). DARBY & JOAN, NOW & THEN, PROP & COP etc.

PARTRIDGE GAME BIRD; **assembly** = covey. [1st day of
Christmas].

PARTY AT HOME, BALL, *DANCE,* DO, FUNCTION,
RECEPTION, SHINDIG. SIDE (leg). **Politics:** ALLIANCE,
CON, DEM, L, LAB, LIB, REP, SDP, TORY, WHIG.

PASS *HAND.* OVERHAUL, OVERTAKE. ACCEPT,
APPROVE, LET GO BY. *COL,* DEFILE. GRADUATE,
SUCCEED; NO HONOURS (crypt). AMOROUS ADVANCE.

PASSENGER FARE. (FELLOW) TRAVELLER. BURDEN,
LIABILITY.

PAST (s/l passed). 1. ANTIQUE, BYGONE, *EX,* FORMER,
GONE BY. 2. Use past tense, e.g. **Past art** = WERT.

PASTE CONFECTION, MIXTURE. GLUE, STICK.
IMITATION *DIAMOND/GEM.*

PATIENCE ENDURANCE, PERSEVERANCE [*Job*]. CARD
GAME. PLANT.

PATRICK *PATRON SAINT* (Ire). [Bishop, Pope Celestine, 17
March].

PATRON SAINT TUTELARY PROTECTOR; **celeb (with feast day)**:
AGATHA (bellfounders, nurses; 5 Feb), ANDREW (Scotland, 30
Nov), ANNE (Brittany; 26 Jul), ANTONY (lost property; poor; 13
Jun), BARBARA (*firemen; gunners;* 4 Dec), BLAISE
(woolcombers; 3 Feb), BRIDGET (*Ireland;* 1 Feb), CATHERINE
(attorneys; *scholars;* wheelwrights; 25 Nov), CECILIA (church
music; 22 Nov), CHRISTOPHER (wayfarers; 25 Jul),
CRISPIN(IAN) (leatherworkers; 23 Oct), *DAVID* (Wales; 1 Mar),
DENYS (*France;* 9 Oct), ELMO/ERASMUS (*sailors;* 2 Jun),
EUSTACE (*hunters;* Madrid; 20 Sep), FRANCIS OF ASSISI
(animals; 4 Oct), *GEORGE* (England; *Portugal;* armourers; 23
Apr), GILES (*beggars;* blacksmiths; *cripples;* 1 Sep), HUBERT
(*huntsmen;* 3 Nov), JOAN OF ARC (*France;* 30 May), JOHN OF

GOD (*booksellers*; printers; 8 Mar), JOSEPH (*workers*; 1 May),
JUDE (afflicted; 28 Oct), LEONARD (*prisoners*; 6 Nov), LUKE
(physicians; 18 Oct), MARGARET (women in travail; 20 Jul),
MAURUS (charcoal burners; 15 Jan), MENAS (merchants; 11
Nov), MONICA (Christian mothers; 27 Aug), NICHOLAS
(*children*; *sailors*; 6 Dec), PANTALEON (physicians; 27 Jul),
PATRICK (*Ireland*; 17 Mar), SABAS (Serbia; 14 Jan), TERESA
(foreign missions; 3 Oct), URSULA (*schools*; 21 Oct),
VALENTINE (lovers; 14 Feb), VITUS (*sickness*; 15 Jun),
WENCESLAS (Bohemia; 28 Sep).

PATTERN (s/l patten). EXAMPLE. DESIGN, MATRIX,
MODEL, MOULD, TEMPLATE, TEMPLET.

PAUL SAUL; *apostle*; b in Tarsus *c.* A.D. 3, ~ was anti-Christian until
converted by *Jesus* in a vision, and became travelling missionary to
the Gentiles (c.f. *Peter* ditto to Jews). Imprisoned by Rom
governor Felix, and later shipwrecked at Malta; martyred by *Herod*
c. A.D. 65 under *Nero*.

PAUL'S LETTERS COLOSSIANS, CORINTHIANS, EPHESIANS,
GALATIANS, PHILEMON, PHILIPPIANS, *ROMANS*,
THESSALONIANS, TIMOTHY, TITUS. P, A, U and L (crypt).

PAUSE (s/l paws). BREVE, *REST* (mus). BREAK,
HESITATION, INACTION, *INTERVAL*. LINGER, TARRY
(**opp** = *go*on*).

PAWNBROKER POP, UNCLE [*pledge*; *weasel*]. *PAWNEE* (crypt).

PAWNEE *AMERICAN INDIAN*. *PAWNBROKER* (crypt).

PAX 1. PEACE. TRUCE! 2. Rom *goddess* of PEACE: **Gk** =
IRENE.

PAY PAYMENT, *SALARY*, *SCREW*, WAGES. DISCHARGE,
RECOMPENSE, RETURN, REWARD, *SETTLE*. CAULK,
STOP (naut).

PAYER PAYMASTER; *SETTLER* (crypt).

PB *LEAD* (chem). PAPERBACK.

PC PARISH COUNCIL. PER CENT. POLICE CONSTABLE.
POST CARD. PRIVY COUNCILLOR.

PD PALLADIUM (*chem*). POLICE DEPARTMENT.

PE PHYSICAL EXERCISE; GYMNASTICS, PT. PERU (*car
plate*).

PEACE (s/l *piece*). 1. ORDER, QUIET, TRANQUILLITY (**opp** =
war); RIVER (Can). 2. **Gk goddesses** = *HORAE*, especially
IRENE (**Rom** = *PAX*).

PEACH *FRUIT*; *TREE*. *BETRAY*. DOLLY-BIRD, SMASHER.

PEAK (s/l pique). *HEAD*; HOLD; TILT (naut). BRIM, APEX, SUMMIT. PINE, WASTE AWAY.

PEAL (s/l *peel*). *RING*. CLAP, LOUD NOISE (thunder). *GRILSE*.

PEAR (s/l *pair, pare*). FRUIT/TREE (genus Pyrus communis); **pl comp** = *apples* (*rh sl*). [**beverage**: perry]; **types**: BERGAMOT, COMICE, CONFERENCE, FERTILITY, JOSEPHINE DE MALINES, LOUISE BONNE, WILLIAMS BON CHRETIEN, WINTER NELIS; ALLIGATOR, AVOCADO; ANCHOVY; PRICKLY.

PEARL *GEM* [oyster]; *anniversary* (30th); 'MARGARET'. PRECIOUS THING. *COLOUR* (white). BEAD, DROP. PICOT (lace). *BUCK* (films). RIVER (US). *TYPEFACE*.

PECK KISS; STAB WITH BEAK/BILL. *MEASURE*. GREGORY (films).

PECULIAR *Anag*. PARTICULAR, SPECIAL. ODD, STRANGE. EXEMPT. PRIVILEGED (eccles).

PEEL (s/l *peal*). PARE, *SKIN*. *JOHN* (*huntsman*; *dogs*). *RIVER* (*Can*). *ROBERT* (*police*). SHOVEL. TOWER.

PEELED (s/l pealed). 1. PARED, SKINNED. 2. Remove first and last letters, e.g. **Called peeled orange** (4) = *RANG*.

PEELER SKINNER (crypt). *POLICEMAN*.

PEER (s/l *pier*). NOBLEMAN: *BARON*, DUKE, EARL, *LORD*, MARQUIS, VISCOUNT. EQUAL, *FELLOW*. APPEAR; *LOOK*, PEEP, PRY. ~ GYNT (mus, Grieg). [Iolanthe (*G & S*)].

PEERESS FEMALE OF PEER. LADY LOOKER (crypt).

PEGASUS 1. Gk myth winged *horse* of *Bellerophon*. 2. *Constellation*. 3. Badge of the Airborne Forces.

PELT *SHY*, THROW. *SKIN*.

PEN BALLPOINT, BIRO, QUILL, STYLO, WRITE(R); **comp** = ink. SCRIBBLE. CAGE, CORRAL, ENCLOSURE, *FOLD*, STY. SWAN (*fem*).

PENELOPE 1. Gk myth wife of *Ulysses* and m of Telemachus who, to deter suitors in her husband's absence, said she could not answer them until she had finished making a *cloak* for Laertes, her f-in-law; each night she undid the previous day's work. 2. A minor *PLANET*. BIRD.

PENNILESS 1. BROKE; BORACIC LINT (*rh sl*). 2. Remove letters D or P from word, e.g. **Encourage to clean out — penniless** (4) = (p)URGE.

PENNY D, P. *COIN*, *COPPER*.

PENNYWEIGHT DWT, *MEASURE*.

PENSION LIFE PAYMENT, RETIREMENT PAY. BOARDING HOUSE. [*football* team].

PENULTIMATE LAST BUT ONE, hence Y (crypt).

PEP *GO*, VIGOUR, ZIP. ENCOURAGE, GINGER.

PEPYS (s/l peeps). DIARIST, NAVY SECRETARY, SAM(UEL), *WRITER* [Evelyn].

PERCH LENGTH, *MEASURE*, *POLE*, *ROD* (5½ yds). BASS, FISH. BALANCE; BAR, RAIL, ROOST. ALIGHT, *REST*, *SETTLE*.

PERFORM ACT, PLAY, *SING*. CARRY OUT, *DO*, *EXECUTE*.

PERFORMING ACTING, ON STAGE; *TURNING* (crypt). DOING.

PERI FAIRY, GOBLIN (Pers myth; Jamshid), IMP, SPRITE [Iolanthe, *G & S*].

PERIOD CLASS, TUITION. FULL STOP (US). PORTION OF TIME (hence TIM, ME etc, crypt), e.g. YEAR, LUSTRUM (5 yrs), QUINQUENNIUM (5 yrs), SEPTENARY (7 yrs), DECADE (10 yrs), CENTURY (100 yrs), MILLENNIUM (1,000 yrs).

PERIODICAL RECURRING, REGULAR. MAGAZINE, WEEKLY. [astronomy; chemistry].

PERIPHITES Gk myth *giant*, too large for his own legs to carry, who beat travellers to death with a massive *club*; he was finally killed by *Theseus*.

PERMANENT LASTING, INDEFINITE. MARCEL, *WAVE*.

~ **WAY** *RAILWAY*; IRON WAY, *TRACK*.

Pers Persian.

PERSEPHONE Also CORA. Gk myth Queen of the *Underworld*; d of *Zeus* and *Demeter*, she was carried off by *Pluto*. Hermes finally got her back, but she had eaten (a pomegranate seed) in the lower world, so she was permitted to spend only 8 months each year in the upper world — in order that Demeter would allow it to produce its fruits. **Rom** = PROSERPINE.

PERSEUS 1. Gk myth s of *Zeus* (who *transformed* into a shower of gold to visit *Danae* and f ~ in her prison cell). ~ slew *Medusa*, helped by *Athene*, the magic sword Herpe, the helmet of *Hades*, winged sandals, a magic bag and a mirror (he looked at Medusa only in the mirror, put her severed head in the bag, and escaped on winged heels, wearing the helmet which made him invisible). Mar to *Andromeda*, he eventually fulfilled a prophecy by (accidentally) killing Acrisius, his own grandfather. 2. *Constellation*.

PERSIAN IRANIAN [Xerxes, Darius, Satrap]. *CAT*, CATTY, FELINE; MIAOW.

PERT *ARCH*, JAUNTY, SAUCY (**opp** = *retiring*).

PET CARESS, PAT; *DARLING*, FAVOURITE, MASCOT. FONDLE, TAME (animal). TANTRUM, TIFF; ILL-HUMOURED, OFFENCE.

PETER 1. CORDITE, DYNAMITE, EXPLOSIVE, TNT. PRISON CELL; SAFE, STRONGBOX; WITNESS BOX (all sl). FADE, GIVE OUT. BLUE ~ (flag). BOY'S NAME; 'A ROCK'; **celeb**: ~ the Great (Russ *emperor*, tsar); ~ the *Hermit* (Fr monk); ~ Pan (*Barrie*); servant (R & J, *Shak*). 2. Known as Simon originally, St ~ was the s of Jonas and br of Andrew; he was a fisherman. A leading disciple who became a missionary (to the Jews; c.f. *Paul*), and one of the 12 *apostles*, he was the first Pope. Probably martyred in Rome *c*. A.D. 66 under *Nero*.

PETERBOROUGH **Episcopal sig** = PETRIBURG.

PETRIBURG *Episcopal sig* of PETERBOROUGH.

PG PARENTAL GUIDANCE (film *censorship*). LODGER, PAYING GUEST. [*monkey*].

PH ACIDITY, ALKALINITY (Sorensen).

PHAETON 1. CARRIAGE. BIRD. 2. Gk myth s of *Helios* and Clymene. He drove his f's *chariot* so dangerously that *Zeus* struck him down with a thunderbolt. [*Jehu*].

-PHAGY Eating of . . ., e.g. **hippophagy** = horses, **ichthyophagy** = fishes.

PHALANX INFANTRY, LINE, *SOLDIERS* (Gk; hoplite). *BONE*. STAMENS (bot).

PHANTOM GHOST, SPECTRE. *AIRCRAFT*.

PHARAOH (s/l faro). KING OF EGYPT (= GREAT HOUSE) [*Ptolemy*].

PHIL (s/l fill). PHILADELPHIA. PHILHARMONIC (mus). PHILOSOPHY. PHILIPPIANS. FLUTER.

PHILOGYNIST *Lover* of women.

PHILOSOPHER WISDOM SEEKER; MORALIZER, THEORIZER; **celeb**: ANAXAGORAS (Gk), ANISTHENES (Gk), THOMAS AQUINAS (It), ARISTIPPUS (Gk), ARISTOTLE (Gk), CATO (Rom), CHRYSIPPUS (Gk), DEMOCRITUS (Gk), DESCARTES (Fr), DIDEROT (Fr), DIODOTUS (Rom), *DIOGENES* (Gk), EPICTETUS (Gk),

EPICURUS (Gk), ERASMUS (NL), EURIPIDES (Gk), HEGEL (Ger), KANT (Ger), LEUCIPPUS (Gk), MONTAIGNE (Fr), NEWTON (Eng), NIETZSCHE (Ger), PASCAL (Fr), *PLATO* (Gk), RUSSELL (Eng), SANTAYANA (Sp), SCHWEGLER (Ger), SCHWEIZER (Swi), SENECA (Rom), SOCRATES (Gk), SPINOZA (NL), *SWIFT* (Eng), VOLTAIRE (Fr), XENOCRATES (Gk), ZENO (Gk). [~'s stone, alchemy; metaphysical ~, moral ~, natural ~].

PHLEGETHON *PYRIPHLEGETHON*.

PHOBIA *AVERSION*.

PHOEBE 1. A Titaness, Gk d of *Uranus* and *Ge*. 2. Associated with Artemis/*Diana* as goddess of the *moon* (MND, *Shak*). 3. A minor *planet*, the smallest satellite of *Saturn*. *BIRD*.

PHOEBUS Rom *god* of the *SUN*; also SOL. **Gk** = *APOLLO*, HELIOS; **Egy** = HORUS, RA; **Nor** = FREY; **Pers** = MITHRA; **Phoen** = BAAL.

Phoen Phoenicia, ~n.

PHOENIX 1. Fabulous bird which, every 500 years, built a pyre and burned itself to death; it was then reborn from the ashes. FUM (Ch). 2. A *constellation*. 3. DATE *PALM*. *THEATRE*. 4. US *State* capital.

PHOSPHORUS 1. Gk name for *VENUS* when seen as the *MORNING STAR* (**Rom** = Lucifer); **opp** = *Hesperus*. 2. *MINERAL*, P (*chem*).

PI (s/l *pie*). 1. DEVOUT, OVER-RELIGIOUS, PIOUS. 2. Gk letter; in maths, the ratio of the circumference of a circle to its diameter.

PIANO P, *QUIET* (mus); and see *music* (3). INSTRUMENT (mus).

PIE (s/l *pi*). *Anag*. COTTAGE ~, PIZZA, SHEPHERD'S, TART. *BIRD*, MAGPIE. *DOG*, MONGREL. CHAOS.

PIECE (s/l *peace*). 1. *BIT*, MORSEL; **pl comp** = bits. 2. Hidden word, e.g. **Piece of Spanish amateur pretence** (4) = SH*AM. 3. Constituent part of object indicated, e.g. **Dollar piece** = CENT.

PIER (s/l *peer*). *JETTY*. BRIDGE SUPPORT.

PIG POLICEMAN (sl). BILLET, LUMP (iron). Quadruped (genus Suidae), SWINE; **assembly** = drove, herd; **male** = BOAR; BARROW (castrated ~); **female** = SOW; **offspring** = PIGLET, SHOAT. [*Ch calendar*]. **Celeb**: MAJOR, MINIMUS, *NAPOLEON*, SNOWBALL, *SQUEALER* (Animal Farm, *Orwell*); BLAND, ROBINSON (*Potter*); BLANDINGS, Empress of (*Wodehouse*). **Breeds**:

BABIRUSSA	LANDRACE	SADDLEBACK
BERKSHIRE	LARGE BLACK	TAMWORTH
BUSH	LARGE WHITE	WARTHOG
ESSEX	*LINCOLN*	WESSEX
		WILD BOAR

PIGEON BIRD; HOMER (crypt); NUN ~, POUTER ~, TURBIT; **assembly** = flock, loft. MARK, SUCKER. [~ **pair** = one of each (boy and girl)].

PIGS EAR BEER (*rh sl*).

PIKE *FISH*, GAR, JACK. HILLTOP. ROAD, TOLL, TOLL-BAR. BILL, HALBERD, *WEAPON*. *DIVE* (swim).

PILATE PONTIUS. Mar to Procula; a bibl Rom *judge* and *governor* of Judea and Samaria, who tried *Jesus*. Ruled harshly, recalled to Rome, sui.

PILE CASTLE, HEAP, STATELY HOME. *POST*, STAKE. *NAP*. NUCLEAR FURNACE. **Pl** = HAEMORRHOIDS.

PILE-UP ACCIDENT, COLLISION, SMASH. CARPET (crypt). ELIP (dn, crypt).

PILGRIM 1. HOLY VOYAGER, TRAVELLER, VOYAGER [Haj (Mos); Islam; Mecca. Canterbury Tales (*Chaucer*); scollop/scallop]. MAYFLOWER SETTLER [~ Fathers (Plymouth, Mass, 1620)]. 2. From Bunyan's Pilgrim's Progress (from City of Destruction to Celestial City): CHRISTIAN, FAITHFUL, HOPEFUL [Apollyon (angel), Greatheart (guide to Christiana), Giant Despair (lord of Doubting Castle), Slough of Despond].

PILLAGE LOOT, PLUNDER, *SACK*. DISPENSARY (crypt).

PILLARS OF HERCULES Old name for ABYLA (CEUTA) and CALPE (GIBRALTAR).

PILOT AVIATOR, FLIER (**Union** = BALPA). *DOG* (Brontë). GUIDE, NAVIGATOR, *STEERSMAN*. TEST PRODUCT. *FISH*.

PINAFORE FROCK, PINNY; GREMIAL (*church dress*); OVERDRESS (crypt). LIGHT OPERA (*G & S*).

PINCH *STEAL* [*robber*]. GRIP, NIP, SQUEEZE. SMALL QUANTITY. EMERGENCY. ARREST. DRUDGE (Martin Chuzzlewit, *Dickens*); *SCHOOLMASTER* (C of Errors, *Shak*).

PINE LANGUISH, LONG, YEARN; PEAK, WASTE. *TREE*; DEAL, TIMBER.

PINK *FLOWER*, CARNATION; *COLOUR*, PALE RED, *ROSE*.

SNOOKER BALL (score 6). RED HUNTING COAT.
PERFECT. PRICK, WOUND. KNOCK, PRE-IGNITION.
BOAT (sailing).
PINKERTON Lieutenant Benjamin Franklin ~, USS *Lincoln* (Mme
Butterfly, Puccini). *DETECTIVES* (US).
PIOUS *PI*, RELIGIOUS.
PIPE BRIAR, CHURCHWARDEN, CLAY, COB,
MEERSCHAUM [*Holmes*]. TUBE [*Pluto*]. DRESS, TRIM.
MEASURE (beer, port). REED (mus). CONDUIT, *SEWER*.
PIPER BAGPIPE PLAYER, MUSICIAN [10th day of *Christmas* in
song]. BOATSWAIN (crypt). HANDKERCHIEF (crypt).
SMOKER, SHERLOCK *HOLMES* (crypt). PAN (crypt).
PIRATE COPY, PLUNDER, STEAL; *BORROW*. BUCCANEER,
CORSAIR, FREEBOOTER, PRIVATEER, ROVER [*cat.
G & S*]; **notorious:**

JOHN AVERY (LONG BEN)
JEAN *BART*
BEN-ALI (*Lofting*)
BLACKBEARD (EDWARD TEACH)
BONITO (BENNETT GRAHAM)
ANNE BONNY (m Rackham)
CALICO JACK (JOHN RACKHAM)
LORD CONRAD (Byron)
WILLIAM DAMPIER
JOHN ESQUEMELING
FLINT (Treasure Island)
FRANCIS *DRAKE*
FREDERIC (*G & S*)
HENRY EVERY
DIRK HATTERAICK
HOOK (Peter Pan)
PAUL JONES
WILLIAM KIDD
LAFITTE
SIR HENRY MORGAN
JOHN RACKHAM (CALICO JACK)
MARY *READ*
BASIL RINGROSE
BLACK BART ROBERTS
LONG BEN AVERY

LONG JOHN *SILVER* (Treasure Island)
BARTHOLOMEW SHARP
SMEE (Peter Pan)
SWAN
EDWARD TEACH (or THATCH)
EDWARD THATCH (or TEACH)
CAPT THOMPSON
LIONEL WAFER
WILLIAM WALKER
Pl = *Football* team (US). ~s of Penzance (*G & S*).

PISTOL (s/l pistil, pistole). DERRINGER, FIREARM, HANDGUN, *WEAPON*. *Shak* character (Merry Wives, H.iv, H.v; mar Ms *Quickly*).
PITCH GROUND, PLAYING FIELD (*cricket, football* etc). *CAST*, THROW; **comp** = toss. ASPHALT, BITUMEN, *TAR*. BLACK (*colour*).
PITCHER *EWER*, URN. DELIVERER, BASEBALL PLAYER. UNSTEADY ONE. ROADMAN, ROAD WORKER (crypt). STALLHOLDER (crypt). DOG (*Orwell*).
PITCHFORK HAYFORK. *CAST*, THRUST. TUNING FORK (mus, crypt).
PITMAN *MINER* (**pl** and **union** = NUM). SHORTHANDED (crypt).
PITY COMPASSION, MERCY; RUTH (arch). *ALAS*; REGRET, SORROW, SORRY.
PL PLURAL. POLAND (*car plate*).
PLACE (s/l *plaice*). PUT, *SET*. *SPOT*. COUNTRY HOUSE, *SEAT, STATELY HOME*.
PLACED PUT, SET. SEATED. LANDED GENTRY (crypt).
PLAGUE AFFLICTION, PESTILENCE, PUNISHMENT. *ANNOY*, BOTHER, NUISANCE, *TROUBLE*. **Gk** and **Rom god** = *APOLLO*. **Bibl** ~s: water into blood; frogs; lice; flies; murrain; boils; hail; locusts; darkness; death of firstborn.
PLAICE (s/l *place*). FLAT *FISH*.
PLAIN (s/l *plane*). CLEAR, EVIDENT, SIMPLE. STITCH (knitting; **opp** = purl). MOURN. LEVEL/OPEN TRACT: KIRGHIZ (USSR), LLANO (S Am), PAMPA (S Am), PRAIRIE (N Am), PUSZTA (Hung), SAVANNAH (tropics), SERENGETI (Tanz), STEPPES (USSR), TUNDRA (Arctic) [*grass*].
PLAN *Anag. CHART*, DESIGN, DIAGRAM, DRAWING,

LAYOUT, MAP. ARRANGE, PLOT, METHOD, SCHEME.
TIMETABLE.

PLANE (s/l *plain*). *TREE*. SCRAPER, SMOOTHER, TOOL.
LEVEL, SURFACE. *AIRCRAFT*; GLIDE.

PLANET 1. CHASUBLE, VESTMENT (eccles). 2. Heavenly body,
revolving round a star, as a satellite. **Major planets** of our own Sun
(in order of increasing distance and with their own satellites or
moons): *MERCURY*, *VENUS*, *EARTH* (Luna/Moon), *MARS*
(Deimos, Phobos), *JUPITER* (Callisto, *Europa*, *Ganymede*, *Io*),
SATURN (Dione, Enceladus, Hyperion, *Iapetus*, Janus, Mimas,
Miranda, *Phoebus*, *Rhea*, Tethys, *Titan*), *URANUS* (Ariel,
Oberon, Titania, Umbriel), *NEPTUNE* (Triton, *Nereid*), *PLUTO*.
There are also thousands of smaller bodies orbiting the Sun, mainly
between Mars and Jupiter, and most of them lumps of rock. Some
2,000 are large enough to be identified and named as asteroids or
minor planets, including: *CERES* (the largest; dia 1,000 km),
VESTA (dia 530 km), *PALLAS* (dia 600 km) and *JUNO* (dia
240 km), plus *CHIRON*, HERMES, *HYGEIA*, *ICARUS*, *IRIS*,
ISIS, KRYPTON (fict), *MINERVA*, *MINOS*, *MNEMOSYNE*,
NEMESIS, *NIOBE*, *PENELOPE*, *TROJANS*.

PLANT 1. FACTORY, MILL, WORKS; MACHINERY, TOOLS.
CONCEAL. HOAX. EMBED, FIX, SET. 2. *FLOWER* (q.v.),
FRUIT (q.v.), *HERB* (q.v.), REED, SHRUB, *SPICE*, *TREE*
(q.v.), *VEGETABLE* (q.v.), *WEED*, *WILD FLOWER/PLANT*
(q.v.); **parts**: carpel (ovary, ovule, stigma, style), nectary, petal,
pistil, root, sepal, stalk, stamen (anther, filament, pollen sac), stem
(bud, leaf, shoot), tendril, torus; **types**:

3-letters	BENE	*HERB*
BOX	BENT	IRID
ERS	*BLUE*	KANS
FOG	COCA	KAVA
HOP	COIX	LING
IVY	DISS	LYME
RYE	DOCK	MOSS
UDO (Ch)	DOOB	REED
	DURA	*RHEA*
4-letters	FERN	RUSA
AIRA	*FLAG*	RUSH
ALFA	GILL	SEGO
ANIL	HEMP	SUNN

TARE
TEFF
TORE
TUTU
VINE
WEED
WELD
WHIN
WOAD
WORT
YARR

5-letters
ABACA
ANISE
AROLD
BHANG
BOHEA
BRIER
BRIZA
BROOM
BUGLE
BUNCH
CAPER
CAREX
COUCH
CUTCH
DURRA
DWALE
ERICA
FURZE
GORSE
GRASS
GUACO
HALFA
HAULM
KEMPS
LIANA
MELIC
ORYZA
PANAX

PANIC
RHYNE
SEDGE
SISAL
SPEAR
SUMAC
THORN
VETCH
VIOLA

6-letters
ALSIKE
ARNICA
ARRACH
ARUNDO
BAJREE
BARLEY
BEDDER
BEJUCO
BETONY
BIBLUS
BLINKS
BOCAGE
BORAGE
BRIONY
BRYONY
BURNET
CACTUS
CASSIA
CEREUS
CICELY
CICUTA
CISSUS
CITRUS
COCKLE
COFFEE
COMFRY
CONIUM
COTTON
COWAGE
CROTON

CUMMIN
DARNEL
DESMID
DODDER
FESCUE
FILAGO
FIMBLE
FIORIN
FRUTEX
FUNGUS
GARLIC
GERVAO
GERVAS
GNETUM
GROMEL
HEDERA
HYPNUM
IBERIS
KALMIA
KNAWEL
KOUSSO
LOLIUM
LUPINE
MADDER
MALLOW
MARRAM
MATICO
MEDICK
MYRTLE
NARDUS
NETTLE
ORACHE
ORCHIL
ORPINE
OX-HEEL
PAIGLE
PAMPAS
PHLEUM
PRIVET
PROTEA
PTERIS

QUITCH
RADISH
RAMSON
REDTOP
RICCIA
RUPPIA
SABINE
SESAME
SESBAN
SESELI
SMILAX
SPURGE
SUMACH
TWITCH
UNIOLA
URTICA
VISCUM

7-letters
ACANTHA
ACONITE
ALE-HOOP
ALFALFA
ALL-GOOD
ALLSEED
ALYSSUM
AMELLUS
ASH-WORT
ATROPIN
AWL-WORT
BLAWORT
BOG-BEAN
BOG-RUSH
BRACKEN
BRAMBLE
BUGLOSS
BUG-WORT
BURDOCK
CALUMBA
CAMPION
CARAWAY

CARLUUS
CASSAVE
CATMINT
CLIVERS
COMFREY
CONEINE
COWBANE
COWSLIP
CUDWEED
DIONAEA
DITTANY
DOGWOOD
ELF-WORT
ESPARTO
EULALIA
FESTUCA
FOGGAGE
FOXTAIL
GENISTA
GINSENG (Ch)
HOGWEED
HEATHER
HEDEOMA
HEMLOCK
HENBANE
JASMINE
LUCERNE
MALACCA
MILFOIL
NAVETTE
OSMUNDA
POP-WEED
RAGWORT
SORGHUM
SPIGNEL
SQUITCH
THISTLE
TIMOTHY
VETIVER
WAGWANT
WHANGEE

ZIZANIA

8-letters
ACANTHUS
AGRIMONY
ANGELICA
BANEWORT
BEDSTRAW
BERBERRY
BINDWEED
BULLRUSH
CAMOMILE
CANWABIS
CLEAVERS
COWBERRY
DEMERARA
DOG-GRASS
DOG-WHEAT
ELEUSINE
FLAX-WORT
FLEABANE
FLEA-WORT
GYNERIUM
MANDRAKE
PLANTAIN
PONDWEED
PUFFBALL
PUSS-TAIL
STAR-WORT
VALERIAN
VERONICA
VIRGINIA
XANTHIUM

9+ letters
BELLADONNA
BLACKBERRY
BLACKTHORN
BLUEBERRY
CHICKWEED
CHOKEBERRY

CORIANDER	HUCKLEBERRY	PUSSY WILLOW
CRANBERRY	LADY'S THUMB	*RASPBERRY*
DANDELION	LIVERWORT	SPEARMINT
FORSYTHIA	LOGANBERRY	SPEEDWELL
GOOSEBERRY	MARIJUANA	STINKWEED
HOREHOUND	MONKSHOOD	TUMBLEWEED
HORSETAIL	PEPPERMINT	WINTERGREEN

PLATE COVER, ENCASE, PROTECTION, VENEER.
ENGRAVING (print). FILM (photo). RAILROAD.
CUTLERY, EPNS, SHEFFIELD. GOLD/SILVER TROPHY.
ASHET (Sc), DISH, PLATTER. FALSE TEETH. *RIVER*
(Braz). **Pl** = FEET (*rh sl*).

PLATINUM *METAL*; PT (*chem*); WHITE METAL; *anniversary*
(70th). BLONDE.

PLATO 1. Gk *poet* of the Old Comedy (*c*. 400 B.C.). 2. Gk
philosopher (*c*. 400 B.C.), the s of Aristo and Perictione. Pupil of
Socrates (who, the night before ~ arrived, dreamed that a *swan*
flew into his lap); ~ later travelled widely and associated with the
tyrant Dionysius, who imprisoned him. Freed later by a friend,
~ taught philosophy in his garden, or the Academy; pupils incl
Aristotle and Xenocrates.

PLAY ACT, DO, DRAMA, *PERFORM*, PIECE, REP, SHOW,
STAGE. BUSK, STRUM. GAMBOL, HAVE FUN.
LATITUDE, MOVEMENT, SLAP. BOWL, *PITCH*, SERVE
(games).

PLAYERS ACTORS, *CAST*, THESPIANS; [*Shak* characters].
BAND, MUSICIANS, OCTET, ORCHESTRA, QUARTET,
SEXTET. SIDE, TEAM. *CIGARETTE*.

PLAYFUL *ARCH*. FROLICSOME, HUMOROUS, SPORTIVE.

PLAYGROUND COURSE, COURT, DIAMOND, FIELD, *LINKS*,
PITCH, RINK, WICKET (all crypt). STAGE (crypt).
NURSERY (crypt). SCHOOL COURTYARD,
QUADRANGLE. And see *cricket*, *football*, *rugby* etc.

PLAYGROUP KINDERGARTEN, NURSERY SCHOOL. *CAST*
(crypt). *BAND*, ORCHESTRA, *PLAYERS* (crypt). *SIDE*,
TEAM, XI, XV (crypt).

PLAYTIME CURTAIN-UP (crypt). RHYTHM, TEMPO (crypt).
BULLY-OFF, FIRST BALL, KICK-OFF, START, WHISTLE
(crypt).

PLAY VIOLIN BOW, *FIDDLE*.

PLEASE (s/l pleas). BEGUILE, *CHARM*, GIVE PLEASURE (opp = *annoy*). THINK FIT. BE GOOD ENOUGH, KINDLY.

PLEDGE BAIL, PROMISE, SURETY. TOAST. ABSTINENCE (TT). HOCK, *PAWN*, *POP* [*weasel*].

PLEIADES Seven d of *Atlas*, placed among the stars and associated with *rain* and *nature*; **names**: ALCYONE, CELAENO, *ELECTRA*, *MAIA* (the eldest), STEROPE and TAYGETE, with one who was invisible, MEROPE.

PLIERS PINCERS. CABDRIVERS, TAXIS (crypt).

PLOT CABAL, CONSPIRACY; CONSPIRE, INTRIGUE, *PLAN*. *CHART*, NAVIGATE. ALLOTMENT, BED, GARDEN, GREEN, LAWN, PATCH, YARD (US).

PLOVER WADING *BIRD*; **types**: AVOCET, CURLEW, DOTTEREL, KILLDEER, LAPWING, OYSTERCATCHER, PE(E)WIT, SNIPE, STILT, TURNSTONE, WHAUP, WHIMBREL.

PLUM (s/l plumb). BEST, GOOD. *COLOUR*, FRUIT TREE genus Prunus: **types**: CATALONIA, GREENGAGE, MIRABELLE, VICTORIA.

PLUTO 1. *DOG* (Disney). Pipe-line under the ocean (acronym); FUEL SUPPLY. 2. Gk and Rom *god* of the *UNDERWORLD* (**Gk** = HADES), br of *Jupiter* and *Neptune*, he carried off Proserpine (**Gk** = *Persephone*). Synonymous with AIDONEUS and DIS. 3. A *PLANET*.

PLUTUS Gk *god* of WEALTH.

PLUVIUS Rom *god* of *RAIN*. **Gk** = *JUPITER*.

PM AFTERNOON, POST MERIDIEM. *PRIME MINISTER*. PROMETHIUM (*chem*). POST MORTEM. PROVOST MARSHAL.

POET BARD, *WRITER*; LINESMAN (crypt); SWAN (of Avon). **Muses** = Calliope (epic ~), Euterpe (lyric ~), Thalia (bucolic ~). [*Argonaut*]. **Celeb** (PL = Poet Laureate):

3-letters

POE, Edgar Allen	US
PYE, Henry James (PL9)	Eng

4-letters

GUNN, Thomson William	Eng

HILL, Geoffrey William	Sc
HOOD, Thomas	Eng
HUNT, James Henry Leigh	Eng
LEAR, Edward	Eng
LI-PO (8th cent)	Ch
MUIR, Edwin	Sc
OWEN, Wilfred	Eng

POPE, Alexander — Eng
ROWE, Nicholas (PL4) — Eng
SADI — Pers
TATE, Nahum (PL3) — Eng
WAIN, John — Eng

5-letters

AUDEN, Wystan Hugh — Eng
BLAKE, William — Eng
BYRON, Lord George
Gordon — Eng
DANTE (Alighieri) — It
DAVID (bibl) — Jew
DONNE, John — Eng
ELIOT, Thomas
Stearns — US/Eng
FROST, Robert — US
GOSSE, Sir Edmund
William — Eng
GOWER, John — Eng
HARDY, Thomas — Eng
HOMER (*c.* 1000 B.C.) — Gk
KEATS, John — Eng
KEYES, Sidney — Eng
LEWIS, Alun — Wal
LEWIS, Cecil Day
(PL16) — Eng
LUCAN, M Annaeus
(A.D. 39–65) — Rom
MOORE, Marianne — US
OLSON, Charles — US
OPPEN, George — US
PATER, Walter — Eng
PLATH, Sylvia — US
PLATO (428–389 B.C.) — Gk
POUND, Ezra Loomis — US
SAADI — Pers
SCOTT, Sir Walter — Sc
WATTS, Isaac — Eng
YEATS, William Butler — Ire

6-letters

AUSTIN, Alfred (PL13) — Eng
BINYON, Robert
Laurence — Eng
BISHOP, Elizabeth — US
CIBBER, Colley (PL6) — Eng
DOBSON, Henry Austin — Eng
DRYDEN, John (PL1) — Eng
EUSDEN, Laurence
(PL5) — Eng
FULLER, Roy — Eng
GRAVES, Robert
Ranke — Eng
HENLEY, William
Ernest — Eng
HORACE (65–8 B.C.) — Rom
HUGHES, Ted (PL18) — Eng
JONSON, Ben (unofficial
PL1) — Eng
LARKIN, Philip — Eng
LOWELL, Amy — US
LOWELL, Robert — US
MILTON, John — Eng
PINDAR (522–442 B.C.) — Gk
PORTER, Peter — Aus
RUSKIN, John — Eng
SAPPHO (*c.* 600
B.C.; fem) — Gk
SEXTON, Anne — US
THOMAS, Dylan — Wal
VIRGIL, Maro
(70–19 B.C.) — Rom
WARTON, Thomas
(PL8) — Eng

7-letters

BENTLEY, Edmund
Clerihew — Eng
BLUNDEN, Edmund
Charles — Eng

BRIDGES, Robert
Seymour (PL14)   Eng
CARROLL, Lewis (see
Alice)   Eng
CHAUCER, Geoffrey   Eng
CORNISH, Sir William   Eng
DARYUSH, Elizabeth   Eng
DOUGLAS, Keith   Sc
EUPOLIS (446–411 B.C.)   Gk
FLECKER, James Elroy   Eng
GILBERT, Sir William
Schwenck   Eng
HERBERT, George   Eng
HERRICK, Robert   Eng
HOPKINS, Gerard
Manley   Eng
JOHNSON, Lionel Pigot   Eng
KHAYYAM, Omar   Pers
KIPLING, Rudyard   Eng
MARVELL, Andrew   Eng
NEWBOLT, Sir Henry
John   Eng
PLAUTUS, T Maccius
(*c.* 250 B.C.)   Rom
SHELLEY, Percy
Bysshe   Eng
SITWELL, Dame Edith   Eng
SITWELL, Sacheverell   Eng
SKELTON, John   Eng
SOUTHEY, Robert
(PL10)   Eng
STEVENS, Wallace   US
TENNANT, Stephen James
Napier   Eng
TERENCE (190–158
B.C.)   Rom
WHITMAN, Walt   US

8-letters
BERRYMAN, John   US

BETJEMAN, Sir John
(PL17)   Eng
CRATINUS (519–422
B.C.)   Gk
DAVENANT, Sir Wm
(unofficial PL2)   Eng
FLETCHER, John   Eng
GINSBERG, Allen   US
LANGLAND, William   Eng
LAWRENCE, David
Herbert   Eng
MALLARME, Stephane   Fr
MENANDER (342–291
B.C.)   Gk
PETRARCH, Francesco   It
PHILAMON (myth)   Gk
PHILEMON (*c.* 360 B.C.)   Gk
SHADWELL, Thomas
(PL2)   Eng
TENNYSON, Alfred Lord
(PL12)   Eng
WILLIAMS, William
Carlos   US

9+ letters
AESCHYLUS (525–456
B.C.)   Gk
ARISTOPHANES (*c.* 444
B.C.)   Gk
CAECILIUS (230–168
B.C.)   Rom
CHESTERTON, Gilbert
Keith   Eng
COLERIDGE, Samuel
Taylor   Eng
CUNSTANCE, Olive   Eng
DOOLITTLE, Hilda   US
FITZGERALD, Edward   Eng
GOLDSMITH, Oliver   Ire
LONGFELLOW, Henry
Wadsworth   US

MASEFIELD, John		SOPHOCLES (495–406	
(PL15)	Eng	B.C.)	Gk
PHILAMMON (myth)	Gk	SWINBURNE, Algernon	
PHRYNICHUS (*c.* 500		Charles	Eng
B.C.)	Gk	WHITEHEAD, William	
SHAKESPEARE,		(PL7)	Eng
William	Eng	WORDSWORTH, William	
		(PL11)	Eng

POETRY 1. LINES, ODE, *VERSE* (**opp** = prose). 2. **Gk myth Muse** = *CALLIOPE*, *ERATO*, EUTERPE.

POINT AIM, GIST, OBJECT. INDICATE, SHOW. HEADLINE, *NESS*, PT. APEX, *TIP*, TOE. NEEDLE, PIN. *CRICKETER*, FIELDER. E, N, S OR W, EAST, NORTH, SOUTH or WEST. PUNCTUATE. REFACE (bricks and mortar). SWITCH (rly).

POINTER *ARROW*, *DIRECTOR*, INDICATION. *DOG*.

POINTLESS 1. MEANINGLESS. NO SCORE. BLUNT. 2. Remove letters indicating cardinal points from word(s) indicated, e.g. **Type of communication that's read is now pointless** (5) = R*ADI**O*.

Pol Poland (*car plate* = PL). Political.

POLE (s/l *poll*). N, S, NORTH, SOUTH. *MEASURE* (length): *PERCH*, ROD. EAST EUROPEAN, SLAV. PILLAR, *POST*, MAST. QUANT.

POLICE CAR BLACK MARIA, PANDA-CAR, SQUAD-CAR, Z-CAR.

POLICEMAN BOBBY (Sir Robert Peel), BOW STREET RUNNER (Henry Fielding), COP, DICK, PEELER (Sir Robert Peel), *PIG*, ROZZER (all sl). *MP*, PC, SP. **Pl** = CID, FBI, FEDS, PD, FORCE, FUZZ, GESTAPO [*detective*]. **Celeb**: DAY (*Kipling*), DIXON (TV), MR PLOD.

POLISH *BUFF*, CLEAN, RUB; SHEEN, VENEER. OF POLAND.

Polit Political.

POLL (s/l *pole*). HEAD. VOTE. *PARROT*. SAMPLE. CUT OFF, LOP.

POLLUX 1. Gk myth *twin* of *Castor*. Skilful boxer and patron of seamen. 2. One of the *Argonauts*.

POLY(HY)MNIA 1. Gk myth; one of the nine *Muses* (hymns). 2. A minor *PLANET*.

POMPEY 1. PORTSMOUTH (sl). FOUR (*rh sl*). 2. Roman leader and general (106–48 B.C.). Maintained an uneasy alliance with *Caesar* (with Crassus, they formed the first triumvirate in 60 B.C.); a great warrior. Mar Julia (d of Caesar). Political ambition finally brought him into open conflict with Caesar, and civil war followed. After being defeated at Pharsalus in 48 B.C., he fled to Egypt, where he was ass by Septimus on the orders of Ptolemy's ministers as he was being rowed ashore. 3. *Shak* characters (A and C); and *clown* in M for M.

PONY *HORSE*, NAG. GLASS. £25 (sl).

POOL KIT BALLS, CUE, CHALK, REST, TABLE. DIVING BOARD, FILTER.

POP *FATHER*. BANG. MUSIC. PAWN, PLEDGE (*weasel*). *DRINK*. SOCIETY (*Eton* prefects).

PORCELAIN *CERAMICS*.

PORPOISE 1. UNDULATE. *CETACEAN* MAMMAL; WHALE (genus Phocaena). **Assembly** = school. 2. Character in *Alice*.

PORT P, LARBOARD (arch), *LEFT*. *WINE*. *GATE*(WAY), HARBOUR. *BEARING*, CARRIAGE. LIGHT, OPENING, WINDOW.

Port Portugal (*car plate* = P). [*patron saint*].

PORTER BEER, *DRINK*. DOOR-KEEPER, GATE-KEEPER. BAGGAGE CARRIER. *POET*, *WRITER*.

PORTUGAL P (*car plate*). [patron saint = St George].

POSEIDON Gk god of the sea (**Rom** = *NEPTUNE*), allied to *Nereus* (**Rom** = Oceanus). Son of Cronos (**Rom** = *Saturn*) and *Rhea*; br to *Zeus* and *Hades*. On dividing the universe with his two brs, ~ got the Seas, Zeus the *Heavens*, and Hades the *Underworld*. Mar *Amphitrite* and f of Triton (*merman*); ~ was also god of *horses*.

POSER PROBLEM. *MODEL*, SITTER.

POSSESSIVE 1. GRASPING, *MISERLY*, RAPACIOUS. *OWN-ING*. 2. Put into the possessive case, e.g. **He is possessive** = HIS.

POST *PILE*, *POLE*, STAKE. *DELIVERY*, MAIL; SEND. APPOINTMENT, JOB, *SITUATION*. *MEASURE* (paper size).

POSTER *AD*, *BILL*, HOARDING, NOTICE, PLACARD. LETTER SENDER (crypt).

POSTHOLDER INCUMBENT. ENVELOPE, LETTERBOX, MAILBAG, MAILBOX, PILLARBOX (all crypt).

POST HOLE LETTER/PILLAR BOX (crypt).

POST SCRIPT AFTERTHOUGHT, PS.

POT COOKPOT, PAN. *DRUG*. POCKET, SINK (billiards, pool, snooker).

POTASSIUM *METAL*; K (*chem*).
POTATO EARTH-APPLE (arch); MURPHY, SPUD, YAM; KING
EDWARD (hence R*ED or R*TED [eyes]).
POTENTIALLY *Anag.* CAN BE, MAYBE; CAPABLE,
POSSIBLY. CHARGED (elect).
POTTER 1. DAWDLE, LOITER, WANDER. WORK
(desultorily). BILLIARD/POOL/SNOOKER PLAYER (crypt).
CLAY WORKER, hence any maker of *ceramics* (q.v.),
BOWLER, THROWER (crypt). *CONDUCTOR* (mus).
~'s Field, see *Judas* (2). 2. Stephen ~, WRITER (humorist;
Lifemanship; One-upmanship). 3. Beatrix ~, WRITER
(children's); **books**: Appley Dapply's Nursery Rhymes; Benjamin
Bunny; Cecily Parsley's Nursery Rhymes; A Fierce Bad Rabbit;
The Flopsy Bunnies; Ginger and Pickles; Jemima Puddle-Duck;
Johnny Town-Mouse; Little Pig Robinson; Miss Moppet; Mr
Jeremy Fisher; Mr Tod; Mrs Tiggy-Winkle; Mrs Tittlemouse; Peter
Rabbit; The Pie and the Patty Pan; Pigling Bland; Samuel
Whiskers; Squirrel Nutkin; The Tailor of Gloucester; Timmy
Tiptoes; Tom Kitten; Two Bad Mice; **characters**: Babbity Bumble
(bee); Cousin Ribby, Mittens, Moppet, Simkin, Tabitha Twitchit,
Tom Kitten (*cats*); Chippy Hackee (chipmunk); John Joiner, Kep
(*dogs*); *Drake*, Jemima & Rebecca Puddle-Duck (*ducks*); Mr
Jackson, Jeremy Fisher (*frogs*); Mrs Tiggy-Winkle (hedgehog);
Farmer *Potatoes*, Mr & Mrs McGregor, Tailor of Gloucester
(humans); Johnny Town-Mouse, Thomasina, Mrs Tittlemouse
(mice); Old Brown (*owl*); Bland, Robinson (*pigs*); Benjamin,
Flopsy, Mopsy, Cotton-Tail & Peter (*rabbits*); Aunt Maria, Samuel
Whiskers (rats); Nutkin, Silvertail, Timmy & Goody Tiptoes,
Twinkleberry (squirrels).
POTTERY *CERAMICS* [*five towns*]; *anniversary* (9th).
BILLIARD/POOL/SNOOKER HALL or TABLE (crypt).
POUCHED BAGGED, CAUGHT, POSSESSED. *MARSUPIAL*.
POUND L, LB, *MEASURE* (weight). COIN, *CURRENCY* (UK);
QUID, SOVEREIGN. PULSATE, THROB; *BEAT*, HAMMER,
PUMMEL. ENCLOSURE, PEN. *MILITARY LEADER*.
POET, WRITER.
POUT *FISH*, WHITING. PROTRUDE, SULKY. [pigeon].
PP *PAGES*. PER PRO, PROXY. PAST PARTICIPLE.
PR PUBLIC RELATIONS, ADVERTISING.
PRECIOUS STONE *GEM*, JEWEL.
PRECIS *SUMMARY*.

PREFIX HANDLE, TITLE. ADD, QUALIFY; INTRODUCE.
[metric ~, see *International units*].
PREMISE INFERENCE, INTRODUCE [logic]. AFORESAID,
FOREGOING. **Pl** = *BUILDING*, HOUSE, OFFICES.
PREPARED *Anag.* COMPOSED, FIT, READY. MIXED (*chem*).
ALREADY PEELED (crypt).
PRESENT NOW; EXISTING, OCCURRING. READY (arch).
AT HAND, ON SITE, THERE. DONATION, GIFT; EXHIBIT,
OFFER. APPEAR, INTRODUCE, RECOMMEND. AIM,
SALUTE (mil). *PUT UP* (petition). **Pl** = DOCUMENT (leg).
~ **DAY** NOW, *AD. ANNIVERSARY*, BIRTHDAY, *CHRISTMAS*
etc (crypt).
PRESIDENT P. MANAGING DIRECTOR (US). GOVERNOR
(arch), HEAD (of Board, State, Country); **~s of the USA since
independence**:

*GEORGE WASHINGTON	Fed	1789–97
JOHN ADAMS	Fed	1797–1801
*THOMAS JEFFERSON	Rep	1801–09
JAMES MADISON	Rep	1809–17
JAMES MONROE	Rep	1817–25
JOHN QUINCEY ADAMS	Rep	1825–29
ANDREW JACKSON	Dem	1829–37
MARTIN VAN BUREN	Dem	1837–41
WILLIAM H. HARRISON	Whig	1841 (d in office)
JOHN TYLER	Whig	1841–45
JAMES K. POLK	Dem	1845–49
ZACHARY TAYLOR	Whig	1849–50 (d in office)
MILLARD FILLMORE	Whig	1850–53
FRANKLIN PIERCE	Dem	1853–57
JAMES BUCHANAN	Dem	1857–61
*ABRAHAM LINCOLN	Rep	1861–65 (ass)
ANDREW JOHNSON	Rep	1865–69
ULYSSES S. GRANT	Rep	1869–77
RUTHERFORD B. HAYES	Rep	1877–81
JAMES A. GARFIELD	Rep	1881 (ass)
CHESTER A. ARTHUR	Rep	1881–85
GROVER CLEVELAND	Dem	1885–89
BENJAMIN HARRISON	Rep	1889–93
GROVER CLEVELAND	Dem	1893–97

WILLIAM McKINLEY	Rep	1897–1901 (ass)
*THEODORE ROOSEVELT	Rep	1901–09
WILLIAM HOWARD TAFT	Rep	1909–13
WOODROW WILSON	Dem	1913–21
WARREN G. HARDING	Rep	1921–23 (d in office)
CALVIN COOLIDGE	Rep	1923–29
HERBERT C. HOOVER	Rep	1929–33
FRANKLIN D. ROOSEVELT	Dem	1933–45 (d in office)
HARRY S. TRUMAN	Dem	1945–53
DWIGHT D. EISENHOWER	Rep	1953–61
JOHN F. KENNEDY	Dem	1961–63 (ass)
LYNDON B. JOHNSON	Dem	1963–69
RICHARD M. NIXON	Rep	1969–74 (resigned)
GERALD R. FORD	Rep	1974–76 (nominated)
JIMMY CARTER	Dem	1976–80
RONALD REAGAN	Rep	1980–

* = Head is carved at Mt Rushmore.

PRESS FOURTH *ESTATE*, NEWSPAPERS, *PAPERS*, *MEDIUM*.
PRINTING MACHINE. API, BUP, GRUB STREET,
REUTER, TASS, UPI, XINHUA. *IRON*; SQUASH,
SQUEEZE. CONSCRIBE, SHANGHAI (naut arch). *URGE*.
~ **CHIEF** ED, PRO.
~ **GANG** RECRUITING PARTY [Andrew Miller, conscription,
draft, national service, **opp** = *volunteer*]. EDITORS, NUJ,
PRINTERS, *REPORTERS* (crypt).
~ **MAN** ED(ITOR), REPORTER. IRONER, LAUNDRYMAN
(crypt).
PRETENDER CLAIMANT, OLD ~, YOUNG ~ (s, grandson of
James II). ACTOR (crypt).
PRIAM Gk myth last king of *Troy*; mar (1) Arisbe, (2) Hecuba, and f
of *Cassandra*, and 50 s, incl *Hector* and *Paris*. [T and C (*Shak*)].
PRICKLY SPINY, THORNY. HEDGEHOG, PORCUPINE,
URCHIN (crypt). TINGLING, UP-TIGHT.
PRIDE 1. AMOUR-PROPRE, ARROGANCE. HUBRIS. BEST,
PICK. [~ and Prejudice (*Austen*); fall]. 2. *Assembly* of lions.
PRIEST CANON, *CHURCHMAN*, MINISTER; [*Chaucer*].
AARON, *ELI*, *ELIJAH*, *ELISHA*, EZEKIEL. *ISLAND*.

PRIMARY COLOURS GREEN, RED, VIOLET (in painting: BLUE, RED, YELLOW).
PRIMATE SENIOR *CHURCHMAN*. APE, HIGH MAMMAL, MAN, *MONKEY*.
PRIME MINISTER PRINCIPAL MINISTER OF STATE, PM; CABINET MAKER (crypt). **British ~s since 1900:**

MARQUIS OF SALISBURY	Cons	1895–1902
A. J. BALFOUR	Cons	1902–05
SIR H. CAMPBELL-BANNERMAN	Lib	1905–08
H. H. ASQUITH	Lib	1908–15
H. H. ASQUITH	Coaln	1915–16
D. LLOYD GEORGE	Coaln	1916–22
A. BONAR LAW	Cons	1922–23
STANLEY BALDWIN	Cons	1923–24
J. RAMSAY MACDONALD	Lab	1924
STANLEY BALDWIN	Cons	1924–29
J. RAMSAY MACDONALD	Lab	1929–31
J. RAMSAY MACDONALD	Nat	1931–35
STANLEY BALDWIN	Nat	1935–37
NEVILLE CHAMBERLAIN	Nat	1937–39
NEVILLE CHAMBERLAIN	War Cab	1939–40
WINSTON S. CHURCHILL	War Cab	1940–45
CLEMENT ATTLEE	Lab	1945–51
SIR WINSTON CHURCHILL	Cons	1951–55
SIR ANTHONY EDEN	Cons	1955–57
HAROLD MACMILLAN	Cons	1957–63
SIR ALEC DOUGLAS-HOME	Cons	1963–64
HAROLD WILSON	Lab	1964–70
EDWARD HEATH	Cons	1970–74
HAROLD WILSON	Lab	1974–76
JAMES CALLAGHAN	Lab	1976–79
MARGARET THATCHER	Cons	1979–

PRIMUS ELDEST, FIRST. BISHOP (Sc).
PRINCE(SSE)S ROYALS. *THEATRE*.
PRINCIPAL (s/l *principle*). CHIEF, *HEAD*, MAIN. *CAPITAL*.
PRINCIPLE (s/l *principal*). *LIGHT*, STANDARD, TENET.
PRISE (s/l *prize*). *FORCE*, LEVER, PURCHASE. Also = *PRIZE*.
PRISON *GAOL* [M for M (*Shak*)].
PRISONER GAOLBIRD, LAG, CONVICT, HOSTAGE; [*patron*

saint]; *CELLIST* (crypt); **celeb**: COL ALTAMONT (Pendennis, Thackeray); SAMUEL BURTON (Kingsley); COUNT OF MONTE CRISTO (Dumas); *LIONHEART* (Eng king); MAGWITCH (Great Ex, *Dickens*); DR MANETTE (shoemaker, 105 North Tower, 2 Cities, *Dickens*); MAN IN THE IRON MASK (Dumas); JEAN VALJEAN (Les Misérables, Victor Hugo); ~ OF ZENDA (Elphberg, *Hope*).

PRIVATE PERSONAL, RESTRICTED, RETIRED, SECLUDED, SECRET; ARCANE, ESOTERIC (**opp** = public). GI, PFC (US), RANKER, SOLDIER, TOMMY (ATKINS).

PRIZE (s/l *prise*). CUP, *REWARD*, TROPHY. CAPTIVE. Also = *PRISE* (arch).

PRO PUBLIC RELATIONS OFFICER, ADMAN. PROFESSIONAL (**opp** = amateur). FOR (**opp** = *anti*, con). PUBLIC RECORD OFFICE.

PROCEED GO, GO ON, MAKE WAY. *ACT*, SUE. *ISSUE*, ORIGINATE. **Pl** = *Anag*. MONEY, RECEIPTS.

PROCESSED *Anag*. *TREATED*. PROGRESSED, TRAVELLED.

PROCRUSTES Gk myth *robber*, who tailored his victims to his *bed* (by amputation or stretching, as appropriate); killed by *Theseus*.

PRODUCT *Anag.*, e.g. **Nuclear product** = UNCLEAR. GOODS, LINE, OUTPUT, RESULT. MULTIPLIED.

PROFIT (s/l *prophet*). ADVANTAGE, BENEFIT, GAIN, RETURN.

PROMETHEUS Gk myth *TITAN*, who stole fire from Mt *Olympus* to give to mankind. Chained by *Vulcan* to a rock, where a vulture (Ethon) fed daily on his liver, only for it to grow again each night. Rescued by *Hercules*.

PRONOUNCED DECIDED, MARKED. DELIVERED, SOUNDED, UTTERED. See *Pronunciation* below.

PRONUNCIATION Many words sound like others which are spelled differently, and this can affect the meaning of a clue, or otherwise lead to the correct answer. 'Court' and 'caught' can introduce an obvious play on courtship and being caught in matrimony; sometimes there are three different interpretations, such as 'cruise', 'crews' and 'cruse'. Such words are often hinted at by use of phrases like '. . . we listen to . . .', '. . . it sounds as though . . .', '. . . a pronounced . . .', or some such in the clue. Thus: **We hear of a sea voyage — unending for widows** (5) means that, when read aloud, the answer sounds like a sea voyage, or cruise; **unending for widows** reveals that it should be the widow's CRUSE which, in biblical times, never emptied.

But don't necessarily think that all is as straightforward even as this. If the puzzle setter can turn a word to his advantage, he will do so. An obvious example is 'flower' which, besides meaning a plant, can mean something which flows, i.e. a river. Even if you are prepared for this kind of deviousness, you may allow your mind to be programmed to accept the wrong pronunciation. The clue **Rows of beans cultivated by our forefathers?** (6, 4) may lead to the following train of thought: 'Rows could be tiers, ranks, lines or files; beans could be haricot, runner or broad.' But the popular phrase 'a row of beans' has been deliberately suggested in order to mislead, for rows can also mean 'dins, noises, battles, fights, or shindies'. This clue requires the answer FRENCH WARS.

The moral is to examine clues for words or phrasing which might imply alternative spelling to produce a similar sound, or alternative sound to produce a different meaning. Where an entry in this Companion sounds like another word, its explanation starts (s/l . . .). Those words capable of unusual interpretation, not always through different pronunciation (but frequently), are too many to list separately but they have been noted in their individual entries, usually by the addition of the word (crypt) to show that a cryptic interpretation is necessary. Besides **flower** = plant and river, and **row** = tier or din mentioned above (or paddle), examples include **banker** = financier or river (between two banks), **sewer** = drain or seamstress, **number** = digit or anaesthetic (makes one numb), **fast time** = high speed or lent/ramadan, **crew** = ship's complement or the past tense of crow (like a cockerel). There are many, and the puzzle setter will usually be one jump ahead of you, so be alert. See also *punctuation*.

PROOF OF DEBT BILL, INVOICE, IOU, MARKER.

PROPERTY ATTRIBUTE, CHARACTERISTIC, *QUALITY*. BELONGINGS, CHATTELS, POSSESSIONS; OWNING; REAL ESTATE. COSTUME, FURNITURE (theat).

PROPHECY FORETELLING. **Gk god** = *APOLLO* [Cassandra; Macbeth (*Shak*), A and C (*Shak*); *Oedipus*; *Perseus*].

PROPHET (s/l *profit*). FORECASTER, DIVINER, *SEER*, SOOTHSAYER, VISIONARY. [Old Moore]. **Celeb, Gk myth**: AMPHIARUS (*argonaut*); CALCHAS (*Troy*; he d when he met superior ~ (Mopsus) as foretold by oracle); MELAMPOS (first *doctor*); MOPSUS (*argonaut*); PHINEUS (*blind*; *harpies*); TIRESIAS (*blind*; golden *staff*). **Biblical**:

AMOS	JEREMIAH
DANIEL	JEREMY
ELI	JOEL
ELIJAH (ELIAS)	JONAH
ELISHA	MALACHI
ENOCH	MICAH
EZEKIEL	NAHUM
HABBAKKUK	OBADIAH
HAGGAI	*SAMUEL*
HOSEA	ZACHARIAH
IDDO	ZEPHANIAH
ISAIAH	ZOROASTER

PROPHETESS Fem *Prophet*, *SIBYL* (q.v.), SOOTHSAYER
  [*oracle*]; **celeb (bibl)**: ANNA (Luke 2); DEBORAH (Judges 4, 5);
  celeb (myth): AMALTHEA; *CASSANDRA*; SIBYL (of Cumea);
  celeb (other): MOTHER SHIPTON; *JOAN* (of Arc).
PROSERPINE 1. Rom eq of *PERSEPHONE*. 2. A minor *PLANET*.
PROSPERITY God: Gk = AGATHODAEMON. **Rom** = GENIUS.
PROVERB ADAGE, APHORISM, BYWORD, MAXIM, SAW,
  SAYING. **Pl** = BOOK (bibl). GAME.
PROVINCE 1. AREA, BRANCH, BUSINESS, DEPARTMENT,
  FIELD, SPHERE. 2. DISTRICT (eccles), ADMINISTRATIVE
  DIVISION, TERRITORY. 3. **Specifically of Canada**:

ALBERTA	AL
BRITISH COLUMBIA	BC
MANITOBA	MAN
NEW BRUNSWICK	NB
NEWFOUNDLAND	NF
N W TERRITORIES	NWT
NOVA SCOTIA	NS
PRINCE EDWARD ISLAND	PEI
ONTARIO	ONT
QUEBEC	Q
SASKATCHEWAN	SAS
THE YUKON	YUK

PS POST SCRIPT, AFTERTHOUGHT. POLICE SERGEANT.
  PRIVATE SECRETARY. PROMPT SIDE. PSALM.
PSYCHE 1. MIND, SOUL, SPIRIT. 2. MOTH. 3. Gk and Rom

myth maiden; *Venus* envied her *beauty* and sent *Cupid* to make her fall for the most contemptible of all men, but Cupid fell in love with her himself. Enslaved by a jealous Venus, ~ eventually became a goddess and was reunited with Cupid. Is often represented with *butterfly* wings. 4. A minor *PLANET*.

PT PHYSICAL TRAINING; PE, GYMNASTICS. PLATINUM (*chem*). *POINT*.

PTOLEMY KING OF EGYPT. Successive kings (I-IX) reigned from 323–81 B.C., notable chiefly for their cruelty, incest (they regularly married their sisters or mothers, who were as regularly called *Cleopatra* and as cruel as their husbands), and the loss of territory. Particularly notable were ~ V (Epiphanes; 205–181 B.C.) who is the subject of the *Rosetta Stone*; ~ X (Alexander II; 81 B.C.) who married his cousin Cleopatra Berenice and immediately had her assassinated, whereupon rioters did the same for him; ~ XI (Auletes; 80–51 B.C.) who was expelled to Rome, where he bribed *Pompey* to reinstate him in 55 B.C. (he murdered his own daughter Berenice); ~ XII (son of ~ XI; 51–47 B.C.) who reigned jointly with his sis Cleopatra (the well-known one) with whom he quarrelled and, when *Caesar* took her side, he was drowned escaping; ~ XIII (br of ~ XII; 47–43 B.C.) who was appointed by Caesar to marry his sis Cleopatra and rule jointly, but she had him assassinated during the Alexandrine war.

PUB *BAR*, BISTRO(T), INN, *LOCAL*, PH (abbr), *TAVERN*. *PUBLIC*. PUBLISHED.

PUBLICAN *HOST*, INNKEEPER, *LANDLORD*. TAX-GATHERER (bibl).

PUBLICATION *ISSUE*. BOOK, MAGAZINE, PAPER, WEEKLY.

PUBLIC SCHOOL BOARDING-, ENDOWED-, PRIVATE-SCHOOL; **celeb**:

ALLEYN'S		founded 1619
ALLHALLOWS		16th century
AMPLEFORTH	(Fr 1608)	1802
ARDINGLY		1858
BEDALES		1893
BLOXHAM		1860
BLUECOAT		1553
BLUNDELLS		1604
BRYANSTON		1928

CANFORD	founded	1923
CHARTERHOUSE		1611
CHRIST'S HOSPITAL		1553
CHURCHER'S		1722
CLIFTON		1862
CRANLEIGH		1863
DAUNTSEY'S		1543
DOUAI	(Fr 1615)	1903
DOWNSIDE	(Fr 1606)	1789
EPSOM		1853
ETON		1440
FELSTED		1564
GORDONSTOUN		1934
GRESHAM'S		1555
HABERDASHERS'		1690
HAILEYBURY		1862
HARROW		1571
HURSTPIERPOINT		1849
LANCING		1848
THE LEYS		1875
LORETTO		1862
MALVERN		1862
MARLBOROUGH		1843
MERCHANT TAYLOR'S		1561
MONKTON COMBE		1868
OSWESTRY		1407
OUNDLE		1556
RADLEY		1847
REPTON		1557
ROSSALL		1844
RUGBY		1567
SAINT PAULS		1509
SEDBURGH		1525
SHERBORNE		1550
SHREWSBURY		1552
STONYHURST		1593
STOWE		1923
TONBRIDGE		1553
UPPINGHAM		1584
WELLINGTON		1841
WESTMINSTER		1560

WHITGIFT   founded 1596
WINCHESTER   1382
WORKSOP   1890
WREKIN   1880
WYCLIFFE   1882

PUCK 1. *SPRITE* (MND, *Shak*); IMP. 2. Ice hockey disc.
PUDDING *Anag.* AFTERS, *COURSE*, SWEET; **types**: APPLE ~,
   BLACK ~, FRUIT ~, HASTY ~, MILK ~, PLUM ~, SPONGE
   ~, STEAMED ~, YORKSHIRE ~, ROLY POLY, SPOTTED
   DICK. FAT PERSON. PAD, PROTECT (naut).
PULLER DRAWER, EXTRACTOR; DENTIST (crypt). TOWER,
   TUG.
PUMP BALE, DISCHARGE, EMPTY. *SHOE*. INTERROGATE,
   QUESTION.
PUNCH *DRINK*, NEGUS. BLOW, HOOK, JAB, KNOCK,
   SWING, UPPERCUT. [~ and Judy].
PUNCTUATION Commas and even full stops are ruthlessly used by
   the puzzle setter to mislead. The object, as with use of words with
   different *pronunciation*, is to brainwash the reader into putting a
   certain interpretation on a word, particularly one which may have
   two or more meanings. Note how the clue **Offers more doubt, is**
   uncertain (7) points to lack of sureness or confidence, but moving
   the comma (and this has to be done mentally, because the puzzle
   setter won't do it for you) from after the word 'doubt' to before it,
   changes the complexion of things: 'Offers more, doubt is uncertain'
   gives a word which must mean 'offers more' and must be an
   'uncertain' rendering (thus an anagram) of 'doubt is'; the answer =
   OUTBIDS. See also *Question mark*.
PUNT *BET*, WAGER. *BOAT*; QUANT. COUNTRY (pre-bibl
   [Queen Hatshepsut]). KICK. CURRENCY (Ire).
PUP PUPPY; *offspring* of dog. DUD. *AIRCRAFT*.
PUPIL L, STUDENT, SCHOLAR [*class*, *form*]. IRIS, EYE
   CENTRE (hence Y, crypt); *SEER* (crypt).
PURPLE *COLOUR*; *PURPURE* (herald). [Idmon, f of Arachne].
PURPURE *COLOUR*; *PURPLE* (herald).
PUSSYFOOT LURK, PROWL, SNEAK. OVERCAUTION. *TT*,
   PROHIBITIONIST [W. E. Johnson]. CATSPAW (crypt).
PUT *PLACE*, *SET*.
~ **BACK** DEMOTE. REPLACE. DEFER. TES, TUP (crypt).
PUTTER *CLUB*; *GOLFER*. PLACER, SETTER.

PUTTING *GOLF*, HOLING. PLACING, SETTING.

PUT UP BUILD, CONSTRUCT, ERECT. TOLERATE.
EMPLOY (jockey). *FLUSH* (game bird). *LODGE* (guest).
OFFER (fight, prayer). *PRESENT* (petition). PROPOSE
(candidate). *RAISE* (price). SHEATHE (sword). TUP (dn).

PYGMALION Gk myth king of Cyprus, who fell in love with the
ivory statue he had sculpted. He persuaded *Aphrodite* to give it
life, and mar her as *Galatea*. [G. B. Shaw].

PYRIPHLEGETHON Gk myth underworld river; literally: flaming
with fire.

PYROMANIA *Obsession* with fire-raising.

PYROPHOBIA *Aversion* to fire.

PYTHEAS Gk navigator, 4th cent B.C. Sailed the N coast of Eur, incl
Britain and Thule (possibly derived from tales of Nor and its frozen
seas), in two voyages, reaching a river he called Tanais (possibly
the Elbe), which ~ took to be the division between Eur and Asia
(c.f. the Don/Volga). Originated derivation of latitude through
sun's shadow.

PYTHON 1. *SNAKE*. 2. Gk myth *DRAGON* or *SERPENT* which
was formed from primeval ooze after the *Deucalion* deluge. Slain
by *Apollo*, who founded the Pythian *games* in commemoration.

Q QUEBEC (*Province*, Can). QUEEN. QUESTION. HEAD OF
MI5.

QC QUEEN'S COUNSEL, SILK.

QT ON THE QUIET, QUIET(LY).

QUAIL FLINCH. GAME *BIRD*; **assembly** = bevy. *INSTRUMENT*
(mus).

QUAKE ROCK, SHAKE, SHIVER, TREMBLE. EARTHQUAKE
[Richter]. *GRASS*.

QUAKER FRIEND, FRY; **pl** = FRIENDLY SOCIETY [Fox].
EARTHQUAKE, TREMBLER (crypt) [Richter]. GUNPORT.

QUALITY ACCOMPLISHMENT, APTITUDE, ATTRIBUTE,
CHARACTERISTIC, FACULTY, *PROPERTY*, SKILL,
TIMBRE. DEGREE, EXCELLENCE. GENTRY, *RANK*,
STANDING.

QUARREL *Anag.* ARGUE, -MENT, CONTEND, DISPUTE,
FALL OUT, FIGHT, FIND FAULT, SCRAP, WAR. *ARROW*,
BOLT (arbalest, cross-bow). Diamond-shaped pane in *window*.

QUARTER E, N, S, W, NE, SE, *NORTH*, *EAST* etc. *MERCY*,
PITY. TRAVERSE. FOURTH PART, *MEASURE*. COIN
(US). AREA, NEIGHBOURHOOD. **Pl** = BILLET,
LODGING.

~ **DAYS** D, A, Y or S (crypt). **England/Ireland**: LADY DAY (25
Mar), MIDSUMMER (24 Jun), MICHAELMAS (29 Sep),
CHRISTMAS (25 Dec); **Scotland**: CANDLEMAS (2 Feb),
WHITSUN (15 May), LAMMAS (1 Aug), MARTINMAS (11
Nov).

~ **HOUR** H, O, U or R (crypt).

~ **PINT** P, I, N or T (crypt). GILL, *MEASURE*.

QUAY (s/l *key*). BUND, *DOCK*, *JETTY*, *MOLE*, PIER, WHARF.

QUEEN 1. CARD (*Alice*). *CAT* (fem). CHESSPIECE. 2. King's
wife, *MONARCH* (fem; q.v.), REGINA, SOVEREIGN (fem);
EII, ER, HM, Q, R; **celeb**: AETHELFLED (Mercia), ANNE
(Eng), BESS (Eng), BILKIS (Sheba), *BOADICEA*, CANDACE
(bibl), CATHERINE (Eng, Fr, Russ), *CLEOPATRA*,
CLYTEMNESTRA, *CORA*, ELEANOR (Eng [Charing Cross,
Waltham Cross, etc]), ELIZABETH (Eng), ESTHER (bibl),
GERTRUDE (*Shak*), *GUINEVERE*, HATSHEPSUT (Egy
[Punt]), *HECUBA*, *HELEN*, *HERA*, HEPHZIBAH (bibl),
HERMIONE (*Shak*), *HIPPOLYTE*, ISABELLA (Sp), JEZEBEL
(bibl), *JOCASTA*, *JUNO*, LEDA (*Helen*), MARIA THERESA
(A), MARIE ANTOINETTE (Fr), MICHAL (bibl), NEFERTITI
(Egy), *NIOBE*, PASIPHAE (*Minos*), *PERSEPHONE*,
PROSERPINE, TITANIA (*Shak*), VASHT (bibl), *VICTORIA*.
Pl = *THEATRE*.

QUEENS OF ENGLAND *See* Monarchs.

QUEER *Anag.* *ODD*, PECULIAR [*Chesterton*]. *FAIRY*, GAY.

~ **STREET** BANKRUPTCY, INSOLVENCY; CAREY STREET.
DEAD END (crypt). Anag. of 'street', e.g. TESTER.

QUESTION Q; PROBLEM (**opp** = answer). INTERROGATE,
GRILL, *PUMP*.

~ **MARK** A question mark is used when the puzzle setter is feeling
benevolent and wishes to draw attention to a double meaning. In
effect, it warns that the answer, while relating well to one half of
the clue, only responds to the other half in a punning or cryptic
way. One of the shortest examples is **Regal liner?** (5) = RULER
(where the answer = 'regal' because it means a king, but it = 'liner'
because it may be said to help in ruling lines); another instance is
Bulls-eye at the mortuary? (4, 6) = DEAD CENTRE (where the

answer = 'bulls-eye' happily enough, but must be looked at
cryptically to arrive at a centre for dead people, or 'mortuary').

It can also be used to indicate that a different meaning should be
put on a word by giving it a different spelling, e.g. **Purchaser for
the old cow shed?** (4) = BYRE (where the answer is an old-fashioned
word for 'cowshed', but it has to be turned into BUYER before it can
mean 'purchaser'). See also *punctuation*.

QUEUER (s/l *cuer*). ONE WHO QUEUES/WAITS IN LINE;
WAITER.

QUICK *ALIVE*. RAPID, *SMART*. SUBCUTANEOUS
TENDERNESS.

QUICKLY RAPIDLY, *SMARTLY*, SPEEDILY. *ALIVE* (crypt).
Shak character.

QUID *NOTE*, *POUND*. TOBACCO WAD.

QUIET P, PP, SH; HUSH, LOW, PIANO, SILENT, WHIST (**opp** =
loud). EASE, REST, TRANQUIL.

QUIETLY P, PP, QT, SH.

QUINCE *FRUIT* (tree). CARPENTER (MND, *Shak*).

QUIT DEPART, *GO*, LEAVE, PART. SHOT.

QUIXOTIC IDEALISTIC, LOFTY, VISIONARY [Cervantes;
Rosinante (horse)].

QUOD *GAOL*. WHICH (Lat).

QV QUOD VIDE, WHICH SEE.

Q without U ABU QIR (Egy), AL QAFA (Egy), AL QATIF (Arab),
AL QATRUN (Libya), AL QAYARA (Iraq), AQABA (Jor),
AQIQ (Sudan), AQRABA (Jor), ASH QELON (Isr), COQ,
DAQM (Oman), IQBAL, IQZALUIT (Eskimo; was Frobisher
Bay), IRAQI, LUQA (Malta), NQA, NQING, NQONG (little,
med, big, Aus gods, Just So Stories, *Kipling*), PETAL TIQWA
(Isr), Q-BOAT, QADDAFI/QADAFFI (Libyan leader), QADI
(Arab, Pers, Turk *judge*), QAFAR (Arab), QAIYA (Arab),
QALA (Afghan), QALA MASHIZ (Iran), QALAT (Yemen),
QAMA BAY (Arab), QANTAS (*airline*), QARA (Egy), QARA
QUM (USSR), QARDAHA (Syria), QARTABA (Lebanon),
QASIM (Arab), QASR (Iraq), QASRQAND (Iran), QA'TABA
(Yemen), QATANA (Syria), QATAR (Isr), QATIF (Arab),
QATTARA (Egy), QAYEN (Iran), QAZRAN (Iran), QAZVIN
(Iran), *QC*, QED, QESHM (Isr, Iran), QEYS (Isr, Iran), QIBLA
(direction of Mecca), QIKIQTALUK (Eskimo; was Baffin Is),
QING (*Ch dynasty*), QINTAR (Albanian *currency*), QISHM
(Iran), QISHN (Arab), QISHRAN (Isr, Arab), QIZAN (Arab),

QIZIL UZUN (Iran), QOM (Iran), QOPH (Heb letter), QOTUR
(Iran), QOZ BAL AIR (Arab), Q-SHIP (mil), *QT*, QTO (quarto),
QTY (quantity), *QV*, SAWQIRAH BAY (Oman), SHAQA
(Arab), SHUQRA (Yemen), TAQAH (Oman), URUMQI (Ch).

R *RAILWAY*. RAND. REAMUR. RECTO. REGIMENT.
REGINA. *RESTRICTED* (film *censorship*). REVEREND.
REX. RIGHT. *RIVER*. *ROYAL*. RUMANIA (*car plate*).
RUNS. KING (= EDWARD, GEORGE, HENRY etc).

RA RADIUM (*chem*). ROYAL ARTILLERY, GUNS. ROYAL &
ANCIENT (*golf club*). ROYAL ACADEMICIAN, ARTIST,
PAINTER (q.v. for list) [Burlington House; Tate]. SUN *GOD*
(Egy) [Cleopatra's needle]. **Pl** = Abyssinian king.

RABBIT (s/l rabbet, rarebit, rebate). CHATTER, TALK (sl).
DUFFER, POOR PLAYER. BOTHER, CONFOUND, DRAT.
ISLAND. BURROWING RODENT, HARE; BUNNY,
CONEY; **assembly** = warren; **breeds**: ANGORA, LOP-EARED;
celeb: BENJAMIN BUNNY (Beatrix *Potter*); BRER RABBIT
(Uncle Remus; Joel Chandler Harris; Brer Fox, Tar-Baby); BUGS
BUNNY® (cartoon); FIVER; HAZEL (Watership Down);
FLOPSY, MOPSY, COTTONTAIL, PETER (Beatrix *Potter* [Mr
McGregor]); HARVEY (invisible, Mary Chase); RABBIT (*Milne*
[Friends and Relations]); MARCH HARE, WHITE RABBIT
(*Alice* in Wonderland); THUMPER® (Bambi®) [*Ch calendar*;
habitation; myxomatosis; playboy].

RAC ROYAL ARMOURED CORPS. ROYAL AUTOMOBILE
CLUB [AA, cars].

RACE *BREED*, ETHNIC GROUP. *TIDE-RIP*. GINGER ROOT,
SPICE. *CLASSIC*, COMPETITION, EGG AND SPOON,
EVENT, GRAND PRIX, INDY, MARATHON, OBSTACLE,
RELAY, *TT*, SACK ~. [*Atalanta*].

~ **OF MAN** HOMO SAPIENS. *TT* (crypt).

RACETRACKS 1. **Celeb (horses):**

AINTREE (Eng)	BATH (Eng)
ASCOT (Eng)	BEVERLEY (Eng)
AUTEUIL (Fr)	BRIGHTON (Eng)
AYR (Sc)	CARTMEL (Eng)
BANGOR ON DEE (Wal)	CAMPTOWN (US)

CATTERICK (Eng)
CHANTILLY (Fr)
CHELTENHAM (Eng)
CHEPSTOW (Wal)
CHESTER (Eng)
CHURCHILL DOWNS (US)
CRAVEN (Ire)
CURRAGH (Ire)
DEVON & EXETER (Eng)
EDINBURGH (Sc)
EPSOM (Eng)
FOLKESTONE (Eng)
FONTWELL PARK (Eng)
GOODWOOD (Eng)
HAMILTON (Sc)
HAYDOCK PARK (Eng)
HEREFORD (Eng)
KEMPTON (Eng)
LEICESTER (Eng)
LINCOLN (Eng)
LONGCHAMPS (Fr)
LUDLOW (Eng)
MAISONS-LAFFITTE (Fr)
MARKET RASEN (Eng)
NAAS (Ire)
NETHERHAMPTON (Eng)
NEWBURY (Eng)
NEWMARKET (Eng)
NEWTON ABBOT (Eng)

PERTH (Sc)
RIPON (Eng)
SAINT-CLOUD (Fr)
SANDOWN PARK (Eng)
STRATFORD (Eng)
UTTOXETER (Eng)
WARWICK (Eng)
WINDSOR (Eng)
WOLVERHAMPTON (Eng)
YARMOUTH (Eng)
YORK (Eng)

2. **Celeb (motor cars)**:

BRANDS HATCH (Eng)
BROOKLANDS (ex Eng)
DAYTONA BEACH (US)
GOODWOOD (Eng)
LE MANS (Fr)
MONACO (Fr)
MONTLHERY (Fr)
MONZA (It)
NURBURGRING (Ger)
RICHMOND (US)
SILVERSTONE (Eng)
SPA (Belg)
THRUXTON (Eng)
ZANDVOORT (NL)

RACKET DIN, NOISE, UPROAR. *DODGE*, SCHEME.
  ORDEAL. *BAT*; **Pl** = *GAME*.
RADIO *BROADCAST*, WIRELESS; *MEDIUM*.
RADIUM *METAL*; RA (*chem*).
RAFFIA PALM FIBRE, *PALM* [bass].
RAF TYPE AC, AIRMAN, FO, *PILOT* etc.
RAG CHAFF, RIB, *TEASE*. FROLIC, GAMBOL. CLOTH,
  SCRAP; **comp** = *bone*. BAD PRESS, GUTTER PRESS.
  SLATE; STONE. CLUB (sl: Army & Navy).
RAIL BR, RLY, RY; IRON WAY; TRACK; HARD LINES
  (crypt). LOCOS, ROLLING STOCK. *BIRD*. ABUSE, RAGE,

RANT, RAVE, *THUNDER*. BAR, FENCE, GUIDE, PERCH,
ROD. [Bluebell, Severn Valley, Volks (elect), Watercress. *cat*].
RAIL GUIDE ABC®, BRADSHAW®.
RAILWAYMEN LOCOMEN; TRAINERS (crypt); **Unions** =
ASLEF, NUR. TOBY VECK (The Chimes, *Dickens*).
RAIN (s/l *reign*, *rein*). 1. PRECIPITATION, DELUGE, *SHOWER*;
DRENCH [piano wires, stair-rods]. 2. Put RA in word indicated,
e.g. **Rainbox for crystalline salt** (5) = BO*RA*X. 3. **God: Gk** =
JUPITER, *ZEUS*; **Rom** = PLUVIUS; **Egy** = OSIRIS; **Ind** =
INDRA; **Mayan** = CHAC; **Goddesses, Gk** = *HORAE* [Hyades;
Pleiades].
RAINBOW 1. ARCH [REFRACTION] (**colours in order**: red,
orange, yellow, green, blue, indigo, violet). 2. **Goddess: Gk** =
IRIS.
RAISE (s/l raze). 1. ELEVATE, ERECT, HOIST, *PUT UP* (**opp** =
lower). 2. Word in dn clue, written up, e.g. **Raise Cain** = NIAC.
RALLY BANTER, *CHAFF*. REASSEMBLE, RECOVER,
REVIVE. *RACE*. DEMONSTRATION, PARADE.
RAM SHEEP (male), TUP; sign of *Zodiac* (1st, ARIES). BEAK,
PROD (battering, mil). PISTON, PLUNGER (mech). BEAT
DOWN, CRAM, DASH, DRIVE, PACK, PUSH, SHOVE,
STRIKE, STUFF, TAMP. ROYAL ACADEMY OF MUSIC. **Pl**
= *Football* team (UK/US).
RANGER GIRL GUIDE. FORESTER, PARK WARDEN.
COMMANDO (US). COWBOY (crypt). **Pl** = CAVALRY. 8 in
song.
RANK *CLASS*, GRADE, QUALITY, STANDING; **mil** = CAPT,
COL, LT etc. LINE, QUEUE, *ROW*, *TIER* (**opp** = file);
ARRAY, ORDER. COARSE, CORRUPT, FOUL, GROSS,
INDECENT, LOATHSOME, OFFENSIVE. LUXURIANT.
RAPT (s/l rapped, wrapped). ABSORBED, CARRIED AWAY,
ENGROSSED, ENRAPTURED, INTENT.
RASH HASTY, IMPETUOUS, OVERBOLD, RECKLESS.
ERUPTION, *GATHERING*, *SPOTS*.
RASPBERRY BRAMBLE, SOFT *FRUIT*; *PLANT*. BIRD,
DERISION, DISAPPROVAL.
RATE *LEVY*, LOCAL TAX. MPH, SPEED. COST, VALUE;
CONSIDER, ESTIMATE, *RANK*, REGARD. CLASS; MAN
OF WAR (arch naut). DRESS DOWN, *REPRIMAND*, SCOLD,
SLANG.
RATING AB, JACK, *SAILOR*, TAR. ABC, TAM, GALLUP®.

HANDICAP (naut). (HOUSE) TAX.

RAVEN 1. PILLAGE, PLUNDER, LOOT. BOLT, DEVOUR, WOLF (food). *BLACK*. 2. BIRD, family corvidae (ill-omen); N Am god of *tricky* deceit; **celeb**: GRIP (*Dickens*); HUGIN (*reflection*) and MUNIN (*memory*; *Odin*) [*Elijah*; *Noah*; Tower of London].

RAW UNRIPE. UNCOOKED (**opp** = *done*). *GREEN*, UNTRAINED. PART-MADE (hence MAD). BITING, CHILLY. SKINNED, SENSITIVE, SORE.

RAY *BEAM*, *LIGHT*, SHAFT [hope]. *FISH*: MANTA, *SKATE*, STING. NOTE (mus; also RE).

RC RED CROSS. ROMAN CATHOLIC. **Pl** = Royal College of Surgeons.

RD BOUNCE, DUD CHEQUE [refer to drawer]. RURAL DEAN. ROAD. RNR DECORATION.

RE RHENIUM (*chem*). *ABOUT*, CONCERNING, DESCRIBING. AGAIN. ROYAL ENGINEERS, SAPPERS. NOTE (mus; also RAY). Egy *god*.

REACTOR Nuclear power plant; **types**: AGC, BWR, PWR: **celeb**: CALDER HALL, CHERNOBYL (USSR), CULCHETH, CULHAM, DOUNREAY, HARWELL, RISLEY, SELLAFIELD, SIZEWELL, SPRINGFIELDS, THREE-MILE ISLAND (US), THURSO, WINDSCALE, WINFRITH.

READ (s/l reed, *red*). 1. INTERPRET, STUDY, UNDERSTAND [books]. *PIRATE*. 2. Word reads differently if split (or read differently), e.g. **A measure of justice, we read** (8, 5) = FREEZING POINT (just*ice).

READY APT, FACILE, INCLINED, PREPARED, PROMPT, QUICK, WILLING. *CASH*. OUT (e.g. **Happen to be ready to cook** (3, 3) = PAN OUT).

RECEDING 1. DECLINING, SHRINKING, WITHDRAWING. 2. Answer reads backwards, or partly backwards, e.g. **The Hittite's top hair is receding** (5) = U*RIAH.

RECEIVER BANKRUPTCY OFFICIAL. RADIO, HEADPHONES, TV SET. FENCE. HOST. ACCEPTER, TAKER (**opp** = giver, donor).

RECKONING AC, *ACCOUNT*, *BILL*, *NOTE*, SUM, TOTAL.

RECLUSE *HERMIT* (q.v.), INTROVERT. **Celeb**: MISS HAVISHAM (*Dickens*); HOWARD HUGHES.

RECORD DISC, EP, LP. ANNAL, ARCHIVE, *CHART*, DIARY, *ENTER*, ENTRY, LIST, *LOG*, *NOTE*, REGISTER, ROLL,

TAPE, WRITE. BEST PERFORMANCE, CHAMPIONSHIP.
TIE AGAIN (crypt). **Pl** = ALBUM.

RECORDER TAPE. DIARIST. LOGGER. CHAMPION,
WINNER. FLUTE. *INSTRUMENT* (mus). JUDGE.

RED (s/l *read*). BILLIARD/SNOOKER BALL (score 3/1).
BOLSHEVIK, COMMIE, COMMUNIST, LEFTIE,
REVOLUTIONARY, RUSSIAN; MARX(IST), STALIN,
TROT(SKY); IVAN. *SEA*. ERIC. *COLOUR*; GULES (*herald*)
[*blush*; Elphberg (*Hope*); *Esau*]. *CASTLE*. OVERDRAWN.
RIVER (Can; US; Viet). **Pl** = (*football* team).

REDCAP MILITARY POLICEMAN, MP, SP. *BIRD*.

REDCOAT HUNTING PINK. SOLDIER (arch); **pl** = BRITISH
ARMY, LOBSTERS (arch). HOLIDAY CAMP GUIDE
(Butlins).

REDHEAD COPPERNOB; **celeb**: ELPHBERGS (*Hope*); *ESAU*.
COMMUNIST LEADER (crypt); hence C. R (crypt).

RED INDIAN See *AMERICAN INDIAN* for **tribes**.

REDSKIN *AMERICAN INDIAN* (q.v. for **tribes**). **Pl** = *football*
team (US).

REEFER JOINT (*drug*). *SAILOR* (crypt). JACKET.

REEL *Anag*. DANCE, LURCH, STAGGER, SWAY. COIL,
SPOOL: *WIND*.

RE-ENACTED *Anag*. REPEATED, REPLAYED, RE-RUN.

REEVE MAGISTRATE, SHERIFF. THREAD (naut). *FEMALE*
RUFF (*bird*). *Chaucer* character.

REFERENCE MARK Direction sign referring reader to note, e.g.
ASTERISK (*), DAGGER/OBELISK (†), DOUBLE OBELISK
(‡), PARAGRAPH (¶), PARALLEL (‖), SECTION (§).

REFERENCE WORK BOOK, CONSULTATION DOCUMENT,
FILE; *DEVILRY* (crypt); **celeb (many ®)**: ABC (rly),
ALMANACH DE GOTHA (genealogy and statistics),
BAEDEKER (countries and travel), MRS BEETON (cook),
BLUE BOOK (US aristocracy), BRADSHAW (rly),
BRITANNICA (encyclopaedia), BURKE'S (aristocracy),
CHAMBERS (dictionary), COLLINS (dictionary),
CROCKFORDS (*churchmen*), DEBRETT'S (aristocracy),
LLOYDS (shipping, yachts), MEDICAL REGISTER (doctors),
NAUTICAL ALMANAC (naut tables and ephemera), OED
(dictionary), OLD MOORE (statistics, prophecy), REEDS (naut
ephemera), ROGET (thesaurus), STUD BOOK (racehorses),
WHITAKER'S ALMANAC (statistics), WHO'S WHO (people).

REFLECTION 1. CENSURE. RECONSIDERATION, THOUGHT [Hugin (*raven*)]. (MIRROR) IMAGE. *ECHO*. 2. Word reads backwards, or is a palindrome, e.g. **On reflection, I lead to a certain amount of evil-smelling** (7) = NO*I*SOME.

REFRAIN ABSTAIN, CURB, DESIST, RESTRAIN. (RECURRING) PHRASE/*TUNE*.

REFORM *Anag.* ABOLISH, CORRECT, CURE. FORM AGAIN (hence FROM, crypt).

REFUSE 1. *DECLINE*, DENY, REJECT, SAY NAY, SHUN, *SHY* (**opp** = *allow*). GARBAGE, LEAVINGS, ORT, RUBBISH, SCRAP, TRASH. 2. In Gk myth, suitors were ~d by: *Atalanta*, *Cassandra*, *Daphne*, *Dido*, *Narcissus*, *Penelope*.

REGENT 1. Ruler in absentia or minority, e.g. ANTIPATER (Macedonia), ADMIRAL HORTY (Hung), and for George III (Eng), LOUIS XV (Fr). 2. *THEATRE*.

REGINA QUEEN, R.

REGIONS OF SCOTLAND See *Divisions*.

REGRET APOLOGIZE, GRIEVE, RUE; [Miss Otis].

REHOBOAM 1. *BOTTLE* (wine = 6 normal). 2. Bibl s of *Solomon* and Naamah, who mar Maacah. When king of Isr (975–957 B.C.), ~ refused reform ('my f chastised you with whips, I shall chastise you with scorpions'), so that ten N tribes seceded to *Jeroboam*.

REIGN (s/l *rain*, *rein*). RULE, SOVEREIGNTY, SWAY; REALM, SPHERE. HOLD ROYAL OFFICE, BE KING/QUEEN/MONARCH/SOVEREIGN.

REIN (s/l *rain*, *reign*). 1. *CONTROL*, CURB, GOVERN, RESTRAIN. *HARNESS*. 2. Put RE in word indicated, e.g. **The little man's horserein** (4) = G*RE*G. 3. **Pl** = KIDNEYS, LOINS (arch). CONTROLS.

REINDEER CARIBOU, SUBARCTIC DEER; **celeb**: BLITZEN, *COMET*, *CUPID*, *DANCER*, DASHER, DONDER, PRANCER, *VIXEN* (Moore); *RUDOLF*. *LAKE*.

REJECT 1. EVACUATE, VOMIT. *DECLINE*, *REFUSE*, TURN ASIDE. 2. Letter or word dropped, e.g. **Treaty rejecting the French fever** (4) = (le)AGUE. 3. In Gk myth, suitors were ~ed by *Atalanta*, *Cassandra*, *Daphne*, *Dido*, *Narcissus* and *Penelope*.

RELATED AGNATE; ALLIED, KIN, KITH. NARRATED, TOLD.

RELATION CONNECTION, FAMILY, KIN, KITH. ACCOUNT, NARRATIVE, STORY, TALE.

RELIEF WORK AID TO POOR, OXFAM, UNICEF. CAMEO

(**opp** = intaglio), ENGRAVING; BAS, FRIEZE. BRAILLE
(crypt).

RELIGION DIVINE RECOGNITION, FAITH, PIETY,
WORSHIP; MONASTIC LIFE [*church, friar, monk*]. **Celeb
vedantisms**: HINDUISM (**gods**: Shakti, Shiva, Vishnu; **goddesses**:
Durga, Lakshmi; **priest**: brahmin); BUDDHISM (**versions**:
Mahayana, Theravada, Ch'an (Ch), Zen (Jap); **founder**: Gautama;
Nirvana (bliss); **priests**: monks); BABISM; BAHAISM, JAINISM
(non-violence); LAMAISM (Tibet); PARSISM (**founder**:
Zoroaster); SAKTIISM (Tantras); SIKHISM (**founder**: Guru
Nanak); ZOROASTRIANISM. **Celeb oriental**:
CONFUCIANISM (**concepts**: chan-tza, hsaio, jen, li, shu, tao,
t'ien); SHINTOISM (**concept**: kami); TAOISM (**concepts**: tao, te,
we, wei, yang, yin). **Celeb Judaisms**: CHRISTIANITY (**founder**:
Jesus); ISLAM (**founder**: *MOHAMMED*; **prophets**: Abraham,
Adam, Jesus, Moses, *Mohammed*, Noah); ZIONISM (**founders**:
Abraham, Isaac, Jacob [**Israel**]). **Celeb paganisms/atheisms**:
MARXISM (communism); SATANISM (black magic); VOODOO
(ju-ju); *WITCHCRAFT* (magick, wicca).

RELIGIOUS HOLY, *PI*.

REMEDY *Anag.* *CURE*, NOSTRUM, PALLIATIVE.

REMOVE 1. ABSTRACT, TAKE AWAY/OFF. DISMISS.
CHANGE, DEPARTURE, DISTANCE, DISTANT, REMOTE.
DISH. DEGREE. PROMOTION (school); *CLASS*, FORM
[*Bunter*]. 2. Take away letters indicated, e.g. **Remove the
courtesan's curves in this joint** (5) = MI(s)TRE(ss).

REMOVED 1. APART. TAKEN AWAY. 2. Remove letter D from
clue, e.g. **Dart removed skill** (3) = *ART. 3. Remove letters RE
from clue, e.g. **Refuse removed igniter** (4) = **FUSE.

REMUS 1. Uncle ~ (book, Joel Chandler Harris; Brer *Fox*, Brer
Rabbit, Brer Terrapin, Tar-Baby). 2. Rom myth *twin* br of
Romulus, s of *Mars* and *Rhea* (Silvia). They were suckled by
wolves, and Romulus later slew Remus.

RENT CLEAVE, RIP, TEAR; CLEFT, FAULT, FISSURE. LET;
HIRE CHARGE, PAYMENT.

REP *MATERIAL*. REPERTORY. REPRESENTATIVE;
CONGRESSMAN, MP. *CHAPMAN*, DRUMMER,
SALESMAN, TRAVELLER. REPUBLICAN.

Rep Republican [donkey].

REPAIR *Anag.* MEND, OVERHAUL, PATCH, *SERVICE*. GO,
HIE.

REPEAT 1. BIS, ENCORE. DO/SAY AGAIN, IMITATE, RECITE, REHEARSE, REPRODUCE. RECUR. BELCH, BURP. 2. Write word/letter again, e.g. **Flower is repeated** (4) = IS*IS.

REPEATER FIREARM, *WEAPON*. CLOCK, *WATCH*. DUPLICATE DIAL/SIGNAL; RELAY, RETRANSMITTER. ACTOR, RECITER, REPETITEUR, SOLILOQUIST (crypt).

REPEL 1. BEAT BACK, REPULSE, WARD OFF. DISPLEASE, BE DISTASTEFUL (**opp** = *attract*). 2. Word(s) read backwards, e.g. **Little Sarah is repellent to Eliot's weaver** (5) = SI*LAS (Marner).

REPORTER ACCOUNTANT, NARRATOR. ED, JOURNALIST. *BANGER*, BOMB, EXPLOSIVE, GUN, RIFLE (crypt).

REPRIMAND *CARPET*, DRESS DOWN, REPROVE, *ROCKET*, TELL OFF (**opp** = praise).

REPTILE Genus reptilia: CROCODILE, LIZARD, SNAKE, TORTOISE, TURTLE, **especially**: ALLIGATOR, CAYMAN, GECKO, IGUANA, MONITOR.

REPUBLICAN PRO-REPUBLIC. POLITICIAN [donkey]. SOCIAL.

RE-ROW REPECHAGE. RE-ARGUE.

RESERVE *BOOK*. POSTPONE, WITHHOLD. SERVE AGAIN [let; tennis]. COOLNESS, RETICENCE. **Pl** = REINFORCEMENTS; TERRITORIALS (mil).

RESOLVE *Anag*. ANALYSE, SOLVE, *SETTLE*; DISSIPATE, DISSOLVE. DECIDE, DETERMINE.

REST (s/l wrest). DREGS, LEES, REMAINS. HOLIDAY; BREAK, PAUSE. *BAR* (mus). BRIDGE, CUE-PROP, SPIDER (pool/snooker).

RESTRICTED CONFINED, LIMITED, NUMBERED. OFF-LIMITS. R (film *censorship*).

RESUME CARRY ON, CONTINUE. *SUMMARY*.

RETAIL NARRATE, RECOUNT, RELATE. SELL, TRADE.

RETIRED 1. *LEFT*, RECEDED, RETREATED, WITHDRAWN. PENSIONED. ABED, SLEEPING. 2. Word reads backwards, e.g. **Retired officer is sweet** (3) = JAM. 3. Word/letter is put into 'bed', e.g. **Retired woman is disbarred** (6) = B*ANN*ED. 4. Because ~ can mean 'in bed', it thus refers crypt to gardening.

RETIRING As *Retired* and: SHY, UNSOCIABLE, WITHDRAWN (**opp** = *pert*).

RETORT 1. CHEMICAL VESSEL, *STILL*; ALEMBIC (arch).
REPARTEE, REPLY, RETALIATE. 2. Word reads backwards,
e.g. **Mad retort stops the flow** = DAM.

RETRIBUTION 1. RECOMPENSE, REQUITAL, VENGEANCE.
2. **Goddess: Gk** = ATE, NEMESIS; **Other** = MENI (Bab).

RETURN 1. COME/GO/SEND BACK (hence EMOC/OG/DNES,
crypt); CONVEY/GIVE/PAY/PUT BACK (do). DIVIDEND,
INTEREST, PAY, PROFIT. COME-AND-GO, DOUBLE
JOURNEY. [boomerang; Miolnir (*Thor*)]. 2. Reads backwards,
e.g. **Beat in return game** (4) = FLOG. 3. Turn letters RE = ER, e.g.
Go and return for a quick one (4) = GO*ER.

REVEALS 1. BETRAYS, DISCLOSES, DIVULGES, MAKES
KNOWN, *SHOWS*. 2. *Hidden word*.

REVERSE 1. DEFEAT, MISFORTUNE. CAPSIZE. VERSO,
TAIL (coin); **opp** = obverse, head. CONTRARY. ANNUL,
REVOKE. TRANSPOSE. 2. Reads backwards, e.g. **Gained some
ground? Now reverse** (3) = WON.

REVISE *Anag.* AMEND, CORRECT, EDIT, IMPROVE.
CHANGE, RECONSIDER. SECOND SIGHT (crypt).

REVOLUTIONARY *Anag.* AGITATOR, REBEL, RED; CHE.
SPINNER, *TOP*, *WHEEL* (crypt).

REVOLVER COLT®, PISTOL, *WEAPON*, WEBLEY®. *TOP*,
TURNSTILE, WHEEL, (WIND)MILL (all crypt).

REWRITE *Anag.* *EDIT*, *REVISE*, SUB-EDIT.

REX KING, R.

RHEA (s/l rear). 1. Gk *goddess* of FERTILITY; d of Uranus and
Ge; mar *Cronos*, m of *Hades*, *Poseidon* and *Zeus*. In Rom myth (as
~ Silvia) m by *Mars* of *Romulus* and Remus. Synonymous with **Gk**
= CYBELE, *DANAE*; **Rom** = *CERES*, *DIANA*, OPS. 2. A
satellite of the planet Saturn. 3. *BIRD* (*ostrich*).

RHINESTONE IMITATION *DIAMOND* [paste].

RHINO PACHYDERM, TOXODON (ex); **assembly** = crash.
NOSE. MONEY (sl).

RHYMING SLANG Form of cockney slang code, which involves
paired words, the second of which rhymes with the meaning (and is
often not spoken — this is indicated below by the use of
parentheses)

Slang	Meaning
Apples (and pears)	STAIRS
Ball of chalk	WALK

Bangers and mash	CASH
Barnet (Fair)	HAIR
Bees and (honey)	MONEY
Bird (lime)	TIME
Boat race	FACE
Boracic lint	SKINT
Bull and cow	ROW
Burnt cinder	WINDOW
Butcher's (hook)	LOOK
Cain and Abel	TABLE
Cherry (Ripe)	PIPE
Cobbler's (awls)	BALLS
Dicky (dirt)	SHIRT
Frog and toad	ROAD
Jam roll	DOLE
Lady Godiva	FIVER
Loaf (of bread)	HEAD
Mince (pie)s	EYES
Mutt and Jeff	DEAF
North and south	MOUTH
Pen and ink	STINK
Pig's ear	BEER
Plates (of meat)	FEET
Pompey (whore)	FOUR
Pot and pan	OLD MAN
Rosie (Lee)	TEA
Rub a dub (dub)	PUB
Sexton (Blake)	FAKE
Square (and round)	POUND
Tea leaf	THIEF
Titfer (tat)	HAT
Tod (Sloan)	OWN
Trouble (and strife)	WIFE
Whistle (and flute)	SUIT

Meaning	Slang
Balls	COBBLER'S (awls)
Beer	PIG'S EAR
Cash	BANGERS AND MASH
Deaf	MUTT AND JEFF
Dole	JAM ROLL

Eyes	MINCE (pie)S
Face	BOAT RACE
Fake	SEXTON (BLAKE)
Feet	PLATES (of meat)
Fiver	LADY GODIVA
Four	POMPEY (whore)
Hair	BARNET (fair)
Hat	TITFER (tat)
Head	LOAF (of bread)
Husband	POT AND PAN
Look	BUTCHER'S (hook)
Money	BEES AND (honey)
Mouth	NORTH AND SOUTH
Old Man	POT AND PAN
Own	TOD (Sloan)
Pipe	CHERRY RIPE
Pound	SQUARE (and round)
Pub	RUB A DUB (dub)
Road	FROG AND TOAD
Row	BULL AND COW
Shirt	DICKY (dirt)
Skint	BORACIC LINT
Stairs	APPLES (and pears)
Stink	PEN AND INK
Suit	WHISTLE (and flute)
Table	CAIN AND ABEL
Tea	ROSIE (Lee)
Thief	TEA LEAF
Time	BIRD (lime)
Walk	BALL OF CHALK
Wife	TROUBLE (and strife)
Window	BURNT CINDER

RHYTHM *BEAT*, SEQUENCE [scan verse for each *foot*].

RI RELIGIOUS INSTRUCTION. RHODE ISLAND. ROYAL INSTITUTION.

RIB BONE [*Eve*]. CHAFF, *TEASE*. RIVER (Eng).

RICH ABUNDANT, COSTLY, FATTY, SPLENDID, SUGARY, WEALTHY (**opp** = *broke*); VALUABLE [*Croesus*, Mammon, *Midas*, Dives]. LAUGHABLE, LUDICROUS.

RIDER ABACK, BACKED, UP (crypt), EQUESTRIAN,

JOCKEY, *MOUNTED.* ADDITION, CODICIL, EXTRA, PS. *HAGGARD* (writer).

RIG *DRESS*, GEAR. PROVIDE. DODGE, FIX, MANIPULATE. *STAY.* BARK, BARQUE, BERMUDAN, BRIG, CUTTER, GAFF, GUNTER, KETCH, LATEEN, LUG, SCHOONER, SLOOP, SPRIT, SQUARE, YAWL.

RIGGING FIXING, MANIPULATION, TRICKERY. STAYS, WIRES: BACKSTAY, BRAIL, BUNTLINE, CLUELINE, FORESTAY, *GARNET*, *JUMPERS*, MARTNET, REEF, RUNNERS, SHROUND, TRIATIC.

RIGHT (s/l *rite*, write). R, RT, S; DEXTER, STARBOARD (**opp** = *left*, port, larboard, *sinister*). **Comp** = left. CORRECT (**opp** = *wrong*). OP (theat). UPTURN, LIEN. TORY. *WHALE.* **Pl** = CHARTER.

~ **AWAY** 1. IMMEDIATELY, NOW. 2. Delete letter(s) R or RT, e.g. **Smooth part right away** (3) = PA*T.

~ **ONE** *CASE*, CAUTION, WAG. R*ONE, R*I (crypt).

RING O (crypt). BUZZ, *CALL*, *DIAL*, PHONE, TOLL [STD]. ARENA, CIRCLE, CIRCUS. CARTEL, CLIQUE, GANG, SET. *CASTLE.* ENGAGED SIGNAL (crypt). AUREOLE, CORONA, DISC, GLORIOLE, HALO, NIMBUS. HOOP. [Wagner].

RINGED CIRCLED, MARKED. AFFIANCED, ENGAGED (crypt).

RINGER *BELL*; CAMPANOLOGIST. COPY, DOUBLE, DUPLICATE. QUOIT. FIANCE (crypt).

RINGING 1. CALLING, PHONING. MARKING. TINNITUS. 2. Word round another, e.g. **Hot and bothered, Fred's ringing the First Lady** (7) = F*EVE*RED.

RINGLEADER AGITATOR, INSTIGATOR. R (crypt). DIALLING (crypt).

RINGMASTER CIRCUS MC. *BOXER*, CHAMPION, PRIZE FIGHTER, PUGILIST (crypt). JEWELLER (crypt).

RITE (s/l *right*, write). CEREMONY, PROCEDURE, LORE.

RIVAL 1. COMPETITOR, COMPETE, VIE. COMPARABLE. 2. Three in *song*.

RIVER R; BECK, *BOURN*, BROOK, BURN, CREEK, EA, ESTUARY, RILL, RIVULET, STREAM, TRIBUTARY, WATERCOURSE; **crypt:** *BANKER*, CURRENCY, *FLOWER*, *RUNNER*; **myth:** *ACHERON*, COCYTUS, LETHE, *OCEANUS*, PYRIPHLEGETHON, *STYX*. [Cebren (god), *Cerberus*,

Charon]. **Comps** = ABANA & PHARPAR (bibl ~s of
DAMASCUS). **Celeb**:

1-letter
E (Sc)

2-letters
AA (Fr, USSR)
II (Finn)
OB (USSR)
PO (It)

3-letters
AAR (Sw)
AHI (Ger)
ALN (Eng)
ALT (Eng)
AXE (Eng)
AYR (Sc)
BUG (Pol, USSR)
CAM (Eng) [Granta]
CAN (Eng)
CHU (USSR)
DAL (Swe)
DEE (Ire, Sc, Wal)
DJA (Cam)
DON (Eng, Sc, USSR)
DUA (Z)
ELY (Eng)
EMS (Ger)
ESK (Eng)
EXE (Eng)
FAL (Eng)
FLY (Papua)
HAY (Aus, Can)
ILI (USSR)
JIU (Rum)
KUR (Iran)
LEA (Eng)
LEK (NL)
LIM (Y)

LOT (Fr)
MOY (Ire)
NAR (Eng)
OBI (USSR)
ORD (Aus)
OKA (USSR)
PIC (Can)
PUR (USSR)
RED (Cam, US, Viet)
RIB (Eng)
ROE (Ire)
RYE (Eng)
SIR (USSR)
TAF (Wal)
TAW (Eng)
TAY (Sc)
TYE (Eng)
USK (Wal)
VAR (Fr)
VER (Eng)
WEY (Eng)
WYE (Eng)
YEO (Eng)

4-letters
AARE (Swi)
ADUR (Eng)
AGRA (Sp)
AGRI (It)
ALPH (Gk)
ALTA (N)
AMOO (USSR)
AMUR (USSR)
ARNO (It)
ARUN (Eng)
AUBE (Fr)
AUDE (Fr)
AVON (Eng, Sc)

BACK (Can)
BANN (Ire)
BENI (Bol)
BRUE (Eng)
BURE (Eng)
BUSH (Ire)
CARY (Eng)
CHER (Fr)
CHEW (Eng)
CHIR (USSR)
COLN (Eng)
CREE (Sc)
DART (Eng)
DOON (Sc)
DOVE (Eng)
EARN (Sc)
EBRO (Sp)
EDEN (Eng, Sc)
ELBE (Ger)
ELWY (Wal)
ERNE (Ire)
EURE (Fr)
FINN (Ire)
GILA (US)
GLAN (Ger)
GLEN (Eng)
GREY (NZ)
HASE (Ger)
HULL (Eng)
IRIN (A)
ISIS (Thames, Eng)
ISLA (Sc)
JUBA (Som)
KAMA (USSR)
LEAF (Can)
LECH (Ger)
LENA (USSR)
LIMA (Port)
LUNE (Eng)
LYON (Sc)
MAAS (NL)

MAIN (Ger)
MEON (Eng)
META (Venez)
MILK (US)
MOLE (Eng)
MOTH (NZ)
NENE (Eng)
NILE (Egy)
ODER (Pol)
OHIO (US)
OISE (Fr)
ORNE (Fr)
OUSE (Eng)
OXUS (USSR)
PEEL (Can)
PLYM (Eng)
QENA (Egy)
RENO (It)
ROCK (US)
RUHR (Ger)
SAAR (Ger)
SEAL (Can)
SPEY (Sc)
STYX (myth)
SUIR (Ire)
SWAN (Aus)
TARA (USSR, Y)
TAWE (Wal)
TEES (Eng)
TEST (Eng)
TOWY (Wal)
TYNE (Eng, Sc)
TYWI (Wal)
UGIE (Sc)
URAL (USSR)
VAAL (SA)
VIRE (Fr)
WAAG (Cz)
WAAL (NL)
WEAR (Eng)
WICK (Sc)

WOLF (US)
WYRE (Eng)
YALN (Ch)
YARE (Eng)
YORK (US)
YSER (Belg)
ZORN (Fr)

5-letters
ABANA (bibl)
ADIGE (It)
ADOUR (Fr)
AERON (Wal)
AGANO (Jap)
AISNE (Fr)
ALDAN (USSR)
ANNAN (Sc)
APURE (Venez)
AVOCA (Ire)
BOYNE (Ire)
BRORA (Sc)
BRIDE (Ire)
CAIRN (Sc)
CAMEL (Eng)
CEDAR (US)
CLARE (Ire)
CLWYD (Wal)
CLYDE (Sc)
COLNE (Eng)
CONGO (Zaire)
CONWY (Wal)
DEBEN (Eng)
DERRY (Ire)
DOURO (Port)
DOVEY (Wal)
DVINA (USSR)
ELLEN (Eng)
FLEET (Eng, Sc)
FLINT (US)
FORTH (Sc)
FOWEY (Eng)

FOYLE (Ire)
FROME (Eng)
GABON (Gab)
GARRY (Sc)
GRAND (Can)
GREEN (US)
HONDO (Mex)
INDRE (Fr)
INDUS (Pak)
ISERE (Fr)
ISHIM (USSR)
JUMNA (Ind)
JURVA (Braz)
KINGS (Ire)
LETHE (myth)
LIPPE (Ger)
LOIRE (Fr)
LOTTA (USSR)
MARNE (Fr)
MEUSE (Belg)
MIAMI (US)
MOSEL (Ger)
NAIRN (Sc)
NEATH (Wal)
NEGRO (Arg, Braz)
NIGER (Nig)
PAYNE (Can)
PEACE (Can)
PEARL (US)
PELLY (Can)
PIAVE (It)
PLATE (Braz)
PRUTH (Rum)
PURUS (Braz)
RHINE (Ger)
RHONE (Fr)
ROPER (Aus)
SARRE (Fr)
SEINE (Fr)
SIONT (Wal)
SLAVE (Can)

SNAKE (US)
SNOWY (Aus)
SOMME (Fr)
SPREE (Ger)
STOUR (Eng)
SWALE (Eng)
TAGUS (Port)
TAMAR (Eng)
TARIM (Ch)
TEIFI (Wal)
TEIGN (Eng)
THAME (Eng)
TIBER (It)
TRENT (Eng)
TWEED (Eng)
VITIM (USSR)
VOLGA (USSR)
WAHGI (Papua)
WESER (Ger)
WHALE (Can)
WHION (Wal)
WHITE (US)
XINGU (Braz)
YANDA (Aus)
YAQUI (Mex)
YARTY (Eng)
YONNE (Fr)
YTHAN (Sc)
YUKON (Can, US)

6-letters
ALBANY (Can)
AMAZON (Braz)
ANGARA (USSR)
ARAGON (Sp)
BARCOO (Aus)
BARROW (Ire)
BIO-BIO (Chile)
BOURNE (Eng)
BUCHAN (Sc)

BULLOO (Aus)
CALDER (Eng)
CARRON (Sc)
CONWAY (Wal)
COQUET (Eng)
CUIABA (Braz)
DANUBE (Aus)
ESCAUT (Belg, Fr)
FRASER (Can)
GAMBIA (Gam)
GANGES (Ind)
GRANDE (Mex)
GRANTA (Cam, Eng)
HUDSON (US)
HUELVA (Sp)
HUMBER (Eng)
HWAN-HO (Ch)
IRTYSH (USSR)
ITCHEN (Eng)
JAPURA (Braz)
JAVARI (Peru)
JORDAN (Jor)
KENNET (Eng)
KIKORI (Papua)
KOLYMA (USSR)
LIDDEL (Sc)
LIFFEY (Ire)
MAMORE (Bol)
MEDINA (Eng)
MEDWAY (Eng)
MEKONG (Viet)
MERSEY (Eng)
MOHAWK (US)
MOISIE (Can)
MOSKVA (USSR)
MURRAY (Aus)
NECKAR (Ger)
NEISSE (Ger, Pol)
NELSON (Can)
NOATAK (US)
ORANGE (SA)

ORWELL (Eng)
OTTAWA (Can)
PARANA (Arg)
PARROT (Eng)
PRIPET (USSR)
QUOILE (Ire)
RIBBLE (Eng)
ROTHER (Eng)
RUPERT (Can)
SABINE (US)
SALMON (US)
SCHELD (Belg, Fr)
SEIONT (Wal)
SEVERN (Can, Eng)
TANANA (US)
TEVIOT (Sc)
THAMES (Eng) [Isis]
THURSO (Sc)
TIGRIS (Iraq)
TUGELA (SA)
TUMMEL (Sc)
TURKEY (US)
UMPQUA (US)
USSURI (USSR)
VIENNE (Fr)
VILYNY (USSR)
WABASH (US)
WEAVER (Eng)
WENSUM (Eng)
YAMUNA (Ind)
YARROW (Sc)
YELLOW (Ch)

7-letters
ACHERON (myth)
ALABAMA (US)
ANALONG (Ire)
BERMEJO (Arg)
BIG HORN (US)
COCYTUS (myth)

DARLING (Aus)
DERWENT (Aus, Eng)
DEVERON (Sc)
DNIEPER (USSR)
DOUGLAS (Eng)
DURANCE (Fr)
ETTRICK (Sc)
GARONNE (Fr)
GIRONDE (Fr)
HOANG-HO (Ch)
LIMPOPO (Moz)
LA PLATA (Braz)
MADEIRA (Braz)
MEANDER (Turk)
MERANON (Peru)
MOSELLE (Fr)
OCEANUS (myth)
ORINOCO (Venez)
OWENBOY (Ire)
PHARPAR (bibl)
POTOMAC (US)
RED DEER (Can)
ROANOKE (US)
SALWEEN (Bur/Ch)
SCHELDE (Belg, Fr)
SELENGA (Mong)
SHANNON (Ire)
SUNDAYS (SA)
SUNGARI (USSR)
TAPAJOS (Braz)
TRINITY (US)
UCAYALI (Peru)
WELLAND (Eng)
XANTHUS (Turk)
YANGTSE (Ch)
YENISEI (USSR)
YSTWYTH (Wal)
ZAMBESI (Zam)

8-letters
AMU-DARYA (USSR)

ARAGUAIA (Braz)
COLORADO (Arg; US)
COLUMBIA (US)
DELAWARE (US)
EVENLODE (Eng)
FINDHORN (Sc)
FLINDERS (Aus)
GUIVIARE (Venez)
HAMILTON (Can)
ILLINOIS (US)
MISSOURI (US)
MITCHELL (Aus)
PARAGUAY (Arg)
PARNAIBA (Braz)
PUTUMAYO (Braz)
SAVANNAH (US)
STINCHOR (Sc)
SUWANNEE (US)
TORRIDGE (Eng)
TUNGUSKA (USSR)
VICTORIA (Aus)
WANSBECK (Eng)

9+ letters
BLACKWATER (Ire)
BRAMAPUTRA (Pak)
ESSEQUIBO (Guy)
EUPHRATES (Iraq)
HACKENSACK (US)
HELMSDALE (Sc)
INDIGIRKA (USSR)
IRRAWADDY (Bur)
MACKENZIE (Can)
MADRE DE DIOS (Bol)
MISSISSIPPI (US)
PILCOMAYO (Arg/Para)
PYRIPHLEGETHON (myth)
QU'APPELLE (Can)
RICHELIEU (Can)
RIO GRANDE (Mex)
ROOSEVELT (Braz)
SAO FRANCISCO (Braz)
ST LAWRENCE (Can)
TENNESSEE (US)
TOCANTINS (Braz)
TROMBETAS (Braz)
YANGTSEKIANG (Ch)

RIVERSIDE *BANK*; ON EDGE.
RLY *RAILWAY*.
RM ROYAL MARINES; JOLLIES. [Irish ~, Major Yeates]. Malagasy Rep (*car plate*).
ROACH *CARP*, *FISH*. CONVEX PART OF SAIL. COCKROACH.
ROAD (s/l rowed). AVE, RD, MI, MIV, ST. DRAG, HIGHWAY, PIKE, STREET, WAY (q.v.). FROG AND TOAD (*rh sl*).
ROBBER BANDOLERO, BURGLAR, CRACKSMAN, PILFERER, SHOPLIFTER, *STEALER*, SWAGMAN, THIEF, YEGG; TEA LEAF (*rh sl*); [*cat*]. **Gk god** = *Hermes*; **celeb**: *AUTOLYCUS* (Gk myth); *BARABBAS* (bibl); *CACUS* (Rom myth); COL BLOOD (Crown Jewels); DANE, WILLIAM (Silas Marner, Eliot); DIDDLER, JEREMY (Raising of the Wind, Kenny); DODGER, ARTFUL (Oliver, *Dickens*); DOONES (Lorna Doone, Blackmore); FAGIN (Oliver, *Dickens*); FILCH

(Beggars Opera, Gay); KAMAL (East and West, Kipling); MEG
MERRILIES (Guy Mannering, Scott); *PROCRUSTES* (Gk myth);
SCIRON (Gk myth); *SINIS* (Gk myth); SIKES, BILL (Oliver,
Dickens); *TOM* (Piper's son); *WILD*, JONATHAN (~, Defoe,
Fielding).

ROBERTSON WILLIAM I (crypt).

ROBIN *BIRD*, REDBREAST, RUDDOCK. CHRISTOPHER
(*Milne*). GOODFELLOW, PICK. *HOOD, OUTLAW.* **Pl** =
BRISTOL CITY, CHARLTON ATHLETIC (*football* teams).

ROCHESTER **Episcopal sig** = ROFFEN. *CASTLE. MEDWAY
TOWN.* Character in Jane Eyre, who goes *blind* [*Mason*]
(*Brontë*).

ROCKERY GARDEN (ROCK/STONE). QUARRY (crypt).
CRADLE, NURSERY (crypt).

ROCKET BAZOOKA, BANGER, CONGREVE, FIREWORK,
FLYING BOMB, FLARE, *SPACECRAFT, WEAPON.*
CARPET, REPRIMAND. RAILWAY ENGINE [Stevenson].

ROCK SINGER ELVIS. LORELEI, SIREN (crypt). NANNY,
NURSEMAID [Lullaby] (crypt).

ROD SYMBOL; BAR, CANE, *POLE*, SWITCH, WAND [*Aaron's*
and *Moses'* ~s. *Garter*]; **comp** = *line*. SHAFT. GUN, PISTOL,
REVOLVER (sl). EYEPIECE, RETINA. *PERCH, MEASURE.*

ROFFEN *Episcopal sig* of *ROCHESTER*.

ROLLING STONE NOMAD, WANDERER [no moss; *Sisyphus*]. **Pl**
= POP GROUP.

Rom *Roman*; (and see *Roman Place Names*).

ROMAN 1. LATIN. *TYPEFACE*. UPRIGHT TYPE. OF ROME
(**noblest** ~ = Brutus). 2. Put into Latin, e.g. **He is Roman** = EST.

~ COIN AS, DENARIUS, SOLIDUS, TALENT.

~ GOD LAR (and see *god*).

~ GODDESS See *goddess*.

~ PLACE NAME The following are some of the better known names
of Roman towns in Britain, with their modern equivalents.

4-letters
DEVA *Chester*
ISCA Caerleon
~ (Dumnuniorum) *Exeter*
MONA Anglesey

DANUM Doncaster
ITIIS (Ins) St Michael's
  Mount
NIDUM Neath
RATAE Leicester
SARUM *Salisbury*
VENTA Caistor

5-letters
BANNA Bewcastle

~ (Belgarum) *Winchester*
~ (Silurium) Caerwent

6-letters
ABONAE Sea Mills
ALABUM Landovery
ALAUNA Learchild
ARBEIA South Shields
BREMIA Llanio
DUBRIS Dover
GLEVUM Gloucester
LINDUM *Lincoln*
MAGNIS Kenchester
OTHONA Bradwell
SPINIS Speen
VECTIS (Ins) *Isle of
  Wight*

7-letters
BINOVIA Binchester
BURRIUM Usk
CALLEVA Silchester
CAONIUM Rivenhall
CICUTIO Y-Glaer
CONDATE Northwich
CUNETIO Mildenhall
ISURIUM Aldborough
LEMANIS Lympne
MONAVA (Ins) *Isle of
  Man*
SALINAE Droitwich

8-letters
AD PONTEM East Stoke
ANDERITA Pevensey
BLESTIUM Monmouth
CANOVIUM Caerhun
CARINIUM Cirencester
EBORACUM *York*
LINDINIS Ilchester
MAMUCIUM Manchester

RUTUPIAE Richborough
SEGENTUM Caernarvon
VERLUCIO Sandy Lane

9-letters
ARDOTALIA Melandra
LAGENTIUM Tadcaster
LONDINIUM *London*
MORIDUNUM Carmarthen
REGULBIUM Reculver
URICONIUM Wroxeter
VAGNIACAE Springhead
VONDOMORA Ebchester

10-letters
AQUAE SULIS Bath
BRANODUNUM Brancaster
CLAUSENTUM Southampton
DORNOVARIA Dorchester
DURNOVARIA *Chesterton*
DUROBRIVAE *Rochester*
DUROLIPONS *Cambridge*
DUROVERNUM *Canterbury*
GORBANNIUM Abergavenny
LACTODORUM Towcester
LUGUVALIUM Carlisle
MEDIOLANUM Whitchurch
NOVIOMAGUS *Chichester*
~ Crayford
VERULAMIUM *St Albans*
VIROCONIUM Wroxeter

11+ letters
CAESAROMAGUS
  Chelmsford
CAMULODUNUM
  Colchester
CATARACTONIUM
  Catterick
DUROCOBRIVAE
  Dunstable

DUROVIGUTUM
  Godmanchester
LONGOVICIUM
  Lanchester

MAGIOVINIUM
  Dropshort
SERVIODUNUM Old
  Sarum
VINDOCLADIA Badbury

ROMAN ROADS The following are some of the better known Roman roads in Britain:

AKEMAN'S ST
ASHWELL ST
DERE ST
DEVIL'S CAUSEWAY
ERMINE ST
FOSSE WAY
ICKNIELD WAY

PEDDAR'S WAY
PILGRIM'S WAY (path)
PORTWAY
RIDGE WAY
RYKNILD ST
STANE ST
WATLING ST

~ **SOLDIER** See *SOLDIER*.

~ **TRIBES** See *TRIBES*.

ROME (s/l roam). 1. ETERNAL CITY, SPQR [*Aeneas*, *AUC*, Seven Hills, *Romulus* and *Remus*; A and C, Cor, Titus (*Shak*)]. 2. Implies Latin, e.g. **They go out in Rome** (6) = EXUENT.

ROMULUS Rom myth *twin* br of *Remus*, s of *Mars* and *Rhea* (Silvia), suckled by wolves, founded *Rome*. Slew his br.

ROOK *BIRD*, *CROW*. *CHEAT*, *ROB*. *CHESSPIECE* (*CASTLE*).

ROOKERY HABITATION (penguins, *rooks*, seals). BURGLARY, *ROBBERY* (crypt).

ROSE (s/l roes, *rows*). *FLOWER*, *TREE*; [St Dorothy; St *Elizabeth* of Hungary (bread into ~s); *Abraham* (fire into bed of ~s in Mos faith)] 'RHODA'. ASCENDED, *MOUNTED*, SOARED; GOT UP (hence TOG, dn crypt). REBELLED. SPRINKLER. BADGE (polit; Lab). *WINDOW*. *WORLD-GIRDLER*. *WRITER*. **Comp** = *crown*.

~ **BOWL** FLOWER VASE. *FOOTBALL* GROUND/COMPETITION (US college).

ROSETTA STONE Memorial inscription to *Ptolemy* V (205–181 B.C.) in hieroglyph, demotic (coptic) and Greek languages on a slab of black basalt, discovered in 1799 by a French officer in the Nile delta. It proved the key to the meaning of hieroglyphics.

ROSE WATER SCENTED WATER, COMPLIMENT [gentle handling]. *SHOWER*, SPRAY (crypt).

ROSIE LEE *TEA* (*rh sl*).

ROSINANTE NAG, *HORSE*, *SCREW* (Don *Quixote*).

ROT DECAY, PUTREFACTION. BOSH, NONSENSE, RUBBISH. BANTER, CHAFF, *TEASE*.

ROUGH (s/l *ruff*). *Anag*. CRUDE. SHAGGY, UNEVEN. BOISTEROUS, RIOTOUS, SEVERE, VIOLENT.

ROUND 1. O (crypt). DRINKS, TURN, TREAT. SANDWICH. CONTINUOUS, ENTIRE, UNBROKEN. CANDID, GENUINE. CIRCULAR, REVOLVING, ROTUND, SPHERICAL. BULLET, SHELL. GAME (golf). **Pl** = INSPECTION ROUTE, VISITS (med). 2. Word round another, e.g. **He's round at the sports eliminators** (5) = HE*AT*S. 3. Letter A before any synonym for 'round', e.g. A*BOUT, A*CIRCLE, A*DISC, A*RING, A*WHEEL, A*NIL, A*ZERO (crypt).

ROUNDABOUT 1. C, CA, CIRCUMLOCUTION. ROAD JUNCTION. CONVOLUTED. MERRYGOROUND (fairground). 2. Word round synonym for 'about', e.g. **The roundabout between two and four** (5) = TH*RE*E. 3. Word or letter plus synonym for 'round' placed about word or letter indicated, e.g. **When roundabout fifty, too** (4) = A*L*S*O.

ROUNDHEAD 1. PARLIAMENTARIAN (**opp** = Cavalier). SKINHEAD. R (crypt). 2. Place letter O before synonym for 'head', e.g. OHEAD, OPATE, ONUT. 3. Place letter O before any word or letter indicated, e.g. **At Roundhead fodder** (3) = O*AT.

ROUNDSMAN *DELIVERY MAN*: MILKMAN, PAPERBOY, POSTMAN. GOLFER (crypt).

ROUND TABLE BUSINESS ASSOCIATION, ROTARY CLUB. ORDER OF CHIVALRY (hist) [*Camelot*, *King Arthur*; **knights**: Bedivere (Tennyson), Bors (Tennyson), Calidore (Spenser), *Galahad* (Tennyson), Gawain (Tennyson), Geraint (Tennyson), *Lancelot* (Tennyson), Launfal (Lowell), Mordred (Tennyson), Pelleas (Tennyson), Percivale (Tennyson), Tristram (Malory); **Ladies**: Elaine (loved Sir *Lancelot*), Enid (wife of Geraint), Ettarre (loved Gawain, loved by Pelleas), Guinevere (wife of *King Arthur*, loved *Lancelot*), Iseult (Tristram), *Lady of the Lake* (Vivien), Lady of Shalott (*weaver*), Morgan le Fey (*sorceress*)].

ROUSE (s/l rows). AWAKEN, INFLAME, PROVOKE, STARTLE, STIR (UP), WAKEN. BUMPER, DRAUGHT; DRINKING BOUT, REVEL, TOAST. HAUL. CURE FISH.

ROW (s/l roe). OAR, PULL, SCULL. ALIGNMENT, DRESSING, FILE, LINE, RANGE, RANK, TERRACE, *TIER*.

BATTLE, DISAGREEMENT, FIGHT, WAR. DIN, NOISE,
RACKET, SHINDY.

ROWER OARSMAN, SCULLER, *STROKE*, WET-BOB.
ARGUER, FIGHTER, SCOLD, SHREW (all crypt). DRILL
SERGEANT (crypt).

ROWING SCULLING, STROKING; PADDLING.
ALTERCATION, ARGUING, DISAGREEING, FIGHTING.
ALIGNING, DRILLING, LINING-UP (crypt).

ROYAL R; MAJESTIC, REGAL. *COLOUR* (blue). *THEATRE*.
ANTELOPE. *SAIL*. *MEASURE* (paper). **Pl** = ROYAL
FAMILY. HORSEGUARDS, HOUSEHOLD CAVALRY.

~ **AIR FORCE** RAF. *AIRMEN*.

~ **AND ANCIENT** RA. *GOLF CLUB*.

~ **ARMOURED CORPS** RAC. TANKERS (crypt).

~ **ARTILLERY** RA. *GUNMEN*, GUNNERS.

~ **AUTOMOBILE CLUB** RAC. CARMEN.

~ **ENGINEER** RE. SAPPER. EMINENCE GRISE (crypt;
Richelieu).

~ **FAMILY** *HOUSE*, RULING LINE [court cards; *Ch dynasty*; *mad
king*; *monarch*; *noble*]; **celeb**:

Country	Family
Abyssinia	MENELUK (Solomon/Sheba)
Austria	HABSBURG/HAPSBURG
Bavaria	WITTELSBACH
Belgium	COBURG
China	HWAN, MANCHU, MING, TANG
Denmark	OLDENBURG
France	BOURBON, CAPET, VALOIS
Franks	CHARLEMAGNE
Germany	HOHENZOLLERN
Greece	SCHLESWIG-HOLSTEIN
Holy Roman Empire	HABSBURG/HAPSBURG, HOHENSTAUFEN
Hungary	HABSBURG/HAPSBURG
India	GUPTA
Ireland	DESMOND, MCCARTHY, O'BRIEN, O'CONNOR, O'NEILL
Italy	*SAVOY*
Monaco	GRIMALDI
Morocco	ALAOUITE

Netherlands	*ORANGE*
Poland	JAGELLON
Portugal	BRAGANZA
Prussia	HOHENZOLLERN
Rumania	HOHENZOLLERN
Ruritania	ELPHBERG (fict)
Russia	ROMANOFF
Scotland	STUART
Spain	BOURBON, HAPSBURG
Sweden	BERNADOTTE, VASA
UK	HANOVER, PLANTAGENET, STUART, TUDOR, WINDSOR
Wales	GLYNDWR, LLEWELLYN, MORTIMER, TUDOR

ROYAL SOCIETY RS. THE *COURT*, PALACE ENTOURAGE (crypt).

RR RIGHT REVEREND, hence *BISHOP*.

RRR BASIC EDUCATION, THREE R'S.

RT RIGHT. RADIO TELEPHONE.

RUBBISH BOSH, *ROT*. REFUSE.

RUBY *GEM*, PRECIOUS STONE; BALAS, CORUNDUM; *anniversary* (40th). *COLOUR* (red). *DOG* (John Peel). *TYPEFACE*.

RUDE COARSE, IMPOLITE, INSOLENT, OFFENSIVE, UNCIVILIZED. CRUDE, PRIMITIVE, SIMPLE. ABRUPT, SUDDEN, VIOLENT. HEARTY, VIGOROUS.

RUDOLF *LAKE*. *REINDEER*. RASSENDYLL (Prisoner of Zenda, *Hope*).

RUFF (s/l *rough*). FRILL, NECK-PIECE, PARTLET. *BIRD*, PIGEON, SANDPIPER (**female** = reeve). *FISH*. TRUMP (cards) hence *TRUMPERY* (crypt).

RUGBY FOOTBALL. RUGGER [**Grounds**: Cardiff Arms Park (Wal), Lansdowne Road (Ire), Murrayfield (Sc), Twickenham (Eng)]. [2 for conversion; 3 for try]. *PUBLIC SCHOOL*. *SERVANT* (to Dr Caius, Merry Wives, *Shak*).

~ **MAN** FOOTBALLER. SCHOOLBOY. DR ARNOLD, TOM BROWN, FLASHMAN. W. W. ELLIS. **Pl** = ALL-BLACKS, LIONS, SPRINGBOKS, WALLABIES.

RUIN *Anag*. 1. DOWNFALL. REMAINS, RESIDUE. HAVOC, IMPAIR, MAR, SPOIL. BANKRUPT, BREAK, WRECK.

2. Put RU in word before or after, e.g. **Did ruin Welsh priest**
(5) = D*RU*ID.

RULER AMEER, AMIR, KING, MONARCH, SOVEREIGN,
SULTAN; CHIEF (**opp** = *subject*). *MEASURE*, STRAIGHT-
EDGE; LINER (crypt). *GORGON*.

RUM *DRINK*, LIQUOR, SPIRIT; NELSON'S BLOOD, TOT.
DANGEROUS, DIFFICULT. *ODD*, QUEER, STRANGE.
ISLAND.

Rum Rumania, ~n.

RUN DOUBLE, LOPE, SCAMPER, SPEED, STREAK; **comp** =
hit. COURSE, FLOW. MANAGE, ORGANIZE. SINGLE
(*cricket*). CAGE, PEN. SMUGGLE. *LADDER*. CRESTA. **Pl**
= SCORE (*cricket*).

RUNNER *FLOWER*, RIVER, R (crypt). SMUGGLER.
ATHLETE. BEAN.

~ **UP** *SECOND*, SILVER MEDALLIST. DRESSMAKER. NAEB
(dn, crypt).

RUN UP APPROACH, INTRODUCTION. (DRESS) MAKE.
NUR (dn, crypt).

RURAL DEAN RD. *CHURCHMAN*.

RUSH ADVANCE PRINT, CLIP (film). MARSH PLANT, REED,
STRAW (and see *GRASS*). ASSAULT, CHARGE, DASH,
DRAG, FORCE, IMPEL, STAMPEDE, SWARM.
OVERCHARGE. FALL, FLOW, HURRY. **Pl** = see *song*.

Russ Russia, ~n (as opposed to USSR).

RUSSIAN RED. IVAN, SERGE.

RUSTLER CATTLE-THIEF, HORSE-THIEF; STEERSMAN
(crypt). FORAGER. *SILK*, TAFFETA (crypt).

RUTH 1. COMPASSION, PITY. 'A FRIEND'. BABE (*baseball*).
G & S. 2. Moabite who mar (1) Mahlon (2) Boaz [Naomi (Mara)
mother-in-law. *Tears* amid the alien corn (Keats)].

RV REVISED VERSION, BIBLE. RENDEZ-VOUS, MEETING
PLACE, TRYST.

RYE *DRINK*, WHISKY. CORN. *GRASS*. CINQUE PORT.
RIVER (Eng).

S *SAINT*. SAN, SANTA. SATURDAY. *SECOND*.
SINGULAR. SMALL. SOCIETY. SOLIDUS, SHILLING.
SON. *SOUTH*. ST. STARBOARD. SULPHUR (*chem*).

SUNDAY. SWEDEN (*car plate*). BRIDGE PLAYER. DOLLAR.

SA SEX APPEAL; *CHARM*, IT. SOUTH AFRICA.

SABLE BLACK (*herald*). DREAD, DUSKY, GLOOMY. MARTEN. PAINTBRUSH.

SABRE CUTLASS, SWORD, *WEAPON*. *AIRCRAFT*.

SACK *DISCHARGE*. PILLAGE, PLUNDER. *BAG*. *DRESS*. FABRIC, *MATERIAL*. *MEASURE* (wool). SHERRY, *WINE*.

SADDLE *MOUNT*, RIDE (**in the** ~ = UP); BACK-SEAT (crypt). BURDEN. *COL*.

SADLY *Anag*. REGRETFULLY, RUEFULLY, SORROWFULLY.

SAGE DISCREET, JUDICIOUS, WISE; MAGUS (**Pl** = MAGI), MAHATMA (Ind), MENTOR, SAVANT, WISEACRE, WISEMAN [Nestor (*Argonaut*), Solomon, Solon]. *HERB*. *CHEESE*. And see *Seven ~s*.

SAID 1. RECITED, SPOKEN, UTTERED; ORAL; **comp** = *done*. PORT (Egy). 2. *Sounds like* another word.

SAIL (s/l sale). CANVAS, PROPELLANT (naut), **types**: BONNET, COURSE, DRABBLER, DRIVER, FLYING JIB, FORESAIL, GENOA, JIB, GAFF, GUNTER, LATEEN, LUG, MAINSAIL, MIZZEN, ROYAL, SKYSAIL, SPANKER, SPINNAKER, SPRIT, SQUARESAIL, STAYSAIL, STUDDING SAIL, TOPGALLANT, TOPSAIL, YANKEE. COLLECTION/*ASSEMBLY* OF SHIPS, SHIP; JOURNEY, NAVIGATE, VOYAGE (**opp** = *steam*). DORSAL FIN (fish). BLADE (windmill [Don Quixote]). SOAR (aero).

SAILOR AB, CREW, DECKHAND, GOB (US), *HAND*, JACK, OS, RATING, SALT, TAR; (**Union** = NUS), CRAFTSMAN (crypt), *REEFER* (crypt). RN, USN. YACHTSMAN. **Celeb**: CAPT *AHAB* (*Moby Dick*), ANCIENT MARINER (Coleridge), TOM BOWLING (Smollett), BILLY BUDD (Melville), CHUCKS (Marryat), LONG TOM COFFIN (Fenimore Cooper), CAPT CUTTLE (*Dickens*), DICK DEADEYE (*Pinafore*, *G & S*), MIDSHIPMAN EASY (Marryat), LEMUEL GULLIVER (Swift), RAPHAEL HYTHLODAY (More), DANIEL & HAM PEGGOTTY (*Dickens*), LT *PINKERTON* (Mme *Butterfly*, Puccini), SHIPMAN (*Chaucer*), SIN(D)BAD (Arabian Nights), DISCO TROOP (Kipling), SALVATION YEO (Kingsley); [*military leaders*, *world-girdlers*, *patron saint*].

SAINT S, ST. *ANGEL*. GOODMAN (crypt). [*patron ~*]. **Pl** = *Football* teams (UK & US).

ST ALBANS 1. **Episcopal sig** = ALBAN. 2. VERULAMIUM (*Rom*).

ST CATHERINE Virgin martyr of Alexandria (4th century). Tradition represents her as tied to a *wheel* [*firework*].

ST ELMO'S FIRE CORPOSANT. Glowing corona, like fire, caused by elect discharge around ch spires and ship masts (and more lately aircraft wings or propellers), associated in Gk myth with *Dioscuri* and *Helen*. Derived from *Elijah* = Elias = Elmo, who confounded the priests of *Baal* and *Astarte*, when only he was able to call down to Mt Carmel fire from heaven; c.f. *ignis fatuus* (which is chem different).

ST LEGER *CLASSIC* (horserace).

SALAMIS Site of a great sea *battle* near Athens in 480 B.C., in which 300 Gk ships under Themistocles defeated over five times their number of *Xerxes'* invading fleet.

SALARY EMOLUMENT, INCOME, PAY, *SCREW*, STIPEND, WAGE.

SALISBURY 1. **Episcopal sig** = SARUM. 2. HARARE (ex-*capital* of Rhodesia/Zimbabwe. SARUM (*Rom*).

SALLY BELL ROPE. COCONUT SHY. OUTBURST, WIT. SALVATION ARMY. SORTIE. STONE-FLY. WREN. SARAH. LUNN [tea-cake].

SALMANAZAR 1. *BOTTLE* (wine = 12 normal). 2. Bibl king of Assyria *c*. 725 B.C., who conquered Isr and captured Samaria.

SALMON RIVER (US). *FISH* (genus salmonidae); **stages:** ALEVIN (fry), BAGGIT (after spawning), KELT (spent), SAMLET (young), SMOLT (1st sea migration), SPRAG (young), SPROD (2nd year); **types:** BARRAMUNDI (Aus, NZ), BLUE-BACK, BLUE-CAP, CAPLIN, COHO(E) (Pacific), FORKTAIL, GWINIAD (fresh water), KIPPER, KOKANEE (N Am), OUANANICHE (Can), PALLAN (Ire), PARR, QUINNAT (King ~), RED ~, SEWIN (Wal), SMELT, SOCKEYE, SPARLING; **male** = cock, **fem** = hen, **offspring** = grilse, peal.

SALOME 1. Bibl sis of Mary (m of *Jesus*) and mar to Zebedee. 2. Herodias' d (bibl), who danced (seven veils) before her step-f *Herod* Antipas and, at her m's behest, exacted the head of John the Baptist. 3. Play by *Wilde*.

SALT SEASONING; BRINE, *MINERAL*, SODIUM CHLORIDE (NACL, *chem*) [*Lot's* wife]. ARMS TALK. *ISLAND*. PUNGENCY, STING, WIT. *SAILOR*. ~ meat = *JUNK*.

SALUTE *BOW*, *GREET*, *HAIL*, *KISS*; ACCOST (Aloha, Ave,

Hallo, Hi). HOMAGE; GUNFIRE.

SAM BROWNE (mil). SMALL (theat). MISSILE (*rocket*), *WEAPON*.

SAME DITTO, DO, IDEM. MONOTONOUS, UNIFORM, SIMILAR.

~ **PLACE** IB(ID).

SAMPHIRE *HERB*; CLIFFHANGER (crypt), CLIMBER (crypt).

SAMSON 1. Bibl Jew s of Manaoh, he mar a Phil, trad enemies of Isr. Endowed with great *strength*, he was betrayed by the *courtesan* Delilah, who sapped his powers by cutting off his hair. Captured and blinded by the Phil, his strength was miraculously restored so he could pull down the temple of Dagon. 2. Servant (R & J, *Shak* [Sampson]). 3. ~ Agonistes; blind wrestler (Milton). 4. Guillotine operator (2 Cities, *Dickens*). *PARSON*. 5. Mooring post for *painter* (naut).

SAMUEL Bibl s of Elkaneh and Hannah, who lived with *Eli* and travelled widely as a *judge* and *prophet*; he defeated the Phil and established Isr as a nation (*c.* 1000 B.C.). In response to demand for a king, ~ chose *Saul* (q.v.), but the latter's qualities did not last, so ~ chose *David* to succeed him. Before his final overthrow, Saul consulted the prophecy of ~'s *ghost* via the Witch of Endor.

SANDHURST ACADEMY, RMA (mil).

SANDWICH PICNIC LUNCH, SNACK; SQUARE MEAL (crypt); SARNIE (sl). LAYER CAKE. INSERT, SQUEEZE IN. *CASTLE. CINQUE PORT. GOLF COURSE.*

SAN(TA) S. SPANISH SAINT. (FATHER CHRISTMAS).

SAPPER RE; ENGINEER. LEECH (crypt).

SAPPHIRE *GEM*, PRECIOUS STONE (blue), CORUNDUM; *anniversary* (45th). *COLOUR* (blue).

SARAH *SAL(LY)*.

SARD *GEM*; SEMI-PRECIOUS STONE, CORNELIAN (orange).

SARDINE FISH, SARDELLE, YOUNG PILCHARD [herring]. *GEM*, SEMI-PRECIOUS STONE. **Pl** = *GAME* [tight-packed].

SARDONYX *GEM*, mix of *sard* and *onyx* (orange and white); *birthstone* (August).

SARK CI, CHANNEL ISLAND. SHIRT. ROOFBOARDING.

SARUM SALISBURY (*Rom*). *Episcopal sig* of SALISBURY.

SAS SPECIAL AIR SERVICE. SCANDINAVIAN AIR SERVICE (*airline*®).

SATAN *DEVIL*, IMP, LUCIFER, OLD NICK (lit = adversary).

SATELLITE 1. FOLLOWER, HANGER-ON, HENCHMAN.

DEPENDENT COUNTRY. 2. Moon or other body orbiting a *planet* or star. 3. A *SPACECRAFT*.

SATIRIST CYNIC, LAMPOONIST [irony, ridicule, sarcasm]; **celebrated**: BUTLER (Eng), BYRON (Eng), DRYDEN (Eng), HOGARTH (Eng), HORACE (Rom), JUVENAL (Rom), LA BRUYERE (Fr), POPE (Eng), RABELAIS (Fr), *SWIFT* (Eng), VOLTAIRE (Fr).

SATURDAY S, SA, SAT. Day of *Saturn*. ~s child = works hard for its living. [Solomon *Grundy*].

SATURN 1. Rom *god* of agriculture, after whom Italy was called Saturnia at one time; mar to Ops. **Gk** = CRONOS. [Saturday]. 2. *PLANET*.

SATYR Gk myth woodland deities, half man half *goat*, with horned head, pointed ears and a tail. Chief among them was *Pan*. Representatives attended *Bacchus*, at the feasts staged by humans to him. **Rom** = FAUN.

SAUCE (s/l *source*). CHEEK, IMPERTINENCE, IMPUDENCE. RELISH, KETCHUP: HP®, PARSLEY, TOMATO, WORCESTERSHIRE® etc. DRINK (US sl).

SAUCY *ARCH*, CHEEKY, IMPUDENT (**opp** = *retiring*, *shy*). SEASONED (cook, crypt).

SAUL 1. Bibl s of Kish and f of Ishbaal and Jonathan, whom *Samuel* chose as first king of Isr (*c*. 1000 B.C.). Power corrupted him and he went *mad*, so that *David* was chosen to succeed, but ~ retained much influence. ~ persuaded the Witch of Endor to call up the *ghost* of Samuel for a prophecy before the fateful battle of Gilboa, at which both ~'s s were k, and ~ suffered severe defeat by the Phil; sui. 2. Name of *Paul* (q.v.) before his conversion.

SAVE DELIVER, PRESERVE, PROTECT, RESCUE. BUT, EXCEPT, UNLESS.

SAVOY CABBAGE. HOTEL. *ROYAL FAMILY* (It).

SAW NOTICED, SPOTTED. SERRATED/TOOTHED TOOL; **types**: BAND ~, COPING ~, CROSS-CUT ~, CIRCULAR ~, FRET ~, HACK ~, JIG ~, TENON ~; CUT, RIP. ADAGE, MAXIM, PROVERB, *SAYING*.

Sax Saxon.

SAY EG, FOR INSTANCE. *Sounds like* . . .

SAYING ADAGE, APHORISM, BON MOT, BYWORD, DEFINITION, MAXIM, MOTTO, PROVERB, QUOTATION, SAW.

Sc Scotland, ~ish. For ~ regions, see *Division*. SCANDIUM (*chem*).

SCALE 1. CLIMB, *MOUNT.* CLASSIFICATION,
GRADUATION [vernier]. PITCH ARRANGEMENT
(chromatic, diatonic, *major*, *minor*, pantatonic; A–G). FLAKE,
HUSK, PLATE, POD, SCAB. INCRUSTATION, RUST.
BALANCE, WEIGHING INSTRUMENT. 2. A *constellation*
(Libra); sign of the *Zodiac* (7th).

SCAMPER *DASH*, *RUN.*

SCAN EXAMINE, LOOK AT, OVERLOOK. RESOLVE. READ
RHYTHMICALLY (test verse by examining each metric *foot*).
SCANDINAVIA.

SCENE (s/l *seen*). STAGE. ACTION, INCIDENT.
LANDSCAPE, LOCATION, PAINTING, PLACE, VIEW,
VISTA. LIFESTYLE. QUARREL, *ROW.*

SCENT (s/l *cent*, sent). AROMA, FRAGRANCE, ODOUR,
PERFUME, SMELL. SPOOR, TRACK, TRAIL. CLUE,
DETECT, SNIFF, SUSPECT.

SCH *SCHOOL.*

SCHOLAR BA, MA, L; SCHOOLBOY/GIRL. SECOND AGE
(AYLI, *Shak*). LEARNED PERSON, CHELA (Ind),
DISCIPLE, SAVANT [*patron saint*]; *Chaucer* character,
ERASMUS.

SCHOOL DISCIPLINE, TAME, TEACH, TRAIN. DISCIPLES,
FOLLOWERS, IMITATORS. *Assembly* of cardplayers, fish,
porpoises, whales. ALMA MATER, CLASS, PLACE OF
EDUCATION, SCH [*patron saint*]; **celeb (fiction)**: BROOKFIELD
(Goodbye Mr Chips, James Hilton), DOTHEBOYS HALL (Nich
Nick, *Dickens*), GRANGE HILL (TV), GREYFRIARS (*Famous
Five*, Frank Richards), LOWWOOD (Jane Eyre, C. *Brontë*), ST
TRINIANS (Ronald Searle), SALEM HOUSE (Copperfield,
Dickens); **celeb (public)** ~s: see *Public Schools*.

SCHOOLMASTER BEAK, DOMINIE (Sc), *MASTER*, TEACHER,
TUTOR; SIR (**opp** = *miss*); **celeb**: DR ARNOLD (*Rugby*); DR
BLIMBER (Dombey, *Dickens*); BROCKLEHURST (Jane Eyre,
C. *Brontë*); CHIPPING (Goodbye Mr Chips, James Hilton);
CREAKLE (Copperfield, *Dickens*); GRADGRIND (Hard Times,
Dickens); HOLOFERNES (LLL); PARTRIDGE (Tom Jones,
Fielding); PINCH (C of Errors); QUELCH (*Greyfriars*, Richards);
SQUEERS (Nich Nick, *Dickens*); DR STRONG (Copperfield,
Dickens).

SCHOONER *BOAT*, (SAILING) VESSEL, SHIP. GLASS (sherry).

SCIRON (s/l *Skiron*). Gk myth *robber* who kicked all strangers over a cliff where they were devoured by a *tortoise*; slain by *Theseus*.

SCOFF GIBE, MOCK, TAUNT. EAT, *WOLF*; FOOD, GRUB, MEAL (sl).

SCOLD NAG, RAIL, REBUKE, *UPBRAID*; SHREW, SPITFIRE, TERMAGANT, VIRAGO [Kate (*Shak*). *Xanthippe*].

SCORE BLAZE, *MARK*, *NICK*, NOTCH, SCRATCH, SLASH. TWENTY, XX. COMPOSE, *MUSIC*, *NOTED*. (MAKE) *RUNS*, POINTS, POT, TOTAL.

SCOREBOARD DISPLAY, TALLYWAG. MUSIC STAND (crypt).

SCORPION 1. ARACHNID (*insect*). BALLISTA (hist). GIBRALTARIAN (sl). TANK (mil). *WHIP* (bibl). 2. *Constellation* (Scorpio); sign of the *Zodiac* (8th).

SCOT NATIVE OF SCOTLAND; IAN, JOCK, MAC, MC, MON. *TAX*. **Pl** = Scottish (for ~s Regions, see *Division*).

SCOTCH SCOTS, SCOTTISH; GAELIC; CELTIC. DRINK, WHISKY. BRAKE, WEDGE (mech). MARK, *SCORE*, WOUND. END, FRUSTRATE.

SCOTT (s/l *scot*). 1. Sir Giles Gilbert ~; archit. 2. Capt Robert Falcon ~; *explorer*. 3. Sir Walter ~; *poet*, *writer*; **books**: Bride of Lammermoor, Guy Mannering, Ivanhoe, Kenilworth, *Lady of the Lake*, Lay of the Last Minstrel, Marmion, Rob Roy, Rokeby, Talisman, Two Drovers, Waverley novels. 4. Gloria ~ (*Holmes* case). 5. Sir Peter ~, s of (2); naturalist and *painter*.

SCOUT SERVANT, VALET (Oxford [C = gyp]). REJECT, RIDICULE. ADVANCE PARTY, FORAGER, RANGER, RECCE, RECONNOITRE, TRAIL-BLAZER, VANGUARD (mil). FIGHTER (*aircraft*). CHAP, FELLOW. CADET, BOY. PATROLMAN. BIRD.

SCRAMBLE *Anag*. e.g. **Scrambled eggs** = GEGS, SEGG etc. CLAMBER, CRAWL. *MIX*, *STIR*. *FLY*, TAKE OFF (av sl).

SCRAP *BATTLE*, CONTEST, DISPUTE, FIGHT, QUARREL, *ROW*, SCRIMMAGE. *REFUSE*, WASTE. DISCARD. FRAGMENT, ODDMENT, PIECE, *RAG*, REMNANT.

SCRATCH NOTCH, *SCORE*. ITCH, SCRAPE. PAR, UNHANDICAPPED. ERASE, WITHDRAW. *DEVIL*.

SCREEN DISPLAY, PROJECT (films, radar). *BLIND*, PARTITION, REREDOS, SHADE. GRID, MESH, SIEVE. CHECK, *TEST*. *CONCEAL*, HIDE, PROTECT.

SCREW *GAOLER*. PAY, *MONEY*, SALARY, WAGES. COUPLING, FASTENING. PROPELLER [Archimedes].

REVOLVE. CONTORT, DISTORT. SQUEEZE. NAG,
POOR *HORSE* [Rosinante].

SCRIBE AMANUENSIS, ARCHIVIST, CLERK, COPYIST,
SCRIVENER, WRITER. MARKER, STYLE. JURIST,
THEOLOGIAN (bibl, Jew) [Pharisee]; **celeb**: EZRA.

SCULL (s/l *skull*). OAR, *ROW*. *BIRD*, SKUA.

SCULLERY KITCHEN, WASHROOM. ROWING [Henley]
(crypt).

SCYLLA 1. Six-headed sea monster on a rock which, with *Charybdis*,
formed a hazard for seafarers in the Straits of Messina. 2. A minor
PLANET.

SE SELENIUM (*chem*). SOUTH EAST; HOME COUNTIES,
KENT (crypt).

SEA (s/l *see*). 1. MAIN, SALT WATER. *COLOUR* (blue). **The
Seven Seas** = ANTARCTIC, ARCTIC, INDIAN, N. ATLANTIC,
S. ATLANTIC, N. PACIFIC, S. PACIFIC OCEANS. 2. **Gods:
Gk** = NEREUS, *POSEIDON*; **Rom** = NEPTUNE; **Nor** =
AEGIR. **Goddess: Gk** = *AMPHITRITE*. **Celeb seas:**

3-letters	6-letters	SOLOMON
RED	AEGEAN	
	BALTIC	**8-letters**
4-letters	BERING	ADRIATIC
ARAL	CELTIC	AMUNDSEN
AZOV	FLORES	BEAUFORT
DEAD	IONIAN	BISMARCK
JAVA	LAPTEV	HEBRIDES
KARA	TASMAN	LIGURIAN
SULU	WADDEN	*SARGASSO* (weed)
5-letters	**7-letters**	**9+ letters**
BANDA	ANDAMAN	CARIBBEAN
BLACK	ARABIAN	EAST CHINA
CERAM	ARAFURA	EAST SIBERIAN
CORAL	BARENTS	HUDSON BAY
CRETE	CASPIAN	MEDITERRANEAN
IRISH	CELEBES	NORWEGIAN
JAPAN	GALILEE	SOUTH CHINA
NORTH	MARMARA	TRANQUILLITY (moon)
TIMOR	MOLUCCA	TYRRHENIAN
WHITE	OKHOTSK	

SEAFOOD Any fish or shellfish eaten at a meal: CLAMS, COCKLES, CRABS, *FISH*, *LOBSTER*, MUSSELS, OYSTERS, PRAWNS, SHRIMPS, SQUID, WINKLES. MAIN COURSE, MAIN MEAL, HARD TACK (crypt).

SEAL 1. *CLOSE*, FASTEN, PLUG, SECURE, *STOP*. APPROVE, ATTEST, CLINCH, FINALISE, RATIFY, SETTLE, SIGN, VALIDATE; AUTHENTICATION, *AUTHORITY*, IMPRIMATUR, INSIGNIA, SIGNET (RING), *STAMP*; *WAX* [Great ~ (Mark *Twain*)]. 2. Pinniped aquatic mammal, eared or earless; **male** = bull, **fem** = cow, **offspring** = pup, **assembly** = herd, pod, rookery; **breeds of** ~: Atlantic, Californian, Caspian, common, crabeater, elephant, fur, grey, harbour, Lake Baikal, leopard, Monk, ringed, Weddel; sealion [walrus].

SEASON AUTUMN, *FALL*, *SPRING*, *SUMMER*, WINTER; **Gk goddesses** = *HORAE*. (PROPER) TIME; PERIOD. ACCLIMATIZE. ADD PIQUANCY (jests, wit; pepper, salt etc).

SEASONAL SUITABLE, TIMELY. CONDIMENTS, MUSTARD, PEPPER, *SALT* (crypt).

SEAT BENCH, CHAIR, STOOL, THRONE; BOTTOM, BUTTOCKS. POSTURE. SIT. ABIDING PLACE, COUNTRY HOUSE, PLACE, *STATELY HOME*.

SEATED ASTRIDE; *CHAIRED*, *MOUNTED* (crypt). SAT (UPON). LANDED GENTRY (crypt).

SEAWEED ALGA(E); **types**: AGAR, BROWN, CARRAGEEN, CEYLON MOSS, CLADOPHORA RUPESTRIS, CORALLINE, CORAL WEED, DEVIL'S APRON, DIATOM, GRASS KELP, IRISH MOSS, (PURPLE) LAVER, OARWEED, OREWEED, SARGASSO, SEA LETTUCE, SUGAR KELP, THONG WEED, BLADDER-, CHANNELLED-, FLAT-, KNOTTED-, SERRATED-WRACK.

SEC SECANT. SECOND(ARY). SECRETARY. *DRY* (Fr).

SECOND 1. S, SEC, TIC, TIME. B; AFTER FIRST, LATTER, NEXT BEST, NUMBER TWO, RUNNER UP, SECUNDUS; SILVER MEDALLIST. TRANSFER. ATTENDANT. D (mus). *BACK*, *SUPPORT*. FAULTY GOODS, SUB-STANDARD. 2. Second letter of previous or following word, e.g. **Second rate** = A.

~ **CLASS** B. E (*Lloyds*). L (crypt).

~ **HAND** USED, PART-WORN. MATE (naut, crypt). A (crypt).

SECRET ARCANE, CLOSE, DARK, ESOTERIC, *HIDDEN*,

MYSTERY, PRIVATE, PRIVY, RETICENT. RESTRICTED, CONFIDENTIAL.

SECRET AGENT BOND, *MOLE*, SPY.

~ POLICE Secret force allegedly to combat subversion, but usually to maintain dictatorship, much given to ruthless cruelty. **Notorious examples**: *BOSS* (S Af); CHEKA, GPU, OGPU, NKVD, NKGB, KGB (USSR); GESTAPO (Ger); PSB (Ch); TON-TON MACOUTE (VSN, Haiti).

SECURE CLOSE, FORTIFY, LATCH, LOCK. CONFIDENT; IMPREGNABLE, RELIABLE, SAFE. GET, OBTAIN.

SEE (s/l *sea*). 1. DESCRY, DISCERN, ESPY, LO, LOOK, *NOTE*, NOTICE, OBSERVE, REFLECT, *SPOT*, *WATCH*; **comp** = wait. REFER TO, VIDE. BISHOPRIC, DIOCESE, hence CHESTER, ELY etc [*episcopal sig*]. 2. Means that the answer is then visible, i.e. if you . . . you will see . . ., e.g. **Miss Chan is outside to see the President** (8) = CHA*IRMA*N.

SEED GRAIN, MILT, PIP, SEMEN. DESCENDANTS, *OFFSPRING*, PROGENY. BEGINNING, CAUSE, GERM, ORIGINS. SCREENED COMPETITOR (tennis).

SEEDSMAN *SOWER*. MILLER (crypt). HANDICAPPER, SCREENER (crypt, tennis).

SEEN (s/l *scene*). *NOTED*, NOTICED, REMARKED, *SPOTTED*.

SEER (s/l sear, sere). *PROPHET*. FISH (Ind). *MEASURE* (Ind). EYE, PUPIL; SPECTATOR, VIEWER (crypt). SEE RIGHT (crypt).

SEE RIGHT ENSURE FAIRNESS. OBSERVE CORRECTLY. *SEER* (crypt).

SEETHE BOIL, COOK, SIMMER. FESTER. NOTE THE . . . (crypt).

SELECT CHOICE, ELITE, PICK. CHOOSE, ELECT.

SELENE Gk *goddess* of the *Moon* (**Rom** = LUNA); d of Hyperion and sis of *Helios* (Sun) and Eos (Dawn). Loved Endymion. Identical with *ARTEMIS*.

SELF 1. ME, NUMBER ONE. INDIVIDUALITY, PERSON. *UNIFORM*, SAME, ALL ONE (colour). **Pl** = FLOWERS (natural coloured).

~ HELP DIY. SELF-SERVICE. BURGLARY, *ROBBERY*, SHOP-LIFTING (crypt).

SENSE APPRECIATION, JUDGEMENT, MEANING, PERCEPTION, SENTIMENT, WISDOM. Any of the five senses: HEARING, SIGHT, SMELL, TASTE, TOUCH (**sixth** =

INTUITION). SANITY, WIT. DIRECTION. [~ and Sensibility, *Austen*].

SENTENCE CONSIGN. GAOL TERM, STRETCH, *TIME*, PUNISHMENT; DEATH, FINE, LIFE. GRAMMATICAL CONSTRUCTION, QUOTATION; *SAYING*.

SENTRY *GUARD*, LOOK-OUT, SENTINEL, *WATCH*, WATCH-KEEPER. BOXED, *BOXER*, BOXMAN, CAVEMAN (crypt). CAPT ~ (Addison).

SEPTEMBER 9th month, M, SEPT (seventh Rom month, before *Caesar* reorganized the calendar). **Birthstone** = chrysolite.

SEPTENTRIO Rom myth N *WIND* (**Gk** = BOREAS).

SERGEANT NCO, RSM, SGT. **Celeb**: BUZFUZ (*Dickens*), CUFF (Moonstone, Collins), KITE (Farquhar), ~ AT LAW (*Chaucer*), TROY (Hardy). ['This fell ~ Death' (Hamlet, *Shak*)].

SERIES (s/l *Ceres*). *ORDER*, *ROW*, SEQUENCE, *SET*, SUCCESSION [seriatim].

SERPENT REPTILE, *SNAKE* (q.v.); **celeb**: APEP (Egy god); KAA (*Kipling*); MIDGARD (*Loki*); *PYTHON*; QUETZALCOATL (*Mayan* god); URAEUS (Egy god); WYVERN (*herald*) [caduceus; Cadmus and Harmonia; *Moses* and *Aaron* (*Pharaoh*)]. *Constellation*. *DEVIL*; TEMPTER. FIREWORK. *INSTRUMENT* (mus).

SERVANT *AGENT*, FACTOR. BUTLER, *COOK*, *DOMESTIC*, *FOOTMAN*, *GARDENER*, GOVERNESS, *MAID*, *NANNY*, *SEWER*, TWEENY, VALET. *CONSTABLE*, FACTOTUM, MAJOR DOMO, (MAN) FRIDAY. GYP (C sl), *SCOUT* (O sl). [*Six*]. **Celeb**: ADAM (AYLI); ADMIRABLE CRICHTON (Barrie); *AMPHITRYON* (Molière); CALEB BALDERSTONE (Scott); *BALTHAZAR* (R & J, *Shak*); *BUNTER* (Dorothy Sayers); CROMWELL (H.viii); HUMPHREY CLINKER (Smollett); JOHN GRUEBY (*Dickens*); GUMBO (Thackeray); HUDSON (TV); JEEVES (*Wodehouse*); JOSEPH (E. *Brontë*); LITTIMER (*Dickens*); BETTY MUXWORTHY (Blackmore); SANCHO PANZA (Cervantes); PAROLLES (All's Well); PASSE-PARTOUT (Jules Verne); CLARA PEGGOTTY (*Dickens*); PETER (R & J); PETO (H.iv); RUGBY (Merry Wives); SIMPLE (Merry Wives); SCAPIN (Molière); SPEED (2 G of V); CPL TRIM (Sterne); JOB TROTTER (*Dickens*); SAM WELLER (*Dickens*); SIMPLE (Merry Wives).

SERVICE *ACE*, FAULT (tennis). DEAL. ARMED FORCE: AIR FORCE, ARMY, NAVY, RAF, RN, USAF, USN. CHURCH

MASS, MASS-MEETING, WORSHIP. MAINTAIN, OVERHAUL, REPAIR. *CHINA*, DISHES, PLATES. TREE.

SERVICEMAN *AIRMAN*, *SAILOR*, *SOLDIER* (**opp** = civilian, civvy). PARSON, PRIEST, VICAR, *CHURCHMAN* (crypt).

SESAME *HERB*, PLANT. PASS-WORD [open].

SET 1. FIRM, GO OFF, RIGID. GAME. CABAL, CLIQUE, COTERIE, ESTABLISHMENT, GROUP, *SERIES*. *DANCE*. BATCH, CLUTCH. EQUIPMENT. PLACE, PUT. BOX, RADIO, TELLY, TV. SCENE, STUDIO (film, theat). 2. *Habitation* of badgers. 3. *Egy god* of DARKNESS.

SETH ADAMSON (crypt).

SET OFF *Anag.* BEGIN, *START*. *Anag.* of 'set', e.g. STE, TSE. COMPLEMENT, ENHANCE, FOIL, *GRACE*. CARDED, MOUNTED, ORNAMENT.

SET ON ENCOURAGE, SICK, *URGE*.

SET OUT *Anag.* BEGIN, *START*. *Anag.* of 'set', e.g. STE, TSE, EST etc.

SETTLEMENT *AC*, *BILL*; PAYMENT. *CAMP*, COLONY, OUTPOST, HOMESTEAD. SUBSIDENCE.

SETTLER COLONIST, HOMESTEADER, IMMIGRANT. ARBITER, COMPOSER, JUDGE, PEACEMAKER. *COIN*, CHECK (US), CHEQUE, PAYER (crypt).

SEVEN See *number*. HEPTAD. BLACK BALL (snooker). *Stars* in the sky (song). *Swans* a-swimming (*Christmas* song) [~ maids with ~ mops (*Alice*; Walrus)].

~ **AGES** (AYLI, *Shak*): (1) INFANT (mewling and puking); (2) SCHOOLBOY (whining; snail); (3) LOVER (sighing like furnace); (4) SOLDIER (bubble reputation); (5) JUSTICE (full of wise saws); (6) PANTALOON (lean and slipper'd); (7) SECOND CHILDISHNESS (oblivion; sans teeth, sans eyes, sans taste, sans everything).

~ **DEADLY SINS** ANGER, AVARICE, ENVY, GLUTTONY, LUST, PRIDE, SLOTH.

~ **HILLS** (of Rome): AVENTINE, CAELIAN, CAPITOLINE, ESQUILINE, PALATINE, QUIRINAL, VIMINAL.

~ **SAGES** BIAS (of Priene), CHILON (of Sparta), CLEOBULUS (of Lindus), PERIANDER (of Corinth), PITTACUS (of Mitylene), SOLON (of Athens), THALES (of Miletus).

~ **SEAS** ANTARCTIC, ARCTIC, N and S ATLANTIC, INDIAN, N and S PACIFIC *OCEANS*.

~ **SISTERS** HILLS, WHITE CLIFFS (of Dover).

SEVEN WONDERS COLOSSUS (of Rhodes), HANGING
   GARDENS (of Babylon), *MAUSOLEUM* (at Helicarnassus),
   PHAROS (at Alexandria), STATUE OF *JUPITER* (at *Olympus*),
   PYRAMIDS (of Egypt), TEMPLE OF DIANA (at Ephesus).
SEWER CONDUIT, DRAIN. MACHINE, *SINGER* (*invention*);
   NEEDLE(R), SEAMSTRESS; MIMI (Puccini — crypt).
   BUTLER, *SERVANT*, FOOD TASTER, PLACE SETTER,
   TABLE LAYER (arch).
~ COVER MANHOLE LID. THIMBLE (crypt).
SEWN STITCHED. *NEEDLED* (crypt). COMPASS POINTS
   (crypt).
SEX APPEAL CHARM, IT, OOMPH, *SA*.
SEXY ATTRACTIVE, PROVOCATIVE, SENSUOUS. X (film
   censorship).
Sh Shetlands.
SHADE *COLOUR*, HUE. BLIND, *SCREEN*; UMBRAGE.
   GHOST.
SHAKESPEARE THE BARD, DRAMATIST, SWAN OF AVON
   (1564–1616), mar Ann Hathaway (2 d:; Susanna, Judith; 1 s:
   Hamnet). Fake play = VORTIGERN (W. H. IRELAND).
   Characters:

   3-letters
   NYM   (*coward*; H.v, Merry Wives)
   SLY   (tinker; Taming)
   4-letters
   ADAM   (*servant*; AYLI)
   BONA   (sis to Fr queen; H.vi)
   CADE   (rebel; H.vi)
   DULL   (*constable*; LLL)
   FANG   (*sheriff's* officer; H.iv) [*Dickens*]
   FORD   (mistress; Merry Wives)
   HERO   (Much Ado)
   IAGO   (villain; Othello)
   JAMY   (Sc *soldier*; H.v)
   JOHN   (*king*; ~)
   KATE   (*shrew*; Taming ~)
   LEAR   (*mad king*; ~)
   LION   (play character; MND)
   MOTH   (*fairy*; MND. page; LLL)
   PAGE   (mistress; Merry Wives)

PETO	(servant; H.iv)
PUCK	(*sprite*; MND)
SNUG	(joiner; MND)
WALL	(play character; MND)
WART	(recruit; H.iv)

5-letters

ARIEL	(*sprite*; Tempest)
BAGOT	(toady; R.ii)
BATES	(soldier; H.v)
BELCH	(Sir Toby; 12th N)
BLUNT	(Sir Walter; H.iv)
BUSHY	(toady; R.ii)
CAIUS	(*doctor*; Merry Wives)
CASCA	(*conspirator*; J. Caesar)
CELIA	(AYLI)
CINNA	(*conspirator*; J. Caesar)
COURT	(*soldier*; H.v)
DIANA	(All's Well)
ELBOW	(*constable*; M for M)
FESTE	(*jester*; 12th N)
FLUTE	(*bellowsmender*; MND)
GOBBO	(*clown*; M of V)
GOWER	(Eng soldier; H.v. Chorus; Pericles)
GREEN	(toady; R.ii)
HELEN	(beauty; T and C)
HENRY	(king; H.iv, v, vi, viii)
JULIA	(beloved of Proteus; 2 G of V)
MARIA	(*maid*; 12th N)
MOPSA	(shepherdess; W Tale)
OSRIC	(courtier; Hamlet)
PARIS	(nobleman; R and J; T and C)
PERCY	(Hotspur; H.iv)
PETER	(*servant*; R & J)
PHEBE	(*shepherdess*; AYLI)
PINCH	(*schoolmaster*; C of Errors)
POINS	(*servant*; H.iv)
PRIAM	(king of Troy; T and C)
REGAN	(graceless d; Lear)
ROBIN	(page; Merry Wives)
ROMEO	(Montague; R and J)

RUGBY	(*servant*; Merry Wives)
SNARE	(sheriff's officer; H.iv)
SNOUT	(tinker; MND)
SPEED	(*servant*; 2 G of V)
TIMON	(nobleman; ~ of A)
VIOLA	(impersonates man; 12th N)

6-letters

AENEAS	(commander; T and C)
ANTONY	(triumvir; J. Caesar, A and C)
BANQUO	(general and *ghost*; Macb)
BIANCA	(Kate's sis; T of S; courtesan; Othello)
BOTTOM	(*weaver*; MND)
BRUTUS	(*conspirator*; J. Caesar)
CAESAR	(general, orator; J ~)
CIMBER	(*conspirator*; J. Caesar)
COBWEB	(*fairy*; MND)
DORCAS	(shepherdess; W Tale)
DROMIO	(*twin servants*; C of Errors)
DUNCAN	(king of Sc; Macb)
FEEBLE	(recruit; H.iv)
HAMLET	(prince of Denmark; ~)
HECTOR	(nobleman; T and C)
IMOGEN	(princess, Cymb)
JAQUES	(cynic; AYLI)
JULIET	(Capulet; R and J. minor lady; M for M)
LAUNCE	(clownish *servant*; 2 G of V)
MOULDY	(recruit; H.iv)
NESTOR	(commander; T and C)
OBERON	(king of *fairies*; MND)
OLIVIA	(countess; 12th N)
ORSINO	(nobleman; 12th N)
PISTOL	(*coward*; Merry Wives, H.iv, v)
POMPEY	(general; A & C. clownish *servant*; M for M)
PORTIA	(impersonates man, *lawyer*; M of V. w of Brutus; J. Caesar)
QUINCE	(*carpenter*; MND)
SCROOP	(archbishop; H.iv. Lord; H.v, R.ii)
SHADOW	(recruit; H.iv)
SILVIA	(beloved of Valentine; 2 G of V)
SIMPLE	(*servant*; Merry Wives)

THISBE	(play character; MND)
TYBALT	(Capulet; R & J)
VERGES	(*constable*; Much Ado)
YORICK	(*jester* and skull; Hamlet)

7-letters

ANTONIO	(merchant; M of V. Also minor parts Much Ado, Temp, 12th N, 2 G of V)
CALIBAN	(*monster*; Temp)
CAPULET	(head of house; R & J)
CASSIUS	(*conspirator*; J. Caesar)
COSTARD	(*jester*; LLL)
GONERIL	(graceless d; Lear)
GREGORY	(*servant*; R & J)
HORATIO	(friend of Hamlet; ~)
HOTSPUR	(Percy; H.iv)
JESSICA	(Shylock's d; M of V)
LAERTES	(s of Polonius; Hamlet)
LAVACHE	(*jester*; All's Well)
MACBETH	(general; ~)
MALCOLM	(s of Duncan; Macb)
MIRANDA	(d of Prospero; Temp)
MONTJOY	(Fr *herald*; H.v)
NERISSA	(*maid*; M of V)
OPHELIA	(d to Polonius; Hamlet)
ORLANDO	(Rosalind's lover; AYLI)
OTHELLO	(*Moor*; ~)
PERDITA	(princess; W Tale)
PROTEUS	(one of the 2 G of V)
PYRAMUS	(play character; MND)
QUICKLY	(landlady; Merry Wives, H.iv, v)
SAMPSON	(*servant*; R & J)
SHALLOW	(*justice*; Merry Wives, H.iv)
SHYLOCK	(Jew; M of V)
SILENCE	(*justice*; H.iv)
SLENDER	(*clerk* to justice; Merry Wives)
SYCORAX	(*witch*; Temp)
TITANIA	(queen of *fairies*; MND)
TROILUS	(s of Priam; T and C) [*Chaucer*]
ULYSSES	(commander; T and C)

8-letters

ACHILLES	(commander; T and C)
BARDOLPH	(*coward*; Merry Wives, H.iv, v)
BASSANIO	(Antonio's friend; M of V)
BULLCALF	(recruit; H.iv)
CLAUDIUS	(king of Denmark and *ghost*; Hamlet)
CORDELIA	(dutiful d; Lear)
CRESSIDA	(d of Calchas; T and C) [*Chaucer*]
CROMWELL	(*servant*; H.viii)
DOGBERRY	(*constable*; Much Ado)
FALSTAFF	(drunken knight; Merry Wives, H.iv)
FLUELLEN	(Wal soldier; H.v)
GERTRUDE	(queen of Denmark; Hamlet)
HERMIONE	(queen of Sicilia; W Tale)
MALVOLIO	(*constable*; 12th N)
MERCUTIO	(prattler; R and J)
OVERDONE	(mistress, a bawd; M for M)
PAROLLES	(*servant*; All's Well)
POLONIUS	(pontificator; Hamlet)
PROSPERO	(noble *magician*; Temp)
ROSALIND	(impersonates man; AYLI)
TRINCULO	(*fool*; Temp)
WILLIAMS	(soldier; H.v)

9-letters

AGAMEMNON	(general; T and C)
AUTOLYCUS	(rogue; W Tale)
CASSANDRA	(prophetess; T and C)
CLEOPATRA	(Queen of Egy; A and C)
DESDEMONA	(w of Othello; ~)
DONALBAIN	(s of Duncan; Macb)
FERDINAND	(nobleman; Temp; king, LLL)
FREDERICK	(nobleman; AYLI)
KATHARINA	(shrew; Taming)
MACMORRIS	(Ire soldier; H.v)
MOONSHINE	(play character; MND)
PETRUCHIO	(tames Kate; Taming)
SEBASTIAN	(nobleman; Temp; 12th N)
TEARSHEET	(Doll, a bawd; H.iv)
VOLTIMAND	(courtier; Hamlet)

10+ letters

FORTINBRAS	(prince of Norway; Hamlet)
HOLOFERNES	(*schoolmaster*; LLL)
MUSTARDSEED	(*fairy*; MND)
PEASBLOSSOM	(*fairy*; MND)
STARVELING	(tailor; MND)
TOUCHSTONE	(*jester*; AYLI)

Shakespeare's Plays:

ALL'S WELL THAT ENDS WELL (*abbr*: All's Well. France, Tuscany; Florentine war).

ANTONY AND CLEOPATRA (*abbr*: A and C. *Rome*, Egypt. *Asp*; *Pompey*).

AS YOU LIKE IT (*abbr*: AYLI. Forest of Arden. *Adam*, Rosalind).

THE COMEDY OF ERRORS (*abbr*: C of Errors. Ephesus. *Twins*).

CORIOLANUS (*abbr*: Cor. *Rome*).

CYMBELINE (*abbr*: Cymb. Britain, Italy).

HAMLET, PRINCE OF DENMARK (*abbr*: Hamlet. Elsinore. *Madness*. Horatio, Ophelia, Polonius).

JULIUS CAESAR (*abbr*: *Caesar*. Rome, Sardis. *Conspirators*: Brutus, Cinna etc).

KING HENRY THE FOURTH (*abbr*: H.iv. England. Two parts. Plot. Harry Hotspur, Owen Glendower, Mistress *Quickly*, Falstaff, Bardolph, *Pistol*).

KING HENRY THE FIFTH (*abbr*: H.v. England, France, Agincourt. Nym, Bardolph, *Pistol*, Mistress *Quickly*).

KING HENRY THE SIXTH (*abbr*: H.vi. England, France. Three parts. *Joan* of Arc).

KING HENRY THE EIGHTH (*abbr*: H.viii. London, Westminster. Anne Bullen, Queen Katherine, Cardinal Wolsey).

KING JOHN (*abbr*: John. England, France. Bastard).

KING LEAR (*abbr*: Lear. Britain. *Madness*, ingratitude. Goneril, Regan, Cordelia).

THE LIFE AND DEATH OF KING RICHARD II (*abbr*: R.ii. England, Wales. Bolingbroke, John of Gaunt).

THE LIFE AND DEATH OF KING RICHARD III (*abbr*: R.iii. England. Hunchback. Princes in the Tower. Richmond. Horse).

LOVE'S LABOUR'S LOST (*abbr*: LLL. Navarre. Court life, letters).

MACBETH (*abbr*: Macb. Scotland. Murder, *prophecies*. Three *witches*, *ghost*; damned spot).

MEASURE FOR MEASURE (*abbr*: M for M. Vienna. *Prison*. *Elbow*).

THE MERCHANT OF VENICE (*abbr*: M of V. Belmont. Shylock, pound of flesh; Portia, male impersonator, pleads. **Saying**).

MERRY WIVES OF WINDSOR (*abbr*: Merry Wives. Falstaff, Bardolph, Nym, *Pistol*, Mistress *Quickly*).

A MIDSUMMER NIGHT'S DREAM (*abbr*: MND. Athens, woods. *Fairies*, Oberon, Titania; Cobweb, Moth etc; *Puck*; Snug, Bottom etc. Pyramus, Thisbe).

MUCH ADO ABOUT NOTHING (*abbr*: Much Ado. Messina, Padua. Dogberry, Verges).

OTHELLO, THE *MOOR* OF VENICE (*abbr*: Othello. Cyprus. Desdemona, Iago).

PERICLES, PRINCE OF TYRE (*abbr*: Per. Antioch, Pentapolis).

ROMEO AND JULIET (*abbr*: R and J. Verona, Mantua. *Lovers*. Capulet, Montague).

THE TAMING OF THE SHREW (*abbr*: Taming. Katharina, Petruchio, Bianca).

THE TEMPEST (*abbr*: Tempest. Island. *Ariel*, Caliban, Miranda, Prospero).

TIMON OF ATHENS (*abbr*: Timon. *Athens*).

TITUS ANDRONICUS (*abbr*: Titus. *Rome*).

TROILUS AND CRESSIDA (*abbr*: T and C. *Troy*. War. *Priam*, *Hector*, *Helen*, *Agamemnon*, Menelaus, *Cassandra*).

TWELFTH NIGHT; or, WHAT YOU WILL (*abbr*: 12th N. Illyria. Olivia, Viola, Malvolio, cross-garters, Sir Toby Belch, Sir Andrew Ague-Cheek).

TWO GENTLEMEN OF VERONA (*abbr*: Two G of V. Milan. Julia, male impersonator; Proteus).

THE WINTER'S TALE (*abbr*: W Tale. Sicilia, Bohemia. Perdita; *shepherd*/ess).

SHANGHAI CARRY OFF, IMPRESS, PRESS. CITY (Ch).
SHAPE *FASHION*, *FORM*, FIGURE. MAKE, MOULD (**saying**).
   HQ, HEADQUARTERS (mil).

SHARK 1. ADVENTURER, SWINDLER. 2. *FISH*; **breeds:**
ANGEL ~, BASKING ~, *BLUE* ~, GREAT WHITE ~, GREY
NURSE, HAMMERHEAD, HORN ~, MACKEREL ~, MAKO,
MAN-EATING ~, *NURSE*, PENNY-DOG, PORBEAGLE,
PORT JACKSON ~, SELACHE, SPUR-DOG, SUNFISH,
SWORDFISH ~, THRESHER ~, *TIGER* ~, TOPE, *WHALE* ~
(biggest fish), WHITE ~, WHITE POINTER, WOBBEGONG
(Aus), *ZEBRA* ~, ZYGAENA [pilot fish, remoru, shagreen,
squaloid].
SHARP-EYED see *KEEN-EYED*.
SHARPSHOOTER 1. MARKSMAN, SNIPER. *GUN*. 2. Crooked
dicer, hence CIDER, RICED etc (crypt).
SHAW (s/l shore, sure). 1. THICKET, WOOD (arch). 2. George
Bernard ~, Irish dramatist. **Plays:** Androcles and the Lion, The
Apple Cart, Buoyant Billions, Caesar and Cleopatra, Candida,
Doctor's Dilemma, Heartbreak House, Pygmalion, Saint Joan, Too
True to be Good. 3. Aircraftsman ~ = Lawrence of Arabia =
Ross.
SHE FEMALE SUBJECT, WOMAN. [~ who must be obeyed,
Haggard].
SHEBA 1. Kingdom of S Arabia; modern Yemen. 2. SABA, the
kingdom of Joktan. AAZIZ; BILKIS, a Queen of ~, visited
Solomon to check on the rumours of his wealth; 'Behold the half
was not told unto me.' The Abyssinians adopted her as the Cushite
or Ethiopian ~, making her and Solomon joint ancestors of the
royal family of Ethiopia. 3. Bibl s of Bichri, who rose against
David and exhorted '. . . every man to his tents O Israel.' Pursued
to the city of *Abel* and k by *Joab*.
SHED CAST, DOFF(ED), DROP(PED), HIVE(D) OFF,
PART(ED) WITH, SPILL(ED). DIFFUSE(D), DISPERSE(D).
REDUCE(D). HUT, SHELTER, STORE. *FOOTBALL
GROUND* (Chelsea). SHE WOULD (crypt).
SHEEP 1. BASHFUL/DOCILE PERSON, NONENTITY.
ISLAND. 2. Horned ruminant, genus ovis. HOGGET, RAM,
TEG, TUP, WETHER. *Constellation*; sign of Zodiac (9th).
Breeds: AOUDAD (N Af), ARGALI (Asia), BHARAL (Ind),
BLACKFACE, BORDER, CARACUL, CHEVIOT,
COTSWOLD, DORSET, HAMPSHIRE DOWN, HERDWICK,
HIGHLAND, JACOB'S, JUMBUK, LEICESTER, MERINO,
MUFFLON (wild), ROMNEY MARSH, ROUGH FELL,
SCOTTISH BLACKFACE, SOAY, SOUTHDOWN, SUFFOLK,

SWALEDALE, ST KILDA, URIAL (Asia), WELSH
MOUNTAIN, WENSLEYDALE, ZUNA (Angola) (**assembly** =
flock, herd; **male** = ram; **female** = ewe, theave; **offspring** = lamb).
SHEER (s/l shear). PERPENDICULAR, PLUMB, VERTICAL.
HOIST, JURY CRANE. RISE OF DECKLINE. YAW (naut).
MERE, OUT AND OUT, SIMPLE, UNDILUTED. BREAK,
SNAP. DEPART, PART COMPANY. RAKE, WOMANIZER
(crypt).
SHEET *LAYER*, STRATUM. ROPE (naut). PANE. *MEASURE*
(paper); F, FOLIO, PAGE. COVERING. Pl = BED LINEN,
COVERS.
SHELF LIFE STAY-FRESH PERIOD, STORAGE TIME.
SPINSTERHOOD (crypt).
SHELL BOMBARD, FIRE AT, LAY BARRAGE, STONK.
CARTRIDGE, PROJECTILE, *WEAPON*. PETROL; OIL
COMPANY®. SHE WILL (crypt). *FORM*, SEMBLANCE,
SHOW. CARAPACE, CASE, CRUST, HUSK, *NUTCASE*
[*kernel*], POD; [*collector*; crustacean, *study*]; **types** (**marine**):
ABALONE, BARNACLE, COCKLE, CONCH, COWRIE,
GAPER, LAVER, LIMPET, MUSSEL, ORMER, *OYSTER*,
PERIWINKLE, RAZOR, SCALLOP (pilgrim), SEA EAR, SEA
SNAIL, SNAIL, SPIRAL LAVER, SPIROBIS, WAMPUM,
WHELK, WINKLE. **Comp** = *shot*.
SHEPHERD 1. FARMER, *TENDER*; MARSHAL, TEND; **celeb**:
Astrophel (Spenser); *Abel*; *David*; Lycidas (Milton); *Moses*;
Stiggins (Pickwick, *Dickens*); in Winter's Tale (foster-f of Perdita,
Shak). CHURCHMAN, MINISTER, PARSON, VICAR. 2. **Gk
god** = PAN. 3. *Constellation* (Bootes).
SHEPHERDESS Fem *shepherd*; *COWGIRL* (crypt), GIRL GUIDE
(crypt); **celeb**: BO-PEEP (trad); DORCAS (W Tale, *Shak*);
MARY (had a little lamb, trad); MOPSA (W Tale, *Shak*); PHEBE
(AYLI, *Shak*).
SHIELD PROTECT, *SCREEN*. *ARMOUR*, BUCKLER; AEGIS
(*Athene*). BADGE, ESCUTCHEON [coat of arms (*herald*)].
SHIFT *Anag*. MOVE. GANG, SPELL, TURN, WATCH.
DODGE, TRICK. CONTRIVE. CHEMISE, SARK, SHIRT.
SHINER BLACK EYE. *FISH* (US). Nine bright, in *song*. Pl =
MONEY.
SHIP SS; *BOAT* (q.v.), SQUARE RIGGER, *VESSEL* (q.v.).
AIRCRAFT (US). STOW, TAKE ABOARD. DELIVER,
SEND. EMBARK.

SHIPMAN *Chaucer's* sea captain. *SAILOR.*

SHIPWRECK FOUNDERING, SINKING, STRANDING. Any anag of SHIP.

SHIRT CHEMISE, JERSEY, SARK, SHIFT.

SHIVA Chief Ind *god*; mar to Devi.

SHOCKER ELECTRICITY (crypt). *JAR*, JERK, JOLT. MURDER MYSTERY, THRILLER.

SHOCKING DISGUSTING, HORRIFYING, IMPROPER, SENSATIONAL. ELECTRIC, LIVE. STOOKING.

SHOE (s/l *shoo*). *BOOT*, BROGUE, CLOG, FOOTWEAR, *MULE, OXFORD, PUMP*, SABOT, SLIPPER, TOPBOOT, *TRAINER, WELLINGTON*, ZORI (Jap) [cobbler, heel, last, snob, sole, tongue, upper, vamp]. HORSE ~. FERRULE, SOCKET. KEEL-BAND, MAST-STEP (naut). IRON STRAP; SPRIG, WHEEL DRAG. Pl = SHOON (arch).

SHOOT (s/l chute). DISCHARGE, EMIT, *FIRE*, LOOSE OFF. KILL. BUD, SUCKER. *FILM*, PHOTOGRAPH, TURN. SCORE. SPEAK!

SHOP BUY, PURCHASE. EMPORIUM, SALEROOM, SUPERMARKET. BUSINESS. *BETRAY.* WOOLWICH (mil sl).

SHOPPER PURCHASER. *BETRAYER.*

SHORN (s/l Sean). 1. CLIPPED, CUT; DISTRESSED (crypt). 2. Remove synonym for hair from word, e.g. **German shorn huntress** (3) = HUN(tress).

SHORT 1. BRIEF, CONCISE, CURTAILED, CUT, RUNT, SMALL (**opp** = *long*, tall). CURT. OWING, SHY. BREAK INSULATION, UNEARTH (elect). CRUMBLING, FRIABLE (cook). Pl = BERMUDAS. Pl = *DRINKS*, SPIRITS. 2. Use any abbr, short or diminutive word, e.g. **Short ton** = T; **Short test** = EXAM; **Short measure** = TOT.

SHORT TIME HR, MIN, MO, SEC (crypt). QUICKLY.

SHOT CANNON, CUT, DRIVE, GLANCE, MASSE, POT, PULL, PUTT (games). *FIRED*, LOOSED OFF, POTSHOT; KILLED. FILMED, SNAPPED; VIEW (photo). *GO*, TURN. **Comp** = *shell*.

SHOUT BAWL, CALL, *CRY*, HAIL (**opp** = whisper). TREAT, TURN.

SHOW *CONDUCT*, GUIDE. DEMONSTRATE, PROVE. DISCLOSE, DISPLAY, EXHIBIT, EXPO, MANIFEST, OFFER. EXHIBITION, PAGEANT, PANTO, *PLAY*, RODEO,

SPECTACLE. PROJECT, SCREEN.

SHOWER DOWNPOUR, HAIL, PEPPER, PRECIPITATION, RAIN; DOUCHE, ~ BATH [*Danae*]. DEMONSTRATOR, EXHIBITOR (crypt); *CONDUCTOR*, DRAGOMAN (crypt).

SHOWPLACE CINEMA, THEATRE (crypt). SIGHT, TOURIST SPOT.

SHREW INSECTIVORE (~ mouse). GRIMALKIN, SCOLD, SPITFIRE, TERMAGANT, VIRAGO; **celeb**: EPICOENE (Ben Jonson), KATE (Taming, *Shak*), *XANTHIPPE* (Gk).

SHRUB DRINK. PLANT (q.v.), WILD PLANT (q.v.).

SHUN AVOID, ESCHEW, EVADE. CUT, SNUB. ATTENTION (mil).

SHUT *BAR*, CLOSE, FASTEN. GAG, *SILENCE*. **Comp** = *open*.

SHUTTLE BOBBIN, WEFT-CARRIER. BIRD (badminton). BRANCH LINE, COMMUTE, FEEDER SERVICE, TRAVEL TO AND FRO. *SPACECRAFT* (Challenger, Columbia).

SHY *ARCH*, CHARY, COY, NEBBISH, RETIRING, TIMID. REAR UP. ELUSIVE, UNEASY. *CAST*, FLING, *PELT*, THROW; AUNT SALLY. OWING, *SHORT*.

SI SYSTEME INTERNATIONALE, *INTERNATIONAL UNITS*. SILICON (*chem*). STAR OF INDIA (*order*). **Pl** = *SISTER*.

SIB AKIN, RELATED; *BROTHER*, SISTER (hence SIBLING, one of two or more children with the same parent or parents).

SIBYL FORTUNE TELLER, *PROPHETESS* (q.v.), ORACULAR MOUTHPIECE; **celeb**: AMALTHEA (cornucopia), ~ of CUMEA (Tarquinius and the Sibiline books), DEIOPHOBE, DEMO, DEMOPHILE, HEROPHILE, PHEMONOE. HAG, *WITCH*. Girl's name.

SIC (s/l *sick*). SO, THUS.

SICK (s/l *sic*). AEG(ROTAT), *ILL*, INDISPOSED [*patron saint*]. VOMIT. ENCOURAGE, SET ON, *URGE*. [~ as a *parrot* = *upset* (**opp** = over the moon)].

SIDE 1. ELEVEN, FIFTEEN, II, XI, XV; PLAYERS, TEAM. BOASTING, SWANK. 2. Use either or both sides (i.e. end) of word indicated, e.g. **Both sides of some Kentish area** = S**E; **This side of the moon** = MO**. 3. **Pl** = any common pair of items which may be on either side, e.g. ON and OFF, L and R, E and W.

~ **LINE** ALTERNATIVE, SECOND STRING [moonlighting]. *BAY*, SIDING; TOUCH, TRAMLINES (games).

SIDING SWITCH-LINE (rly). PARTISANSHIP.

Sig Signature.

SIGN (s/l sine). CROSS, MARK; GUARANTEE, PASSWORD, *SEAL*, TOKEN. OMEN, PORTENT. SYMPTOM. PLUS, MINUS, MULTIPLY etc. ARROW, BOARD, POSTER. UNDERWRITE. [*Zodiac*].

SIGNAL *SIGN*, INDICATION. *ARROW*, *DIRECTOR*. MORSE, SEMAPHORE [*aldis*, *flag code*]. FLARE, PYROTECHNIC, ROCKET. OUTSTANDING, REMARKABLE.

SILENCE NOISELESS, PEACE, QUIET. P, PP, SH; HUSH, MUM, WHIST [*oyster*, *Shak character*].

SILICON SI (*chem*).

SILK 1. KC, QC; BARRISTER, COUNSEL. GOWN; RACING COLOURS. *MATERIAL*: BOMBAZINE, TAFFETA, TULLE; RUSTLER (crypt). 2. *Anniversary* (12th).

SILVER *METAL*; AG (*chem*). *ARGENT* (*herald*). *Anniversary* (25th). CHANGE, *COINS* (nickel) [*Judas*]. *HORSE*. *PIRATE* (Treasure Island, *Stevenson*).

SIMPLE ARTLESS, *ATTIC*, BASIC, EASY, PLAIN, UNCOMPLICATED (**opp** = *involved*). ABSOLUTE. *MERE*. FOOLISH. HUMBLE, LOWLY. HERBAL REMEDY, HERB. SERVANT (*Shak*).

SIN 1. DO WRONG, ERR, SLIP, TRANSGRESS. 2. **Seven deadly, or mortal, sins**: ANGER, AVARICE, ENVY, GLUTTONY, LUST, PRIDE, SLOTH. 3. Bibl city (Egy); wilderness. 4. Moon god (Ur).

SINGER DIVA, CROONER, *SONGSTER*, TROUBADOUR, VOCALIST; ALTO, BARITONE, BASS, CONTRALTO, SOPRANO, TENOR; **celeb**: BLONDEL (minstrel), CARUSO, GIGLI, *JENNY* LIND, LORELEI, MELBA, ORPHEUS (*Argonaut*), *SIREN* (myth). *BETRAYER* (sl). BURNER, TOASTER (crypt). *SEWER* (crypt).

SINGLE 1. *ACE*, I, ONE, UNIT. BACHELOR, SPINSTER, UNMARRIED, UNWED. R, RUN (cricket). **Pl** = game of tennis. 2. Remove indication of marriage (i.e. letters 'm' or 'wed') from clue, e.g. **Secure single wedlock** (4) = ***LOCK.

SINGULAR S. ODD, PECULIAR, STRANGE. INDIVIDUAL, UNIQUE; ONE ONLY (**opp** = plural).

SINIS Gk myth *robber* who tied his victims to twin bent fir trees, and split them on release. Slain by *Theseus*.

SINISTER EVIL, MALIGNANT, VILLAINOUS. *LEFT* (**opp** = *dexter*); BASTARDY (*herald*).

SIRE *FATHER*, GOVERNOR (arch), PA, POP. BEGET. LORD,

MASTER, MAJESTY.
SIREN 1. HOOTER, SIGNAL, WARNING [*police*]. SINGER,
TEMPTRESS. 2. Sea nymphs whose sweet singing lured sailors to
shipwreck. *Ulysses* filled his sailors' ears with wax and had himself
tied to the mast. *Orpheus* surpassed them in singing, so they threw
themselves into the sea and were turned into rocks. A siren also
lured sailors at Lorelei on the Rhine.
sis Sister.
SISTER *CHURCHWOMAN*, NUN. *SIB* (**opp** = *brother*). *NURSE*.
Pl = CONVENT, NUNNERY; ~ OF MERCY. **Celeb**:
ANDREWS, BEVERLEY, NOLAN (all theat).
SISYPHUS Gk myth king of Corinth, condemned to atone for his sins
in the *Underworld*, by rolling a boulder uphill, at the top of which
it always rolled down again. [*Autolycus*].
SITTER EASY, FACILE. *MODEL*, POSER. BABYMINDER.
SITUATION APPOINTMENT, JOB, POSITION, *POST*.
LOCATION. PASS.
SIX See *number*. HEXAD, SICE, VI. BOUNDARY,
UNBOUNCING (*cricket*). *PINK BALL* (*snooker*). *Proud
walkers* (*song*). *Geese* a-laying (*Christmas song*). [*Holmes* case; ~
honest serving men: What, Why, When, How, Where, Who
(*Kipling*)].
~ **FOOTER** ANT, *INSECT* (crypt).
~ **NATIONS** Iroquois confederation of *American Indian* tribes, west
of New York (1770).
SKATE ICE ~, ROLLER ~. *FISH*, *RAY*.
SKIN FELL, FLEECE, *HIDE*, PELT. PARE, PEEL, RIND,
CICATRIZE, FLAY. PLANKING, PLATING (naut). **Comp** =
bones.
SKINNER FURRIER. *PEELER*. [~'s Horse (mil)].
SKINT BROKE; BORACIC LINT (*rh sl*); **opp** = *flush*.
SKIPPER *BOSS*, CAPT. *BUTTERFLY*. *DEER*. *FISH*.
ABSCONDER, RUNAWAY (crypt). *LAMB* (crypt). [bowls,
curling].
SKIRON (s/l *Sciron*). Gk myth NW *WIND* (**Rom** = CAURUS).
SKULK 1. LURK, SHIRK DUTY. 2. *Assembly* of foxes.
sl Slang.
s/l *Sounds like* (and see *Pronunciation*).
SLACK IDLE, LAZE, LAZY. LATITUDE, MARGIN, PLAY.
COAL DUST. **Pl** = TROUSERS.
SLANG 1. ARGOT (Fr), IDIOM, JARGON (denoted in this

Companion by the abbr: 'sl'); *common* or vulgar speech. ABUSE, BERATE, INSULT, RAGE, *RAIL*, RANT, RAVE, *THUNDER* AT. 2. The solver should be prepared for clues which seek to divert attention through the use of words which have a ~ meaning different from their more usual interpretation, e.g. **He's got plenty of coppers to afford the drug** (4) = HE*MP (note the use of **afford**, which encourages consideration of coppers as money, rather than **to provide** the answer. 3. The answer itself may be a ~ word, not necessarily indicated in the clue, e.g. **Point to a fish with some hesitation, and run for it** (7) = S*CARP*ER. 4. Employ ~ for word(s) in clue, e.g. **Slang talk for fast breeder** (6) = RABBIT.

SLAVE DEPENDENT UNIT (mech/tech). SUBORDINATE ANT. DRUDGE; VICTIM; BONDSMAN, HUMAN CHATTEL, SERF, UNPAID SERVANT; **celeb**: AESOP (when young; fables), ANDROCLES (lion, thorn), CALIBAN (Tempest, *Shak*), GUMBO (Virginians, Thackeray), JIM (Huckleberry Finn, *Twain*), MORGIANA (Arabian Nights), SPARTACUS (Rom), TOPSY, UNCLE *REMUS* (Harris), TOUSSAINT L'OUVERTURE (Haiti '*Napoleon*'), UNCLE TOM ('I 'spects I growed', Uncle Tom's Cabin, H. B. *Stowe*). HELOT (Gk). RIVER (Can).

SLEEPER KIPPER, NAPPER (sl) [*Morpheus*]. EAR-RING. RAILBED.

SLEEPY DOZY, DROWSY, SOMNOLENT. INATTENTIVE, INDOLENT, UNOBSERVANT. *DWARF* (Snow White).

SLIGHT LITTLE, SLIM, *SMALL*. INSULT.

SLING BALLISTA, CATAPULT [David and Goliath (bibl)]. *DRINK*. HOIST, SUPPORT, SUSPEND. BANDAGE, BELT, STRAP.

SLIP *FALL*, SLIDE. ESCAPE. ERROR, FAULT, GAFFE, MISTAKE. QUAY, LANDING, RAMP, WAY (naut). PETTICOAT, UNDERSKIRT. DROP. *CRICKETER*, FIELDER.

SLIPPER INDOOR *SHOE*, *MULE*. BEAT, CHASTISE, LEATHER, WALE. BRAKE, SKID (mech). CLAY. EEL, SKATE, SKI, SLEDGE, TOBOGGAN (all crypt).

SLOPING *INCLINED*, LEANING, LISTING, SLANTING. ITALIC.

SLOTH IDLENESS, INDOLENCE, LAZINESS. TREE MAMMAL; **2-toed**: CHOLEOPUS, UNAU; **3-toed**: AI, BRADYPUS. ~ BEAR (Ind); ~ MONKEY (loris). [And see *lemur*].

SMACK BLOW, SLAP. *BOAT*. HEROIN, *DRUG*. TASTE; LICK (lips).

SMALLHOLDING ACRE, ALLOTMENT. MINORITY SHARE. BRIEFCASE, ETUI, RETICULE (crypt).

SMALL VOLUME CC, VOL (crypt). QUIET (crypt), hence P.

SMART A LA MODE, CHIC, DAPPER, FASHIONABLE, IN, MODISH, SWELL, TONISH. HURT, STING. CLEVER, EFFICIENT [Alec]. QUICK. *PAINTER*.

SMASHED BROKEN, SHATTERED. *DRUNK* (sl).

SMEE (s/l It's me). *DUCK*. *PIRATE* (*Barrie*).

SMELT FISH, *SALMON*. EXTRACT, MELT (tech). SNIFFED; STANK.

SMITH METAL WORKER; FORGER (crypt); *IRONER* (crypt); **celeb**: JAMES BURTON (Kingsley); JOE GARGERY (Great Ex, *Dickens*); THE VILLAGE BLACKSMITH (Longfellow); FE ~ (Lord Birkenhead). SMUDGER (*nickname*).

SMOKER COMPARTMENT (rly). CIGARETTE, CIGAR, PIPE(R), *DRAWER* (crypt). CHIMNEY, FIREPLACE, FLUE, FUNNEL, LUM, STACK (all crypt).

SMUGGLE AVOID DUTY, RUN; CONCEAL, *HIDE*, STASH [contraband, Customs].

SN *TIN* (*chem*).

SNAFFLE *STEAL*. *BIT*, *HARNESS*.

SNAKE 1. SWAY, WIGGLE. EMF (European Monetary Fund). RIVER (US). 2. Limbless reptile, ASP; **breeds**: *ADDER*, ANACONDA, BASILISK, BOA, BOLOBI, COBRA, COCKATRICE, CORAL, CRIBO, DABOIA, FER-DE-LANCE (S Am viper), GLASS ~ (lizard), *GRASS*, GWARDAR, HABU, JIBOYA, KARUNG (water ~), KING, KRAIT, *MAMBA*, MOCCASIN, *PYTHON*, RATTLER, RING-HALS, TAIPAN (Aus), VIPER. **Celeb**: KAA (Kipling), A and C (*Shak*), MIDGARD (*Loki*); **k by** ~ **bite**: *Cleopatra*, *Eurydice*, Laocoon (*Troy*) [*Ch calendar*]. **Pl comp** = *ladders*. 3. *Constellation* (Serpens).

SNAP *BREAK*. *CARD* GAME. PHOTO, PICTURE. QUICK, SPUR OF THE MOMENT.

SNEAK *BETRAY*. *CREEP*.

SNEEZY *DWARF* (Snow White).

SNIPE AMBUSH, ATTACK [*sharpshooter*]. GAMEBIRD; **assembly** = wisp.

SNOOKER POOL [billiards; pyramids; *black*, *blue*, *brown*, *green*,

pink, *red*, *yellow* balls]; BLOCK, OBSTRUCT. DEFEAT,
THWART. GESTICULATOR (crypt).

SNOW ICE CRYSTALS. COCAINE, *DRUG*. *BOAT*.
SILVER/NICKEL *COINS*.

SNUB CUT, *SHUN*. PULL, TUG (naut).

SO SOUTH. STANDING ORDER. STATIONERY OFFICE.
ERGO, SIC, THUS; AS. NOTE (mus; also SOH). KING (bibl).
Pl = MAYDAY.

SOCIETY S. ASSOCIATION, *CLUB*, ORGANIZATION.

SOCRATES Gk philosopher, mar *Xanthippe* in self-penance.
Condemned to death, he chose to drink hemlock in front of his
friends.

SODIUM *METAL*; NA (*chem*).

SOFA SETTEE, UPHOLSTERED SEAT; ~ TABLE; and see
furniture.

SOFT B (pencil); P, PP (mus), SH; HUSH, QUIET; DULCET.
EASY, GIVING (**opp** = *hard*).

SOILED DIRTY, UNWASHED. EARTHY; BEDDED, LAID
OUT, PLANTED (crypt).

SOL Rom *god* of the SUN; also PHOEBUS (**Gk** = APOLLO, HELIOS).

SOLDIER 1. Any rank in the Army, usually abbreviated, e.g. *BRIG*,
CAPT, *COL*, CPL, *GEN*, LT, MAJ, RSM, SGT. 2. POILU (Fr);
HOPLITE (Gk); BERSERKER (ON); KERNE (Ire);
CENTURION, LEGIONARY, PRIMUS PILUS (Rom);
LOBSTER (arch), PBI, PONGO, REDCOAT (arch), SWADDY,
TOMMY ATKINS (UK); DOUGHBOY, GI, PFC (US). **Celeb**:
ALEXANDER (the Great), ANTIPATER (Macedon), BEN
BATTLE (Faithless Nelly Gray, Hood), *CLUBS* (*Alice*),
FOURTH AGE (The *Seven Ages* of Man, *Shak*), MONTY (Lord
Montgomery), OLD BILL (Bruce Bairnsfather), and, all from H.v
(*Shak*): BARDOLPH, BATES, COURT, FLUELLEN (Wal),
GOWER (Eng), JAMY (Sc), MACMORRIS (Ire), NYM,
PISTOL and WILLIAMS; [*military leaders*]. **Pl** = ARMY,
INFANTRY, MEN, TROOPS, ~s of the Queen. **Gk** =
PHALANX, **Rom** = LEGIONARY (100) CENTURY, MANIPLE
(6) COHORT [eagle, vexillum] [10] LEGION (commanded by a
Legatus); **Irregulars** = AUXILIA (Rom); FENCIBLES, HOME
GUARD, LDV, MILITIA, TA, TERRIERS, VIGILANTES.

SOLE EXCLUSIVE, ONLY. UNMARRIED (leg). *FISH*, FLAT-
FISH. BASE, BOTTOM, FOUNDATION; SHOE-TREAD.
Comp = *heel*.

SOLICITOR BEGGAR, IMPORTUNER, TOUT. LAWYER
[Sampson and Sally Brass, *Dickens*]. See *law*.
SOLIDARITY COMMUNITY INTEREST,
INTERDEPENDENCE. *UNION* (Pol).
SOLIDUS S. *COIN* (Rom) [£ s d]. OBLIQUE STROKE,
VIRGULE.
SOLOMON 1. Second s of *David* and Bathsheba (bibl), third king of
Isr (*c.* 990–930 B.C.). He then had his half-br Adonijah (who
coveted his step-m Abishag) ass, and also *Joab*. Endowed with
great *wisdom* (decision on custody of baby), ~ is renowned for the
number of his 'wives' or concubines, incl the Queen of *Sheba* (by
whom he started the *royal family* of Abyssinia. [Rider *Haggard*].
2. ~ Pross, alias John Barsad, prison *spy* who lets Carton into
Darnay's cell (2 Cities, *Dickens*). 3. ~ *Grundy*. 4. Br *painter*.
5. Musician.
SOLUTION ANSWER, *KEY*, RESOLUTION, SOLVING,
DISSOLUTION, SEPARATION.
SOLVE ANSWER, PUZZLE OUT. DISSOLVE, LOOSEN, UNTIE.
Som Somalia.
SOME (s/l *sum*). 1. A FEW, APPROXIMATELY. A QUANTITY,
AT LEAST. WONDERFUL. 2. Hidden word, as *part* (2). 3.
Part of word following, e.g. **Some money for my Scots friend** (3) =
MON**.
SON (s/l *sun*). 1. S; BOY, LAD. 2. Used after a name to indicate
'the son of ', e.g. **Adamson** = CAIN or ABEL or SETH [*Ap*].
SONG 1. AIR, ARIA, *CATCH*, CHANSON, DITTY, *GLEE*, *LAY*,
LIED, SHANTY, TUNE. CHEAP. 2. **Gk goddess** =
TERPSICHORE. 3. **Celeb**: Green grow the rushes-oh:

  (1) All *alone* and evermore shall be so;
  (2) Lilywhite *boys*;
  (3) *Rivals*;
  (4) *Gospel* makers;
  (5) *Symbols* at your *door*;
  (6) Proud *walkers*;
  (7) *Stars* in the sky;
  (8) Bold *rangers*;
  (9) Bright *shiners*;
(10) *Commandments*;
(11) Who went to *Heaven*;
(12) *Apostles*.

Twelve days of *Christmas*:
  (1) *Partridge* in a pear-tree;
  (2) Turtle *doves*;
  (3) French *hens*;
  (4) Calling *birds*;
  (5) Gold *rings*;
  (6) *Geese* a-laying;
  (7) *Swans* a-swimming;
  (8) *Maids* a-milking;
  (9) *Drummers* drumming;
  (10) *Pipers* piping;
  (11) *Ladies dancing*;
  (12) *Lords* a-leaping.

SONGSTER *BIRD*. CROONER, *SINGER*; POET; COMPOSER, LYRICIST.
SOON 1. *ANON*, PRESENTLY, SHORTLY. WILLINGLY. ETC (crypt). 2. Add 'so' to word, e.g. **Lace and so on brings comfort** (6) or **Lace soon brings comfort** (6) = SO*LACE.
SOOTHSAYER See *PROPHET*.
SORCERER ENCHANTER, ~RESS, *WITCH*, *WIZARD*. LIGHT OPERA (*G & S*). *ISLAND* (*Swift*).
SORRY APOLOGIZE, CARE, DEJECTED, LAMENTATION, PENITENT, REGRETFUL, REPINING, RUEFUL, SELF-REPROACH, UNHAPPY. PALTRY, SHABBY, WRETCHED.
SORT SIEVE, SIFT. *LOT*. KIND, TYPE. MANNER, WAY. **Pl** = HEALTH, SPIRITS, TEMPER.
SOUND 1. DIN, NOISE, *RACKET*, *ROW*, TONE. *DIVE*, FIND DEPTH, PLUMB (naut). *FIRM*, *FIT*, HALE. 2. Implies that the sound invoked by the following word is required, e.g. **Sound asleep** = SNORE or ZZ.
SOUNDER MORE STABLE. FITTER. LEAD-LINE (naut). *Assembly* of swine.
SOUNDS LIKE Indicated in this Companion by use of the letters s/l at the appropriate entries, it means that other spellings may sound similar, e.g. BORN, BORNE, BOURN all have *pronunciation* (q.v.) which is similar. Can also require the sound made by . . . (onomatopoeic), e.g. **Sounds like a sheep** = BAA.
SOUP *Anag*. BOUILLON, BROTH, CONSOMME, STEW, STOCK; *COURSE*. NITRO-GLYCERINE (sl).

SOURCE (s/l *sauce*). *Anag.* EMITTER, ORIGIN.
FOUNTAINHEAD, SPRING, *WELL*.
SOUTH S, SO; POINT, POLE. *BRIDGE PLAYER* (crypt).
~ **WIND Gk** = NOTOS, **Rom** = AUSTER.
SOVEREIGN GOLD *COIN*, POUND. *MONARCH*.
SP SERVICE POLICEMAN. STARTING PRICE: BETTING ODDS.
Sp Spain, ~ish.
SPA (s/l *spar*). 1. HEALTH RESORT, SPRING, WATERING
PLACE (town in Belgium). *RACETRACK* (cars). 2. **Celeb
resorts**: AIX LES BAINS, BADEN BADEN, BATH, BUXTON,
CONTREXEVILLE, CHELTENHAM, DROITWICH,
HARROGATE, OSTEND, TUNBRIDGE WELLS, VICHY,
WIESBADEN.
SPACECRAFT *ROCKET*, *SPACE TRAVELLER*, SPACE
VEHICLE [NASA]. SCIENCE OF SPACE. **Celeb (US)**:
APOLLO, AQUARIUS, ARIEL, *ATLAS*, CHALLENGER,
COLUMBIA, COURIER, *DISCOVERER*, *ECHO*,
EXPLORER, *GEMINI*, MARINER, *MARS*, *MERCURY*,
MIDAS, NIMBUS, PIONEER, RANGER, SAMOS, SHUTTLE,
SKYLAB, SPACELAB, TELSTAR, VANGUARD, VIKING,
VOYAGER. **Celeb (USSR)**: COSMOS, LUNA, LUNIK,
SALYUT, SOYUZ, SPUTNIK, TIROS, VOSHKOD, VOSTOK.
SPACE TRAVELLER ASTEROID, COMET, METEORITE,
MOON, *PLANET*, SHOOTING STAR. *SPACECRAFT*.
ASTRONAUT, COSMONAUT. **Celeb (US)**: ALDRIN (2nd on
moon), ARMSTRONG (1st on moon), BORMAN,
CARPENTER, CERNAN, COLLINS, CONRAD, COOPER,
GLENN (1st US), GORDON, GRISSOM, LOVELL,
MCDIVITT, SALLY RIDE (1st US fem), SCHIRRA, SCOTT,
STAFFORD, *WHITE*, *YOUNG*. **Celeb (USSR)**: BELYAEV,
BYKOVSKY, FEOKTISTOV, GAGARIN (1st man in space),
LAIKA (*dog*; 1st space traveller), LEONOV (1st *EVA*),
NIKOLAYEV, POPOVICH, TERESHKOVA (1st woman),
TITOV, YEGOROV [Jules Verne; H. G. Wells].
SPAIN SP. E (*car plate*).
SPANIARD DON, SENOR, SR.
SPANNER TOOL, WRENCH. *ARCH*, *BRIDGE* (crypt).
SPAR (s/l *spa*). BOOM, GAFF, MAST, SPRIT, *YARD*. *BOX*,
FIGHT. *MINERAL*. HOOP, STAPLE (thatching).
SPEAKER ORATOR (chairman; Commons). *LIP*, MOUTH,
TONGUE (crypt).

SPEAR HALBERD, HARPOON, JAVELIN (Meleager), PIKE, *WEAPON*. RUN THROUGH, SPIKE, SPIT. MALE (**opp** = distaff). EAR, SPRIG [asparagus (bot)]. *GRASS*. *PAINTER*.

SPECTACLE EXHIBITION, *SHOW*, SIGHT. **Pl** = BIN(N)S, GLASSES [*Company* (livery)].

SPECTATOR ONLOOKER, VIEWER, WATCHER. **Pl** = *CROWD*.

SPECULATOR *BEAR*, PUNTER, *STAG* (comm).

SPEECH *ADDRESS*, *DELIVERY*, LECTURE, TALK. LANGUAGE.

SPEED KNOT, KPH, LICK, MPH, *RATE*, *TEMPO*. DRUG. SERVANT/JESTER (2 G of V, *Shak*).

SPELL ATTRACTION. CANTRIP, CHARM, INCANTATION. DUTY, PERIOD, TURN, *WATCH*. RELIEVE. INVOLVE, PRESAGE, RESULT. MAKE or FORM WORDS.

SPELLER *WITCH* (crypt).

SPELLING 1. CHARMING, INCANTATION, WITCHCRAFT (crypt). RELIEVING (naut watch). INVOLVING. ABC, WORD FORMATION. 2. The clue setter will sometimes vary the breakdown of letters in an answer, so as to offer a different meaning (which should be alluded to in the clue) e.g. **Cheeky aroma some puddings possess** (5, 5) = AFTER SHAVE; this responds to the first two words of the clue, whereas changing the position of the letter 'S' from the second word to the first (to give AFTERS HAVE) responds to the last three clue words — thus providing the secondary indication.

SPENT *TIRED*. PASSED (time), STAYED. BLEW, BLUED, EXPENDED, SQUANDERED.

SPHINX 1. Egy male *monster* (head human, body lion; strangler) representing the god Horamkhu. Also Gk female counterpart who put a riddle to the Thebans and killed all who could not solve it. *Oedipus* solved it and the Sphinx committed suicide. The riddle was 'A being with 4 feet has 2 feet and 3 feet, and only one voice; but its feet vary, and when it has most it is weakest. Who or what is it?' Oedipus' answer was 'Man, who in infancy crawls on all fours, then stands up on two feet, and in old age supports himself with a stick.' 2. Monkey (strangler).

SPICE FLAVOUR, MALICE, ZEST: ARTEMISIA, CARAWAY, CAYENNE, CHILI, CHIVE, CINNAMON, CLOVE, CORIANDER, CURRY, GARLIC, GILLYFLOWER, GINGER, MACE, MOULI, MUSTARD, NUTMEG,

OREGANO, PAPRIKA, PEPPER, PIMENTO, RACE,
SAFFRON, TURMERIC [*herb*].

SPIDER ARANEIDA. 8-LEGGED ANTHROPOID: BLACK
WIDOW, *COB*, MONEY ~, SOLPUGA, TANT,
TARANTULA, *WOLF*; *SPINNER*, WEBSTER (crypt). [Anansi
(W Af ~ god), *Arachne*, Robert the Bruce]. CUE-REST.
CRAB. CARD GAME. *MONKEY*.

~ **GIRL** *ARACHNE*. MISS MUFFET.

SPILL *Anag*. LIGHTER, TAPER. SHED, UPSET.

SPINNER FISHERMAN, TROLLER. TOP. DRIER.
GYROSCOPE. *SPIDER*. SCHEHERAZADE (crypt).
RUMPLESTILTSKIN (Grimm).

SPIRIT *DRINK* (q.v.); HARD STUFF (sl); AQUAVIT, ARAK,
ARRACK, BOURBON, BRANDY, COGNAC, GIN, GRAPPA,
HOLLANDS, RUM, RYE, SAKE, -I, SCHIEDAM,
SCHNAPPS, SCOTCH, VODKA, WHISKEY (Ire), WHISKY
(Sc) [*liqueur*]. *GHOST*, SHADE, SOUL. ELAN, GO, LIFE,
MORALE, PEP, VERVE, VIM. AFREET, AFRIT, ANGEL,
ARIEL, BANSHEE, BROWNIE, DEMON, DJINN, ELF,
FAMILIAR (witch), GENIE, GOBLIN, HOBGOBLIN, IMP,
KELPIE, PERI, PIXY(IE), PUCK, *SPRITE*, WILI (Giselle
ballet). ELIXIR, ETHOS.

SPITFIRE *SHREW*, TERMAGANT. *AIRCRAFT*; **comp** =
Hurricane.

SPLIT CLEAVE, DIVIDE. CLEFT, CRACK, FISSURE, RENT.
BREACH, RUPTURE, SCHISM. *BETRAY*. *DRINK*, MIXER.
BOTTLE. DISH. TOWN (Y).

SPOIL DAMAGE, *MAR*, *RUIN*. BOOTY, LOOT.

SPONDEE *FOOT*.

SPOON UTENSIL; **comp** = fork. SCOOP. BILL AND COO,
CANOODLE, WOO. *GOLF-CLUB*.

SPORT 1. JOKING, PLAYFUL; MOCKERY. GAMBOL,
FROLIC, SKIP. MUTATION (biol, zool). COBBER, FRIEND,
MATE, PAL (Aus sl). GOOD LOSER, FAIR PLAYER. 2.
(competitive) ACTIVITY, EXERCISE, *GAME*. PASTIME.
GREYHOUND-, HORSE-RACING (the ~ of kings; and see
racetrack); CAR-, MOTOR-RACING (and see *racetrack*),
CYCLING, CYCLO-CROSS, DIRT-TRACK, SPEEDWAY
RACING. *BOXING* (q.v. for weights); *WRESTLING* (q.v. for
types). BLOOD ~ (for so-called pleasure): COURSING,
FISHING, HUNTING, SHOOTING, STAG-HUNTING. **Pl** =

ATHLETICS (q.v. for field and track events), *GAMES* (Asian ~,
Commonwealth ~, Olympic ~) e.g. **Indoor** ~: any *GAME* or
EXERCISE played or taken indoors, usually competitively and
often with a *ball* (q.v.) or on a *board* (q.v.). CANOODLING,
LOVE-MAKING, PETTING (sl). **Outdoor** ~: any *GAME* (q.v.)
or EXERCISE played or taken outdoors, usually competitively
with a *ball* (q.v.); any blood ~. And see *BALL GAME* and
GAME for lists of such ~. **Water** ~: AQUALUNG, *DIVING*
(q.v. for positions), *SAILING* (q.v. for rigs), SKIN DIVING,
SUB-AQUA, SURFING, *SWIMMING* (q.v. for styles), WATER
POLO, YACHTING. **Winter** ~: BOBSLEIGH, CURLING,
LUGEING, SKATING, SKIING (cross-country, down-hill,
jumping, langlauf, slalom), SLEDGING, TOBOGGANING
(Cresta Run).

SPORTING CLUB MCC, RFU, FA etc. BAT, *RACKET* (crypt).

~ JUDGE REFEREE, UMPIRE.

~ SET *SIDE*; TEAM.

SPOT 1. PLACE, LOCALITY. ACNE, PIMPLE. MARK, SOIL,
STAIN. CIRCLE, PATCH. *DASH*, DROP, *LITTLE*. BEAM,
FLOOD (light). DETECT, ESPY, LOCATE, SEE. 2. May
indicate a location connected with the following word(s) in the
clue, e.g. **Spot of gambling** (5, 5) = MONTE CARLO.

SPOTTED SEEN. DAPPLED, SPECKLED.

SPRING BOUND, JUMP, LEAP. COIL ~, LEAF ~. *SEASON*.
FLOW, WELL [*spa*]. *Assembly* of teal.

SPRINGBOK *ANTELOPE*. *RUGBY* PLAYER.

SPRINGTIME SEASON; MARCH, APRIL, MAY.

SPRITE *SPIRIT*; PUCK (MND, *Shak*), ARIEL (Temp, *Shak*).

SPRUCE *TRIM*. *TREE*.

SPUR URGE. **Pl** = *FOOTBALL* TEAM.

SPY *AGENT* (q.v.). SEE, SPOT. SNOOP. *CARTOONIST*.

SQUARE 1. *DATED*, OLD FASHIONED. PLACE, PIAZZA.
RIGHTANGLED ['you broke a Br ~'; Fuzzy Wuzzy (*Kipling*)].
T-, SET-. 2. Any square number, 9, 100 etc, hence IX, C.
[*measure*].

~ MEAL GOOD SPREAD. BISCUIT, SANDWICH (crypt).

SQUASH CORDIAL, *DRINK*. *VEGETABLE*. CRUSH,
SQUEEZE. *GAME*.

SQUEALER *BETRAYER*, *GRASS*, SNEAK, TELL-TALE. PIG
(*Orwell*).

SS *SAINTS*. *SHIP*. GESTAPO, *SECRET* POLICE.

ST *SAINT*; GOODMAN (crypt). *STREET. STONE.* STUMPED
(cricket).

STABLE 1. *FIRM*, SOUND, STEADY. RACEHORSE. STRING;
habitation of horses. 2. Gk myth stable of *Augeus*, the subject of
one of the labours of *Hercules*.

STAFF 1. *ROD*, VERGE (eccles), WAND [authority, office; Black
Rod, Gold Stick; *Aaron*; Tiresias (*prophet*)]; CADUCEUS
[*Asclepius* (medicine); *Hermes*, *Mercury*]; PEDUM (*shepherd*);
THYRSUS (*Bacchus*, *Dionysus*). QUARTER ~, STAVE,
STICK [Kendo (Jap), Little John (Robin *Hood*)]. 2. Framework
for written *music* (STAVE).

STAG 1. Male *DEER*, BROCKET (2nd year), CERVUS. MALE
(party). BEETLE. SHARE BUYER, SPECULATOR. **Pl** =
Football team. 2. Gk myth *ACTAEON*. 3. One of the labours of
Hercules.

STAGE DAIS, PLATFORM, STEP, SCAFFOLD. ACTING
PROFESSION, *BOARDS*, DRAMA, THEATRE. ARRANGE,
PRESENT, PRODUCE. BUS-STOP, LEG, PERIOD, POINT,
STATION, STOP-OVER. *CARRIAGE*, COACH.

STAIRS FLIGHT, STEPS [ladder]. APPLES (*rh sl*).

STAKE (s/l steak). ANTE, *BET*, RISK, *WAGER*. POST, SPIT,
STICK. *ANVIL*. FASTEN, *SECURE*.

STAMP FRANK, IMPRESS(ION), IMPRINT; (HALL)MARK,
SEAL. BANG, CLUMP, THUMP, TRAMPLE, TREAD,
TRUDGE. POSTAGE ~; **coll** = philatelist. [Roland *Hill*].

STANDARD BANNER, EAGLE, ENSIGN, *FLAG*, FLIER (crypt),
PENNANT. DEGREE, LEVEL, *MEASURE*, NORM, PAR,
QUALITY, REGULAR, YARDSTICK.

STANDING ORDER SO. ATTENTION, GET UP (crypt).

STAR 1. ASTERISK, *MARK*; 17 (*tarot*). *CASTLE*. ACTOR,
ACTRESS, CELEBRITY, *LION*, VIP; ACT, FEATURE, PLAY
LEAD. MAIN, OUTSTANDING, PRINCIPAL.
DECORATION. 2. NEBULA; CELESTIAL/HEAVENLY
BODY, NOVA, SUN; SKYLIGHT (crypt): (binary-, day-,
double-, *evening*-, falling-, *morning*-, multiple-, pole-, shooting-
[black hole, *planet*, pulsar, quasar, white dwarf]). 'ESTHER'.
3. **Pl** = *CONSTELLATION*. Seven ~s in the sky in *song*.

STARBOARD S; RIGHT (**opp** = *port*, larboard). PLAYBILL.

STARLING *BIRD* (*assembly*). YOUNG ACTOR (crypt).

START FRIGHT, JUMP. SCRATCH. BEGIN, FOUND,
INITIATE (**opp** = *end*). OPENING. *GO*, OFF, *REPAIR*.

EASE, LOOSEN (naut).

STARTER 1. *BEGINNER.* APPETIZER, *COURSE*, ENTREE (cook). JUMPER (crypt). GUNMAN (sports, crypt). A, ALPHA (crypt). ADAM, EVE (crypt). 2. First letter of word concerned, e.g. **Race starter** = R; note that this could also be GUNMAN or ADAM/EVE.

STARTING 1. BEGINNING. JUMPING (crypt). 2. First letter, e.g. **Starting time** = T; but note **Failure starting with a cry (7)** = W*A*SHOUT, which is revealed by the secondary word **failure**.

STAR TURN MAIN ITEM, LEAD PART. Anag. 'star' as RATS, TSAR etc.

STATE ANNOUNCE, SAY. CONDITION. ANXIOUS, EXCITED, UNTIDY. DIGNITY, POMP, RANK. GOVERNMENT, COMMUNITY, NATION. **Pl** = *LEGISLATIVE BODY* (CI). **Division of Aus:**

Aus State	Nickname
NEW SOUTH WALES	Ma ~
NORTHERN TERRITORY	White Ant ~
QUEENSLAND	Bananaland
SOUTH AUSTRALIA	Wheat ~
TASMANIA	Apple Isle
VICTORIA	Cabbage Patch
WESTERN AUSTRALIA	Groperland

Division of the USA:

State	Abbr	Abbr	Capital
ALABAMA	ALA	AL	Montgomery
ALASKA	ALAS	AK	Juneau
ARIZONA	ARIZ	AZ	Phoenix
ARKANSAS	ARK	AR	Little Rock
CALIFORNIA	CALIF	CA	Sacramento
COLORADO	COLO	CO	Denver
CONNECTICUT[13]	CONN	CT	Hartford
DELAWARE[13]	DEL	DE	Dover
DISTRICT OF COLUMBIA		DC	Washington
FLORIDA	FLA	FL	Tallahassee
GEORGIA[13]		GA	Atlanta
HAWAII		HI	Honolulu
IDAHO	IDA	ID	Boise

ILLINOIS	ILL	IL	Springfield
INDIANA	IND	IN	Indianapolis
IOWA		IA	Des Moines
KANSAS	KANS	KS	Topeka
KENTUCKY		KY	Frankfort
LOUISIANA		LA	Baton Rouge
MAINE		ME	Augusta
MARYLAND[13]		MD	Annapolis
MASSACHUSETTS[13]	MASS	MA	Boston
MICHIGAN	MICH	MI	Lansing
MINNESOTA	MINN	MN	St Paul
MISSISSIPPI	MISS	MS	Jackson
MISSOURI		MO	Jefferson City
MONTANA	MONT	MT	Helena
NEBRASKA	NEBR	NE	Lincoln
NEVADA	NEV	NV	Carson City
NEW HAMPSHIRE[13]		NH	Concord
NEW JERSEY[13]		NJ	Trenton
NEX MEXICO	N MEX	NM	Santa Fe
NEW YORK[13]		NY	Albany
NORTH CAROLINA[13]		NC	Raleigh
NORTH DAKOTA	N DAK	ND	Bismarck
OHIO	O	OH	Columbus
OKLAHOMA	OKLA	OK	Oklahoma City
OREGON	OREG	OR	Salem
PENNSYLVANIA[13]	PENN	PA	Harrisburg
RHODE ISLAND[13]		RI	Providence
SOUTH CAROLINA[13]		SC	Columbia
SOUTH DAKOTA	S DAK	SD	Pierre
TENNESSEE	TENN.	TN	Nashville
TEXAS	TEX	TX	Austin
UTAH		UT	Salt Lake City
VERMONT		VT	Montpelier
VIRGINIA[13]		VA	Richmond
WASHINGTON	WASH	WA	Olympia
WEST VIRGINIA	W VA	WV	Charleston
WISCONSIN	WISC	WI	Madison
WYOMING	WYO	WY	Cheyenne

[13] = one of the original 13 states.

STATECRAFT DIPLOMACY. PRESIDENTIAL YACHT, ROYAL *BARGE* (crypt).

STATELY HOME *COUNTRY HOUSE* (q.v. for **celeb, fict**), PLACE, SEAT (dignified, grand, imposing; open to the public); **celeb (fact)**:

APSLEY HOUSE
ARUNDEL CASTLE
BEAULIEU
BELVOIR CASTLE
BERKELEY CASTLE
BLAIR CASTLE
BLENHEIM PALACE
BODIAM CASTLE
BROADLANDS
BURGHLEY HOUSE
CAWDOR CASTLE
CHARTWELL
CHATSWORTH HOUSE
COMPTON WYNYATES
FALKLAND PALACE
GLAMIS CASTLE
HAMPTON COURT
HAREWOOD HOUSE
HATFIELD HOUSE
HEVER CASTLE
HOLKHAM HALL
KNEBWORTH HOUSE
LEEDS CASTLE
LONGLEAT
LUTON HOO
PETWORTH HOUSE
POWDERHAM CASTLE
SCARISBRICK HALL
SCONE PALACE
STRATFIELD SAYE
SUDELEY CASTLE
WARWICK CASTLE
WILTON HOUSE
WINDSOR CASTLE
WOBURN PLACE
WOOLATON HALL

STATESMAN POLITICIAN. AMERICAN (crypt).

STAUNCH FIRM, LOYAL, TRUSTWORTHY. CHECK, DAM, STEM, STOP. AIRTIGHT, WATERTIGHT.

STAY AVAST (naut); REMAIN, STOP (**opp** = *go, go on*). PREVENT. GUY (ROPE), PROP, RIG, *SUPPORT*. **Pl** = CORSET.

STEAL (s/l *steel*). *BONE* (sl), BURGLE, FILCH, NICK, PINCH, PURLOIN, *ROB*. SNAFFLE, THIEVE. CREEP, GLIDE (AWAY).

STEAMER *BOAT*, LINER, SS (**opp** = *sailing* craft) [see *Comet* (2)]. ENGINE, TRAIN. COOKER, COOKPOT.

STEEL (s/l *steal*). 1. METAL [Bessemer]. HONE, SHARPENER. BRACE, HARDEN, RESOLVE. 2. Alloy of carbon, iron and manganese, hence (crypt) letters CFEMN. 3. *Anniversary* (11th).

STEEP PRECIPICE, SHEER, VERTICAL. IMMERSE. DRENCH, SOAK. DEAR, EXPENSIVE.

STEEPLECHASER *HORSE*; JUMPER; FENCER (crypt).

STEER *CON*, CONDUCT, DIRECT, DRIVE, HELM. *COW*.

STEERSMAN HELMSMAN, NAVIGATOR, PILOT, TILLER-MAN; CONMAN, WHEELER (crypt). *COWBOY* (crypt). GLAUCUS (*Argonaut*).

STELLA GIRL, 'STAR'. *AWARD* (Br film)®.

STEM CHECK, DAM, *STA(U)NCH*, *STOP*. BOW, FRONT (naut). ADVANCE. LINE, ORIGIN, STALK.

STEP (s/l *steppe*). MARCH, PACE. DANCE. RISER, TREAD. **Pl** = FLIGHT, LADDER, STAIRS.

~ **DOWN** DECLINE, GIVE WAY, CEDE. DESCEND. RESIGN. DEMOTION.

STEPPE (s/l *step*). *PLAIN* (q.v.).

STERLING L, POUND. HIGH QUALITY.

STEVENSON (s/l Stephenson). 1. Engineer (Sc), lighthouse builder (not steam engines — he was -ph-); Bell Rock. 2. Robert Louis, writer; **celeb books**: The Black Arrow, Catriona (sequel to Kidnapped), Inland Voyage (his first), Kidnapped (sequel: Catriona), The Master of Ballantrae, The Strange Case of Dr Jekyll and Mr *Hyde*, Travels with a Donkey in the Cevennes, Treasure Island (ex The Sea Cook) [Benn Gunn (marooned), Billy Bones, Black Dog, Blind Pew, Capt Flint (*parrot*; *pirate*), Israel Hands (coxswain), Jim Hawkins, Dr Livesey, Long John *Silver* (one-legged *pirate*, cook 'Barbecue', *parrot*), Capt Smollett, Squire Trelawney; the black spot (death sentence), Hispaniola (ship), Admiral Benbow (inn), the Spyglass (inn)].

STEW *Anag*. BOIL, COOK, FERMENT, *SEETHE*. DISH. *STUDY*. ANGER, ANXIETY, BOTHER, FUSS, WORRY. BROTHEL (*sl*). FISH-POND.

STILL EVER, YET. DISTILLERY, RETORT [moonshine (*sl*)]. CALM, MOTIONLESS (**opp** = *moving*). EVEN.

STILTED BOMBASTIC, POMPOUS. AWKWARD, GRALLATORIAL, HIGH-STANDING, TALL (crypt).

STING NETTLE, HURT, PROVOKE. OVERCHARGE. *FISH*, RAY.

STINGY MEAN, MISERLY, NEAR, TIGHT. HURTFUL, INSULTING, WOUNDING. BEE, WASP (crypt).

STIR *Anag*. AROUSE, INFLAME. *ADMIX*, *MIX*, WHIP. COMMOTION, EXCITEMENT, TO-DO. *GAOL* (sl).

STOAT ERMINE, *WEASEL*.

STOCK CREDIT, REPUTATION. PROVIDE, RESERVE,

STORE. BREED, BLOOD, FAMILY, *STRAIN*; ANIMALS, *CATTLE*. BASE, BUTT, HANDLE, STÜMP. *FLOWER*. SHIPYARD WAY/SLIP. CRAVAT, SCARF, TIE. BRICK. **Pl** = wooden punishment device. **Pl comp** = shares.

STOCKTAKING COUNTING, REVIEW. RUSTLING (crypt).

STOIC 1. AUSTERE, COURAGEOUS, SELF-CONTROLLED. 2. *Philosopher* of Athens school founded by ZENO; **celeb**: ANISTHENES, ANTIGONUS, *BRUTUS*, *CATO*, CHRYSIPPUS, *CICERO*, CLEANTHES, DIODOTUS, EPICTETUS, MARCUS AURELIUS, SENECA.

STOLEN *ROBBED*; HOT [*steal*].

STONE COBBLE, GRANITE, PEBBLE, ROCK (Norman, Portland). *AGATE*, *GEM*. AGE. *MEASURE* (weight), *ST*. [*Andromeda, Atlas, Medusa, Niobe, Perseus*].

STONED DRUGGED, DRUNK. PELTED. SCULPTED (crypt).

STOOL PIGEON *BETRAYER*, GRASS, SNEAK, SHOPPER.

STOP 1. ARREST, BAR, CLOSE, CUT OFF, GAG, OBSTRUCT, PARRY, PREVENT, STAUNCH, STIFLE. CEASE, CHECK, DESIST, GIVE OVER, HALT, PAUSE. CALL AT, REMAIN, SOJOURN, *STAY*. HALT, STATION (rly). APERTURE, DIAPHRAGM, ORGAN CONTROL, VALVE. PUNCTUATE: COLON, COMMA etc. MAKE FAST. CAULK, PAY (naut). *CARD GAME*. 2. Word with last letter(s) removed, e.g. **Drink stops play** (4) = DRAM(a).

~ **TALKING** BUTTON UP, CLAM UP. GAG, SILENCE.

STOREY (s/l *story*). FLOOR, LEVEL.

STORM *Anag*. 1. ASSAULT. RAGE. SHOWER. GALE, HAILSTORM, HURRICANE, RAINSTORM, SNOWSTORM, TEMPEST, THUNDERSTORM, TORNADO. 2. **Rom god** = FULGURATOR. **Gk goddesses** = *HARPIES*.

STORY (s/l *storey*). ACCOUNT, NARRATION, NARRATIVE, *RELATION*. FIB, LIE, TALE.

STOUT *BRAVE*, DOUGHTY, RESOLUTE, STAUNCH, STUBBORN, STURDY [Cortes]. BULKY, CORPULENT, FAT, OBESE (**opp** = *thin*). *BEER*, GUINNESS®.

STOVE COOKER [oven]. BREACHED, BROKEN.

STOWE (s/l *stow*). 1. *PUBLIC SCHOOL*. TOWN. 2. Harriet Beecher ~, writer; **book**: Uncle Tom's Cabin (Legree, *bully*; Li'l Liza; Topsy [*slave*; I 'spects I growed]).

STRAIN AIR, MUSIC, SONG, TONE, TUNE. INJURE, OVER-TASK, PULL STRESS, STRETCH. FILTER. BREED, *STOCK*.

STRAIT (s/l straight). RIGOROUS, STRICT. CONFINE,
LIMITED, NARROW. **Pl** = DISTRESS, NEED. PASSAGE
OF WATER; **celeb**:

4-letters
BASS
COOK
PALK

5-letters
BANKS
CABOT
DAVIS
DOVER
KERME
KOREA
LUZON
NARES
SUNDA

6-letters
BERING
HORMUZ
HUDSON
TORRES

7-letters
DENMARK
FLORIDA
FORMOSA
FOVEAUX
MALACCA
MESSINA
OTRANTO

8+ letters
BELLE ILE
BONIFACIO
BOSPHORUS
GIBRALTAR
LA PEROUSE
MAGELLAN
MAKASSAR
PENTLAND
SINGAPORE
SKAGERRAK

STRANGER ALIEN, FOREIGNER. TEA LEAF (fig). MORE
PECULIAR, RUMMER.
STREAK BAND, LINE, STRIPE. ELEMENT, SERIES, SPELL,
STRAIN. DASH, RUN; RUN NAKED.
STREET ST; DRAG, *ROAD*.
~ **MARKET** BRICK LANE, FLEA-MARKET, MARCHE DES
PUCES (Fr), MIDDLESEX STREET, PETTICOAT LANE,
PORTOBELLO ROAD; AGORA (Gk), SOUK (Mos),
MONOPOLY® (crypt, game).
STRENGTH QUALITY. COGENCY; INTENSITY: NUMBERS,
SUCCESS (mil); FIRMNESS, FORCE, POTENCY, POWER;
celeb possessors (male): ANTAEUS, CHARLES *ATLAS*,
BROBDINGNAGIANS (*Swift*), BRIAREUS, COLOSSUS,
CRATOS, *CYCLOPES*, GOLIATH, HERACLES/*HERCULES*,
KWASIND (*Hiawatha*), POLYPHEMUS, *SAMSON*, SANDOW,

SUPERMAN, TARZAN, TITAN; ~ (**fem**): AMAZONS,
STHENO (*Gorgon*).

STRIKE BAT, HIT, INNINGS, *KNOCK*, RAM, SMACK,
SWING. IMPRESS. DIVERGE. LEVEL. FIND (gold/oil).
LOWER FLAG, SURRENDER. STOP WORK, TAKE
(industrial) ACTION.

STRIKER BATTER, HITTER. FLINT, FUSEE, LUCIFER,
MATCH (crypt). PROSPECTOR. YIELDER.
NON-WORKER. LIGHTNING (crypt).

STRIKING BATTING, HITTING, INNINGS (*cricket*). LIGHTING
(match). YIELDING. IDLING, OUT. EYE-CATCHING.
UNCO (Sc).

STRING CORD, PULL, TAG, TIE. *STABLE* (racehorses). **Pl =**
OBLIGATION.

STRIP DENUDE, DOFF, UNDRESS (**opp** = *dress*). SHEAR.

STROKE CARESS, FONDLE. OARSMAN, *ROWER*.
APPROACH, CHIP, DRIVE, HOOK, LOFT, PUTT, SLICE,
SWING (golf); BLOCK, CUT, DRIVE, HOOK, GLANCE,
LOFT, PULL, SLASH, SWING (*cricket*). BRAIN STORM.

STUCK UP SUPERCILIOUS, SUPERIOR. BILLED, POSTED
(crypt).

STUDENT L, LEARNER, *PUPIL* (**Union** = NUS).

STUDIO WORK ROOM (artist/painter/cinema/film/movie/music/
photographic/radio/sculptor's/TV); and see *FILM* ~ for list.

STUDY DEN, SANCTUM. *CON*, EXAMINE, READ, *SCAN*,
SCRUTINISE; OVERLOOK (arch and crypt). Any subject thus
investigated, e.g.

animals	ZOOLOGY
antiquities	ARCHAEOLOGY
beetles	COLEOPTEROLOGY
birds	ORNITHOLOGY
blood (med)	H(A)EMATOLOGY
bones (med)	OSTEOLOGY
caves	SPEL(A)EOLOGY
character	ETHOLOGY
China (geog)	SINOLOGY
clouds	NEPHOLOGY
coins	NUMISMATOLOGY
culture	SOCIOLOGY
disease (body)	PATHOLOGY

disease (mental)	PSYCHOLOGY
~ (female)	GYNAECOLOGY
earth's crust	GEOLOGY
Egypt (ancient)	EGYPTOLOGY
ferns	PTERIDOLOGY
fossil life	PAL(A)EONTOLOGY
handwriting	GRAPHOLOGY
heart	CARDIOLOGY
insects	ENTOMOLOGY
languages	PHILOLOGY
life (fossil)	PAL(A)EONTOLOGY
mankind	ANTHROPOLOGY
medals	NUMISMATOLOGY
mind (med)	PSYCHOLOGY
minerals	MINERALOGY
mountains	OROLOGY
old age	GERONTOLOGY
religion	THEOLOGY
shells (zool)	CONCHOLOGY
sleep	HYPNOLOGY
soil management	AGRONOMY
teeth	ODONTOLOGY
tissue (med)	HISTOLOGY
weather	METEOROLOGY
weevils	COLEOPTEROLOGY
wine	OENOLOGY ·
words	ETYMOLOGY
writing	GRAPHOLOGY
~ (ancient)	PAL(A)EOGRAPHY

STUVW S*TO*W (crypt).

STY (s/l *stye*). ENCLOSURE, PEN; *habitation* (pigs).

STYE (s/l *sty*). *EYESORE*, IRITIS.

STYX Gk myth principal river of the Underworld, d of *Oceanus* and Tethys [*Acheron, Charon, Cocytus, Lethe, Pyriphlegethon*].

SU SUNDAY. SOVIET UNION (*car plate*).

SUBJECT SUBDUE; VASSAL (**opp** = *ruler*). EXPOSE, INFLICT, TREAT. LIABLE TO. NOUN, NOMINATIVE (e.g. **My subject** = I). THEME. EGO, MIND. PHOTO, PIC, POSER, MODEL, STILL LIFE.

SUBMIT *BOW*, GIVE WAY, SURRENDER, YIELD. OFFER,

PRESENT, RENDER.

SUBSCRIBE CONTRIBUTE, ENGAGE, RAISE (money). SIGN, UNDERWRITE (arch).

SUBSOLANUS Rom myth EAST *WIND* (**Gk** = APELIOTES).

SUBSTITUTE 1. DEPUTY, EXCHANGE, REPLACE(MENT), SURROGATE. 2. Exchange a letter, usually in anag, e.g. **I substitute a revision of pure ideas for a dramatist** (9) = EURIPIDES (anag of 'pure ideas' with 'a' substituted by 'I').

SUCCEED ENSUE, FOLLOW, INHERIT. ACCOMPLISH, GET ON, PROSPER, WIN.

SUCCESSOR One who succeeds, e.g. HEIR, FOLLOWER, WINNER.

SUCKER (s/l succour). BARNACLE, LEECH, LIMPET. BUD, SHOOT. GREENHORN, GULLIBLE FELLOW, MARK, PIGEON.

SUIT ADAPT, FIT, SATISFY; *BECOME*. SET (*armour*, clothes, sails). ACTION, CLAIM, COURT CASE, ISSUE, PETITION. CLUBS, DIAMONDS, HEARTS, SPADES. WHISTLE (*rh sl*).

SUITABLE 1. APPROPRIATE, FITTED, FITTING, MEET, PROPER. 2. In a *suit* [*bridge, cards*].

SUITED CLOTHED, DRESSED. COURTED, WOOED (crypt). ACCOMMODATED, SATISFIED. FLUSH (*cards*).

SULKY MOROSE PET(ULANT), POUTING, SULLENLY. *CARRIAGE*.

SULLIVAN 1. Sir Arthur ~, *COMPOSER*, MUSICIAN (Eng); co-op with *Gilbert* in operettas (for details, see *G and S*).

SULPHUR S (*chem*).

SULTRY *HOT*. PROVOCATIVE, PASSIONATE, SENSUAL.

SUM (s/l *some*). *ADD UP*, TOT, TOTAL. AMOUNT. SUBSTANCE, SUMMARY. I AM (Lat).

SUMMARY (s/l summery). ABSTRACT, DIGEST, PRECIS, RESUME, SUBSTANCE, SYNOPSIS.

SUMMER SEASON. HORIZONTAL BEAM, JOIST, RAFTER. ADDER, CALCULATOR, COUNTER (crypt).

SUN (s/l son). 1. *SUNDAY*. STAR; SKYLIGHT (crypt); 19 (*tarot*). NEWSPAPER®. YEAR (crypt). SUNBATHE, TAN. 2. **Gods: Gk** = APOLLO, HELIOS; **Rom** = PHOEBUS, SOL.

SUNDAY S, SU, *SUN*. Day of the *Sun*; day of rest. *ISLAND*. ~'s **child** = bonny & blithe, good & gay [Solomon *Grundy*]. **Pl** = RIVER (SA).

SUPERIOR ABOVE, HIGHER, UPPER. BETTER, MORE, U.

(GREAT) LAKE; GITCHE-GUMEE, BIG SEA WATER (*Hiawatha*).

SUPERMAN IDEAL/SUPERIOR MAN. CLARK *KENT* [Krypton; Lois Lane].

SUPPLIED *Anag*. 1. FUNDED, FURNISHED, PER, PROVIDED (BY). 2. Hidden word, e.g. **Food is supplied by great ingenuity** (6) = (gr)EAT*ING(enuity).

SUPPLY FURNISH, MEET, PROVIDE; **comp** = *demand*; **pl** = PROVISIONS, STOCKS, STORES. FLEXIBLY, NUBILE, PLIANTLY.

SUPPORT 1. CARRY, CONFIRM, HOLD UP, *SECOND*. BRA, CORSET, TRUSS. BACK, BRACKET, GUY, LEG, PROP, SLING, STAY. 2. Directs attention to second half of dn answer, e.g. **Age supports us by custom** = US*AGE.

SUPPORTER BACK, FOOT, LEG, PROP, SLING, STAY. BELT, BRA, BRACES, SUSPENDERS. FAN, FOLLOWER.

SWAGMAN AUSSIE, DIGGER. *ROBBER* (crypt).

SWALLOW 1. ABSORB, DOWN, EAT, ENGULF. GULLET, WEASAND. REPRESS, SUPPRESS. *BIRD* [Sea ~ = tern]. 2. Word put into another, e.g. **We are swallowed by me, a patron of the arts** (4) = M*US*E; the same answer is given more cryptically by **A patron of the arts, I engulf** (or, **take in**) **America**.

SWAN 1. RUBBER-NECK, SIGHT-SEEING (RAF sl). *RIVER*. *THEATRE*. *ISLAND*. *PIRATE*. *Constellation* (Cygnus). **Comp** = Edgar. 2. Waterbird of genus CYGNUS; BEWICK ~, BLACK ~, MUTE ~; **assembly** = wedge; **male** = COB; **fem** = PEN; **offspring** = CYGNET. [*Graeae*. *Leda/Zeus* (qq.v.). *Plato*. Ugly Duckling (Hans *Andersen*)]. 3. Seven ~s a-swimming in *Christmas* song. ~ of Avon (*Shak*).

SWARM 1. CLUSTER, LARGE GROUP. CONGREGATE. ABOUND, BE OVERRUN, CLAMBER, CLIMB, SCRAMBLE. 2. *Assembly* of bees; e.g. TUC, WORKERS (crypt).

Swe Sweden, ~ish.

SWEDEN S (*car plate*). Swe (abbr).

SWEETHEART DONAH, FLAME, *LOVER*, POPSIE (RAF sl). HARD/SOFT CENTRE (crypt). E (crypt).

SWELL *SMART*, TOFF. HEAVE, SCEND, SURGE, WAVES. BULGE, CRESCENDO, DILATE, EXPAND, RISE [*organ*].

Swi Switzerland, Swiss. For ~ cantons, see *Swiss canton*.

SWIFT 1. FAST, PROMPT, QUICK, RAPID, SOON. FRAME

(winding yarn). *LIZARD*. *BIRD* [*swallow*, martin]; DEVIL'S
BIRD (arch). 2. Jonathan ~, Ire writer and *satirist*; ordained.
Books: Battle of the Books, The Drapier's Letters, Journal to
Stella, Meditation on a Broomstick, Tale of a Tub, and esp
Gulliver's Travels, the Journals of Lemuel Gulliver, Surgeon and
Captain; Book 1: Lilliput (dwarfs), Big-endians (catholics), Little-
endians (protestants), blundercrad (book of lore); Book 2:
Brobdingnag (tall and strong people); Book 3: Laputa (flying
island, science), Balnibarbi (projectors), Luggnagg (Struldbrugs,
immortal), Glubbdubrib (sorcerers and magicians), Japan; Book 4:
Houyhnhms (intelligent horses), Yahoos (degenerate humans).

SWIMMER *FISH* (crypt). BATHER [natation]; **celeb**: *LEANDER*
(Gk), 7 swans (*Christmas* song), ESTHER WILLIAMS (films),
TARZAN (Edgar Rice Burroughs), CAPT WEBB (Eng Channel
1875). And see *dive* and *sport (water)*.

SWIMMING *Anag*. DRENCHED, STEEPED. BATHING,
NATATION, WATER *SPORT*; **styles**: back stroke, breast stroke,
butterfly, crawl (trudgen), dogpaddle, freestyle, medley, overarm,
sidestroke. And see *DIVE*; *SPORT*.

SWINDLE *Anag*. CHEAT, CON, COZEN, *DO*, *FIDDLE*,
RACKET, *RAMP*.

SWINE BEAST, BRUTE, CAD, GLUTTON, HEEL, LOUT,
SCOUNDREL. HOG, *PIG*; **assembly** = herd, sounder; **male** =
BOAR; **fem** = SOW; **offspring** = PIGLET. [pearls before ~].
Patron saint = Anthony.

SWISS CANTON **Division of Switzerland**: AARGAU,
APPENZELL, BASELAND, BERN, FRIBOURG,
GRAUBUNDEN, GLARUS, LUCERN, NEUCHATEL,
OBWALDEN, ST GALLEN, SCHWYZ, SOLOTHURN,
THURGAU, TICINO, UNTERWALDEN, VALAIS, VAUD,
ZURICH.

SWITCHED *Anag*. DEVIATED, EXCHANGED, SWAPPED (rly
lines). TURNED OFF/ON (elect). BEATEN, CANED (rod).

SWITZERLAND CH (*car plate*). Swi (abbr). For cantons of ~, see
Swiss canton.

SYMBOL (s/l cymbal). ANALOGY, ASSOCIATION.
CHARACTER, LETTER, NOTATION, SIGN. CREED. 5 ~s
at your door in *song*.

SYNOPSIS *SUMMARY*.

T (s/l *tea*, *tee*). TENANT. TERA (*Int unit*). *TIME*. TON.
TUESDAY. TURN. JUNCTION, SQUARE. CAR, FORD.
SHIRT.

TA (s/l *tar*). TITANIUM (*chem*). TERRITORIAL ARMY.
THANKS.

TABARD *CLOAK* (knight), COAT (*herald*). INN (*Chaucer*).

TABLE DUMMY (*bridge*). FACET. COLUMN, LIST,
SCHEDULE. *FURNITURE* (q.v. for **types**), CAIN AND ABEL
(*rh sl*); BOARD, FOOD, KEEP, MEALS.

TACITUS Cornelius, Rom historian b A.D. 55, d A.D. 120. A friend of
Pliny, ~ mar the d of Agricola. Only five of his works survive.

TACK BOARD, COURSE (naut). BISCUIT, FOOD (naut).
GEAR, *HARNESS*. FASTENING, PIN. STITCH.

TAIL BACKSIDE, BOTTOM, REAR. SCUT, WAGGER. FIN
AND RUDDER (av). WAKE. DOG, SHADOW, TRACK.
RAIL, TRAIN. REVERSE (coin **opp** = obverse). DOCK. **Pl** =
EVENING DRESS (**opp** = heads).

TAILED FOLLOWED, TRACKED; hence *COMET* (crypt).
FADED. EVENING DRESS, WHITE TIE (crypt). DOCKED;
hence remove last letter, e.g. **Pete is tailed, the dear boy** (3) = PET*.

TAIL ENDER SCUT; RABBIT. L (crypt). LAST MAN.

TAKE OVER 1. BUY OUT, COMMANDEER, SEQUESTER.
RELIEVE. *BOWL* (crypt). 2. Add OVER to word, e.g. **Sir
Thomas takes over, besides** (8) = MORE*OVER.

TALENT ABILITY, APTITUDE, FACULTY, GIFT. *COIN*,
MONEY; WEIGHT (Gk, Rom).

TAN BRONZE, BROWN, SUNBURN, SUNTAN. *COLOUR*
(brown). BEAT, CANE, THRASH, WHIP. BARK. CURE.
TANGENT.

TANNER SIXPENCE; hence SHIL or LING (crypt).
LEATHERWORKER, -CURER. SUN(SHINE), UV rays
(crypt).

TANTALUS Gk myth s of *Zeus*. Stood to his neck in water, which
receded when he tried to drink; food above his head wafted out of
reach when he tried to take it. Father of *Niobe* and Pelops
(tantalize).

TAP DRAW OFF, SIPHON. FAUCET (US). EAVESDROP,
MONITOR. BROACH, PENETRATE. SOLICIT. CUT
THREAD. KNOCK, RAP, STRIKE. **Pl** = LIGHTS OUT (US
mil). *AIRLINE* (Port).

TAR (s/l *ta*). AB, JACK, GOB (US), *SAILOR*, SALT. ASPHALT,

BITUMEN, PITCH.

TAROT TAROC; card game; fortune telling cards; 78 in pack, 22 trumps.

0 = *fool/jester*	11 = *strength*
1 = juggler	12 = *hanged* man
2 = female pope	13 = *death*
3 = *empress*	14 = temperance
4 = *emperor*	15 = *devil*
5 = pope	16 = *tower*
6 = *lovers*	17 = *star*
7 = *chariot*	18 = *moon*
8 = *justice*	19 = *sun*
9 = *hermit*	20 = day of *judgement*
10 = wheel of *fortune*	21 = *world*

TART ACID, BITING, CUTTING. PROSTITUTE. PASTRY, PIE, SWEET; **celeb**: apple, Bakewell, cherry, custard, fruit, jam, mince, peach, walnut.

TARTAN PATTERN, PLAID (Sc); *MATERIAL. BOAT.* GENERAL (bibl).

TARZAN Jungle-dwelling character of Edgar Rice Burroughs, 'real' name Lord Greystoke [Jane. Cheta (monkey)].

TATTOO NEEDLEWORK (crypt). MARK, STAIN; DECORATE. DRUMMING, SIGNAL. PAGEANT.

TAUNT RAG, REPROACH, RIB, *TEASE*, UPBRAID.

TAVERN *BAR*, INN, PH (abbr), PUB; **celeb**: Admiral Benbow (Treasure Island, *Stevenson*); Boar's Head (H.iv, H.v, *Shak*); Garter (Merry Wives, *Shak*); *Mermaid* (Cheapside 1666); Spyglass (Treasure Island, *Stevenson*); Tabard (Canterbury Tales, *Chaucer*). *CRICKET CROWD* (Lord's).

TAW LEATHER, *WHIP*. MARBLE (game). RIVER (Eng).

TAX (s/l *tacks*). DUTY, EXCISE, LEVY, PAYE, SCOT, TOLL, VAT [*customs, smuggle*]. ASSESS, DEMAND, DRAIN, *TEST*, TRY. [~ **gatherer** = PUBLICAN (bibl)].

TB TERBIUM (*chem*). TORPEDO BOAT (mil). TRIAL BALANCE. TUBERCULOSIS.

TE NOTE (mus; also TEE, TI). TELLURIUM (*chem*).

TEA (s/l t, *tee*). *MEAL*. DRINK (genus camellia); CHA, CHAR, CUPPA, ROSIE LEE (*rh sl*); **types**: CEYLON, CHINA (BOHEA, CONGOU, EARL GREY, JASMINE, KEEMUN,

LAPSANG, OOLONG, ORANGE PEKOE, SUCHONG);
INDIAN (DARJEELING, KASHMIRI, NILGIR). [Jap ~
ceremony (Chanoyu, Koicha, Ususha)].

TEA GIRL POLLY (nursery rhyme).

TEAM (s/l teem). 1. II, XI, XV, ELEVEN etc. GANG,
PLAYERS, *SIDE*, SQUAD. YOKED OXEN. 2. *Assembly* of
young ducks, oxen.

TEA-MAKER KETTLE, POT, SAMOVAR. POLLY. ATE, EAT
(crypt).

TEA-PARTY AT-HOME, ENTERTAINMENT. FRACAS (sl).
CHAR-LADY, POLLY (crypt) [Mad Hatter (*Alice*); Boston].

TEAR (s/l tare, *tier*). *DASH*, HURRY, *RUN*. PULL, REND, *RIP*.
DRIP, DROP, LACHRYMA [*Niobe*, *Ruth*].

TEASE (s/l t's, *teas*, *tees*). *CHAFF*, CHIP, *RAG*, RIB, TAUNT,
TWIT. PICK FIBRES. IRRITATE, VEX.

TEASING *ARCH*, COY. *CHAFF*, TAUNTING. PICKING,
SEPARATING FIBRES.

TED EDWARD. TEDDY BOY. DRY/MAKE HAY. HEATH
(Prime Minister).

TEE PROP, SUPPORT (golfball). PIPE JOINT, ROAD
JUNCTION (as letter T). NOTE (mus; also TE, TI). TARGET
(curling, c.f. bowls jack).

TEETH CHAMPERS, MASHERS, MOLARS [*study*]; DENTURES
(see *bone*, *tooth*). COGS (mech).

TEETOTAL AA, ABSTAINER, TT; RECHABITE. [Richard
Turner].

TEG *SHEEP* (young). GET UP (dn). GET BACK.

TELEPHONE BELL (sl), CALL, DIAL, PHONE, RING [STD].

TELEVISION BOX, MEDIUM, SET, TV. [BBC, IBA, ITA, ITV;
ABC, CBS, NBC (US)].

TELL RECOUNT, RELATE, NARRATE. *COUNT*. BOWMAN
(crypt), WILLIAM [Rossini]. LINTEL (crypt: L*in*TEL).

~ **OFF** CARPET, *REPRIMAND*. COUNT, *NUMBER*.

~ **TALE** FIBBER, LIAR. *BETRAY*. INDICATOR, SIGNAL.
RELATE, NARRATOR.

TELLUS Rom eq of *GE* (also TERRA).

TEMPER ANGER, IRE. HARDEN. MITIGATE, RESTRAIN;
TUNE.

TEMPEST STORM, *WIND*. *AIRCRAFT*, FIGHTER. Play by
Shak.

TEMPLE 1. Part of head/skull. STRETCHER (weaving).

SHIRLEY ~ (film). 2. *INNS OF COURT* (Knights Templar). 3.
FANE, PLACE OF WORSHIP (*oracle*); **architecture**: adytum,
cella, mecaron, naos, portico, posterula, propylaeum, propylon,
sekos, thalamos, vestibule; **celeb**: ABU SIMBEL (Nile), *APOLLO*
(Delphi; Palatine), *ARTEMIS* (Ephesus), *DELPHI* (*Apollo*),
DIANA (Aricia), KARNAK, LUXOR, MICAH (Jewish),
PARTHENON (Athens), PHILAE (Aswan Dam), SOLOMON'S
~ (Jerusalem), THE TEMPLE (Jerusalem, Solomon).
TEMPO RHYTHM, TIME (mus): ACCELERANDO, ADAGIO,
ALLEGRETTO, ALLEGRO, ANDANTE, ANIMATO,
COMODO, LARGAMENTE, LARGO, LENTO, MAESTOSO,
MORENDO, MOSSO, PRESTO, PRESTISSIMO,
RALLENTANDO, RUBATO, STRINGENDO, VIBRATO. **Pl**
= TEMPI. And see *Music* (3).
TEMPTRESS ENCHANTRESS, HOURI, SEDUCTRESS, VAMP.
TEMU Egy *god* of gods, Creator. **Gk** = *ZEUS*; **Rom** = JOVE,
JUPITER.
TEN See *number*. DECADE, IO, VV, X. TWE or NTY (crypt).
[tithe]. *Commandments* in *song*; pipers piping, in Christmas *song*.
~ green bottles.
TENANT T. HOLDER, LESSEE, OCCUPANT; **comp** = *landlord*.
[*Brontë*].
TEN COMMANDMENTS Spoken by God to Moses: (1) Thou shalt
have no other gods before me. (2) Thou shalt not make unto thee
any graven image. (3) Thou shalt not take the name of the Lord thy
God in vain. (4) Remember the sabbath day, to keep it holy. (5)
Honour thy father and thy mother. (6) Thou shalt not kill. (7)
Thou shalt not commit adultery. (8) Thou shalt not steal. (9) Thou
shalt not bear false witness against thy neighbour. (10) Thou shalt
not covet thy neighbour's house, his wife . . . nor anything that is
his.
TEND *APT*, CONDUCE, INCLINE, SERVE. CARE, *NURSE*,
WAIT ON.
TENDER OFFER, PRESENT, PROFFER. SOFT, SORE.
NEEDING CARE, TICKLISH. AFFECTIONATE,
CONSIDERATE, FOND, LOVING, SOLICITOUS.
ATTENDANT BOAT/WAGON, GUARDIAN. SHEPHERD
(crypt). MATRON, NANNY, *NURSE*, SISTER (crypt).
TENNE/TENNY BROWN (*herald*).
TENNIS BALL GAME; **venues**: Forest Hills, Flushing Meadows,
Queen's Club, Stade Roland Garros, Wimbledon. DECK ~,

LAWN ~ [WCT], REAL ~ [dedans, grille, hazard side,
penthouse, service side, tambour], RING ~, TABLE ~.
TENT CANOPY, (CANVAS) SHELTER. WOUND PLUG,
WAD. (RED) WINE.
~ MAKER CANVAS WORKER. BREWER, VINTNER; OMAR
(KHAYYAM). NETT (crypt, anag).
TERM BOUNDARY, LIMIT, PERIOD, *SENTENCE*, SPAN.
CONDITION, FOOTING, RELATION, STIPULATION.
CALL, DENOMINATE; LANGUAGE. HALF, SEMESTER:
Easter (C), Hilary (O), Lent (C, O), Michaelmas (C, O), Trinity
(O). For music terms, see *Music* (3).
TERMITE *INSECT*, (WHITE) ANT. SCHOLAR, SCHOOLBOY,
-GIRL (crypt).
TERPANDER The first historical *musician*, who lived at Antissa in
Lesbos 700–650 B.C.
TERPSICHORE Gk myth, one of the nine *Muses* (*dance* and *song*).
TERRA Also TELLUS. Rom eq of *GE*, *goddess* of EARTH.
TERRITORIAL ARMY TA, TERRIERS (hence *football team*).
RESERVES.
TERRY BOY, MAN. TOWEL.
TEST EXERCISE, TAX, TRIAL, *TRY*; EXAMINE. ASSAY,
REFINE. *MATCH* (games). *RIVER*.
TESTER ANALYST, ASSAYER, EXAMINER. (BED)
CANOPY. *COIN* (Eng). CRICKETER (crypt).
TESTING GROUND LABORATORY, LAB, WIND TUNNEL,
CRICKET GROUND.
TH *THORIUM* (*chem*). *THURSDAY*.
THALIA 1. Gk myth, one of the nine *Muses* (comedy and bucolic
poetry). 2. A minor *PLANET*.
THAMES RIVER. *ISIS*. LONDON BANKER (crypt). CAPITAL
CURRENCY (crypt). **Bridges of the** ~ (in order from the sea):

Barrier	Charing Cross (rly)
Tower	*Westminster*
London	*Lambeth*
Cannon St (rly)	Vauxhall
Southwark	Grosvenor Rd (rly)
Blackfriars (rly)	Chelsea
Blackfriars	Albert
Waterloo	Battersea
Hungerford (foot)	Battersea (rly)

Wandsworth	Chiswick
Putney (rly)	Kew (rly)
Putney	Kew
Hammersmith	*Twickenham*
Barnes (rly)	Richmond

THANKS *GRACE*, GRATITUDE, TA.
THANKSGIVING Expression of gratitude, usually to God; specifically 4th Thursday in Nov (US) and 2nd Mon in Oct (Can).
THAT YON.
~ **FRENCH** CA, CELA.
~ **IS** ID EST, IE.
~ **LATIN/ROMAN** ID, ILLE.
~ **ONE** HE, SHE.
THAT'S ID EST, IE.
~ **RIGHT** IER (crypt).
THEATRE 1. ARENA, FIELD, SCENE, BATTLE-, WAR-ZONE (mil). OPERATING ROOM (med). LECTURE HALL; *STUDIO*. 2. AUDITORIUM, MUSIC-HALL, PLAYHOUSE, STAGE. ART, DRAMA, REP, SHOW BIZ, THE STAGE, VAUDEVILLE [*awards. Apollo, Athene, Minerva, Muse* (all q.v.)]; **celeb**:

ABC	DUCHESS
ADELPHI	DUKE OF YORK'S
ALBERY	EMPIRE
ALDWYCH	ESSOLDO
ALHAMBRA	EVERYMAN
AMBASSADORS	*FORTUNE*
APOLLO	GAIETY
BARBICAN	GARRICK
COLISEUM	GAUMONT
COMEDY	GLOBE
CONNAUGHT	GRANADA
COTTESLOE	*GRAND*
COVENT GARDEN	GREENWICH
CRITERION	HAYMARKET
CURZON	HER MAJESTY'S
DALYS	HIPPODROME
DOMINION	HIS MAJESTY'S
DRURY LANE	HOLBORN EMPIRE

KINGSWAY   PROMENADE (US)
LA SCALA (It)   *QUEEN'S*
LIBERTY   *REGENT*
LITTLE ~   RIALTO
LYCEUM   *ROYAL*
LYRIC   ROYAL COURT
LYTTLETON   ROYALTY
MARQUIS (US)   SADLER'S WELLS
MAYFAIR   ST MARTINS
MERMAID   ST JAMES
METROPOLITAN   SAVOY
MUSIC HALL   SHAFTESBURY
NATIONAL ~   STOLL
NEW ~   STRAND
NEW LONDON ~   STRATFORD
NEW OXFORD ~   *SWAN*
ODEON   THEATRE ROYAL
OLD VIC   TIVOLI
OLIVIER   TROCADERO
OPERA HOUSE   *VARIETY*
PALACE   VAUDEVILLE
PALLADIUM   *VICTORIA* PALACE
PAVILION   VIRGINIA (US)
PHOENIX   *WESTMINSTER*
PICCADILLY   WHITEHALL
PIT   WINTER GARDEN
PLAYHOUSE   WYNDHAM'S
PRINCE EDWARD   YOUNG VIC
PRINCE OF WALES   YVONNE ARNAUD
PRINCE'S

THEATRE GOER PLAY-WATCHER. PATIENT, SURGEON (crypt).

~ **WORK** ACTING, PLAYING. MEDICINE. OPERATION, SURGERY (crypt).

THE FRENCH LA, LE, LES.

~ **GERMAN** DAS, DER, DIE.

~ **ITALIAN** IL.

THERMOPYLAE Narrow defile in the mountains 100 miles north of Athens, where 300 Spartans under Leonidas withstood *Xerxes* and his army of about 1,000,000 men for three days. They only failed in

the end because the treachery of Ephialtes revealed a secret path
through the hills to their rear. The sole Gk survivor was received in
Athens with reproaches for having fled.

THESE TIMES AD, NOW(ADAYS).

THESEUS Gk myth hero, to whom *Ariadne* (d of king *Minos*) gave a
ball of string so he could find his way back out of the labyrinth after
he had killed the *Minotaur*. He was one of the *Argonauts* and, on
his successful return to *Attica*, he neglected to hoist the white sail
which was the signal of his triumph; Aegeus, his father, thought
him dead so he leaped into the sea and was drowned — thus
jumping to a *conclusion*. [*Cercyron*; *Periphites*; *Procrustes*; *Sciron*].

THE SPANISH EL.

THEY PEOPLE, PERSONS. AUTHORITY, THE
ESTABLISHMENT. OPPONENTS (*bridge*).

THIEF *ROBBER* (q.v.); TEA LEAF (*rh sl*). [Ali Baba].

THIN CULL, DILUTE. LEAN, SKINNY, SLENDER (**opp** = fat,
stout). FINE, NARROW. BALDING. INSUBSTANTIAL,
INSUFFICIENT. FLIMSY, SCANTY, SHALLOW,
TRANSPARENT (**opp** = thick).

THING OBJECT; RES (Lat). CONVENTION. OBSESSION.
LIFESTYLE. *LEGISLATIVE ASSEMBLY* (ON). **Pl** =
BELONGINGS, PROPERTY.

THIRD Next to second, hence 'a second before'; BRONZE.
E (mus). INTERVAL (mus). DIVISION, RIDING.

~ **CLASS** C. A (crypt).

~ **MAN** ABEL (crypt). *CRICKETER*. HARRY LIME. N (crypt).

~ **PERSON** CAIN (crypt). HE, SHE, THEM. R (crypt).

THIS 1. Indicates near at hand (**opp** = that). EXISTING,
PRESENT. 2. Ancient Egy town (TINI). 3. Answer is added to
preceding or following word, to make a further word as also
indicated, e.g. **Play no to this remedy** (5) = (no)STRUM; or **Elevated
this way for the main road** (4) = HIGH(way). 4. This side of . . .
indicates the first part of the next word, e.g. **Musical instrument
this side of violence** (4) = VIOL(ence).

~ **MONTH** INST. Current month, as JAN, FEB etc.

THOR (s/l thaw). 1. Nor *god* of THUNDER, s of *Odin*. He
possessed a magic throwing hammer called Miolnir. **Rom** =
TONANS. [Thursday]. 2. HEYERDAHL (Kon-Tiki).

THORIUM TH (*chem*).

THOROUGHBRED HIGH-SPIRITED, METTLESOME,
PURE-BRED (**opp** = mongrel) [**original horse studbook ancestors**

= BYERLY TURK, DARLEY ARABIAN, GODOLPHIN
BARB].

THOUSAND See *number*. K, KILO; M (Lat). CHILIAD.

~ **GUINEAS** *CLASSIC*: LML (crypt).

THREE See *number*. TRIAD. GREEN BALL (snooker). *Rivals* in
song. French *hens* in *Christmas song*. [*Holmes* cases]. ~ Men in a
Boat (George, Harris, J and the dog Montmorency) by Jerome K.
Jerome.

~ **ESTATES** COMMONS, LORDS SPIRITUAL, LORDS
TEMPORAL [**fourth estate** = *press*].

~ **FEET** YARD, *MEASURE*. TRIPOD.

~ **QUARTERS** BACKS, WINGS (*rugby*) [*Holmes* case]. 75%. Any
3 of E, N, S and W (crypt).

THRICE TER, THREEFOLD, THREE TIMES.

THRILL FRISSON, PULSATION, THROB, TREMOR; EXCITE,
WOW.

THROUGHWAY BY-PASS, FLYOVER. ARCH, TUNNEL
(crypt).

THROWER BALLISTA, CATAPULT, SLING, TREBUCKET.
GARDENER; POTTER (crypt). *THOR*.

THUG 1. ROUGHNECK, RUFFIAN, TOUGH GUY, YAHOO
(*Swift*). 2. Indian religious fanatic of 19th century, who garotted
victims as sacrifice to *Kali*, Hindu *goddess* of Destruction.

THUNDER 1. CLAP, CRASH, LOUD NOISE; **comp** = *lightning*.
ADVANTAGE, CREDIT. RAIL, THREATEN. 2. **Gods: Gk** =
ZEUS; **Rom** = JOVE/*JUPITER*, *TONANS*; **Nor** = *THOR*. 3.
BOANERGES (James and John, sons of ~; bibl).

THUNDERBOLT DESTRUCTION, LIGHTNING, SHAFT,
THREAT. *AIRCRAFT*. [Jove, *Jupiter*, *Tonans*, *Zeus*].

THUNDERER *THOR*, *TONANS*. THE TIMES®.

THURSDAY TH, THURS; day of *Thor*. ~'s **child** = far to go
[*Chesterton*, Solomon *Grundy*].

TI *TITANIUM* (*chem*). BACK IT (crypt). NOTE (mus, also TE).
TREE (Polynesia, NZ).

TICK CR, CREDIT. CHECK OFF, MARK. CASE, COVER.
BLOODSUCKER, *INSECT*, PARASITE. CLICK. INSTANT,
MO, MOMENT, SEC. GROUSE, GRUMBLE (sl).

~ **OFF** 1. CHECK, MARK. BERATE, CHASTISE,
REPRIMAND. STOPWATCH. 2. Delete any synonym for 'tick'
from clue, e.g. **Tick off sector hill** = ***TOR.

~ **OVER** IDLE, RUN SLOWLY. STOPPED CLOCK (crypt).

TIER (s/l *tear*). LINE, RANGE, RANK, *ROW*. DRAWER,
EQUAL WINNER. BINDER, KNOTTER.

TIGER TANK, *WEAPON*. CHEER. *LEPIDOPTERA* (moth).
SHARK. MANELESS FELINE; BIG CAT; SHERE KHAN
(Kipling); **offspring** = cub. [*Ch calendar*; Tora (*Jap*)]. **Pl** =
Football team.

TIGHT CLOSE, FIRM. IMPERMEABLE (**opp** = porous).
NEAR, MEAN, MISERLY. STRETCHED, TAUT, TENSE,
TENSIONED. DRUNK. **Pl** = HOSE, UNDERWEAR;
CATSUIT, LEOTARD.

TILBURY *DOCK. CARRIAGE. CASTLE.*

TILDE ACCENT (ñ = ng).

TILL UNTIL, UP TO. CASHBOX. CULTIVATE, FARM,
PLOUGH, TURN UP. CLAY.

TILLER SALESMAN/WOMAN (crypt). *FARMER* (crypt).
HELM. DANCING GIRL.

TILT AWNING. *CANT*, *LEAN*, LIST, SLOPE. JOUST.

TIM BOY. SPEAKING CLOCK. LITTLE TIME (crypt).

TIMBER (s/l timbre). *FOREST*, TREES, WOOD [*measure*].
FRAME, RIB (naut).

TIME T; *DATE*, HOUR, MOMENT, SECOND. EST, GMT etc.
ENEMY (sl). CLOCK, RECORD, REGISTER. PERIOD;
DAY, *MONTH*, *SEASON*, *WEEK*, *YEAR*; *AGE*, AEON, EON,
ERA. BIRD, GAOL TERM, PETER, *SENTENCE*,
STRETCH. *TEMPO*. **Pl** = PAPER®, THUNDERER.
TYPEFACE. X, MULTIPLY BY. [O tempora, O mores
(Cicero)].

~ **OUT** BREAK, BREATHER, INTERVAL. EMIT, ITEM (crypt,
anag).

~ **WARP** FOURTH DIMENSION [Einstein]. EMIT, ITEM (crypt,
anag).

TIN 1. *METAL*; SN (*chem*); *anniversary* (10th). CAN. MONEY.
2. Put letter 't' in word(s) following, e.g. **Tin spoon precisely** (4, 2)
= SPO*T*ON.

TINY 1. MINUTE, SMALL, WEE (**opp** = *giant*). [*Dickens*]. 2. Use
diminutive or offspring of, e.g. **Tiny Tom** = KITTY or TH.

TIP 1. EDGE, END, POINT, RIM. CUE, HINT. WRINKLE.
CANT, TILT, TOPPLE. GRATUITY. 2. First or last letter of
word, e.g. **Asparagus tip** = A or S.

~ **OFF** 1. CUE, HINT. WRINKLE. 2. First or last letter removed,
e.g. **Communist Fred's tip-off** (3) = *RED.

TIRE (s/l *tyre*). BORE, EXHAUST, FATIGUE, WEARY. US =
TYRE (UK). ATTIRE, DRESS.

TISIPHONE One of the *Furies*.

TIT NIPPLE. CONTROL, KNOB (av). BIRD; bearded ~, blue ~,
coal ~, crested ~, great ~, longtailed ~, marsh ~, willow ~.

TITAN (s/l tighten). 1. Gk myth children of *Uranus* and *Ge*
(sometimes incorrectly confused with the *giants* or *monsters* called
Gigantes): OCEANUS and TETHYS (sea), HYPERION and
THEA (sun and moon), COCUS and PHOEBE (light), CREIOS
and EURYBIA (strength), CRONOS and RHEA (heaven and
earth), THEMIS and MNEMOSYNE (law and memory),
IAPETUS (father of mankind). 2. A satellite of the *planet*
SATURN.

TITANIUM *METAL*; TI (*chem*).

TITFER HAT (*rh sl*).

TITLE HANDLE, NAME. BARON, COUNT, DUKE, EARL,
LORD, VISCOUNT etc. DEED, RIGHT.

TO (s/l too, two). 1. AS FAR AS. TOWARDS; **comp** = fro.
COMPARED WITH. BY WAY OF, FOR. CONTAINED,
INCLUDED, INVOLVED. 2. Letters or word put before word
indicated, e.g. **As to this, it's in pieces below** (5) = (as)UNDER.

TOAD (s/l toed, towed). CAD, SYCOPHANT. Amphibian of
genus bufo: FROG [Grahame; Badger, Mole, Ratty, Wind in the
Willows].

TOAST BROWN, COOK, HEAT, SCORCH, SINGE, WARM;
COOKED BREAD; **comp** = butter, marmalade. CHEERS,
CHIN CHIN, PROSIT, SANTE, SKOLL; ROUSE.

TOASTER COOKER; *SINGER* (crypt). HEALTH-DRINKER
(crypt).

TOBACCO Plant genus Nicotiana: VIRGINIA, TURKISH. QUID,
SNOUT (sl), TWIST [chewing, snuff].

TOD *MEASURE* (wool). ALONE (*rh sl*).

TODAY MON, TUES, WED etc according to date.

TOM *CAT*. ~ *BROWN*; ~ DICK and HARRY; ~ SAWYER
(*Twain*); ~ THUMB. *BELL* (Oxford). DR or UM (half of tom-
tom).

TOMMY LAD, SMALL BOY. BAR. GUN. TUCKER.
ATKINS, SOLDIER.

TON (s/l tun). C, T. 100 (mph). CENTURY, HUNDRED.
FASHION.

TONANS Rom *god* of THUNDER.

TONE PITCH, QUALITY, MODULATION; SOUND. FITNESS, CHARACTER. HARMONIZE. SHADE, TINT.

TONIC BRACING, INVIGORATING. TREATMENT. KEYNOTE, TONAL (mus). *DRINK*, MIXER; **comp** = *gin*.

TONY *AWARD* [Antoinette Perry] (theat)®. ANT(H)ONY.

TOOTH *BONE* (q.v.), CHAMPER, *FANG*, IVORY, MASHER. MOLAR [caries]; **comp** = *nail*. COG, SPROCKET.

TOP 1. ACE, ACME, APEX, *HEAD*, SUMMIT, UPPER, U. COVER, PIECRUST. BEST, OVERCOME. BEHEAD, EXECUTE. DIABOLO, SPINNING TOY. BEST, FIRST CLASS. 2. Omit first letter, e.g. **Top gear for listener** (3) = EAR. 3. **Pl** = DOUBLE TWENTY, hence FORTY, XL (darts).

TOPAZ *GEM* (blue, green, white, yellow). *Birthstone* (November). Sir ~ (*Chaucer* character).

TOPAZOLITE *GEM* (green, yellow); GARNET.

TOPE *DRINK*, TIPPLE. MANGO-GROVE. *SHARK*. SHRINE.

TOPLESS 1. BALD. BAREBREASTED. 2. Remove letters 'bra' from word, e.g. **Topless bravery is extreme** (4) = ***VERY. 3. No first letter in dn answer.

TOPPING A1, FIRST CLASS, FIRST RATE. HALO, *HAT*, ROOF, TIARA (crypt).

TORTOISE 1. Reptile with carapace or shell; land version of TURTLE or TERRAPIN [Achilles and ~ (Zeno); Aechylus (k by ~); hare and ~ (Aesop); *Sciron's* ~ (myth)]. 2. Tank-like formation of Rom soldiers protected by shields held overhead or alongside; TESTUDO.

TORY C, POLITICIAN, RIGHT WING. *ISLAND* (Ire).

TOT CHILD. *DRINK*, MEASURE. SUM; *COUNT*, TELL. SCAVENGE.

TOUCH *SENSE*; BRUSH, CONTACT, FEEL. REACH. INJURE, MARK. AFFECTED, CRAZY. SYMPATHY. SIDE-LINE (games).

TOWED (s/l *toad*, toed). DRAWN, PULLED, TUGGED. HEMPEN. TO *MARRY* (crypt).

TOWER TALL BUILDING, SKYSCRAPER. 16 (*tarot*). CITADEL, FORTRESS. SOAR. *DRAWER*, PULLER, TUG (crypt). *THAMES* BRIDGE.

TOXIPHOBIA *Aversion* to poisons.

TOYMAKER MASTER CHERRY (Pinocchio), DR COPPELIUS (Coppelia, Delibes), CALEB PLUMMER (Cricket, *Dickens*), TACKLETON (Cricket, *Dickens*). OTY, YOT etc (crypt, anag).

TRACE *SIGN*, VESTIGE. DELINEATE, *MARK*, SKETCH,
WRITE; *COPY*, FOLLOW. ASCERTAIN, OBSERVE,
PURSUE, TRACK. *HARNESS*, STRAPS.

TRACK COURSE, FOOTPRINTS, PATH, SCENT.
RACECOURSE. *DOG*, FOLLOW, TAIL, TRACE. GROOVE
(disc, EP). TREAD (tank, tractor). GAUGE, WIDTH; *EM*, *TT*,
Z (wheels, rails); BR, RLY, RY, IRON WAY: HARD LINES
(crypt).

TRACT GROUND, PLOT, STRETCH. HAND-OUT,
PAMPHLET.

TRADE TERMS DISCOUNT. GATT. CIF, EX WORKS, FAS,
FOB (crypt).

TRADING COMPANIES MUSCOVY ~ (1555), EASTLAND ~
(1579), LEVANT ~ (1581), AFRICA ~ (1588), EAST INDIA ~
(1600), HUDSON BAY ~ (1670).

TRAGEDY 1. CALAMITY, DRAMA. 2. Any celebrated play of
tragic nature, e.g. KING LEAR. 3. **Gk Muse** = MELPOMENE.

TRAIN KEEP FIT [PE, PT]. *COACH*, *DRILL*, INSTRUCT,
PREPARE. CORTEGE, RETINUE, SKIRT, STRING, TAIL.
APT, BR, HST, RLY, RY ENGINE, *LOCAL* [commuting].
EXPLOSIVE CHARGE, *FUSE*.

TRAINEE APPRENTICE, LEARNER. COMMUTER,
PASSENGER, RAILMAN, TRAINER (all crypt).

TRAINER *COACH*, TEACHER. COMMUTER (crypt). *SHOE*.
Pl = RAILMEN (**Unions** = ASLEF, NUR).

TRAINING COACHING, LEARNING, TEACHING. EXERCIS-
ING, KEEPING FIT, REGIME. COMMUTING (crypt).

TRAITOR DESERTER, RAT, RENEGADE, TURNCOAT. SIR
MORDRED (Knight of the *Round Table*, Tennyson). [Quisling].

TRAMP BAGLADY (US sl), BUM, HOBO, SUNDOWNER.
BOAT, CARGO SHIP. FOOTSLOG, *MARCH*, STAMP,
TRAMPLE, TREAD, TRUDGE, WALK, YOMP.
GOLDDIGGER.

Trans Translate.

TRANSFER *Anag*. CONVEY, HANDOVER, REMOVE.
CHANGE, MOVE, SWITCH. WATERCOLOUR.

TRANSFORMATION *Anag*. ALTERATION, CHANGE,
METAMORPHOSIS; e.g. *insects* (caterpillar's ~ into pupa, into
imago); *ballet* or pantomime actors' ~ into players in subsequent
harlequinade or play-within-a-play, e.g. in Nutcracker ballet); also
in Gk myth, esp ~s of *Zeus* (q.v., usually for amatory purposes).

See also: *Aaron's* rod (into *serpent*, and to almond tree; bibl); *Acheron* (into river; myth); *Actaeon* (into *stag*; myth); *ants* (into men; Myrmidons, myth); *Arachne* (into *spider*; myth); *Argus* (eyes to peacock's tail; myth); *Atlas* (into stone; myth); *Autolycus* (all he touched; myth); bread (into roses; St *Elizabeth*); Cadmus and Harmonia (into *serpents*; myth); *Daphne* (into laurel; myth); dragon's teeth (into soldiers; Cadmus, myth); father (into son; Vice Versa, Anstey); fire (into roses; *Abraham*, bibl); frog (into prince; trad); *Galatea* (from ivory statue to life; myth); head (into that of an ass; Bottom, *Shak*); hand (withered; *Jeroboam*, bibl); *Io* (into heifer; myth); ivory statue (into *Galatea*; myth); Dr Jekyll (into Mr *Hyde*; *Stevenson*); *Lot's* wife (into a pillar of salt; bibl); *Medusa* (others to stone; myth); mice and pumpkin (into coach and horses; Cinderella, trad); *Midas* (all to gold; myth); *Moses'* rod (into *serpent*; bibl); *Narcissus* (into flower; myth); *Niobe* (into stone; myth); *Sirens* (into rocks; myth); son (into father; Vice Versa, Anstey); stones (into people; *Deucalion*, myth); Ugly Duckling (into *swan*; *Andersen*); water (into wine; *Jesus*, bibl); *witch* (into black cat; trad).

TRANSLATION *Anag.* 1. *TRANSFER*, TRANSFORM. INTERPRET. 2. Put into foreign language, e.g. **My French translation at the beginning of the week** (3) = MON. 3. Reverse the syllables, **Translate the German stable** (6) = MAN*GER.

TRANSPORT EMOTION, RAPTURE. CONVEY, MOVE; BR, CAB, CAR, *CARRIAGE*, BUS, *LORRY*, RLY, *TRAIN*, TRAM, VAN (**Union** = TGW).

TRAP CATCH, *GIN*, SNARE. *CARRIAGE*. **Pl** = *BAGGAGE*, CASES, GRIPS, LUGGAGE. DRUMS, *INSTRUMENTS* (mus).

TRAPPIST BENEDICTINE, CISTERCIAN MONK [silence]. HUNTER (crypt). DRUMMER (crypt).

TREAT *Anag.* MANIPULATE, MINISTER, NEGOTIATE, PROCESS. REGALE, ROUND, SHOUT, STAND. EXCURSION; PLEASURE.

TREBLE ALTO; CLEF. *BET*.

TREE 1. ANCESTORS, GENEALOGY. FRAME-WORK. BOOT-BLOCK. Celebrated actor. 2. PERENNIAL PLANT; [*branch*, sapling, stem; *Absolom*, Charles I] **types:**

2-letters	3-letters	
BO	ASH	*BAY*
TI	*ASP*	BEN
		BOX

ELM

FIG

FIR

GUM

JAK

KOA

OAK

SAL

YEW

4-letters

ACER

AKEE

BAEL

COCO

DALI

DATE

DHAK

DOUM

EJOO

GEAN

HOLM

ILEX

JALA

KOLA

LANA

LIME

MORA

NIPA

PALM

PEAR

PINE

PLUM

POON

RATA

ROSE

SAGO

SAUL

SHEA

SORB

TEAK

TEIL

TOON

UPAS

5-letters

ABELE

ABIES

ALDER

APPLE

ARECA

ARENG

ASPEN

BALSA

BEECH

BIRCH

BODHI (sacred)

BUNYA

CACAO

CAROB

CEDAR

EDONY

ELDER

HAZEL

HOLLY

IROKO

JAMBU

JUDAS

LARCH

LEMON

LILAC

MAPLE

OLIVE

OSIER

PAPAW

PEACH

PLANE

ROHAN

ROWAN

SALIX

TAXUS

TIKUL

TILIA

TINGI

TUCUM

WITHY

YACCA

ZAMIA

ZANTE

6-letters

ACACIA

ACAJOU

ALMOND

ANTIAR

BAMBOO

BANANA

BANIAN

BANYAN

BAOBAB

BOG-OAK

BOMBAX

CARAPA

CARICA

CASHEW

CERRIS

CHERRY

COHUNE

CONKER

COWDIE

DEODAR (sacred)

ELAEIS

FUSTIC

GINGKO

GINKGO

GOMUTI

GOMUTO

GOPHER

JARRAH

JUJUBE

JUPATI

KITOOL

KITTUL

LAUREL
LINDEN
LOCUST
LONGAN
MABOLA
MACACO
MALLEE
MASTEL
MIMOSA
NARGIL
OBECHE
ORANGE
PEEPUL (sacred)
PLATAN
POPLAR
PRUNUS
QUINCE
RATTAN
RED-BUD
RED-GUM
RED-OAK
RHAPIS
SAPELE
SAPIUM
SISSOO
SORBIN
SORBUS
SPRUCE
TUPELO
WALNUT
WATTLE
WILLOW
YARRAH

7-letters
AILANTO (sacred)
ARBUTUS
BACTRIS
BAY-TREE
BAYWOOD
BEBEERU

BEE-TREE
BURR-OAK
CAJEPUT
CALAMUS
CAMPHOR
CANELLA
CARYOTA
CEDRELLA
CHAMPAC
COCONUT
COG-WOOD
CONIFER
COQUITO
CORYPHA
CYPRESS
DURMAST
ELK-WOOD
EMBLICA
FAN-PALM
FILBERT
QUIACUM
HICKORY
HOLM-OAK
JUGLANS
JUNIPER
MORICHE
MORINGA
OIL-PALM
PALMYRA
PAXIUBA
PHOENIX
PLATANE
QUERCUS
REDWOOD
ROBINIA
SAPLING
SEQUOIA
SERVICE
SHITTAH
SUNDARI
TALIPAT

TALIPET
TALIPOT
TALIPUT
TANGHIN
WALLABA
WAX-PALM
WYCH-ELM
YEWTREE
ZALACCA

8-letters
AGUE-TREE
ALGAROBA
BEDEWEEN
BLACK-GUM
BOURTREE
CARNAUBA
CASTANEA
CHESTNUT
COCOANUT
COKERNUT
CORKWOOD
CRABWOOD
DATE-PALM
HAWTHORN
HEMP-PALM
HORNBEAM
JACKWOOD
KINGWOOD
LABURNUM
MAGNOLIA
MAHOGANY
MANGROVE
MULBERRY
PALMETTO
PIASSABA
PIASSAVA
PINASTER
ROSEWOOD
SAGO-PALM
SCRUB-OAK

SYCAMORE	FLAME OF THE
WITCH-ELM	FOREST
ZIZYPHUS	FRANGIPANI
	MONKEY PUZZLE
	SILVER BIRCH
9+ letters	SPINDLETREE
BLACKTHORN	TURKISH OAK
CLUSTER-PINE	*WELLINGTON*
COPPER BEECH	YGGDRASIL (Nor myth)

TREMBLER VIBRATOR (elect). *BIRD* (W Ind).
EARTHQUAKE (crypt).

TRENT BRIDGE *CRICKET GROUND*.

TRIANGLE FIGURE (geom); **types:** EQUILATERAL ~,
ISOSCELES ~, SCALENE ~, OBTUSE/ACUTE ANGLED ~,
[Bermuda; eternal]. INSTRUMENT (mus).

TRIBE GROUP (zool). FAMILY, NUMBER, SET. CLAN,
DIVISION [see *African*; *American Indian*; *Israel*; and see
TRIBESMAN]. **Roman Britain:** ATREBATES, BELGAE,
BRIGANTES, CANTII, CARVETII, CATUVELLAUNI,
CORITANI, CORNOVII, DECEANGLI, DEMETAE,
DOBUNNI, DUMNONII, DUROTRIGES, ICENI,
ORDOVICES, PARISI, REGENSES/REGNI, SILURES,
TRINOVANTES; **chiefs:** *Boudicca*, Cartimandua (f);
Cara(c)tacus, Cunobelinus, Epilus, Togodumnus, Verica (m).

TRIBESMAN BARBARIAN, NOMAD, SAVAGE; JOLLIGINKI
(*Lofting*), YAHOO (Gulliver's Travels, Swift). CLANSMAN,
NATIVE; **celeb:** ANGLE (Eur), ARAB (Af), ASHANTI (Af),
BANTU (S Af), BERBER (NW Af), BELGA (Eur), COSSACK
(Russ), DORIAN (Gk), FRANK (Eur), GAUL (Fr), GOTH
(Ger), HITTITE (bibl), HOTTENTOT (Af), HUN (Asia),
HYKSOS (Egy), JUTE (Eur), KIKUYU (Af), MAGYAR (Eur),
MASAI (Af), MEDE (bibl), MONGOL (Asia), MOOR (NW Af
[Othello]), OSTROGOTH (Ger), PARTHIAN (Asia),
PHOENICIAN (bibl), PYGMY (Af), SAXON (Eur), SPARTAN
(Gk), TARTAR (Russ), TAUREG (Af), VANDAL (Ger),
VISIGOTH (Ger), ZOUAVE (Af), ZULU (Af) [*American
Indian*; impi; *Israel*; and see *TRIBE*].

TRICKY ADROIT, CRAFTY, DECEITFUL, DELICATE,
TICKLISH; **N Am god** = *raven*. RESOURCEFUL. *CARD
GAME* (bridge, solo, whist etc; crypt).

TRIFLE BAGATELLE, CIPHER, MODICUM [*Autolycus*].
NEGLECT, PLAY/TOY WITH, SKIMP. CONFECTION,
PUDDING, SWEET. PEWTER.
TRILBY *HAT*. BOOK, CHARACTER (Gerald du Maurier,
inspiration).
TRIM NEAT, SMART, *SPRUCE*, TIDY. ADORNMENT,
DECORATION, PIPING. BALANCE, BALLAST; *TUNE*.
CUT, PARE, PRUNE, WHITTLE. FIT, GOOD SHAPE.
SERVANT (Sterne).
TRIP EXPEDITION, JOURNEY, OUTING, TOUR, VOYAGE.
FALL, STUMBLE. RELEASE, TRIGGER.
HALLUCINATION (drugs).
TRIPOD STAND, STOOL, TABLE (3 feet; hence YARD, crypt).
ALTAR (*Delphi*).
TRIPPER GROCKLE, HOLIDAYMAKER, RUBBERNECK,
TOURIST. DANCER (crypt). TRIGGER (crypt).
PROJECTION, SNAG (crypt). DRUG TAKER.
TROCHEE *FOOT* (—).
TROJAN 1. FIGHTER. CITIZEN OF TROY. 2. **Pl** = minor
planets.
TROT GAIT, PACE, RUN. FISHING LINE. PRODUCE.
COMMIE, *RED*, REVOLUTIONARY. DAVID
COPPERFIELD (*Dickens*).
TROUBLE *Anag*. ADO, BOTHER, DO, FUSS, RIOT, TO-DO.
AIL, FIX. WIFE (*rh sl*).
TROUSERS BAGS, DUCKS, PANTS (US), SHORTS, SLACKS.
TROY 1. System of weight *measure* (precious metals). 2.
HISSARLAK, also ILIUM. According to *Homer's* Iliad, a city of
Asia Minor, scene of 10 years' war (*c*. 1250 B.C.), when Gks under
Agamemnon beat the Trojans under King Priam's s Paris (whose
abduction of *Helen*, w of Menelaus, started it all), by means of
hiding soldiers (as suggested by *Ulysses*) in a wooden horse, which
was taken into the city by the unsuspecting defenders. 3. Scene of
T and C (*Shak*).
TRUE ACCURATE, GENUINE, REAL; STRAIGHT.
CONSTANT, HONEST, LOYAL (**opp** = *false*). *DOG* (John
Peel). 'VERA'.
TRUMPERY BRIC-A-BRAC, NONSENSE, RUBBISH.
DELUSIVE, SHALLOW, WORTHLESS. BRIDGE, WHIST
(crypt); RUFFING (crypt).
TRUMPETER BUGLER, MUSICIAN. AGAMI, *BIRD*, CRANE,

ELEPHANT, *FISH*, HERON, HOOPOE, PIGEON, SWAN.

TRURO Episcopal sig = TRURON. CITY (SW Eng).

TRURON *Episcopal sig* of TRURO.

TRUTH 1. ACCURACY, HONESTY, LOYALTY. 2. **Egy god** = MAAT.

TRY THREE POINTS (hence any 3 of E, N, S and W, crypt); SCORE, TOUCHDOWN. ATTEMPT, EXPERIMENT, ESSAY, GO, TEST. INVESTIGATE. ARRAIGN, JUDGE.

TRYING ATTEMPTING. IRRITATING. *RUGBY* (crypt). IN COURT, JUDGING (crypt).

TT ABSTAINER, DRY, *PUSSYFOOT*, TEETOTAL [Richard *Turner*; W. E. Johnson]. BIKE RACE, MANX RACE. GAUGE (model rly). MILK. DOUBLET (crypt).

TUB FATSO, FATTY. BATH. BARREL, VAT [*Diogenes*].

TUC TRADES UNION CONGRESS, WORKERS. Dn = CUT UP, hence CHOPSTICKS (crypt). CUT BACK (crypt).

TUESDAY TUES. Day of Tiw, Ger *god* of war. ~**s child** = full of grace. [Shrove ~; Solomon *Grundy*].

TUN (s/l *ton*). *MEASURE* (beer, wine).

TUNA *FISH*, TUNNY. EEL (NZ). PRICKLY PEAR.

TUNE AIR, CATCH, LILT, REFRAIN, *SONG*, STRAIN. ADJUST, BREATHE ON, *TRIM*, TWEAK (mech).

TUP *SHEEP* (male), RAM. PUT UP (dn, crypt).

TUPPENCE DD, PP (crypt).

Turk Turkey, ~ish (abbr); (**car plate** = TR).

TURKISH OFFICIAL AGHA, BEG, BEY, DEY, EGA, EMIR, PASHA, SATRAP, WALI [*Eastern official*].

TURN (s/l tern). 1. T, TN. U~. ADAPT, CONVERT, DIVERT, INVERT, REVERSE, REVOLVE, TWIST, *WHEEL*. BEND, CORNER, DEFLECTION. CHANGE, CURDLE, NAUSEATE, SHOCK. SPASM, STATE. CHARACTER, DISPOSITION, TENDENCY. DRIVE, RIDE, STROLL, WALK. ACT, PERFORMANCE. *GO*, OCCASION, OPPORTUNITY, PRIVILEGE, PURPOSE, SPELL, *TIME*, TRICK [Buggins' ~ (*unseen*)]. COIL, WRITHE. 2. Word reads backwards, e.g. **Gratuities for the turnspit** (4) = TIPS; or, in conjunction with another word, e.g. **It turns colour when sleepy** (5) = TI*RED.

TURNER 1. ACROBAT, ACTOR, ARTISTE, GYMNAST, PERFORMER, TUMBLER. *PAINTER*, CARPENTER, WOODWORKER [*Company* (livery)]. AXLE, LATHE,

ROTOR, SPINNER, TOP, WHEEL (crypt). BIRD. 2. Reverse, or turn, word, e.g. **Jolly Mr Turner** = RM. 3. Richard ~, who coined the word *teetotal*, because he stammered when describing t-total abstinence.

TURNING CORNER, JUNCTION; T. MACHINING, WOODWORKING. ACTING, PERFORMING (crypt). **Pl** = SHAVINGS (mech).

TURNKEY *GAOLER.* YEK (crypt).

TURN-OUT APPEAR. PRODUCE. DRESS, GEAR, KIT, OUTFIT, RIG. TOU, UTO (anag, crypt); RUNT, TRUN (anag, crypt).

TURNOVER *Anag.* ROLL, UPSET. BUSINESS, THROUGHPUT. PIE, TART. REVO, ROVE, VORE etc (crypt).

TURN UP APPEAR, ARRIVE. [Micawber, *Dickens*]. PLOUGH, PLOW (US), TILL. CUFF (clothes). PU (crypt). NRUT (dn, crypt).

TURQUOISE *GEM*, PRECIOUS STONE (blue/green). *Birthstone* (December). *COLOUR* (blue/green).

TV BOX, BROADCASTING, IDIOT'S LANTERN, MEDIUM, SET, TELEVISION, TELLY. BBC, IBA, ITA, ITV.

TWAIN Mark (pseudonym of Samuel Langhorne Clemens); *writer* (US) b 1835; became riverboat pilot, then took to journalism ('mark ~' indicates the two fathoms necessary depth for riverboats); mar Olivia Langdon (2 d, Susy and Jean). **Books**: The Celeb Jumping *Frog* of Calaveras County (first); The Innocents Abroad; Roughing It (autobiographical); The Gilded Age (with C. D. Warner); A Tramp Abroad; The Prince and the Pauper (Prince Ed — later ED VI — changes place with Tom Canty, his *double*, and only regains the throne when he can produce the Great *Seal* — which Tom has been using as a nutcracker); The Adventures of Tom Sawyer (with Huckleberry Finn, Tom witnesses a murder by Injun Joe, and they hide; later the Indian is found dead and they obtain his money); Life on the Mississippi (autobiographical); The Adventures of Huckleberry Finn (Tom and Huck escape on a raft down the Mississippi with Jim the *slave*); Pudd'nhead Wilson; Personal Recollections of *Joan* of Arc (as though written by 'Sieur Louis de Comte' and translated by 'Jean François Alden'); Following the Equator; The American Claimant; Tom Sawyer Abroad; Tom Sawyer Detective; The Mysterious Stranger.

TWELVE See *number*. DODECA, DOZEN, XII. *Apostles* in
song. *Lords* a-leaping in *Christmas song*.

TWENTY See *number*. SCORE, XX, JACKSON (sl).

TWENTY-FIVE See *number*. £~ (PONY). XXV.

TWICE 1. BIS, ENCORE. TWO TIMES, DOUBLY. 2. Letter or
word repeated, e.g. **The priest is twice a small boy** = A*A*RON; but
beware **Is twice the river**, which is not THE*THE, but = IS*IS.

TWICKENHAM *RUGBY GROUND*; TRYING PLACE (crypt).
THAMES BRIDGE.

TWIN 1. DUPLICATE, EXACT *COPY*, FACSIMILE, MIRROR
IMAGE, REPLICA. TWO-ENGINED (Av). COUPLE, PAIR.
'THOMAS'. 2. Two children born at the same time; **celebrated**:
AMOREL/BELPHOEBE (Faerie Queene, Spenser),
ANTIPHOLUS bros (C of Errors, *Shak*), *APOLLO/ARTEMIS*
(myth), *CASTOR/POLLUX* (myth), CHEERYBLES (Nich Nick,
Dickens), DROMIO bros (C of Errors), ESAU/JACOB (bibl),
DIOSCURI, *GEMINI* (stars), *HELEN/CLYTEMNESTRA*
(myth), *ROMULUS/REMUS* (myth),
TWEEDLEDUM/TWEEDLEDEE (*Alice* in Wonderland, Lewis
Carroll), VALENTINE/ORSON (Legends of Charlemagne). 3.
Constellation (*Gemini*); sign of the *Zodiac* (3rd).

TWIST *Anag*. CHANGE, DISTORT, WARP. CURL. *DIVE*.
INTERWEAVE, SPIRAL. ROPE, TWINE. *DANCE*.
SWINDLE. TOBACCO. OLIVER ~ [ask for more; *Dickens*].

TWISTER *Anag*. CHEAT, SWINDLER. ROPE-,
THREAD-MAKER. BALL, DELIVERY, SPINNER.
TORNADO, *WIND* (US). EEL, *SERPENT*, *SNAKE* (crypt).

TWO See *number*. BIS, DUO, TWAIN. YELLOW BALL
(snooker). Lilywhite *boys* in *song*. Turtle *doves* in *Christmas
song*.

~ **BITS** 25 cents (US), from two bits, or pinches, of gold dust as
payment in a bar during the gold rush.

~ **HUNDRED** CC, TWO TON.

~ **PENCE** DD, PP.

TWO THOUSAND See *number*. MM. KK (crypt).

~ **GUINEAS** *CLASSIC*: LMMC.

TYNESIDE NE (crypt).

TYPE CHARACTERISTIC, EXAMPLE, GENUS, KIND, *SORT*.
TAP, WORD-PROCESS. GOTHIC, ITALIC, PICA, ROMAN.

TYPEFACE Design, size or style of printing; *FACE*,
LOWER/UPPER CASE; **sizes** (in order, smallest first):

EXCELSIOR, BRILLIANT, *GEM*, *DIAMOND*, *PEARL*, *AGATE* (US), *RUBY*, NONPAREIL, MINION, BREVIER, BOURGEOIS, ELITE, LONG PRIMER, SMALL PICA, *CICERO*, *ENGLISH*, COLUMBIAN, GREAT PRIMER, PARAGON, *CANON*; **styles:** ANTIQUE, *BASKERVILLE*, BOLD, CASLON, CENTURY, CLARENDON, CURSIVE, DORIC, *ELECTRA*, FUTURA, GARAMOND, GOTHIC, GRANJON, IONIC, ITALIC, JANSON, OLD ENGLISH, *ROMAN*, SANS SERIF, SCRIPT, *TIMES*, TYPEWRITER.

TYPHON Gk myth *monster* with 100 heads; embodiment of earthquakes and volcanoes, breathing fire and hurricane winds. Father of *Chim(a)era* and the inclement *winds*.

TYPHOON STORM, *WIND*. *AIRCRAFT*, FIGHTER.

TYPICAL CHARACTERISTIC, SYMBOLIC. PRINTING, TYPESETTING (crypt).

TYRANT *BULLY*, OPPRESSOR, THUG; **celeb:** *ATTILA*; *CALIGULA*; *CERCYON*; DIONYSIUS; GELON, HIERO (Syracuse); *NERO*; PHALARIS (Rom).

TYRE (s/l *tire*). CROSSPLY, RADIAL, SOLID. *BIBLICAL TOWN*, PORT (Phoen) [Sidon].

U (s/l *ewe*, you). URANIUM (*chem*). UNIVERSAL (film *censorship*). UPPER CLASS; ACCEPTABLE, DONE, SUPERIOR, TOP (**opp** = *low*). BEND, *TURN*.

UD UT DICTUM; AS DIRECTED.

UGLY (s/l ugli). *Anag.* DISCREDITABLE, UNPLEASANT, VILE; THREATENING, UNPROMISING. REPULSIVE, UNPLEASING; DUCHESS (*Alice*); ~ DUCKLING (*swan*, *Andersen*) (**opp** = *attractive*). BONNET, SHADE.

UHT ULTRA HEAT TREATED (milk).

UK UNITED KINGDOM.

ULSTER *HERALD*. KING OF ARMS. COAT. NI, N IRELAND. *UNIVERSITY*.

ULT ULTIMO. LAST MONTH.

ULTIMATE FINAL, LAST, OMEGA, Z. MAXIMUM. FUNDAMENTAL, PRIMARY.

ULYSSES (Gk = ODYSSEUS). 1. Rom myth s of Laertes, mar to *Penelope*. In the Odyssey, Homer describes his return from the Trojan war, how he blinded Polyphemus, one of the *Cyclopes*, then

navigated between the *monsters* on the rocks *Scylla* and *Charybdis*,
and was tempted by the *sirens*. Only he could bend the black bow
of Eurytus. 2. T and C character (*Shak*).

UMBRAGE INJURY, OFFENCE, SLIGHT. SHADE.

UMLAUT ACCENT (").

UN 1. UNITED NATIONS, A FRENCH (crypt). 2. As prefix
indicates 'lacking'. 3. Often implies anag when used as a prefix,
e.g. 'undone', 'uneven' or 'unwrapped'. 4. Remove synonym for
word indicated, e.g. **Uncertain gratification** (4) = PLEA(sure) or
Uncatalogued medallist (5) = MEDAL****.

UNCIVIL ILL-MANNERED, IMPOLITE, RUDE. MILITARY
(crypt).

UNCLE RELATION [*Remus*; Sam]. PAWNBROKER; POPIST,
POPPER (crypt) [pledge, three balls]. BOB (catchphrase).

UNDER 1. BELOW, BENEATH, LESS THAN, LOWER. 2. Word
under another in dn clue, e.g. **Little man has under 100** (4) =
C*HAS. 3. Indicates what goes under, or beneath, the word
indicated, e.g. **Underclothes** (4) = BODY or SKIN; or **Underrider** (6)
= SADDLE.

~ **CANVAS** CAMPING. SAILING. INTENT (crypt), hence
TE . . . NT.

UNDERCURRENT 1. INFLUENCE. HIDDEN ACTIVITY. 2.
Any of the rivers of the Underworld = *ACHERON, COCYTUS,
LETHE, PYRIPHLEGETHON, STYX*.

UNDERSTANDING 1. COMPREHENSION, *GRIP*,
INTELLIGENCE. AGREEMENT, CONVENTION,
HARMONY. 2. Anything beneath the legs (crypt), e.g. DAIS,
FEET, *FOOT*, PAWS, PLATFORM, SHOES, SOLES, *STAGE*.

UNDERTAKER BURIAL/FUNERAL DIRECTOR; **celeb**:
WILLIAM BANTING (dietician), MOULD (Chuzzle, *Dickens*),
OMER (Copperfield, *Dickens*). DOER, GUARANTOR (crypt).
PROCUROR (arch).

UNDERWEAR UNDERCLOTHES; e.g. BELT, *BLOOMERS*,
BRA, BRIEFS, BUST-BODICE, COMBS, CORSET,
DRAWERS, GIRDLE, HOSE, KNICKERS, PANTS, PANTIES,
SOCKS, SPENCERS, STOCKINGS, *TIGHTS*, UNDERPANTS,
VEST. But also: PANTS, SHOES, SKIRT, SOCKS, TROUSERS
or any garment worn on nether part of the body (crypt).

UNDERWORLD ABODE OF THE DEAD, *HELL*, NETHER
REGIONS, **specifically**: ABADDON (Hebr), ABYSM, ABYSS
(Heb), EBLIS (Asia), EREBUS (Gk myth), GEHENNA (bibl),

HADES (Gk myth), INFERNO (Dante), ORCUS (Rom myth), TARTARUS (Gk myth) [asphodel meadows; *Cerberus*, *Charon*, *Hecate* and, for all ~ rivers, see *Styx*]. **Gods: Gk** = *HADES*; **Rom** = *DIS*, ORCUS, *PLUTO*; **Egy** = OSIRIS, SERAPIS; **goddesses: Gk** = *HECATE, PERSEPHONE*; **Rom** = PROSERPINE; **judges** = AEACUS, MINOS, RHADAMANTHYS. **Hebr** = BOR, SHAHAT, SHEOL; **Nor** = HEL; ANTIPODES. ATLAS (crypt). GANGLAND, ORGANIZED CRIME.

UNDERWRITE ACCEPT LIABILITY. SIGN (crypt).

UNEARTH DISCLOSE, DISCOVER, FIND (**opp** = *hide*). DIG UP. FUSE, SHORT CIRCUIT (crypt).

UNEATABLE BAD, INEDIBLE. *FOX* [*unspeakable* (Wilde)].

UNFAIR BIASED, CHEATING. ROUGH, UNEVEN. *UGLY*. BRUNETTE, DARK, REDHEAD (crypt).

UNIFORM CONSTANT, SAME, UNVARYING. CONFORMING. MILITARY/SCHOOL DRESS (**opp** = mufti, civvies). *SELF*.

UNION COALITION, JUNCTION. *MARRIAGE*, MATRIMONY, WEDDING, WEDLOCK. ENGLAND/SCOTLAND; GB/IRELAND. AGREEMENT, CONCORD. PIPE JOINT. WORKERS' ASSOCIATION; **celeb**: APEX (professional and executive), ASLEF (locomotive *engineers* and *firemen*), ASTMS (scientific technical and *managerial*), AUEW (*engineering* workers), BALPA (air line *pilots*), COHSE (health service), ETU (*electricians*), GMBU (boilermakers), ISTC (iron and steelworkers), NALGO (local government officers), NATSOPA (operative printers), NFU (farmers), NGA (printers), NUJ (*journalists*), NUM (*miners*), NUPE (public employees), NUR (*railwaymen*), NUS (seamen, students), NUT (teachers), POEU (Post Office Engineers), SLADE (graphical and allied trades), SOLIDARITY (Polish workers), TGW (*transport* and general workers), TUC (Trades Union Congress).

~ **CARD** MARRIAGE LICENCE (crypt).

~ **MAN** TRADE UNIONIST, WORKER. (BRIDE) GROOM, BEST MAN, USHER (crypt).

UNIT I, INDIVIDUAL, *ONE*. FACTORY. And see *International units*.

UNIVERSAL *U* (film *censorship*). GENERAL, WIDESPREAD. PAN-.

UNIVERSITY FURTHER EDUCATION ESTABLISHMENT. BAs. **Celebrated**:

3-letters
CUA (US)
MIT (US)
USC (US)

4-letters
BATH (Eng)
CUNY (US)
HULL (Eng)
IOWA (US)
KENT (Eng)
OPEN (Eng)
OXON (Eng)
UCLA (US)
YALE (US)
YORK (Can, Eng)

5-letters
ASTON (Eng)
ESSEX (Eng)
KEELE (Eng)
LAVAL (Can)
LEEDS (Eng)
PADUA (It)
POONA (Ind)
WALES (Wal)

6-letters
ACADIA (Can)
BOMBAY (Ind)
BRUNEL (Eng)
DUBLIN (Ire)
DUNDEE (Sc)
DURHAM (Eng)
EXETER (Eng)
LONDON (Eng)
MCGILL (Can)
OTTAWA (Can)
OXFORD (Eng)
PRAGUE (Cz)
QUEBEC (Can)

QUEEN'S (Can, Ire)
SURREY (Eng)
SUSSEX (Eng)
ULSTER (Ire)
VASSAR (US)

7-letters
ALBERTA (Can)
BELFAST (Ire)
BOLOGNA (It)
BRISTOL (Eng)
CALGARY (Can)
CARDIFF (Wal)
CHICAGO (US)
CORNELL (US)
FLORIDA (US)
GLASGOW (Sc)
HARVARD (US)
LEIPZIG (Ger)
LOUVAIN (Belg)
LUCKNOW (Ind)
MONCTON (Can)
NEW YORK (US)
READING (Eng)
SALERNO (It)
SALFORD (Eng)
TORONTO (Can)
WARWICK (Eng)

8-letters
ABERDEEN (Sc)
ADELAIDE (Aus)
AUCKLAND (NZ)
BRADFORD (Eng)
CALCUTTA (Ind)
CAPE TOWN (SA)
CARLETON (Can)
CARNEGIE (US)
COLUMBIA (US)
FLINDERS (SA)
FREIBURG (Ger)

ILLINOIS (US)
MANITOBA (Can)
MICHIGAN (US)
MONTREAL (Can)
SORBONNE (Fr)
STAMFORD (Eng)
STIRLING (Sc)
SYRACUSE (US)
TASMANIA (Aus)
VICTORIA (Aus)

9-letters
CAMBRIDGE (Eng)
DALHOUSIE (Can)
EDINBURGH (Sc)
FRANKFURT (Ger)
GOTTINGEN (Ger)
JAMES COOK (Aus)
LANCASTER (Eng)
LEICESTER (Eng)
LIVERPOOL (Eng)
MELBOURNE (Aus)
MINNESOTA (US)
NEWCASTLE (Eng)
NOTRE DAME (Can)
PRINCETON (US)
ROCHESTER (Eng)
SHEFFIELD (Eng)
SINGAPORE (S'pore)
ST ANDREWS (Sc)
WISCONSIN (US)

10+ letters
BIRMINGHAM (Eng)
CALIFORNIA (US)
CANTERBURY (NZ)
CINCINNATI (US)
CITY COLLEGE (US)
CONNECTICUT (US)
EAST ANGLIA (Eng)
GOETTINGEN (Ger)
HEIDELBERG (Ger)
HERIOT-WATT (Sc)
LETHBRIDGE (Can)
LOUGHBOROUGH (Eng)
MANCHESTER (Eng)
MASSACHUSETTS (US)
MILTON KEYNES (Eng)
MOUNT ALLISON (Can)
NEW BRUNSWICK (Can)
NEW ENGLAND (Aus)
NOTTINGHAM (Eng)
PENNSYLVANIA (US)
PITTSBURGH (US)
SASKATCHEWAN (Can)
SHERBROOKE (Can)
SIMON FRASER (Can)
SOUTHAMPTON (Eng)
S CALIFORNIA (US)
STRATHCLYDE (Sc)
WASHINGTON (US)

UNIVERSITY COLLEGE Colleges of Cambridge (C) and Oxford (O):

3-letters
NEW (O)

5-letters
CAIUS (C)
CLARE (C)
JESUS (C, O)

KEBLE (O)
KINGS (C)
ORIEL (O)

6-letters
DARWIN (C)
EXETER (O)

GIRTON (C)
MERTON (O)
QUEENS' (C)
QUEEN'S (O)
SELWYN (C)
WADHAM (O)

7-letters
BALLIOL (O)
CHRIST'S (C)
DOWNING (C)
LINCOLN (O)
NEWNHAM (C)
ST ANNE'S (O)
ST HUGH'S (O)
ST JOHN'S (O)
TRINITY (C, O)

8-letters
ALL SOULS (O)
EMMANUEL (C)
GONVILLE (C)
HERTFORD (O)
HOMERTON (C)

MAGDALEN (O)
PEMBROKE (C, O)
ROBINSON (C)
ST HILDA'S (O)
ST PETER'S (O)

9-letters
BRASENOSE (O)
CHURCHILL (C)
MAGDALENE (C)
WORCESTER (O)

10+ letters
CHRISTCHURCH (O)
CORPUS CHRISTI (C, O)
FITZWILLIAM (C)
LADY MARGARET HALL (O)
PETERHOUSE (C)
SIDNEY SUSSEX (C)
SOMERVILLE (O)
ST CATHARINE'S (C)
ST EDMUND HALL (O)
TRINITY HALL (C)
UNIVERSITY (O)

UNIVERSITY GRANT BURSARY, EXHIBITION, SCHOLARSHIP. DEGREE (crypt).

UNKNOWN STRANGE, UNFAMILIAR. X,Y (maths).

UNLIMITED 1. GREAT, UNRESTRICTED, VAST. 2. Delete both end letters, e.g. **Old money is unlimited cash** = *AS*.

UNLOCKED OPENED, UNBOLTED, UNFASTENED. *CUT*. DISTRESSED, SCALPED, SHORN (crypt).

UNMARRIED 1. BACHELOR, SINGLE, SPINSTER. 2. Delete **m** or **wed** from clue, e.g. **Unmarried man** = *AN.

UNORDERED HIGGLEDY-PIGGLEDY, RANDOM, SCATTERED, UNTIDY. SPONTANEOUS, VOLUNTARY. LAY, NON-CLERICAL (crypt).

UNQUALIFIED 1. UNRESTRICTED. INCOMPETENT. UNTRAINED. COMPLETE, PERFECT, UTTER. 2. Remove any letters implying technical or educational qualification (BA,

FCA, MB etc), e.g. **Early South African unqualified bomber** (4) = BO**ER.

UNQUIET 1. UNEASY. NOISY, F. 2. Delete any indication of quiet from clue (e.g. **p**, **sh** etc), e.g. **Unquiet tipper leads to row** (4) = TI**ER.

UNREADY UNPREPARED. LACKING ADVICE, RASH; ETHELRED.

UNSAINTLY 1. UNHOLY. 2. Delete letters **st** from word, e.g. **Ernest is unsaintly bird** (4) = ERNE**.

UNSEEN 1. INVISIBLE, NOT NOTICED, NOT READ [*eminence grise*]. 2. ~ characters in literature: BUGGINS (~ turn); BUNBURY (The Importance of Being Earnest, *Wilde*); *MRS GRUNDY* (Thos Morton); MRS HARRIS (Chuzzle, *Dickens*); HARVEY (*rabbit*, Mary Chase); INVISIBLE MAN (H. G. Wells); LT KIJE (Troika, Prokofiev); MACAVITY (*cat*, T. S. Eliot); MRS PARTINGTON (Sydney Smith).

UNSPEAKABLE OBJECTIONABLE, REPULSIVE. HUNT, HUNTERS, HUNTSMEN [*unbeatable* (*Wilde*)].

UNSUPPORTED 1. SECONDARY, SOLO, UNAIDED, UNSUBSTANTIATED. DESTITUTE. CANTILEVER. 2. Remove synonym for 'support' (bra, guy, prop, stay), e.g. **Prohibit unsupported staybar** (3) = ****BAR.

UNWATERED 1. DRY, PARCHED; DESERT, NOT IRRIGATED. NEAT, UNDILUTED. 2. Delete synonym for **water** from clue (hoo, sea etc), e.g. **Volume of unwatered choochoo** = C**C**.

UNWILLING RELUCTANT. INTESTATE (crypt).

UP 1. ON HIGH, TO HIGHER PLACE (**opp** = *down*). AT UNIVERSITY. FINISHED. RISEN. MOUNTED, RIDING, SADDLED. 2. Dn answer reads backwards, or upwards, e.g. **Dickens lived up** (5) = DEVIL.

UPAS *TREE*. EVIL INFLUENCE, MALEVOLENCE. SA (dn, crypt).

UPBRAID CHIDE, SCOLD. PUT UP HAIR [bun] (crypt).

UPHOLD 1. CONFIRM, MAINTAIN, SUPPORT. 2. In dn answer, word holds another inside, and one or both reads backwards, e.g. **Every account he upholds** (4) = E*AC*H.

UPIS 1. Egy chief *goddess*, and of *NATURE*. 2. *SI* (dn, crypt).

UP-MARKET SOPHISTICATED. TRAM (dn, crypt).

UPPER HIGHER, TOP. SHOE TOP, VAMP. REP (dn, crypt).

UPPER CLASS U; ARISTOCRACY, GENTRY. FIRST FORM, SIXTH FORM, SENIOR.

UPRIGHT CORRECT, RIGHTEOUS. VERTICAL (**opp** = *leaning*). PIANO. ROMAN TYPE. TR (dn, crypt).

UPSET *Anag.* 1. CAPSIZE, DISTURB, OVERTURN, SPILL. ANXIOUS, WORRIED [*parrot*]. TES (dn, crypt). 2. Answer reads up (dn). 3. RIDING SCHOOL (crypt).

UPSTART NOUVEAU RICHE. U (crypt).

URANIA 1. Gk myth, one of the 9 *Muses* (astronomy). 2. A minor *PLANET*.

URANIDS Gk myth sons of *Uranus* and *Gaea*, identified with the *GIGANTES*, who conquered the *Titans* when the latter made war on the gods; they were *monsters* with 100 arms and 50 heads: AEGAEON or BRIAEREUS, COTTUS and GYGES or GYES.

URANIUM *METAL*; U (*chem*).

URANUS Gk *god* of HEAVEN, f (by Ge) of the *Titans* and the *Uranids*. When he was killed, *Aphrodite* sprang from the sea foam where his limbs were thrown.

URGE ABET, ADVOCATE, EGG, ENCOURAGE, ENTREAT, EXHORT, IMPEL, SET ON, SICK, SPUR, STIMULATE. DRIVE, DESIRE, WISH, YEARNING.

URIAH HEEP (David Copperfield, *Dickens* ['umble]). HITTITE.

US WE (**opp** = them). UNITED STATES OF AMERICA.

USA UNITED STATES OF AMERICA (*car plate*).

USS US SHIP, *BOAT*.

USSR SOVIET RUSSIA (as opposed to **Russ** = Russia).

UTHERSON *KING ARTHUR* (son of Uther Pendragon) [*Guinevere, Lancelot, Round Table*].

UTTER EXPRESS, SAY, SPEAK. CIRCULATE, ISSUE (money). COMPLETE, *UNQUALIFIED*, TOTAL.

UTTERLY COMPLETELY, TOTALLY. Sounds like . . ., *pronounced* like . . . (crypt).

V VANADIUM (*chem*). VATICAN CITY (*car plate*). VERSUS, VS; AGAINST. VICTORY SIGN. SEE, VIDE. VOL(UME). VOLTS. *FIVE*.

VALE CHANNEL, VALLEY (**opp** = *hill*). FAREWELL.

VALHALLA Nor myth; *Odin's* great hall, the house of warriors slain in battle [*Valkyries*].

VALKYRIES Nor myth; *Odin's* handmaidens, who selected those to be slain in battle and thus go to *Valhalla*.

VAMP ADVENTURESS, FLIRT. ALLURE, EXPLOIT, SEDUCE. UPPER (shoe). FURBISH, REPAIR. IMPROVISE, STRUM (mus).

VANADIUM *METAL*; V (*chem*).

VARIETY *Anag*. DIVERSITY, CHANGE. SPECIMEN, TYPE. SHOWBIZ, *THEATRE*, VAUDEVILLE. [spice of life].

VAT CISTERN, CONTAINER, TANK, TUB, VESSEL. TAX.

VAULT JUMP, LEAP, *SPRING*. *ARCH*, CELLAR, CRYPT, FIRMAMENT.

VEGETABLE 1. MONOTONOUS, UNEVENTFUL. APATHETIC, CATALEPTIC, INCAPACITATED. 2. PLANTLIFE (**comps** = animal, mineral or abstract). **Pl** = GREENS. **Types:**

3-letters	SPUD	MARROW
COS		PHASEL
DAL	**5-letters**	PORRET
OCA	APIUM	*POTATO*
PEA	CHARD	PYROLA
SOY	CHICH	RADISH
UDO	CRESS	RUNNER
YAM	MAIZE	SPROUT
ZEA	NAVEW	*SQUASH*
	ONION	TOMATO
4-letters	ORACH	TURNIP
BEAN	PEASE	
BEET	PULSE	**7-letters**
COLE	SWEDE	CABBAGE
CORN	TUBER	CHICORY
DOHL		GHERKIN
EDDO	**6-letters**	LETTUCE
FABA	BATATA	PARSNIP
KALE	CARROT	PUMPKIN
KOHL	CELERY	SALSIFY
LEEK	CYNARA	SEAKALE
OKRA	DAUCUS	*SEAWEED*
PEAR	ENDIVE	SHALLOT
RAPE	LENTIL	SPINACH
SOYA	LOMENT	TRUFFLE

8-letters	9+ letters
BEETRAVE	ARTICHOKE
BEETROOT	ASPARAGUS
BORECOLE	AUBERGINE
BRASSICA	BROAD BEAN
CELERIAC	BRUSSELS SPROUT
CHICK-PEA	CAULIFLOWER
CHOW-CHOW	COLOGASSI
COLERAPE	COURGETTE
COLEWORT	FRENCH BEAN
CUCUMBER	JERUSALEM ARTICHOKE
EGG-PLANT	MANGE-TOUT
	RUNNER BEAN
	SWEET CORN

VEHICLE AUTO, CAB, CAR, *CARRIAGE*, LORRY. BUS, CHARABANC, MINI-BUS, MINI-CAB. TRUCK, VAN. AIRBUS, AIRCRAFT, PLANE. *BOAT*.

VENETIAN OF VENICE; MARCO (POLO). BLIND.

Venez Venezuela.

VENUE RENDEZVOUS. GAME PARK, MATCH SITE; AWAY, HOME. GROUND (*cricket*, *football*, *rugby*, *tennis*).

VENUS 1. Rom *goddess* of *LOVE*; m of *Aeneas* by Anchises and of *Cupid* by Jupiter. **Gk** = *APHRODITE*, HESPER (US); **Phoen** = ASTARTE; **Nor** = *FREYA*; **Bab** = ISHTAR; **Egy** = *ISIS*. 2. *PLANET*. As *evening star* = *HESPERUS*; as *morning star* = *LUCIFER*.

VERSE POEM, POETRY, STANZA. FURROW. VERSICLE (bibl).

VERSED EDUCATED, SCHOOLED, *TRAINED*. POETIC, IN POETRY (crypt).

VERSION *Anag*. ACCOUNT. BOOK. VARIANT. TURNING (crypt).

VERSUS V, VS; AGAINST.

VERT VERTICAL. GREEN (*herald*).

VERY BIG OS.

VERY LOUD FF.

VESSEL *BOAT* (q.v.), *CRAFT*, SHIP; HMS, SS, USS. **Celeb**: ARK (Noah), BEAGLE (*Darwin*), *BELLEROPHON* (Napoleon), BOUNTY (Bligh), *CINQUE PORTS* (*Crusoe*), *DISCOVERY* (Cook, Scott), ENDEAVOUR (Cook), FRAM (Nansen),

GOLDEN HIND (ex Pelican, *Drake*), HISPANIOLA (Treasure
Island), USS LINCOLN (*Pinkerton*), MARY ROSE (Henry VIII),
MAUD (Amundsen), NINA (Columbus), PELICAN (later
Golden Hind, *Drake*), PEQUOD (*Ahab*), PINTA (Columbus),
RESOLUTION (Cook), REVENGE (Grenville), *VICTORY*
(Nelson). *BOWL*, CROCK, CRUSE, CUP, DISH, *EWER*,
GLASS, LAVER, PAN, POT, STOUP, URN.
VESTA 1. MATCH®, LUCIFER. 2. Rom *goddess* of the HEARTH;
Gk = *HESTIA*. 3. A minor *PLANET*.
VESTMENT *CHURCH DRESS*, GARMENT, ROBE.
BLOCKADE, SIEGE (mil; arch).
VETO BAN, BAR. WRONG VOTE (crypt).
VI SIX. VIOLET. BUZZBOMB, DOODLEBUG, FLYING
BOMB, *ROCKET*, *WEAPON*.
VICTOR CONQUEROR, WINNER. *AIRCRAFT*, BOMBER.
VICTORIA 1. *QUEEN*; REGINA; *EMPRESS*. RLY STATION.
CARRIAGE. LAKE. RIVER (Aus). *STATE* (Aus).
THEATRE. UNIVERSITY. 2. Rom *goddess*, eq of *NIKE*. 3. A
minor *PLANET*.
VICTORY 1. TRIUMPH, WIN. WARSHIP [Nelson].
CIGARETTE. 2. **Goddesses: Gk** = *NIKE*; **Rom** = VICTORIA.
~ **SIGN** LAUREL, MEDAL, PALM, GARLAND; V.
Viet Vietnam.
VIGORN *Episcopal sig* of WORCESTER.
VINTNER WINE-MERCHANT. NABOTH, *NOAH* (bibl) [f of
Chaucer].
VIOLIN *FIDDLE, INSTRUMENT*, ROCTA (mus) [viol, viola];
parts: back, bass bar, belly, block, bout, bridge, button,
fingerboard, fret, head, neck, nut, peg-box, rib, scroll, sound-hole,
string, tail-piece, waist. [Strad(ivarius)].
VIOLINIST FIDDLER; *BOWER*, BOWMAN, SCRAPER (crypt).
HOLMES. [Amati, Strad(ivarius)].
VIP VERY IMPORTANT PERSON; CELEBRITY, LION,
NOTABLE, *STAR*.
VIPER *ADDER*.
VIRGINITY 1. INNOCENCE (patron saint: Agnes). FLORIMEL
(Faerie Queene, Spenser). 2. **Goddess: Gk** = ARTEMIS. 3.
Constellation (Virgo); sign of the *Zodiac* (6th).
VIRGO *Constellation* (Virgin); sign of the *Zodiac* (6th).
VIRTUE EXCELLENCE, MORALITY, QUALITY,
RIGHTEOUSNESS; CHASTITY; **celeb cases**: *Atalanta*,

Cassandra, *Daphne*, *Dido*, *Narcissus*, *Penelope*. **Cardinal** ~s:
FORTITUDE, JUSTICE, PATIENCE, PRUDENCE,
TEMPERANCE; **theological** ~s: CHARITY, FAITH, HOPE.
Pl = 5th of the nine orders of angelology.

VISIT CALL, GO TO SEE, STAY. ATTACK; PUNISH (bibl).
BLESS, COMFORT (arch).

VIXEN FOX (*female*). SCOLD, TERMAGANT. *REINDEER*.

VO/VOL VOLUME. BOOKLET, SHORT BOOK (crypt).

VOLCANO ERUPTING MOUNTAIN; HOT SPOT (crypt). [active,
dormant, extinct; igneous rock; magma; lava; crater]. **Celeb**:
ETNA, FUJIYAMA, MT ST HELENS, KRAKATOA,
MAHARA, MAUNA LOA, PARICUTIN, MT PELEE,
STROMBOLI, SURTSEY, SUSWA, TANGSHAN, VESUVIUS.

VOLTS V; SHOCKING (crypt).

VOLTURNUS Rom myth SE *WIND*; **Gk** = EUROS.

VOLUME BOOK, TOME, VOL. CAPACITY, CC, CL, GAL,
MEASURE, *PECK*.

VOLUNTEER OFFER, UNDERTAKE; ENLIST, JOIN UP (**opp** =
conscribe, conscript, *press gang*). Type of snooker. **Pl** = DAD'S
ARMY, HOME GUARD, LDV, TA, TERRIERS [*soldiers*].

VOTE BALLOT, CROSS, POLL, X; CHOOSE, ELECT,
SUGGEST, VOICE.

VOWEL A, E, I, O, U (Y). Open sound of speech capable of
forming a syllable. Word with all ~s in correct order: FACETIOUS;
word with five ~s consecutively: QUEUEING; 6-letter word with no
~s: RHYTHM; 9-letter word with only one ~: STRENGTHS. **Opp** =
consonant [word without ~s: CRWTH (*instrument*)].

VS V; AGAINST, VERSUS. FIVES (crypt).

VULCAN 1. *AIRCRAFT*, BOMBER. 2. Rom *god* of *FIRE*; **Gk** =
HEPHAESTUS.

VULGAR 1. COARSE, COMMON, LOW, PLEBEIAN (**opp** = U).
FREQUENT, PREVALENT, POPULAR. 2. Use slang or
abbreviation, e.g. **Quiet! Isn't Edward vulgar made up like that (7)**
= P*AINT*ED.

W WATTS. WED, WEDNESDAY. WEST. WHITE. WICKET.
WIDE. WIFE. WITH. WOLFRAM (*chem*). WOMEN'S
(size). TUNGSTEN (*chem*). *BRIDGE PLAYER*.

WAGE CARRY ON, CONDUCT. REQUITAL. PAY, *SCREW* [salary].

WAGER COMBATANT (crypt). *BET*. PAID WORKER (crypt).

WAIF ABANDONED CHILD, MITE, SCRAP. TINY TIM.

WAIT (s/l *weight*). ATTEND, AWAIT, REMAIN, *STAY*; **comp** = see. CAROL SINGER. AMBUSH.

WAITER ATTENDANT, COMMIS, GARCON, MAITRE D'HOTEL. RUNNER (Stock Exchange). CAROL SINGER (crypt). QUEUER (crypt).

Wal Wales, Welsh. Cambria, ~n. [*patron saint*]. For ~ counties, see *Division*.

WALK BALL OF CHALK (*rh sl*), FOOTPATH, PERAMBULATE, PROMENADE, PATH; CONSTITUTIONAL, OUTING; AMBLE, TRAIPSE. [*Enoch* '~ed with God'].

WALKER PEDESTRIAN, PERAMBULATOR; 6 proud ~s in *song*. WALKING AID.

WALRUS SEA-MAMMAL, MORSE; **male** = *bull*; **female** = *cow*; **offspring** = *calf* [seal, sealion]. *Alice* character; **comp** = *carpenter*.

WANDERING *Anag*. ERRING, MEANDERING, WINDING [*Jew*].

WAR BELLIGERENCE, CONTENTION, FIGHT, HOSTILITIES, STRIFE, STRUGGLE (**opp** = *peace*). **Gods: Gk** = *ARES*, **Rom** = MARS, **Ger** = TIW; **goddesses: Gk** = *ATHENE*, PALLAS, **Rom** = *MINERVA*, **Nor** = *BRUNHILDA*.

WARCRY 1. Salvation Army broadsheet. 2. Battlecry used in action, e.g. BANZAI (Jap); GERONIMO (US para); GUNG HO (Ch, US); HARAMBEE (Kenya); TO ARMS (gen); TORA TORA (Jap, Pearl Harbor); VAE VICTIS (Rom); UP GUARDS AND AT 'EM (*Wellington* at Waterloo).

WARD (s/l *warred*). CONFINEMENT, CUSTODY. CHARGE, MINOR. LOCK FLANGE. DEPARTMENT, DISTRICT, DIVISION; ROOM; NURSERY (crypt). DEFENCE; BAILEY. AVERT, PARRY. DRAWBACK (crypt). *CARTOONIST*.

WARDER *GAOLER*. DOCTOR, HOUSEMAN, INTERN (US), *NURSE*, PATIENT (all crypt).

WAR OFFICE WO; OPS ROOM, BUNKER, COMMAND POST.

WASP *INSECT*; STINGER (crypt). WOMEN'S AIR FORCE (US).

WATCH ATTENTION, GUARD, LOOK-OUT, OBSERVATION, VIGILANCE; CAVE-MAN (crypt). CARE FOR, OBSERVE. DUTY SPELL. STREET PATROL. VIGILANTE [posse].

CLOCK, (HALF) HUNTER, REPEATER, TIMEPIECE.
Assembly of nightingales.

WATCH CASE SENTRY BOX (crypt).

WATCHMAN 1. GUARD(IAN), SENTINEL, SENTRY [cave,
curfew]. PEEPING TOM, VOYEUR (crypt). SAILOR.
HOROLOGIST, JEWELLER (crypt). SPECTATOR (crypt).
2. ~ **of the gods** = HEIMDAL (Nor) [*Cerberus*].

WATER *GULF*, LAKE, RAIN, *RIVER*, *SEA*, SPRING, STREAM,
WELL; ADAM'S ALE: HOO (crypt). DRIBBLE, SALIVATE.
DILUTE. **Comp** = *fire*.

~ **CARRIER** 1. AQUEDUCT, GOURD, MAINS, PIPE [Gunga Din
(Kipling)]. 2. *Constellation* (Aquarius); sign of the *Zodiac* (11th).

WATERFALL CASCADE, CATARACT, FALLS, RAPIDS
[Minnehaha]; **celeb falls**: *ANGEL* (S Am), ANGRABIES (S Af),
BOYOMA (W Af), CEDAR (USA), CHURCHILL (Can),
GRAND (Can), IGUACA (S Am), IROQUOIS (Can),
KABALEGA (Af), NIAGARA (Can/USA), NGONEYE (Af),
OWEN (Af), PARK (USA), REICHENBACH (Swi, *Holmes*),
SIOUX (USA), SMITHS (Can), VICTORIA (Af).
RAIN(DROP) (crypt). TEARS (crypt).

WATERLOO *BATTLE*; FINISH, UNDOING. STATION (rly);
~ and City Line = THE DRAIN. THAMES BRIDGE.

WATER SPORTS See *SPORT*.

WATER TOWER MAIN SUPPLY, TANK. TUG (crypt).

WATTS W.

WAVE BREAKER, BRINY, COMBER, FOAM, RIPPLE,
ROLLER, SEA, SURF, WHITE HORSE; BORE, EAGRE.
CURL, HAIR, LOCK, MARCEL [permanent]. BRANDISH,
FLUTTER, VIBRATE; CURVE, UNDULATE.

WAVING OSCILLATION, SIGNALLING. HAIRDRESSING
(crypt). SURFING, SWIMMING (crypt).

WAX (s/l whacks). BEESWAX, RESIN [*Daedalus*, Icarus]. *SEAL*.
POLISH. GROW, INCREASE. FIT OF ANGER, TEMPER.

WAY (s/l weigh). AVENUE, CUL-DE-SAC, LANE, PASSAGE,
PATH, RAIL, *ROAD* (q.v.), ROUTE, STREET, TRACK
[Appian, Fosse, Icknield, Pilgrim's (*Roman roads*); Milky].
MANNER, METHOD, SYSTEM. MOMENTUM [kinetic
energy]. SLIPWAY, STOCK. N, E, S, W.

WEALTH 1. ABUNDANCE, OPULENCE, PROFUSION,
RICHES [*Croesus*, Dives, *Midas*]. 2. **God: Gk** = PLUTUS.

WEAPON INSTRUMENT; WAR MATERIAL:

Clubs
COSH
CUDGEL
MACE
MERE

Blades
BATTLEAXE
BROADSWORD
CUTLASS
DAGGER
EPEE
FOIL
HANGER (arch)
JAVELIN
KNIFE
LANCE
RAPIER
SABRE
SPEAR
STILETTO
SWORD

Launchers
ARQUEBUS
AUTOMATIC
BAZOOKA
BIG BERTHA
BOW
BREN
BROWNING
CANNON
CARBINE
CATAPULT
COLT
CROSSBOW
DERRINGER
FLAMETHROWER
FOWLING PIECE
GAT
GATLING

GUN
HOWITZER
LUGER
MONS MEG
MUSKET
PIAT
PISTOL
REPEATER
REVOLVER
RIFLE
SHOTGUN
SLING
STEN
WALTHER
WEBLEY
WINCHESTER

Missiles
ARROW
BOMB
BULLET
GRENADE
GUIDED *MISSILE*
ICBM
MILLS BOMB
MINE
MISSILE
ROCKET
SAM
SHELL
SLINGSHOT
TORPEDO
VI

Vehicles (manned)
AIRCRAFT
ARMOURED CAR
BATTLESHIP
BOMBER
CARRIER
CRUISER

DESTROYER	Q-BOAT
FIGHTER	SHUTTLE
FRIGATE	SUBMARINE
MONITOR	TANK
MTB	WARSHIP

WEASEL EQUIVOCATE, QUIBBLE. TRACKED VEHICLE (mil). QUADRUPED: *FERRET*, GLUTTON, MARTEN, MEERKAT, MINK, MONGOOSE, *OTTER*, POLECAT (fitch; US skunk), STOAT (ermine), SURICATE, WOLVERINE. *PLEDGE* (*pawn*; *pop* goes the ~).

WEATHER (s/l whether). CURE, DRY, EXPOSE, SEASON; DISCOLOUR. OVERCOME, PASS; WINDWARD (naut). ATMOSPHERE, CONDITIONS, METEOROLOGY; **forecast areas**: Bailey, Biscay, Cromarty, Dogger, Dover, Faeroes, Fair Isle, Fastnet, Finisterre, Fisher, Forth, Forties, German Bight, Hebrides, Humber, Irish Sea, Lundy, Malin, Plymouth, Portland, Rockall, SE Iceland, Shannon, Sole, Thames, Tyne, Viking, Wight, Trafalgar, N and S Utsire.

WEAVER CLOTH/TAPESTRY MAKER; [*company* (livery); Aubusson]; **celeb**: *ARACHNE*, *BOTTOM* (MND, *Shak*), *Chaucer* character, LADY OF SHALOTT (Tennyson), *PENELOPE*, SILAS MARNER (G. Eliot/Marian Evans). PLOTTER, SCHEMER. AMADAVAT, TAHA, *BIRD*. RIVER (Eng). *SNAKE* (crypt). *SPIDER* (crypt).

WEBSTER DICTIONARY®. *SPIDER* (crypt).

WED WEDNESDAY. HITCHED, JOINED, MARRIED, MATCHED, MATED, PAIRED, SPLICED, WEDDED [*union*, matrimony]. WE WOULD.

WEDDING *MARRIAGE*, MATRIMONIAL, *UNION*.
~ **PRESENT** DOT, DOWRY. GIFT.

WEDGE V-SHAPE. JAM, PACK, SQUEEZE IN. *GOLF CLUB*. *Assembly* of swans.

WEDNESDAY W, WED. Day of *Odin*, *Woden*. ~**'s child** = full of woe. [Ash ~; Solomon *Grundy*].

WEED (s/l we'd). WILD HERB, *WILD PLANT*. LANKY, WEAK PERSON. *DRUG*, MARIJUANA; TOBACCO. **Pl** = mourning clothes.

WEEK (s/l weak). SEVEN *DAYS*, SENNIGHT. MON–FRI. PERIOD, *TIME*.

WEEP CRY, GREET (Sc), KEEN. DRIP, EXUDE, SWEAT. DROOP.

WEIGHT (s/l *wait*). 1. EFFECT, IMPORTANCE. HEAVINESS, MASS, *MEASURE*: CWT, DWT, KG, KILO, LB, *OUNCE*, OZ, *POUND*, TON, *TROY*. LONDON DISTRICT (W8; crypt). **Pl** = *CIGARETTE*. 2. **Boxing** ~s: see *Boxing*.

WELL ARTESIAN, FOUNTAIN, GUSHER, SOURCE, *SPA*, SPRING. INKPOT. FIT, HALE, NOT ILL, SOUND. CAREFULLY, EASILY, PROBABLY, SATISFACTORILY, THOROUGHLY, WISELY (**opp** = *badly*). WE WILL (crypt). ER, UM.

WELLINGTON *BOOT*. IRON DUKE, NOSEY, *MILITARY LEADER* [Wellesley]. *PUBLIC SCHOOL*. *CAPITAL* (NZ). WIMPY (aircraft nickname).

WELSH (s/l welch). CELTIC, CYMRIC [leek, Taffy]. ABSCOND, DECAMP, FLIT.

WELT SHOE LEATHER; RIBBING, TRIM. BLOW, CUFF, SMACK. WORLD (Ger).

WEMBLEY *FOOTBALL GROUND*, STADIUM.

WENDY DARLING [Peter Pan]. CURVY, SINUOUS (crypt).

WEST 1. W, OCCIDENT. MAE. *PAINTER*. *WRITER*. *BRIDGE PLAYER*. 2. Reads from right to left, e.g. **Childish seat of learning looks west** = SKOOL.

~ **END** LONDON, MAYFAIR, WI.

WESTERN W, OCCIDENTAL. COWBOY FILM, B MOVIE [*outlaw*].

WESTMINSTER *LEGISLATIVE ASSEMBLY*, PARLIAMENT. *PUBLIC SCHOOL*. *THAMES BRIDGE*. *THEATRE*.

WH ONLIE BEGETTER (*Shak*).

WHALE (s/l wail). BEAT, THRASH, WHACK. HUGE, LARGE. *ISLAND*. RIVER (Can). CETACEAN MAMMAL: **types**: ARCTIC ~, BALEEN, -EIN, BELUGA, BLUE ~, BOOPS, BOTTLE-NOSE ~, BOWHEAD, CACHALOT, DOLPHIN, FIN ~, GRAMPUS, GREY ~, HUMP-BACKED ~, KILLER ~, LEVIATHAN (bibl), MINKIE, NARWHAL, ORC, ORCA, PILOT ~, POTHEAD, RIGHT ~, RORQUAL, SEI, SINGING ~, SPERM ~, TOOTHED ~, WHITE ~, ZEUGLODON (zool); **assembly** = pod, school, **offspring** = *calf* [Ahab, Moby Dick; Jonah; ambergris].

WHALER (s/l wailer). WHALE HUNTER; AHAB [Moby Dick, Herman Melville]. BOAT, CUTTER, GIG.

WHEEL (s/l weal). BALANCE, CATHERINE, COG, FLY, MILL, PADDLE, POTTER'S, SPINNING, STEERING [*Company*

(livery); *Ixion*. *St Catherine*, *tarot*]. PIVOT, *TURN* (mil).
REVOLVER (crypt). *WINDOW*.

WHIG (s/l *wig*). PARLIAMENTARIAN, LIBERAL [BURKE,
FOX, *GREY*: *Prime Minister*].

WHIP DART, *DASH*, JERK, NIP, SNATCH. BIND, SEIZE,
SERVE (naut). BURTON, HANDY-BILLY, *HOIST*, PULLEY,
PURCHASE (naut). BEAT, FLOG, LASH, LEATHER, *URGE*;
CANE, *CAT* (O'Nine-Tails), QUIRT, ROD, ROMAL,
SCORPION, SCOURGE, STRAP, *TAW* [bolas, lariat, lasso].
COACHMAN, HUNTSMAN. DISCIPLINE, ORDER (polit).

WHISKER BEARD, BEAVER, BRISTLE, HAIR. SHORT
DISTANCE. EGG-BEATER (crypt).

WHISKEY *DRINK*, USQUEBAUGH (Ire); POTEEN.

WHISKY *DRINK*, SCOTCH; **comp** = soda; splash. *CARRIAGE*.
MOUSSE, SNOW (cook, crypt). WHIPPY (crypt).

WHIST *CARD GAME*; TRUMPERY (crypt). P, PP, SH; HUSH,
QUIET, SILENCE.

WHISTLE SHRILL; **comp** = *pig*. THROAT (sl). *SUIT* (*rh sl*).

WHITE *COLOUR*. BILLIARD/SNOOKER BALL.
CAUCASIAN. *COMPOSER*. *ISLAND*. RIVER (US). *SEA*.
SPACE *TRAVELLER*. *WRITER*. 'BLANCHE'. **Pl** =
CRICKET TROUSERS, CREAMS.

WHITEFRIARS CARMELITES.

WHISTABLE NATIVE, *OYSTER* [Colchester].

WHO DOCTOR, DR. WORLD HEALTH ORGANIZATION
[*six*].

WI LONDON, MAYFAIR, WEST END. WEST INDIES.
WOMEN'S INSTITUTE. WILLIAM THE CONQUEROR.

WICKED EVIL, MISCHIEVOUS, SINFUL, SPITEFUL.
CANDLE, OIL LAMP (crypt).

WIDELY BROADLY. ABROAD, FOREIGN, TRANSLATED
(crypt).

WIDOW SHORT LINE (print). BEREAVED WIFE, surviving fem
spouse; **celeb**: BRADY (Garrick); CLIQUOT (Veuve,
champagne); TWANKY (theat) [cruse (*Elijah*); grass ~; ~'s mite;
~'s peak; ~'s weeds].

WIFE CONSORT, HELPMEET, MATE, PARTNER; BETTER
HALF, DUTCH, MRS, OLD WOMAN, *RIB*; TROUBLE (*rh sl*).

WIG (s/l *whig*). TOUPEE; RUG (sl). **Comp** = gown.

WILD *Anag*. ANGRY, BARBAROUS, DESOLATE,
DISORDERLY, EAGER, IRREGULAR, RASH, UNTAMED,

WAYWARD. [joker]. *ROBBER*.
WILD CAT HOT TEMPERED, IMPROMPTU, RECKLESS, SNAP, VIOLENT. UNOFFICIAL. *AIRCRAFT*. And see *CAT*.
~ **FLOWER** WILD PLANT. CASCADE, WATERFALL, WHITE WATER (crypt).
~ **PLANT** UNCULTIVATED FLOWER, WEED (and see *plant*).
Breeds:

4-letters
FLAG
LING
REED
RUSH
WELD
WORT

5-letters
AVENS
DAISY

6-letters
BALSAM
BURNET
CLOVER
MEDICK
NETTLE
SORREL
SPURGE
SUNDEW
TEASEL
YARROW

7-letters
BISTORT
BOG-BEAN
BUGLOSS
CAMPION
COMFREY
EELWORT
FROGBIT
HEATHER

LUCERNE
MAYWEED
RAGWORT
RAMSONS
SPURREY
VERVAIN

8-letters
ASPHODEL
BILBERRY
BINDWEED
CHARLOCK
COW-WHEAT
CROW-FOOT
FLEABANE
HAREBELL
HAWKWEED
KNAPWEED
MARJORAM
MILKWORT
PLANTAIN
SCABIOUS
SCULL-CAP
SELFHEAL
SOAPWORT
TOADFLAX
VALERIAN

9-letters
BUCKTHORN
BUTTERCUP
CHICKWEED
COLTSFOOT

DANDELION	CRANESBILL
EYEBRIGHT	CUCKOOFLOWER
GIPSYWORT	DEADLY NIGHTSHADE
GOLDEN ROD	DEADNETTLE
GROUNDSEL	GOATS BEARD
LOUSEWORT	HERB ROBERT
MARESTAIL	LOOSESTRIFE
PIMPERNEL	MEADOWSWEET
SPEARWORT	RAGGED ROBIN
SPEEDWELL	RESTHARROW
STONECROP	SILVERWEED
TORMENTIL	SNEEZEWORT
WOUNDWORT	SOWTHISTLE
	STITCHWORT
10+ letters	STORKSBILL
BUTTERWORT	WATERCRESS
CINQUEFOIL	YELLOW RATTLE

WILDE Oscar (Fingal O'Flahertie Wills); b 1854 Dublin; mar Constance Lloyd (2 s Cyril and Vyvyan Holland). Libel action v Lord Alfred Douglas' f; imprisoned 2 years for immoral practices 1895; d Paris 1900. *Writer* and wit; **plays**: Vera, or the Nihilist; The Duchess of Padua; *Salome*; Lady Windermere's *Fan*; A Woman of no Importance; An Ideal Husband; The Importance of being Earnest; **books**: The House of Pomegranates; The Picture of Dorian Gray; The Ballad of Reading Gaol (by C3.3, ~'s prison number); De Profundis.

WILL IMPULSE, INTENTION, VOLITION. TESTAMENT [legacy]. BILL, WILLIAM. [*ignis fatuus*]. **Pl** = *CIGARETTE*.

WILLIAM BILL, WILL, WM; 'A DEFENDER'. KING. CONQUEROR. ORANGE, HALF-SOVEREIGN (~ and Mary, crypt; **comp** = Mary); TELL; WILBERFORCE. Old Father ~ (*Alice*). Just ~ (*Outlaw*, Richmal Crompton).

WILLING CONSENTING, GAME, *KEEN*, READY. DEVISING, LEAVING, TESTATOR (crypt). [Barkis is willin' (*Dickens*)].

WILL O' THE WISP IGNIS FATUUS (q.v.).

WIMBLEDON *TENNIS VENUE*. *COURTED* (crypt). [Wombles].

WINCE FLINCH, START. ROLLER. CWE (crypt).

WINCHESTER 1. RIFLE, WEAPON. VENTA BULGARUM (*Rom*). *CASTLE*. *PUBLIC SCHOOL*. 2. **Episcopal sig** = WINTON.

WIND 1. COIL, CRANK, REEL, TURN, TWIST; MEANDER [serpent, *snake*]. EMBRACE, ENTWINE. AIR, BREATH, FLATULENCE. BREEŻE, BLOW, CYCLONE, GALE, GUST, HURRICANE, MUZZLER (sl), NOSER (head ~), PUFF, SOLDIER'S ~ (naut), SQUALL, STORM, TEMPEST, TORNADO, TYPHOON, WUTHER (N Eng dial), ZEPHYR (**opp** = calm, doldrums, horse latitudes). [~y City = Chicago]. **Celeb**: AFER (Milton, SW), ANTANE (Toulouse), BAGLIO (Sp Pac), BERG (S Af), BISE (Alps), BORA (Adriatic), BUSTER (Aus), CANDELIA (Sp Am), CAPE DOCTOR (S Af), CHINOOK (Rocky Mts), CHOCOLATE GALE (W Ind naut), CIERZO (Sp N), DUST DEVIL (Ind), ETESIAN (Mediterranean), EUROCLYDON (Medit), FOHN (Alps), FREMANTLE DOCTOR (Aus; cricket); GARBI (Sp S), GHIBLI (Libya), GREGALE (Malta), HARMATTAN (W Af), HELM (Lake District), HIPPALUS (Arab Gulf), KAMIKAZE (Jap), KHAMSIN (Egy), KUBAN (Java), LEVANTER (E Med), LIBECCHIO (Corsica), LLEBEIG (Sp SW), MELTEMI (Aegean), MIGJORN (Sp S), MISTRAL (Fr), MONSOON (Ind Ocean), PAMPERO (Andes), PASSAT (N Atlantic), PEESASH (Ind), PONIENTE (Sp W), PUNA (Peru), ROARING FORTIES (Antarctic), ROGER (E Anglia), SAMIEL (Turk), SANTA ANNA (Nevada), SHAITAN (Ind), SHAMAAL (Pers), SIMOOM, -N (Arab), S(C)IROCCO (Libya), SNOW EATER (US), SOLANO (Sp), SUMATRA (Sing), SURES (Chile), TRADE ~ (Cancer, Capricorn), TRAMONTANA (Adriatic), TWISTER (US), VENAVAL (Mex), WILLI-WAW (US/S Am), WILLY-WILLY (Aus), XALOC (Sp E), ZONDA (Arg) and, all *Hiawatha*, KABIBONOKKA (N), SHAWONDASEE (S), WABUN (E), MUDJEKEEWIS (W). 2. **Gk myth god/king** = AEOLUS; **beneficial** ~s: N, NE, S, W (sons of *Aurora*/Eos by Astraeus); **storm** ~s: *HARPIES* (q.v.; dd of *Electra* by Thaumas or by *Typhon*). **Other god** = ENLIL (Sumerian). [Mt Haemus. Typhoeus. Sleipner (Nor *horse*)]. **Individual winds: N** = BOREAS (Gk), SEPTENTRIO (Rom); **NE** = KAIKAS (Gk), AQUILO (Rom), ARGESTES; **E** = APELIOTES (Gk), SUBSOLANUS (Rom); **SE** = EUROS (Gk), VOLTURNUS (Rom); **S** = NOTOS (Gk), AUSTER (Rom); **SW** = LIPS (Gk), AFRICUS (Rom); **W** = ZEPHYRUS (Gk), FAVONIUS (Rom); **NW** = SKIRON, THRASCIAS (Gk), CAURUS (Rom).
WINDOW LIMITED PERIOD, TIME SLOT. CHAFF, FOIL,

RADAR JAMMING, RCM (mil). CLEAR VIEW, OPENING, LIGHT, PORTHOLE (naut), TRANSLUCENT/TRANSPARENT PANE or PANEL, *QUARREL*; **types**: ATTIC ~. BAY ~, BOW ~, BULLSEYE, CASEMENT ~, CHURCH ~, DORMER ~, FANLIGHT, FRENCH ~, GEORGIAN ~, GOTHIC ~, GRILLE, *JUDAS* ~, LANTERN, LANCET ~, LATTICE ~, LOUVRE ~, NEO-GOTHIC ~, NORMAN ~, OEIL DE BOEUF, OGEE ~, ORIEL ~, PANE, PATIO ~, PERPEN-DICULAR ~, PICTURE ~, PORT, -HOLE, -LIGHT, ROMAN ~, ROSE ~, SASHCORD ~, SHOP ~, SKYLIGHT, SLIDING ~, STAINED GLASS ~, TRANSOM, TROMP-L'OEIL, *WHEEL* ~, WICKET [roller/venetian blind, curtain, jalousie, shutters; double glazing; ~ box; ~ envelope; ~ shopping. And see *architecture*; *cathedral* (*parts*)].

WINE (s/l whine). 1. *COLOUR* (dark red). FERMENTED DRINK, GRAPE JUICE [*study*]; TENT (arch); **celeb** (most ®): ASTI SPUMANTE, BARSAC, BEAUJOLAIS, BEAUNE, BORDEAUX, BORDELAIS, BURGUNDY, CHABLIS, CHAMPAGNE, CHATEAUNEUF DU PAPE, CHATEAU YQUEM, CHIANTI, CLARET, COTE DU RHONE, COTE D'OR, GRAVES, HOCK, LIEBFRAUMILCH, MACON, MALAGA, MARSALA, MEDOC, MOSELLE, MUSCADET, NUITS ST GEORGES, POMAGNE, PORT, POUILLY FUISSE, POUILLY FUME, REISLING, RETSINA, RIESLING, RIOJA, OUSO, SAKE, ST EMILION, SANCERRE, SAUTERNES, SHERRY, TOKAY, VOUVRAY. **Lover of** ~ = oenophile. **Gods: Gk** = DIONYSUS, **Rom** = *BACCHUS*, IACCHUS (*Hebe*). [*Noah*; mulled ~, glogg, gluhwein].

WING 1. PINION [bird; *Daedalus*, Icarus]. PROJECTING ARM (arch). FORWARD, STRIKER (football). Group of fighter *aircraft*. **Comp** = prayer. **Pl** = PILOT'S BADGE. 2. Myth endows *Hermes* (Gk) and *Mercury* (Rom) with winged sandals as messengers of the *gods*, *Pegasus* with winged hooves, and *Hades* with a winged helmet (borrowed by *Perseus*); the caduceus was a winged wand or staff (*Asclepius*).

WINGER *FOOTBALLER*. *BIRD* (crypt).

WINTER SPORTS See *SPORT*.

WINTON *Episcopal sig* of WINCHESTER. TOWN (crypt: W in TO()N).

WIRELESS 1. *BROADCAST*, MEDIUM, RADIO; SET. 2. Word with letters 'wire' or synonym removed, e.g. **Wireless sage is in**

command (4) = (wi)SEAC(re).

WISDOM 1. EXPERIENCE, KNOWLEDGE, PRUDENCE, SAGACITY [Confucius, *Daniel*, Mentor, Methuselah, Nestor, *Paris*, *Solomon*]; *TOOTH*. 2. **Goddesses: Gk** = *ATHENE*, **Rom** = MINERVA.

WISEMAN MAGUS (**pl** = magi), SAGE [Confucius, *Daniel*, Mentor, Methuselah, Nestor, *Paris*, *Solomon*].

WISP BUNDLE, TWIST. SMOKE. *Assembly* of snipe.

WITCH (s/l which). GRIMALKIN, HAG, SIBYL, SORCERESS; SPELLER (crypt); **male** = warlock; **assembly** = coven; **celeb**: ARMIDA (Tasso), ~ OF ENDOR (Saul), MORGAN LE FEY (Malory), SYCORAX (Temp), VIVIEN (Tennyson), 3 in Macbeth (*Shak*) [*HECATE*, Salem, Walpurgis night]. **Comp** = black cat; broomstick.

WITCHCRAFT 1. CHARM, SORCERY; OBEAH, OBI, VOODOO; SPELLING (crypt). BROOMSTICK (crypt). 2. **Goddess: Gk** = *HECATE* [Macbeth. Walpurgis night. Hallowe'en].

WITH 1. AMONG, BESIDE, IN COMPANY. AGREEABLY, HARMONIOUS. CARRYING, CUM, HAVING, POSSESSING, IN CARE OF, BY MEANS (**opp** = sine). CONCERNING. AGAINST, DESPITE, NOTWITHSTANDING. 2. Two words to form one, e.g. **Victoria, for example, with 'er provider of newspapers** (9) = STATION*ER.

WITHIN Hidden word. INSIDE, INTERNALLY.

WITHOUT 1. LESS; SINE (**opp** = cum). OUTSIDE. 2. Word outside another, e.g. **Hen without trouble colliding** (4, 2) = HE*AD O*N. 3. Delete word or letter(s) indicated, e.g. **No railway is without trouble in this country** (6) = NOR***WAY. 4. Start answer with letters 'no', e.g. **Seen without Edward** (5) = NO*TED.

WIZARD SUPER. *MAGICIAN*, SORCERER; MAGUS, MERLIN, OZ (cowardly lion, tin man, Frank Baum). *COMIC*.

WODEHOUSE Pelham Grenville, writer; broadcast for enemy in World War II. **Books**: Big Money, Blandings Castle, The Code of the Woosters, The Inimitable Jeeves, Leave it to Psmith, Money in the Bank, Quick Service, Spring Fever. **Characters**: Aunt Agatha, Bertie Wooster, Lord Emsworth; Jeeves, Aunt Julia, Bingo Little, Lord Uffenham, Oofy Prosser, Pongo Twistleton, Ukridge, Psmith.

WODEN A-Sax chief *god*. One-eyed, he looked after warriors. **Gk** = *ZEUS*, **Rom** = *JUPITER*, **Nor** = *ODIN* [Wednesday].

WOLF GOBBLE, SCOFF. FLOW BACK (crypt, hence EBB).
COMPOSER. RIVER (US). *SPIDER*. CANIS LUPUS,
COYOTE (US); **offspring** = cub [Isengrim (Reinecke Fuchs);
Little Red Riding Hood; Lycaon; cry ~]. *Constellation*. Fenris
(*Loki*). **Pl** = *Football team*.

WOLFRAM *METAL*; W (*chem*); TUNGSTEN.

WOMAN EVE, HER, SHE [**Little women** = AMY, BETH, JO,
MEG (Louisa May Alcott) or, more generally, any abbreviated
girl's name].

WOMANIZER LECHER; SHEER (crypt). CASANOVA (It);
DON JUAN (Byron); LOTHARIO (The Fair Penitent, Rowe).

WOMAN WARRIOR *AMAZON, ARTEMISIA, BOUDICCA,*
BRITOMART (Spenser), *BRUNHILDA*, HIPPOLYTE, JOAN
OF ARC, THE MAID, PHILOSTRATE (MND, *Shak*),
VALKYR **pl** = ~IES (Nor). **Goddess of War** = ATHENE (Gk),
BELLONA, MINERVA (Rom).

WOMEN'S ORGANIZATION ATS, RWI, WAAF, WASP (US),
WAVE (US), WI, WRAC, WRAF, WRNS, WRVS.

WONDER MIRACLE. PONDER, THINK. [*Seven* ~s].

WOOD *CONDUCTOR* (mus). *PAINTER*. DRIVER, *GOLF
CLUB* (**opp** = *iron*). BIASED BALL (bowls). *FOREST*,
GROVE; *anniversary* (5th). TIMBER.

WOODEN CLUMSY, EXPRESSIONLESS, STIFF, STILTED.
SILVAN, TIMBER. *XOANON*; *anniversary* (5th).

WOODPECKER *BIRD*, genus picidae; **breeds**: AWLBIRD, BLACK
~, GREATER SPOTTED ~, GREEN ~, HICKWAY, LESSER
SPOTTED ~, NICKER, PICUS, SASIA, WOODPIE,
WOODWALL, WRYNECK, YAFFIL, YAFFLE, YUCKER.

WOOL ALPACA, ANGORA, LAMBS, MOHAIR, MERINO,
WORSTED [measure]; *MATERIAL*; *anniversary* (7th).

WORCESTER **Episcopal sig** = VIGORN. CATHEDRAL.
CERAMICS. UNIVERSITY COLLEGE.

WORK 1. LABOUR, EFFORT [Saturday's *child*]. BOOK, PLAY,
MUSIC, OP, OPUS. 2. When associated with author's name,
requires the title, e.g. **More work** (6) = UTOPIA. 3. **Pl** =
FACTORY, MILL. FUNCTIONS, GOES, RUNS.

WORKER ARTISAN, HAND, LABOURER [*patron saint*]; ANT,
BEE. **Pl** = TUC.

WORKSHOP ATELIER, STUDIO. DISCUSSION GROUP.
FIRM'S DANCE (crypt).

WORLD 1. *EARTH*, GLOBE, ORB; 21 (*tarot*). 2. **God: Rom** =

ATLAS (see also *earth*).

WORLD GIRDLER EQUATOR, LATITUDE, LONGITUDE. MOON, SATELLITE. **Celebrated**: ARIEL (Temp), CHICHESTER (Gypsy Moth), COOK (Endeavour), DRAKE (Golden Hind), PHILEAS FOGG (80 days, Verne), MAGELLAN (Trinidad, Vittoria), PUCK (MND), *ROSE* (Lively Lady), SLOCUM (Spray).

WORST BAD, BADLY, POOREST (**opp** = *best*). BEST, BEAT, DEFEAT, OUTDO, OVERCOME. SCUM, YEAST.

WORSTED BUNTING, *MATERIAL*, WOOLLEN YARN. DEFEATED, OUTDONE.

WRECK *Anag.* DESTRUCTION, RUIN. REMAINS. REMNANT.

WREN *ARCHITECT. BIRD. CARTOONIST.* Fem sailor (RN).

WRESTLING *Anag.* FIGHTING, GRAPPLING (*sport*); **styles**: catch-as-catch-can; Cornish; Cumberland; Devon; dinnie (Sc); freestyle; glima (Iceland); Graeco-Roman; judo (Jap); jujitsu (Jap); karate (Jap); kempo (Jap); kushti (Pers); pankration (Gk); sambo (USSR); schwingen (Swi); sumo (Jap); tag; Westmorland; yagli (Turk); **celeb wrestlers**: Antaeus; *Cercyon*; Charles (AYLI, *Shak*); H.I (Fr) and H.VIII (Eng) (Field of Cloth of Gold); Milo (of Croton); Muldoon (US); Samson Agonistes (Milton); Sukune (Jap); Theseus (Gk rules); Theogees (of Thasos; Gk); character in *Chaucer* (the Miller).

WRITER BALLPOINT, BIRO, PEN, PENCIL, QUILL, STYLO. AMANUENSIS, AUTHOR, GHOST, SECRETARY, STENOGRAPHER. **Celebrated**:

1-letter

Q	(Sir Arthur Quiller-Couch), Eng

2-letters

AA	(Milne), Eng
YY	(Robert Lynd), Ire

3-letters

BOZ	(Charles *Dickens*), Eng
FRY	Christopher, Eng
POE	Edgar Allan (Bostonian), US

4-letters

AMIS	Kingsley, Eng
BELL	Acton (Anne Brontë), Eng
BELL	Currer (Charlotte Brontë), Eng
BELL	Ellis (Emily Brontë), Eng
BIRD	Cyril Kenneth (Fougasse), Eng
BUCK	Pearl Sydenstricker, US
CARY	Joyce, Ire
DAHL	Raoul, Eng
ELIA	(Charles Lamb), Eng
GIDE	Andre, Fr
GRAY	Thomas, Eng
HOPE	Anthony (A. Hope Hawkins), Eng
HOWE	Edgar Watson, US
HUGO	Victor Marie, Fr
KERR	Jean, US
KNOX	John, Sc
LAMB	Charles (Elia), Eng
LAMB	Mary Ann, Eng
LEAR	Edward, Eng
LIVY	(Titus Livius), Rom
LYLY	John, Eng
LYND	Robert (YY), Ire
MANN	Thomas, Ger
MARX	Karl, USSR
NASH	Ogden, US
OVID	(Publius Ovidus Naso), Rom
PHIZ	Hablot K. Browne
POPE	Alexander, Eng
QUIZ	(Charles *Dickens*), Eng
ROSE	Alexander, US
ROSS	(T. E. Lawrence), Eng
SADE	Marquis de, Fr
SAKI	(H. H. Munro), Sc
SAND	George (Amandine Dupin, Baronne Dudevant), Fr
SHAW	(T. E. Lawrence), Eng
SHAW	George Bernard, Ire
WEST	Rebecca (Cicely Maxwell Andrews), Eng
ZOLA	Emile (Fr)

5-letters

ADAMS	Franklin, US
ADAMS	Henry, US
AESOP	Gk
AGATE	James Evershed, Eng
AUDEN	Wystan Hugh, US
BACON	Francis, Eng
BEHAN	Brendan, Ire
BEYLE	Marie Henri (Stendhal), Fr
BLAIR	Eric Arthur (George Orwell), Eng
BLAKE	Nicholas (C. Day Lewis), Eng
BLAKE	William, Eng
BREDE	Baron de la (Montesquieu), Fr
BURKE	Edmund, Eng
BURNS	Robert, Sc
BYRON	Lord George Gordon, Eng
CAMUS	Albert, Fr
CHASE	James Hadley (Rene Raymond), US
COOKE	Alistair, Eng/US
DANTE	Alighieri, It
DEFOE	Daniel, Eng
DONNE	John, Eng
DOYLE	Sir Arthur Conan, Eng
DUMAS	Alexandre (fils), Fr
DUMAS	Alexandre (pere), Fr
DUPIN	(George Sand), Fr
ELIOT	George (Mary Ann Evans), Eng
ELIOT	Thomas Stearns, US/Eng
EVANS	Mary Ann (George Eliot), Eng
GORKY	Maxim (Alexei Peshkov), USSR
HARDY	Thomas, Eng
HENRY	O (William Sydney Porter), US
HOMER	Gk
HOYLE	Edmond, Eng
IBSEN	Henrik Johan, Nor
INNES	Hammond, Eng
JAMES	Henry, US
JAMES	P.D., Eng
JOYCE	James, Ire
KEATS	John, Eng
LEWIS	Cecil Day (Nicholas Blake), Eng

LUCAN	(Marcus Annaeus Lucanus), Rom
MASON	William, Eng
MILNE	Alan Alexander, Eng
MUNRO	Hector Hugh (Saki), Sc
O'HARA	John, US
PAINE	Thomas, Eng
PEPYS	Samuel, Eng
PLATO	Gk
PLINY	(Caius Plinius), Rom
POUND	Ezra Loomis, US
ROCHE	Mazo de la, US
SAGAN	Francoise (Quoirez), Fr
SCOTT	Sir Walter, Sc
SHUTE	Nevil (Norway), Aus
SMITH	Dodie (C. L. Anthony), Eng
SMITH	Sydney, Eng
SOLON	Gk
STAEL	Anne Louise (Necker), Swi/Fr
STEIN	Gertrude, US
STOWE	Harriet Elizabeth Beecher, US
SWIFT	Jonathan, Eng
TWAIN	Mark (Samuel Langhorn Clemens), US
VERNE	Jules, Fr
VIDAL	Gore, US
WAUGH	Auberon, Eng
WAUGH	Evelyn Arthur St John, Eng
WELLS	Herbert George, Eng
WHITE	Gilbert, Eng
WILDE	Oscar Fingal O'Flahertie Wills, Ire/Eng
WOOLF	Virginia, Eng
YATES	Dornford (Cecil William Mercer), Eng
YEATS	William Butler, Ire
ZWEIG	Arnold, Ger
ZWEIG	Stefan, A

6-letters

ANSELM	Saint, Eng
ARCHER	Jeffrey, Eng
ARNOLD	Matthew, Eng
AROUET	Francois Marie (Voltaire), Fr
ASCHAM	Roger, Eng

AUSTEN	Jane, Eng
BALZAC	Honore de, Fr
BARRIE	Sir James Matthew (Gavin Ogilvie), Eng
BELLOC	Hilaire, Eng
BORROW	George, Eng
BRECHT	Bertolt, Ger
BRONTË	Anne (Acton Bell), Eng
BRONTË	Charlotte (Currer Bell), Eng
BRONTË	Emily Jane (Ellis Bell), Eng
BROOKE	Rupert Chawner, Eng
BUNYAN	John, Eng
BURNEY	Fanny Frances (Mme D'Arblay), Eng
BURTON	Sir Richard Francis, Eng
BUTLER	Samuel, Eng
CAESAR	Gaius Julius, Rom
CICERO	Marcus Tullius, Rom
COFFIN	Joshua (H. W. Longfellow), Eng
COLTON	Charles Caleb, Eng
CONRAD	Joseph (Teodor Konrad Korzeniowski), Pol
COWARD	Sir Noel, Eng
COWPER	William, Eng
DARWIN	Charles Robert, Eng
DRYDEN	John, Eng
EVELYN	John, Eng
FRANCE	Anatole (Jacques Anatole François Thibault), Fr
FULLER	Thomas, Eng
GEORGE	Henry, US
GIBBON	Edward, Eng
GOETHE	Johann Wolfgang von, Ger
GRAVES	Robert, Eng
GREENE	Graham, Eng
HARRIS	Joel Chandler (Uncle Remus), US
HERZOG	Emile (André Maurois), Fr
HOLMES	Oliver Wendell, US
HORACE	(Quintus Horatius Flaccus), Rom
HUXLEY	Aldous Leonard, Eng
IRVING	Washington, US
JEROME	Jerome Klapka, Eng

JONSON	Ben, Eng
KELLER	Helen Adams, US
KRUTCH	Joseph Wood, US
LANDOR	Walter Savage, Eng
LAOTSE	(Laotzu or Latze), Ch
LARKIN	Philip, UK
LONDON	Jack (John Griffiths), US
LOWELL	James Russel, US
LUCIAN	Gk
MAILER	Norman, US
MALORY	Sir Thomas, Eng
MERCER	Cecil William (Dornford Yates), Eng
MILLER	(Agatha Christie), Eng
MILLER	Arthur, US
MILLER	Henry, US
MILTON	John, Eng
NATHAN	George Jean, US
NEWTON	Sir Isaac, Eng
NORWAY	Nevil Shute, Aus
O'NEILL	Eugene Gladstone, US
ORWELL	George (Eric Arthur Blair), Eng
PARKER	Dorothy Rothschild, US
PASCAL	Blaise, Fr
PINDAR	Gk
PINERO	Sir Arthur Wing, Eng
PIOZZI	Hester Lynch (Mrs Thrale), Eng
PORTER	William Sydney (O. Henry), US
POTTER	Stephen, Eng
PROUST	Marcel, Fr
RACINE	Jean Baptiste, Fr
RUSKIN	John, Eng
SARTRE	Jean-Paul, Fr
SAYERS	Dorothy L., Eng
SENECA	Lucius Annaeus, Rom
SEWELL	Elizabeth M., Eng
SONTAG	Susan, US
STEELE	Richard, Ire/Eng
STERNE	Laurence, Eng/Ire
STOKER	Bram, Eng
THOMAS	Dylan Marlais, Wal
THRALE	Hester Lynch (Piozzi), Eng

VIRGIL	(Publius Virgilius Maro), Rom
WALTON	Isaak, Eng
WARNER	Charles Dudley, US
WILCOX	Ella Wheeler, US
WILDER	Thornton Niven, US
WINSOR	Kathleen, US

7-letters

ADDISON	Joseph, Eng
ANDREWS	Cicely (Rebecca), Eng
ANOUILH	Jean, Fr
ANTHONY	C. L. (Dodie Smith), Eng
AQUINAS	St Thomas, It
BAGNOLD	Enid, Eng
BALDWIN	James, US
BARNETT	Lincoln, US
BECKETT	Samuel, Ire
BEECHER	Henry Ward, US
BENTLEY	Edmund Clerihew, Eng
BOSWELL	James, Sc
BRIDGES	Robert, Eng
BURNETT	Frances Hodgson, Eng/US
CARLYLE	Thomas, Sc
CARROLL	Lewis (Dodgson), Eng
CHAPMAN	George, Eng
CHAUCER	Geoffrey, Eng
CLEMENS	Samuel Langhorn (Mark *Twain*), US
COLLINS	William Wilkie, Eng
COCTEAU	Jean, Fr
COLETTE	Sidonie Gabrielle, Fr
COOKSON	Catherine, Eng
D'ARBLAY	Mme (Frances Burney), Eng
DA VINCI	Leonardo, It
DICKENS	Charles John Huffam (Boz, Quiz), Eng
DICKENS	Monica, Eng
DIDEROT	Denis, Fr
DODGSON	Rev Charles Lutwidge (Lewis Carroll), Eng
DOUGLAS	Lord Alfred, Eng
DUHAMEL	Georges, Fr
DURRELL	Lawrence, Eng/Ire

EMERSON	Ralph Waldo, US
FLEMING	Ian Lancaster, Eng
FORSYTH	Frederick, Eng
FRANCIS	Dick, Eng
GALLICO	Paul William, US
GILBERT	Sir William Schwenck, Eng
GLASGOW	Ellen, US
GRAHAME	Kenneth, Eng
HAGGARD	Sir Henry Rider, Eng
HAKLUYT	Richard, Eng
HAWKINS	A. H. (Anthony Hope), Eng
HAZLITT	William, Eng
HERBERT	Sir Alan Patrick, Eng
HERRICK	Robert, Eng
HOPKINS	Gerard Manley, Eng
HOUSMAN	Alfred Edward, Eng
HOWELLS	William Dean, US
HUBBARD	Albert Green, US
JOHNSON	Dr Samuel, Eng
JUVENAL	(Decimus Junius Juvenalis), Rom
KHAYYAM	Omar, Pers
KIPLING	Rudyard, Eng
LE CARRE	John (D. J. *Cornwall*), Eng
LOFTING	Hugh, Eng
MACLEAN	Alastair, Eng
MARLOWE	Christopher, Eng
MAUGHAM	William Somerset, Eng
MAURIAC	François, Fr
MAUROIS	André (Emile Herzog), Fr
MENCIUS	Gk
MENCKEN	Henry Louis, US
MOLIERE	(Jean Baptiste Poquelin), Fr
MURDOCH	Dame Iris, Eng
OGILVIE	Gavin (J. M. Barrie), Eng
PEACOCK	Thomas Love, Eng
PESHKOV	(Maxim Gorky), USSR
PUBLIUS	Syrus, Rom
QUOIREZ	(Françoise Sagan), Fr
RAYMOND	Rene (James Hadley Chase), US
ROLLAND	Romain, Fr
RUSSELL	Earl Arthur William, Eng

SALLUST	(Gaius Valerius Sallustius Crispus), Rom
SHELLEY	Mary, Eng
SHELLEY	Percy Bysshe, Eng
SIMENON	Georges, Belg/Fr
SOUTHEY	Robert, Eng
SPENSER	Edmund, Eng
TACITUS	Cornelius, Rom
TENNANT	Stephen James Napier, Eng
THOREAU	Henry David, US
THURBER	James Grover, US
TOLKIEN	John Ronald Renel, Eng
TOLSTOI(Y)	Count Leo, Russ
VACHELL	Horace Annesley, Eng
WALLACE	Edgar, Eng
WALPOLE	Earl Horace, Eng
WHITMAN	Walter, US

8-letters

BEERBOHM	Sir Max, Eng
BETJEMAN	Sir John, Eng
BROWNING	Lady (Daphne Du Maurier), Eng
BROWNING	Elizabeth Barrett, Eng
BROWNING	Robert, Eng
CALDWELL	Erskine Preston, US
CATULLUS	Gaius Valerius, Rom
CHILDERS	Erskine, Ire
CHRISTIE	Agatha (Miller), Eng
CLERIHEW	(Edmund Clerihew Bentley), Eng
CONGREVE	William, Eng
CORNWALL	D. J. (Le Carre), Eng
CRATINUS	Gk
CYNEWULF	A-Sax
DAY-LEWIS	Cecil, Ire
DE LA MARE	Walter John, Eng
DISRAELI	Benjamin (Earl of Beaconsfield), Eng
DUDEVANT	Baronne (George Sand), Fr
FAULKNER	William, US
FIELDING	Henry, Eng
FLAUBERT	Gustave, Fr
FOUGASSE	(Cyril Kenneth Bird), Eng

FRANKLIN	Benjamin, US
GINSBERG	Allen, US
GINSBERG	Louis, US
GONCOURT	Edmond, Fr
GONCOURT	Jules, Fr
GRIFFITH	(Jack London), US
HOUSEMAN	Alfred Edward, Eng
KINGSLEY	Rev Charles, Eng
LANGLAND	William, Eng
LAWRENCE	David Herbert, Eng
LAWRENCE	Thomas Edward (Ross, Shaw), Eng
LIPPMANN	Walter, US
LOVELACE	Richard, Eng
MACAULAY	Lord Thomas Babington, Eng
MCCARTHY	Mary, US
MARQUAND	John Phillips, US
MELVILLE	Herman, US
MENANDER	Gk
MEREDITH	George, Eng
MITCHELL	Margaret, US
MOREHEAD	Alan, Aus
PHAEDRUS	Rom
PLUTARCH	Gk
RABELAIS	François, Fr
RATTIGAN	Sir Terence Mervyn, Eng
ROSSETTI	Christina, Eng
ROUSSEAU	Jean-Jacques, Swi/Fr
SANDBURG	Carl, US
SCHILLER	Johann Christoph Friedrich von, Ger
SHERIDAN	Richard Brinsley, Ire/Eng
SOCRATES	Gk
STENDHAL	(Marie Henri Beyle), Fr
STOPPARD	Tom, Eng
TEASDALE	Sara, Eng
TENNYSON	Lord Alfred, Eng
THIBAULT	(Anatole France), Fr
TROLLOPE	Anthony, Eng
VOLTAIRE	(François Marie Arouet), Fr
WESTCOTT	Edward Noyes, US
WILLIAMS	Tennessee (Thomas Lanier Williams), US

XENOPHON	Gk

9+ letters

AESCHYLUS	Gk
ALLINGHAM	Marjorie, UK
ANTIPATER	of Sidon, Gk
ARISTOPHANES	Gk
ARISTOTLE	Gk
AYCKBOURN	Alan, UK
BAUDELAIRE	Charles, Fr
BEACONSFIELD	Earl of (Disraeli), Eng
BURROUGHS	John, Eng
CERVANTES	Miguel de, Sp
CHATEAUBRIAND	Viscomte de, Fr
CHESTERFIELD	Lord, Eng
CHESTERTON	Gilbert Keith, Eng
CHURCHILL	Sir Winston Leonard Spencer, Eng
CLAUSEWITZ	Karl von, Ger
COLERIDGE	Samuel Taylor, Eng
CONFUCIUS	Ch
CORNEILLE	Pierre, Fr
DE LA ROCHE	Mazo
DELDERFIELD	E. M., US
DE MAUPASSANT	Guy, Fr
DICKINSON	Emily Elizabeth, US
DOSTOEVSKY	Fyodor Mikhailovich, USSR
DU MAURIER	Daphne (Lady Browning), Eng
EHRENBURG	Ilya, USSR
EURIPIDES	Gk
FITZGERALD	Francis Scott Key, US
GALBRAITH	Paul William, Can
GALSWORTHY	John, Eng
GOLDSMITH	Oliver, Ire/Eng
LONGFELLOW	Henry Wadsworth, Eng
LUCRETIUS	(Titus Lucretius Carus), Rom
MACMILLAN	Sir Maurice Harold, Eng
MONTAIGNE	Michel Eyquem, Fr
MONTESQUIEU	Charles de Secondat (Baron de la Brede), Fr
NIETZSCHE	Friedrich Wilhelm, Ger
OMAR KHAYYAM	Pers

PARKINSON	Cecil Northcote, US
PASTERNAK	Boris Leonidovich, USSR
PETRONIUS	Gaius, Rom
PRIESTLEY	John Boynton, Eng
SHAKESPEARE	William, Eng
SOLZHENITSYN	Alexander Isayevich, USSR
SOPHOCLES	Gk
STEINBECK	John Ernst, US
STEVENSON	Robert Louis Balfour, Eng
STREATFEILD	Noel, Eng
STRINDBERG	John August, Swe
SWINBURNE	Algernon Charles, Eng
TARKINGTON	Newton Booth, US
THACKERAY	William Makepeace, Eng
THEOCRITUS	Gk
THUCYDIDES	Gk
WODEHOUSE	Pelham Grenville, Eng
WORDSWORTH	William, Eng

WRITE-UP 1. CRIT, *NOTICE*, PUFF, REVIEW. 2. A dn answer written upwards, e.g. **Press's bad write-up** (3) = DAB.
WRITING MS. PS. TS. (*study*).
~ OFF 1. CANCELLING, STRIKING OFF. 2. Delete letters meaning 'writing' (MS, PS, TS) from the clue, e.g. **Writing-off terms, in triplicate?** (3) = TER(ms).
WRONG *Anag.* INCORRECT, IN ERROR, OUT OF ORDER; NOT RIGHT (hence delete letters 'r' or 'rt' from clue, e.g. **Divert wrong plunge** (4) = DIVE(rt).
WRY *Anag.* ASKEW, DISTORTED, SKEW. DISAPPOINTED. *BIRD*.
WYVERN WINGED *DRAGON* (myth). WINGED SERPENT [*Asclepius*, caduceus, *herald*, viper].

X (s/l ex). 10, TEN. ANTEPENULTIMATE. CHRIST. EXTRA LARGE. KISS. OVER 18 (film *censorship*). UNKNOWN QUANTITY; graph co-ordinate. ABSCISSA (**opp** = y or ordinate). VOTE. WRONG.
XANGTI Ch chief *god*.
XANTHIC *COLOUR* (*yellow*).

XANTHIPPE 1. Wife of *Socrates*, notorious for her peevish and nagging nature. It is said that Socrates mar her as a penance. 2. SCOLD, SHREW, SPITFIRE, TERMAGANT.

XANTHUS City and river of Lycia (E Turk). Horse of *Achilles*.

XAU LAKE (Af).

XE XENON (*chem*).

XEBEC *BOAT*.

XENOPHILE *Lover* of foreigners/strangers.

XENOPHOBIA *Aversion* to foreigners/strangers.

XER- Prefix for DRY, e.g. **xeransis** = desiccated; **xerophilous** = adapted to dry climate.

XERES SPANISH SHERRY, WINE.

XERXES King of Persia 485–465 B.C. Conquered Egypt and then invaded Greece (480 B.C.) by crossing the *Hellespont* on a bridge of boats. Checked by the Spartans at *Thermopylae*, he was finally forced to withdraw after his fleet was beaten by the Greeks at *Salamis*. He was ass in 465 B.C.

XHOSA BANTU, TRIBE (SA).

XINGU RIVER (Braz).

XINHUA Newsagency (Ch).

XIPHOID SWORD-SHAPED.

XOANON Gk myth wooden god, supposedly fallen from Heaven.

X-RAYS RONTGEN RAYS.

XX TWENTY.

XYLONITE CELLULOID.

XYLOPHONE *INSTRUMENT* (mus), MARIMBA.

XYSTUS EXERCISE AREA (Gk). TERRACE, WALK (Rom).

Y (s/l why). PENULTIMATE. UNKNOWN QUANTITY; graph co-ordinate, ORDINATE (**opp** = x or abscissa). YTTRIUM (*chem*). YUGOSLAVIA.

YAMA Ind *god* of Dead.

YANKEE AMERICAN (**opp** = Confederate). *BET*. JIB, *SAIL*. **Pl** = *BASEBALL TEAM*.

YARD AREA; GARDEN (US). *MEASURE*, THREE FEET; hence TRIPOD (crypt). SPAR (naut).

YARN THREAD. STORY, TALE.

~ SPINNER BOBBIN, SPOOL. NARRATOR, STORY TELLER.

YEAN *KID*, LAMB.

YEAR AD, BC. Either of these added to Rom numerals to make a word, e.g. **year 1009** (5) = ADMIX.

YEARN HANKER, LONG, PANT FOR.

YEGG *ROBBER*.

YELLOW *COLOUR*. *SNOOKER* BALL (score 2). AFRAID, *COWARDLY*. RIVER (Ch). *SEA*. CRY OUT, SHOUT 'OW' (crypt).

YES AY, AYE, CERT, SURE; NOD; AGREE; ROGER, WILCO (mil). DA (USSR); JA (Ger); OUI (Fr), SI (It, Sp).

YIELD CEDE, GIVE WAY, SUBMIT. AMOUNT, OUTPUT, PRODUCE. CONSENT.

YMIR Frost giant (Nor).

YOKE (s/l *yolk*). BAR, CROSS-BAR, *HARNESS*, LINK; WAIST; TEAM. BOND, DOMINION, SWAY.

YOLK (s/l *yoke*). YELK. SECRETION, WOOL OIL. EGG CENTRE (hence G, crypt).

YORK 1. HAM. BOWL OUT (*cricket*). 2. EBORACUM (*Rom*). **Episcopal sig** = EBOR. *CASTLE*. *UNIVERSITY*. *RACETRACK* (horses). RIVER (US). [white rose]. 3. *HERALD*.

YOU HEAR . . . The answer is *pronounced*, but not spelled, like the word indicated, e.g. **Shaggy bird you hear** (5) = ROUGH, whereas **You hear shaggy bird** (4) = RUFF; place a semi-colon mentally between 'shaggy' and 'bird' in each case, and the principle will be clear.

YOUNG 1. BABY, YOUTHFUL; *OFFSPRING*; **comp** = old. *SPACE TRAVELLER*. 2. Put name in diminutive, e.g. **Young David** = DAVE.

YOU SEE Hidden word, e.g. **You see gold in Gothic origins** (5) = IN*GOT(hic).

YOUTH 1. ADOLESCENCE. INEXPERIENCE (**opp** = *age*). [Picture of Dorian Gray (Wilde)]. 2. **Goddesses: Gk** = *HEBE*, **Rom** = JUVENTAS.

YTTRIUM Y (*chem*).

YU YUGOSLAVIA (*car plate*).

YUX HICCOUGH.

Z Zanzibar. GAUGE (model rly). FINAL, LAST (crypt).

ZA SOUTH AFRICA (*car plate*).

Z-CAR *POLICE CAR*.

ZEBRA STRIPED ANIMAL (genus equus), **breeds**: COMMON ~, GREVY'S ~, MOUNTAIN ~, QUAGGA (ex) [okapi]. *SHARK*. BELISHA/PELICAN CROSSING; CROSS-PATCH (crypt).

ZECHIN *COIN*.

ZENITH HIGH POINT, OVERHEAD, TOP (**opp** = nadir).

ZENO *STOIC*.

ZEPHYRUS Gk myth WEST *WIND*; mar *Iris*. **Rom** = FAVONIUS.

ZERO O, DUCK, EGG, LOVE, NIL, NOTHING, ZILCH. Mr ~ (The Adding Machine, Elmer Rice).

ZEST GUSTO, KEENNESS, RELISH. LEMON PEEL.

ZEUS Gk chief *god*; s of *Cronos* and *Rhea*, mar to his sis *Hera* as his chief among many wives; br of *Demeter*, *Hades*, Hera, *Hestia* and *Poseidon* (**Rom** = JOVE, JUPITER). On dividing the universe with his two brs, Hades got the *underworld* and Poseidon the *seas*; Zeus obtained the heavens and upper regions, and lived on *Mt Olympus*; his shield was called *Aegis*. He had many children by his various wives, but his marriage to Hera remains the archetype. **Transformations**: 1. Acrisius confined his d *Danae* in a brazen tower lest she should conceive a child who would k him as prophesied; ~ visited her in a shower of gold and fathered *Perseus* (who did indeed eventually k Acrisius). 2. ~ transformed into a swan to seduce *Leda* and thus f *Helen* and the *Dioscuri*. 3. ~ also transformed into a bull and carried off *Europa*, who became the m of *Minos*. 4. ~ transformed into an eagle to carry off *Ganymede*. 5. ~ transformed into a cloud (*Io*). 6. ~ transformed to *Amphitryon* (to seduce Alcmene, his w).

ZILCH ZERO (sl).

ZINC *METAL*; ZN (*chem*).

ZINNIA *FLOWER*.

ZIRCON *GEM*; HYACINTH, JARGON.

ZIRCONIUM *METAL*; ZR (*chem*).

ZLOTY *CURRENCY* (Pol).

ZN *ZINC* (*chem*).

ZODIAC 1. FULL CYCLE. 2. HEAVENLY BELT (*constellations*), TRIGON. **Signs**: ARIES (the *Ram*), TAURUS (the *Bull*), GEMINI (the *Twins*), CANCER (the *Crab*), LEO (the *Lion*), VIRGO (the *Virgin*), LIBRA (the *Scales*), SCORPIO (the *Scorpion*), SAGITTARIUS (the *Archer*), CAPRICORNUS (the *Goat*), AQUARIUS (the *Watercarrier*), PISCES (the *Fishes*).

ZONDA *WIND* (Arg prevailing northerly).
ZR ZIRCONIUM (*chem*). ZAIRE (*car plate*).
ZULÚ TRIBE (Bantu, SA). **Pl = IMPI.**